IMPRINTS ON HISTORY

Imprints on History

Book Publishers

AND AMERICAN FRONTIERS

BY

Madeleine B. Stern

1956

INDIANA UNIVERSITY PRESS

BLOOMINGTON

Acknowledgment is made to *Publishers' Weekly* for the use of articles published by it in the years indicated: "James Redpath and His 'Books for the Times,'" 1945; "The Rise and Fall of A. K. Loring," 1946; "Elliott, Thomes and Talbot and Their Blue Backs," 1946; "G. W. Carleton: His Mark," 1946; "Hilliard, Gray & Company: Booksellers to the University," 1946; "Dick and Fitzgerald, The Troupers of Ann Street," 1946; "George W. Childs: Poor Richard the Second," 1946; "The Leslies of Publishers' Row," 1947.

TO THE ETERNAL TRIANGLE

Author · Publisher · Bookseller

ACKNOWLEDGMENT

I WISH TO thank the editors of *The Boston Public Library Quarterly, California Historical Society Quarterly, New York History, The North Carolina Historical Review,* and *Publishers' Weekly* for permission to reprint chapters which appeared originally as articles in those periodicals.

Acknowledgment of the author's deep gratitude to the many individuals who have provided information and assistance in connection with the preparation of this book is made at appropriate points in the section, "Notes on Sources."

The author's gratitude to Leona Rostenberg may be acknowledged, but can neither be adequately expressed nor adequately repaid.

CONTENTS

ILLUSTRATIONS

IMPRINTS ON HISTORY

For my part I wonder that among the variety of subjects on which authors have employed themselves, no one of them has ever bethought himself of writing the Lives of Eminent Booksellers. The life of an eminent bookseller is the history of the literature of his time.

WILLIAM CULLEN BRYANT

The publisher and the bookseller are both, in a peculiar sense, conservators of an advancing civilization. Upon no other department of purely commercial enterprise do the enlightenment and intelligence of the world so largely depend. It is especially through their active agency that a continued impulse is given to all educational interests; and to their method of adapting the means and capacities of trade to the needs of the people much of the intellectual progress of the world is due. . . . The publisher, . . . has for his sphere of action the whole world.

GROWOLL COLLECTION OF American Book Trade History

In America it was a century of frontiers. The turbulent, exhilarating years raced in swift course from 1800 to 1900, leaving in their traces the blazing of trails, the conquest of wilderness, the building of cities, the leveling of roads, the rounding out of a union, the creation of a nation's character. In America, it was a century when all things were possible, when all things, whatever the cost, were accomplished. The hunter and trapper, the man with the axe who cut down the timber, cleared the way for those who would follow. The farmer followed, sowing the ground; the merchant followed, his stand a cabin where, days before, there had been an Indian camp, the loneliness of tangled forest. The doctor followed, the preacher, the lawyer, the teacher, the brazen speculator in land so lately broken from the wild. People followed, and with the people, and often in their vanguard, came one who carried neither axe nor spade nor hoe nor gun, a pioneer whose tools were type and printing press. Without him, what were farmer and doctor, teacher and lawyer, children and merchant? If schools rose in the wilderness, what were they without the printer's wares? What was a nation without the printed word to herald its progress, to record its history?

In America, it was a century of many frontiers—frontiers in space, East and West on the map; frontiers in the mind of a people, whose will stormed all barriers, whose initiative evolved gradually into democracy, a people fighting in war and building in peace, a people through whom a great creative impulse surged, a people who could fling a gage at fortune and, by the end of the century, win their gage, win fortune too.

In all the frontiers of space and of the mind, the printer takes his place. He, too, broke ground and cleared the wilderness. He, too, built schools and planted seed, laid the railroad tracks and built the cities. He, too, advanced the reaches of a nation's mind. With plowman and hunter, with merchant and trapper, he made the nation's history. But, above and beyond those others, he recorded that history as well.

Here, a few of those printers, and their allies, the publishers and booksellers, live again, recording the history they helped to make. Once again they clear the frontiers of a continent, marching with type and composing stick from East to West across the land, marching with newspaper and pamphlet and book across a nation's mind. They live again, as they have always lived, part of the nation whose wilderness they helped to break, whose aspirations they shared and set in words upon their presses during a century that saw so many wildernesses cleared, so many aspirations realized.

1

FRONTIERS OF SPACE

I. CLEARING EASTERN FRONTIERS

James D. Bemis

PIONEER PRINTER

AMERICA's first frontier lay not in the West, but in the East, and by the close of the Revolution it was to be found in upstate New York. By the year 1800, the settlements of the western part of the State consisted of a few rude log dwellings, along with a saw and grist mill, one or two stores, a tavern. The villagers wanted news of the world, but it required a week to get intelligence from Albany, two weeks from New York, and two months from Europe. None the less, the postrider brought them the news, riding on horseback over muddy roads that had been broken through forests over Indian trails, carrying parcels in his neat pouch, carrying newspapers, a few books and pamphlets in his saddlebags. As he drew up before a store or tavern in a sparsely populated settlement, his arrival was announced by the sounding of a long tin horn, and the blasts attracted the villagers who came to learn the news from this "herald of a noisy world."

The books and pamphlets in his saddlebags had been printed by a pioneer who had joined the farmer in the westward march, for everywhere the axe and plow had been followed by the schoolhouse and the printing press. The printer, too, had come through a near-wilderness, with perhaps "as much type as a squaw could carry in her bag," and had printed those pamphlets and newspapers on an old Ramage press with a short screw and lever, after the pattern used in the days of Franklin. With four solid jerks he printed one page at a pull, while his apprentice made balls of wool covered with green sheepskin to ink the type, and the printer's wife folded the sheets and stitched the pamphlets. So, the pioneer printer, paying his apprentice thirty or forty dollars a year to tread pelts, make the

5

fires, and cut the wood, produced the books for the schools that were rising in the wilderness, books to spread the Gospel among the Indian tribes—Bibles and primers, grammars and spelling books. Only the nearest villagers could congregate at his bookstore, where he began to assemble imports from New York and where the neighbors could discuss the topics of the day—the timely visit of Bonaparte to the Directory, the resolutions passed in honor of George Washington's memory. Most of the printer's wares had to be distributed by postriders and colporteurs, on wagons and pack-horses. By those means, the printed word reached to the farthest settlements of the State, forming public opinion at the same time as it mirrored the life of the people. So the pioneer printer lived history and made it, too. So he helped clear a wilderness and conquer one more frontier.

In January of 1804, Canandaigua was just such a small settlement in the wilderness of Western New York. On the fourteenth of the month, a light snow fell upon the courthouse, the fine jail, the tanyard, as a three-horse sleigh carrying a young man with a stock of books and stationery turned into the village. There was, at the moment, little to indicate that James D. Bemis would one day be known as the "patriarchal editor" and "father of the press" of Western New York. All that was known of him was that he was a twenty-year-old employee of Backus and Whiting, an Albany firm of booksellers, and that he was on his way to Little York, Canada, where he planned to set up a bookstore with a partner's interest. Yet there must have been some mark of promise in him, for a few "gentlemen of respectability" of the village persuaded him to open his store in Canandaigua and remain there for the winter at least.

Soon after his arrival, Bemis wrote a letter to his sister, telling of his journey, his adventures, and his plans. He did not write that he was helping to clear a frontier, but his words paint a graphic picture of a pioneer journey along the muddy roads of Western New York. Sixty-two days before, he had set out from Albany.

After being detained at Utica, upwards of seven weeks, my patience was so far exhausted, that I determined, notwithstanding the badness of the roads, to make one more attempt to gain the place of my destination; and accordingly hired two wagons to take me to Canandaigua. They had proceeded about fifty rods, when one of them got mired to the hub! — "Good start" you will say. Well! we got out in about an hour, and travelled *eight miles* the first day.

Next morning, after taking a warm breakfast, I again "weighed anchor," and trudged in solitude along the muddy waste, (for it is indeed solitary to have no company but swearing teamsters) 'till we reached Oneida village, an Indian Settlement, where, about dark, both wagons got again mired to the hub! Zounds and alack!—what a pickle we were in! How did I invoke the aid of old Hercules to give one tug at the wheel! However, after lifting, grumbling, hollowing, and tugging three hours and a half, with the assistance of an Indian, we once more got on land. It was now ten o'clock, and no tavern within our power to reach. Cold, fatigued, and hungry, we were glad to get under shelter, and accordingly stopped at the first Indian hut we found, where there was no bed, and no victuals except a slice of rusty pork. After a night spent in yawning, dozing and gaping, we again got under headway, . . . and we went on to Onondaga, where we arrived about ten at night. Here the house was full; and I obtained the privilege of sleeping with two strangers, by paying for their lodgings, and giving them a glass of bitters—an odd bargain, to be sure! But I thought it cheap, had it been my last shilling. . . . At . . . Onondaga, the waggoners got discouraged, and despaired of the practicability of travelling! They accordingly stored the goods, and made the best of their way home again. Here I was obliged to remain *two* weeks; when a fine snow falling, I hired a man with a three horse sleigh, to carry me to Canada, and arrived at this place on Saturday Evening, the 14th of January, after a "short and pleasant passage" of sixty two days from Albany! Here I put up for the night only, expecting to depart early in the morning for Canada— but receiving sound advice here from gentlemen of respectability which deserved my attention, I was persuaded to open my store in this village, for the winter at least. How I shall succeed, is yet among the secrets of fate; but as yet I have had no reason to repent of having stopped in Canandaigua; for, such is the encouragement I have already found, that I think it probable I shall continue here.

Bemis had arrived in Canandaigua on January 14. On February 7 a notice, dated January 24, appeared in the *Western Repository,* advertising a new book and stationery store: "Whiting, Backus & Whiting (of Albany) and James D. Bemis, under the firm name of Whiting, Bemis & Co. Respectfully inform their Friends and the Public in general, that they have opened a Book and Stationary [sic] Store in Canandaigua, at the Store of Mr. Henry Chapin, where they have for sale, a Large and Gen'l Assortment Of Books, in the

Various Branches." The "various branches" ranged from divinity to anatomy, from novels to agriculture, from law to physic, and the villagers might also obtain from Whiting, Bemis an assortment of stationery that included ledgers, alphabets, wrapping paper, pen-knives, corkscrews, toothbrushes, seals and wafers, quills and ink-stands, playing cards, slates, pencils, scales, and mathematical instruments. Despite the hardships of his journey and the sudden change in his plans, James D. Bemis had made his own opportunity and, with the enterprising nature that was to characterize his diverse activities, had begun a career that was to be of the utmost importance in clearing an eastern frontier.

From his earliest days he had manifested the same boldness and energy. He had been born in Spencer, Massachusetts, on July 1, 1783, the son of Benjamin and Rebekah (Draper) Bemis. His father, a merchant and farmer, had failed in 1790 and removed to Worcester, where he kept a tavern. At the age of ten James had gone to Boston to learn printing. After ten months at the trade, he had left to resume his schooling, but, irresistibly drawn to the craft of printing, he returned to it, completing seven years of apprenticeship in Albany. At eighteen he had become a journeyman, working hard by day and studying at night. Though he had had only two years of schooling, he taught himself in the printing office and was so well qualified both in printing and bookselling that Backus and Whiting proposed to give him a partner's interest in a new bookstore.

Though the plans of the Albany firm were destined to be checked, Bemis's projects were to expand and multiply until they influenced the entire book world of Western New York. The faithful apprentice, the efficient and painstaking journeyman, was soon to become a sovereign master not in printing alone but in every aspect of the book trade. For ten months Bemis continued the management of the bookstore in the chambers over Wyvill's tailor shop, but though his stock, worth four or five thousand dollars, seemed sufficiently varied, selling books and stationery to the villagers of Canandaigua began to pall. In October, 1804, Bemis sold out to the abolitionist, Myron Holley, and bought one half of a printing establishment, an old press, and types, for which he paid seven hundred dollars. Six years were to pass before Bemis bought back his book stock, but in that interim he was to learn another trade, that of newspaper editor, and to realize that, in order to attain full success and exercise a strong influence upon public opinion and taste, a pioneer bookseller must also be a printer and a publisher of books.

In 1803 the weekly *Western Repository* was the only medium west of Utica for the distribution of public intelligence. Though its equipment was "rude and uncouth," it was at this establishment that all the job work was done for land offices, together with legal and business advertising for the region west of Onondaga. The newspaper's circulation was about one thousand, and James D. Bemis saw in the *Repository* an excellent opportunity for molding popular opinion and developing the unworked resources of Western New York.

With the issue of October 30, 1804, Bemis joined John K. Gould as proprietor of the *Western Repository*. After Gould's death in 1808, Bemis became sole publisher of the paper, the title of which he later changed to the *Ontario Repository*. Perhaps one of the most interesting issues is that of July 7, 1812, when the President's manifesto recommending war with Great Britain gave to the publisher an opportunity to sway the minds of the readers. The terms of the paper (the price to village subscribers was $2.50 a year, to those who called for their papers only $2.00) together with advertisements of the Canandaigua Hat Factory, a saddling business, Mrs. Robb's Millinery Store, and Rogers's Vegetable Pulmonic Detergent adorned the first page. The second carried Madison's message to Congress, and the third, the publisher's editorial on the war, which incidentally revealed his journalistic policy. Bemis minced no words when dealing with the "calamitous" event. "Our Rulers have plunged the country into War . . . and are accountable to the People for the issue. . . . *The evil is upon us*—and there is but *one* remedy for its removal—that remedy is prescribed by the Constitution. It is for the People to apply it—and it is the duty of public journalists to spread before them such information as will enable them to act correctly." Believing, too, that "a sketch, taken on the spot, is . . . gratifying to common readers," Bemis proceeded to supply whatever information was available, printing news items on "False Alarms" about Indian dangers, and intelligence "From the Frontiers." On page 4, between advertisements and announcements of mortgage sales, might be found the moral lesson of the day: "If we delay till tomorrow what ought to be done to-day, we overcharge the morrow with a burden which belongs not to it."

Through agents in Buffalo, Palmyra, Geneva, and Batavia, the paper was carried to distant readers, pushing back a frontier with every issue. Postriders were supplied on liberal terms and represented the most common mode of circulation, which was described by Bemis himself in colorful manner: "The most important route was the western, . . . Imagine a small, humpback, cross-eyed, deaf old man—and you may see honest Ezra Metcalf, . . . mounted on a skunk horse, and you have the post-rider. . . . In an old-fashioned pair of saddlebags, were stowed from 150 to 200 papers. On the top of this was a small portmanteau, containing the U.S. Mail, with a padlock. . . . Thus mounted, with tin horn in hand, which he blew when he got in the saddle, he set off. . . . The arrival and departure of 'old uncle Ezra,' was an event."

Fording the Genesee River, passing New Amsterdam on Buffalo Creek, an Indian trading place, "old uncle Ezra" carried through Western New York James D. Bemis's newspaper and James D. Bemis's opinions. The *Repository* was a fine vehicle for the proprietor's point of view on the politics of the day. A strict Federalist, he made every effort to keep the "Republican *form* from being thrown into *pi.*" But Bemis's interests embraced more than the politics of his country. Consciously or unconsciously he knew that he was playing a part in clearing an eastern frontier. He was engrossed in every development of Western New York, the history of which he hoped one day to write. Though he never wrote that history, he did help to make it. Through his newspaper and his public activities Bemis was identified with nearly every movement of the day for promoting the prosperity of Western New York, from its turnpikes and canals to its literary and benevolent institutions. He became a director of the Ontario Bank, the first president of the Auburn and Rochester Railroad, treasurer of the Ontario Agricultural Society, a trustee of the Ontario Female Seminary, treasurer and librarian of the Literature, Science Society, and president of the village of Canandaigua—a prime mover in advancing the progress of his region, a sower in the flowering of a wilderness.

Yet it was less through his public offices than through his newspaper and printing establishment that Bemis spread abroad his interest in the development of the State. And, more particularly, it was through his apprentices that his plans and purposes were carried to the settlements of the frontier. Through the young men trained at his office, bookstores and printing presses were established from Onondaga to Detroit, and it was to him that Erie, Wayne, Livingston, and Onondaga counties were indebted for many of their literary beginnings. For many years there were from forty to sixty workers dependent in various ways upon Bemis's "old establishment." They were, to judge from Bemis's agreement with Elisha Loomis, indentured for a period "during which term the said apprentice his said master shall faithfully serve, his secrets keep, and his lawful commands everywhere gladly obey. He shall not waste the property of his master, nor give nor lend it to any person without his master's orders. With his own goods or money or those of any other person he shall not traffic or in any manner buy or sell during said term unless he have license from his master for that purpose. He shall not go to taverns or any other places of resort nor otherwise absent himself day or night from his master's service without his leave." In return, the master covenanted "to teach and instruct or cause to be taught and instructed the said apprentice in the art, trade or mastery of printing, and to find unto his said apprentice meat, drink, lodging, washing, medicines, and good and sufficient clothing."

Many of these "said apprentices" Bemis set up in business, with the result that his policies as well as his wares reached the remotest sections of the State. Among those who, under his supervision, learned the craft of printing, from treading pelts to setting type, were (besides Loomis, who carried his trade to the Sandwich Islands) Smith H. and Hezekiah A. Salisbury, who ventured to Buffalo, where they established its first paper and printed its first book, and Oran Follett, who planted *The Spirit of the Times* in Batavia. There were others, too—Roswell Haskins, who found his way to Rochester; Chauncey Morse, who left for Geneseo; Thurlow Weed —a notable roster of printers, publishers, and editors who had been trained by Bemis and spread afield his techniques and his policies, pushing back yet a step further a more remote frontier. The relations of the Canandaigua editor with his apprentices may best be described by the methods he used with one of his boys, Lewis H. Redfield. Redfield, having served his six-years' apprenticeship on the *Ontario Repository,* purchased on credit from his employer a suit of second-hand type and other printing material and set out for Onondaga Hollow, much as Bemis had once set out for Canan-

daigua. There he established the *Onondaga Register* in partnership
with Bemis, opened the first bookstore there, paid off his debt, and
in his turn became an influential figure in the State whose limits he
had helped expand.

By that time, the *Ontario Repository* was regarded by many as
"the greatest of all the weekly papers of the country," and Bemis
himself was well on his way to becoming the "father of the Western
New York Press." By that time, also, the Canandaigua editor had
realized that through his numerous apprentices as well as through
the influence he exerted, he could turn to his bookselling activities
with far greater promise of success than the young man in the three-
horse sleigh had felt when he entered the village in 1804.

In 1810 Bemis repurchased Myron Holley's bookstore for $1,200.
Having married Ruth Williams, the daughter of a Revolutionary
soldier, in 1807, he had set up in the corner of Captain Israel Chapin's garden a two-story building, which housed his office, store, and
family. Later the proprietor added a wing, in the garret of which
the boys of his printing office slept; the front lower rooms became
his bookstore. There the villagers of Canandaigua might find a varied assortment of books, and there they gathered often, making of
those lower front rooms a meeting place where the latest literary
or social developments of the day could be discussed. There the
pastor of the First Congregational Church in Canandaigua doubtless cast an appraising eye over Bemis's stock of Bibles, Testaments,
Psalms, Hymns, and Prayer Books, of all qualities, sizes, and prices,
debating whether to take with him Hannah More's *Practical Piety*
or a *Life of Bishop Porteus*. There the members of the Ontario
Agricultural Society must have lingered over the shelves devoted
to husbandry, where Forsyth on *Fruit Trees,* Mills's *Farriery,* and
Wakefield's *Botany* offered many a suggestion for the improvement
of their daily pursuits. The county clerks and sheriffs surely visited
Bemis's establishment to browse through his excellent stock of legal
reports and digests, nisi prius trials and attorney's companions, that
ranged in price from 38¢ to $30, while the ladies of Canandaigua
dropped in for a look at Marmontel's *Moral Tales* or *Precaution, A
Novel,* priced at $2. The *Dying Confession of John Van Alstine
Who was executed at Schoharie* gave food for much speculation,
and *The Maniac,* or a work with the intriguing title, *Fragments of
Miss Smith,* must have attracted many an eager village reader. There

were periodicals to thumb through also, for Bemis was the agent for *Niles' Weekly Register* and other reviews of the day. The "beautiful miniature London copies" or the two hundred plays of the most celebrated dramatic writers may have tempted one or two Canandaiguans along the road to serious book collecting, and certainly there were few tastes of a frontier community that were not satisfied in one way or another by Bemis's varied stock.

Of all the books for sale at the Canandaigua Bookstore, from the historical to the medical, from travel and science to poetry and biography, the most salable must have been the schoolbooks. As a trustee of the Ontario Female Seminary, the proprietor was in an excellent position to know which books were needed there as well as in all the academies and seminaries of Western New York, and he proceeded to supply them on liberal terms. There were few branches of learning not represented by his texts, from Gibson's *Surveying* to Blair's *Chemistry,* from Willett's *Geography* to Ainsworth's *Latin Dictionary,* from Ferguson's *Astronomy* to Pike's *Arithmetic.* First Lessons, Practical Calculators, rhetorics, readers, spellers, ciphering books, vocal and instrumental music books, all the current "preceptors for learners" were available, along with tracts and school certificates. There were children's books, too, for Maria Edgeworth's *Moral Tales* or *Galateo, A Treatise on Politeness* might at the same time whet the appetites of juvenile readers and increase the returns of the astute pioneer bookseller.

Bemis's bookselling methods indicate in a marked manner his characteristic shrewdness. His endeavors, he announced, should be encouraged, as long as he furnished books "of as good editions, and on as low terms, as those brought from a distance." Besides, it was to the interest of individual purchasers to save "the risk and expenses of transportation" by patronizing their neighborhood store. What was more, his books were sold at New York prices, from which discounts were made to those who purchased in quantity. Libraries would be furnished on liberal terms; orders, postpaid, would be promptly filled; and catalogues might be had gratis at the Canandaigua Bookstore.

Bemis was not only a bookseller, but a stationer as well. His stock of ledgers and journals, day-books and ink-powders, globes and mathematical instruments was as varied and extensive as his assortment of books. From surveyor's chains to scales and dividers, from morocco pocketbooks and purses to inkstands and penknives, from pencils and slates to lottery tickets and "uncurrent money," there was little in the line of stationery that was not to be obtained by applying at Bemis's stand. Some idea of the variety of his stock may be derived from the following order sent from a Rushville customer in 1832:

The knife which you sent me is a very good one, but I find that I had rather have one with an additional blade which shall be a size larger, even at an additional expense of .25 or .50cts. If you have none such or are unwilling to exchange return the same. I also wish to procure a very large peice [sic] of sponge or two smaller ones—also I wish to become a subscriber for the Ontario Repository for a quarter, for all which the bearer will pay.

So extensive did his book and stationery business become that, before the opening of the Erie Canal in 1825, Bemis was a wholesaler for the entire western country, supplying merchants throughout the West with the books and office stationery they had previously purchased from New York. His sales swelled from twenty to thirty thousand dollars a year, and his wares reached towns as far west as Detroit and Mackinac.

In 1812 the astute bookseller added a bindery to his business, announcing that "Ledgers, Journals and all other kinds of Account Books" would be "rul'd to any pattern," old books would be "rebound at short notice," and "any other work in that line" would be "executed in a neat and faithful manner." Magistrates and surrogates would be furnished with blankbooks of good paper, ruled and bound in the best style, and, in order to facilitate his new enterprise, Bemis was ready to pay in cash, books, or stationery for clean linen and cotton rags.

His firm was one not only of booksellers, stationers, and binders, but of printers, too, and, boasting a good assortment of type, Bemis neatly executed orders for job printing, producing handbills and blanks at short notice. Besides making his own ink, he was the agent for ink makers, press manufacturers, and typefounders, including Ronaldson's Philadelphia foundry and Bruce's New York foundry. In 1820 Bemis extended his activities still further by establishing a circulating library at his stand.

The Canandaigua Bookstore, with its printing establishment, its book and stationery departments, must have been a bustling center for the village. The mild, even-tempered, dignified but genial proprietor had become everyone's friend in Canandaigua, and his store, as he himself described it, became "a sort of rendezvous, and I was in the way of being in all that was going on. . . . It was this, the papers, the business, the headquarters—not myself—that made up all the reputation and all my comfort. I had rather continue as I was to my end than to have been Governor of the State." Actually, it may be questioned whether, through his far-reaching influence as a pioneer bookseller, he did not exert as great an influence upon his section of the country as the governor himself. Certainly, when he turned to printing and publishing books as well as to selling them, he gave as strong an impetus to the development of Western New York as any man in public office.

The first work bearing Bemis's imprint was a theological item of local interest. The *Minutes of the Cayuga Baptist Association, holden at Palmyra, September 26th and 27th, 1804* was printed by Gould and Bemis as early as 1805 and paved the way for numerous publications of a similar nature. The ministers of Canandaigua and near-by villages found in James D. Bemis a reliable printer and successful publisher of their sermons, and Bemis, in turn, perceived enough local interest in such works to be encouraged to produce them. When Henry U. Onderdonk, rector of St. John's Church in Canandaigua, delivered a discourse on baptismal regeneration or the forms of prayer, when Pastor A. D. Eddy spoke at the Brick Church in the village, or the Rev. Mr. Hickox delivered a New Year's sermon, Bemis seemed the most likely person for setting their phrases in print. His publications included the works of theologians of neighboring towns also, a sermon by the rector of St. Luke's Church in Rochester, a scriptural commentary by the pastor at Bristol, New York, a discourse given at the ordination of a minister in East Bloomfield. Bemis widened the scope of his theological enterprises, reprinting Baxter's *Call to the Unconverted* and Isaac Watts's *Plain and Easy Catechism for Children,* until he served as a kind of publisher to the frontier church, with benefit of clergy.

It was not only local theological organizations such as the Ontario and Cayuga Baptist Associations that Bemis represented as printer-publisher. From its first meeting in 1819 through 1824, the Ontario Agricultural Society assigned publication of its annual addresses to him, and he also printed a broadside on the Society's premiums for 1827. The proposed canal from Lake Erie to the Hudson was as significant and lively a topic at the time as agricultural developments in Western New York, and at the request of members of a convention of the people of Ontario County in 1817, Bemis published Gideon Granger's speech on the subject, and later a *Report, on . . . a communication, between Canandaigua lake and the Erie canal.*

The Indians were still subjects of considerable interest when, in 1809, Bemis printed the speeches of Farmer's Brother and Red Jacket, two Seneca Chiefs, and two years later, issued *Native Eloquence* after the Buffalo Creek council regarding purchase of Indian rights to reservations in the Holland Purchase.

With his strong Federalist principles, Bemis naturally took occasion, by the choice of his publications, to exhort his readers to adopt his convictions. As early as 1808, when Timothy Pickering wrote *The Dangers of the Country! . . . Exhibiting . . . The Imminent Danger of an Unnecessary And Ruinous War,* it was Bemis whose name appeared on the imprint of the work. It was he, too, who printed in 1811 Eleazer Fairbanks's *Message to the Military* in which the chaplain of the regiment boldly queried, "What has clipped our national wings?" Myron Holley's *Oration,* delivered on February 22 in the eventful year of 1812, an *Address of Members of the House of Representatives, . . . on the Subject of the War with Great-Britain* were both printed by Bemis, and for the Washington Benevolent Society, organized by the Federalist Party to promote the principles of Washington, he issued a reprint of the *Farewell Address* in 1813.

Though schoolbooks were not a medium for a political point of view, they were as important in the development of the State as any partisan publication. Bemis fully realized their significance, advertising that, "Having considerably increased the Printing of Books, and extended his intercourse with other Publishers, in different parts of the United States," he was "enabled to furnish Merchants, Teachers, and others who buy in quantities, with all School Books in use, on as liberal terms, as can be afforded by any booksellers in the State." He was warranted in giving this assurance, "as well by the above circumstances, as by the rapidly increasing demand for School Books in this country." He published and sold, both at wholesale and at retail, therefore, such books as were designed for American academies and common schools, from Ezra Sampson's *Brief Re-*

marker on the Ways of Man to Walker's *Critical Pronouncing Dictionary,* from Ostrander's *Elements of Numbers* to Webster's *American Spelling Book. The Child's Instructer, A Gamut or Scale of Music,* Murray's *English Reader,* Willson's *American Class Reader,* all bore the Bemis imprint. As publisher and as trustee of the Ontario Female Seminary, Bemis printed not only the books recommended for the pupils of that institution but also its *Catalogue,* which, incidentally, contained a list of those approved books. Pope's *Essay on Man* and Goldsmith's *Roman History* rounded out his publications for schools, bearing a Canandaigua imprint that indicated the clearing of the frontiers of Western New York.

Three words that follow the Bemis imprint in many of his publications suggest the reasons for his success as printer and publisher as well as the methods used in pushing back those frontiers: "Sold also at." The list of bookstores at which his works were "also sold" includes those of many of the apprentices who had been taught in his establishment and then went forth to set up their own businesses in other parts of the State. Several of the books printed and sold by Bemis were "sold also by" S. H. and H. A. Salisbury of Buffalo, L. H. Redfield in Onondaga, Chauncey Morse at Geneseo, and others who had learned their trade from Bemis and now not only carried on his business methods but purveyed his wares as well.

The imprints themselves reveal the changes in his firm name, indicating the partners whom, from time to time, he took on in his establishment. The early Gould and Bemis imprint became, after the former's death, James D. Bemis, and that in turn changed to Bemis and Beach, while the firm of L. H. Redfield and Company was a co-partnership in which the master was associated between 1814 and 1817. When the "and Company" was added in 1819 to Bemis's name, it signified a partnership with Chauncey Morse, his brother-in-law, and Samuel C. Ward, his nephew, whose names were later linked with Bemis's in books bearing the imprint of Bemis, Morse and Ward. After 1828 Morse's name disappeared, leaving those of Bemis and Ward, and still later the imprint of Bemis and Son indicated the entrance of George W. Bemis to his father's establishment.

James Bemis appears to have been somewhat disillusioned by his various associations. "During my business career," he wrote, "I had ten partners, and I am satisfied that I never was a good judge of character, and my devotion to the pleasures of editing ruined my business experience." None the less, his publications continued for some time to roll from his press, and Bemis's success and influence increased hand in hand.

For the most part, any Canandaigua imprint, and therefore any Bemis imprint, is rare today. The books and pamphlets that arose in a near-wilderness answered the needs of a frontier community and hence were often either ephemeral in nature or else thumbed to death by avid local readers. Yet there is an added interest to three of Bemis's publications that gives them a greater significance than his sermons, political tracts, or schoolbooks. In addition to his activities as newspaper and book publisher, Bemis was also a publisher of almanacs, those fascinating paper-bound pamphlets that reveal so much of the social life and interests of a frontier settlement. *The Farmers' Diary, Or Western Almanack, For The Year Of Our Lord, 1814 . . . The 14th Year of the Nineteenth Century And of American Independence, . . . the 38th Year* was printed and sold, wholesale and retail, at Canandaigua by James D. Bemis. It is as interesting a contribution to American social history as many other almanacs and, because of its imprint, more interesting than some. With the calculations of Andrew Beers, a table of interest, a depiction of the anatomy of man's body as governed by the twelve constellations, it appeared before a public avid enough to permit its continuance for some thirty years. The villagers found much to elevate them in its account of "The Ancient City of Tyre," much to instruct them in its report of "A Remedy for the Apoplexy" or a brief discourse on "Cucumbers," and much to entertain them in an amusing extract entitled "I can't help it.—But have you tried?" As the years passed, the calculations for the latitude and longitude of Canandaigua, serving also for the adjacent country, were supplied either by Beers, Oliver Loud, or Loud and Wilmarth; recipes for a lady's dress or a cure for the toothache continued to instruct its readers; Bemis found a conspicuous place on the verso of the back cover to advertise his numerous bookselling and publishing activities; and *The Farmer's Diary* steadily provided "a great variety of useful and entertaining pieces." "Sold also by" Oran Follett in Batavia, Chauncey Morse in Geneseo, Redfield in Onondaga, R. W. Haskins in Buffalo, the *Almanacs* were carried through the State until copies were all but thumbed out of existence. With the deepening sense of their importance as social and historical documents, the few copies that are extant have taken on an increased significance and interest to scholars and book collectors, to all who find in the clearing of a nineteenth-century wilderness a vital part of their own history.

Another work printed by Bemis has had an unusual record. The first bound book, as distinguished from a pamphlet, printed in Western New York was Timothy Pickering's *Political Essays. A Series of Letters Addressed To The People Of The United States,* printed and sold at Canandaigua by James D. Bemis in 1812. The work was priced at 56¢ in boards or 75¢ bound and lettered, and was advertised as "a lucid exposition of the conduct and policy of the present administration of the general government." Politically it was a volume of much interest, for it typified not only the author's but the publisher's point of view in its denunciation of the Democratic Party for its subservience to Napoleon and its anathemas against John Quincy Adams for the desertion of his Federalist friends.

Two most interesting copies of the work are now in the possession of the New York Historical Society, one presented by the family of James D. Bemis, and the other by Henry O'Reilly, the first local historian of Rochester, who over-enthusiastically described it as "the 'first bound book,' printed between Seneca Lake and the Pacific Ocean." When Lewis H. Redfield learned of O'Reilly's intention of presenting the Society with a copy, he wrote the following etter dated March 10, 1858, to O'Reilly, telling the story behind the publication. The letter is of interest not only because it relates to a book that made frontier history, but because it reveals the methods in use at a pioneer printer's establishment in 1812.

I did most of the compositives, & with Chauncey Morse, I believe all of the Press work. I think it was set up in *pica,* and worked off on an old . . . Press, the same that I afterwards removed to Onondaga, and was the *first Book work* I ever attempted. I shall remember it as long as I recollect any thing connected with Printing at that early day. The work was 8 pages to the form, . . . and in correcting one of the forms (I think the 3 or 4th) it became necessary to make room for an "out" of two lines. In doing which I removed two lines from the bottom of the page, intending to put them on the top of the next, or succeeding page & so on thro' the form; but instead of doing this, I very carelessly placed them on the standing galley, thinking I wd. do the "overrunning" when I had corrected the other pages, but by the time I had finished correcting the proof, and revised it, I had forgotten all about the two lines which I had placed on the galley. The paper being in readiness, I locked up the forms, made ready the Press, and proceeded to work off the edition, which was accomplished that afternoon and evening. In the morning, having occasion to notice the galley, what was my astonishment on beholding the unlucky lines. I was dumbfounded and frightened out of what little sense I had, and what to do I knew not. Mr. Bemis came into the office about this time, looking, as I tho't, abnormally stern. I saw there was no other way but to put on the best face I could. I concluded to make a clean breast of it and to confide plainly the whole matter. I told him how it had all occurred. He looked, as we boys used to say, very *"dry,"* and after a few minutes said—"Well, Lewis, this is a bad job," (of which I was already quite sensible), "the paper is spoiled, and the Press work must be done over again"—the form was yet standing. I replied that I was willing to do that, and pay for the paper too, if he wd. overlook it and say no more about it. I suggested, however, that perhaps something might be done whereby the paper might be saved and the Press work too, and proposed to fasten the two lines firmly into an imposing stick while the paper was yet damp, and to go thro' the whole edition and stamp them on the bottom of the page to which they belonged. He tho't it could not be done *decently,* but was willing I should try. I did try, & succeeded so well that the "signature" was saved, and the work was thus bound up and offered for sale. . . . The Book I have not seen in many years, but this incident in its printing is yet fresh in my recollection. It was a high-toned . . . production & J presume the first cost of printing the work was never realized from i' sales.

The book, however, did make history as the first bound volume printed in Western New York, though its record cannot be compared with that of another Bemis imprint which has become both historically and bibliographically one of the most interesting items that ever stemmed from a pioneer press. In the same year that Lafayette was wined and dined in Blossom's Hotel in Canandaigua, James E. Seaver's *Narrative of the Life of Mrs. Mary Jemison* was printed by J. D. Bemis and Company under the date of 1824. In November, 1823, the story had been taken down from the lips of Mrs. Jemison herself, and it is that episode rather than the details of subsequent editions of the work that still leaves room for discussion.

According to the introduction to the first edition, one Daniel W. Banister, prompted to add to the fund of useful knowledge, had resolved in the autumn of 1823 to collect and publish an accurate account of Mrs. Jemison's life. Little appears to be known about Banister except that he settled in Township 11, Range 1, of the Holland Purchase in 1806, that around 1812 he purchased land in the township of Bethany, Genesee County, and that he apparently was a prominent local man of affairs. James E. Seaver, who had practiced physic and surgery, was "employed to collect the materials, and prepare the work for the press; and accordingly went to the house of Mrs. Jennet Whaley in the town of Castile, Genesee co. N.Y. in company with the publisher, who procured the interesting subject of the following narrative, to come to that place . . . and there repeat the story of her eventful life." The question arises whether by his words "the publisher" Seaver wished to designate Banister or Bemis. While there is room for some doubt on the subject, certainly the possibility exists that it was Bemis rather than Banister who in November, 1823, accompanied Seaver for that most interesting rendezvous.

Whoever it was, there is no doubt about the presence of Mrs. Jemison herself. De-he-wa-nus, the White Woman of the Genesee, had gone on foot from her home on the west bank of the Genesee River to the house of Mrs. Jennet Whaley, four miles distant, and there, dressed as an Iroquois squaw, she met Seaver and his companion. Short, wrinkled, with head bent forward, arrayed in the Indian fashion complete with moccasins and blanket, she recounted the story of her eventful life. Of the raiding of her childhood homestead, of the massacre of her family, and her own life among the Indians in the valley of the Genesee, of her marriage to two Indians, of her children, and her sufferings she spoke, and though only two or possibly three men heard her words, they were destined to be carried to a host of readers through the years in what has been called "the most interesting book descriptive of Indian life in western New York that has ever been written."

The first edition of that book consisted of only about five hundred copies. Priced at 37½ cents, the work comprised 189 pages and measured 3⅜ x 5½ inches, a small enough volume for so large a history. The book's early success increased through the years, edition following edition until it has averaged better than a reprint every five years. Copies of the first edition are no longer available at 37½ cents. Between 1941 and 1945 they have ranged at auction for from

$50 to $120 depending upon condition, while a perfect copy may bring considerably more. James D. Bemis has many claims to fame, but not the least notable is that he has supplied libraries and collectors of Americana with a *pièce de résistance* for their bookshelves, and—more important perhaps—that in 1824 he provided to a frontier settlement of Western New York a reminder that it still had links with a tribe of Indians.

By 1824 when the *Narrative* was published, Bemis had set up a building at his old stand, and today one of the most important commercial buildings of Canandaigua, bearing the name of Bemis, has been erected on the site of the printing press that produced the first edition of the *Life of Mary Jemison*. Through the years his business, with its various branches, had expanded until he was compelled to work all day, superintending the apprentices of his printing establishment and managing his bookselling and publishing activities, and to write half the night, keeping up his private correspondence and the editorial department of his newspaper, which remained in his control until 1828. It is little wonder, therefore, that under the great responsibilities he had assumed his health began to give way.

In the fall of 1834 Bemis, accompanied by his daughter, journeyed to Europe, remaining there fourteen months in his search for renewed health, but as soon as he resumed work he found himself unfitted to continue as he had before. As he himself pitifully described his state, he was "a wreck upon the society he had so faithfully served, and by which he had been so often honored." He could still attend the Printers' Festival of 1847, when he was toasted as "the father of the Press in Western New York: May his noble *form* long withstand the *pelts* which are *beating* it, and his *last edition* be *well bound* in the book of life." That hope was not destined to be fulfilled. The years that followed brought misfortune and infirmity to Bemis until they affected not only his stately and manly form, but his well-balanced mind. As a result of his severe malady, and after two sessions at the Utica State Hospital, he was admitted on August 3, 1850, to the Vermont Asylum for the Insane. Though no diagnosis is given in his record, "in all probability he was what we understand today as a schizophrenia." At that asylum Bemis remained until his death, in his seventy-fifth year, on November 2, 1857.

Neither his death notice nor the inscription on his grave gives any indication of Bemis's manifold accomplishments. Not very long before he died, he himself wrote, "I only wanted two things in my power to do, namely, to die as the oldest Editor in Western New York (which I am,) and to write its History." Though that history was given to others to write, the name of James D. Bemis must appear in bold letters in its text if not on its title-page. By fair and upright dealing through the years he did indeed become the "Father of the Western New York Press," spreading his business through the country until fifteen bookstores had been sent abroad in the various counties of the State. "I established," he could write, "the first presses and bookstores in Erie, Wayne, Livingston, and Onondaga counties at a pecuniary loss to myself of from 20,000 to $25,000 but with the satisfaction of knowing that I had put a goodly number of young men into active and successful business." He might have added that he had combined the offices of editor, publisher, and bookseller in the person of a pioneer printer, and through his varied activities had given an impetus to the development of Western New York State. He did not write the history of the clearing of a wilderness. Instead, armed with tools of type and ink, he was a pioneer who helped to clear that wilderness and make that history.

J. D. BEMIS,
Printer, Bookseller and Bookbinder,
CANANDAIGUA,

KEEPS for sale, Ledgers, Journals, and all other kinds of Account and Blank Books; Cyphering and Writing Books, Memorandum do. Blank do. rul'd for Music; Attorney's Registers, &c. Books for Recording Deeds, Town business, &c. and all work in the Binding line, executed in a neat and faithful manner.

William Hilliard & His Firm

BOOKSELLERS TO THE UNIVERSITY

B ETWEEN the clearing of a wilderness and its flowering, the gulf seems wide. Between the breaking down of a frontier in space and the broadening of a frontier of the mind, the gulf seems all but impassable. Yet between the two there is a bridge, and the name of the bridge is the printing press.

At the turn of the century in the East, when much of New York State was still a wilderness surrounding tiny settlements, Massachusetts was beginning to assume its role as cultural arbiter of a new nation. As one printer—James D. Bemis of Canandaigua—helped to clear a wilderness, another printer and bookseller—William Hilliard of Boston—helped to expand the awakening intellectual forces of the East. Both men used for their differing purposes the same device, the printed word. Bemis used it to lighten and encourage the labors of a pioneer people engaged in clearing an Eastern frontier. Hilliard used it to expand and illumine the mind of an already cultivated people engaged in broadening an Eastern culture. With the shift in geography, if not in time, the emphasis, and with it the needs of the people, had changed. Where the people of Western New York State required books on husbandry or agriculture and primers for their rising schools, the people of Massachusetts, having long since pushed the wilderness behind them, needed volumes for the advancement of their already distinguished learning. In Harvard College the Augustan Age would be relived, and its effulgence would in time be reflected far beyond the reaches of the State. Still in the East, but farther south, Thomas Jefferson would plant the seeds of another great university in Charlottesville. In the development of Harvard College and in the building of the University of Virginia, the printer-bookseller would play his part. As the geographical frontiers of the East could not have been cleared without the printer and his press, so the intellectual advance of the East could not have been effected without the bookseller-publisher and his wares.

William Hilliard, the printer, was the instrument through whom this tremendous task was, in part at least, accomplished. He did not work alone. His firm, changing its style at various times through the years, reflected the names of his many associates: the schoolmaster, the young apprentice and his brother, the clerk trained in a shipping house, the Swedenborgian, the bookbinder, the domestic servant. The fortunes of many men were interwoven with the career of William Hilliard and with the annals of his firm, and together they carried to success an enterprise that had many claims to fame. Enjoying a thriving existence for thirty years in Boston, Hilliard's firm had subsidiary connections in Cambridge, Massachusetts, and in Charlottesville, Virginia. As publisher of lawbooks and of textbooks designed for Harvard University, it increased the educational facilities of New England. As agent supplying books for the new University of Virginia, it gave an impetus to the development of learning in the South. Technically the firm takes its place in history, too, for it published one of the first books in America with colored engravings printed from copper plates. It bore good fruit, for from its branches sprang the first type and stereotype foundry in Boston, the Old Corner Bookstore, and the company of Little, Brown. Hilliard's firm exerted a powerful and important influence upon its age, for, with its many ramifications, it extended the intellectual capacities of the East during the first half of the nineteenth century.

Son of the pastor of the First Parish Church in Cambridge, and himself a reputable young deacon, William Hilliard was aware that very little printing had been carried on in that town since Mather's *Daughters of Zion* graced the press in 1692. To fill the gap, he established a printing house in Cambridge in 1800. His enterprising nature could scarcely have been satisfied, however, by the printing of hymnbooks; perhaps because his father had once served as tutor in Harvard College, or perhaps simply because of his own intelligence and enterprising qualities, William Hilliard perceived that a bookstore which published and sold texts for the benefit of the young students of the Yard would be a profitable as well as a significant undertaking. For such a purpose he would need a partner, and who could know the needs of students better than a schoolmaster? Jacob Cummings was the schoolmaster, born in Hollis, New Hampshire, and a graduate of Harvard. Plodding his way between his home on Oliver Street and his private school at Chauncy Place, this industrious and amiable master surely ruminated often upon the dearth of good texts in geography and Scripture, and upon his own qualifications as a "superior teacher" for supplying them. His brief association with the bookbinder and bookseller, William Andrews, at the Boston Bookstore, No. 1 Cornhill, had been terminated; he needed a partner, and who was more likely for such an enterprise than a printer?

On May 16, 1812, the *Columbian Centinel* carried the following simple announcement:

Jacob Abbott Cummings, of Boston, and William Hilliard of Cambridge, have this day formed a connection in the Bookselling business, and have taken that wellknown stand No. 1 Cornhill, where they offer for sale, a great variety of Books and Stationery, upon as advantageous terms, as can be procured in Boston.

While William Hilliard continued to superintend his Cambridge establishment, the new firm, inheriting a business originally founded by Ebenezer Battelle, who had opened a little bookstore in Marlborough Street in 1784, offered its wares in Boston at the corner of Spring Lane and Washington Street. At the Boston Bookstore, despite the fact that war with England was declared in June, customers seemed eager for the blank books and paper, the quills and penknives, the scissors, pocketbooks and paint boxes sold by Messrs. Cummings and Hilliard. Members of the bench and bar, schools and colleges might leave letters for their friends at No. 1 Cornhill, and, more important, they, along with the "cultivated folk purchasing for private libraries," might buy books to advance their cultivation.

The firm lost no time in supplying textbooks for its customers. Jacob Cummings's *Ancient and Modern School Geography,* published in 1813, was "constantly for sale," being almost exclusively used in most of the principal academies of New England and being required reading for admission into Harvard College. The printer and schoolmaster together had struck a vein of gold in the Cambridge mine, for the *Geography* at 75 cents (with an Atlas, priced at 87½ cents) went into edition after edition, with agents extending its fame from Portland to New Haven and from Salem to Keene. Cummings's *Questions on the New Testament* was another steady source of income, and surely if the schoolmaster-author-publisher achieved such success with his own productions, the firm could expand and issue the works of other textbook writers. Mastery of nearly every text published by Cummings and Hilliard was described as a requirement for admission into Harvard College, from Valpy's *Greek Grammar* to Worcester's *Elements of Geography* or *An Introduction to Algebra*. It might almost seem that a young scholar could not walk across Harvard Yard without a volume bearing the Cummings and Hilliard imprint under his arm.

Having thus cornered the textbook market in Cambridge, the firm took advantage of its connections with the University. During the presidency of John Kirkland many professors eagerly gave their manuscripts to Cummings and Hilliard for publication. John Quincy Adams, introduced as "Late Professor of Rhetoric and Oratory in Harvard College," gave to the firm his *Lectures on Rhetoric and Oratory,* and Levi Hedge, "Professor of Logic, Metaphysicks and Ethicks," his *Elements of Logic*. It was a perfect circle established by a progressive business, this publishing of important texts by Harvard professors to be sold to Harvard students—a circle, incidentally, not unlike a golden nimbus.

Over one of the works thus published by Cummings and Hilliard still shines a golden light, for it is one of the first American books with plates printed in color. Jacob Bigelow, Rumford Professor at Harvard, undertook the responsibility of furnishing for his *American Medical Botany* sixty plates and sixty thousand colored engravings. At the period of publication, 1817–20, both lithography and photography were comparatively unknown. Bigelow's account of his enterprise is of no little technical interest:

I came to the conclusion that the only mode of extricating myself from the difficulty was to invent some new mode of printing the impressions at once in colors from the copperplates. After many . . . experiments a tolerably successful mode was discovered, which consisted in engraving the plates in *aqua tinta,* thus producing a continuous surface, to the parts of which separate colors could be applied, and the surplus wiped off in different directions, so as not to interfere with each other. . . . The principal difficulty was found in the surface of green leaves, . . . After many trials, a compound of gamboge and Prussian blue ground in nut oil was found to answer the purpose . . . and a workman could strike off a hundred complete copies in a day.

Appropriately dedicated to President Kirkland, the three-volume manual of medical botany with its new style of color engraving has become not only a collector's item, but a reminder of its publishers' enterprise.

In addition to their own publications, Cummings and Hilliard offered books for sale to customers who, though they might not boast a Harvard degree, were none the less eager for scholarly works—the *Letters of Junius,* Lord Bacon's *Works, Elegant Extracts of Epistles.* Readers without benefit of scholarship might purchase *Tears of the Novel Writers* and *Pleasures of Hope* at 1 Cornhill, while a private collector might find upon the shelves the *Works* of Anselm, "lately received from Germany" and dated 1491, and carry it off for $3.75. The volumes themselves, often purchased by Hilliard from the ancient monastic libraries of Germany, were sometimes superior to their descriptions in the catalogues issued by the firm, for when an invoice of foreign works was received the eager booksellers simply listed them alphabetically by title with very few dates and with no prices. Yet, as the years passed, the rare book department grew along with the publication of texts, and a customer needed $179 to purchase Agincourt's *Histoire de l'Art* of 1823, although Bryant's *Poems* (Cambridge, 1821) might be his for only 37 cents.

In time the firm itself had been enlarged, for Timothy Harrington Carter, a native of Lancaster, Massachusetts, having spent a rather inventive childhood making teapot handles and washboards, was apprenticed to Cummings and Hilliard at the age of sixteen. In return for his labors, which included the printing of maps, the making of writing-books, the folding and stitching of pamphlets, and the manufacture of liquid blacking and inks, he received forty dollars a year plus board. The young Massachusetts clerk was a decided asset, for during his apprenticeship he expanded the business, selling at his own discretion some $20,000 worth of books while on a trip to Baltimore. For this he was rewarded when he came of age by admission as a partner into the new firm of Cummings, Hilliard and Company. In March, 1823, the *Columbian Centinel* carried the announcement:

The Partnership lately existing under the firm of Cummings and Hilliard, was dissolved on the 26th of February last. WILLIAM HILLIARD, Surviving Partner. The business of the establishment will be continued as heretofore under the firm of CUMMINGS, HILLIARD, & CO. the subscriber having admitted into the firm MR. TIMOTHY HARRING-TON CARTER.

Though Jacob Cummings had died, the "and Company" filled his place adequately and quickly proved his worth by inducing his partner to branch out into the publication of law books. William Hilliard did not know then that his son Francis would become a noted legal writer, but he seems to have shared Carter's interest in the law, an interest evinced by the publication of various Digests of Cases and Common Laws that would one day start the firm of Little, Brown upon its way.

No sooner had Carter come of age than he found an opening for his brother Richard. In Virginia, where he had been sent to widen the firm's market, the prompt and efficient Richard may have taken a part in shaping one of the most important roles to be played by Cummings, Hilliard and Company. There is no doubt at all that Joseph Coolidge of Boston did take such a part. Coolidge, a Harvard graduate of the class of 1817, was shortly to become the grandson-in-law of Thomas Jefferson, and fortunately he recognized the enterprising qualities of William Hilliard and his firm. By 1824 Thomas Jefferson's great achievement, the University of Virginia, was well on its way to completion. It still needed, however, a library and a bookstore. Joseph Coolidge suggested to Thomas Jefferson the name of William Hilliard, and upon that "recommendation . . . and explanation of the means he had established of procuring books from the several book-marts of Europe," Jefferson accepted the proposition that Hilliard supply books for the University of Virginia.

Jefferson's part in establishing the University of Virginia and in outlining the nature of its library has been described in full. The part taken by William Hilliard and his firm merits a more complete accounting than it has received. It was an outstanding enterprise by which a Boston bookseller helped not merely to build the library of a great University, but, in that building, to extend one step further the intellectual frontiers of the East. He had helped develop Harvard. Now he could help establish the University of Virginia.

On July 14, 1824, William Hilliard of Boston addressed to the

Hon. Thomas Jefferson, Late President of the United States, a letter indicating not only his willingness and ability to undertake the task, but his awareness of that task's significance in advancing "the republic of letters":

By the politeness of Mr. Cooledge [sic] of this city, I have recently received an application to supply your University with such Books as may be wanted for your course of studies, when in operation. I rejoice for the republic of letters, that an Institution of this description is to be established in the ancient dominion, independent of all personal advantages, I may receive. I have for many years supplied Harvard College with their Classical Books, as well as many other Universities; & have published most of the late French course of Mathematics, translated by the professor at Cambridge; also . . . Hedge's Logic, Enfield's Philosophy, Gorham's Chemistry, . . . &c &c. . . . In a recent tour through Europe, I have purchased a large stock of English, French, & German Literature, ancient & modern; & have established such a correspondence, as will enable me to procure a regular supply of the best works, either for individuals & corporate bodies. The advance, which I have received in importations of this description has been 10 pr ct upon the cost & charges, . . .

I herewith send you a Catalogue of a small part of my recent importations, & whether you should select from this, or give orders for the importation of others, you may depend upon the prompt & faithful execution of such orders, & upon the lowest terms.

From more than 20 years experience, as a Bookseller, & from my highly respectable correspondence in Europe, I presume it will not be considered as vanity to state that I shall be enabled to give satisfaction to your Excellency, & to such others, as may see fit to favor me with their commands.

This letter, signed with the "veneration & respects" of William Hilliard, marked the beginning of a relationship, a correspondence, and an undertaking that would clearly testify to the part played by a printer-bookseller in advancing the learning and cultivation of his times.

On April 8, 1825, an historic agreement was drawn up between Thomas Jefferson, Rector of the University of Virginia, and William Hilliard of Boston:

The said University having occasion for the purchase of a large collection of Books, to the amount, as is expected of fifteen thousand dollars, be it more or less, to constitute a library for the purposes of the Institution; & it being believed, that by picking them in the different book markets of Europe; as well as America, they may be obtained in better forms, & on cheaper terms, the said Rector, duly authorized by the visitors of said University, does hereby appoint and constitute the said William Hilliard, Agent for the said University, to procure the said books, and attend to their care, transportation and delivery, at the said University.

A catalogue of the books, specifying their titles, and, where deemed important, their particular editions, is to be delivered to the said William Hilliard; but, as it may happen, in some cases, that no particular edition may be specified, or an older & inferior, when not known, that there is a newer and better one to be had; it is confided to the discretion and judgment of the said agent to procure of preference, the newer & better one; & he is in all cases, to use every exertion to make the purchases at the lowest cash prices.

The purchase of the said Books, package, transportation, insurance, port & contingent charges, are to be at the expence & risk of the University; & a commission of five pr. Cent on the purchase and all the said charges and expences is to be allowed to the said Agent, in full compensation for his personal labour, trouble and expences in the performance of his Agency.

Where books are purchased unbound, they are to be bound where it can best be done, & at eligible prices, in good solid half binding, with back & corners in calf, & properly lettered.

Due diligence and dispatch is to be used by the said Agent in the execution of this Agency; & after he shall have received the catalogue before mentioned, & the money, as next to be stipulated, there is to be no unnecessary tardiness or delay in any part of his transactions.

A sum not exceeding fifteen thousand dollars, as wanted by the said Agent, is to be deposited, on behalf of the University, in a bank or banks, in Richmond, subject to his order, so soon as he shall have given good and satisfactory security to the Rector and Visitors of the said University for its due and faithful application to the purposes of this agreement.

In witness whereof, the said Thomas Jefferson, as Rector of the University, & the said William Hilliard, have hereto set their hands, this 8th day of April, 1825.

Jefferson's Catalogue was sent to the Boston firm in June, and was later supplemented with another catalogue of periodical publications that were to be supplied annually. The Catalogue, listing the books in forty-two chapters according to their classifications, covered an enormous range of works in law, theology, literature, philosophy, mathematics, history, travel, philology and language, botany and medicine. It represented a wide variety of authors, from Grotius to Pascal, from Rousseau to Mather, and included such titles as Barlow's *Columbiad,* Butler's *Hudibras,* the *Journals of Congress,* Gibbon's *Roman Empire,* and Stewart's *Philosophical Essays.* Many languages were represented, and the Catalogue presented to the agent considerable problems in assembling so varied and inclusive a library. "It contains," he remarked, "many, which I fear, cannot be obtained"; and again, "Many of the works upon American History will be procured with much difficulty, if at all. . . . From the great variety of works contained in your Catalogue it is altogether impossible to ascertain the cost: We have therefore ordered the whole, & must take the hasard of any excess of the funds."

Although in May of 1825 Hilliard had sent by Joseph Coolidge a bond for the fulfillment of the contract, with Samuel H. Walley as surety, he had at the same time expressed the hope that "it will be found practicable to extend the amount to ten or fifteen thousand dollars more, as my commission is considered as extremely low. I considered it so at the time; but other considerations of some advantage resulting from the supply of the students operated as an inducement to close the bargain[.] I trust that a reference to these circumstances, will induce the faculty to favor me with such farther orders, as they may need." Hilliard's suggestion was followed in part, an "additional purse of three thousand dollars" being granted to supplement the original fifteen thousand, and the money deposited, again at Hilliard's suggestion, in the Bank of the United States in Philadelphia. The purchase funds were deposited in the banking house of Mr. Williams of London, and subsequently orders were subjected to considerable delay because of the failure of that bank.

The "considerations of some advantage" for which Hilliard hoped were centered principally in the branch bookstore which his firm established in Charlottesville about a half mile from the University. As Hilliard put it, "We will readily comply with the suggestion, . . . of sending an agent to Charlottesville, by way of experiment. We think this will be the best method, as it will thereby give us an opportunity of judging of the expediency of forming a more permanent establishment. It will be important, however, in this connection, that no person should previously be introduced." Mr. M. W. D. Jones, who served as Hilliard's representative in Charlottesville, proved in time "well worthy the confidence reposed in him." Books sent from Boston that were not retained by the library could be transferred to Jones for disposal elsewhere, and Jefferson's belief that "in time you may draw here much of the demand of the state for respectable books, leaving only novels and poetry to the other bookshops generally," was not without foundation. Indeed, at one time he feared that the supply of Coke on Littleton might be exhausted "by the country lawyers buying it up before our law school opens," and that thus the University would "lose much of the benefit of it."

Hilliard himself planned to visit Charlottesville "as soon as the roads are better & the season opens," but his plans were for a time forestalled. He had also planned to go abroad to execute the order, and Jefferson had reported that the Boston bookseller would "proceed immediately to England, France and Germany on that business." This, however, had been agreed to only when Hilliard expected a commission of ten per cent. When the commission was reduced to five per cent, he did not feel that such an expedition would be justified. "It was the intention of Mr Hilliard to have gone to Europe to execute your order, at the commission first proposed 10 pr.Ct. This, with his own business, would have justified the enterprise." As Hilliard viewed the matter, "The commission which I finally accepted was too small to indemnify me; but it was agreed to in consideration of an establishment at Charlottesville in the sale of Books, and the future supplies of the Library."

Although Hilliard refrained from going abroad in person at this time, many of the books desired for the library were obtained from abroad. One of the most interesting aspects of this important phase of his career is indeed the method, revealed in his correspondence, by which a Boston bookseller was able to assemble so varied a collection of works between 1824 and 1826. Some of the books ordered by Jefferson were supplied from the firm's stock, and Hilliard could boast, "We can supply a considerable proportion of the order received, without sending to Europe." As he explained, "Such Books upon your Catalogue as can be procured upon what I conceive, from a comparison with foreign Catalogues, better terms, than in Europe, here, will be sent, as soon as those in boards can be bound." Some of the books procured in America or already in the firm's stock had been obtained at auction "very low, compared with the usual prices." Others were conveniently purchased at "a discount of 25 pr.Ct. . . . of our College Library."

Most of the items, however, Hilliard was forced to import from abroad. Even the works relating to America which he "had supposed would be found in this country," were not so found and had to be ordered from Europe. Many of the imported books, such as the *Philosophical Transactions,* were "purchased in Europe at Auction, & could not probably be again procured upon the same terms." From England Hilliard ordered the "Saxon Books," and when he was informed that they were "not to be had," he renewed the order. "The set of Year Books was purchased at Clark's, when . . . Mr. Hilliard was in London." The delay often attendant upon a foreign supply necessitated the countermanding of one order from abroad when a shipment ordered the previous year and including Hilliard duplicates was unexpectedly received at the University from Bohn of London. Not only from England, but from Germany and France, Hilliard ordered cases of books. The *Anthologia Graeca* he purchased in Leipzig. "Our correspondents in France & Germany," he reported, "have advised us, that the auctions, during the winter season, of several private Libraries, will give them the opportunity of purchasing many valuable Books, not otherwise to be had." Actually, some works "could not be procured, except as opportunities occurred of purchases from private libraries; & perhaps some of this description may embrace some of the most valuable & expensive works." By purchases at auction, by orders from the principal book marts of England, France, and Germany, by supplying works from his own shelves, Hilliard assembled the collection that was to form the basic library of the University of Virginia, shaping from the literary and cultural centers of the world the nucleus of yet another "republic of letters" in America.

The books so assembled were frequently shipped directly from New York to Jefferson's agent, Col. Bernard Peyton, at Richmond. Others were packed in boxes by the firm itself and shipped, some aboard the *Enterprise.* By July of 1825, five hundred twenty volumes had been sent. By January of 1826, invoices for cases 10 to 14 had been forwarded. In April, an additional five cases were ready, and

Jefferson, examining fifteen numbered boxes of books that had arrived at the University, remarked that "all appear in good order except one which being tumbled carelessly by a waggoner at Richm^d.
burst, without falling asunder or losing any thing as far as we can
judge." On May 8, 1826, the firm reported, "We shipped to the
care of Col. Peyton, 3 Cases Books from England, 1 from France, &
2 from Germany; & yesterday one other case from Germany. These,
with what are now on their way from Europe, and the addition of
some American works, which have not, as yet been found, will
make about the full amount of our commission." Hilliard had trusted
that "if the order is completed within one year from its reception it
will be all that is expected," an expectation that proved fairly accurate.

Some delay had been caused by the necessity of having books
bound. Other delays arose from a difference of opinion regarding
editions ordered and sent. Jefferson felt strongly that "it would be
lamentable . . . if, after recieving [sic] from our legislature so handsome a donation, we should waste it on obsolete editions." Hilliard
had asked for explicit details regarding editions: "You will have the
goodness to forward particular instructions . . . in regard to the editions, especially in the Law & Medical departments, as the American editions in these two branches are generally subject to much
greater alterations, if not improvements, than those of any other."
With good judgment he inquired, "Is it not important, that in the
Law Books, you have those that contain references to American
decisions." When Jefferson complained about the editions sent, the
firm countered with the explanation that "In some instances the
Books we have procured here vary from the precise editions ordered, from the circumstance, that we considered those sent, best &
cheapest." In regard to Voltaire, they had "consulted one of our
first literary characters . . . who recommended the one sent, as the
best edition." Anatomical plates were sent in sheets, since they were
"generally sold & preserved in this form in Port-folios. They are preferred in this way in our own College Library. You will find them
very splendid."

Such criticism as Hilliard received, he had invited. "We beg you to
be free in any criticisms, which may justly be made in regard to price,
style of binding, & c. as we wish to give perfect satisfaction in this
negotiation, as well as in all others." There was little criticism of

prices, the reasonableness of which was frequently pointed out by the Boston dealer. "I had a favorable opportunity to purchase a set of Wilson's Ornithology, Eighteen dollars below the subscription price. . . . Biglow's [sic] Botany & Barton's are at about half-price, the former being 25 dollars in boards & the latter thirty. The Anthologiae [sic] Graeca, I . . . have fixt . . . at cost." Although Albertus Magnus and Fleury's *Ecclesiastical History* were not in the Cata-logue, the former would be available at $2 a volume and the latter at $1 a volume. The major dissatisfaction was found in the firm's failure to supply a sufficient number of classbooks in the branch bookstore. Time and time again Jefferson commented upon this deficiency. "The want of books for the schools and most of all of the proper Spanish books in your store here is much complained of by the Students and Professors." "The Professors complain that while your bookstore is furnished with books and editions they mean not to use, those they have desired are not sent." When the Visitors pointed out the "very serious obstacles to the purposes of our in-stitution from the want of the particular books and editions of them which our Professors wish to use in their classes and to recommend to their pupils," the firm explained away the criticism: "We feel mor-tified, at the course, which the faculty of College have felt themselves obliged to adopt, in relation to a supply of class books and believe, at the same time, that upon a proper representation of the facts, in the case, not so much blame would attach itself to us, on account of the deficiency. Most of the Books, ordered, in the first instance, were of such a kind, as are not generally used in other Colleges; and con-sidering the uncertainty of the number to be called for by your in-stitution, it would have been imprudent in us, to order them from Europe in any considerable quantities. As soon as we found, at the commencement of the second term, the prodigious increase of the pupils, and received a particular designation of the Books wanted, we sent our orders out for them, by the hundred, and may soon ex-pect a supply of those, which have not already been sent in quantities. We are confident, that no house in the United States can furnish Books at a lower rate, or with greater facility than ourselves; and our future operations, we hope, will have a tendency to convince the faculty, that the particular circumstances, and embarrassments, un-der which we have hitherto laboured in the supply, will operate, in some small degree, as an apology for what may now appear to be negligence. We will however, endeavor, to atone for the past, by doing better for the future."

Despite the criticisms and complaints, Hilliard and his Company did assemble the library, completing an historic commission and indicating that a bookseller may be the instrument whereby intellectual boundaries are broadened and enlarged. In July, 1826, the cases of books were opened in Virginia. Death had deprived Thomas Jefferson of the opportunity to be present at this splendid occasion. William Hilliard was there, however, surveying the works he had assembled, the small "republic of letters" he had helped establish in the "ancient dominion."

It was an age of intellectual awakening in the East, and Cummings, Hilliard and Company were part of that age. As early as 1824 the firm had inserted in the Boston papers the announcement of their intention "to devote themselves more exclusively to the publication of such works as are connected with studies in the literary institutions of our country. . . . From the exertions they have heretofore made and from such as they will in future make, to raise the standard of the American Press, they confidently anticipate continued patronage."

As the patronage continued, the pattern of the firm gradually changed. Timothy Harrington Carter, besides having planted the legal seed in the soil of the business, had also established a type and stereotype foundry in Boston, which would one day be rather closely associated with the firm's productions. Since the concern was expanding so rapidly, Carter had advertised for a clerk and engaged a young man from Maine who had been trained in a Boston shipping house. Charles C. Little, who married Hilliard's daughter, proved himself of enormous service in supervising the legal publications of the company. Energetic, sagacious, upright, and prudent, Mr. Little was, as Mr. Hilliard had doubtless perceived, a man to watch.

One by one, Hilliard's associates made their entrances into the firm. Not long after the shipping clerk had appeared, the Swedenborgian made his bow. John Hubbard Wilkins hailed from a ministerial family and after his graduation from Harvard had spent a year as a preceptor in the Bristol Academy in Taunton. Unable to resist the lure of the church, he had studied at the Theological School in Cambridge, devoting his attention principally to the works of Swedenborg. A member of the Boston Society of the New Jeru-

salem, he had attracted the attention of Mr. Carter, who, with his
brother Richard, displayed a similar interest in the New Church
dispensation.

Wilkins offered more specific assets when Carter engaged him as
a nominal partner in charge of a special department of the firm.
Like Jacob Cummings he was the author of a textbook, *Elements
of Astronomy,* published by Cummings and Hilliard in 1822. Like
Hilliard he enjoyed suitable Harvard connections, for he married
the sister of Professor Bond of the Cambridge Observatory. In business he displayed talent, industry, and stern integrity, though it must
be admitted that the catalogue issued under his direction would not
meet the demands of present-day bibliographers. After a business trip to London, he listed the works he had purchased minus
prices and in most cases minus dates and sizes for the rather odd
reason that the books had not yet arrived in Boston. Between the
success of his own astronomical textbook and his ardor for the New
Church, he seems to have satisfied Carter none the less, and for
several years he continued to lend a Swedenborgian tone to the
Boston Bookstore.

One more member was to be introduced before Carter left the
firm—Harrison Gray, a man of charitable inclinations and temperance convictions, who had plied his trade as a bookbinder on Spring
Lane and later as a bookseller on Washington Street. Having admitted him, like Wilkins, as a nominal partner in charge of a special
department, Timothy Harrington Carter was ready to leave a business now yielding $25,000 in annual profits, and turn his direction
to fresh fields among the expanding frontiers of the day. Those
fields eventually led him to the Old Corner Bookstore which the
Carter brothers established in 1829 under the firm name of Carter &
Hendee, and thus sprang forth a flourishing scion from the roots of
Hilliard's establishment.

Both Cummings and the "and Company" had left Cummings,
Hilliard and Company. The time had come for a change in the pat-
tern and the formation of a new firm name. In 1827, reorganized as
Hilliard, Gray and Company, Messrs. Hilliard, Gray, Little, and Wil-
kins continued to devote themselves to raising the standard of
American taste. Their address had been changed to 134 Washington
Street, and there, opposite the newly founded firm of Carter &
Hendee, they published works that reflected the interests of the

partners and carried on the established traditions of the old concern.

Dominated by Little and Hilliard, the company expanded its legal publications, carrying "an extensive stock of the most valuable Law Books." The student of the bar might purchase at 134 Washington Street Coke's *Reports* or Roper *On Wills,* Perkins *On Conveyancing* or Finch's *Precedents in Chancery,* while any volume of the Massachusetts or Pickering *Reports* might be supplied to complete sets.

Continuing the tradition established by Cummings, Wilkins displayed a keen interest in the circulation not only of his own textbook, but of all the miscellaneous schoolbooks published or imported by Hilliard, Gray. Colburn's *Arithmetic,* Gould's *Grammar,* Professor Farrar's *Algebra,* Pietro Bachi's *Italian Grammar* were offered with liberal discounts to school committees and found their way to Harvard or the Boston Latin School. Gardner's twelve-inch globes at $26 a pair were sold along with the texts, carrying an endorsement by Professor Farrar.

Hilliard continued his Harvard connections in the reorganized firm, publishing the works of any literary don in Cambridge, from Professor Felton's edition of the *Iliad* to Thomas Nuttall's *Manual of Ornithology,* from Judge Story's *Commentaries* to Josiah Quincy's *Memoir* of his father. Harvard found in Hilliard, Gray the same publishing outlet it had found in Cummings, Hilliard.

Henry Wadsworth Longfellow had not yet succeeded Ticknor at Harvard when his *Outre-Mer No. I* was published by Hilliard, Gray and Company in 1833. The manner in which that work was issued casts light not only upon the firm's policies, but upon the author's interest in publishing. *Outre-Mer No. I* had apparently been printed completely, except for the title-page, at Joseph Griffin's press in Maine, before a publisher was found. The offer made by Hilliard, Gray and Company was better than Longfellow had expected, though he declined it because of his obligation in respect to future numbers of the work. Instead, he requested the firm to act as agent for the work, and proceeded to enlarge upon his demands. With the retail price fixed by the author at 62½ cents per number, he allowed the publishers a discount of 35 per cent. Five hundred copies had already been printed, of which 425 were to be sent to Hilliard, Gray, 25 of them for gratuitous distribution. Moreover, Longfellow wished the copyright taken out in the firm's name as he did not wish to appear as the author of the work. Finally, because he had given preference to Hilliard, Gray over Allen and Ticknor, he requested that the arrangement be kept secret. So it was that the pamphlet in marbled covers, printed in a large type like the numbers of the *Sketch Book,* made its bow to the public. On July 16, 1833, Longfellow wrote to George W. Greene a commentary that has become familiar as far as author-publisher relations are concerned: "I do maintain, that the publishers of our country are as niggardly a set as ever snapped fingers at a poor devil author. If the whole edition of Outre Mer No. I sells I shall make fifty dollars!"

The work of another Harvard professor led to one of the most interesting enterprises of the firm. Jared Sparks, having undertaken the editorship of a series of works in American Biography, was allowed by Hilliard, Gray 70 cents a page for every page of his own composition and 30 cents for every page written under his editorial supervision. Two thousand copies of each biography were to be published. Though the terms changed from time to time, it was more or less under such a contract that the ten volumes of the first series of American Biographies were produced, a series that brought to the American public the *Lives* of John Ledyard, Jonathan Edwards, Cotton Mather, John Eliot, "a whole Pantheon of American heroes." The Library of American Biography established Sparks as the American Plutarch and was proof positive of Hilliard, Gray's endeavor to raise the standard of American literature, and with it the intellectual life of the public.

Still another important series is associated with the firm—Specimens of Foreign Standard Literature, edited by George Ripley before he wandered off to Brook Farm. Tempering their Americanism with the motto, "As wine and oil are imported to us from abroad, so must ripe understanding . . . be imported into our minds from foreign writings," Hilliard, Gray sponsored the publication of translations from Continental literature by Ripley, William H. Channing, Professor Felton, Margaret Fuller, James Freeman Clarke, and others whose efforts introduced the New England Transcendentalists to the original documents of their philosophy.

Many volumes in this series, as well as many of the texts that appeared under the Hilliard, Gray imprint, were now being stereotyped at that Boston Type and Stereotype Foundry with which T. H. Carter had been associated. Indeed, though Carter had sold the foundry, the firm's connections with it had solidified as the years passed, for at one time Charles C. Little became its President, and orders might be left at the Boston Bookstore for work to be produced at the foundry. This particular offshoot of Hilliard, Gray helped the firm to increase its circulation and to stereotype one after another of its editions.

As a medium for business expansion, the firm circulated the *Literary Advertiser,* a sheet containing notices of the company's "valuable *Copy-right Books."* Since the publishers were not "interested in any periodical publication" in which they could have their works suitably publicized, they availed themselves of this device. Issued semi-annually in July and January, the *Advertiser* was sent "free of expense to all persons interested in education." Glancing at this rather formal "browser," the pedagogue could find a variety of historical or mathematical, botanical or geographical works at reasonable prices, and he, along with all persons into whose hands the *Advertiser* might come, was requested to extend its circulation.

At the Boston Bookstore or at the Cambridge branch might be met such celebrities as Jacob Bigelow or R. H. Dana, Ralph Waldo Emerson or Edward Everett, Amos Bronson Alcott, Daniel Webster, and George Ripley, searching out the latest tomes in the various branches of learning or turning from the folios and quartos to consider the quality of the paper and quills, the wafers and wax that could be purchased at the bookstore and used for the writing of manuscripts that would develop into other learned tomes under the now eminent imprint. Among their patrons the firm counted Peter Force, supplying him with books that doubtless found their way eventually to the Library of Congress.

The Cambridge branch of Hilliard, Gray had kept pace with the Boston Bookstore. Several years before, Professor Levi Hedge had recommended to William Hilliard a young man then serving him as a domestic. James Brown, he assured the publisher, had taken readily to the instruction he had given him in Latin and mathematics, and would be a creditable assistant in the Cambridge Bookstore. And so it was that James Brown began his noted publishing career by opening and shutting William Hilliard's door, running errands, pressing the sheets that emerged from the printing office, and selling books at retail. With his vigorous tread and erect bearing he electrified the

Cambridge Bookstore, and his own insatiable love of knowledge
was probably enjoyed by the bigwigs of Harvard as much as his
affable manners. Brown's admirable literary tastes and excellent
judgment appealed to his employer, who gradually gave him a larger
share in the management of the business until he was admitted as a
co-partner in the Cambridge branch. Finally, Brown formed a new
connection with the Boston firm of Hilliard, Gray, where he delighted in a friendship with Charles C. Little, a friendship that was
one day to bear significant results.

The nature of Hilliard's firm was changing now, not only by the
addition, but by the departure of its members. John Wilkins was
ready to abandon publishing to establish himself as a paper dealer,
a pursuit in which he was later joined by Richard Carter, and amass
more funds to be contributed to the Boston Society of the New
Jerusalem. In his place, Charles Brown was admitted as a member,
and the firm finally assumed a definite shape.

Meanwhile, however, many interesting collateral connections had
been established, like shoots from the publishing family tree. Hilliard and Brown, advertising themselves as booksellers to Harvard
University, were selling at Cambridge, at wholesale prices, Abiel
Holmes's *Annals of America* and Nuttall's *Ornithology,* and publishing, like the father firm, the works of the Harvard professors.
Hilliard and Brown's *Catalogue of Books, with the Prices Annexed at
which They Are Furnished to the Students of Harvard College* offered works in modern and ancient languages, mathematics, and
philosophy to the "Gentlemen of the University," along with a fair
price for any books in the college course that students might wish to
sell. Supplying, in addition, new publications and stationery, the firm
expressed the hope that it would "continue to . . . receive that patronage" so liberally extended to it. Still another subsidiary business was
that set up by James Brown and Lemuel Shattuck, who was to become famous later on as the founder of the American Statistical
Association. Precise, slightly pompous, Shattuck shared with Brown
his business acumen, selling to the County of Middlesex or the Concord Latin School, the Cambridge Book Club or Harvard College,
texts for the advancement of learning.

Although Brown, Shattuck sold out within a short time to James
Munroe and George Nichols, Hilliard had continued his old University Press at Cambridge with Eliab W. Metcalf and Charles Folsom.

Folsom, who had served as librarian of Harvard Library, was engaged by Hilliard and Metcalf to correct proofs of their classical works, and he devoted his time to examining, correcting and editing manuscripts and proofs. Known as the "Harvard Aldus," he superintended the printing of works in Hebrew, Greek, Latin, French, Italian, German, and Spanish, and thus helped to foster the growth of classicism during Harvard's Augustan Age. Hilliard and Metcalf had printed at the University Press of Cambridge many of the works published under the Cummings, Hilliard imprint, and for a time there seems to have been room in Cambridge for all these subsidiary firms to flourish. While Metcalf printed the town's circulars, Hilliard and Brown issued its "Stationery for Selectmen" and Brown, Shattuck its tax books. Hilliard, Gray had a whole network of associations at Cambridge, serving town and college, printing the works that illumined the past and heightened the culture of the present.

No living thing stands still or remains constantly at a peak: time and changing interests alter the pattern. In 1836, the enterprising founder of the firm, William Hilliard, died, and in 1837, a decisive year in the history of publishing, the pattern of Hilliard, Gray was metamorphosed even more completely by the withdrawal of James Brown, following the departure of Charles C. Little, who together formed their own partnership. Taking the old stand of Hilliard, Gray, at the changed address 112 Washington Street, Little and Brown took over also their law, foreign, and miscellaneous stock, along with several uncompleted publishing projects including Sparks's Library of American Biography. A new shoot had burgeoned forth that was to develop into a century plant.

Not much was left for Hilliard, Gray. Its two least colorful members remained, Harrison Gray and Charles Brown. At addresses changed first from the College Buildings at 112 Washington Street, which they had vacated for Little and Brown, to 10 Water and finally 107 Washington, they were actually back where the founders had started in 1812, back to the publishing of schoolbooks. They announced after 1837 that they were "extensively engaged in the publication of School and Classical Books." The subsidiary connections had been broken. Having planted the seeds of Little, Brown and the Old Corner, the firm was ready to retire, giving way to the offshoots that were to overgrow it. In 1843, after the departure of

Charles Brown, Harrison Gray joined the bookselling business of T. H. Webb and Company. Little and Brown had depleted Hilliard, Gray of much of its stock, and James Munroe, at the old address of 134 Washington Street, took much of what was left, including Ripley's Specimens of Foreign Literature.

A street in Cambridge was eventually named after William Hilliard, and that may be considered by some sufficient claim to fame. Yet the summary of his achievements is imposing. To no small extent it was through the efforts of Hilliard and his firm that the library of the University of Virginia was assembled and that Harvard flourished during its Augustan Age. Out of his firm emerged the Old Corner, the Boston Type and Stereotype Foundry, Little, Brown, which in their turn would continue the work of intellectual growth. In the hands of William Hilliard, printer, publisher, and bookseller, a torch had brightly burned, illuminating the corridors of the mind.

III. THE PERSISTENCE OF
NEW ENGLAND TRANSCENDENTALISM

James P. Walker & Horace B. Fuller

TRANSCENDENTAL PUBLISHERS

IN THE East, by the time of the mid-century, frontiers in space had been conquered, and revolutionary ideas had challenged the mind. In New England particularly a concept had arisen which eventually released the liberated conscience of man to do its work in the world. Labeled Transcendentalism, it had reacted against orthodoxy, upholding the Unitarian belief that God was immanent in man, and, supported by a faith that in this world all things were possible, it had clothed itself in a humanitarianism that led to militant accomplishment. This renaissance, this "adventure in liberalism," this "flowering" asserted "the inalienable worth of man" for several decades, during which New England's intellectuals arose from their studies to enter the lists on behalf of all the causes of the time, from the rights of slaves and freedmen to the rights of women and children.

In this crusade the publishers played their part, even those minor publishers who eventually failed in business. Indeed, by reason of a smaller and more specialized output, the minor publisher often cast a keener light upon the peculiar interests of his age than the larger publisher whose comprehensive lists reflected everything in general and therefore nothing in particular. And the publisher who failed in business represented, perhaps better than the publisher who succeeded, a time when all causes, including those that were eventually lost, flourished bravely in a crusading New England.

Both James P. Walker and Horace B. Fuller, Boston publishers whose careers paralleled each other and for a time coincided, failed in business. Yet the imprints of both men illumine the period of plain living and high thinking in which they lived. For that reason, having enjoyed a kind of success in failure, they demonstrated the persistent idealism of New England's renaissance.

On a winter day before the turn of the century, Horace B. Fuller died by his own hand in a Boston boardinghouse. A man in his early sixties, he had for the last fifteen or twenty years led a precarious existence, "earning a scant living by peddling books." The boardinghouse was located at 29 Pinckney Street. The date was January 12, 1899.

Little was known at the time and little is known today of his private life, but Horace B. Fuller had in his prime made a notable contribution to Boston's publishing history. Although even in his heyday he could not vie with the larger houses of Roberts Brothers or Lee and Shepard, his imprints reflected both the tastes of New England children and the interests of the later Transcendentalists. His chequered career illumines the story of other Boston publishing houses, too. Though no monument of any kind has been erected above his grave at Mount Auburn Cemetery, he is entitled to a niche among the lesser Boston publishers whose limited output highlights the affirmations of their age.

On that street of publishers, Boston's Washington Street, where Little, Brown, and Gould and Lincoln, and Crosby, Nichols plied a vigorous trade, the firm of Hickling, Swan and Brown occupied number 131 on the westerly side of the street, over the Old Corner Bookstore, and just below the corner of School Street. The firm was one of the oldest in the city, having been founded in 1792 by John West. Reorganized by W. H. Jenks as Jenks, Hickling and Swan, it had succeeded to the present owners by the year 1856, when a twenty-year-old gentleman named Horace B. Fuller embarked upon his clerkship there. For seven years he continued his "apprenticeship," daily entering number 131, opposite the firm of James Munroe and close to Ticknor and Fields. During those years, Hickling, Swan and Brown sustained many changes in style, their signboard appearing as Hickling, Swan and Brewer; Swan, Brewer and Tileston; and finally Brewer and Tileston. The name Fuller was conspicuous by its absence. Horace B. Fuller never attained a partnership, though he did profit from his experience with the company. Famed on two counts—as publisher of Worcester's Dictionaries and as the oldest and most extensive schoolbook publishers in New England—the house over the Old Corner had an enviable reputation, and young

Mr. Fuller must have learned much, during his association with the firm, of the type of book that would appeal to a juvenile reader in Boston after the mid-century. While he never was to use his experience with Worcester's Dictionaries after he set up for himself, nor to re-enter the textbook field, nevertheless his knowledge of youthful literary appetites would serve him well in the future.

In 1864, William D. Swan, who had conscientiously replied to the attack of the Messrs. Merriam upon the character and Dictionaries of Dr. Worcester, died. If Fuller had waited a little longer, he might perhaps have become a partner in the firm, and his career would have been quite different. Instead, in 1864 he joined a younger firm on the same street and began the association that was to influence his publishing career for nearly a decade.

Years before, when Fuller was still clerking at 131 Washington Street, James P. Walker, a slender, delicate gentleman in his late twenties, who had already had a varied though unsuccessful career in the book business, talked with a Boston friend at tea and hatched a plan for a publishing house that would be connected with the American Unitarian Association, which, as early as 1854, had embarked upon a publishing program of its own. On December 23, 1858, Walker wrote the following letter, outlining his project:

What is wanted is an *Unitarian Association Bookstore,* where not only such books as the Association publish may be found, but all Unitarian books, and these especially and primarily. Then a miscellaneous book and stationery business may, and should, be added thereto. . . . Let the present copyrights, stereotypes, and printed stock be turned over to an agent, and a sum of say $3,000 for working capital, and, after a year, the store would take care of itself; *i.e.,* pay the agent, furnish rooms for the meetings of the clergy, print and circulate Unitarian books at a low rate, besides being a depot and headquarters for the denomination, and an actual power for the promulgation of liberal Christianity.

On May 2, 1859, the plan was realized, James P. Walker and Daniel W. Wise organizing the firm of Walker, Wise and Company at 21 Bromfield Street in the rooms of the American Unitarian Association. Unitarianism was a far cry from a narrow denominational creed. A spur to Transcendentalism in New England, it had become the catch-all for a variety of liberal and humanitarian beliefs. And so, though Walker, Wise may have set up business as handmaids to

Unitarianism, they would progress as liberal Christianity progressed, becoming in their own right publishers of tracts on anti-slavery, transcendental reflections, the advancement of women, and especially of works designed to open the eyes and ears of the young. It was to this firm that Horace B. Fuller, weary perhaps of dictionaries and textbooks, turned in 1864.

Walker, Wise had set up their stand at 245 Washington Street, sandwiched between a trimmings store and a "hair jeweller" and opposite the drygoods establishment of Jordan, Marsh. Henry May Bond, a relative of Louisa May Alcott, after serving as salesman for the firm, had been admitted to partnership. By 1863, Bond had joined the Cadets and was off to the War. There was an opening at Walker, Wise which Horace B. Fuller filled in good time. When, at the age of twenty-eight, he entered their employ, Fuller found, in the same building with the publishers, the American Unitarian Association, *The Christian Examiner,* and the Sunday School Society. The Walker, Wise imprints naturally reflected, though they were not limited by, this close association.

It pleased James P. Walker to present under his imprint a new volume by so liberal a Unitarian as James Freeman Clarke, or a collection of *Stories of the Patriarchs* by Octavius B. Frothingham. Frederic Henry Hedge's *Reason in Religion,* Theodore Parker's *Prayers,* and Channing's *Works* represented the Unitarian credo, but went beyond it, too, reflecting the larger philosophy of the day, which flourished under the name of Transcendentalism. Walker, as the new employee soon discovered, was a great admirer of Emerson, whom he read along with his Thomas à Kempis and Fénelon. Perhaps, in the weighty abstractions of transcendental thought, he found solace for a career that had been—like Bronson Alcott's—one of success in failure.

It was a career that Horace Fuller's would one day parallel. Walker, born in Portsmouth, New Hampshire, in 1829, had earned his first money by driving cows to pasture. At the age of twelve he had left school and served an apprenticeship in a bookstore, opening the premises early in the morning, fetching keys and account books, making and selling ink. Four years later he had left Portsmouth to seek his fortune in Boston. After a term with Little, Brown, he had opened a store in Lowell, but trade "fluctuated," and, closing out the Lowell store, he had gone on to Albany to assist the law-bookseller, W. C. Little. The Albany enterprise proved a "disappointment." It was followed by another "disappointment" in Mansfield, Ohio, and by yet another period of employment with Leavitt and Allen of New York, whose retail department Walker had supervised. Certainly, though his experience had been unsuccessful, it had been varied, and Horace Fuller heard with interest the story of Walker's wanderings as his slender, delicate-looking employer, with a mass of chestnut hair and grayish hazel eyes, told in a serious, self-conscious manner, marked with weariness and lassitude, the tale of so many failures. He seemed at last to have wrested triumph from defeat, for, by 1864, Walker, Wise and Company had developed from an agency for Sunday school books into a firm whose imprints were as varied as they were significant.

Having arranged with the American Unitarian Association to assume the publishing department of their business, Walker, Wise offered a Theological Library of "stereotyped" works in "a neat and attractive style," including James Martineau's *Studies of Christianity,* Andrews Norton's *Statement* against the Trinitarians, John Wilson's confirmation of *Unitarian Principles,* along with treatises on athanasia and regeneration. In addition, they kept a full stock of Unitarian books, which they supplied by mail order, and, having bought or leased the plates of the majority of denominational books in print, they could present in their catalogue the largest selection of Unitarian literature ever grouped under one imprint. The "eminent Unitarian divines" who visited the Association in the rear of 245 Washington Street, would find, in the front part of the building, their own works for sale. Clarke and Hedge and Alger, browsing through the stock, would note not only the Sunday school manuals and hymn books and liturgies, but works by Dr. Orville Dewey and Dr. Furness, Ephraim Peabody and Cyrus Bartol, at prices agreeably ranging from 16¢ to $4.

They could note other works as well, for while Walker, Wise served the American Unitarian Association on the one hand, they served all of progressive New England on the other.

After his stay in the West, James P. Walker had returned to Boston more and more alive to the importance of providing women with the means for earning their own support and of advancing their general welfare. His deep sympathy with the cause of women's rights was evinced by his publication of such works as Mrs. Caroline H.

Dall's *Woman's Rights under the Law,* Dr. Zakrzewska's *Practical Illustration of Woman's Right to Labor,* and Virginia Penny's *Employments of Women.* Boston's "strong-minded" women could find in the rooms of Walker, Wise and Company almost as much food for thought as the "eminent Unitarian divines."

By the year of Fuller's entry into the firm, the Civil War had given the partners an equally glorious and timely cause to champion, and Walker, Wise entered the lists on the side of abolition, sponsoring such works as Hosmer's *Color Guard,* Hepworth's *The Whip, Hoe, and Sword* (on paid plantation labor), and a *Life-Sketch* of Chaplain Fuller, brother of the illustrious Margaret. All three authors were clergymen, but, like their publishers, they had developed beyond the confines of denominationalism to an interest in the larger aspects of world history and struggle. Styled as the Popular War Series, the volumes sold at $1.50 each, and formed "a three-sided presentation of the new experience which the Rebellion has afforded." To their Civil War imprints, the company added Cochin's well-known works on *The Results of Slavery* and *The Results of Emancipation,* along with Moncure Conway's *Rejected Stone; or, Insurrection vs. Resurrection in America.* To Wendell Phillips's *Speeches, Lectures, and Letters* the publisher prefaced an advertisement that reflected a far-sighted policy in respect to the Rebellion:

The only liberty the Publisher has taken with these materials has been to reinsert the expressions of approbation and disapprobation on the part of the audience, . . . and to add one or two notes from the newspapers of the day. This was done because they were deemed a part of the antislavery history of the times, and interesting, therefore, to every one who shall read this book,—not only now, but when, its temporary purpose having been accomplished by the triumph of the principles it advocates, it shall be studied as an American classic, and as a worthy memorial of one of the ablest and purest patriots of New England.

Children could be encouraged in their patriotism also, and Horace Fuller noted with interest the manner in which Walker and Wise appealed to the youth of New England in the books they published as well as in those they sold. The Walker, Wise imprints were a far cry from the Hickling, Swan and Brewer textbooks, but both taught him how to capture and retain the attention of Boston children. That the attention of children was worth capturing was an inherent part of a credo that upheld the dignity and the rights of childhood. *A Youth's History of the Rebellion* by William M. Thayer and the four-volume Union Series were timely juveniles, while, among the books sold by Walker, Wise for Sabbath school libraries, they tucked in the *Child's Anti-Slavery Book,* suggesting only, "Let it be read." In a charming catalogue, profusely illustrated with cuts that some Boston child probably filled in with water colors, the firm advertised its *Standard Books for the Young Published by Walker, Wise, & Co. Spectacles for Young Eyes,* with forty woodcuts, neatly bound in bright-colored cloth, made an immediate appeal at 60 cents a copy, while All The Children's Library offered at 50 cents such attractive titles as *Noisy Herbert* and *Bessie Grant's Treasure,* whose morals were made alluring by being presented in great primer type with copious illustrations. All The Children's Library, according to the publishers, was an "entirely new and original series of Juveniles," since, besides being printed on fine paper from clear and handsome type, attractively illustrated and neatly bound in muslin and put up in pasteboard boxes, the books were graded according to the age and reading ability of the children. The Silver Penny Series, at 25 cents a volume, met the "demand for good but cheap juveniles," with its *Story of the Princess Narina* and *Nobody's Child.* Then there was the Pioneer Boy Series, including *The Pioneer Boy, The Ferry Boy,* and *The Farmer Boy,* along with Home Story Books "of character and intelligent design, not mere patched up collections." The children of Boston must have been lured from play as easily as the clergymen from their pulpits to browse at 245 Washington Street, and Horace Fuller must have imbibed, during his year or two with Walker, Wise and Company, as much experience in making transcendental and humanitarian beliefs attractive as in appealing to the little humanitarians of the future. He was soon to put his knowledge to use in his own right.

Two significant undertakings of general interest, which were launched by Walker, Wise, but continued by their successors, engrossed the firm during Horace Fuller's association with it. Of Henri Martin's *History of France,* translated into English by Mary L. Booth with the help of George Bancroft and sold exclusively by subscription, seventeen "elegant octavo volumes" were planned, but only two were published. Seventy-five copies of a large paper edition were printed and seem to have had a ready sale. Because of what the publishers called its "most immediate interest," they began the set with *The Age of Louis XIV*. Walker's awareness of the value of "immediate interest" is indicated also by his second major enterprise, the launching of Harriet Martineau's *History of the Peace*.

Previous to undertaking the republication of the "History of the Peace," we wrote to Miss Martineau soliciting from her pen a Preface for this edition.

She responded with promptness, not only supplying the desired Preface, and making sundry corrections in the text of the work, but proposing to write, Expressly For This Edition, An Entire New Book, continuing the History of the Peace down to the Russian War in 1854. . . . This offer we gladly accepted. The present publication has, consequently, a value and completeness largely in advance of the English edition.

The reproduction of this work may be regarded as peculiarly opportune at the Crisis through which this Nation is now passing. Our people are studying anew . . . questions connected with an Extension of the Suffrage; the Emancipation of the Blacks; a Paper Currency; the Removal of Restrictions on Trade; the Increase of Taxation and of the National Debt.

The first two volumes of this set bear the imprint of Walker, Wise, and Company. By the time the third and fourth volumes were ready for the press, the imprint of the firm had undergone a metamorphosis.

In February, 1865, Daniel Wise left the company, and from that date to the time of its failure in the autumn of 1866, the style of the house was Walker, Fuller, and Company. Horace B. Fuller, at the age of twenty-nine, had at last come into his own with a full partnership. During the brief period of their association as Walker, Fuller, the publishers continued along the lines laid down by Walker, Wise, issuing from 245 Washington Street books that asserted "the inalienable worth of man." Not only Martin's *History of France* and Miss Martineau's *History of the Peace,* but many of the Civil War works that had appeared under the earlier imprint were published now by Walker, Fuller. Hosmer's *Color Guard,* Hepworth's *The Whip, Hoe, and Sword,* and Chaplain Fuller's *Life-Sketch* were grouped together as The Patriot's Library, and to them was added another volume by Hosmer, entitled *The Thinking Bayonet*. The volumes

by Cochin and Wendell Phillips were augmented by a history of
Massachusetts in the Rebellion, sold by subscription, along with
Lincoln's *Second Inaugural,* Hale's *Sermons of a War,* and other
works of immediate interest in the national crisis.

Walker, Fuller's insistence upon continuing Thayer's *Youth's
History of the Rebellion* among its juveniles incurred the wrath of
the *American Literary Gazette,* where it was asserted:

We trust this sort of books [sic] will now come to an end. War is bad
enough at the best, but to have it served up to us in a perverted partisan
story-telling and sensational style, and thrust in our faces in the nursery
and at the fireside, all for the good of small writers, speculating publishers, and insidious propagandists, is adding to it an additional and
more protracted terror.

When Walker, Fuller objected, the *American Literary Gazette* re-
treated a bit:

The publishers . . . are displeased with our observations, and they have
written to us a note in which they speak of us as being "unjust," and
construe our language as an "offensive allusion" to their firm. These
gentlemen wholly misunderstand both our object and what we expressly
said. We should extremely regret to be "unjust" or to make an "offensive
allusion" to a house of such recognized character and energy in the
trade, and deserving of such success as that of Walker, Fuller & Co. We
simply referred to a general class of recent juvenile literature . . . without . . . particularizing the work . . . or its publishers.

Despite such trials, the Walker, Fuller juveniles fared well. Miss
Lander's Spectacle Series, "detailing . . . life in some of the chief
cities of the world," had by 1866 reached a sale of "some 30,000
volumes." Nearly as many copies had been sold of the juvenile
biography of Lincoln, *The Pioneer Boy,* and 10,000 copies of Chief
Justice Chase's early life, *The Ferry Boy.*

In their larger interests, Walker, Fuller did not forget that they
had begun as Unitarian publishers. In this field, also, they continued
publishing the liberal works originally offered by Walker, Wise,
broadening a list that included *The Christian Examiner* and the
treatises of Hedge and Clarke by sponsoring Wasson's *Radical
Creed.*

For all their efforts, however, Walker and Fuller were not destined
for success. Early in 1866 the American Unitarian Association de-

cided to resume its own publishing, arranging that Walker, Fuller of Boston and James Miller of New York become the selling agents of the Association and attend to the retailing of its publications. By the same arrangement, *The Christian Examiner* was transferred to New York, and a great number of works were withdrawn from the Walker, Fuller list. For its own enterprise of denominational publishing, the American Unitarian Association collected $100,000, a sum of money that Walker, Fuller could have used to full advantage. As it was, the firm was left in the subordinate position of acting as selling agents where once they had been publishers. Without more solid support from the Association that had once taken them under its wing, they apparently could not continue. After a few months, Walker, Fuller failed, and the partners separated.

Walker analyzed his own part in the failure when he wrote: "I am not a trader, and never was. I hate bargaining, and lack about as many qualifications for success in business as I possess, unless I could be associated with some one who would complement my qualities." He obviously had not found such a "complement" in Horace B. Fuller. In addition to a personal lack of bargaining ability and the withdrawal of substantial support by the American Unitarian Association, other factors had been involved in the failure of Walker, Fuller, including "want of capital" adequate to meet unforeseen emergencies and the "general commercial stagnation" occasioned by the War. The enterprise had failed. Yet Walker's remarks, delivered long before in a lecture, still held:

Though fortune may frown upon our endeavors, and the position of the prosperous business-man be not our lot, if possessing the unfailing resource of an elevated taste, a cultivated intellect, and a well-stored mind, we shall never despair. We may not become successful merchants: we can become successful men.

In the longer historical view, they had both been successful publishers, despite their failure in business, for they had reflected and advanced the timely interests of an age that had taken up many great challenges, from anti-slavery to liberal Christianity, from the advancement of women to the enlightenment of children.

Walker moved, after the failure, to 26 Chauncy Street, where, as secretary of the Sunday School Society, he kept for sale samples of Sunday school equipment—scriptural mottoes, textbooks, and hymn cards—and also served as editor of the *Sunday-school Gazette*. On March 15, 1868, at the age of thirty-nine, he died—a man who, even in the eyes of his contemporaries, presented "a noble illustration of success in non-success."

While Walker had been sorting Sunday school mottoes in his pleasant room on Chauncy Street, Horace B. Fuller had become a publisher in his own right. At first continuing at 245 Washington Street, then moving to number 383, a few doors south of the Adams House, and finally establishing himself at 14 Bromfield Street, Horace B. Fuller, "successor to Walker, Fuller and Company," was on his own. For the next five or six years, between 1867 and 1873, he would serve both juvenile and later transcendental Boston well, proving that even a minor publisher may make a memorable mark in his trade and that failure and success are often two sides to a single coin.

Like Washington Street, Bromfield Street, a few doors away, was a publishers' row in the early 1870's, where Nichols and Hall, Virtue and Yorston plied their trade. At number 14, opposite the antiquarian dealer, S. G. Drake, and in the same building with the temperance publisher, Samuel W. Hodges, Horace B. Fuller set up his stand. Besides his experience with James P. Walker, he had inherited some of the Walker imprints, including a few theological items by Frothingham and a few juveniles by William M. Thayer and Dr. Harley. Fuller's theological interests were, however, less pronounced and less denominational than Walker's had been. In that field he concentrated upon publishing the works of Theodore Parker, which he printed from the old stereotype plates, but "on better paper and in better style than before." To the many volumes by the great Unitarian preacher that appeared under his imprint, Fuller added the writings of another eminent Bay Stater, the educator Horace Mann, proving by his presentation of the works of those two great figures that, in its broader ramifications, Transcendentalism in the church and in the school still flourished.

It was the children of Massachusetts who interested Horace B. Fuller primarily; it was their dignity that he upheld, their rights that he proclaimed, their pleasure that he fulfilled. It was for them that he issued in 1867 his Morning Glory Series, consisting of four volumes of juveniles by Auerbach, Miss Lander, Mrs. Follen, and Louisa May Alcott. It was for them that he published two stories by Mrs. Mary G. Darling, *Battles at Home* and *In the World,* and it was for them that he undertook his major juvenile enterprise— publishing *Merry's Museum.*

Merry's Museum, established in 1841 by "Peter Parley," was, in 1867, the oldest magazine for boys and girls. In October of 1867 Fuller announced that he had purchased the periodical and would issue it "in a superior style."

This number of the Museum goes to subscribers with a change of publisher. . . . Mr. Fuller, the present publisher, has the ability and advantages (in connection with a large bookstore and acquaintances) to make the Magazine better than it ever has been. . . . Several important changes are contemplated in the management of Merry's Museum. . . . The Museum is the oldest magazine for young people published in America; it will be our aim to make it the best.

It would sell for $1.50 a year or 15 cents a number. Club rates were offered. In November Fuller outlined his plans in greater detail. The *Museum* would be "clearly printed, on fine white paper, from new and handsome paper prepared expressly for our own use." The new volume would be "beautifully illustrated with original designs," and for its contributions the services of "some of the best and most popular writers for the young" had been engaged. One thousand canvassers were wanted to obtain subscriptions. The following month Fuller continued his advertising campaign by promising that with the January number, *Merry's Museum* would appear "ENLARGED, IMPROVED, & REJUVENATED," and that "Louisa M. Alcott, the brilliant author of 'Hospital Sketches,'—who has hardly an equal, and who has no superior as a writer for youth in the country," had been engaged as editor.

In January, 1868, with a new series number and a cover design executed by Miss E. B. Greene, *Merry's Museum* made its bow to the public under the new proprietorship. The issue included two stories by Miss Alcott, "Tilly's Christmas" and "Grandmother's Specs," as well as two poems by the editor, installments of the serials, "Little Pearl" and "The Loggers," adventures and articles adorned with Miss Greene's illustrations, and educational bits of information, acrostics, and rebuses under the titles of "Aunt Sue's Scrap-Bag" and "Aunt Sue's Puzzle Drawer." To this pleasant medley was added an editorial section called "Merry's Monthly Chat with His Friends," to which Miss Alcott, disguised as "Cousin Tribulation," contributed an episode that was later to appear in her *Little Women.* With premiums for those who secured new subscribers and advertisements of Turner's Tic Douloureux, or Universal Neuralgia Pill, the issue was complete.

For her services, the editor received $500 a year, along with the appreciation of a publisher who could declare that "A young-folks Magazine is nothing, if not lively; and we have in our editor, Louisa M. Alcott, one of the most charming and brilliant writers for young people that our country has hitherto produced." Besides fulfilling his aims of making the *Museum* "sprightly and entertaining; and, at the same time, to preserve in all its lessons a healthful moral tone," the publisher enjoyed the satisfaction of increasing his juvenile clientele and of using his periodical as an advertising medium for his own publications, especially those designed for the young. Special premiums for new subscribers frequently included old Walker, Wise imprints, and *Merry's Museum,* filled with "pleasant pictures and good stories," continued for several years to whet children's appetites for Alcott narratives and Aunt Sue's puzzles, educational serials, and animal tales.

In time, Miss Alcott came to feel that her industry was not adequately rewarded, writing to her uncle:

Merry is not what I wish it was, but little Fuller does his best on a small capital & hopes to improve. If you know of any one who wields a sprightly & sensible pen pray ask them to drop us a line now & then, for Fuller mildly suggests that I should write the whole magazine, which was not in the bargain.

Nor was it "in the bargain" for Fuller to publish, unbeknown to the author, a book by Miss Alcott which had appeared serially in the pages of his *Museum.* He did so, none the less, adding a curious and not altogether savory episode to his career as juvenile publisher.

In 1870, while the *Museum* still flourished, Horace B. Fuller lent his imprint to what he called the Dirigo Series, consisting of four anonymous volumes which had appeared serially in his magazine: *The Loggers; or, Six Months in the Forests of Maine; Will's Wonder Book* (actually by Louisa May Alcott); *Mink Curtiss; or, Life in the Backwoods* (erroneously supposed author, Emerson Bennett);

and *Famous Dogs* (by M. G. Sleeper). Issued in green cloth, with green and gilt lettering, and announced as encased in a "neat box," the Series was priced at $1 a volume and, with frontispieces and illustrations, the books are charming examples of nineteenth-century juveniles at their best. The Series, however, was unauthorized, and indicates the publishing tactics of a period when the rights of authors came far behind the rights of freedmen and the rights of women in the humanitarian hierarchy. Fuller's interest in women's rights seems to have faltered in this instance, and yet his inconsistency was less real than apparent. He exploited Louisa May Alcott not because she was a woman, but rather because she was an extremely popular author.

The last number of *Merry's Museum* was presented to the public in November, 1872, after which it was merged into *The Youth's Companion*. In the same month the Boston fire "exercised a very depressing effect on the book-business." Horace B. Fuller's days as a publisher were numbered. One of his last imprints, issued in 1873, was a work by Daudet, appropriately entitled *The New Don Quixote*.

The remaining years of Horace B. Fuller were to parallel the early years of his one-time partner, James P. Walker. By 1877 he was back where he had started, a clerk once more, working for the bookseller William B. Clarke. Two years later he served as salesman for Albert W. Lovering—a poor choice for a man on the downward path, since Lovering, the "gift-bookseller of Boston," had failed in 1876 and again in 1879. In order to dispose of a heavy stock of books, Lovering had devised the system of giving prizes with book purchases, a plan which necessitated the outlay of some $50,000. In January, 1875, he had $19,000 in the bank; in January, 1876, he had 62 cents, along with *Publishers' Weekly*'s endorsement of him as one of the "predestined bankrupts." The gift enterprise was born and buried in a marble-front store in Boston, and at number 336 Washington Street, where Horace B. Fuller acted as salesman, it was said that "pianos, gold watches, and other luxuries too numerous to mention" were daily given to the customers. It is no wonder that little remained either for the publisher or his salesman.

By 1883, Horace B. Fuller had dissociated himself from the publishing business and worked for a few years as superintendent of Jordan, Marsh. Then began those precarious years when he earned a "scant living by peddling books," until, on January 12, 1899, he turned on the gas in his boardinghouse at 29 Pinckney Street, and took his life.

James P. Walker and Horace B. Fuller illustrate the "success in non-success" that merits some memorial. Through their publications they championed the causes of transcendental New England. Their imprints, few by comparison with those of the great rival houses, mirror the New England renaissance that endorsed the perfectibility of man and worked for its fruition. Even their failure fits the pattern of an age that buoyantly embraced lost causes.

IV. THE BROTHERHOOD
OF THE ANTE-BELLUM SOUTH

John Russell

"LORD JOHN" OF CHARLESTON

BEFORE the Civil War, when New England was trumpeting abroad the rights of man and enlisting in militant crusades to champion those rights, the South was uttering wood-notes of its own in a milder tone and with results less practical but no less characteristic. The ideal of the North lay in the future—a goal toward which all mankind, with plain living and high thinking, could and must advance. The ideal of the ante-bellum South lay in the past—a roseate region toward which the flower of mankind might, with civilized living and cultivated thinking, make a leisurely retreat. The Southern ideal has been identified with that of "the Greek democracy," which "in its blend of romanticism and realism . . . fitted exactly the temper of the plantation mind." It was an ideal unhampered by the need for practical accomplishment, unfettered by economic necessities, undisturbed by rights and isms. It was an ideal of tranquillity, civilized and ivory-towered, an ideal of gentlemen generous and humane among themselves. If the concept of slavery intruded occasionally upon the ideal, then that "peculiar institution" was defended without bitterness and to the satisfaction of its defenders. For, long before secession, the South was intellectually independent, not in a bristling, hostile sense, but in an independence of Southern brotherhood. And, as that brotherhood turned to the past in quest of its ideal, it became, perforce, a literary brotherhood, a brotherhood of poets whose songs were inscribed upon a palimpsest, whose words were writ in water. For the ideal—urbane and polished, refined and cultivated—had little relationship with the crying world around it. The ideal was impossible, though it took a war to prove its impossibility. While the North rode forth into its vistas of the future, the gentlemen of the South took their pleasure on the landscaped playing field of the past. So, for a little while, pursuing its ideal, the brotherhood of Southern litterateurs created an oasis in history.

Since no literary brotherhood, however independent, could express itself effectively without a publisher, the Southern brotherhood sought and found one in Charleston, the intellectual capital of the South. Sharing the ideals and the way of life of the ante-bellum men of letters, the publisher became himself an impetus to the literary independence of the South until that impossible ideal and the brotherhood itself were annihilated by the war of all the brothers.

In Charleston, one autumn evening in the 1850's, a group of young men might have been seen walking along narrow King Street until they paused at number 251, a large store with handsome plate-glass windows and a name in prominent gilt letters above the main door. The young men had already earned enviable reputations in Southern society, and whatever careers they had embarked upon, they were all, in addition, of a literary turn. There was the handsome Basil Gildersleeve, who had received his doctor's degree from Göttingen and was about to enter upon a long and honorable life as professor of Greek at the University of Virginia; there was young Dr. John Dickson Bruns, soon to teach physiology at the New Orleans School of Medicine; there was the vigorous young lawyer, Samuel Lord; and there were others who, in the leisurely fashion of Charleston in the '50's, met at number 251 King Street, to talk perhaps of shooting and riding, of racing and the Cecilia Society, to talk surely of life and letters and the Southern culture they were themselves creating.

The gilt letters above the door should have spelled the name of the "Globe" or the "Cocoa Tree" or of some academic Arcady, but though the store at number 251 was in reality the mecca of culture in a city that was itself the center of the cultural South, it was, after all, only a bookstore, and the sign above the door spelled simply the name of the proprietor, John Russell.

As the young men entered, they were greeted by Russell, a brisk, active, self-confident man in his early forties, eager to show them a pocket Elzevier or black-letter work imported from abroad, hospitably beckoning them past the counters and heavily laden shelves to his sanctum in the rear of the store. There the young men would see their elders gathered on chairs and sofas about a large comfortable stove, and there they would find a salon that rivaled the famous breakfasts of Poinsett or the equally famous suppers of William Gilmore Simms. Simms himself was, by the divine right of poetry, king among those who flocked to Russell's bookstore, and his tall, vigorous form dominated the scene as he played Dr. Johnson to a group of ardent, versifying Boswells that included Paul Hamilton Hayne and Henry Timrod. In another corner one might see James Petigru, the social lion whose magnificent voice and dark eyes had helped make him the Nestor of the Charleston bar. The gray-headed, guileless planter, William J. Grayson, was ready to discourse pleasantly upon the South's "peculiar institution," while the beetle-browed Mitchell King buttonholed Russell to repeat in his Scottish brogue long passages from the Latin poets, and that "man of air and fire," James W. Miles, dilated upon philosophy. Among them all the host of number 251 moved, accepting a pinch of snuff from Father Lynch, discussing a new botanical work with Dr. Porcher, fetching a medical tome for Dr. Dickson. Among them all the spirit of poetry moved, a Pegasus whose wings carried them swiftly into the past.

Here, in the rear room of a Charleston bookstore, seated at a fire or standing up for rhetorical effectiveness, were gathered the brightest lights in the Southern constellations. Had John Russell achieved nothing else in his life beyond drawing them together, he would have merited a claim to fame. Actually, he did considerably more than that for his patrons, and hence for Southern letters.

Who was the man who attracted the illuminati of the South, whose bookshop was their favorite rendezvous in the leisurely ante-bellum days of Charleston, who displayed to them his latest shipment from abroad during the golden afternoons and glorious evenings of the fifties? John Russell has suffered the paradoxical fate of being remembered as a famous man about whom little else is known. The Southerner recalls his celebrated bookstore, the Northerner may associate him with *Russell's Magazine;* but with these points, memory fails. In reality, Southern literature owes an important debt to John Russell, for he not only provided the literati of his time with books, but supplied them with a means of self-expression by publishing their books. He was a bookseller and publisher whose influence was felt throughout the literary South at the time of its apogee. As such he deserves a more substantial memorial than he has received.

John Russell was born in Charleston in 1812, shortly before war with England was declared, and though he was not to die until 1871, another, more dreadful war was to mark the finis to his career. After the death of his father, his mother appears to have remarried, taking the name of Rachel Jones. Two sons born of that second marriage were to be associated with Russell in the book business, and a daughter of that second marriage was to become Russell's sole heir at his death. In other words, the hospitality and generosity that the bookseller extended to his patrons were also bestowed upon his half-brothers and half-sister. According to Paul Hamilton Hayne, Russell was "educated in the book-trade" and "had mastered, at a comparatively early age, its requisitions and technicalities." It was in the bookstore of John P. Beile, the predecessor of Samuel Hart of Charleston, that Russell learned the rudiments of the trade. Through the *Charleston Directory* his career may be followed as he rose "from grade to grade in the service." According to the *Directory* for 1835-36, when Russell was in his early twenties, he was located at 172 King Street as an accountant. At the same address appeared the military and fancy store of John S. Bird, where Russell doubtless became acquainted not only with a general assortment of spectacles but with Bird's fine French looking-glass plates and his engravings and paintings direct from Paris. His familiarity with art objects probably proved useful when he joined Jacob K. Sass to form the firm of Russell and Sass, auctioneers and commercial merchants, for it is under that heading that he is listed in the *Directory* of 1840 and 1841. When, at length, Russell acquired the necessary capital, he opened his own "literary emporium." Though he never left King Street, he did move at least three times, appearing in 1848 at number 256, moving later to number 251, and still later to number 285. He strayed farther, however, in his travels. As early as 1847 he was in Philadelphia on a business trip, two years later he traveled to New York bearing a letter of introduction from William Gilmore Simms to E. A. Duyckinck, and at least once he journeyed to Europe, for on the Channel packet he was mistaken for Lord John Russell, and the sobriquet, "Lord John," clung to him for the remainder of his life. In 1859 he seems to have planned an extended absence from the country, but perhaps the growing anti-slavery excitement dissuaded him from the project. The Civil War itself was not only to change his plans, but to have a most disastrous effect upon his business as well.

Before that time, however, Russell had developed business methods that were to provide him with a notable reputation. He was a man of bright, quick mind, in whom native shrewdness joined with a kind heart and generosity. The information he had acquired made him a clever and witty conversationalist, suited to be "Lord John" of the Charleston literati. Enterprising, intelligent, popular, he could preside easily over the illustrious group that met in the rear of his store. What is more, his knowledge of books made him one of the most successful booksellers of the South, until Augustus Flagg of Little, Brown could state that he sold more fine books in proportion to the population than almost any other, and Trübner of London declared him one of the most accomplished bibliopoles in the United States.

Perhaps more telling than any other token to his reputation is a letter written as early as February, 1846, by William Gilmore Simms, introducing Russell to the publishers Carey and Hart:

Let me bring to your knowledge my friend, Mr. John Russell, who is on his way to establish a personal and business intercourse with the publishers. He is about to establish for himself, having been for several years the chief clerk in the establishment of our friend Saml. Hart. Mr. R. is an old acquaintance & friend of mine though not an old man. He begins auspiciously & according to his deserts, which are worthy of the best friends hopes—with a cash Capital, and the countenance of many of our best men, literary & professional. Perhaps, no person in our State is more highly competent to, or more familiar with, the business than himself. Personally & considerably acquainted with books, he knows something about selling them & is highly popular in the bargain.

Three years later, in September, 1849, Russell carried another letter from Simms to Duyckinck, bringing the New Yorker "to a personal knowledge of my friend, Mr. John Russell, of this city, whom you perhaps already know as a bookseller of great worth & intelligence." Later in the same month, Simms, who had previously described Russell as "a worthy and intelligent person upon whom you can rely," wrote again to Duyckinck, characterizing his Charleston friend as "a very worthy Gent. and a first rate Bookseller." Simms wrote authoritatively, for Russell was not only his friend, but his bookseller and his publisher.

As a bookseller Russell had earned his reputation. His store was not merely a rendezvous for his literary patrons, but an unofficial post office as well. The poet Simms in writing to Northern bookmen wished to be addressed in care of Russell, and other facilities were also provided for customers. At a table in the back of the store the literati of Charleston were welcome to sit and examine new books, while careful young men were given the privilege of taking home a new book over-night to look it over and decide if they wished to keep it. But perhaps, in addition to such bookstore delights, the greatest advantage of trading with Russell arose from the wide range and variety of his stock. A single extant catalogue and his newspaper advertisements enable the latter-day scholar to return the lost books to the shelves, brush off the dust of a century, and walk again through the King Street emporium.

Basil Gildersleeve—and all the Southerners who yearned for the Arcadian past—probably found the most interesting section of "Lord John's" bookstore that devoted to the classics, and even within that category the range was great. Lemaire's *Collection of the Latin Classics,* consisting of 144 calf-bound volumes, might be theirs for $250, while Bodoni's edition of the *Iliad,* in three royal folio volumes, was offered for $50, and the first volume of Rawlinson's *History of Herodotus* sold for only $2.50.

Despite their absorption in the academic past, Russell's followers had their posts in the present, and to their professional needs the bookseller also catered. For young Dr. Bruns, or Dr. Porcher, or any other of the medicos who strolled through the King Street bookstore, there was a fine selection of medical works, from Carpenter on *The Microscope* to Rokitansky's *Manual of Pathological Anatomy,* while those of a turn for pure science might consider Hugh Miller's *Sketch Book of Popular Geology* cheap at $1.50, or Loomis's *Recent Progress of Astronomy* a most enlightening acquisition.

There was a happy hunting ground for Father Lynch and his colleagues in other denominations in Russell's excellent assortment of theological works, for the firm acted as agent for the Protestant Episcopal Church Book Society and the Evangelical Knowledge Society, carrying a full stock of all their publications. In addition, Russell received from London a wide variety of foreign theological works, from the *Liturgies of Queen Elizabeth* to Maimbourg's *History of Arianism.* Strickland's *History of the American Bible Society,* Baird's *Religion in America,* catechisms, psalms, hymns, and sermons gave Russell's theological section the air of a complete Bibliotheca Biblica for all patrons of a clerical turn. James W. Miles and those who, like him, indulged in metaphysical speculation would find more to their interest in the shelves devoted to philosophy, from which Blakey's *History of the Philosophy of the Mind* could be carried off for $9 or Sir William Hamilton's *Lectures on Metaphysics* for $3.

As grandson of the famous historian, young David Ramsay might have found much to interest him in Russell's historical selections, where the original subscriber's copy of Hume's *History of England* at $150 vied with Brougham's *Historical Sketches of Statesmen under George III* and Gurowski's *Russia As It Is*. For only $1 he might own a *Life of Peter the Great,* for $1.25 Gretton's *Vicissitudes of Italy Since the Congress of Vienna,* and for $2 White's *History of France.*

Young Ramsay did not know, when he visited Russell's, that he was destined to lose his life at Fort Wagner, but perhaps he was attracted none the less by the growing collection of works that reflected contemporary history, the military tomes which in the early '60's found their way to the bookstore—manuals for volunteers, instructions for field artillery, Mahan's *Treatise on Field Fortification,* books on rifle practice, outpost duties, and cavalry tactics.

Young scholars returned from Göttingen might have enjoyed "Lord John's" display of travel books in which they could browse, transported by Richard H. Dana to Cuba, by Kane to the Arctic, by others to the mysteries of Fiji.

Charles Fraser, the celebrated miniaturist, doubtless headed directly for the fine collection of art books that included a brilliantly illustrated four-volume *Galerie de Florence* for $125, and a select variety of other *Galleries,* from that of the *Pictures at Grosvenor House* to the finely engraved *Galerie de Dusseldorff.* Appleton's *Cyclopædia of Drawing* and Mrs. Ellet on *Women Artists in All Ages* probably pleased him also, giving him food for interesting talk of art with the proprietor, who as early as 1849 had taken in charge Mr. Fraser's own exquisite paintings. It was not without reason that the King Street dealer advertised his firm as importers of books, stationery, and works of art.

Of all the books, however, that were offered by Russell, probably the most popular were his literary works. Hayne and Simms and

Timrod, with all the Southern poets, must have found their keenest pleasure in turning the pages of Tennyson's latest verses or Duyckinck's *Cyclopædia of American Literature,* in browsing through Sir William Temple's *Works* or seeing proudly displayed on the shelves the tales and poems of William Gilmore Simms himself.

In selling books Russell believed in a varied stock. For the numismatics addict he could provide Humphreys's *Coin Collector's Manual;* for the children there was a charming array of juveniles among which *Granny's Wonderful Chair* vied with *Pussy's Road to Ruin.* For the Southern ladies who delighted in novels there was no dearth of stories by Charles Reade or "Marion Harland." For readers who wanted the latest in periodicals there was *Harper's* or *Blackwood's* or the *English Quarterly Review.*

Even in selling books, however, Russell could never forget that he himself was a Southerner, and that, in the wide range of works he offered, Southern books would always be given a place of distinction. W. J. Rivers's *Sketch of the History of South Carolina, The Old Plantation* by James Hungerford of Maryland, and *Gardening for the South* found their proud place, therefore, among John Russell's varied wares.

Selling Southern books was one way of encouraging Southern letters, but providing an organ for the expression of Southern thought was perhaps a more effective way. Out of the *petits soupers* at which Simms presided, and out of the enthusiastic meetings in the rear of Russell's bookstore, there emerged finally the suggestion for launching a magazine that would reflect Southern sentiment and defend Southern institutions. Paul Hamilton Hayne and W. B. Carlisle, the Charleston journalist, were ready to serve as editors, and Russell, approached with the idea, eagerly agreed to act as publisher, taking on the business management of the new scheme. On January 1, 1857 —the same year that saw the launching of *The Atlantic Monthly*— an announcement appeared in the *Charleston Daily Courier* regarding the new venture, which was to be dubbed *Russell's Magazine.*

We hope to make it a faithful representative Organ of Southern Genius, Taste and Opinions in every branch of Literature, Art, and General Politics. . . .

In regard to its *form,* we shall make Blackwood's Magazine the model of our own, . . .

Having adopted a system of liberal remuneration, we can ensue [sic] the services of the ablest writers.

The price would be $3 a year, and single numbers would be furnished and subscriptions received by agents throughout the Southern states.

The magazine fulfilled its promise, though its career was destined to be short. In April, 1857, backed by a joint stock concern organized by Russell, the first number appeared, a neat, thin octavo by, for, and of the South. The issue opened with an attack on antislavery doctrines by William J. Grayson, and included the first part of J. E. Cooke's "Estcourt," a poem by Timrod, and Hayne's review of Poe's "Arthur Gordon Pym." Throughout its three years of existence *Russell's Magazine* served as a "depository for Southern genius, and a new incentive, . . . for its active exercise." "Believing that an organ of Southern genius and opinion was imperatively demanded, . . . we have undertaken to supply this great want." In publishing the best of Timrod's earlier poems and essays, the works of Samuel Henry Dickson, King, and Simms, the magazine became an excellent organ of expression for the habitués of Russell's bookstore and hence for the literati of the South.

Russell's part in the enterprise was more than that of publisher. With the second number, after Carlisle had proved a disappointment to the staff, Russell became connected with the editorial management also, and at least one letter from the proprietor of the bookstore to a contributor survives, expressing his appreciation and acceptance of a review of *Aurora Leigh*. The publisher's keen interest in the enterprise is indicated by the fact that he kept an annotated copy of the issues in bound volumes on his desk, in which he recorded the names of authors over their articles. That very set, having survived the Civil War, at length found its way to the New York Public Library, where it serves as a reminder of John Russell's close connection with the magazine that bore his name.

The interest of the proprietor and his magazine—indeed, of the South itself—in the lyrical past is reflected by Simms in his "Literary Docket," where, on July 12, 1859, in the fanciful role of judge, he arraigned John Russell before the bar:

Russell's Magazine, . . . [was] . . . represented in court . . . by Mr. John Russell himself; who had, for his supporters,—or in the language of the ring, his bottle-holders—Mr. Hurlbut, Mr. Hayne, Mr. Carlyle [sic], and a goodly group in the back-ground, among whom we recognize the amiable features of Mr. Grayson, and the trim, though poetical face of Mr. Timrod—the one holding up Lives of Burr, Hamilton, and others, with long, well written sheets of commentary; the other bringing out occasionally, from a little cithera, which he carried gracefully in his hand, the languishing notes of a new lyric, dedicated to the proper *Eros;* which, we take for granted, will soon be sweetly sounding in all the ears musical of the South.

Mr. Russell himself wore a most triumphant aspect, in consequence of a recent discovery of huge masses of valuable antique matter in literature, such as a passionate Bibliop is apt to go into exstacies [sic] over; crying, with Dominie Sampson, Prodigious! Mr. Paul Hayne recited to the court, . . . a poem of rich, sensuous, purple and golden character, called "Avolio," which the court at once pronounced to be one of the most beautiful samples of American poetry which has been produced in American magazines during the last five years. "It is almost faultless," cried his Honor. "It is worthy of the fancies of Apuleius of old times, and of the fountain-lapsing musing of Keats, in our own day. As long, sir," he continued, addressing Mr. Russell, "as long, sir, as you can persuade such poetry into your pages, you will deserve well of your country. Go, sir, and see that you provide your poet daily with a bottle of Rhenish, in summer; of Madeira in winter; so shall you never lack true poetry in your pages."

The time for persuading poetry into the pages of *Russell's Magazine* was all too short. In October, 1859, Russell, planning a protracted absence from the country, offered the periodical for sale, but there seems to have been no purchaser for what was described as "a highly profitable investment in the hands of a person of energy and talent." In the last number of March, 1860, the publisher yielded "to the necessity which constrains us to discontinue . . . publication." He had provided the South, and particularly the brotherhood of Southern poets, with an important vehicle for self-expression, and posterity with a notable record of sectional thought. But though his scheme was short-lived, there were other means, John Russell knew from experience, for supplying Southern literati with an audience.

Though Russell's connection with the magazine is still remembered, there are few who recall that in his day he was also an influential book publisher. The South had need of such a publisher. In 1858 *Russell's Magazine* itself expressed that need. "The papers have recently been filled with articles in reference to Southern Publishing Houses; and much regret has been expressed that the expenses of book-printing at the South should be so great, as to deter an author from patronizing the publishers in his own section." The events of every week indicated to Southern writers the need for the South "to declare, and to attempt to establish, her literary independence." Simms bemoaned the fact that

Hitherto, . . . in literature there was no publisher, . . . and the very publication of a book (which might hardly sell) could not be undertaken save at the expense of the author, himself, or by a humiliating subscription of the funds of unwilling friends.

We have not in all the Southern States a single publisher!

For to Simms, a publisher was "never a mere Printer," but "a merchant, in as high a sense of the term as it is known. . . . He imports the literature of foreign countries, and transmits that of his own in exchange. He exercises a large discrimination in both. He has to decide upon the merits, or rather upon the possible popularity, of the books he publishes. He has to determine upon the original productions of his own country in the first instance."

As early as 1852, Walker, Richards of Charleston had tried to establish a large Southern publishing house for the encouragement of Southern authors and the dissemination of Southern books, but the plan had not materialized. By the time the Civil War began, the difficulty of importing Northern and European publications into the Confederate States, coupled with the increased demand for reading matter, heightened the need for a substantial Southern publisher. The ideas and ideals that characterized Southern culture needed not only the exposition of a new literature, but the underwriting of a Southern publisher.

Although it cannot be said that John Russell supplied that great need, by branching out into publishing he did serve the South, issuing —in a spasmodic fashion to be sure—the works of some of its most illustrious citizens. Every book bearing his imprint was, like his magazine, by, for, and of the South. The names of his authors read like a roll-call of those who frequented the literary sessions in the rear of his store, and since they were also the names of the most eminent among Southern literati, Russell's service in publishing their works is far from negligible. Between 1846 and 1855 he lent his name to a series of books in neat format and dignified typography, all of which echoed the voices of the brotherhood of Southern poets.

The first book undertaken by Russell was, characteristically, William Gilmore Simms's *Areytos: or, Songs of the South,* a duodecimo that appeared in 1846, and which was followed two years later by Simms's *Cassique of Accabee* and his *Lays of the Palmetto,* and by the publication in 1853 of the subscription edition of Simms's two-volume *Poems Descriptive, Dramatic, Legendary and Contemplative.* Russell's prospectus, announcing that the collection would be published "in a style unsurpassed by any similar production of the Northern press," stressed the regional importance of Simms's works which "recommend themselves peculiarly to the South, as illustrating its history—its traditions and legends—its scenery and its sentiments." As Simms put it, "Mr. Russell has the hope of presenting me to our home public in full. To save himself from loss, in an experiment so full of peril as a couple of volumes of native poetry, I have counselled him to resort to private subscriptions." A few weeks later Simms repeated his desire that "John Russell who publishes at his own risk, should not suffer loss. Of course, no money is to be made out of such an experiment. If this had been my object I should publish at the North. But in truth," he added significantly, "this is one of the phases by which we are to secure home independence." When the volumes appeared, they were welcomed as a "tribute to native genius—to a true son of the South, and of South Carolina, whose pen has done so much, not only to illustrate the history and promote the literary reputation and educational interests of this State; but has ever been wielded fearlessly and efficiently in the great cause of Southern Rights and Southern institutions." Southern poetry that would "secure home independence" was a favorite literary form with "Lord John," who also sent forth a curious work by Catharine Poyas entitled *Huguenot Daughters and Other Poems,* as well as *The Hireling and Slave,* a versified apology for slavery by William J. Grayson, described by the publisher as "a Poem of considerable merit," for which he hoped eventually to obtain a wider circulation north of the Mason and Dixon line.

For one of his loyal patrons, James W. Miles, Russell published a number of discourses and orations, as well as his important work, *Philosophic Theology; or, Ultimate Grounds of All Religious Belief Based in Reason.* When Russell's friend, Louisa C. McCord of South

Carolina, translated Bastiat's *Sophisms of the Protective Policy,* "Lord John" was ready to join his name with that of George P. Putnam of New York in sponsoring the undertaking. When W. H. Trescot of Charleston desired a publisher for his *Thoughts on American Foreign Policy,* when Miles or Porcher eulogized Calhoun after his death in 1850, they turned to Russell to handle publication. Russell himself was particularly interested in seeing through the press books of a local or sectional quality, publishing Ramsey's *Annals of Tennessee;* Charles Fraser's *Reminiscences of Charleston; House and Home; or, The Carolina Housewife By a lady of Charleston;* and, replete with finely engraved colored plates, Holbrook's *Ichthyology of South Carolina.* For local societies he proved a willing publisher, lending his name to Samuel Henry Dickson's *Speech at the Dinner of the New England Society of Charleston,* or to Miles's oration before the literary societies of the South Carolina College.

By 1857, the year which saw the launching of *Russell's Magazine,* there had been a change in the firm name and in the imprints of Russell's publications. James C. Jones, Russell's half-brother, who had worked as a clerk in the bookstore, apparently had become a partner, and the firm's name was changed to Russell and Jones. It is possible, too, that another half-brother, Edward C. Jones, the Charleston architect, entered the firm at this period, perhaps to supervise its fine arts department. At any rate, it was the name of Russell and Jones that appeared as publishers of *Russell's Magazine,* and, between 1857 and 1860, of other Southern publications, all of which followed the trends established by Russell earlier in his career. Grayson's poem, *The Country,* took the place of *The Hireling and Slave; The South Carolina Jockey Club* whetted local interest, as did Simms's *History of South Carolina,* while the new firm sponsored the publications of such local organizations as the Elliott Society of Natural History of Charleston, of which John Russell was a member.

One work, published in 1857 by Russell and Jones, typifies the firm's desire to serve as what might be called publishers indigenous to the South. *Pleiocene Fossils of South-Carolina* by Tuomey and Holmes had previously appeared without plates, but at the "urgent solicitation" of Agassiz, Bache, and Gould, it was published now as a folio with twenty-nine plates. Its artistic merits would "challenge the severest criticism." What is more, the work was offered to the public as "a good specimen of what can be done by our artists at home." The drawings on stone were executed at the College of Charleston by C. G. Platen; the letterpress was, in part, the work of Halper and Calvo and James and Williams, native Charleston printers. Since there was no press for printing the plates in Charleston, that work had to be done elsewhere, but otherwise the volume, for two hundred copies of which the legislature subscribed, was indeed an excellent example of Southern workmanship, as well as of the publishing ideals and purposes of John Russell.

By 1860, the last date when a Russell and Jones imprint appeared, the firm's stock of goods was valued at $20,000. Russell and Jones could afford to turn some of their profits from bookselling into book publishing, could undertake more or less unremunerative enterprises, and could give to the South such finely illustrated works as Holmes's *Post-Pleiocene Fossils of South-Carolina.* Their relations with Northern publishers had been established on a firm foundation, and they appear to have served as agents for the publications of Redfield, Appleton, and Harper in New York, and Bentley in London. Although Simms asserted that "the success of their issues has been greatly affected by the simple fact, that, not contemplating publication *as a business,* they have not established, and cannot establish, the proper agencies for the general circulation of their books," perhaps in time Russell and Jones might have developed into that great Southern publishing house of which the region felt so sore a need. Fort Sumter, however, was soon to signify more than a place, and the year 1860 was to make way for the more eventful year of 1861. The guns were to be fired over Charleston, presaging ruin to the "Globe," the "Cocoa Tree" of King Street, dooming the antebellum ideals of the brotherhood of Southern literati.

Just before the outbreak of the war, Russell suffered a personal loss in the death, by drowning, of his half-brother, James C. Jones. Not long after, in December, 1861, his mother died. No more books bearing the imprint of Russell and Jones would appear, and only a very few works remained to be published by John Russell. Those few would attest, however, to his determination to carry on his purposes in the face of the havoc that surrounded him.

In order to save his stock from the effects of bombardment, Russell, like so many of the book dealers of more recent times, stored his wares beyond the reach of shot and shell. But Camden, the town he selected, was to prove a poor choice, for it lay in the line of Sherman's march. Russell himself, besides serving as the adjutant of a battalion of reserves, found the time and courage to publish what proved to be "the most elegant book, as to paper, printing and binding, which appeared in the South during the war." *The Life and Times of Bertrand Du Guesclin: A History of the Fourteenth Century* by D. F. Jamison of South Carolina was "Lord John's" last attempt to recapture the past and its chivalric ideals. He published it in Charleston in 1864, a two-volume set with a frontispiece portrait of Sir Bertrand, dedicated by the author to William Gilmore Simms—a final testimony to a dream that had already been proven impossible.

John Russell, returning to Camden to claim his stock at the close of the war, was confronted by a sorry and disheartening sight. Sherman's soldiers had recklessly broken open the cases, scattering or destroying the contents, and when the remnants were gathered there was little left of his once valuable wares. With that meager stock John Russell set up business again, at number 285 King Street, but the days of the "Globe" and "Cocoa Tree" were over. Charleston, the proudest city of the South, had been bombarded and fired. By the time the war was over, it was a place of vacant houses, rotting wharves, and lifeless, grass-grown streets, where yawning walls and shattered windows were reminders of the disaster that had befallen it. The proprietor himself had but five more years to live, surrounded by shadows of a former greatness. At least twice he undertook book publication, in 1867 issuing Ephraim Seabrook's *Ariel Refuted. A Complete Exposure. Of A Pamphlet Entitled "The Negro,"* and in 1870 sending forth William Trescot's *Memorial of the Life of J. Johnston Pettigrew, Brig. Gen. of the Confederate States Army.* To the end Russell remained faithful to his desire to give expression to the voice of the South. But that voice was, by 1871, all but stilled.

Few were left to recall those brilliant sessions that had taken place in the rear of another bookstore on King Street during the proud mid-century. Paul Hamilton Hayne remembered, however, and during a journey from New York to "Copse Hill," he passed through Charleston, visiting John Russell. The superb collection of beautifully bound books had disappeared, and in their place stood empty shelves. The proprietor had grown old, although he was not yet sixty. The brisk, active, confident "Lord John" had vanished.

With a melancholy greeting Russell welcomed Hayne, waving his hand around the store and by that gesture conveying a sense of the desolation that surrounded him. It was a place of ghosts, ghosts of people and ideals as well as of books.

Before his death, part of the remnants of Russell's stock was sold at a sacrifice. On November 21, 1871, the proprietor died of heart disease, leaving his estate to his half-sister, Eliza Catherine Jones. The stock, once assessed at $20,000, was valued after his death at $2,500. There were intangibles, however, disregarded by the "Inventory of Goods and Chattels of John Russell, Deceased." There is no mention in that document of his attempt to provide an organ for Southern thought by selling and publishing Southern books and by giving to the writers of the South a meeting-place and a spring-board for self-expression. Yet much of the literary work produced in the South in ante-bellum days owes a debt to John Russell, the book-seller-publisher who played his significant role behind the scenes. Although the ideal for which he, and all the Southern illuminati sought, was sought in vain, still, in the seeking, he left a more substantial estate than he could realize, for he bequeathed a heritage to history.

V. CIVIL WAR & ABOLITION

James Redpath

AND HIS "BOOKS FOR THE TIMES"

THE Civil War, which annihilated the ante-bellum dream of the South, brought to fruition a quite different dream in the North. The Transcendentalists of New England, whose conscience had long since been awakened to humanitarian impulses, could not remain indifferent to slavery. And those who did not entirely share the transcendental creed found themselves at one with many Transcendentalists in their struggles for abolition. The firing of Fort Sumter brought the issue—brought so many issues—to a crux. The guns over Sumter, scattering the brotherhood of Southern poets, breaking the pattern of their lives and their thoughts, united New England as it had never been united before, and established there a pattern of life and of thought that had been long in the making. Against the "peculiar institution" and secession of the South, New England inscribed upon its banner two mighty watchwords: Emancipation and Union, wrote the words in blood and in fire, but wrote them also in a medium far more enduring. The printed word, published abroad, had awakened the North to the crying needs of humanity. Now, when the Civil War dissipated and then effaced the ante-bellum ideals of the South, the printed word—two printed words: Emancipation and Union—rallied the North, stirred it as it had never been stirred, gave it a cause and a creed, set its jubilant feet on the crusaders' march to freedom.

Now, if ever, there was need in New England for men who would publish those words abroad. James Redpath, who styled himself a "Roving Editor," had never published a book. But he had been, and still was, a Republican, Emancipationist, American, Abolitionist, Peace-Man, Non-Resistant, and Democrat. He had long before "en-

rolled himself a Crusader of Freedom until slavery ceased to exist."
He did not fear the label of "ultra-fanaticism" with which he had
been branded. He had written and fought for abolition. In 1863 he
decided to publish for abolition, for emancipation, for union. The
Civil War, which had caused John Russell of Charleston to store
his wares in the hope of safety, caused James Redpath to open a
publishing office in Boston from which he could issue his inflammatory "Books for the Times." The times needed those books. And as
always, when the need arose, a publisher arose with it, to supply
the need fearlessly and forcefully until the need ceased to exist.

Because James Redpath served so effectively as Boston's wartime
publisher, it is surprising to discover that, in the numerous works
that delineate other phases of his many-sided career, there is scarcely
a mention of that significant fact. A full-length biography is devoted
to Redpath, and sketches of his life appear in several other works.
Yet none of these important sources assigns more than a phrase to
James Redpath's fiery though short-lived activity as the reform publisher of New England.

Perhaps this rather startling omission may be explained by the
very versatility of James Redpath's career, which at every stage was
occupied with the varied reforms of the zealot. Certainly, by the
time he decided to include publishing among his activities, he had
prepared himself well for the great crusade that marked the outbreak
of the war. He had not merely crystallized his creed, but carried it
out as well.

Born in August, 1833, at Berwick-on-Tweed, on the Scottish side
of the river, young Redpath had emigrated with his family during
the period of the gold rush to Allegan, Michigan. The ambitious boy
found work in a printing office at Kalamazoo, and later moved to
Detroit, where his writing attracted the attention of Horace Greeley,
who offered him a position on the staff of the *Tribune*. From that
time on the spirit of reform dominated his life and his work. He
traveled through the Southern states to "see slavery with his own
eyes and learn what bondmen said and thought of their condition."
He reported upon the affairs of Kansas as special correspondent,
meeting John Brown in the eventful "interview" of May 30, 1856,
and subsequently being subpoenaed by the Senate for complicity in
the Harpers Ferry plot. He visited Haiti and established the Haytian
Bureau of Emigration. During the Rebellion he served with Sher-

man's armies as correspondent for a newspaper syndicate, and at the close of the war he founded a Negro orphan asylum in Charleston and inaugurated the first regular decoration of soldiers' graves in May. Redpath owes his greatest fame to the Lyceum Bureau which he established in Boston in 1868, having as clients such renowned reformers as Emerson, Greeley, Beecher, Sumner, and Wendell Phillips, through whose voices he could plead his varied causes. Toward the end of his career he took up his pen to champion Ireland, denouncing English rule and landlordism, and founding *Redpath's Weekly* in support of the Land League. The Anti-Poverty Society claimed his attention until he was appointed managing editor of *The North American Review*. On February 10, 1891, Redpath's many-faceted career came to an end in St. Luke's Hospital, New York. He had spoken and written vigorously upon every significant cause of the times, and as a publisher he had swayed public opinion during a crisis in American affairs.

After his return from Haiti, Redpath set up the Haytian Bureau of Emigration in Boston's Washington Building. There he sponsored the immigration of American Negroes into that republic, believing, both as abolitionist and as republican, that a cordon of free Negroes in the Island would serve as a barrier to the expansion of slavery in the Southern states. "As the agent of the Government of Hayti," he wrote to Secretary of War Cameron on June 1, 1861, "I offer to provide every negro whom you may confiscate with a comfortable home and a farm in Hayti." In his Boston office he provided certified copies of governmental guarantees, journals of Haiti, reference books, maps, and specimens of the ores and staple cultures of the Island. In addition, he founded a weekly newspaper, *Pine and Palm,* to advance the cause, and edited *A Guide to Hayti,* issued in 1860 by the "courageous" publishers, Thayer and Eldridge.

It was that firm which in 1860 also published *Echoes of Harper's Ferry,* in which Redpath pledged *"Success to the next Negro Insurrection!";* his pamphlet, *Southern Notes for National Circulation;* and his fiery *Public Life of Capt. John Brown*—a book written because the author "could not resist it" and denounced by the press as "detestable," expounding "the most ultra-fanaticism." The following year Thayer and Eldridge failed. It was then that the Haytian Bureau of Emigration published another edition of the *Guide to*

Hayti, and it was doubtless also then that Redpath decided to become a publisher in his own right.

It was a career that must have held forth great appeal to one who "could concoct more schemes over night than half a dozen men could manage." Here was a "scheme" whereby a man could turn pens into swords through the medium of printer's ink, could inflame the North whether it gathered round a camp fire or a hearth fire, could take an active part in the great Rebellion of the times by publishing "Books for the Times." Redpath's magnetic personality, his understanding of popular taste, and his indefatigable nature augured well for the new enterprise. The short, wiry, alert young man, "electrical in mind and body," decided to take on where Thayer and Eldridge had left off, and play the role of Boston's reformer publisher.

In Room 7 of the Washington Building at 221 Washington Street, Redpath set up his publishing office. He shared the building not only with Brown's millinery and King's trimming goods establishment, but with the more congenial offices of *The Liberator* and the Massachusetts Anti-Slavery Society. There Redpath proceeded to apply the creed he had announced in his *Roving Editor.* In publishing, as in living, he would be "a Crusader of Freedom until slavery ceased to exist."

It was as such a crusader that James Redpath sent forth his "Books for the Times." They were books that few conservative publishers would have included on their lists, but they were indeed books for the times. They comprised primarily such anti-slavery works as William Wells Brown's *The Black Man,* containing biographical sketches of fifty-eight distinguished Negroes by a Negro, Redpath's own *Public Life and Autobiography of John Brown,* Wendell Phillips's *Speeches, Lectures, and Letters,* Beard's *Toussaint L'Ouverture,* and Louisa Alcott's *Hospital Sketches.* The works of Phillips and Beard had no little bearing upon Redpath's emigrant agency and his championship of the Black Republic, for it had been Phillips's lecture on Toussaint L'Ouverture that first interested the publisher in Haiti. Other publications, equally timely, were *Shall We Suffocate Ed. Green? By a Citizen of Malden,* directed against capital punishment, and Cochin's *Results of Emancipation.*

Redpath not only advertised his "Books for the Times" in the

Boston Almanac and *American Publishers' Circular,* and sent free lists to any address, but issued the volumes in editions that would have a wide popular appeal. *Hospital Sketches* at 50 cents, *The Black Man* and *Life of John Brown* at $1 each, the biography of *Tousaint L'Ouverture* at $1.25 were reasonably priced, while Phillips's *Speeches* was offered in three separate editions at three different prices, the Library Edition "in a luxurious style of book-making" at $2.25, the Trade Edition in cloth and boards at $1.50, and the People's Edition in paper at $1. Liberal terms were offered to agents, books were mailed to any address, and arrangements were made with Lippincott in Philadelphia and Miller, Francis, and Low in New York to supply the trade with Redpath's "Books for the Times."

The publisher's handling of *Hospital Sketches* illustrates his methods in dealing with his authors. Louisa Alcott's letters from the Union Hotel Hospital in Georgetown, D. C., where she had served as nurse, had been revised upon her return home and published in *The Commonwealth* between May 22 and June 26, 1863. In June, 1863, Redpath requested permission to reprint the *Sketches* in book form. She was to receive 5 cents on each copy of the edition of 1,000, and he to have 10 cents, out of which he was to pay for the cost of the book and give something to charity. Redpath carried on the publishing "vigorously, sending letters, proof, and notices daily, and making all manner of offers, suggestions, and prophecies concerning the success of the book and its author." On August 25 Miss Alcott received her copy, "a neat little affair," a "green-covered 18mo. of 100 pages, handsomely printed," though "fussy people said the margin should be wider and the cover darker." By September Redpath began to ply the author with requests for another book as well as with payments that eventually amounted to $200. It was because he had made what in popular opinion was "a good success" with *Hospital Sketches* that Redpath was named as a possible publisher of Channing's memoir of Thoreau. He chose timely works on his own side of the political fence, issued them with speed, and lived up to his monetary promises to authors.

Since Redpath was a concocter of schemes, there is little to marvel at in his next major publishing venture. If the more highly priced "Books for the Times" had sold well, a series of "Books for Camp and Home," priced much lower, would, no doubt, have even greater popularity, and both by their nature and design would reach not only readers at home, but soldiers in the field. Accordingly, Redpath announced on March 1, 1864, a series of ten-cent "Books for the Camp Fires," "of a much higher class than the dime publications now in the market." They were to contain from 96 to 124 pages, to be printed in new type, on good paper, "neatly bound in greenbacks." So the war gave a special *raison d'être* to Redpath's paper-covered pocket books which in 1864 found their way to the distant battlefields of the North.

The first of Redpath's new series was another work by Louisa M. Alcott, *On Picket Duty, and Other Tales,* containing "On Picket Duty," "The King of Clubs and the Queen of Hearts," reprinted from the Concord *Monitor,* "The Cross on the Old Church Tower," and "The Death of John," reprinted from *Hospital Sketches.* For the second issue of the series, Redpath again turned to William Wells Brown, publishing his *Clotelle, A Tale of the Southern States.* The next three works were, like so many pocket editions, reprints of foreign books—Balzac's *Vendetta,* Swift's *Gulliver's Travels . . . to Lilliput,* and Hugo's *Battle of Waterloo.* An army edition of *Hospital Sketches* followed, along with *Legends of the Infancy and Boyhood of Jesus Christ.* There it was announced that "The flattering reception of the first five numbers of these [Books for] the Camp Fires, by the trade, the press, and the people, [indicates] that a higher style of literature than has hitherto been issued [in the] cheapest form, will find a ready support for them." The reception of the press was indeed flattering, the papers lauding the series as "just the books for the soldier in camp." "They will be welcome visitors in the camp, and the friends of our patriotic soldiers should endeavor to supply them with a copy." "Our soldier boys will find them just the thing to beguile an otherwise tedious hour."

Each number was guaranteed to be "complete and unabridged." Ten cents sent to the publisher would secure a specimen copy with postage paid to any home or camp address. Redpath's "Books for the Camp Fires" were on sale by all newsdealers, and were sold to the trade, sutlers, peddlers, and retailers at a rate of $60 per thousand. Advertised as "the cheapest books of real merit in the market," the "Camp Fire Series" indicated what a wartime publisher, who had issued timely reform works for home consumption, could accomplish in the way of giving pleasure and enlightenment to men in the field.

Like all publishers, Redpath added to his books for "the Times" and for "Camp Fires" a few works of a more general nature, offering to the public Captain Mayne Reid's *Croquet* at 50 cents—almost as timely during the '60's as his anti-slavery publications, *The Morals of Epictetus* and Louisa Alcott's fairy tale, *The Rose Family,* each at 25 cents, Madame Guyon's *Spiritual Torrents* at 75 cents, and Sala's *Breakfast in Bed* at $1.

On April 15, 1864, Redpath's last advertisement appeared in the *American Publishers' Circular.* In May Sherman began "his campaign to subjugate Georgia," and the publisher turned from his office on Washington Street to join the men in blue as army correspondent in the South. He was with Sherman at Atlanta, and sent the first report of the capture of Charleston to the North. There, the perpetual concocter of schemes was to organize South Carolina's school system before he returned home.

Though his career as publisher had ended, his career as reformer had not. Many schemes were to whet his interest before his death in 1891, from the Lyceum Bureau to Ireland's politics, from the United Labor Party to the Anti-Poverty Society. Whenever a reform was needed, Redpath seemed to rise to the occasion. In 1880 he went to Ireland as special correspondent of the *New-York Tribune,* publishing his *Talks About Ireland* the following year and earning for his radical championship of Irish rights the title of "adopted Irishman." In 1883 he addressed a mass meeting of newsdealers at Cooper Institute after a price reduction of New York papers, and as a consequence of this "newsdealers' war," the *Herald* announced its intention to establish stands for the sale of all morning papers at established rates, "an entirely new system of newspaper service." Strangely enough, one of Redpath's latter-day activities was helping Jefferson Davis in the preparation of his histories and assisting Varina Davis with the *Memoir* of her husband. The pen had, in this instance at least, turned the sword into the ploughshare.

Of all Redpath's enterprises, the Lyceum Bureau was his most famous. As the leading lecture agent, he managed nearly all the platform celebrities of the day. From 1868 to 1875, when George H. Hathaway and Major J. B. Pond assumed control of the Bureau, Redpath numbered among his clients Mark Twain, who addressed him as "Dear Red," magicians, and musical soloists, as well as the reformers Greeley, Julia Ward Howe, Mary Livermore, and others, with whom Redpath ever felt a kinship and through whose varied voices his many causes could be championed.

In all his undertakings the current reform was his dominating motive. Yet it is of special significance that, when the current reform was anti-slavery, and the current scene that of the American Civil War, James Redpath chose to abet that reform not merely by writing, but by publishing. Both the reform and the publishing trade owe a salute to James Redpath, who, in his "Books for the Times" provided the Civil War public with works to indoctrinate civilians and in his "Camp Fire Series" supplied enjoyment to men in the field. Author, reformer, journalist, lecturer, founder of the Lyceum Bureau, James Redpath was also Boston's wartime publisher. He demonstrated, indeed, how a publisher could be Emancipationist, American, and Abolitionist, and could "enroll himself a Crusader of Freedom until slavery ceased to exist." When slavery was abolished, his publishing reforms were no longer needed. But until that time he proved that a courageous publisher could advance a cause and help resolve a nation's struggle.

VI. RECONSTRUCTION & THE
POST-WAR SOUTH

Charles W. Clark

"SOUTHERN KNIGHT" OF NEW ORLEANS

THE end of the Civil War brought an end to the fighting, but
not to the hatred. Still girded for battle, the defeated South
faced the dozen years that followed the close of the war, that period
from 1865 to 1877 which has been called Reconstruction. It was
not the war's end alone that led to the severities of Reconstruction.
The bloody 1866 Convention that resulted in a riot between the
Negroes and the white police intensified the drastic program until
the dreaded Reconstruction Acts stripped the South of everything
but hatred. Its state governments abolished, the South was placed
under military control. Only thus, at the point of the bayonet, did
it accept the Fourteenth Amendment, which assured the Negro of
equal rights, and the Fifteenth Amendment, which granted him the
ballot. Shattered, destroyed, confused, the South stood apart from
the Union while fortune-hunters from the North intruded, setting
up new state governments. In all the welter of new words, where
was the New South? Not in Warmothism—so-called after the administration of Governor Henry Clay Warmoth; not in carpetbag
government and the political machinations of northern adventurers.
Somehow the New South would come into being, its agricultural
economy and its social institutions renewed, its relationship with
the Union restored—but not before the havoc of Reconstruction
had taken its toll. The idealistic brotherhood of the ante-bellum
South was a brotherhood of hatred now. The guns might be silenced,
but troops still paraded the streets. The plantation slave was
an equal, a voter, a candidate for office. The South shook its
futile fists and could not understand. The nation might call it
Reconstruction; to the South, it was a dozen years of antag-

JACOB W. CRUGER

ROBERT FERGUS

JAMES REDPATH

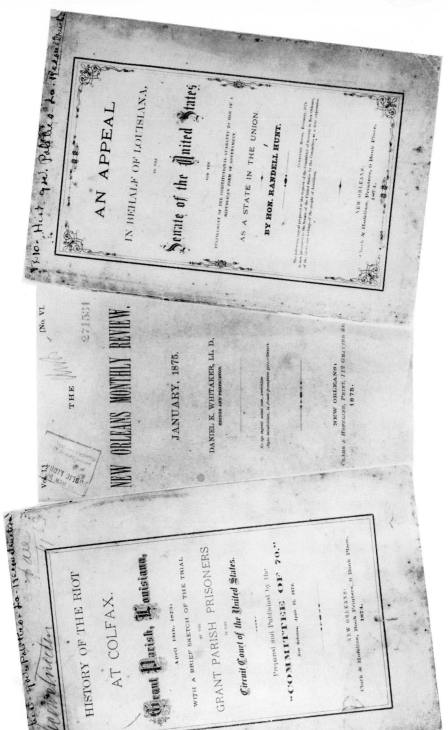

CLARK TITLE-PAGES OF RECONSTRUCTION WORKS

onism and confusion that followed the ruin and destruction of war.

Of all Southern cities overwhelmed by the turmoil of the post-war years, none represents better the antagonistic forces, the hatred, the bewilderment than New Orleans. New Orleans was the battle-ground where, from 1865 to 1877, radical and conservative tides swept back and forth, revealing the flotsam of confusion and rancor that the war had not buried. And in New Orleans, none could present a sharper reflection of those years of disturbance than the printer whose name appeared modestly on the books and the pamphlets that revealed the heart of the South. If the South was confused, the printer gave a name to that confusion. If the South was embittered, the printer echoed that embitterment. If, over-shadowed by confusion and embitterment, there was a New South that would some day arise, the printer, more ably perhaps than the politician, gave it form and substance and voice.

On Gravier Street or Camp Street or Commercial Place, the printing house rows of New Orleans, many a craftsman rose up to lend his imprint to a book or a pamphlet during Reconstruction—rose up, but seldom flourished. Here and there, their names appear on local addresses or legal briefs, medical reports or war reminis-cences, but their appearances are desultory, their imprints few. During the dozen years of Reconstruction, the Propagateur Catho-lique, the Renaissance Louisianaise, the Plume de Bronze, the Daily Republican, L. Graham & Co., the Picayune Book and Job Office, all strove to keep the public informed by printing books and pam-phlets of and for Louisiana. Their task was difficult, and it is amazing not that so few but that any imprints bear their names. The dreaming ante-bellum days were over; no brotherhood of poets swarmed to set their effusions in print. Lyrical effusions were meta-morphosed now into political fulminations that found their way into ephemeral pamphlets. In the confusion of the times, the printers often became shadows behind their imprints. Newspapers arose and were silenced. Directories, especially when they desig-nated the color of the citizens, were destroyed. History was made, but the records of that history were not always treasured. Only the confusion and the embitterment remain, set in type by an obscure printer.

Many of the books and pamphlets printed in New Orleans during those years of Reconstruction bear the imprint of a firm named

Clark and Hofeline. Leading the ranks of Reconstruction printers, quantitatively at least, their imprint appears on works that reflect the hatred and bewilderment of the times. Through their imprints, those times can be anatomized. But the men themselves, unlike Russell of Charleston or Redpath of Boston, escape the hand of the historian who would bring them to life. Their only substance lies in the books and periodicals that bear their imprint. For they worked in the nighttime of confusion, and the light that would pierce the darkness of their lives is dim.

At number 70 Camp Street, with the office of the *Delta* on one side and the office of the *Picayune* on the other, Charles W. Clark made his first public appearance in New Orleans. There, in 1857, he set up shop in partnership with the printer, W. W. Brisbin, beginning his Southern career as proprietor of the Crescent Job Office, one of a host of job printers who plied their trade in the city's newspaper row. Yet two curious facts distinguish him from many of his fellow printers of the Crescent City. Clark was a native, not of Louisiana, but of Pennsylvania, and at the age of 37, when he made his entry into the printing annals of New Orleans he was no apprentice, but a master in his own right. He appears fullblown, so to speak, his past shrouded in darkness, if not in mystery. His present seems to have been fruitful. Not long after his arrival in New Orleans, Clark was initiated into Quitman Lodge, No. 76, at the annual communication of Free and Accepted Masons in February of 1858. From his home on Carondelet Street, he found his way to the Grand Lodge Masonic Hall on the corner of St. Charles and Perdido Streets, and for the fifty years that remained to him he was to continue a faithful member of his order. Clark, apparently a joiner, was also a member of Typographical Union No. 17. Combining business with pleasure through the years, he would in time lend his firm name to the imprints of Masonic proceedings, and between his organizations and his family life—Clark was married and had a son who also followed the printing trade—he seems to have settled contentedly in the South.

Over the Crescent Job Office, the Clark and Brisbin establishment was fitted up "with a large and extensive assortment of plain and ornamental job type, presses, etc.," and was "prepared to execute every variety of book and job printing, . . . every description of commercial and mercantile printing, in the best style of typography, at satisfactory prices." The firm was ready to fill orders for all varieties of printing, from books to bill heads, from checks to dray receipts, from pamphlets to bills of lading, from insurance policies to steamboat bills, and, "having on hand a large assortment of beautiful Scotch Face type, carefully selected with especial reference to printing books, pamphlets, etc.," the partners announced that their patrons could "rely on having their work executed in a style unsurpassed by any other office in the city." Since both were experienced "Practical Printers," who devoted "their personal attention to all orders entrusted to them," and since their facilities enabled them to undertake "any and every description of plain, fancy and ornamental job printing," they advertised that their work could not be excelled by any other local establishment. They could execute "book binding and ruling, in connection with printing," and their printing was "Neat! cheap!! quick!!!"

Until the outbreak of war Clark and Brisbin flourished, printing minor works of local interest. For the New Orleans Board of School Directors they printed the *Annual Report of The Directors of the Public Schools, of the First District of New Orleans,* for the city's Protestant Episcopal Church, the *Constitution and By-Laws of The Children's Home,* and when the Rev. Dr. Illowy delivered an *Oration . . . for Jewish Widows & Orphans,* Clark and Brisbin issued the work. Moving from Camp Street to 19 Commercial Place, the firm continued its services as local job printers, and it is possible that the partners were associated with the *Commercial Advertiser,* which in 1858 had been published at 70 Camp Street and in 1860 was issued from their later address. The following year, their imprint appeared on *The Volunteers' Friend,* an eight-page paper edited by the girls of Fourth District High School "for the purpose of aiding our brave volunteers."

By August 13, 1861, however, Clark's active partnership with Brisbin had been terminated, for on that day, as one of New Orleans's "brave volunteers," Charles W. Clark appeared at Camp Moore to enlist in the 12th Battalion of Louisiana Infantry. Despite the fact that he had been born in Pennsylvania, he evinced by this act his complete affiliation with the Confederate cause—an affiliation that would be confirmed by his printing activities during Reconstruction. His partner joined him the following March, serving in the Confederate Guards Response Battalion, as the 12th Louisiana

Infantry was also known, but Brisbin's army career was destined to be short-lived. After a few months he was detailed to the printing office at Corinth, Mississippi, and in July of 1862 he was discharged for being "over age." Meanwhile, Charles W. Clark was "present on all rolls" until December, 1863, an indication that he fought through the dire campaigns of the Army of Tennessee. In the battle of Kenesaw Mountain, Georgia, Clark was captured on June 27, 1864. The following year he was sent from Chattanooga to the Military Prison at Louisville, and finally interned at Camp Douglas, Illinois. On June 20, 1865, he was discharged in accordance with General Orders from Washington.

The war had ended. Charles W. Clark, aged 45, was a defeated Confederate soldier and a printer in search of employment. Like all the South, he faced the ruin and destruction that had come in the wake of the war. While his former partner, Brisbin, became foreman of the Bulletin Job Office, Clark turned quite naturally to the Crescent Office of which he had early in his New Orleans career been proprietor. Now, however, he served as foreman.

The *Crescent* had had an interesting history. Established in 1848, the newspaper had been purchased in 1854 by "gallant old" James O. Nixon, a popular civic leader before the war, a lieutenant colonel with Scott's cavalry during the war, and a leader of the conservative press after the war. The *Crescent,* which had been the official city journal, was declared a rebel sheet and was confiscated and sold at public auction by General Butler during the Federal occupation of New Orleans. In 1865 Colonel Nixon revived the paper, and a year later spent several thousand dollars in remodeling the offices, job shop, press and engine rooms, and installing a new printing machine and lithographic business.

We have, at an expense of several thousand dollars, remodeled and refitted the whole Crescent office, from the first story to the fourth, as well as the job printing, press and engine rooms in the rear of the main building. We have gone to this expense in the confident belief that in a great metropolitan city like New Orleans, a first-class printing establishment was an absolute necessity, and that the public would not fail to appreciate and sustain our exertions in behalf of the journalism of this city and the South. We are gratified to be able to say that our expectations have not been disappointed. The steadily increasing business of the Crescent, in subscriptions, advertisements and job work, prove to us that enterprise is sure of its reward, and that the people of New Orleans, as well as those of Paris, London and New York, know how to appreciate a first-class metropolitan newspaper establishment.

As there is one branch of our business which is comparatively new here, we will be excused for making special reference to it. We mean the lithographic business, which we have lately connected with the office. In this line we safely challenge and defy competition—and the specimens of our work are the tests by which we are willing to be judged. We foresee that this is a business destined to be hereafter an important one, and we have provided for the future by organizing a lithographic establishment at which we are very certain work can be done, not to be surpassed in any city in this country or any other.

It was as foreman of this office that Clark resumed his place in the printing history of New Orleans. He doubtless agreed with the policy voiced by Nixon in the newspaper two months before the passage of the first of the Reconstruction Acts: as a temporary expedient, Negro suffrage might be tenable, even advisable, but the South would never accept it unless at the point of the bayonet. The carpetbaggers were in time rebuked, but rather with humor than with rancor. Since the *Crescent* for a time had the contract for state printing, Clark was well occupied during his brief employment as foreman of the office. From 94 Camp Street he doubtless supervised the printing of Lusher's *Compilation of the Laws Of Louisiana, . . . For The Organization And Support Of Free Public Schools, Acts of the Legislature for Leveeing, . . . Swamp Lands in . . . the Parishes Of Orleans And Jefferson,* a *Report* on the Military Reconstruction Bill, General Assembly Acts, committee reports, Senate and House of Representative Journals, as well as the more literary *Southern Sketches* of Mrs. Helena J. Harris, a native of Alabama. Between blue wrappers, "Cecil Gray; Or, The Soldier's Revenge" and "Rosa Sherwood; Or, The Avenger" still bear testimony not only to the point of view of the foreman of the Crescent Job Office, but to his neat and careful craftsmanship.

Clark's technical skill and typographical interests are most notably reflected in *The Phonographic Magazine,* a periodical "devoted to the interests of phonographers and students of shorthand." Edited by H. C. Manley and J. O. Nixon, Jr., the journal was printed at the Crescent Book and Job Office at 94 Camp Street in 1868, while Clark was foreman. Its object was "the dissemination of a knowledge of the art of Phonography by means of a series of lessons, one in each number, presenting its principles in so full and clear a manner as to enable any persons who choose, to acquire the knowledge of it, without any other instruction." The printing of such lessons in phonographic symbols presented rather serious problems for the typographer. The second issue of the weekly, the terms of which had been optimistically set at $9 a year, explained the difficulties and pinned a feather on the cap of the foreman:

In order to exonerate ourselves from the charge of neglect or carelessness, . . . on account of the delay in issuing our first number, and the rather inartistic work upon the lithographic portion, we herewith submit a description of the process by which the phonographic part is produced.

Having explained the intricacies of the various methods—the difficult and expensive technique of engraving upon lithographic stone and printing from it, and the device of copper plate relief engraving —the editors concluded that

The most facile, and the cheapest method . . . is by . . . *transfer lithography*. In this the characters are simply *written* upon a page of paper prepared for the purpose, which does not absorb the ink, but holds it upon the surface, . . . This writing is then *transferred* to a smooth stone, which . . . leaves the characters *reversed,* so that when printed from they are brought back to their original position, right side up. . . . We prefer this method to any other, for the reason that it "holds the mirror up to nature" and gives an exact copy of the writer's style, and though from several vexatious circumstances, such as not having the kind of *transfer paper* and lithographic ink best suited for the purpose, etc., our phonographic department is not as clear and well executed as we could wish, we are confident, after a few trials and patient experiment, to make it so.

The editors completed their remarks to subscribers by announcing that

For what we consider the very neat appearance of the typic portion, we are indebted to Mr. Clark, the careful and accommodating foreman of the Crescent Job Office.

Despite their confidence, *The Phonographic Magazine* did not outlast the year, and although Colonel Nixon changed his policy, urging in the *Crescent* that the South grant the Negro equal rights, the

Radical legislature for 1868 decided to void the office's contract for state printing.

Perhaps it was for these reasons that Charles W. Clark terminated his services as foreman. Perhaps he simply preferred the status of master. At any rate, by 1870 he had severed his connections with Nixon and established his own Lithographic, Book and Job Printing House at 106 Gravier Street, corner of Bank Place. There he boasted that he could supply "Lithography at New York Prices!" and advertised:

The attention of Cotton Factors, Commission Merchants, Druggists, and the mercantile community generally, is invited to an examination of our Lithographic & Letter Press Specimens, Feeling assured that with the most experienced workmen, and all the necessary material, we can turn out work equal to any done at the North; and that there may be no necessity of sending work to be done elsewhere, we are determined to do it at New York Prices.

For "Specimens of Drug and Liquor Labels," Clark referred prospective customers to his "printed Price List." For specimens of his book printing, he might have referred them to his issue of the *Charter; and Rules And Regulations* of the Bank of Lafayette, or the *Act Of Incorporation and By-Laws of the Loan and Pledge Association* of New Orleans. His masonic brothers certainly availed themselves of his services, for it was the imprint of Clark's Lithograph, Book and Job Print that appeared on the *Proceedings* of the M.˙.W.˙.Grand Lodge of the State of Louisiana at its fifty-eighth and fifty-ninth annual communications, as well as on the *Proceedings* of the Grand Commandery of Knights Templar and Appendant Orders and of the Royal Arch Masons of the State of Louisiana. Perhaps, too, Clark had a hand in the printing of the elusive *New Orleans Democrat,* which was issued from his address at 106 Gravier Street in 1871.

During that year Albert D. Hofeline, a twenty-three-year-old New Orleans printer and one of the Knights of Pythias, worked with Simmons and Company, stationers and printers of Camp Street, and subsequently served as a printer on the New Orleans *Picayune.* By 1873, Clark had formed a partnership with Hofeline and had set up a printing establishment that would during its brief history reflect all the antagonisms and embitterment of the Reconstruction period in New Orleans.

At 112 Gravier Street, near his former office and in the same building that had housed the Plume de Bronze, Clark took his stand with Hofeline. From there, or the alternate address, 9 Bank Place, they sent forth for nearly a decade the books and pamphlets that still reveal to the patient historian the preoccupations and requirements, the confusion and disturbances that beleaguered a city in the travail of transition from war to peace.

The establishment of the firm of Clark and Hofeline all but coincided with the race riot at Colfax, Louisiana, on April 13, 1873. Among their earliest imprints reflecting the turmoil of Reconstruction politics is the firm's fourteen-page pamphlet printed for the Committee of Seventy of Louisiana and entitled *History Of The Riot At Colfax, Grant Parish, Louisiana, . . . with a brief sketch of the trial of the . . . Prisoners in the Circuit Court of the United States.* The anti-Northern point of view of the Committee of Seventy—and indirectly of the printers—is unmistakably apparent. "Throughout the length and breadth of the State anarchy, confusion and disorder reigned, and the utmost bitterness of feeling between the partisans of the rival governments prevailed." The Committee deplored "the bloody affair at Colfax" and could regard it "in no other light than affording another evidence of the results of the misrule and oppression of the Southern States at the hands of the Federal power." The riot had its lesson, they believed, both for Negro and for white, for it "teaches the former what he may expect, if in obedience to the develish [sic] teachings of the Radical emissary, he arrays himself in hostilty [sic] to the whites of the South," and it "teaches the latter that acts of violence, no matter what the provocation, are construed into hostility and hatred of the National Government, and retards the day of conservative triumph."

From the start Clark and Hofeline indicated their unfailing allegiance to the South and their determination to print the works that would reveal to the world at large the struggles and conflicts of postwar Louisiana. They followed their account of the race riot with Randell Hunt's *Appeal In Behalf Of Louisiana, to the Senate of the United States for the fulfillment of the constitutional guaranty to her of a republican form of government, As A State In The Union.* Prepared at the request of the Committee of Seventy in New Orleans, the *Appeal* was presented to the Senate of the United States "as a true expression of the views and feelings of the people of Louisiana."

It depicted a Louisiana "wronged and oppressed: . . . subjected to the rule of a faction, tyrannically set over her by judicial usurpation, supported by the military forces of the United States." It appealed for that Louisiana "in the name of a violated constitution . . . to restore to her the republican form of government to which, . . . she is entitled by express guaranty of the Constitution of the United States." Its stand on States' rights was firm. Its definition of the carpetbaggers as "flocks of greedy and unprincipled adventurers from the North" minced no words. The *Appeal* candidly declared that there was "no republican government in Louisiana," and reminded the Senators that when they "participated, during the war, in the emancipation of the slaves of the South, and struck off the fetters of the black man, it was not to fasten them on the white man."

The restoration of Louisiana to the Union was a culminating effort of the Reconstruction period in which Clark and Hofeline thus played their part. At the same time, they issued the Hon. F. C. Zacharie's *Review of The Constitutional Points in the Louisiana Case,* in which it was declared that

The loyalty of the Union readily yielded, during our late civil war, extraordinary powers to the General Government, in order to save the life of the Nation, and shut its eyes, if it did not approve, constitutional infringement, with a view to render more effective the operations in the field of the national arms. That emergency has, fortunately, passed away, and if we purpose to perpetuate civil freedom on this continent, it is high time to . . . gather up the disordered strands of the Constitution.

Having thus aligned themselves against the "usurpation," the partners continued their campaign for the re-emergence of the South by printing the *Arguments of Henry M. Spofford, before The Senate Committee on Privileges and Elections*. The pamphlet, concerned with "returning-officers" and the "returning-board law," was dedicated "To Those Citizens Of Louisiana Who respect the Traditions of the Founders Of The Republic, And Who Hope That Constitutional Government Within The United States Is Still A Possibility And Not A Dream."

Substituting for the direct attack the instrument of satire, Clark and Hofeline varied their imprints by publishing James Dugan's *Doctor Dispachemquic; A Story of the Great Southern Plague of 1878.* Supposedly centered about the epidemic of 1878, the story is sharpened with the double edge of satire, as is the Publishers' Notice regarding the book:

In presenting "Doctor Dispachemquic" to the favorable consideration of the reading public, the publishers desire to state that, in this work, the author has opened up a phase of life hitherto untouched by any novelist. . . .
   It is a satire, in the sense that it remorselessly depicts the follies and crimes of a certain class of people and so-called physicians, but underneath it all there is so much that is instructive and practical that the reader will rise from its perusal with a feeling that he has not only been well entertained but greatly benefitted.

Printed in double columns and bound in gilt-lettered purple cloth, *Doctor Dispachemquic* was sent forth as a healing agent for Louisiana's festering wounds. Less healing, but no less essential to place before the public, were other Clark and Hofeline imprints, the *Argument of Dr. D. W. Brickell . . . in reply to the representatives of the bondholders,* the *Speech* of delegate Warmoth on the public debt of Louisiana, delivered at the Constitutional Convention in 1879, and the *Argument* of delegate Forman on the same occasion, in which the orator asked:

What is slavery? Is it not the essence of slavery that one man, the master, shall take all the earnings of the slave. If the so-called public creditor is to continue, with the office-holder, to take all the rewards of our industry, are we not continuing to be slaves, and are we here to rivet those chains forever, and to permit those felonious fingers that manipulated the ballots to reach into the pockets of posterity and rob the children whose fathers are yet unborn?

   In their engrossment with the turbulent affairs of the present, the printers of the South would not and did not forget the affairs of the past. To remind the reading public of the roseate days that were dead, they issued Valcour Aime's *Plantation Diary,* and to stir up—if they needed stirring up—recollections of a more recent and violent past, they printed for subscription Napier Bartlett's *A Soldier's Story of the War; including the marches and battles of the Washington Artillery, and of Other Louisiana Troops.* The author prefaced his story with a word to subscribers that reveals the printing problems of New Orleans in 1874, for he asked their "indulgence . . . for not having prepared a more costly work—an omission due to the present disturbed financial and political condition of the city. This narrative was not written with any hope of profit; but should the reception given indicate an interest on the part of the public in the State troops during the war, or justify the expense, this will be followed by a more complete work, giving incidents of the return home of the disbanded army." An Appendix, containing Camp Stories and Tales Of The Crescent City before and since the war, was "added to the edition intended for subscribers, at the request of old army friends. . . . they were most of them in their original shape put together while living in small tents, around camp-fires, or read aloud during the intervals of guard mounting. . . . 'Under the Yoke,' was New Orleans, as it was misgoverned immediately upon our return, and as it has been ever since." Clark, himself a Confederate veteran, must have felt a particular interest in these camp stories, an interest paralleled by that of James Redpath in his own Camp Fire tales for the North. Even in an anonymous collection of verse issued by the Steam Book and Job Printers, Clark and Hofeline, in 1878, and entitled *The Muse, As I Have Found Her,* were included a poem, "The Rebel—A Carolina Tale," and a Dedication that expressed the forlorn condition of the times:

In an age and country where publications of the nature of this are so unusual, it is as impossible to anticipate success as it would be rash to say that it is deserved. Poets are rare, philosophers do not even starve, for they do not exist, and the arts, at least in our remote corner, live upon the grudging charity of the few.

In the "remote corner" that was New Orleans, more pressing publications were needed during the seventies, brochures and pamphlets and books that reflected current local economic and legal conditions. These also Clark and Hofeline printed, issuing the *Charter, Constitution, By-Laws And Rules of the New Orleans Cotton Exchange* and the *Report Of The Committee of the Chamber of Commerce Of New Orleans to the Senate Transportation Committee,* in which the commercial needs of the port of New Orleans were stressed, together with the relief that would be afforded by the Fort St. Philip Canal. For the Crescent City's Bar Association, the firm lent its imprint to the *Constitution and By-Laws,* and for the profession in general to Thomas J. Semmes's *History of the Laws of Louisiana and of The Civil Law* and Louque's *Digest of Decisions of the Supreme*

Court of Louisiana. Legal successions and briefs were printed at
one dollar a page, large octavo, by Clark and Hofeline, who occasionally styled themselves "Law Printers" with whom brief printing was "A Specialty." For his fellow Masons, Clark continued his
services by issuing proceedings of their convocations, together with
James B. Scot's compilation of the *Outline of the Rise And Progress
Of Freemasonry In Louisiana.*

No work, however, that appeared over the Clark and Hofeline
imprint reflects more acutely the local reaction to the times than a
periodical undertaken by the veteran editor, Daniel K. Whitaker,
and innocuously dubbed *The New Orleans Monthly Review.* Despite
its colorless title, that magazine, filled with the fulminations of a
South disarmed but far from propitiated, still bears testimony to the
bitterness with which New Orleans faced Reconstruction and to the
one-sided conviction with which the printers of the Crescent City
gave voice to that bitterness. This was no *Russell's Magazine,* in
which a brotherhood of poets joined to share their dreams, but a
periodical clamoring with invective, excoriating the North, demanding redress for the indignities and humiliations of a Reconstruction
effort it refused almost to comprehend.

Although the first numbers of *The New Orleans Monthly Review*
were issued by the Steam-Power Print of W. A. Weed, the Editor's
Salutatory of April 1874 indicated not only his own purposes, but a
point of view that would be intensified when Clark and Hofeline
took over.

The pride of New Orleans has, heretofore, consisted in her commerce.
No people were ever more enterprising, . . . than the merchants of
New Orleans. But no class of men among us has been more affected by
the disorganization in the social system of the South, and the evils thence
resulting to labor and capital, than our merchants. The agriculture of
the country must be reinstated by an infusion of new life into it. . . .

In a word, we are, at the present time, in a state of great depression
in the Crescent City. Money is scarce; confidence is slack, . . .

Commerce will receive our special attention. It is the great and leading interest of this important metropolis. . . . We shall have an eye, also,
on what the General Government does, and what, . . . it omits doing,
which it ought to do, for the restoration of our depressed commerce.

Despite this intention, the editor insisted that the *Review* would be
a "literary Monthly," for which contributions would be solicited

from "the educated ladies of the South" as well as from the "dissertations and lectures that are weekly submitted to our Academy of Sciences." Indeed, it had been "by an unanimous vote of that learned body" that the *Review* had been selected for such a purpose. Literature, of course, was "neither partisan nor sectional," and the editor was not loath to promise a non-partisanship he would never uphold:

While we are devoted to the principles of a free government and to freedom of inquiry, we shall studiously avoid everything like partisanship in politics and religion, using the press, (always a mighty engine when in honest and able hands,) for the great purpose for which it was originally designed by the framers of the Federal Constitution, viz: the publication of the truth from good motives, and for justifiable ends. These, as we understand, are the only limitations to the freedom of the press in America.

Yet the political preoccupations of the monthly were such that, even at the outset, partisanship could not be avoided:

A great political convulsion has occurred, by which the foundations of the fabric of American society have been shaken and its integrity imperilled. . . . While many are overwhelmed with despair, turning their attention to the past, . . . others, . . . think they see rays of gold light, . . . from which they draw favorable inferences in respect to the future. It is certainly not a time for idle retrospects, neglected opportunities of action, and gloomy forebodings. Much is to be done, if not in retracing our steps, yet in moving forward courageously in new directions. We should never abandon our principles in any contingency, but reasserting them, at all times, with dignity and firmness, study to ascertain how we may extricate ourselves from existing difficulties, how we may recover the ground we have lost, and maintain liberty and independence without losing self-esteem. . . . The conductors of the Daily, Weekly, Monthly and Quarterly press have duties imposed upon them in this crisis, of a more serious character than ever before devolved on them.

It was this magazine, promising an impossible non-partisanship while it was pledged to the reassertion of Southern principles, that Clark and Hofeline printed in 1875 and 1876. It is true that some attention was given in the monthly to such uncontroversial subjects as "The Head Waters Of The Savannah," "Authors Read By Our Grandmothers," and "The English Drama." Poems on "Orange

Flowers" or "Thoughts Of The Beautiful" brightened the pages now and then, while articles on evolution or the origin of species lent a scientific air to its issues and critical notices of books submitted through the courtesy of the Canal Street bookseller, R. G. Eyrich, gave the numbers a literary flavor. By and large, however, the magazine existed neither for literary nor for scientific purposes, but for the reinstatement of Southern rights, and in its efforts to bring those rights to fruition, the monthly was to prove itself not only primarily political in nature, but vehemently partisan in tone.

As early as January, 1875, when Clark and Hofeline were serving as printers, the magazine presented its views on one of the most vital issues of Reconstruction, the Negro in the role of constitution-maker. Opposed to the "leveling up doctrines" contained in the "so-called Civil Rights Bill" introduced by the Radical party, it noted the "folly of Federal interference" in placing the Negro over the "free and intelligent white people of Louisiana." In April it pursued the theme more furiously, declaring that "the transformation of slaves into magistrates and rulers" was one of the "disastrous consequences" of Reconstruction. "The Government ordains not only that Africans—of a race different from our own—shall be voters and fill the highest offices, but that they shall be our guests and companions in social circles." The magazine proceeded to air its opinion that the Fifteenth Amendment was nothing but a punitive measure against the South on the part of the North.

Whether the extension of suffrage to the negro was intended as a punitive or as a party measure, . . . it has up to this time proved a terrible curse to the country. . . . These imbecile but passionate beings, have, as is well-known, been ready tools in the hands of ambitious and grasping demagogues. . . . They have not intelligence enough to judge of the qualifications of candidates for office—much less to perform the duty of rulers, but under the present arrangement they have votes to dispose of for party purposes, and, when in a numerical majority, their influence is very commanding. . . . His [the Negro's] muscular strength fits him for toil, and for manual and mechanical labor, and this appears to be the sphere for which Providence designed him, and not that of statesmanship. His color separates him, *longo intervallo,* from the white race, . . .

In our opinion, the peace of the country cannot be restored, . . . until steps are taken by the Federal Government, . . . to remove the whole

African population, . . . to some part of the public domain, where they may live apart by themselves. . . . The 14th and 15th Amendments of the Constitution were violently, not to say fraudulently, introduced into the body of that instrument, and, in due time, will we trust, be subject to democratic revision.

Since the monthly was of the opinion that the Fifteenth Amendment was devised merely as an instrument of punishment, it is not remarkable that it viewed the Civil War itself as treason on the part of the North. This casuistry was given free expression in an article entitled "Were The Confederates Guilty Of Treason?" in the February, 1875, number.

The truth is, the late war, was a war between the masses of people who composed the Northern States, on one side, acting without right, and without the authority of a legitimately organized government, and the Confederate States, with a regular government, against which as sovereign powers, treason could be committed, on the other side. The object of the war was to overthrow the sovereignty of the Southern States, and reduce them to the condition of conquered provinces, which the assailants were able to accomplish, . . . by the force of overwhelming numbers. This was treason to the Southern States.

Turning to the issues of Reconstruction, *The New Orleans Monthly Review* voiced, loud and shrill, the embitterment, the confusion, the antagonism of the South.

The approaches of tyranny are slow, silent, and at first imperceptible. . . . One breach after another is made in the ramparts of the Constitution until at length the whole edifice is seen to totter. We do not mean the new Constitution, a thing of shreds and patches, botched and framed— so to speak, not by the States, but by the Reconstruction Committee, now so famous, or rather infamous in history—but we mean the old Constitution.

Federal interference with States' rights was another "treasonable" act, a natural target for the periodical's arrows, as were all postwar efforts at Reconstruction.

The forcible assault upon the sovereignty of the States was of a treasonable character. . . . It is a lamentable passage in the history of our country . . . but not more so than the undisguised exhibition of usurpation and tyranny by a professedly American Congress since the war, and the farcical and utterly contemptible attempt of a committee in Congress to reconstruct sovereign States of this Union, and prescribe limitations to their powers of action—to define for the information of those who had been freemen and republicans all their lives, the doctrines of civil liberty and of civil rights.

Carpetbag ascendancy loosened some of the magazine's most violent invective:

For the space of nine years, we have had carpet-bag ascendancy—that of a vile set of men, without honor, principle, or humanity—who followed in the wake of the Federal Army after the war, and carried the trail of the serpent and the sting of the scorpion wherever they went. . . . the carpet-bagger and the negro, congenial associates, enter into a compact . . . to share all the laurels and all the spoils of office. . . . When is this farce to cease?

Corruption in public office was denounced as "the canker . . . consuming the national life." The voluntary surrender by a State of its sovereignty was regarded as "a suicidal act." The entire object of Reconstruction was flayed in a burning excoriation. "The object of the reconstruction measures was, in the first place—not the good of the country, but the cruel, inhuman and indecent punishment of brave and conscientious men, who were guiltless of wrong to civil liberty."

Despite this stubborn opposition, this unyielding partisanship, the *Review,* and through it not only the printers, Clark and Hofeline, but the South itself, saw "light in the distance." Better times were coming. The Young South, fighting gallantly "for liberty and independence," no longer afraid to earn its living by the sweat of its brow, would in time bring the New South into being. Meanwhile, however, the South would reiterate its insistence upon the constitutionality of States' rights and the unconstitutionality of every Reconstruction measure it wished to defy.

To this magazine Clark and Hofeline lent their imprint at the height of Reconstruction, and through this magazine the vicissitudes of the printers and of the South in general may be relived. To its friends and patrons the *Review* expressed the "regret that the stringency of the money market, . . . arising from heavy taxation and the protracted misgovernment, State and Federal, of the country, rendered it difficult, if not impossible, for many of our best subscribers to pay even the small amount of their subscription to this work, . . . Had these terms been promptly complied with, *there would have been no occasion for the temporary suspension of the work*. As matters, however, stood, its suspension became necessary." Priced at $5 a year, and optimistically described as a magazine "always to be found upon the centre tables and in the offices of our wealthiest and most influential citizens," the *Review* weathered some of the storms of Reconstruction, but not all. Although it was termed "an excellent medium through which to advertise," it attracted few advertisers other than Soulé's Commercial College and Literary Institute, the Crescent Mutual Insurance Company, and Dr. Bradfield's Female Regulator. Its circulation was never large, there were many "defaulting subscribers," and the publication of the magazine was marked by irregularity until its last appearance in August, 1876. In January, 1878, it was superseded by the *New Orleans Quarterly Review,* which, in turn, gave way in 1880 to the *Southern Quarterly Review* also printed by Clark and Hofeline. Despite its ephemeral nature and short life, *The New Orleans Monthly Review* was an important and highly articulate vehicle for the opinions of its editor, Daniel K. Whitaker, its printers, Clark and Hofeline, and the bewildered, irreconcilable South of the Reconstruction period. More markedly than any other Clark and Hofeline imprint, it represented the Southern approach to Reconstruction, the hatreds that persisted after the war had ended, the distrust, coupled with a faint and glimmering hope for the future, that characterized the South during the difficult decade of the 1870's. It is a museum piece that still depicts the Reconstruction period and the printer's part in that period.

There were other periodicals with which Clark and Hofeline may have been associated. From their address at 112 Gravier Street were issued between 1878 and 1882 the *Daily City Item,* the *New Orleans Observer,* and the *Southwestern Churchman.* But, apparently even more ephemeral than *The New Orleans Monthly Review,* these publications exist only in Directory listings, the shadows of their names. With one other ephemeral periodical Clark and Hofeline were definitely associated, not only as printers but as proprietors—a publication intriguingly entitled *Southern Knight.* It, too, lives only in a Directory listing where, in 1882, the names of Clark and Hofeline appear as proprietors of the magazine, which was issued from their address at 112 Gravier. It is a temptation to speculate upon the nature of a *Southern Knight* known only by its name and the character of its printers. Did it continue along the lines laid down in *The New Orleans Monthly Review,* reasserting an allegiance to States' rights, a condemnation of Negro suffrage and carpetbag ascendancy, an invective against the "punitive" measures of the North? Or did it, instead, become more resigned to a Reconstruction already historical, more mellow in its approach to the postwar problems of the South? Better still, did it grasp at that faint glimmering of hope in the future that had been adumbrated in *The New Orleans Monthly Review,* and set forth to champion the causes of the New South? By 1882 the New South had begun to emerge from the ashes of war and the holocaust of Reconstruction. In that year, the last of the association between Clark and Hofeline, a *Southern Knight* donned armor under their auspices. It is to be hoped that his crusade plunged him forward into the future rather than backward into the past, into the promise of the New South rather than into the confusion of the Old.

The future severed the partnership between Charles W. Clark and Albert D. Hofeline. By 1883 Hofeline was employed as foreman of the stationer-printers, J. S. Rivers, and Clark was serving as a printer with L. Graham & Son, a firm which had been established after the war and which had prospered until it employed about forty men and offered special facilities for "fine book and job work." Subsequently, Clark appears in the New Orleans Directories as a bookbinder or printer, while Hofeline appears first in partnership with Alexander Malus in the firm of Malus and Hofeline, and finally on his own as Albert D. Hofeline, engraver and printer of Chartres Street. Charles W. Clark survived as a New Orleans printer until his death in 1907, Albert D. Hofeline until 1928. At Clark's funeral the members both of Quitman Lodge and Typographical Union No. 17 attended the services in a body. He had been, the *New Orleans Item* declared, "one of the best known printers in the City."

He had been more than that. Born in the North, he had affiliated himself through the greater part of his long life with the plans and purposes of the South. He had served the Confederacy during the war, and after the war he had helped to give expression to the voice of the South. Although he worked as a printer for some fifty years, the most fruitful and most significant part of his career had the Reconstruction as background. He was primarily a Reconstruction printer, setting his imprint upon the books and pamphlets and periodicals that expressed the demands and needs, the perplexities and humiliations, the opposition and intransigence of the postwar South. His imprints reflect Reconstruction in all its phases. Through them the negations of hatred and defiance are boldly mirrored, and through them also glimmers a more positive hope in the future when a New South, struggling to take shape, would at last find form and embodiment.

VII. CULTURE FOR THE MIDDLE WEST

Robert Fergus

PRAIRIE PRINTER

B Y THE 1830's the American frontier had pushed on beyond the Middle West. And because it was a later frontier than that in the East, it was characterized by swifter and more self-conscious transformations. Only five years after the last Indian War between the Sacs and Foxes, Chicago became a city. Talk of Indian claims was still rife when it adopted as its motto, "Urbs in Horto," a rather euphemistic description of a muddy little town on the low banks of a sluggish bayou. On Chicago's unpaved streets, the green turf of prairie grass reminded the "Garden City" of its origins. Its sidewalks were planks of wood. Its only water supply was the peddler and his pail. Wolves abounded; bears were occasionally seen; and a deer could be shot within a mile or two of the new settlement. Prairie chickens and quail invaded the town, along with horse thieves, and fires sprang up continually in its flimsy dwellings. But Chicago had emerged swiftly from the wilderness, surviving fire and boom and panic. Work on the Illinois and Michigan Canal had begun. Hides and grain, beef and pork rolled from the city. Schools sprang up, and the seal of Hercules seemed suddenly not inappropriate for a city that had risen out of swamp and mud on the shores of the Chicago River. Of the 4,000-odd inhabitants who, by 1839, were that city, many would survive to find their muddy little settlement one of the greatest and richest metropolises in the world. One of those 4,000-odd, destined to share in and record that incredible metamorphosis, was a printer by trade, a Scot named Robert Fergus.

Born in 1815 in the Gallowgate of Glasgow, the son of Margaret and John Fergus, organist and composer of glees, young Robert had been early orphaned. He was committed to the charge of William

Leckie, at whose small school four miles northwest of Glasgow Cross, in the village of Maryhill, the boy was grounded in the rudiments. His studies were rounded off at William Lindsay's Commercial School in Glasgow, and at the age of fifteen Robert was apprenticed to Messrs. Hutchison and Brookman, printers in Villafield. His career had begun.

Robert Hutchison, a printer and stereotyper, and George Brookman, a skilled operative printer, were well qualified to teach the boy his specialized trade. In May 1831 Messrs. Hutchison and Brookman were appointed printers to Glasgow University, and Robert's proficiency as a compositor was of such note that his galley proofs were tacked on the outside door of the printing office, where students of the University would see them and read the notice that had been placed above: "A guinea for an error." The following year, upon the dissolution of the partnership, Fergus continued his apprenticeship at Villafield with George Brookman, who served in association with the publisher and bookseller, John Blackie. Along with readings in Scott and Burns and Allan Ramsay, he worked at the case, setting type for editions of Scott's *Marmion, The Lady of the Lake,* and *The Lay of the Last Minstrel,* as well as for Sturm's *Reflections* and Meadows' French, Italian, and Spanish dictionaries. By the time his apprenticeship had been served, he was equipped for the future with a wife, Margaret Scott, whom he had married in 1836, and with a thorough knowledge of a trade that he was to follow all his life. It was by accident, however, that instead of continuing as a Glasgow printer, Robert Fergus became a pioneer in an as yet unknown village called Chicago four thousand miles away.

Francis Metcalf, a young Englishman who had just returned from Milwaukee, gave Fergus so glowing an account of the American West that he decided to pull up his roots and become a journeyman in the largest sense of the word. With his wife he made the long voyage, setting sail from Glasgow by paddle-wheel steamer for Liverpool, and thence by the packet-ship, *Orpheus,* for New York. By steamer, Erie Canal packet, and again by side-wheel steamer he journeyed west to Milwaukee. There the business arrangements proposed by Metcalf seemed unsuitable, nor did Fergus accept Harrison Reed's offer of a half interest in the Milwaukee *Sentinel.* Instead, hearing of a settlement to the south named Chicago, he embarked on the side-wheel steamer, *Anthony Wayne,* and arrived in the city on Monday, July 1, 1839, nearly two months after he had left Glasgow.

On the southeast corner of Lake and Clark Streets a three-story brick building had been erected three years before. Because it had been designed as a meetinghouse, it was called the Saloon Building, and already it boasted a colorful history, since Stephen Douglas had debated there. It boasted a few offices, too, among them that of the engravers and printers, Rudd and Childs, with whom Fergus took a position as journeyman printer. There he met the man destined soon to become his partner.

William Ellis, two years Fergus's senior, had been born in Montreal and had learned the printing business in a newspaper office there before the August day in 1840 when he set up in Chicago as a "jour" in Ryan's *Tribune* office. Later that year Ellis purchased in New York the materials for a job office, and after Fergus had worked for a time on the *Chicago American* and the *Chicago Democrat,* the two young printers joined forces as Ellis and Fergus with offices on the third floor of the Saloon Building. The house bustled with temperance lectures and concerts, with an intelligence agency, a land office, and a bookbindery. But the stir in the rooms of Ellis and Fergus, the first job office in the city, was destined to reverberate beyond the third story of a brick building in a small Midwestern community. The time and the place and the characters had met at a point of destiny. It was a time and a place for "firsts"—and Robert Fergus and William Ellis grasped the time and gloried in the place, producing in rapid succession one landmark after another to expand and cultivate an American frontier.

Even before his association with Ellis, Fergus had issued one of those memorable "firsts." In September of 1839, only two months after his arrival in Chicago, the Common Council had ordered the printing, in pamphlet form, of the city's laws and ordinances. The work had been assigned to Fergus's employers, Rudd and Childs, but since that firm could not find sufficient funds to complete the printing for thirty-three cents a copy, they offered to transfer their contract to Robert Fergus. When the work had been put into type, it was noticed that there were six blank pages at the end. On those pages were inserted the names of the business men of the city, Fergus setting each name directly in type as it occurred to him, without previous canvassing or written copy, until the six pages were filled, with a covering title, "Chicago Business Directory." There were no numbers on any street except Lake Street. The brief business directory, set up in that primitive manner by Fergus, became, for all its inadequacies, the first Chicago directory. Although *The Laws and Ordinances of the City of Chicago. Passed in Common Council* bears on its title-page the name of Edward H. Rudd as printer, it was actually printed by Fergus, whose name appears nowhere in it. The city paid $25 for fifty copies, and about fifty copies were sold to the citizens at fifty cents each. The remainder of the five hundred printed were never used, and in time were lost. Robert Fergus, however, remembered this first of his many firsts, and, mindful of its significance in Chicago's history, was to revise and reprint it in 1876, when the printer, like his work, had become a landmark.

At the moment, when he had just joined forces with William Ellis, the landmarks were all before him. Their names alone are sufficient reminders that the key to the present lies in the past, that the printer setting type in a straggling village can help make of that village a city of overwhelming proportions and magnificent power. In the order of their appearance, then, the Ellis and Fergus "firsts" included the first volume of poetry printed in Chicago: Horatio Cooke's *Gleanings of Thought,* printed by the firm of book and job printers in 1841, just six years after the Indians had danced their last great dance in what was to become a city, just seven years after the last wild bear had been killed in a wilderness of woods soon to be identified as a street. Not long afterward Ellis and Fergus pursued their efforts at bringing culture to the Middle West by issuing in blue-gray wrappers the earliest poem separately printed in Chicago, William H. Bushnell's *Knowledge is Power,* a poem pronounced before the Junior Lyceum of Chicago in 1843.

The following year became an *annus mirabilis* for the firm and for the city. Few buildings were numbered in the "Queen City of the Northwest" when Ellis and Fergus presented to that city its first regular directory—the first book compiled, printed, bound, and issued in Chicago. On December 1, 1843, the preface was written: "The Directory of Chicago, now presented to the public, may be regarded as an experiment. It must be decided by those for whose use and benefit it has been prepared, whether it is required, and can be sustained. The sudden rise, and unexampled prosperity of Chicago, have created a curiosity in regard to its early history, and the incidents connected with its rise and progress, which considerations of interest, if nothing else, impel us to embrace every suitable opportunity to gratify." This *General Directory and Business Advertiser of the City of Chicago, For the year 1844; together with a historical sketch and statistical account to the present time* was compiled by the attorney J. Wellington Norris, and printed, with the seal of the city on its title-page, by Ellis and Fergus in 1844. The volume, for which Fergus set the type and Ellis did the presswork, bears evidence of the fact that it was prepared from a careless canvass, for sailors were made tailors, and tailors sailors, names were "spelled at" and locations guessed. None the less, it made history as the first of a long line of regular Chicago directories. Chicagoans were aware that its publication was an event, for on June 5, 1844, when the cornerstone of Trinity Church was laid, several articles, including that directory, were deposited in a leaden box beneath—a surviving testimonial to a city that was springing up in less than a generation, almost before the very eyes of the printer who had set the type as he stood before the case.

As an illustration of the "favorable auspices" under which Chicago's bookmaking and publishing business had been commenced, the compiler of the directory alluded to another work printed by Ellis and Fergus and "now about ready for publication," the third volume of "Mr. Scammon's Reports of the Supreme Court." The first and second volumes of Scammon's *Reports of Cases Argued and Determined in the Supreme Court of the State of Illinois* had been printed in the East. With the third volume (and the fourth as well) Ellis and Fergus of Chicago undertook the printing, marking another landmark by producing the first work of its kind completed and issued from the local press. As J. Wellington Norris put it, "The fact that the execution of this volume is equal, if not superior to the two former ones, which were issued from two of the best presses in the East, is highly creditable to our city, and must be gratifying to the profession generally."

But it was a simple octavo pamphlet that climaxed the significant year of 1844 for Ellis and Fergus. The first historical work printed in Chicago, Mrs. Kinzie's *Narrative of the Massacre at Chicago, August 15, 1812,* has become not only a milestone in local annals, but a *pièce de résistance* for book collectors. The story it told was unique. John Kinzie, a silversmith by trade, had come to Chicago in the spring of 1804, the first permanent white settler in the place. Despite his personal friendship with the Indians, who dubbed him "Shaw-nee-aw-kee," the settlement at Fort Dearborn became in 1812 the scene of a frightful massacre in which men and women fought hand to hand with the Indians, in which hundreds of painted savages surrounded the stockaded fort and tomahawks glistened in the summer air. Kinzie and his family owed their safety to two friendly Potawatomis and a half-breed, and Kinzie's daughter-in-law, having viewed the slaughter from across the river, was able to write her first-hand account of the massacre in a half-bound blank book of about four quires, from which Ellis and Fergus set the type of a rare and incomparable thirty-four-page pamphlet. Complete with a frontispiece map of the settlement and printed wrappers, Mrs. John Kinzie's *Narrative of the Massacre at Chicago* was issued from the Saloon Building in 1844, "the only printed account by an eye-witness" of the troubled time from which a great city was at length to emerge. The pamphlet would be reprinted, discussed, and para-phrased, but in its original form it remains a rare tribute both to a city and to the printer who realized its worth and set down its story. Nearly fifty years after its appearance, Robert Fergus was to attend the ceremonies held near the "Massacre Tree" for the unveiling of a bronze group of the Chicago Massacre, when he must have thought far back to the time when a half-bound blank book was turned into a small and unpretentious pamphlet that made history.

Through the years, as Ellis and Fergus prospered, dealing in printers' materials and operating the first printers' paper and supply house in Chicago, the firm produced other "firsts." In 1845 *The Rosarist's Companion: or, Manual of Devout Exercises* appeared, not merely an "unusual early Chicago product of book-making," but a "first" in local Catholic printing. Two years later Robert Fergus issued the "first item of typographical interest" in the form of John E. Wheeler's *Address . . . before the Printers of Chicago, on the 18th of January, 1847, the anniversary of Franklin's Birth-Day*. The next year, when he himself attended the birthday celebration, his toast was "The festival of St. Benjamin—The first on the American Calendar."

During his entire career, the festival of St. Benjamin remained the first on Fergus's calendar. With his partner he had issued, besides some epoch-making books and pamphlets, a four-page newspaper, the *Quid Nunc,* the first penny paper published west of the Alleghenies. Its purpose, like that of the publishers, was to "advance the cause of Literature, the Fine Arts, Science, Commerce, Agriculture, and the Mechanical Arts; combined with such other topics, of local and general interest as circumstances may . . . give rise to. . . . It will give no currency, nor encouragement to personalities, in any shape whatever; nevertheless, as a vehicle, or instrument of general reform, it will be its pride and cue to lash folly, and expose oppression." This lofty purpose the *Quid Nunc* sustained for only thirty-seven numbers, from July to August, 1842, being discontinued after the proprietor, one David D. Griswold, was unable to provide the $131.33 owing to the printers! Two years after the untimely demise of the *Quid Nunc,* the firm of Ellis and Fergus printed another periodical destined to have a longer life—*The Illinois Medical and Surgical Journal,* the first medical journal issued in Chicago, begun in the interests of the newly founded Rush Medical College.

It was a time of newness, a time of beginnings in Chicago during the 1840's. And the firm of Ellis and Fergus, boasting that "every variety of book and job printing" would be done in the "best style and on the most moderate terms," shared in the newness and in the beginnings. The city, having been born, was growing, and the printers fostered its growth with their publications. Education was paramount as schools arose on the prairies, and Ellis and Fergus were on hand to print an address on the *Education of Young Men* or a treatise on *Phreno-Mnemotechny, (or Art of acquiring Memory).* Medically, too, Chicago was developing, and for Rush Medical College, which had opened with a class of twenty-two students, the firm printed not only the early issues of *The Illinois Medical and Surgical Journal,* but numerous lectures, announcements, and catalogues. For a local sermon or a local lodge, a local Baptist association or a local engine company, Ellis and Fergus served as book and job printers to their adopted city. Fergus especially served his city in many ways. Attending the River and Harbor Convention, he shared in the improvement of western waterways and harbors on the Great Lakes. Establishing the *Democratic Advocate and Commercial Advertiser,* he became, with his partner, a corporation printer who could send couriers to Michigan to obtain an advance copy of the President's Message, or announce the election of Polk when the news arrived as a "special" way-bill, along with the letter sack, at his office. By the end of the forties, the city had shaped itself. The time of beginnings was over. And toward the end of the decade the firm of Ellis and Fergus was dissolved. After a brief session with Stewart and Wheeler, William Ellis during the height of the gold fever abandoned Chicago for California, becoming a foreman at a salary of $100 in gold per week, but still investing his money in Chicago real estate. Fergus remained, investing not only his money but his life in the city of his choice. Opening a printers' warehouse, he survived two fires in '49, after which he was compelled to work as a compositor. By 1852 he was back in harness as a printer in his own right, continuing along the lines laid down by Ellis and Fergus. For the educational advancement of his city, Robert Fergus produced a treatise on *Industrial Universities for the People;* for its medical progress he issued the *Transactions* of the Illinois State Medical Society; for its literary entertainment, *Prairie Fire! A Tale of Early Illinois;* and for its general enlightenment he printed *Sloan's Garden City,* a weekly newspaper issued not merely in the interests of Sloan's patent medicines, but in the larger interests of "pro-western" literature.

With his city, as the decades passed, Robert Fergus faced the trials and hardships of the years: the panic of '57, the Civil War, the Great Fire. During the war his firm was carried on by his sons, particularly George H. Fergus, who served also as a Zouave Cadet during the conflict. With offices on Clark Street, George H. Fergus continued along the lines set down by the founder, printing works of local interest, announcements of the Chicago Medical College, and reports of the Chicago Charitable Eye and Ear Infirmary, and trying his hand at a latter-day Kinzie *Narrative* with the *Life and Adventures of William Filley, who was stolen from his Home . . . by the Indians.* Robert Fergus's friendship with the great detective Allan Pinkerton, whom the printer had first welcomed to the city, received a testimonial of sorts when his son printed *Tests on passenger conductors, made by the National Police Agency* of which Pinkerton was principal.

And so the past set the pattern of the present, until the Great Fire of 1871 destroyed much of both. On October 8 and 9 the conflagration raged through the wooden city, a searing calamity that spared little except the bravery of the desolate. Fergus, with his predilection for statistics, doubtless found a grim satisfaction in collecting the estimates of destruction after the roaring flames had died to embers and the embers to cold ash. Wiping out almost every building in the city, the fire had burned over 2,100 acres of land and rendered 100,000 people homeless. It had brought destruction to industry of all types, and not the least to the book trade. Many of the smaller dealers were so overwhelmed by the catastrophe that they were forced out of business. Though the actual loss of plates and manuscripts was comparatively light, the general loss to publishers was so great that for a time they were discouraged from the experiment of issuing new books that did not bear an Eastern imprint. Nearly every publisher was burned out, and many of the largest bookstores fell in smoking ruin. The loss in stationery was estimated at $1,110,000, and in books at $864,000. The great Book House of Griggs & Company, the Western News Company's Block, the publishers, Keen & Cooke—all went down with their companions in the trade, went down temporarily until they could start again in other quarters. The "Burnt District" became a geographical reality. Booksellers' Row had been devastated, and the fire had not spared locally printed books and pamphlets. Those that did survive were given a new name and were enhanced with a special value. They became "ante-fire imprints."

Robert Fergus not only surveyed the destruction of the fire, but suffered personally from it, for it had deprived him of his home on Dearborn Avenue. On the other hand, it had given him a new purpose, a new ambition. While Chicago was rising physically from the ashes, Robert Fergus set himself a great task. He would rescue from complete oblivion the early history of a city that had gone down in flame. During the forties he had helped make that history. Now, during the seventies and eighties, he would help to record it, reminding the world of beginnings that were lost to sight and might otherwise have been lost to memory. And so, the career of Robert Fergus—like the annals of his city—divides itself into two parts. The more or less unconscious shaper of history had become, in a way, the conscious historian. The maker had become recorder.

With the great project of what was, in time, to be known as the Fergus Historical Series, Robert Fergus came into his own. He had grown, it was said, faster than the city; from being a simple citizen he had expanded into a corporation. For he rescued from oblivion the history of early Chicago, part of which he was. While Fergus's office became now a rallying place for survivors of pioneer days, Fergus himself became a fountainhead spouting forth the streams of history. The first number of the Fergus Historical Series was printed in 1876, a republication of Joseph N. Balestier's *Annals of Chicago,* a lecture which had been delivered before the Chicago Lyceum in the Saloon Building in 1840, a lecture which Robert Fergus had doubtless heard. The original edition had been printed by his old associate, Edward Rudd, and now, thirty-six years later, Fergus, having heard that a copy was extant at the Wisconsin State Library, decided to reprint it. From then on the Fergus Historical Series was on its way. Over thirty issues would appear through the years, their paper wrappers colored pink or yellow, blue or gray. Carefully indexed and illustrated, they offered to the citizenry of Chicago, in exchange for prices ranging from 25¢ to $1.50, the rich mine of the city's history. For years, the old business directory of 1839 had lain upon the imposing stone, and now, revised and corrected until even the "Old Settlers" pronounced it complete, *Fergus' Directory of the City of Chicago, 1839* was reprinted as the second pamphlet of his Series.

As the years passed, the pamphlets increased. Lectures delivered before the Chicago Historical Society, of which Fergus became a member, were introduced in the Series. Biographical sketches of early settlers, reminiscences of early Chicago, accounts of early medical and legal Chicago, Fergus's own compilation on the Chicago River and Harbor Convention which he had attended, a reprint of Mrs. Kinzie's *Narrative,* papers on early Illinois railroads, Congressional reminiscences, and local Indians all rolled from the Fergus press to remind the city of its beginnings. Early directories were reprinted, with errors corrected and omissions filled. On his eighty-first birthday Fergus wrote the introduction to the reprint of the *Directory of the City of Chicago Illinois, for 1843,* which he had first printed when he was twenty-nine! So the past was drawn into the present by a man whose life spanned so much of both. "The Fergus Printing Company of Chicago," it was announced, "is doing an excellent work and one that has received too little recognition in bringing out, in suitable form, the lectures, essays, memoirs, etc., that have, from time to time, come into the possession of the Chicago Historical and other Societies, relating to the early history of the City and State. . . .

"These papers are beautifully printed in a large paper pamphlet and sold for the moderate price of 25 and 50¢. . . . All this work is, to a great extent, a labor of love, as it has been unremunerative up to this time. But these volumes will have increasing value as time goes on, and a full set of them will, before many years, be rare. We do not know a worthier undertaking in the line of local publishing, or one which more fully deserves the cordial support of the people of Chicago than this one of the Messrs. Fergus."

Not all of Fergus's conscious efforts at resurrecting the history of his community were confined to his Series. In other works as well, he reminded the city of its roots. The first edition of the "Old Ranger," Governor John Reynolds' *My Own Times,* epitomizing the early history of the State, had been published in 1855, and the work had had an interesting although almost fatal history before Fergus rescued it from annihilation. The manuscript had been taken to a small job office in Belleville, Illinois, which issued some four hundred copies, printing them from a common hand press. "The typography was a miracle of wretchedness. The result was, 'My Own Times' remained unknown." Old Ranger, however, was far from content with such a fate for his book. On an autumn day in 1855 he set out to rectify the matter. "As Mr. D. B. Cooke, then Chicago's leading bookseller and publisher, was standing in the entrance to his establishment, a dray laden with shoe-boxes was backed against the curbing. Perched upon the load sat a tall, gaunt, odd-looking individual who immediately alighted, strode into the store, and, with considerable profanity, inquired for the proprietor. Making himself known he was informed in strong language that his visitor was no less than Governor Reynolds, and, in still stronger language, that he had written a book. The book would not sell. It *must* sell. He had boxed up every copy and brought them along." Cooke proved obliging, giving his receipt for about three hundred fifty copies of *My Own Times,* and the insistent author drove off atop the trundling dray. Two years later, however, in 1857, after only a trifling number of copies had been sold, a fire consumed D. B. Cooke's establishment, along with nearly every existing copy of Governor Reynolds' book. The fire of 1871 completed the work of destruction, until "copies . . . were not to be found save at such prices as would cause the possibly remaining dozen, to realize a larger total sum than the entire Belleville edition would have brought when issued." It was this volume which Fergus reproduced, adding to it a complete index, for he believed, as he wrote, that "no volume can . . . be of greater interest and value than one tracing the early growth . . . of a Commonwealth or a Nation. It need not necessarily be a ponderous tome. . . . But it should glow with the charm surrounding recitals of the every-day experience of those men whose lives are passed in molding the growth, character, and even destiny, of States or Countries." To this work Fergus lent his imprint in the hope that he would "assist in perpetuating the history of the great commonwealth of Illinois."

That hope motivated many of his undertakings, from an eye-witness account of *The Matyrdom of Lovejoy* to Kelton's *Annals of Fort Mackinac,* from the *Reception to the Settlers of Chicago by the Calumet Club* to Hurlbut's *Chicago Antiquities.* As the works devoted to a city and a State in the making had once borne the Fergus imprint, now volumes recording that making rolled from his press. The Chicago Historical Society's *Collections* or addresses, with expenses paid by such notable local leaders as L. Z. Leiter or Marshall Field, carried the Fergus imprint now, along with Moses' *Illinois, Historical and Statistical,* Reynolds' *Pioneer History of Illinois,* and Goodwin's *Discourse* on the eightieth anniversary of the occupation of Fort Dearborn.

In addition to his historical enterprises, Fergus executed job orders for various notable Chicago institutions: Rush Medical College, the Chicago Literary Club, the Fortnightly Club, the Calumet Club. And, now and then, he entered other fields as well. Fergus had never forgotten that he had been born a Scot, and so he was glad to issue Allan Ramsay's *Gentle Shepherd,* which he had loved in childhood, and his own revision of a *Glossary of Scottish Words.* Genealogies published by subscription supplemented his income, along with such works of general interest as Jackson's *Miller of Scrawnton Dale,* the *Dramatic Students' Vade Mecum* or Turchin's *Chickamauga,* one of the "noted battles for the Union during the Civil War." But it is not for these that his name will be remembered. All of the books bearing his imprint are scholarly volumes, indexed and attractively executed. But those that will forever bring lustre to his name are the books that record the history of the city he claimed as his own.

Long after his sons and grandson had joined the Fergus Printing

Company, Robert Fergus continued to set type and arrange the forms for the books that issued from his press. He lived to see the city of his choice grow to be one of the most famous in America and "a center of typographical activity second to none." He lived to see a settlement of wooden houses and unpaved streets withstand fire and flood and panic and develop into a mammoth metropolis. The Garden City of the prairies became the Windy City of stockyards and colossal business ventures before death cut down the man who had helped shape that development. On June 23, 1897, Robert Fergus, the Scot who had migrated to Chicago fifty-eight years before, was struck and instantly killed by a train at the South Evanston crossing during a blinding rainstorm. He did not live to see his city advance into the havoc and turmoil of the twentieth century.

It was, perhaps, as well that he did not. For in 1900, possibly as a result of the panic of 1893, a writ of ejectment brought the oldest printing house in Chicago to a close. The House of Fergus was no more. Its founder was saved the ignominy of seeing its stock removed from the building to the sidewalk. He was saved the ordeal of reading in the Chicago papers that "the mountain of jumbled printing furniture and paper stock that clogged Michigan street was a sight to stir the heart to pity." Yet, Fergus would have agreed with the reporter, who added, "The fickleness of fortune cannot rob the owners of the honors won during three-score years of active business." Robert Fergus, in the books that bear his imprint, left a lasting monument that neither time nor fortune can demolish. For, with his hands on a printer's case, he helped build a city, and after the building was done he helped commemorate the building.

c. J. M. C.

Hilliard and Brown's

CATALOGUE OF BOOKS,

WITH THE

PRICES ANNEXED

AT WHICH

THEY ARE FURNISHED TO THE STUDENTS

OF

HARVARD COLLEGE.

CAMBRIDGE:

HILLIARD, METCALF, AND COMPANY.

1828.

HILLIARD AND BROWN CATALOGUE

THE

Overland Monthly

DEVOTED TO

THE DEVELOPMENT OF THE COUNTRY.

VOLUME I.

SAN FRANCISCO:
A. ROMAN & COMPANY.
1868.

ROMAN'S OVERLAND MONTHLY, SHOWING THE GRIZZLY
ON THE TRACKS OF THE PACIFIC RAILROAD

VIII. MANIFEST DESTINY

Jacob W. Cruger

PUBLIC PRINTER OF HOUSTON

D URING the 1830's, when the Middle West, emerging from wilderness, was attracting emigrants and pioneers to its settlements, a larger expanse of territory, stretching farther south and farther west, drew bands of young adventurers to its borders. The journey from the United States to Texas was long and tedious. Young men and boys from Vermont and New York, starting out on foot, might follow the road to Cincinnati or New Orleans and eventually, by sail or steamboat, arrive at the tiny landings of rivers that flowed into the Gulf. For all its hardships the journey was worth while, for revolution lay at the end of it—the Texas Revolution that sought freedom from Mexican rule. There were other inducements, too, that had been advertised in books and pamphlets published in the East. Back in the village of Bath, New York, young men with restless feet and daring minds might have read Woodman's *Guide to Texas Emigrants* or Edwards's *Texas and Coahuila,* with their stirring details about land grants and colonization. By 1835, the Republic of Mexico was in arms against what might become the Republic of Texas. Chivalrous, impetuous, the young men came from the East, recruiting companies of volunteers or joining the Buckeye Rangers or the Cincinnati Greys. They heard or saw how the dictator Santa Anna was overcome by the Texans until, with the fall of the Alamo, victory was turned into defeat and slaughter. Not until San Jacinto, in April of 1836, was independence assured. Some of the young men arrived too late for San Jacinto. Some of them fell there. Others survived to celebrate the occasion at many a San Jacinto Ball. But most of those who had come to join the Texas

Revolution remained in the Republic—colonists from the United States of America.

For nine years they watched their Republic grow. As one of the colonists put it, "Her lone star became the cynosure of the chivalry of America, and her camps were thronged with young men distinguished for courage and talents of a high order." Another said, "Some had come in the name of freedom to help liberate Texas from what was termed an alien yoke. Some had come to acquire what they could in a new land. Others were adventurers, looking always for whatever might fall into their hands, . . . but these last were few." They watched, as their President appointed an Envoy Extraordinary and Minister Plenipotentiary to the United States— his mission, like theirs, annexation. They debated and worked and planned for nine long years, an independent nation within an independent nation, a sovereign republic within a sovereign republic. And at last, in 1845, overcoming the objections of many citizens of the United States who had no desire to convert a slave-holding Republic into a State or to fight a war with Mexico to retain that State, the Texans became legally what they had always been inherently— Americans. The Lone Star found its place among twenty-seven other stars, and by a joint resolution of Congress Texas became the twenty-eighth State of the Union. The President of the Republic retired; the first Governor of the State of Texas was elected. In a Houston newspaper, an editor gloried in the occasion: "The Independence of Texas passed away amid the joyous acclamations of her citizens, and the event is hailed as the dayspring of her future glory and greatness. . . . It is the great event of the age. . . . No armies were required to effect this Union."

It was an event not only unique, but predestined. Not slavery, not war with Mexico could long forestall this natural territorial expansion of the United States, by which the West was rounding itself out and the Union taking shape. The annexation of Texas was inevitable—a "manifest destiny."

Annexation was inevitable. But it might have been delayed. It was "manifest destiny" only when it was made manifest. And of all those who fought, first for independence from the yoke of Mexico, and then for the statehood of the Republic of Texas, none exposed the issues more loudly or more clearly, none rallied more effectively to the cause than the printer, whose musket was a composing stick, who waved a pamphlet as his banner.

Jacob W. Cruger was not a printer by trade, but printer's ink flowed in his veins. Born in Dansville, New York, in 1819, he was related to Daniel Cruger, Jr., who had learned the printing trade at the Webster office in Albany and had published *The American Constellation* at Union and Owego. Subsequently, Daniel Cruger, Jr., had shifted his interests to the law and had become one of the leading members of the Steuben County bar, traveling from circuit to circuit on his bay horse, Jingle Foot. At Bath, New York, where he settled, he continued his early interest in printing, serving as patron to the establishment of Benjamin Smead. And it was from Bath that the seventeen-year-old Jacob Cruger, with his younger brother James and a friend, Francis Moore, Jr., set out on foot late in 1835 or early in the historic year of 1836 for the Texas Revolution.

Young Cruger had a happy faculty for making friends, and his friendship with Francis Moore, Jr., was destined not only to transform his own life, but to help shape the history of Texas. The son of Dr. Francis Moore, young Francis had been born in Massachusetts in 1808 and had lost one arm in an accident early in life. His family had moved to Western New York State, where the boy had studied medicine, and, settling for a time in the village of Bath, he had taught school and studied law in the office of R. Campbell, Jr. There, too, he had met the Cruger boys, and the trio of crusaders pledged themselves to the life of western adventure and the challenge of western expansion. "A warm & devoted friend to the cause of the Revolutionists," Moore "abandoned *fair prospects* . . . and set out for Texas *on foot,* not as an adventurous speculator but as a friend to Liberty and the rights of man determined to hazard his life, and his all in the cause of Texean patriots." Together they made the journey—the one-armed, "long slabsided, . . . six footer," Moore, filled with staunch convictions and hard-driving determination, and his young companions, the Cruger brothers.

In the spring of 1836 in Cincinnati, Captain James L. Allen was organizing a volunteer company of "emigrants" for service in the Texas Revolution. By June a band of seventy-five to one hundred men had been recruited and dubbed the Buckeye Rangers. It is possible that Moore, who had already been appointed assistant surgeon in the volunteer army, and Jacob Cruger may have both joined the Buckeye Rangers, leaving Cincinnati in the steamboat *Farmer* under the escort of the Cincinnati Greys. It is also possible that in Cincinnati they may have met Gail Borden, destined for fame as the founder of a great milk industry, but at the time publisher of the *Telegraph and Texas Register,* who was busy buying a new press to replace the one that the Mexicans had thrown into Buffalo Bayou. If the meeting did take place, it was an historic one, for before another year had passed Cruger and Moore were to assume publication of the paper. At the time muskets seemed more to the point than composing sticks, and, perhaps with the troupe of Buckeye Rangers, Moore and the Crugers may have arrived at New Orleans in mid-June, sailing for Texas some days later. They were too late for San Jacinto, but not too late to serve until danger of the threatened Mexican invasion had passed. At all events, from June 6, 1836, apparently the date of his enlistment, until September 22, 1836, Jacob W. Cruger was a member of the Army of the Republic of Texas. By September of 1836, having been honorably discharged, he was working as a clerk in the War Department, continuing his duties through December, while Moore was employed as assistant surgeon.

San Jacinto had been decisive. Texas was independent and Sam Houston had been chosen its first president. In the new Republic all things were possible. Up the bayou from Harrisburg, at the tiny hamlet of Frosttown, a headquarters had been established by the pioneering Allen brothers, and there the Crugers, with Gail Borden and a fellow adventurer, Ed Bartholomew, met some time after San Jacinto to journey to a place that would soon be known as Houston. It was a voyage of discovery. To avoid the mud and rain-swept prairie, the explorers went by boat until, abreast the White Oak, they disembarked,

climbed the slippery bank and surveyed the tranquil scene. It was quiet there on the banks of the bayou, in this virgin wooded glen with the undulating prairie stretching to the South. A steady mist was falling, yet we walked about amid the mud and water . . . all giving our views, locating, plots here, a building there, a street running from this place on the bayou to the south, named Main street, as well as entering into other fanciful planning. . . . After a cold lunch of corn doings and cold fried pork, we again entered the boat for the long row back up the misty

stream to the comforts of the little town and the congenial atmosphere
of the store and main meeting place at Frosttown.

. . . It was a historical moment, as later events showed.

An historic moment indeed, for the place that had been pencilled
"X" on a hand-sketched map of the Texas territory was soon to
flourish as Houston, and Jacob Cruger, a boy of seventeen, had
seen Houston before it was Houston, even before it was "Mudtown."
It developed rapidly. On the south side of Buffalo Bayou it stood
upon the edge of a prairie—a place of tents and shanties made of
poles set in the ground, covered with rough split shingles. But soon
it would be the seat of government of the Republic of Texas. Logs
were being hauled in from the forest, workmen were constructing
cabins, hammers and axes were resounding, trees were falling. All
was bustle and animation. The city of Houston was building, and
there were concentrated all the energy and enterprise of Texas.
Emigrants poured in from all directions. Houses could not be built
fast enough, and linen tents were pitched all over the prairie. In a
few months, in a place where the Crugers and their fellow explorers
had located their fanciful plots, streets were laid out, lots were sold,
commission merchants set up their shingles, along with lawyers and
boardinghouse keepers, and even a portrait painter. The Texas Land
Agency bustled with activity. The Franklin Debating Society met
to discuss annexation. The steam packet *Columbia* churned to New
Orleans in forty hours. A place that only a little while ago had not
existed had become the seat of government. But Houston could not
have become Houston without a printing office.

For a short time, Jacob W. Cruger had joined his brother James
in merchandising at Houston, but "the confinement and monotony
of the store and counting-room soon became irksome and distaste-
ful" to the young man who had journeyed all the way from New
York State to join the Texas Revolution, and seeking "an employment more congenial to his active and energetic temperament,"
Jacob Cruger found it in the printing office that issued a newspaper
known as the *Telegraph and Texas Register*.

On March 9, 1837, Francis Moore, Jr., bought an interest in the
Telegraph. On June 20, Jacob W. Cruger bought the remaining
interest, beginning a partnership that was to last fourteen years.
Their paper had already had, as it would continue to have, a sig-

nificant and fascinating history. Established in October, 1835, at San Felipe de Austin by the Borden brothers (Gail and Thomas H.) and Joseph (Don José) Baker, it had served as the organ of the provisional government of Texas. When Santa Anna's invading army had approached San Felipe, the press—a Smith medium hand-press—had been moved by team and wagon to Harrisburg on Buffalo Bayou. There, in April, 1836, a few days before San Jacinto, the forms of Number 22 went to press, but after the sixth copy had been struck off, Santa Anna's advance guard entered the village, seized the printers whom they held as prisoners, and the press which they tossed into the bayou. Gail Borden had subsequently journeyed to Cincinnati, where he purchased a new press and type and resumed publication of the *Telegraph* at Columbia on the Brazos in August of 1836. When it was announced that Houston would be the seat of government of the Republic, the press was moved in April, 1837, from Columbia to Houston aboard the historic steamboat *Yellowstone*. Through the gulf and up the bayou, along boggy river bottoms, the *Yellowstone* plied its way to the new capital, carrying not only the press of the *Telegraph and Texas Register,* but the government archives. Both Gail Borden and Francis Moore, Jr., who had bought Thomas Borden's interest in the paper, were aboard. The *Yellowstone* was held on the bar at Velasco a week and was grounded at Clopper's Bar for a day before it proceeded at two miles an hour to Houston. Both the *Telegraph* and the government had made the trip to Houston on the same vessel. Begun as "a tool to no party," the paper had helped make Texas free. Under the aegis of Cruger and Moore, it would carry as its motto, "We Labor For Our Country," and the press that had been the official organ of the Revolution would become the official organ of the Republic and the mouthpiece for annexation.

It was a grand and high-sounding task for a paper issued from a shanty in a newly laid-out community. At a time when oxen were drawing wooden-axle wagons for hundreds of miles, a pioneer printer was well equipped if he had a few hundred pounds of body type, a few fonts of job type, and a hand-press. His pocketknife was used to cut paper. His cigar boxes made excellent reglets. Strips of tin were used for rules, pieces of cardboard for leads, and every office manufactured its own rollers. The office of the *Telegraph* was no exception. In a small shack on Prairie Street with a leaking roof that dripped water onto the press, Cruger and Moore established their headquarters. The log house had been in almost complete disrepair when the press had been moved there, and, during the first few days, one, then another of the large pine beams holding the roof fell to the floor of the office. One of the beams had destroyed a made-up page of the paper which was on the composing table. Rain poured torrents onto the press and meager stocks of paper. As the paper itself had revealed,

We have been deceived: no building had ever been nearly finished at Houston intended for the press; fortunately, however, we have succeeded in renting a shanty, which, although like the *capitol* in this place,

> 'Without a roof, and without a floor,
> Without windows and without a door,'

is the only convenient building obtainable. . . .

Our troubles have not yet ended, the shanty is falling about our ears, two massive beams have dropped down upon the stands, made a most disgusting *pi,* and driven the workmen to seek safety outside, the *devil* alone looks smiling on the mischief.

But, with the clang of metal against metal, Cruger and his partner Moore worked at the task of repair in the early morning before the bayou mists had disappeared, as "Mudtown" was coming to life. Their roof was sound, and their type-trays were neatly arranged beside the make-up table. The printer stood beside his board dropping type into place. Sheet after sheet of paper was placed on the face of the type, locked in the chase of the press, and the roller was pulled back and forth across the paper until one by one copies of the *Telegraph* were neatly stacked beside the press.

The issue of June 24, 1837, carried for the first time the firm name, Cruger and Moore, Publishers. From that date until April, 1851, when Cruger disposed of his interest to Moore, the firm and their paper were to labor for their country. Published weekly at the City of Houston by Cruger and Moore, proprietors, the *Telegraph and Texas Register* sold for five dollars a year, payable in advance. It carried official government papers and proclamations of the President of the Republic of Texas. It advertised sales of land and of Negroes, and it published estray notices of horses along with announcements of Indians shot in the city. The one-armed Moore proved a bold and forthright editor, crusading for a variety of causes, from attacks upon dueling to excoriations of Sam Houston, vituperating against politicians and gun-fighters, gambling and drinking, bribery and conspiracy and treason. Especially he crusaded for annexation, the "one object" of the people of Texas, whose "march is onward," an object which "they are determined to consummate . . . in spite of every obstacle." While Moore wrote the editorials, his young partner, Jacob Cruger, frequently provided the ammunition, managing the business end of the office and indirectly manifesting his own opinions. Despite allegations that Cruger was a *"Liar,"* he continued his blasts against Sam Houston and for annexation, while traveling agents carried the *Telegraph's* views abroad in Texas and the United States. Threatened with *"the Cow hide,"* Francis Moore, Jr., blandly repeated his fulminations. Labeled a "miserable malcontent," he proceeded to incite his fellow Texans to espouse the cause of annexation. By 1845, Sam Houston, reviewing the San Jacinto Campaign in a speech at Houston, declared, "The lying scribbler of the *Telegraph,* is a one armed man. You never would forgive me for abusing a cripple, but I must confess that one arm can write more malicious falsehoods than any man with two arms I ever saw." Yet, in the same speech, Houston was constrained to admit that he had directed the Texan minister at Washington to withdraw the application of Texas for annexation and commence paying court to England and France. The *Telegraph,* dominated by Cruger and Moore, struggled from the beginning for annexation, and since it was "the only paper which is known, or has an extensive circulation," being "regularly received, and eagerly perused by every family," it swayed the public effectively. Backed by the young and enterprising Cruger, Moore, tall, one-armed, with a pugnacious nose and a shock of prematurely white hair, sat in his office clad in his Kentucky stitchdowns, fearlessly and independently pleading the causes of the Republic of Texas, until, in 1845, he could print the resolutions passed at the Court House in San Felipe, "that the people of Texas with unparalleled unanimity are solicitous of the annexation of their Republic to the great Union of sovereign and independent American States." It was the *Telegraph and Texas Register* which, on March 4, 1846, carried the editorial that hailed annexation as the "dayspring" of the "future glory" of Texas. It was Francis Moore, Jr., who wrote the editorial, and Jacob W. Cruger who saw that it was circulated throughout the Republic that had become a State.

The Houston office of Cruger and Moore was more, however, than a newspaper establishment, and Jacob W. Cruger was more than a newspaper publisher. If "a large and commodious house" or a yoke of work steers were for sale, applications were to be made to Cruger and Moore. A lost pocketbook could be claimed at the same establishment, and a gentleman who wished to take charge of a school might appear at the *Telegraph* to present his qualifications. Even information about "a General assortment of Fresh Medicines" could be obtained at Cruger's office, while at one time the post office was housed in his building on Main Street opposite the White House. A pet bear, captured as a cub, served as an extra-curricular attraction for a while—the first bear in a Texas printing office, and one that succeeded in delaying a week's issue of the *Telegraph* by pieing the forms! When a July Fourth celebration was planned at Galveston, Houstonites were invited by means of a note addressed to Jacob W. Cruger, a gesture proving not only that Texans had not ceased to be Americans, but that Jacob W. Cruger, as proprietor of the Houston printing office, was a mouthpiece and sounding board for his compatriots.

It was not through his newspaper alone that Cruger attained that position. His office issued a journal, but executed all varieties of job printing as well, from letters of citizenship to powers of attorney, from justices' blanks, warrants and estray bonds to sheriffs' summonses, stock and land certificates, and handbills—all the ephemeral printed sheets that were needed in that new country of Texas during the early '40's. But, far more significantly, his establishment was the center from which emerged the books and pamphlets that reflected the demands and activities of a Republic and a State. For Cruger, with Moore and other partners as well, served Texas not only as newspaper proprietor, but as public printer, first to the independent Republic, and then to the sovereign State of Texas—a State which by his work he helped to make.

During the early days of the Republic, the Secretary of State advertised for bids on public printing, and the printer who responded most satisfactorily and reasonably received the contract. It was in this manner that the Bordens had, in October, 1836, been awarded the contract for public printing. When Cruger and Moore bought out their interests in the *Telegraph,* they fell heirs to their contract for public printing as well, and the "Office of the Telegraph" appeared as the imprint on such important government publications as the *Declaration of Independence . . . and the Constitution of the Republic of Texas,* the *Report of the Secretary of the Treasury,* the *Laws of the Republic of Texas,* the *Journals of the Consultation held at San Felipe,* and the various communications, messages, and documents submitted to Congress by President Houston.

Yet almost from the start difficulties arose and animosities developed out of the coveted contract for public printing, and the *Telegraph* was the medium in which Cruger and Moore presented their problems to subscribers. Charged by the *National Banner,* a Houston weekly published by J. Warren Niles, with having "battened upon the Government," Cruger and Moore published in their newspaper on May 12, 1838, a full account of the means whereby they had taken over the contract, the finances involved, and their own efforts to serve honorably as public servants. Accused by Niles of having charged and received from the government $8,640 for work which he would have done for $2,652, they explained that they had neither received that amount nor were they entitled to it. The sum was due them "under the old contract with Messrs. Bordens at Columbia, when the credit of the government was so low, that its Treasury drafts were selling at 20 and 25 cents on the dollar." By a curious legal entanglement, the Secretary of State had refused to accept the Telegraph bill for "the second volume of the laws" because it had been lower than that of the original contract, amounting to only $100 for printing and binding in pamphlet form 2,000 sheets of sixteen pages each. Despite such monetary problems, Cruger and Moore persisted in their initial determination

that while we had one dollar left to pay our workmen we would continue to do the Public Printing, that we should cease only when our hands should become fettered with want, and trust . . . to an impartial Congress for our reward. Fortunately the liberal patronage of a generous people enabled us to continue uninterruptedly the printing for Congress, and for the different departments of government until the meeting of this Congress; during that time, we received nothing from government, except fifteen bundles of paper, . . . furnished by the Secretary of State, . . . and such were our circumstances, that we were compelled to expend nearly all of our available funds, in purchasing materials to conduct the

Public Printing. And what has been the result? to have been first blamed because we were too poor to procure the means of publishing all the laws and journals of Congress, as expeditiously as they would have been published in the United States. And then to be taunted by one who has been laboring incessantly to 'slip into our shoes,' that we have 'battened on the government'!!

The *Telegraph* concluded its startling revelations with a vehement journalistic tirade and a fine flurry of patriotism:

Whatever have been our transactions with government, they have been *open* and *fair*. . . . But when men secretly sneak in, like *'rats,'* to under-mine our business and *sustained by the means of our enemies,* offer to do work lower than actual cost, in order that they may at some after period, . . . raise their prices at pleasure; when such men oppose us, and . . . intoxicated with that importance which the *lackey* feels, in a new livery, snap their fingers and say, 'go poor devil, there is room enough in the world for me and thee,' we shall say to them, go back . . . to 'your Masters, and learn better manners,' . . .
    . . . we fight under the Telegraph, which has never been soiled by a base sentiment, and which has once passed through the fiery ordeal of Tyranny. We bid eternal defiance to the grovelling reptiles who have leagued against us.

The Joint Committee of Congress on Public Printing reported that the statement was correct, that "the only *valid* contract for the ex-ecution of Printing for the Government, is that originally made with the Messrs. Bordens," that Cruger and Moore voluntarily offered to reduce the charges made under the old contract, but that for the future execution of public printing, "sealed proposals will be re-ceived by the Speaker of the House of Representatives, for printing, stitching and folding in pamphlet form, the Laws and Journals of the Republic not contracted for," and that the opening of the pro-posals would be followed by the election of a Public Printer.

Having weathered the storms of public printing in Houston, Jacob W. Cruger, learning that the seat of government was to be trans-ferred to Austin, decided to move to that city. In addition to the *Telegraph,* he had established at Houston the *Morning Star,* the first daily published in Texas, printed at the Telegraph office, and its columns "set to the same measure" as the older sheet. The *Morning Star,* besides being the first daily in the Republic, has another claim to fame since it was printed on that historic press which had been thrown into Buffalo Bayou by the Mexicans and had been subsequently recovered, cleaned, and set up in Houston. When he removed to Austin, Jacob Cruger transferred the management of the *Morning Star* to his brother James and the paper became a tri-weekly. While Moore continued the *Telegraph* and James Cruger the *Morning Star,* Jacob Cruger settled for a time in the new capital, devoting himself not only to public printing, but to the publication of yet another newspaper, the *Texas Centinel.*

For these purposes, during his Austin sojourn, Cruger allied himself with George W. Bonnell, like himself a native of New York, who had come to Texas in 1836 with a company of volunteers whom he had recruited for the Revolution. Bonnell had edited papers in Alabama and Mississippi before he had served as Major commanding the Milam Guards on the frontier. Not many years were left for the lithe, red-haired, gray-eyed Bonnell, whose freckled face appeared from under his slouched hat. He would be killed by the Mexicans at the Battle of Mier in 1842, but before that time he would serve effectively as a member of the firm of Cruger and Bonnell, public printers and proprietors of the *Texas Centinel.*

On December 6, 1839, Bonnell and Cruger submitted their bid on public printing, agreeing "to print the Laws and Journals of the present Congress for thirty per cent less than the sum allowed . . . for printing the laws and journals of the last Congress," and to "give bond . . . in the sum of ten or twenty thousand dollars if required, that they will have a printing office in this city [Austin]." In submitting their proposals at that time, the firm explained "that they have now a complete printing establishment in readiness to be brought to this city [Austin], and have been prevented from bringing it at an earlier day on account of the state of the roads. It will probaly [sic] arrive in a few days." The reason why they could "afford to do the Public Printing cheaper" than their predecessor was, they continued, "that they have a large, Machine Power Press, which diminishes, in a great degree, the expense of the press work." Not quite two weeks later, on December 18, Cruger received the contract to print the translation of the Texas Laws in Spanish, "in small Pica type properly accented and executed in a style equal to the Spanish laws of Coahuila and Texas as printed by me . . . @ One hundred & thirteen dollars for Two Thousand copies of each and every form of eight pages." For this purpose, "a reasonable number of hands" would be employed, the paper would be furnished by Cruger, and the work would be "folded cut and substantially sewed for twenty five cents per one hundred pages for each copy—deducting . . . one and a half per cent."

On January 15, 1840, the first number of the *Centinel* made its bow to the Austin public, and in time the imprint of the Sentinel Office appeared upon a land office *Report* and a presidential *Message,* an *Act* on public revenue and a *Report of the Secretary of State* of the Republic of Texas. By 1841 Cruger's partnership with Bonnell had given way to one with Martin Carroll Wing, a practical printer who had come to Texas from Vermont and worked on the *Centinel*. Like Bonnell's, his life was not destined to be long, for in 1843 Wing was to become one of the seventeen martyrs in Mexico— a victim of the Black Bean Episode in which every tenth man was executed by a Mexican lottery decided by the drawing of beans. The imprint of Cruger and Wing followed the imprint of the Sentinel Office on the *Journals* of the House of Representatives and the *Abstract of land certificates* of the General Land Office, and at the same time the new firm acted as proprietors of the *Texas Centinel,* issuing extra editions during the sessions of Congress and serving as liaison between the public and government.

It was especially as public printer that Cruger could serve most effectively in such a capacity, and the rich mine of Public Printing Papers casts an interesting light upon the work that he performed and the remuneration that he received. For binding six hundred volumes of the Laws and Journals in sheepskin, his charge was $3.33⅓ per volume, while for binding a single volume of the Laws the price was $14. For printing two hundred copies of the Revenue Laws in pamphlet form, he demanded $133.33 in specie or $400 in Texas promissory notes, and a printing bill might run as high as $8,088. In addition, Cruger supplied the Republic of Texas with quires of ruled folio post paper, blank commissions, and subscriptions to the *Telegraph*.

The contract which had been issued in 1839 to Cruger and Bonnell for printing the Spanish translation of the Laws was not fulfilled until 1841, when the *Constitucion, leyes generales, . . . de la República de Téjas,* translated into Spanish by the abolitionist, "universologist," and advocate of free love, Stephen Pearl Andrews, was finally published. It bore the imprint not of Cruger and Bonnell but

of the "Telégrafo," and it was printed not at Austin but at Houston.
Cruger had continued his Houston interests during his brief sojourn
at the capital, and by February of 1844 the firm of Cruger and Moore
once again received the contract for public printing.

In January the partners had deposited their sealed proposals with
the Committee on Public Printing, offering to print the Laws and
Journals of Congress at the rate of *"one half of one cent per page,*
which would make a volume of 100 pages cost your Government
Fifty Cents," and reminding the Committee that their "facilities . . .
for completing the work in the best possible manner, and in the
shortest time allowed, are well known to the . . . Congress." The
firm pointed out particularly the advantages to the government of
electing as public printers men who were proprietors of such a newspaper as the *Telegraph.*

Heretofore it has been customary to pay several hundred dollars for
publishing the laws in the official Journal of the country: We propose to
publish them in the Telegraph, *free of Expense to the Govt.* which from
its extensive circulation will bring within the reach of every citizen of
the country the means of understanding & appreciating the institutions
under which they live, where, otherwise they can only be found in the
possession of some few Government officers.

On February 12, 1844, the contract was signed, Cruger and Moore
agreeing "to print accurately, and in pamphlet form *2000* copies of
the Laws of the eighth Congress; . . . *300* copies of the Journals of
the Senate, and *300* copies of the Journals of the House of Representatives," and to deliver the copies, "properly folded and stiched
[sic], (edges cut) at the office of the Department of State" within
the specified time. For this service they would be paid "at the rate
of *one half of one cent per page,* in Exchequer bills." The printing
was to be in no "wise inferior; . . . the paper . . . shall be of the best
quality; and . . . the volumes shall in reference to the type, the size
of the pages, and in all material respects," correspond with the
pamphlet acts of the sixth Congress. The Act regarding appropria-
tions for the support of government provided that "four thousand
dollars be appropriated, or so much thereof as may be necessary to
pay Cruger and Moore, agreeably to their propositions to this Congress, *provided,* they print, and deliver to the Secretary of State the

laws, within forty days, and the journals, within sixty days, after copies are delivered to them, from the State Department."

Once again, however, difficulties had arisen in connection with the authorization of the contract, and President Sam Houston had written to the House of Representatives in January of 1844 a letter exposing those difficulties as well as his own objections to the "public printers elect." The joint resolution for the relief of Cruger and Moore required, he declared, an impossibility of the Department of State, since copies of all laws could not be furnished the public printers before the adjournment of Congress. The resolution, therefore, was returned to the House without signature. Mindful, no doubt, of the anti-Houstonian policy so frequently aired by Cruger and Moore, the President availed himself of the opportunity to remark

that he has been informed upon good authority, that it was not the design of Messrs. Cruger & Moore to print the laws themselves, but to enter into a subcontract . . . and . . . to delay and perhaps defeat their distribution among the people. The reception of this information has caused the Executive to look with more caution into the seemingly strange and unusual course thus far pursued by the public printers elect.

Despite the animosity of President Houston, thirty-three Ayes carried the joint resolution for the relief of Cruger and Moore against five Noes, and the bill was passed. The troubles of the public printers were by no means ended, however; for, as they had faced the tirades of the *National Banner* in 1838, they were greeted now by the fulminations of the *National Vindicator,* a paper published by Thomas Johnson, a supporter of Sam Houston's policy, who had earned the nickname of the President's "Ramrod." His *National Vindicator,* "that paragon of official journals," was promptly labelled the "National Vituperator" after it had "belched out a tirade of low, disgusting blackguardism" leveled against the eighth Congress. The reasons for the tirade were clear. "The Hon. Congress thought proper to appoint Cruger & Moore printers of the Laws passed by the . . . Congress, and the maw of the expectant patriot being defrauded of its usual feed, his stomach sickened and threw up the putridity. . . . It is wonderful what a substantial sentiment, the patriotism of some men is."

Certainly, although the financial rewards of acting as public print-

ers were not to be disregarded, the patriotism of Cruger and Moore
in that service cannot be questioned. Francis Moore, Jr., who had
been elected the first Mayor of Houston as well as Senator from
his district, was sent as a delegate for Harris County to the great
Convention of 1845, which framed the Constitution of the State of
Texas. The committee on resolutions for annexation had included
his name among its members. Jacob W. Cruger, who had served
the public as postmaster of Houston for a short time in 1837, and
attended the council meeting of April, 1839, as city official, had
found it not only lucrative but congenial to advance the welfare
of his country. By bounty warrants he was amassing land in Texas,
but his coffers were filled not at the expense of his beliefs, but
through the active practice of those beliefs. Cruger had danced at
the San Jacinto Ball in Houston, and on San Jacinto Day of 1845,
Dr. Moore had led the annexation rally. What, then, was more appropriate than that, after Cruger and Joel Miner had printed the
Constitution at the office of the "New Era" in Austin—a paper established to record proceedings of the Convention—the office of
the Telegraph should issue the *Constitution of the State Of Texas.
(Adopted unanimously in Convention, at the City of Austin, 1845.).*
To the words they printed Cruger and Moore subscribed with their
convictions, for they had helped transform those words into an enduring monument: "We, the people of the Republic of Texas, ac-
knowledging with gratitude the grace and beneficence of God, in
permitting us to make a choice of our form of Government,—do, in
accordance with the provisions of the Joint Resolution for annexing
Texas to the United States, approved March first, one thousand
eight hundred and forty-five, ordain and establish this Constitution."
Both Cruger and Moore had helped ordain and establish that *Constitution.* It was supremely fitting that they should print it. The
Constitution, issued from the Telegraph Office in 1845, included the
Bill of Rights, regulations concerning the departments of government, the Land Office and slaves. It included also a list of signers
of the Austin Convention, among them the name of Francis Moore,
Jr.

The Convention had assembled in the city of Austin on the fourth
of July, 1845, for the purpose of framing that *Constitution,* and the
Journals of the Convention had been presented to the public by
Miner and Cruger, printers to the Convention. Joel Miner, Jacob W.

Cruger's associate in this short-lived but significant Austin partnership, had been born in Vermont and had worked as a printer in France before he volunteered in the Texas Army. A term of service in the Office of the Telegraph prepared him for his association with Cruger as printers to the Convention, an association to which the *Journals of the Convention* and the *Constitution* still testify.

It was, however, the imprint of the Telegraph Office at Houston that appeared on most of the statehood publications executed by Cruger, from the *Laws passed by The . . . Legislature* to the *Journals* of the Senate and the House of Representatives. The *Laws passed by The Second Legislature of the State Of Texas,* and printed at the Telegraph Office in 1848, contain not only joint resolutions on slavery and the war against Mexico—a war which the State considered "necessary to the vindication of our national honor"—but "An Act to regulate the Public Printing." The terms of the Act indicate clearly the responsibilities of the public printer of the State of Texas. Elected by joint vote of the two Houses of Legislature on the basis of sealed proposals, he was instructed to print, in small pica type, 2,500 copies of the general laws and 500 copies of the Journals of each House.

The Telegraph Office had developed as Texas had developed. It had printed the *Laws* of Texas when Texas was part of a Mexican State. Its imprint had appeared upon the *Declaration of Independence* of the Republic of Texas and the *Laws* of that Republic. From the Telegraph Office had been issued the *Messages* of President Houston and *The Inaugural Address* of President Lamar. The *Constitution of the State Of Texas* had appeared under its aegis, and in 1848 the *Laws* of the second legislature of that State. Through the changing imprints of the Telegraph Office at Houston, the history of Texas is reflected, from the *Journals of the Consultation . . . at San Felipe* to the *Report* of a provisional government, from the Statutes of a Republic to the *Constitution* and *Laws* of a State. In the course of a decade that printing office had served as the instrument whereby a foreign territory had been transformed into a sovereign State. The Office of the Telegraph had not merely survived through all these changes, but had played a vital part in effecting them. It had borne witness to the swift metamorphoses of a unique history which it had helped to shape.

The Houston of 1848 was no longer the place of tents and shanties that had come to life little more than a decade before. It had weathered a yellow-fever epidemic and a war with Mexico. Its streets were no longer muddy quagmires. The *Telegraph* had developed from an army paper, moving from point to point as the Mexicans advanced, to the organ of the State of Texas, adding to its title the word "Democratic." The want of ink no longer kept its "subscribers in the dark" for a week. There was less need now for such publications as Francis Moore, Jr.'s *Map and Description of Texas* or for George W. Bonnell's *Topographical Description of Texas*. The country was well aware of the resources of its new State.

By 1851, Jacob W. Cruger's self-appointed task had been accomplished. The boy who had journeyed to Texas to help free it from the yoke of Mexico had seen its independence established and its annexation to the United States assured. In April of that year Cruger sold out his interest in the *Telegraph* to his partner, Francis Moore, Jr., and at that time the *Morning Star* was merged with the older paper. Moore held the *Telegraph* for only three years, disposing of his interest to H. H. Allen and Company, and later serving—a man of many parts—as State Geologist. Subsequently the paper passed to Edward H. Cushing, who conducted it through the Civil War, using wallpaper, blank letterheads, billheads, and brown wrapping paper for its issues, and establishing a pony express between Houston and army headquarters in Louisiana to bring war news directly from the front.

The outbreak of war had brought changes not only to the *Telegraph,* but to its erstwhile publishers. Francis Moore, Jr., still hard-driven by his convictions, was Unionist in his sympathies and went North. There he entered the service of a copper mining company which sent him to Lake Superior, and in 1864 he died of injuries suffered from a fall. The one-armed, "long slabsided, . . . six footer" was redoubtable to the end—as effective in his actions as he was staunch in his opinions. Jacob W. Cruger remained as true to his own convictions. While his former partner espoused the cause of the North, Cruger joined the Confederate Army, serving as aide to Richard Montgomery Gano, who led a company of Texas cavalry known as Gano's Squadron, assigned to General Morgan's command in the Trans-Mississippi Division and Indian Territory. On November 30, 1864, not long after the death of Francis Moore, Jr., Jacob W. Cruger died of disease contracted during his military service. He was only forty-five years of age. "He had been constantly in military service almost from the commencement of the war to his death, and . . . the labors and exposure were more than he could bear. . . . he died in the service of his country."

He had also lived in the service of his country, and the office that he had for so many years superintended with his partner Moore survived them both. The *Telegraph* continued in existence until 1877. Four years later the press on which it, and so many of the significant publications of Texas, had been printed, passed into other hands. Its story ended on a cold winter's night during the 1880's when "the most historic press that has ever existed in Texas" was destroyed by fire. It was an historic press indeed, for it had issued, between 1838 and 1851, the books and pamphlets that had borne witness to the emergence of a new State. Jacob W. Cruger, public printer to the Republic of Texas, printer to the Convention, printer of the Texas *Constitution,* had helped carve that State out of what had once been foreign territory. On his composing table had been spread the pages that made history. In the chase of his press had been locked the words that advanced the borders of his country. Through the imprints of his Telegraph Office, the Union was pushed farther south and farther west, fulfilling a destiny that he had helped make manifest.

IX. THE SETTLING OF THE FAR WEST

Anton Roman

ARGONAUT OF BOOKS

A MANIFEST destiny seemed at work not merely upon the lips of statesmen and historians, but upon the whole great continent itself. Fast upon the heels of the peace treaty that concluded the Mexican War came the discovery of gold in the California hills. A new State was in the making, and with the opening of the Far West came the need not only for miners to work the diggings, but for farmers to work the soil, teachers to instruct the new generation of children, writers to lift the hearts and expand the minds of settlers in the far-flung reaches of the country. Settlers and farmers, teachers and tradesmen—all who thronged to the bustling, roaring, colorful communities that sprang up overnight in the wake of the mining camps—needed books almost as much as they needed tools. Books, in fact, were their tools, and in San Francisco as the 1850's rolled their swift, vivid course, the sharp need for men who could publish those books was answered. The Golden Fleece that was California had many Argonauts, not the least of whom was the Argonaut of Books who, purveying wares that would ease the path of pioneers and enlighten and enrich their lives, became himself a pioneer in the distant West whose bloodless conquest rounded out a nation and determined its borders forever.

As always, when the need arose, such an Argonaut was on hand. In December of 1851 he appeared in San Francisco, a bearded miner with thick hair and a prominent nose. His name was Anton Roman. Born in Bavaria some twenty-three years before, he had migrated to America in his youth and in 1849 had crossed the plains to California. He had joined the gold-seekers on the Trinity River at Weaverville, along the Klamath, in Siskiyou, and in the northern regions of Shasta, striking rich diggings at Scott Bar. But Roman had washed more than dust from the sand at Scott Bar. He had lived among traders and prospectors, had worked the rich placers, had been on hand at the Scott Bar decision between rival mining groups, had seen a claim opened, gold extracted with iron spoons, pans filled with solid gold; but he had observed, too, the bustling camps, the stores, the saloons, the hotels. He had seen Ozarkers and York Staters stake their claims and wash dust from the sand. He had heard the sound of shovel on gravel, and in the tents and huts on the banks of the creek he had listened while miners exchanged their tales of rich diggings. He had lived the uproarious days that would soon become history and literature. And, along with a fund of mining anecdotes with which he would one day regale a young man named Bret Harte, he had taken with him his awareness of the need for books among prospectors and tradesmen and lonely men.

And so, in December of 1851, the bearded miner might have been seen strolling about San Francisco. In Brenham Place on the west side of the Plaza he paused before the bookstore of Burgess, Gilbert and Still; and, though he had no clear intention of making any purchases, he entered the shop. The clerk was interested in the visitor's tales of the miners at Scott Bar. More particularly, Roman showed an extreme fondness for books; and in short order the conversation between miner and clerk culminated in a business transaction whereby over a hundred ounces of gold dust, the current earnings of Roman's share of a claim on Scott Bar, were exchanged for books. Though probably neither the miner nor the clerk was aware of it, that little transaction opened an important page in the history of bookselling and publishing on the west coast.

At the moment Roman's problem was not to consider his place in history, but simply to dispose of his books. During the winter months in the Shasta mining region, he knew, prospectors could be induced to exchange their gold for reading matter; and so Anton Roman peddled his wares from camp to camp, with such success that he soon decided to abandon mining for migratory bookselling. From Eureka he moved on to Shasta City, during the golden period when the town was almost as proud of its stores as of its diggings. In the *Shasta Courier* of March 12, 1853, Roman inserted an advertisement of his Shasta Book Store, opposite El Dorado Hotel, where new books might be purchased wholesale and retail, and

where might be found at all times "a large and splendid assortment
of Books and Stationery . . . at the lowest prices. Among the late
works just received are the following: The Necromances [sic], Par-
ricide . . . Fair Rosamond, Amy Lawrence, Mad Cap . . . Stanley
Thorn . . . &c. Also, the works of Shakspeare, Byron, Milton, Gray,
Campbell and other distinguished poets. All the latest newspapers,
both home and foreign, constantly on hand." In addition, musical
instruments were available at the Shasta Book Store, for the proprietor had "just received an assortment of . . . Flutes, Flagelets,
Clarionets," as well as note and song books and violin and guitar
strings. Anton Roman hoped, "by strict attention to his business,
to merit a continuance of the patronage heretofore bestowed on
him," and his hopes were realized, for by the fall of 1853 his purchases in books and stationery for the three counties of Shasta,
Trinity, and Siskiyou amounted to $42,000. It was apparently sim-
pler to extract gold dust from a miner than from a mine.

Yet Roman extracted more than money from his patrons. Before
his eyes rolled the gaudy panorama of the gold mining fields. At
his feet were spread the rude communities of men whose tools were
picks and shovels and gold pans. His comrades were the "sour-
doughs," with their shaggy beards and broad hats, their boots and
rolled-up trousers. Picture after picture flashed before his observant
eyes, a kaleidoscope of history in the making—colorful images of
pack and pan, shovel and rifle, colonies of tents with lofty mountains
in the background. Roman saw the gold-bearing earth washed down,
watched the rush from camp to camp; and his ears were filled with
the twang of the guitar at night and the congenial murmur of tall
tales exchanged by candlelight. Among villain and outlaw, lucky and
luckless, gambler and drinker, he wandered, trading his books and
his pamphlets for gold dust—for more than gold dust—for a rich,
inexhaustible store of adventure from the flashy and crude and notorious days of the Gold Rush.

It was not until 1857 that Roman left the northern counties and,
having purchased a large stock of standard and miscellaneous books
in the eastern cities, set up his stand in San Francisco. Roman's
trade covered about a dozen of the interior counties besides the city,
and by 1859 he had so expanded that, with a still larger stock, he
opened a permanent store on the west side of Montgomery Street,
north of California. The migratory bookseller had settled down, a

fact to which the San Francisco *Directory* of 1860 bears evidence, for there "Anthony" Roman is listed as an "importer and wholesale bookseller" at 158 Montgomery Block and 78 and 80 Merchant. Having provided miners with books to while away their weary hours, he was ready at last to fill the larger needs of the more stable community of settlers who had followed the miners to the West in a second wave of migration.

Roman had learned, in the years that had elapsed since his eventful purchase from Burgess, Gilbert and Still, that demand governs supply and that books to be bought must be needed. The books he sold, therefore, answered the requirements of a newly expanding community on the Pacific coast. The farming settlements near the seaboard were attracting immigrants; prospective settlers would want information about their new home. If books on the subject were not available, they could be printed; and Anton Roman, importer and wholesale bookseller, responded to the needs of his time and his place by entering a new phase of his career, that of publisher.

One of the earliest books bearing the Roman imprint was *An Outline of the History of California, from the Discovery of the Country to the Year 1849.* The Argonaut of Books, who had already helped make the history of California, was ready to record that history and publish it abroad. The little paper volume consisted of an address delivered by Edmund Randolph before the Society of California Pioneers at their celebration of the tenth anniversary of the admission of the State into the Union. Printed at the Alta California Job Office, the work was published by Roman in 1860 and marked the beginning of a long line of books that were designed to instruct gold-seekers and settlers in the history and resources of their new State. Roman was akin with John S. Hittell, who wrote in the preface to the first edition of his *Resources of California:*

I undertake to write the resources of a state, which, though young in years, small in population, and remote from the chief centres of civilization, is yet known to the furthest corners of the earth, and, during the last twelve years, has had an influence upon the course of human life, and the prosperity and trade of nations, more powerful than that exerted during the same period by kingdoms whose subjects are numbered by millions.

The publisher had been quick to seize the opportunity of sponsoring this book, the extended title of which was *The Resources of California, comprising Agriculture, Mining, Geography, Climate, Commerce, . . . and the Past and Future Development of the State;* and his interest was justified, for it passed through several editions, a compendium by, for, and of the Californian. In the third edition of 1867 is an affidavit stating that the "book is exclusively Californian in composition and manufacture," from the paper and pasteboard to the morocco, thread, and gold leaf. The publisher had grown conscious of his place in California's history. Through the years Roman published similar works, from Mowry's *Geography and Resources of Arizona and Sonora* to Ferris's *Financial Economy of the United States Illustrated, and Some of the Causes Which Retard The Progress of California Demonstrated;* from *A Youth's History of California* by "Lucia Norman" [Louise Palmer Heaven]—a volume "Californian in authorship and execution"—to Cremony's *Life Among the Apaches.* The Indian fighter, Cremony, astutely dedicated his book "To the Pioneer and Liberal Publisher, Anton Roman, The Zealous and Enterprising Friend of Literature on the Pacific Coast."

By 1868 Roman had indeed become a pioneer publisher, who watched the expansion of the State and provided books that would inform prospective settlers of the nature of the west coast. In a prefatory note to Hutchings's *Scenes of Wonder and Curiosity in California,* the publisher later explained his point of view:

Since the completion and appointments of the great Overland Railway have made travelling to the Pacific Slope easy, pleasant, speedy, and safe, a general desire has arisen for information concerning its remarkable scenery, the cost of travelling, distances, hotel charges, etc.

This general desire Roman fulfilled, giving to the public in well-printed volumes, bound in cloth or paper, a variety of works ranging from Morse's *Treatise on the Hot Sulphur Springs, of El Paso De Robles* to Stillman's *Seeking the Golden Fleece; A Record of Pioneer Life in California.* Not Stillman's book alone, but, metaphorically at least, all these publications were dedicated to the "Argonauts of California," who, at prices ranging from 50¢ to $3, could receive by mail, post-paid, the literature that would inform them of the resources of their new home. In some of these books, such as *A*

Sketch of the Route to California, China And Japan, via the Isthmus of Panama, Roman's device was printed on the title-page: surmounting his initials was the grizzly bear; below them, in a significant union, the miner's pan, pick, and shovel.

In the broader aspects of his publishing activities, Roman had not forgotten the miners.

The rapid extension of Silver Mining enterprise, in consequence of numerous discoveries of rich and extensive silver-bearing lodes in California, . . . has excited a general desire for information of such methods of extracting Silver and Gold from the . . . ores, as are practical and adapted to our circumstances.

Although the name of Frank D. Carlton, Roman's associate, appeared on the imprint of Küstel's *Nevada and California Processes of Silver and Gold Extraction,* Roman advertised and circulated the book, and, in addition, it was he who published Gregory Yale's important and authoritative *Legal Titles to Mining Claims and Water Rights, In California.* Roman had not forgotten the Scott Bar case, nor the necessity for prospectors to learn the principles governing the laws on mining property. Another volume bearing the Roman imprint was William Barstow's *Sulphurets,* designed to help miners make their own assays. Besides entering the publishing field with such works, Roman had for sale in his Montgomery Street bookstore a remarkable collection of volumes on minerals and their processing. There miners might exchange their gold dust for manuals and reap benefit from the transaction.

As the completion of the "great Overland Railway" stimulated the need for books on Western resources in general, so the discovery of new lodes created a need for books on allied and other phases of mining. Upon the successful pioneer voyage of the Pacific Mail S.S. *Colorado* to Hong Kong in 1867, a third field had opened to publishers. China was brought closer to California than ever before; and this fact, together with the presence of a great many Chinese in the State, emphasized the need for "books to enable one to understand their character." This need the enterprising publisher was eager to fill, his imprint appearing on A. W. Loomis's edition of *Confucius and the Chinese Classics*—the first book printed from stereotype plates in California. As Roman declared, "No question is more frequently asked by curious and thinking people than this:

What is the literature of the Chinese? They are a reading people; then what do they read? They are a peculiar people; what has made them so? They are an unchanging people; what is it that has fixed their habits?" It was to the advantage of Californians that such questions be answered. While Loomis's compilation was designed to supply those answers, still another work published by Roman, Lanctot's *Chinese and English Phrase Book,* was intended "to enable all classes of citizens, especially merchants, shipmasters, contractors, families, and travelers to acquire an elementary and practical knowledge of the spoken language of the Canton dialect . . . the dialect most generally understood by all classes of Chinese immigrants on the Pacific Coast." The author—and, one might add, the publisher—had been induced to undertake the work because of "a daily increasing necessity, consequent upon the extended employment of Chinese, and the now established regular line of communication with China and Japan." In the preface to his own compilation Loomis had stated that, to meet the demands for understanding the Chinese, "a Book Firm of this city has spared no pains or expense to bring together as complete a collection of works on China as was possible. Such as were not to be obtained at home have been ordered from abroad." The name of that book firm must have been apparent to all, for Roman had established in his Montgomery Street bookstore a section devoted to Orientalia. There one might have found Huc's *Travels in Tartary* or Davis's *China and the Chinese,* books on Yedo and Peking, or Upper and Lower Amoor, a dictionary of the Chinese language, or a tome on the Middle Kingdom, books to charm the alien and nostalgic Oriental, and books to help the Occidental understand him.

It was not the merchants only who wished to learn something of the Asiatic industries adapted to California. The fertility of the soil along the western seaboard was attracting farmers to the coast, and for them Roman published Kendo's *Treatise on Silk and Tea Culture.* "As there is, at this time, much attention being paid to the cultivation, in this State, of many trees, shrubs and other vegetable productions heretofore only grown extensively in Japan and the Orient," Kendo's treatise was issued to acquaint the farmers of California with the requirements of the plants named in the title, and to give advice on the growing of mulberry and persimmon trees. For their more general needs, Roman added to his bookstore a section on horticulture that offered works on garden vegetables or greenhouses, facts about peat and grape culture, farm implements or landscape gardening. There were shelves devoted to the mysteries of bee-keeping, to poultry, to horses, cattle, and sheep, simply because the soil and climate of California were attracting homesteaders, just as its placers had attracted the men with pan and shovel.

As the years passed, another need made itself felt among California settlers. They were raising not only horses and grapes and roses, but children, too; and Roman, enterprising and public-spirited as ever, was ready to enrich his own coffers by facilitating the education of youth. For their amusement he published the Inglenook and Golden Gate series; for their instruction he published textbooks. The children's stories that appeared over his imprint were adapted to, and concerned with, California. In them, Roman advertised, Californians would "recognize many familiar places and personages." "Elegantly illustrated from original designs," Roman's California juveniles rolled from the press—May Wentworth's *Fairy Tales from Gold Land,* Carrie Carlton's *Inglenook,* Clara Dolliver's *Candy Elephant*—and with them were issued such texts as Layres's *Elements of Composition,* or Carrie Carlton's *Popular Letter Writer,* "particularly adapted to the wants of California." The children's teachers were urged to call and examine the textbooks and pedagogic apparatus.

Less practical than treatises on mining or agriculture, of less immediate need than works on Oriental customs or school texts, books for relaxation began to find a place on Roman's crowded shelves. Besides selling standard literary treasures, he himself published works of fiction, such as novels by "Laura Preston" [Louise Palmer Heaven] and Mrs. Embury, as well as volumes of poetry, to encourage native talent and to manifest to the world the possibilities of Californiana. James Linen's *Poetical and Prose Writings* included accounts of the missions of Upper California; Patterson's *Onward: A Lay of the West* sketched "a hasty picture of our great and growing West, at this period of its magical progress"; and the poem, *Madrona,* was "conceived and begun during a trip made by the author through the picturesque County of Sonoma." The *Poems* of Charles Warren Stoddard appeared in an elegant edition, illustrated by William Keith and printed by Bosqui on the finest paper, with a subscription list including nearly every well-known name in the professional and social circles of California.

Another verse collection, published by Roman and now a bibliographical rarity, gave rise to as much excitement as the discovery of a new lode and paved the way for a general interest in the literary enterprises of California. The story behind its publication is of extreme interest. One Mary Tingley, having filled a large folder with clippings culled from periodicals, had offered the collection to Anton Roman, who held it for possible publication. Having become acquainted with Bret Harte, the publisher requested the young man to edit the collection and obtain additions to it. The arrangements between them were not very clear, for after its publication Harte was to write to Roman:

From your remarks concerning the cost of the volume . . . am I to infer that you propose to recompense me from the profits of the edition? I do not think we made any agreement whatever as to the amount or manner of remuneration, but I certainly cannot consent to any that is to be *contingent* upon the success of the volume, if that is your intention.

Whatever the intention, the book appeared as a small quarto, beautifully printed on fine, tinted paper, handsomely bound in cloth, priced at one dollar, and entitled *Outcroppings: Being Selections Of California Verse*. Today it is of interest as the first book with which Bret Harte was associated. In December, 1865, when it first appeared, it proved of interest for another reason. "Its contents," Harte's preface explained, "have been selected partly from contributions made by local poets to the California newspapers during the past ten years, and partly from material collected three years ago for a similar volume, by Miss M. V. Tingley."

That Miss Tingley objected to the work, disavowing Roman's right to use her selections, is understandable. That the poems of Ina D. Coolbrith, Emilie Lawson, B. P. Avery, J. R. Ridge, C. H. Webb, and other local littérateurs should have called down upon the head of the compiler a storm of abuse is scarcely comprehensible today. None the less, there was "Commotion on Parnassus" when *Outcroppings* made its bow. Within two hours after its arrival was bruited abroad, a mob of poets besieged Roman's bookstore, all eager to learn whether their effusions had been immortalized among the selected gems. *Outcroppings* had become "the salient literary topic of the day." Heralded as a "beautiful specimen of typography," it was also condemned both for the geological character of its title and the limited nature of its contents. According to one paper, *Outcroppings* was "a Bohemian advertising medium. . . . As a collection of California poetry, it is beneath contempt." The contempt was aired, however, and the newspapers enjoyed a field day at the expense of Roman's little gift book. "All of which," the editor astutely observed, "ought to make the volume sell." It did more than that. While Ward's Furnishing Store, with tongue in cheek, issued "Outcroppings No. 2, by A Rum-Un & Co.," Hubert Howe Bancroft was quick to publish a rival anthology, *Poetry of the Pacific*. Edited by May Wentworth, this collection was, as its title indicates, more complete and ambitious in scope than Roman's undertaking. Though many of the authors were the same as in *Outcroppings,* and though their utterances paid similar tribute to such poetic staples as autumn, love, and trees, *Poetry of the Pacific* was, quantitatively at least, superior to its predecessor. Decades later Harte recalled the excitement attending the publication of *Outcroppings,* in his *My First Book;* but long before that the anthology had spread Roman's reputation abroad and had indicated to him the interest in California that a native literary work might arouse. By 1868 even a Bancroft publication could declare that "the leading publishing houses in California are those of H. H. Bancroft & Co. and A. Roman & Co." It was time for Anton Roman, miner, bookseller, and publisher, to embark upon yet another enterprise, and to prove—if proof were needed—that California was rich not only in its natural resources, but in its literary products as well.

He himself needed no such proof. His bookselling and publishing activities had acquainted him with many of the writers of the coast. Manuscripts were constantly being submitted to him, and he was confident that abundant material, not suitable for publication in book form, would be valuable for use in a magazine. Shortly before his death, Roman explained the purposes behind his entrance into the field of magazine publishing:

I considered the geographical position of San Francisco and California, the large extent of territory surrounding it, its immense seacoast both on the American side and across the Pacific. . . . Here I saw an opportunity for a magazine that would furnish information for the development of our new State and all this great territory, to make itself of such value that it could not fail to impress the West, and the East also.

Financial support and advertising patronage were sought by means of the following circular:

A. Roman & Co. propose taking immediate steps for issuing a first-class monthly magazine, the first number to appear July 1st, 1868.

The nature and character of the magazine will embrace, to the fullest extent, the commercial and social interests of California and the Pacific Coast.

We ask your assistance in this enterprise in the shape of an advertisement of your business for the term of one year, which we think will fully repay you.

Our intentions are to have every article original; to employ only the best talent in the country; to pay for every article; and to distribute 3000 copies monthly, until its permanent circulation reaches or exceeds this number.

The rates of advertising will be $50 per page monthly, or $25 for a half page.

The circular brought in contracts for advertising which would assure the magazine an income of $900 monthly for a year. With such support, and with the confidence that he himself could procure at least half the articles for the first six months of the magazine, Roman was ready to seek an editor.

Charles Warren Stoddard, whose *Poems* Roman had published, recommended the writer who had edited *Outcroppings* and who was then serving as secretary of the U.S. branch mint—Bret Harte. Harte entertained some doubts about the project, and, to win him over, Roman indicated on a map of the two hemispheres in his office the central position of San Francisco on the Pacific coast, and its potential influence upon the entire territory. The prospective editor was convinced. Harte had visited Roman at the moment when the publisher was considering a change of die for the cover. The line-cut of the grizzly now seemed too unadorned and Roman desired some alteration. Harte took out a pencil and drew two lines beneath the bear, placing it on the tracks of the Pacific Railroad. If Roman had had any doubts about Harte's abilities, they were dispelled by this inspired touch. Both editor and publisher were ready to proceed

with a magazine that needed only a title, and this too was supplied
by Harte, who dubbed the periodical *The Overland Monthly*.

The first number of *The Overland Monthly Devoted To The Development of the Country* appeared in July, 1868. Harte's editorial
section, entitled "Etc.," explained the reason for its name:

Shall not the route be represented as well as the *termini?* And where
our people travel, that is the highway of our thought . . . what could be
more appropriate for the title of a literary magazine than to call it after
this broad highway?

Noah Brooks, who had agreed to serve as a joint editor with Harte
and W. C. Bartlett, contributed "The Diamond Makers of Sacramento"; B. P. Avery discussed "Art Beginnings on the Pacific";
and a poem, "San Francisco," was supplied by Harte. The section
on Current Literature included the review of a Roman publication,
Swift's *Going to Jericho. The Overland Monthly,* priced at $4 a
year, with appropriate reductions in the rates for clubs, had been
launched.

Perhaps one of the most interesting concomitants of the enterprise was Roman's relationship with Bret Harte. Roman wished to
obtain from Harte a story for at least every other number. This plan
threw publisher and editor together much of the time; and, as they
journeyed by train up and down Santa Clara Valley or rode across
the Santa Cruz Mountains by stagecoach, Roman shared with Harte
his anecdotes and reminiscences of the gold rush, pointing out to
him their literary possibilities.

The results of this association appeared in the second number of
The Overland in the form of "The Luck of Roaring Camp." At
Santa Cruz Harte had outlined the tale to Roman, and one Sunday
afternoon the duplicate galley proofs arrived on the stagecoach.
Roman's wife, Eliza Fletcher Roman, read the story aloud to him
until she was too affected to continue. The next day, upon his return
to San Francisco, Roman was greeted by his chief clerk with the
announcement that the proofreader, Mrs. Sarah B. Cooper, had
objected to the immorality of "The Luck." Roman decided to print
the story, none the less, and it became the sensation of the day. By
October, 1868, Harte could write in "Etc.":

The prophet has been honored in his own country. Throughout the
Pacific Slope, from San Diego to Portland; on the Sierras and along the

Great Highway ... wherever a printing press has been carried or a ream of printing paper packed, the Overland has been kindly welcomed.

What is more, the local talent of the west coast found in it a medium for their writings, and, through earthquake and sunshine, *The Overland* pursued its successful way, crossing the continent on the completed Pacific Railroad. By the end of its first year, however, Roman fell ill, and at the advice of his physician left San Francisco for a rest, selling out his proprietorship in the magazine to John H. Carmany for $7,500, an amount that represented a profit of $3,000.

By the terms of his contract with Carmany, Roman had agreed not to enter the magazine field again for ten years. Magazine publishing was, however, as he himself described it, "in his bones." At the same time that he had sponsored *The Overland,* his imprint appeared on the *California Medical Gazette,* a monthly devoted to medicine, surgery, and the collateral sciences. As soon as the ten years had elapsed, therefore, Roman returned to the field with another venture in periodicals, *The Californian A Western Monthly Magazine.* The first number of January, 1880, included an editorial section appropriately called "Outcroppings," in which the publisher introduced his new enterprise:

Keenly alive to the fact that we have here on this coast the elements of a literature as strong, original, and characteristic, as the people themselves, the projectors of this periodical warmed it into life ... to stand the exponent of our life and letters, such as they now are, and such as they may in time become. In the language of its prospectus, and indicative of its name, "The Californian will be thoroughly Western in its character, local to this coast in its flavor, representative and vigorous in its style and method of dealing with questions, and edited for a popular rather than a severely literary constituency." ... With ... a sincere desire of arousing a local literary pride among our people, the new magazine clasps hands with all interested in the working out of a common and continued prosperity.

Under the editorship of Fred W. Somers and later of Charles H. Phelps, *The Californian* became a medium for the "outcroppings" of a later generation of the West, publishing the writings of Joaquin Miller and Ambrose Bierce. By May, 1880, however, Roman was again compelled—because of "lack of means to push the enterprise"—to yield his proprietorship in the magazine, this time to the

California Publishing Company for the sum of $275; and, with the revival of the old *Overland Monthly,* which had been suspended, *The Californian* was merged with it. Both magazines had been the offshoots of Anton Roman's ingenuity and confidence in the literary possibilities of California, and though he himself was never to return to the field, he could rest content with the contributions he had made to periodical publishing on the west coast. He could write, "I have always felt grateful to the public and to the many good friends who readily and cheerfully . . . aided my endeavors in magazine publishing, but above all to the many contributors to the early issues, who worked for the success of the enterprise."

In the years that passed between Roman's withdrawal from *The Overland* and his connection with *The Californian,* his bookstore had expanded to such an extent that it offered works not only for miners and farmers, settlers and Orientals, children and littérateurs, but "for the million" as well. As a publisher he had undertaken such travel books as Swift's *Going to Jericho;* he had sponsored the writings of local theologians, publishing the sermons of the San Francisco minister, Charles Wadsworth, and the scriptural commentaries of the California bishop, William Kip. But, in order to attract "the million," Roman was forced to import and sell. As early as 1861 he had issued a 259-page *Catalogue raisonné,* consisting of "a classified collection of prominent standard authors—embracing a wide range . . . and of use to all seeking the best works in any branch of Literature." As the years passed, the Montgomery Street bookstore became a market for books "for the million," books standard and miscellaneous, medical and scientific, legal and theological, books appealing to every class of society and every profession. At Roman's stand might be found, therefore, the works of Eastern publishers—G. W. Carleton and T. B. Peterson, D. Appleton and Harper, Loring, and Lee and Shepard; so many of the books published in New York, Philadelphia, and Boston were sold by Anton Roman in San Francisco that he could advertise "a complete stock in every department of literature." His shelves were filled with "the finest library bound books, embracing all the standard works in the English language." On the center tables might be found "the rarest and most costly editions of the poets and favorite authors of the age, together with the choicest gift-books and other *recherche* publications of the English and American press." Globes, maps,

charts, atlases, school apparatus, toy books, and juveniles completed a stock that increased yearly, and indicated, as it increased,
the development of California's interest from the regional to the
universal. In 1865 Roman's establishment ranked next to Bancroft's
as the leading firm on the Pacific coast. The annual sales for two
years past were represented as between $175,000 and $200,000,
while the stock of books on hand was valued at $75,000 or $85,000.
Here was a far cry from the California of only eighteen years before,
when "there were not probably 300 volumes of English books within
the territory." Now Roman's firm had agents in London and Paris,
as well as in New York, from whom shipments were received. His
relations with the Eastern publishers were generally equal, if not
superior, to those of any other house on the coast, and he advertised
that thus he was able to supply books in larger quantities and at
cheaper rates than other importers.

With one Eastern publisher Roman's relations were more closely
knit. In 1866 he established, for some six years, a residence in New
York, but even before that date the firm of William J. Widdleton had
served as his New York purchasing agent. Widdleton's business was
substantial, and as the publisher of standard books and belles-lettres,
he had earned a fairly solid reputation. Many of Roman's publications appear with a double imprint—that of the Montgomery Street
establishment in San Francisco and that of Widdleton at 17 Mercer
and later at 27 Howard Street, New York. It was through this New
York agency that Roman offered Bret Harte's *Condensed Novels* to
the publisher, G. W. Carleton, and it is on the back of Widdleton's
lists in the *Publishers' Trade List Annual* that Roman's advertisements appear. In addition, Roman could observe publishing conditions in the East. With Widdleton in particular he could discuss the
close affiliation of the book and stationery trades, current methods
of book distribution, publicity devices, seasonal trends in books,
the growth of the reprint field, changes in popular taste, the relative
appeal of English novels or American travel books, juveniles or
household helps, and could cull many ideas for California circulation.

As a west coast publisher and bookseller Roman needed such
an association. The books he sold were carried by semi-monthly
steamer between San Francisco and the East; and his relationship
with Widdleton provided him with the best facilities for obtaining

the latest issues of the American and English presses. In other directions, ships for Japan and China, Honolulu and Australia, Mexico and British Columbia carried heavy shipments of his goods. "We are constantly in receipt of all new publications by steamer," he advertised, "as fast as issued from the press. Books imported to order on shortest notice." Roman catered not only to the interests of the "million," but to their pocketbooks as well, building up his business on the principle of "quick sales and small profits," and advertising that his "extensive and elegant assortment" might be purchased "cheap for cash." The trade was supplied on liberal terms, special inducements were offered to libraries, and particular care was taken "in filling all wholesale and retail orders by mail and express, with promptness and at the lowest cash rates." Roman was prompt, indeed, as a letter of his sent in 1876 to the publishers of the *New-York Tribune* indicates:

Do you propose republishing Chas. Reade's Letters on International Copyright in any form? We have tried to obtain copies of your issues containing the several letters without success, and as we have repeated inquiries for the letters, either in a collected or in the original form, we take this means of finding whether you will republish or not.

Roman's letter shows not only his expeditiousness but the status of his business as well, for it is signed "A. Roman & Co." In his early business career, Roman had associated with himself Frank D. Carlton, who had had his training as a clerk with W. T. Coleman & Co., shipping merchants. Boarding with Frederick McCrellish, publisher of the *Alta California,* he had become interested in printing and in 1862 had joined Roman's company. Later on, after Carlton listed himself as a "capitalist" instead of a publisher in the San Francisco *Directories,* his place in the firm was taken by Joseph A. Hofmann, who had served as Roman's chief clerk and afterwards as salesman in the concern.

In 1871 announcement was made that Messrs. Roman & Co. had removed from their old quarters to "new and larger premises" at 11 Montgomery Street. Equipped in lavish style befitting California's spectacular, silver seventies, the store in the Lick House Block displayed to its customers a ceiling painted in fresco, appointments of white picked out with walnut, and the whole "a magnificent temple of letters." The firm that had long before advertised itself as "the largest miscellaneous book buyers in this country," and "the only exclusive book store on the Pacific Coast," now offered its customers, for the Christmas season of that year, "a royal literary feast." The "noble hall has its long tables covered with the choicest mental food culled from all climes and served up in the most magnificent style of binding." A. Roman & Co. could proudly boast, "Here we are, geographically isolated from the great world's throng, and yet the greatest cities cannot show a more complete establishment than ours." Besides the books, the annuals, the photograph albums of earlier times, 11 Montgomery Street could provide its patrons with Russian leather *porte-monnaies,* and "a complete trousseau of stationery, from the maiden card to the family Bible." Furniture, too, was for sale in the Lick House Block: carved book shelves and brackets, book stands and pouches for the wall, card stands and ink stands of cut glass or ormolu. The window display gave an earnest of the riches within; and by that Christmas of 1871 Anton Roman had reached the zenith of his success. The miner of Scott Bar, the proprietor of the Shasta Book Store, had come a long way in twenty years.

The general panic of 1873, however, resulted in a continued business depression on the Pacific coast, which, by 1879, had affected booksellers as well as farmers and industrialists. In consequence of this economic crisis, an announcement was made in April, 1879, that A. Roman & Co. had made an assignment for the benefit of their creditors. The firm's liabilities were estimated at from $85,000 to $90,000; their nominal assets at $80,000, consisting of about $15,000 in book accounts and the balance in stock and claims in equity. At the same time, W. J. Widdleton disposed of the bulk of his publications to A. C. Armstrong and discontinued his service as Roman's New York agent.

Roman's failure did not overwhelm him. Enthusiastic and venturesome as ever, he emerged from bankruptcy as the A. Roman Publishing Company, 511 California Street, and by 1882 had opened an agency in Room 15, 120 Sutter Street. In order to give the widest possible publicity to his undertaking, the publishers of *The Californian,* which he himself had projected, announced that "Mr. Roman has again started in business as bookseller and publisher . . . and . . . is prepared to supply anything and everything in his line, from a sheet of note-paper to a complete library in bindings warranted to match the carpet. We mention this last with the special purpose of influencing the patronage of our rich men in his favor."

Such patronage, however, does not seem to have been extended to him. It was less as bookseller and publisher that he resumed business than as general agent for subscription books. Roman had earlier in his career served as agent for *The National Almanac and Annual Record,* the publications of the Sunday School Union, and *The California Mail Bag.* He had also handled subscription books, such as Palmer Cox's *Squibs of California* and Hugh Quigley's *Irish Race in California;* he had been the San Francisco agent for the first edition of Mark Twain's *Roughing It,* and his imprint appears, in conjunction with that of the American Publishing Company, on the first American edition of *The Adventures of Tom Sawyer.* Along such lines he continued his business during the 1880's, no longer in a "magnificent temple of letters," but in a single room on Sutter Street. By that decade, however, the handling of subscription books had fallen into disrepute, and this aspect of the book business, impinging as it did upon the regular trade, had not only become the object of attack but was less lucrative than it had once been. Roman's first imprint had appeared in 1860 on *The Still Hour* by Austin Phelps, a work copyrighted by Gould and Lincoln and offering "standard thoughts" on religious subjects. His last imprint appeared in 1886 on a book far more characteristic of his own interests, Walter M. Leman's *Memories of an Old Actor,* for Leman's memories embraced the Sacramento Theater and the San Francisco theatricals of the early days. Though Roman never wrote his "Memories of an Old Publisher," he might well have recorded his history now, for by 1888 he had abandoned the book field forever.

At that time, and until his death in 1903, Roman appears in the San Francisco *Directories* as real estate agent, dealer in city and country property and timber lands, and loan broker. At first with Arthur H. Breed (with whom—as Holcomb, Breed and Bancroft— Harlow P. Bancroft, nephew of H. H. Bancroft, became associated after the turn of the century), Anton Roman sold the land he had loved instead of the volumes that had been written about it.

On June 21, 1903, he accompanied his son and daughter to a funeral, traveling on the North Shore Railroad. A car was derailed near Tomales, and among the victims of the wreck whose injuries proved fatal was the seventy-five-year-old Anton Roman.

Roman had been naturalized in Shasta County during the summer of 1885. In reality he had been naturalized long before that. Although his activities were neither so elaborate nor his reputation so celebrated as Bancroft's, his choice of publications served as a kind of marker to the progress of the Pacific coast. In this way Roman's career was both a parallel and a herald to the story of westward expansion, and the narrative of his life reaffirms the sometimes forgotten American tradition which asserts that every man is a debtor not only to his profession, but to his country. Anton Roman had paid that debt in full. With tools of type and ink he had helped to settle the Far West and round out a nation. The miner from Bavaria, who had crossed the plains to seek gold, had enriched the land of his adoption. When he placed his initials between grizzly bear and pick, pan and shovel, he had taken up the task of Argonaut in a broad sense. He had given to settlers the books they needed to establish a new community, and he had published abroad the literary treasure that could be found in El Dorado. In the settling of the Far West he takes his place, along with miner and farmer and teacher and builder. He, too, was a builder of empire—his masonry the printed word.

2

FRONTIERS OF THE MIND

X. THE SUCCESS OF
RUGGED INDIVIDUALISM

George W. Childs

POOR RICHARD THE SECOND

THE frontier spirit built the American empire, established its boundaries, expanded and rounded out the continent. But even after its geographical task was completed, the spirit itself would still flourish, turning to areas that had neither boundaries nor limits— the regions of the mind.

One idea was particularly inviting to the nineteenth-century mind. It was based upon the belief that an American man could hoist himself by his own bootstraps to the highest position in the land. Owing much to the conception of equality formulated by the Founding Fathers, it was regarded as the birthright of every American, his heritage from the eighteenth century. Indeed, had not Franklin in his little brown almanacs "filled all the . . . spaces . . . between the remarkable days in the calendar with proverbial sentences, chiefly such as inculcated industry and frugality, as the means of procuring wealth, and thereby securing virtue"? Had not his Poor Richard set the pattern with his "God helps them that help themselves," his "Nothing but money, is sweeter than honey," his "A penny saved is two pence clear," his "Every little makes a mickle"? Franklin himself, entering the city of Philadelphia with "a Dutch dollar, and about a shilling in copper," dirty and hungry, knowing "no soul nor where to look for lodging," had set the pattern.

The nineteenth century took up the basic pattern, but rewove it. Democracy came to mean that man was born free to seize or seek out opportunity. The nineteenth-century man could, with the benefit of such opportunity, make himself. Freedom was thus centered upon the individual, and the more rugged the individual, the greater his chances of success. Success itself was material, industrial, mercantile, its symbol the dollar sign. Franklin's Poor Richard had pointed the way. Now the Poor Richards of the nineteenth century followed him.

Born poor—except for their birthright of illimitable possibility—they could, and many of them did, become rich. Born in a log cabin, they could—and three of them did—arrive at the White House. Born with no other heritage than their belief in themselves and the opportunities around them, they could, and frequently did, become captains of industry, self-made men, sovereigns of the mighty dollar. This was the tapestry the nineteenth century manufactured from the pattern of the century that had gone before.

In 1874, Horatio Alger, Jr., who had, in his own typically nine-teenth-century manner, applied the aphorisms of Poor Richard in several series of popular narratives, wrote a novel for boys entitled *Risen From The Ranks.* It was the story of Harry Walton, whose "ambition had been kindled by reading the life of Benjamin Frank-lin." Harry, who first appeared in the novel as printer's devil on the *Centreville Gazette,* ended as joint proprietor and sole editor of the paper. The author, introducing the story, wrote in his Preface: "In describing Harry's rise from the ranks I have studiously avoided the extraordinary incidents and pieces of good luck, which the story writer has always at command, being desirous of presenting my hero's career as one which may be imitated by the thousands of boys similarly placed, who, like him, are anxious to rise from the ranks."

Actually, Horatio Alger, Jr., was telling an oft-told tale. Harry Walton's career might well be imitated in the future, but its outlines had been set in the past. George W. Childs, for one, had also "risen from the ranks" in much the same manner as Harry Walton. A book-seller's errand boy, he was to become a mighty publisher, a host to kings. He is remembered today as the publisher of the Philadelphia *Public Ledger,* an "honorable titan" whose career has become al-most legendary. His name at one time was a talisman; his endorse-ment was honored by the social and financial magnates of Europe and America; he was even recommended for candidacy to the Presi-dency.

Such a man has naturally become the nucleus round whom scores of articles have been written, and at first one might justifiably ques-tion the necessity for another addition to this mass of literature.

Nearly all the material concerning Childs, with one important exception, has been extremely laudatory, and almost all of it deals with his later life, when as proprietor of the *Ledger* the ruddy-faced, stocky magnate reaped the fruits of his shrewd sagacity. The single significant exception to these numerous eulogies is a fourteen-page pamphlet entitled *Review,* anonymous and suppressed, which calls attention to the titan's less honorable traits, and which was probably issued by his father-in-law, Robert Evans Peterson. This—together with a picture from *Truth* depicting Childs at twenty-three with the usual amount of hair, at thirty-eight reduced to baldness, and at sixty-four with a miraculous return of hirsuteness, and demanding, "Whose hair restorer was it?"—is almost the only anomaly in the eulogistic literature that has collected through the years. An addition to Childsiana is, therefore, in order, to extract the truth from the conflicting reports, but primarily to discover the truth about his early career in book publishing which was far more active and varied than his sycophantic eulogizers ever knew, and which laid the foundations for a typical nineteenth-century success story.

It is strange that although Childs's death was front-page news, his background is buried in obscurity; that though we know such singular facts about him as that he presented Mrs. Grover Cleveland with an Alderney calf, we have no information about his parentage. The Superintendent of Laurel Hill Cemetery, where he is buried, states, "We have no record of Mr. Childs' parentage." The *Childs Genealogy,* suspending all disbelief, inserts his name with the following remark: "One of the leading descendants of Henry Child of Colds Hill, England . . . writes us that George William Childs is of their line. For this reason we place him in juxtaposition to this branch. It is pleasant to think that Mr. Childs belongs to so noble a branch." Who his immediate forebears were, however, is a mystery that Childs himself never attempted to dispel. He began life invested with the vague obscurity which—far better than a silver spoon—characterizes the origins of so many nineteenth-century individualists.

Childs was born in Baltimore on May 12, 1829, apparently an unacknowledged son of a father belonging to a prominent family, and he was reared by an aunt who, like his parents, remains anonymous. At thirteen he entered the United States Navy, serving as an apprentice on board the *Pennsylvania* stationed at Norfolk, remaining in the service only fifteen months. It is after this period of ancestral obscurity and nautical endeavor that he emerges as a youthful member of the book trade, and at this point, therefore, his story properly begins.

Franklin took his historic walk up Market Street with a roll in his mouth, his pockets stuffed with shirts and stockings, and his capital consisting of a Dutch dollar. George W. Childs, a boy with ruddy cheeks and large gray eyes, made his entry into the same city, with a capital of similar proportions and with Franklin's principles in mind. Though his antecedents remain anonymous, he surely may claim moral kinship with the venerable publisher of *The Pennsylvania Gazette*.

At the suggestion of a friend of his anonymous aunt, the boy found a position in Philadelphia as clerk and errand boy for Peter Thomson, stationer and bookseller at the northwest corner of 6th and Mulberry Streets. There, for $3 a week, he made the fires, cleaned, swept, washed the pavement, and sold the "general assortment of miscellaneous books in the various departments of literature" offered by his employer, "The Cheap Bookseller." Besides acquainting himself with Mr. Thomson's plain and fancy stationery, juvenile books, albums, and floral keepsakes, Poor Richard the Second began to frequent the evening book auctions, going after his purchases with a wheelbarrow. Finally, he was regularly sent to attend the book trade sales in New York and Boston, where he formed an acquaintance with the Harpers and Appletons, Ticknor and Fields, Little and Brown, and where he learned to strike a bargain by calling for the "balance" of the number offered by the auctioneer after the desired quantity of books had been sold.

After four years of this characteristic nineteenth-century apprenticeship, young Childs had amassed enough capital to set up in business for himself. He did not, however, as so many of the eulogies insinuate, hire a slice of the old Ledger Building for the dissemination of literature. At 320 Market Street, in 1848, under the name of George W. Childs & Company, the young merchant established himself in the confectionery business, offering bon bons, French chocolates, steam refined candies, and calling to the special attention of grocers his new mode of putting up candies in packages. In addition, he announced himself sole proprietor of Dr. Wiley's celebrated cough candy, "the great remedy for coughs, colds, hoarseness, and in fact all diseases likely to terminate in confirmed consumption."

There may have been more cold victims than candy addicts in Philadelphia, for a few months later Childs altered his stock to patent medicines and toilet preparations, for the sale of which he did hire a slice of the old Ledger Building, No. 1. William M. Swain would one day recall the "chubby little fellow hiring an office of me, and boasting that he would own the *Ledger*," a boast which less than twenty years of rugged individualistic enterprise would realize. There the future publisher of the *Ledger* developed his advertising bent, announcing for sale Gouraud's Italian Medicated Soap and Poudre Subtile, Asiatic Golden Life Drops, and Cholera Flower Cordial. Since the cholera, however, failed to invade the city, George W. Childs soon abandoned the sale of medicines designed to prevent it, and consented to accept a position as clerk with R. E. Peterson, the bookseller and cousin of T. B. Peterson, at a salary of $600 a year.

Peterson had had an interesting history. His career had included periods as merchant, conveyancer, and attorney-at-law before he became associated with Daniels and Smith, booksellers. Having broken off relationships with that firm, and having been accused by its members of being an infidel, Peterson, who specialized in theological books, was naturally eager for an assistant who would not offend book-buying ministers. It was for this reason also that the business was placed for a time in the name of George W. Childs.

If the anonymous author of the rather virulent *Review* may be identified with Peterson, his summation of Childs's ability is, to say the least, deprecative: "His . . . knowledge of a general book business was very limited, and of the Theological trade—a most important branch of Mr. Peterson's business—he knew nothing. . . . Childs was at first a mere *makeshift* . . . his knowledge of the business was very limited . . . for he had never been in a position to acquire much knowledge of it."

Nevertheless, the firm of R. E. Peterson seems to have prospered, entering the publishing field in which it sowed the seeds of four different types of books which later were to be carried on by Childs alone. For the theological trade the works of the Reverend B. Dorr were published, along with *The Pastor's Wife, The Closing Scene,* and scriptural commentaries by, of, and for the clerical. For the barristers *Institutes of American Law* by John Bouvier, Peterson's father-in-law, made its appearance in four volumes priced at $15. For the schools *Familiar Science* was edited from Dr. Brewer's work by R. E. Peterson himself, adapted for American consumption, and priced at seventy-five cents—a book destined to reach a circulation of 200,000 copies. Finally, for those in search of information *The National Cook Book* by a Lady of Philadelphia (Hannah M. Bouvier Peterson, the publisher's wife) formed a ready reference work in the kitchen. Theological and law books, textbooks, and informative reference works were to take important places in the lists of George W. Childs, publisher, and it may not be amiss to call attention to the fact that it was R. E. Peterson who, at the northwest corner of 5th and Mulberry, first aroused his assistant's interest in them. In addition, Peterson's publications early indicate that his business was to no small extent a family affair to which his wife and father-in-law as well as he himself contributed. It may be no less amiss to point out here that George W. Childs was one day to join that family circle by marrying Peterson's daughter, Emma Bouvier Peterson, thus acquiring an even stronger interest in the copyrights of his father-in-law and incidentally climbing yet another rung in the nineteenth-century ladder of success.

Though Childs may have been merely a "makeshift" when he entered Peterson's employ, he must have proved his mettle, for, on January 1, 1852, he was admitted to partnership in the publishing business, which was to be conducted under the name of R. E. Peterson and Company. At the same time the stock of books previously sold on the plan of "small profits and quick sales" was transferred to C. G. Henderson and Company, juvenile booksellers. R. E. Peterson and Company was to be associated henceforward with publishing as distinguished from the retail trade.

The new firm continued with a line of publications similar to those originally issued by Peterson, carrying on the informative handbook type of work with *The National Portrait Gallery of Distinguished Americans,* recommended to "the friendly editor, the traveling companion, and the neighbor-associate at the fire-side." The schoolbook publications were expanded with works by Knighton on grammar and composition, along with Enoch Lewis's *Algebra,* and though the firm of R. E. Peterson and Company made little stir in the publishing world, it seems to have prospered on the fruits of its minor publications.

The stir was not made until the firm had once again changed its name, on November 1, 1854, to Childs and Peterson, to prevent confusion with the publishing house of T. B. Peterson. From their headquarters on Arch Street during the next five years, Childs and Peterson were to lend their names to several important undertakings, and George W. Childs, still in his twenties, was to exhibit a mastery of the art of dramatic advertising that would carry him far.

To the schoolbook publications of the new firm, Abby Kimber contributed a text on *Familiar Botany* and Hannah Peterson one on *Familiar Astronomy,* which appeared with testimonials obtained from Sir John Herschel, Lieutenant Maury, and Professor Bond designed to recommend the work to "schools, families, and private students." Childs's hand may be seen in this device of collecting endorsements in return for complimentary copies, a technique he was to exploit to the full later on.

The old law book line was expanded with Sheppard's *Constitutional Text-Book,* Joel Jones's *On Easements,* Bouvier's *Law Dictionary,* for which $40,000 was to be paid for copyright, and Sharswood's edition of Blackstone. It was Childs who suggested that Judge Sharswood prepare an American edition of the *Commentaries,* which appeared in two volumes, royal octavo, heralded by testimonials, encased in the "best law binding," and priced at $6.

Though both the legal and school texts sponsored by Childs and Peterson brought considerable profit to the firm, they were standard works which created little or no furor among general readers. Fortunately, Childs was not content with immediate monetary rewards alone and, with an almost never-failing instinct for success, he was willing to risk both his own and his partner's profits in order to publish more exciting, colorful books that would appeal to a wider public. The opportunity came in the shape of the informative type of work which the firm had handled on a small scale before. There was little excitement in publishing *A New Medical Dictionary* whose only claim to uniqueness was that it contained several thousand more words than were to be found in any other work of the kind. No thrill could be attached to the handling of David Wells's *Year Book of Agriculture,* which, in spite of its colored engravings, failed to result in any *éclat* or financial profit. Childs's mind was too imaginative, his range of interests too wide for him to rest content with the publication of such standard reference books. Yet the public wished to be informed, he knew; but he knew, too, that *"amusement* as well as instruction must be afforded the reader. It will be the *popular* element that will get us the largest no. of subscribers." One man was at hand, who, were he to write his experiences in the form of a colorful narrative of adventure for the general reader, would instruct the public while he thrilled them, appeal profoundly to the popular element, enrich the coffers of the firm, and, last but not least, make the name of the publisher, George W. Childs, as well known as his own.

That man was Elisha Kent Kane, the fair, gray-eyed explorer who had returned from the second Grinnell Expedition to the Arctic in search of Sir John Franklin, and who could, if properly guided, tell a tale of interest not only for geography but for humanity, a tale of perilous adventure and thrilling incident. Childs undertook to guide the explorer, prevailing upon him to write a narrative that would be popular rather than scientific. While engaged, under orders of the Navy Department, in elaborating the results of his expedition, Kane therefore availed himself of the Secretary's permission to connect the passages of his journal that would have interest for the general reader and to publish them as a narrative of his party's adventures. To the explorer, the undertaking seems to have been an arduous task, a "wretched book," an "incubus," to which he was "anxious to write *'Finis.'* " In the course of its preparation he wrote numerous letters to his publisher, expressing his distaste for the task, requesting advances, and revealing illuminating glimpses of author-publisher relations.

Kane's letters reflect particularly his publisher's insistence that he popularize the narrative—a demand which the author found most uncongenial, but to which he tried to conform. Kane's wish was "to make a Centre table book fit as well for the eyes of children as of refined women." His attempt to popularize the narrative by "introducing descriptive anecdote and suppressing scientific and discursive matter" would work to the publisher's advantage, but, as for himself, "Most certainly my efforts to make that book readable will destroy its permanency and injure me.—It is a sacrifice."

Interesting technical details were frequently mentioned by Kane, rounding out the picture of a work in progress. Through his "friends of the Coast Survey" he was "offered the loan of their electrotyping apparatus," which would, he informed Childs, "much increase your facilities and reduce the Costs." Yet, the author reminded the publisher, "The book has thus far cost me in my little way nearly as much as you in your larger operations.—From a Chart to a line of figures;—a Cypher to a penny Whistle every thing had to be paid for." Sketches and illustrative material, paging and proofs, charts and engravings, all presented their problems until at last, "With little spirit of congratulation and much weariness," the author sent to his publisher "the preface which completes my text. . . . now that the holy day is at hand I am ungrateful enough to complain that it finds me without the Capacity to enjoy it." His "slavery" was ended but, he remarked sadly and prophetically, "The book poor as it is has been my coffin."

Meanwhile, the publisher took the liberty of striking from the proofsheet of the preface a paragraph regarding the imperfection of the work, and set himself to advertising it with an energy and skill that surpassed his most elaborate efforts on behalf of Dr. Wiley's cough candy. Having undertaken publication at an expense exceeding $70,000 for the first edition, the firm could spare no opportunity to capitalize upon the investment. When the work was ready to be issued, therefore, Childs took a sample copy to New York to solicit orders from the leading booksellers. Though the largest house ordered only one hundred copies at first, Childs was shortly to be gratified by a later request for five thousand more. To the editors the publisher was quick to send circulars and specimen pages, asking for notices and offering to furnish cuts for illustrated articles. Dr. Griswold, for example, received with his copy of the work an autograph portrait of the author along with a request for a notice to appear preferably "after the Election, as your colums [sic] are over crowded and people haven't time to think of books." Childs was never reticent about placing his publishing cards on the table. "I hope," he wrote to Griswold, "you will always say a good word for us whenever you can. We want your influence. If any of your editorial friends have not received a copy of Kane, please let me know and I shall be pleased to send them one."

Childs did not content himself, however, with trumpeting the book to editors and agents. Through devious machinations he made a grandiose attempt to persuade Congress to purchase 15,000 copies of Kane's narrative—an endeavor which involved the publisher in large-scale hostilities and animosities. Although the effort failed in the end, it reveals the magnitude of Childs's ambitions and the colossal nature of his schemes. In its original form the resolution stated "That the Committee on the Library be authorized to purchase from the publishers fifteen thousand copies of a forthcoming work, by Dr. E. K. Kane, on Arctic explorations, . . . to be distributed among the members of Congress . . . *Provided,* That the price shall not exceed five dollars for the two volumes: *And provided further,* That the material, press-work, illustrations, and binding, shall be approved by the said committee." Kane's own initial enthusiasm for such a Congressional purchase underwent a drastic change which he explained in a forthright letter to his publisher:

I had—like a fool—looked upon my approaching narrative as that of a voyage of discovery undertaken by orders of government—and it seemed to me under the circumstances open to purchase or adoption by our National legislature.—With this view only I had sanctioned an indirect Connection with your movement feeling that it was not a pecuniary recompense but a direct transaction for which a full equivalent was intended in the work itself.

But my views upon that matter have undergone a mortifying Change. . . . Mr. Broadhead [sic] has written a letter to my Father. . . . This letter implies that I am acting with you to carry out a Congressional act of pecuniary reward and in every respect repugnant to my instincts as a gentleman and an officer. . . .

In order to prevent any misapprehension, I have sent my brother to Washington with authority to withdraw my name from any connection with this matter.

Three months later Kane reiterated his distaste for the proceedings, at the same time reflecting Childs's continued and persistent efforts to realize his unusual scheme in the face of Senatorial opposition:

I am really sorry to find you in Washington reviving the book question from which I had so entirely separated myself. . . . a Continuation of the question would be unpleasant to my feelings and prejudicial to my real interests. Besides I have washed my hands of all Connection with the book and therefore with yourself—My Expedition and its merits are neither in your hands nor my own and I beg you to leave unmolested the action of Congress for this Coupling of my name with the book will interfere with any expression of *disinterested* feeling on the part of the Senate and thus stand in the way of that which I value far beyond either books or money viz.—an honorary testimonial in recognition of our party.

As Kane confided to his father, "I understand Mr. Childs—and he is *using* me for his own ends. I do justice to his sympathy, his efficiency, his friendship and the other good qualities Connected with these—but were our interests disconnected there would be none of all this activity."

Childs's efforts ended in failure. Perhaps through the opposition of Senator Brodhead, who, according to the Philadelphia *Ledger,* "would still continue to assert that the Legislature of his native State had been bribed to pass the Kane resolutions," a general law was passed "prohibiting the gratuitous distribution of books among the members, except those of a strictly documentary character," and the section of the resolution regarding the purchase of Kane's work by Congress was, accordingly, stricken out.

Indirectly, however, Childs had achieved no small measure of success. Often under the heading of "Telegraphic News from Washington," the press teemed with news about the explorer and his book. Even before its publication, *Frank Leslie's Illustrated Newspaper* had carried a lengthy article about the Commander of the Arctic Exploring Expedition and the "great work" upon which he was engaged—"a monument of industry and mighty enterprise" that would "cause a thrill of patriotism to run through the country." "Thirty presses driven by steam" were constantly employed in getting out the edition. Advance orders from Boston, New York, Philadelphia, Cincinnati, and Baltimore indicated that 100,000 copies would be "demanded upon the first issue of the work." Enlightened and stimulated by such advance notices, the public was ready to welcome Kane's narrative.

The book itself, entitled *Arctic Explorations: The Second Grinnell Expedition in Search of Sir John Franklin,* appeared in 1856, a two-volume work illustrated from the author's sketches with over three hundred engravings by James Hamilton, bound in cloth, and priced at $5. Childs's advertising exploits had, however, not yet reached their zenith. It was only when Kane's prophetic remark was realized, and the explorer died in Cuba the following year, that the enterprising publisher wrested his most outstanding triumph from the author's misfortune. When the explorer's body was brought back to Philadelphia, its progress became, largely through Childs's machinations, a public event. At every stop along the route city authorities and state militia honored the dead explorer, until at Philadelphia Kane was given a "final" funeral that was "one of the most remarkable in history."

The result of Childs's showmanship was all that the publisher could have desired. By January of 1857 he had expected "to pay Dr. Kane $50,000," and the author's share of royalties for the first year amounted to $65,000. Sixty-five thousand copies were sold, which at the retail price exceeded the sum of $300,000. By 1866 it was said that the Kane family had received $100,000 from the explorer's copyrights. As for the publisher, the foundation of his fortune was made. His stocky figure, ruddy complexion, and hearty manner were soon to become familiar to all of Philadelphia. The man who rose at five in the morning and eschewed strong liquor and tobacco was becoming a personality in the Franklin tradition.

Meanwhile, the firm purchased the stereotype plates of Kane's book on the *First Grinnell Expedition,* and proceeded to exploit the popular demand for informative travel literature by publishing Kidder and Fletcher's *Brazil and the Brazilians,* Frémont's *Explorations,* and William Elder's *Biography of Elisha Kent Kane.*

Childs, however, was interested not only in fortune but in fame. Early in the 1850's he had made an arrangement with S. Austin Allibone to write *A Critical Dictionary of English Literature, and British and American Authors,* offering him $10,000 for his copyright, and by 1854 this magnum opus was described as in a "forward state of preparation." The manuscript, copied by Mrs. Allibone, assumed enormous proportions, until it filled 19,044 large foolscap pages. The zeal with which the publisher advertised Kane's *Arctic Explorations* was matched with that which he applied to the preparation of a book that was to be "to the literature of the language what a dictionary of words is to language itself." To his zeal the publisher added large monetary advances, lending the firm's money and persuading Peterson to lend more on collateral security of the stock of the Bank of Pennsylvania. Though Childs thus furnished the money for the vast number of books required by Allibone in his researches, and though he himself took an active part in the preparation of the work, carrying on a correspondence with numerous informants, neither the publisher's financial investment nor his fine art of advertising could make the tome a monetary success. Having lost a considerable sum on the enterprise, the publisher was forced to consider it in the light of a service to letters and to content himself with Allibone's dedication of Volume I to "George William Childs, the publisher of this Work, who has greatly furthered my labours by his enterprise and zealous and intelligent interest." The super royal octavo, consisting of over one thousand pages of biographies elegantly printed on fine paper, and bearing the testimonials of Dickens, Washington Irving, and Macaulay, was unfortunately not regarded by the public as "indispensably necessary to all who read." Moreover, Volume I covered only the letters *A* to *J,* and it was not until an interval of many years had passed that the second and third volumes were brought out by J. B. Lippincott.

Childs, equipped by nature with the self-confidence essential to rugged individualism, was able to sustain his publishing losses with equanimity, but Peterson, upon being informed that the firm was insolvent, retired in 1860. His partner, having demonstrated both his mastery of advertising and his devotion to letters, formed a brief connection with J. B. Lippincott, whose firm had taken over Allibone's *Dictionary.* As the papers put it, "Mr. Childs has become a partner in the very extensive and thriving firm of J. B. Lippincott & Co. . . . The united business capacity and energy of these gentlemen will make a publishing firm of unsurpassed experience and resources." Childs himself regarded his new partner as "the leading bookseller not only of this country but of the world." According to the anonymous *Review,* their connection consisted of a kind of morganatic contract whereby Childs was to "continue the publication of his own books on his own account, and for his services as a partner J. B. Lippincott and Company were to give him a share of the profits of the firm." The arrangement, whatever its nature, did not last long, for the contracting parties soon found themselves in disagreement regarding their individual rights and privileges.

By the time Childs's long apprenticeship was over, he had outmastered his teachers in the publishing craft and was ready to strike out for himself. His device of the broken sword and quill pen would adorn many a volume that proved the truth of his motto, "The pen is mightier than the sword." In his offices on Chestnut Street, George W. Childs, Publisher, was ready to exhibit his enterprise and liberality, his boldness and energy to the public. He had developed also a publishing credo whereby he continued to stress the necessity for coupling amusement with instruction, for appealing to the popular element, and for paying authors well by sharing profits once his original outlay had been covered.

Childs proceeded to apply his credo in publishing books of every type that his former partner and present father-in-law had launched. The informative reference line was continued and expanded with pocket dictionaries and travel books, with volumes that ranged in subject from parliamentary rules to steam engines, from English literature to cooking. Remembering Peterson's early interest in theology, Childs returned to that type of work, issuing *The Beauty of Holiness, A Manual of Worship,* and *Songs of the Soul.* Schoolbooks were not neglected, for the publisher supplied industrious students with texts on science and elocution, geology and the Constitution. For the legal trade he offered works on common carriers and arbitration, reprinting at the same time Peterson's earlier successes in each field. And characteristically he also announced the publication of a revised edition of Sparks's *Dr. Franklin's Life and Writings* as well as two or three of the Rollo books by Jacob Abbott.

Childs could never remain a follower, however. Any line introduced by him would have to appeal to that popular element in which he so implicitly trusted. The Civil War was a timely theme, and books about it would stimulate reader interest and enjoy financial profit. It was with this in mind that the florid, gray-eyed publisher joined a group of outriders from Philadelphia to meet the eccentric Tennesseean, William G. Brownlow, at Altoona. Childs was aware that the fighting parson of the Southern Highlands could write the kind of book that people wanted to buy, a book that would tell how the South had provoked the war and harried the Union people in East Tennessee. Brownlow agreed, accepting $10,000 for the manuscript. As the *American Publishers' Circular* put it, "Parson Brownlow has accepted the liberal offer of Mr. Childs, . . . and at the request of the Parson, a copy of the book will be given to the editor of every newspaper in the country, so that they can see what it costs to be loyal in Secessiondom." By September, 1862, 100,000 copies had been sold. Applegate & Company of Cincinnati had, it was said, ordered 40,000 copies—the "largest order ever given in the world for one book." *Parson Brownlow's Book,* boldly advertised and thrust before the public at an opportune moment, set another feather in the cap of the enterprising publisher and another fortune in his lap.

The war could be viewed from many angles, and a far-sighted publisher could profit from all of them. By authority of the War Department, Childs issued the *United States Revised Army Regulations* (which had been one cause of his disagreement with Lippincott) and garnered the fruits of a work essential for men in the field and men preparing for army life. The public was eager for war books, whether they were narratives of *The Siege of Richmond* or accounts of *Prison-Life in the Tobacco Warehouse at Richmond,* and Childs was eager to supply them. Even *The National Almanac,* which the nineteenth-century Poor Richard undertook at the same time that he acted as agent for the sale of Wheeler and Wilson's Sewing Machines, could provide military and naval statistics along with information on eclipses and hospitals for the insane. "The primary object of the publisher . . . has been," he informed his readers, "to make it, as far as possible, a thoroughly accurate, reliable, and exhaustive authority. . . . To this end, every effort has been used, and no expense has been spared." "The aim," he pursued, "has been to take nothing at secondhand, but to resort, . . . to the original sources of knowledge." The aim appears to have succeeded, for Childs announced that 15,000 copies of the 1863 *National Almanac* had been sold. Callan's compilation of *The Military Laws of the United States,* along with the *Lives of the Generals of the Union Army* and *The Light and Dark of the Rebellion,* swelled Childs's list of war books, appealed to the popular element, and met a current demand.

For some time the publisher had also been arranging with Benson J. Lossing for a *Pictorial History of the Civil War,* and the author, equipped with camera lucida and portable drawing-board, had been visiting the battlefields and supervising the preparation of engravings. As he had "collaborated" with Allibone, Childs enthusiastically assisted Lossing by soliciting from the country's notables "material bearing upon the war," "facts or incidents relative to the lives and services of . . . the Generals of the Union Army," and "official, newspaper, or other accounts . . . in regard to the battles or sieges in which any of them may have been engaged." Author-publisher relations were in this instance warm and closely knit. Childs was impatient to "get at work" on this "great book,"—"our book," for, as he wrote to Lossing, "They are piling the other histories into every nook and corner of the land, and the masses of the people are not competent to discriminate, and it is with them the heavy sales are made." By the end of 1865 he could inform the author, "I am hard at work and have laid all my plans for a thorough and exhaustive canvass of your great book. I am doing everything on the principle that our book is bound to be the standard history for the next 20 years to come and while I do not expect a great sale at the start I am determined to do the matter up completely in time. It is a big thing and requires to be managed with perseverance and judgment."

Once again letters were sent to the nation's bigwigs announcing the proposed work, and once again the publisher was the recipient of a prefatory eulogy from the author, who could not "refrain from expressing his gratitude to Mr. Childs . . . for his untiring and zealous aid and encouragement from the inception of the work . . . and his generous liberality in bringing it out in the beautiful and costly manner in which it is presented." Once again, it was only the first volume that Childs saw through the press, for by the time the second was ready the publisher had turned his attention to an even more productive field than the battlegrounds of the Civil War.

Before the day that he became proprietor of the *Public Ledger,* however, Childs was to serve an apprenticeship in periodicals and exhibit still another aspect of his versatility in publishing. On April 1, 1863, announcement was made of the termination of Charles R. Rode's connection with the *American Publishers' Circular and Literary Gazette,* and of the transferrence of proprietorship, with the "approbation of the trade," to George W. Childs. That journal, a trade paper, was in time to develop into the present *Publishers' Weekly.*

Childs's connection with it lasted nearly ten years, during which time he broadened its scope, expanding what had been primarily an advertising sheet into a paper of professional and literary interest. His aims and proposed improvements are admirably set forth in the salutatory with which he introduced himself to his patrons in the first number issued by him on May 1, 1863:

We have formed in our mind a very clear and distinct conception of what the Circular should be. . . . Our sole desire is to make the Circular a complete medium of intercommunication between all who are interested in the purchase, sale, collecting, and reading of books. . . . Those who write books, who publish books, who collect books, and who read books, all have interests in common. It is those interests we would serve. . . . It is the manifold activities going on in the great world of books, at home and abroad, that we seek faithfully to seize and record. All that relates to the pecuniary interests of publishing should, of course, merit profound attention. But we must by no means overlook the readers and collectors of books, our professional classes, our recluse students, and our librarians, whose opinions go so far towards stimulating purchases. The publisher's calling is not, in truth, a mere trade. He is the dispenser of knowledge to the community, and even his material interests are best served by whatever excites and appeals unto that desire for knowledge which it is his lofty mission to satisfy.

In order to carry out his broad and high-minded purposes, Childs determined to include in his semi-monthly *Circular* foreign correspondence, a list of new publications, and articles concerned with bookmaking, paper manufacture, copyright laws, the history of publishing houses, rare editions, typograhy, catalogues, and the management of libraries. His Christmas numbers became notable specimens of typography, while his Educational issues extended an appeal to the schools and colleges of the country. Childs's original aim, to make the *Circular* "a first class live journal of its kind," was successfully carried out until it became, at $2 a year, not only an organ for booksellers, but a medium of communication and information for the literary world. Under his direction the journal was known to all the publishers of the country and was acclaimed as the "index of the Republic of letters throughout the world." Dr. Oliver Wendell Holmes gave it a well-deserved accolade when he declared that it fitted "exactly in an empty niche of the temple of letters," a remark worthy of the father of *Publishers' Weekly*. The *Circular* was destined for a success story analogous to that of its publisher.

Not long after Childs had assumed proprietorship of the trade paper, he purchased, with Anthony J. Drexel, in December of 1864, the *Public Ledger* of Philadelphia, its plant of type and steam presses, and *The Dollar Newspaper* from William M. Swain, who recalled at that time the "chubby little fellow" who had once hired an office of him. The *Ledger* quickly became, under Childs's energetic touch, one of the foremost daily family newspapers in the country, while *The Dollar Newspaper,* converted into the *Home Weekly,* combined prize stories, "sterling editorials," and agricultural and horticultural information for the edification of the households of America. Despite his tremendous force and enterprise, Childs as proprietor of three journals did not wish to continue also as a publisher of books. The beginning of his career as a giant of the newspaper world marks, therefore, the end of his career as a potential Napoleon of the book trade.

In 1866, when Childs was apotheosized as one of "The Self-made Men of our Times" in *Frank Leslie's Chimney Corner,* the firm of Sower, Barnes and Potts took over his list of schoolbooks, and the next year the publisher, "being about relinquishing the book business," offered for sale his stereotype plates, including those of *Brownlow's Book,* Lossing's *History* of the Rebellion, and Kane's *Arctic Explorations.* Yet the newspaper magnate could not refrain altogether from keeping a finger in the publishers' pie. He maintained his proprietorship of Sharswood's edition of Blackstone, for example, farming out to others the right to publish it, and the Philadelphia *Directories* list him as publisher of the *Ledger* and of books throughout the '70's. The works issued from the book publication office on the second story of the splendid new Ledger Building, which was appropriately adorned with a statue of Benjamin Franklin, were concerned primarily with the newspaper. They consisted of a book on *The Public Ledger Building* (1868), "beautifully printed on toned and tinted paper" and "richly bound in Magenta and gold," and a series of *Ledger Almanacs* printed annually from 1870 for free distribution among the subscribers of the paper. Childs himself took a hand in the editing of the *Almanac,* displaying the same zeal for first-hand information that had characterized his work with Allibone and Lossing. "Great care," he announced, "and an outlay of several thousand dollars have been bestowed upon the preparation of the Almanac, and it is presented in the hope that it may prove interesting and valuable as a daily reference companion." It would be continued yearly, "and its successive numbers will make a useful series of books well worthy of preservation." Eighty thousand copies of the 1870 *Almanac* were printed for free distribution among *Ledger* subscribers, and this home book of reference takes its place as a nineteenth-century version of another, more famous *Almanac.* And so Poor Richard the Second wrote the finis to his career in the book trade by offering to his patrons an almanac containing familiar quotations and Philadelphia chronology, the signs of the zodiac and useful family receipts.

To his personal career the finis had not yet been written. Childs was to survive until 1894, moving from his magnificent Ledger Building at the corner of 6th and Chestnut to his white marble mansion at the corner of Walnut and 22nd, a mighty and almost legendary figure who talked with kings, yet, as far as his newspaper was concerned, kept the common touch. G. P. Putnam, remembering that Childs had once given him his name as security for $100,000, exclaimed, "You wave your magic wand, and, lo! palaces rise." Rise they did, from his summer residence at Long Branch to his country seat, "Wootton," from the Childs-Drexel Home for Union Printers to his Philadelphia home. There, the princely publishing magnate dined in state, wearing full evening dress in rooms graced by lighted candelabra and powdered footmen. Around a monogrammed table service worth between forty and fifty thousand dollars, and set upon a scarlet cloth fringed with gold bullion that had been brought from the Vale of Cashmere, G. W. Childs, late errand boy to Peter Thomson, entertained the world's dignitaries. During the Centennial Year he was acclaimed as "the first gentleman in the United States" who, at a private reception, could number among his guests the President of the United States, the members of the Cabinet, and the justices of the Supreme Court. The recipients of Childs's royal hospitality made a mighty roster, including Dom Pedro of Brazil, the Count of Paris, General Grant, Lord and Lady Herschel. Their host was their peer—the first citizen of Philadelphia. His position was assured. His claim to be "the richest editor in the country" was unquestioned since he also claimed "to have money enough to back his assertion." He had become a familiar if not an imposing figure as, rosy-cheeked, side-whiskered, portly, he walked briskly to his office with his friend, Mr. Drexel. The name of George W. Childs was one to conjure with. His birthday was journalistic news. His activities had political implications. A trip abroad was for him a triumphal tour in the course of which he was welcomed by Charles Dickens. His generosity to his employees was proverbial. He was hailed as "A Friend to the Workingman" and "The Printer's Patron Saint." His gifts ranged from a cemetery lot to memorial fountains and stained-glass windows. His personal collection of clocks included one originally owned by Napoleon, and his collection of autographs included the manuscript of Poe's *The Murders in the Rue Morgue.*

Into his favorite tree at "Wootton" Childs had a spiral staircase built connecting with a platform, where, of a Sunday, he read the newspapers, hunting for references to "his distinguished self." The references were plentiful. From the Leipzig *Illustrirte Zeitung* to the *Arte Della Stampa,* from the *Pall Mall Gazette* to the New York *Sun,* there were articles about the man who, with "Ben Franklin's principles of thrift in his heart," was "a living proof of the oft-repeated fact that good work, honest endeavor and clean journalism pays. Mr. Childs," according to *The Journalist,* "started without money, without influential friends, without 'backing' of any kind. His capital was brains, energy, industry and integrity of purpose. He made his own position as . . . honored leader."

The publisher agreed. He had been "uniformly successful," and was not averse to recounting the story of his benevolent deeds as he sat back in his comfortable chair in his private office, and in his close-fitting frock coat surveyed a setting that became him—the Queen Anne trappings, the panels and stained glass that his fortune had created. One newspaper article in particular carried the cheerful utterances of the self-made man before the public: "If a man has good principles, and does his best to act up to them, he cannot fail of success, though it may not be success of precisely the same kind or degree as mine." The article was most appropriately headed, "Rising From The Ranks."

George W. Childs had indeed risen from the ranks. When he died in 1894 his estate was valued at some $1,350,000. And on the last day of his life, when Dr. S. Weir Mitchell arrived to attend him, the patient, it was reported, greeted him with the words, "What can I do for you, Dr. Mitchell?"—a question that epitomized not only the publisher's altruism, but the concentrated egoism of the man whose life had been a success story, a trait which doubtless inspired the anonymous author of the *Review.* The boy who had stood on the sidewalk in front of Peter Thomson's store, resting his tired hand upon a broomstick and watching in awe Graham of *Graham's Magazine* roll by in his magnificent equipage, reached the ultimate of satisfaction when he gave to that very man the pension upon which he was able to retire. The legend was complete. Poor Richard had risen from the ranks. From the thread of nineteenth-century opportunity he had woven the tapestry of nineteenth-century success, fulfilling a destiny that seemed almost less personal than national.

The finis to his personal career was also written in a manner becoming the moral heir of Benjamin Franklin, for Childs in 1890 gave to the world his *Recollections* as, about a century before, the *Autobiography* had first made its bow. His success he attributed to industry, temperance, and frugality—those virtues which Franklin had exalted, and which, set against the background of nineteenth-century opportunity, unrolled seemingly endless possibilities at the feet of the self-made man. Indeed, one reviewer went so far as to remark, "For this and coming generations these 'Recollections' are better than Franklin's autobiography." George W. Childs had proven that the pen in the hands of an American individualist was mightier than the sword in the hands of a Napoleon. He had trumpeted abroad yet another variation on the theme of opportunity and success, weaving in the annals of his country a nineteenth-century legend to profit the lowly and spur them to fortune.

XI. THE FAILURE OF
RUGGED INDIVIDUALISM

THE RISE AND FALL OF

A. K. Loring

SOMETIMES the legend faltered, and there was a break in the pattern. A man might start life equipped with the virtues of Poor Richard and the opportunities afforded by the dynamic economy of the nineteenth century, and yet he might end not as a power in the land, but as a ward of the state. Somehow, there were devious by-paths on the golden road from rags to riches. Off the record, the Alger hero did not always rise from the ranks, or, if he rose, he sometimes faltered and fell back. The flaw might lie in the pattern— not always inevitable, not always infallible. Or it might lie in the individual himself who, despite his industry and his ambition, might have a dash of eccentricity that turned him off the glittering "Way to Wealth." Wherever it lay, the flaw—the possibility of failure— was a fact to be faced, even in that exhilarating century when the application of Franklin's ethics was so often rewarded with the pot of gold that had come to mean success. "Bound To Rise" was frequently not only a gratifying state of mind, but a realistic state of affairs. On the other hand, sometimes it was just a phrase—the title of a book by Horatio Alger, Jr.

By all the laws of poetic justice, George W. Childs, who, throughout his life was an Alger hero, should have been the publisher of Alger's books. It is the law of poetic irony, perhaps, that Alger's actual publisher ended in failure instead of in success. Aaron K. Loring, the publisher of the works of Horatio Alger, Jr., began life in strict conformity to the rules of "Bound To Rise." As the son of a Massachusetts saddler, his origins were lowly enough—if not so obscure as those of Childs—to start him forth on a steady rise from the ranks. As Alger's publisher, he had the opportunity and the

shrewdness essential for those who "Strive And Succeed." Yet Aaron
K. Loring ended his life not as a host to kings and the proprietor
of a great newspaper, but in a Home for Aged Men. Unlike the
heroes whose careers he published to the world, he had striven but
had not succeeded. His life marks the failure of rugged individualism, the gap in the pattern, the fallibility of the legend.

It was opposite Doane's Oyster House, and only a step from
Ritchie's Philosophical Instrument Store in Boston, that Aaron Kim-
ball Loring opened his Select Library in June of 1859. The time
and the place augured well for his success. Though Bostonians were
at the moment perhaps more interested in the Public Library on
Boylston Street, still Loring's new private enterprise was almost
bound to succeed in this mid-century when private enterprise seemed
invested with a divine grace. Surely his humble beginnings and his
own ambitious intent insured for him a gilded role in a Gilded Age—
unless, of course, there was alloy hidden in the metal.

A. K. Loring had been born in 1826 in Sterling, Massachusetts,
where his father, Enos, set up as a saddler. Before the thirty-three-
year-old bookman established his own circulating library at 319
Washington Street, he had served the customary apprenticeship as
clerk and junior partner in Phillips, Sampson and Company. There
he must have been grounded in the fundamentals of the trade, for
after the death of Moses Phillips and the dissolution of his firm, Loring was able to enter business for himself, much as George W.
Childs had done, offering at his library books for circulation and for
sale, and installing in addition a full line of stationery.

For two cents a volume for each day, patrons of Loring's Select
Library—including such celebrities as George Ticknor, Wendell
Phillips, and Edward Everett—might borrow the works of Cooper
or Kingsley, Dumas or Thackeray, and they could purchase "very
cheap" the surplus books withdrawn from circulation. In time, Loring's "Up-Town Bookstore, Periodical Counter, Fashionable Stationery Store, and Select Circulating Library" made available to
Bostonians a variety of English and American magazines, fiction,
biography, travels, and history, from the novels of Grace Aguilar
to those of Anthony Trollope, from *The Origin of Species* to *Graver
Thoughts of a Country Parson,* from the Round-Robin Series and
the Leisure-Hour to the Transatlantic. The library's original purpose, "to provide ample supplies of all books of sterling interest and

merit, that will be enjoyed by the great mass of readers, as soon as they are published," was kept steadily in view by the astute proprietor through the years. The juvenile department was "appreciated by parents"; the library became a rendezvous of avid readers; and Loring could boast not without reason that "what Mudie's great London Library is to London, Loring's aims to be for Boston."

His Library Catalogues, issued at various times between the 1860's and the 1880's, announced among the features that gave "very great satisfaction" the famous *Revue des Deux Mondes* of Paris, English magazines representing the Conservative, Whig, Free Church, and Liberal points of view, and the native *Godey's, North American, Atlantic Monthly,* and *Harper's Magazine.* Ranging from a four-page leaflet to a forty-page brochure, Loring's Library Catalogues advertised the books most called for, the English and American fiction in circulation, and the works in constant demand. Between eight in the morning and six in the evening, "every responsible person, whether living in Boston or the Towns surrounding" might take books from the library at the stipulated fee, "cash on delivery." A house-to-house service, first by boys and then by horsemen, was available. One or two copies of each title were ready for circulation, but six were on hand attesting the popularity of Mrs. Delany's *Autobiography.* Among the Anglophilic subscribers, Wilkie Collins vied with Grace Aguilar, Bulwer with Disraeli, Scott with Charles Reade, while those with a taste for native American productions favored, in time, Louisa May Alcott and Horatio Alger, Jr. Loring's Library Catalogues are an illuminating index to the literary predilections of the time. They are also a guide to his own career, for it was through his library experience that Loring developed the power of gauging popular taste, acquiring an ability that could be put to fruitful use when the library proprietor turned publisher. His training was a harbinger of success in a day when wealth was, theoretically at least, so often the reward of industry and ambition, those twin cardinal virtues of a materialistic age.

The rungs of the towering ladder invited, and Loring did not limit himself for long to a career in circulating libraries. As brisk and as business-like as Childs, but perhaps a bit eccentric as well, he determined to sample every type of literary plum in the Boston market, especially the fruits of publishing. In this pursuit he was assisted for a time by George W. Dillingham, that colorful, blasphemous gourmand who subsequently was to enter the employ of G. W. Carleton of New York and still later to become a well-known publisher in his own right. As for Loring, though he was admittedly no scholar, he had developed through his library experience very definite and significant ideas about publishing. He knew the type of book that appealed to his patrons and to himself. Moreover, he was convinced that he could launch such a book with success. By 1864, when he had established himself in the juvenile field as the publisher of Mrs. A. D. T. Whitney's *Faith Gartney's Girlhood,* and had formed an association with Horatio Alger, Jr., the author who was to bring him his greatest opportunity for success, Loring wrote down his demands as a publisher in a letter that reflects not only his own self-confidence, but his extraordinary ability to estimate the popular taste:

I judge a book by the impression it makes and leaves in my mind, by the *feelings* solely as I am no scholar.—A story that touches and moves me, I can make others read and believe in.—What I like is conciseness in introducing the characters, getting them upon the stage and into action as quickly as possible.—Then I like a story of constant action, bustle and motion.—Conversations and descriptive scenes are delightful reading when well drawn but are too often skipped by the reader who is anxious to see what they do next, and its folly to write what will be skipped in reading. The books you have read and admired, the poetry you love, the music that has enchanted, Paintings and Sculpture admired, the heroic words uttered by earnest thinkers who sway the world rightly introduced add greatly to the enjoyment of the story as they revive and refresh the memory of every reader. . . . I like a story that starts to teach some lesson of life goes steadily on increasing in interest till it culminates with the closing chapter leaving you spell bound, enchanted and exhausted with the intensity with which it is written, the lesson forcibly told, and a yearning desire to turn right back to the beginning and enjoy it over again. . . . Stories of the *heart* are what live in the memory and when you move the reader to tears you have won them to you forever.

In this unusual self-revelation Loring manifested a publishing creed that was basically practical. He trusted to his instincts rather than to scholarship when he accepted or rejected a manuscript. He demanded primarily a story of action, and he believed in the necessity of a moral lesson. Formed by his observations of readers' choices in his own Select Library, his credo was realistic. He needed only opportunity in the shape of an author who could unite a story of action with a moral lesson and touch Loring's instincts and the public's heart. In a century of opportunity, such an author must be at hand. By the divine grace that attended rugged individuals engaged in honorable private enterprise, such an author must be made known to a publisher with such a credo.

Indeed, such an author was already known to Loring. Either through the good offices of Joseph Henry Allen, the Unitarian clergyman who for a time published *Student and Schoolmate* on Boston's Washington Street, or simply through patronizing Loring's "Up-Town Bookstore," Horatio Alger, Jr. had formed a friendship with the proprietor. Here was an author to whom the Loring creed applied most pointedly, an author who could adapt that creed with brilliant simplicity, an author who was the golden opportunity that came to all who would be self-made men.

Born in Chelsea, Massachusetts, in 1832, Alger had studied at Harvard Divinity School and had done some editing and had written two books—one a collection of stories and essays, the other a narrative poem. In 1864, the year when Loring articulated his creed, he wrote the first of his full-length novels, *Frank's Campaign*. It was a natural sequence of events that Loring should become Alger's publisher—the first publisher of the juveniles of Horatio Alger, Jr. —especially since *Frank's Campaign*, "intended to show how boys can be of most effectual service in assisting to put down the Rebellion," seemed to fill the publisher's demands for a story of action in which a moral lesson was inherent. Moreover, the author was able to promise that "Should 'Frank's Campaign' have the good fortune to find favor among the class for whom it is written, it will be followed by other volumes devoted to boy-life." His promise was destined for a triumphant fulfillment. *Frank's Campaign* was followed in swift order by *Paul Prescott's Charge, Helen Ford, Timothy Crump's Ward,* and *Charlie Codman's Cruise*—all published by Loring between 1865 and 1867.

In January of 1867 Alger's *Ragged Dick* was begun as a serial in *Student and Schoolmate,* published by Joseph H. Allen on Boston's Washington Street, where Loring still plied his trade. Loring shrewdly realized that here was not only a tale of action with a moral lesson, but a pattern woven from the very fabric of American life, a pattern that could be worked and reworked indefinitely. He "immediately made him [Alger] a liberal offer for a series of six volumes on a similar subject, and the 'Ragged Dick Series' was the result."

Ragged Dick; or, Street Life In New York With The Boot-Blacks appeared in 1868 over Loring's imprint. The preface indicates clearly the crystallization of the author's intent:

"Ragged Dick" was contributed as a serial story to the pages of the Schoolmate, a well-known juvenile magazine, during the year 1867. While in course of publication, it was received with so many evidences of favor that it has been rewritten and considerably enlarged, and is now presented to the public as the first volume of a series intended to illustrate the life and experiences of the friendless and vagrant children who are now numbered by thousands in New York and other cities.

At last the pattern was set. Ragged Dick, frank, straightforward, manly, self-reliant, was self-supporting from the age of seven, but since "in this free country poverty in early life is no bar to a man's advancement," Ragged Dick promptly proceeded to advance. Having rescued Little Johnny from drowning and found employment as a clerk in a countingroom, he was Ragged Dick no longer, but Richard Hunter, Esq., a young gentleman on the great American highroad to fame and fortune. "He has taken a step upward, and is determined to mount still higher"—an ascension that might be followed by readers of the promised sequel, *Fame And Fortune; or, The Progress of Richard Hunter,* a story in which the author (along with the publisher) hoped "to exert a salutary influence upon the class of whom he is writing, by setting before them inspiring examples of what energy, ambition, and an honest purpose may achieve."

Alger had hit upon the perfect interpretation of Loring's demands. Here indeed was a tale of action coupled with a moral purpose. What was more, the action could be varied as easily as the names of the heroes could be changed. The moral purpose—and hence the purport of the story—would remain the same. But what more inspiring moral to present to the youth of America than this message of Poor Richard couched not in aphorisms but in a lively narrative? It was no dry-as-dust sermon, but a living ethic with which the reader could identify himself and his ambitions. It was a moral that had been realized before and could and would be realized again. Nowhere but in America could the tale be told so often, and so often proven true. At no time but in the nineteenth century could the Alger moral inspire so many Ragged Dicks to the action that would bring them to fortune. Author and publisher conspired to re-create a legend. The time and the place conspired to bring the legend to happy fruition.

The stories in the Ragged Dick Series followed fast: *Mark, The Match Boy; or, Richard Hunter's Ward; Rough And Ready; or, Life Among The New York Newsboys*—a history designed to "teach the valuable lesson that honesty and good principles are not incompatible even with the greatest social disadvantages," and to "serve as an incentive and stimulus to the young people who may read it." *Ben, The Luggage Boy; or, Among The Wharves* and *Rufus And Rose; or, The Fortunes Of Rough And Ready* completed the Ragged Dick Series, the "principal object" of which had been "to show that the large class of street boys . . . furnishes material out of which good citizens may be made." In each volume the author had "led his hero, step by step, from vagabondage to . . . respectability." Instead of exceeding truth, he was convinced that he had rather "fallen short" of it, for *"many of our most conspicuous public men* have commenced their careers as newsboys."

The publisher, too, was convinced, for in time "half a million" readers testified to the popularity of Alger's work, at the same time enriching the purse of A. K. Loring. While Joseph H. Allen offered bound volumes of *The Schoolmate* along with a photographic likeness of Alger at $2 a volume, Loring took a short-cut to fortune by issuing the serials in book form at $1.25 each. As for the author, he found that he had "by no means exhausted his subject," and was "induced to announce a second series." One after another, indeed often overlapping each other, the Series rolled from Loring's press: the Luck and Pluck in two series of four volumes each, in the course of which *Bound To Rise* and *Risen From The Ranks* traced the inspiring career of Harry Walton, that second Benjamin Franklin; the Tattered Tom Series; the Brave and Bold Series, in all of which the juvenile public was steadily, fervently, repeatedly, even monotonously reassured that "nowhere . . . are such opportunities afforded to those who wish to rise, as in America."

When Loring's investigations showed him that Alger's popularity was increasing in the West and declining in the East, the astute publisher advised his favorite author to reverse his procedure and write stories about the West for boys in the East. Alger heeded the suggestion to "go West," producing the Pacific Series in which the motif remained the same while only the background shifted. The hero's prosperity was still "chiefly due to his own energy and industry," although it was "also true that he was exceptionally lucky. Yet," Alger reminded his young readers, "his good fortune has been far exceeded by that of numerous adventurous spirits in Colorado, within the last twelve months. Some measure of prosperity generally awaits the patient and energetic worker."

How often the message had been proven true! Andrew Carnegie had started out as a weaver's assistant in a cotton factory, Commodore Vanderbilt as a Brooklyn ferryman, Horace Greeley as a day laborer—now they were golden names in a Gilded Age. Indeed, for a time, the publisher himself could testify to the truth of the message. His coffers were enriched as the Alger Series were devoured, along with the Alger legend. Loring's creed as a publisher had been prophetic. He had, indeed, been able to "make others read and believe in" a story that touched and moved him. He had realized the popularity of "a story of constant action, bustle and motion." He had, most significantly, perceived the appeal of a tale that taught "some lesson of life." Loring's publication of Alger's works proved the reliability of his instincts as well as the fortune gained from books of action with a moral lesson—with the most inspiring lesson of nineteenth-century American life.

The most fertile field in which to sow such lessons is, or should be, the mind of the young. Loring proceeded to develop his juvenile publications, applying to them the same credo that was proving so successful in the case of Horatio Alger, Jr. Along with the boxed Alger Series, the works of "Laura Caxton" [Elizabeth Barker Comins] for girls, with "elegant illustrations" by the author, Virginia F. Townsend's successful Breakwater Series, the Fairy-Folk Series by the authors of *The Fairy Egg,* George Macdonald's books, and Mrs. Whitney's were issued by Loring. Whether they appeared, like Louisa May Alcott's *Proverb Stories,* as Loring's Tales of the Day, in paper copies priced at 50¢, or like Alger's works, boxed and at $1.25 or $1.50 a volume, they were nearly all "best selling juveniles," supplied by all jobbers, yielding a liberal profit not only to the booksellers but to the publisher.

Loring did not, however, confine himself to the publication of juveniles. As early as 1865 he issued Louisa Alcott's *Moods,* which, cut down to his specifications of a book that would make "46 letters to the line, 43 lines to the page, and about 286 pages," brought far greater profit to the publisher than to the author. Miss Alcott received, in addition to the advice to prune the first chapter and make the eleventh less cold, ten cents on each copy in cloth and five on each in paper. What is more, without consulting the then famous author, the publisher issued a new edition of the work in 1870. Louisa Alcott was observant when she noted that Loring was "a brisk, business-like man who seemed in earnest."

He was sufficiently ambitious and "in earnest" to expand his publishing to include, besides his juveniles and Books for Young Ladies, a popular paper-covered Railway Library, Standard English Novels, and Select Novels of the type that was well-thumbed in the equally Select Circulating Library. Loring's Select Novels consisted of thirty "handsome paper" books priced at fifty cents each, and he issued as well a line of Popular Books by Edmund Yates, Anne Beale, M. B. Smedley, Cecil Griffiths, and others. *Erring, Yet Noble. A Tale of, and for Women* and *Pique. A Tale of the English Aristocracy* were not only published by Loring, but included in his circulating library, where they enjoyed an "enduring popularity." The gentleman of Washington Street was indulging in no exaggeration when he advertised that "Booksellers attending the Trade Sale should ask for Loring's publications. They sell."

The third type of book to which the publisher inclined consisted of Home Manuals, Practical Stories similar to the semi-technical works so popular today. Issued in paper and priced at seventy-five cents, Mrs. Warren's Practical Stories gave ever-timely advice on *How to Furnish and Adorn a House with Small Means, How I Managed My House on £200 A Year, How I Managed My Children from Infancy to Marriage,* and *Comfort for Small Incomes.* Charles Barnard's books on *Gardening for Money, $2000 A Year from My Ten Rod Farm,* and *A Simple Flower Garden for Every Home* were equally "practical" for Boston's amateur horticulturists. Edward Mitchell's *$5000 A Year, and How I Made It,* the *Dixie Cookery* by Mrs. Barringer of North Carolina, which vied with Prof. Blot's *Lectures on Cookery,* and Dr. Bowen's *Dyspepsia* ("sensibly treated") enriched the coffers already filled with the profits from juveniles and Select Novels. In all three types, the publisher manifested his astuteness in gauging the demands of the day, as well as his briskness in supplying them.

By the mid-seventies Loring had not only established himself as a publisher, but had expanded his circulating library at the corner of Bromfield and Washington Streets, where he had removed. If his observations of readers' interests in the circulating library had taught him the lessons he applied in publishing, his publications in turn increased the revenue from his library, where the works he issued were among those most in demand. The now celebrated "Corner," near the publishing houses of Estes and Lauriat, Gill, and the American Tract Society, numbered among its patrons Longfellow, Emerson, and Lowell. Between his publishing activity and his library he had developed a kind of mutual-benefit system, and Loring's success as a self-made man seemed inevitable.

Yet, Loring was perhaps not quite so single-minded as a self-made man should be. Like Childs he was brisk, business-like, and earnest. But unlike Childs he was also eccentric, and eccentricity may not always be compatible with the kind of rugged individualism that is rewarded with the gold that in the nineteenth century was manna from heaven. Probably it was a certain eccentricity in Loring that induced him, in 1875 or 1876, when George W. Childs was publishing his *Ledger Almanacs* and entertaining the notables of the world in Philadelphia, to set up a coffee house at 1 Bromfield Street, vying with the Boston restaurant proprietors, Haseltine or Rankin. Certainly it was a singular enterprise for the publisher of the best-selling *Helen's Babies* and the works of Horatio Alger, Jr. Perhaps A. K. Loring was trying to identify himself too closely with an Alger hero in an unwritten version of *Brave And Bold; or, The Publisher In The Coffee House*. A reporter for *Publishers' Weekly* noted dolefully that "It is a sad symptom of dull times in the trade when even the publisher of 'Helen's Babies' does not hesitate to declare that he 'don't care any more about books—the coffee-room is worth the whole of 'em.' " At any rate, there were no "net rates or discounts" on coffee, and there was considerable animation in the "soda-water business." Loring proceeded, therefore, to devote his major efforts to feeding the bodies instead of the minds of his patrons. In addition to coffee, he offered to his indulgent public "our old-fashioned Country Dier-Drink, compounded by Dr. Swett, from roots and herbs." Its medicinal properties were guaranteed to "invigorate the system and correct all derangements caused by excessive heat," a specific most reasonable at five cents "a copy" and somewhat reminiscent of Dr.

Wiley's celebrated cough candy or the Cholera Flower Cordial once purveyed by George W. Childs. Childs, however, had started with cough candy and flower cordial and worked his way up to publishing. Loring seems to have preferred the more erratic course of turning from the book room to the coffee house, marching blindly along one of those devious bypaths that intersected the road from rags to riches. As *Town Topics* put it, "Loring, . . . as clever a book man as Boston had, became . . . fearfully demoralized, and indulged in some of the queerest caprices. He removed his library from one of the best stands in the city to Bromfield street and actually opened a cheap lunch room in the basement, personally attending to it himself, and refusing to attend to his book business, which as a publisher in the wholesale line was large, during the progress of coffee serving at five cents a cup."

From about 1876 to 1881 Loring continued to combine his library and publishing activities with his coffee enterprise. Then the crash came. Perhaps indeed he had devoted too much of his energy to coffee instead of to books. Perhaps Dr. Swett's "Country Dier-Drink" was less invigorating than he had hoped, or Mrs. Daggett's cooking drew the Bromfield Street diners to her own establishment at No. 5. Perhaps the flaw lay in Loring; perhaps it lay simply in the fact that not all who strove inevitably succeeded, that the lowly and ambitious and industrious were not always "Bound To Rise." Even Alger was not infallible. His own publisher was about to prove it.

On June 15, 1881, Loring's bankruptcy was announced. He was compelled, according to *The American Bookseller,* "to succumb to the pressure of financial embarrassment." At a meeting of the creditors held on June 28, Mr. Shepard reported for the committee that the publisher's gross liabilities were placed at $28,514.75 and his gross assets at $19,304.36. Among the assets had been included $10,230 for stereotype plates, "a sum far larger than they would probably bring." The liabilities included $3,000 due on copyright and $8,000 arrears on rent for "his old stand" at the corner of Washington and Bromfield.

At the fall trade sale of September 22 to September 30, Loring's plates were sold, his list scattered among various publishers. In August, in return for "one dollar . . . and for other good and valuable considerations," he had already transferred the copyright of *Moods* to Louisa M. Alcott, who was then free to revise the work for

Roberts Brothers. In October the firm of Porter and Coates was able to advertise that "having purchased the stereotype plates of the famous 'Alger' Books," the company would issue them "as soon as possible, in new and beautiful bindings." Between 1864, when he had published *Frank's Campaign,* and 1880, when *The Young Explorer* appeared over his imprint, Loring had issued about thirty-five of Alger's books and not a year had passed without at least one Alger book on the Loring list. Now, on December 8, 1881, a receipt signed by the bankrupt publisher indicated that he received from Shepard, Sanborn, and Clark, trustees, $1118.80. The plates and copyrights had been transferred. A. K. Loring had "retired" from Boston's publishing scene.

Between 1882 and 1906, the once-successful publisher made sporadic attempts to resume business as stationer, bookseller, and librarian. During those years he changed his address eight times. One could still subscribe at Loring's for any newspaper, magazine, and fashion-book, American, English, or French. He offered, according to his letterhead, "the best stock of magazines, fashion books, newspapers, and note paper in town." From 542 Washington Street to Bromfield Street, "just in the rear of the 'corner' where he was for many years established," he wandered, and from Bromfield Street to Bosworth, under Horticultural Hall. But it was not as publisher or even as coffee house proprietor that he was listed, but as stationer, bookseller, or newsdealer.

On April 30, 1906, the eighty-year-old bookman ceased his efforts to cling to the fringes of Boston's literary life. The *Directory* lists him at a house in the Highlands, 133 West Springfield. The house happened to be the Home for Aged Men. Between 1900 and 1906 he had received "outside aid" from that institution, and there, on September 26, 1911, the aged Loring died, "practically unknown to the present generation." The man who "probably was the most successful retail bookseller and publisher of his time" ended as "the inmate of a charitable institution."

As the first publisher of the juveniles of Horatio Alger, Jr., that same man had time and again reminded the public that nineteenth-century America was caught up in an inspiring legend. The self-made man could start life humble and obscure and end as a prince among the mighty. *Strive And Succeed. Try And Trust. Bound To Rise.* He had endorsed the titles with his imprint. As George W.

Childs had proven the truth of the legend in his rocketing career, A. K. Loring had proven its truth in the books he had published. Now, by his own life as it ended in oblivion, he must prove that the legend was not always true, that a flaw in the pattern or in the man might vitiate the legend even in a Gilded Age.

Loring's Up-Town Bookstore, 319 Washington, between Winter & West Sts.

TERMS CASH, ON DELIVERY.

☞ Below we hand you a statement of your account to date.
Your prompt response to it will greatly oblige me.

Boston, *Dec 31,* 1861.

Mr. J. A. Holmes Ge Depot

In Account with A. K. LORING, *Dr.*

Nov 30.	To Bill rendered to date	6.75
23	" #9 Rob Roy	.50
29	" 1 Holmes' Poems	1.25
Dec 11	" Subs to R Record	.50
26	" #10	.50
		9.50
Jan 29	" " #12	.50
		.50
	Amt of Cards	10.50
	Recd Payment	.50
	A K Loring	

XII. THE NEED FOR LAUGHTER
IN AMERICA

G. W. Carleton

HIS MARK

THE PANGS of failure could be softened, the pomposities of success could be pricked, indeed all the outrages of fortune could be
tolerated, with a touch of humor. Like a man, a nation must learn
to laugh at itself and its own self-consciousness, and that was the
bridge that led to the nation's maturity.

The need for humor in America was never so sharp as in the
nineteenth century when Civil War threatened to divide the country
South from North, when migrations into distant geographical frontiers threatened to divide it East from West. Humor was the clay
that could cement the union once the nation learned to laugh at
itself.

There was much to laugh at—but this the so-called humorists
alone could point out. For they alone, whether they came from
Massachusetts or from Ireland, from New York State or from
Maine, whether their wanderings had carried them to the West or
the South, could gently but pointedly expose the weaknesses of the
country. How many Achilles' heels were ready for their darts: from
the war to political office-seekers, from Yankee notions to frontier
conditions, from Fourth of July orations to the Negro question, from
free love to woman's rights, from scheming Yankees to bragging
Kentuckians, from circuit lawyers to politicians in caucus, from
manifest destiny to every gaudy feather in the spreading wings of
the American eagle. Humbug, quackery, absurdity, and insincerity,
the sentimental and the highfalutin—all awaited the pin that would
prick the empty balloons that floated over the continent.

And it was a pin rather than a barbed arrow that performed the
national operation. It was a genial humor, a mild satire, a combina-

tion of parody and burlesque, tall tales and distorted spellings. It was good humor—compounded partly of the conventions of backwoods wit and partly of a characteristic form of fantastic exaggeration; it was the good humor that Mark Twain eventually inherited, and it was this good humor that led a nation to chuckle at its own foibles. Like most humor, it was topical, contemporary; and though it has therefore suffered the fate of becoming outdated, it has for that very reason become invested with a historical, a documentary importance. The humor may be less funny today; but it is an open window upon the mores of yesterday.

Sometimes the humorist paraded under the disguise of an itinerant showman, and Lincoln enjoyed his extravagances so much that he read them to his Cabinet members before submitting to them the final draft of the Emancipation Proclamation. Sometimes the humorist assumed the character of an Irish private in the Union Army; sometimes he donned an all-revealing pseudonym—"Orpheus C. Kerr" (office seeker); sometimes he began to look, with his sharp features and rustic demeanor, like the country farmer he was impersonating. Whether his name was "Artemus Ward" or "Private Miles O'Reilly," whether it was "Orpheus C. Kerr" or "Josh Billings," he frequently practiced his "trade" or tested the effect of his broad burlesque at one of two rendezvous. One was Pfaff's restaurant in a basement on Broadway near Bleecker Street, where the so-called "Bohemians" gathered to air their witticisms while they downed their beer. Another was perhaps a more significant rallying place, for it was the bookstore of their publisher, George W. Carleton. Like the men whose works he published, Carleton was a humorist of sorts, and by placing their extravagant phrases, their vivid caricatures and atrocious spellings before the public, he helped a stumbling and self-conscious nation to enjoy a laugh at its own expense. Setting his own unmistakable mark upon the humor that he published, he helped America become not only mature, but characteristically American.

During the winter of 1864-65 George Washington Carleton, a young New Yorker with a genial, intelligent face, a long, pointed nose, and a pair of conspicuous lorgnettes, might have been seen tearing through the narrow streets of Havana. On vacation from his publishing office at 413 Broadway, he was employing his time fruitfully, for he was exercising not only his legs but his sense of humor. Besides assisting with domino and false nose at the masquerades in the Tacon Theatre and lounging over ices at the Café Dominica, Carleton sketched many a delicious caricature in pen-and-ink, setting down in humorous fashion the sights of Cuba, from the Havana Flea to the Cuban Tooth-Pick, and his own aspect as he regarded them. The young man had had no little experience with humor—and with its publication.

In his early thirties, Carleton could already look back with satisfaction upon his brief but promising career. Born in New York in 1832, he had studied at St. Thomas Hall in Flushing and served as clerk to Burnham, Plumb and Company, an importing and commission house. During his leisure moments he had varied his occupation of deciphering foreign invoices by designing illustrations for such humorous papers and periodicals as *The Lantern* and *The Picayune*. Some of his work attracted the attention of George Merriam, who asked him to design for his firm an appropriate illustration to head an advertisement of Webster's Dictionary. Carleton's sketch of two chubby little cherubs weighted down with Webster's Unabridged had earned for the artist a copy of the Dictionary bound in full calf. In light of the fact that the sketch was to be used for nearly half a century, the reward was perhaps less weighty than it seemed at first sight. But doubtless it tickled Carleton's sense of humor.

That sense of humor had yielded more substantial results when Carleton had applied it to his more recent interest in publishing. In 1857, with the retirement of Edward Livermore of Livermore and Rudd, he had joined the firm, which was promptly transformed into Rudd and Carleton. Though young Carleton, at the age of twenty-five, could offer to his partner, who had served several years with Barnes and Burr, neither any specialized training nor any considerable capital, Rudd and Carleton had, during its short life on Broadway near Duane, proved successful. Besides publishing B. D. Emerson's *National Spelling Book* and the Rev. W. I. Kip's *Christmas Tree,* the firm had struck a bonanza in *Nothing to Wear,* the poem on fashionable city life in which the lawyer, William Allen Butler, had immortalized Miss Flora M'Flimsey of Madison Square. With illustrations by Augustus Hoppin, the 18mo priced at fifty cents had

had a huge sale even during the panic year of 1857. Readers enjoyed the smooth verses and mild satire about the young lady who had shopped

> For bonnets, mantillas, capes, collars, and
>   shawls;
> Dresses for breakfasts, and dinners, and
>   balls;

but still had "nothing to wear." The sombre note on "Spoiled children of Fashion" with which the poem ended detracted not at all from the good-humored travesty, but merely sharpened the point of the moral. The success of *Nothing to Wear* was followed by the claim of one Miss Peck, daughter of an Episcopal clergyman of Greenwich, Connecticut, to the effect that she had lost the manuscript of the poem in a Madison Avenue stage, where it was found by Butler, who had elaborated upon her idea. Although the controversy that followed did not profit Miss Peck, it did profit Rudd and Carleton, the latter of whom demonstrated his quick-wittedness by offering Mortimer Thomson, the immortal "Doesticks," one dollar a line for a burlesque on the subject entitled *Nothing to Say.* This "Slight Slap at Mobocratic Society," which had "Nothing to Do" with "Nothing to Wear," was issued in the same format and binding as Butler's poem and sported a genial but inverted snobbery on behalf of the villainous rich. Q. K. Philander Doesticks, whose *Plu-Ri-Bus-Tah* "burlesqued *Hiawatha* in meter and the American eagle in attitude," and who had already been "discovered" by Edward Livermore, helped center Carleton's interests upon humor and helped increase the profits of the Rudd and Carleton treasury.

Another poem published by the firm had yielded not only financial profit to Carleton but the trademark by which he was destined to be known throughout the next generation. Exploring Lane's *Arabian Nights* for inscriptions with which to embellish Thomas Bailey Aldrich's Persian poem, *The Course of True Love Never Did Run Smooth,* Carleton and Aldrich had come upon a curious symbol, the Arabic word for "books." Viewed upside down, the symbol seemed to spell the initials, "G. W. C." Besides selling 2,200 copies of Aldrich's versified love story, Carleton had found the trademark that would adorn his advertisements and title-pages for the next three decades. The year 1858 could be marked in red upon his publishing calendar, for that trademark, coupled often with Carleton's personal cipher, a pert little bird drawn with two or three pen strokes, was to symbolize for the reading public not only books but Carleton's books, and most particularly Carleton's books of genial satire and good humor.

The name of Edmund Clarence Stedman had been added to the firm's publishing list, and *The Prince's Ball,* illustrated and printed on tinted paper, sold in the thousands under the imprint of Rudd and Carleton. A similar sale attended another, more enterprising undertaking of the firm—a work that was, moreover, to be accorded a niche in history. *The "Wigwam Edition." The Life, Speeches, and Public Services of Abram Lincoln,* published by Rudd and Carleton in 1860 and issued in paper wrappers for twenty-five cents, was the first campaign biography of Lincoln, the most popular *Life* of the campaign; and today it has become the keystone of any Lincolniana collection.

Then in 1861 Edward P. Rudd had died, and his father, George R. Rudd, retired, leaving Carleton to carry on alone. The genial publisher had gained from his association with Rudd some specialized training in addition to some capital, and, equipped with the fame of his two or three successes and a trademark, he was ready to make the name of G. W. Carleton a synonym for a nation's good humor.

In this enterprise Carleton was assisted by some interesting figures. Thomas Bailey Aldrich served him as clerk and literary adviser for a short period. Carleton's brother Charles was for a time connected with the publishing house, and during the sixties Henry S. Allen left Appleton to share his knowledge of the book business with G. W. C. before joining John K. Allen in the juvenile trade. Finally, George W. Dillingham, who had for some years been associated with Crosby, Nichols of Boston and had worked for A. K. Loring, became a moving spirit in the house of Carleton, first as head clerk and later as partner.

By the time Dillingham had entered Carleton's employ, the publisher had decided upon the types of books that would be associated with his name. The Arabic symbol would appear most significantly beneath humorous titles. The comic fellows who gathered at Pfaff's brought the results of their laughter to G. W. Carleton, aware that he knew wit when he saw it since he possessed such a fund of it himself. Indeed, Carleton's Broadway office could vie with Pfaff's as the rendezvous for American comic writers—for "Corry O' Lanus" or Robert H. Newell, known to his followers as "Orpheus C. Kerr," for all the clever young men who were bent on tickling America's ribs until the country could laugh at its own expense. They rallied at Carleton's establishment to swap stories or cap anecdotes, and they transformed a publisher's office into a headquarters for the humor that would set a slow and knowing smile upon the face of a nation.

The most famous of Carleton's humorists were "Artemus Ward" and "Josh Billings." The publisher had met Charles F. Browne, otherwise known as "Artemus Ward," soon after the author came to New York from *The Cleveland Plain Dealer*. Together they projected a humorous book entitled *Artemus Ward His Book,* the result of which was a sale of over 40,000 copies in six months. *His Book* had been bundled into a green baize bag, in which the publisher had found a blotted, almost illegible manuscript stuck with mucilage and plastered with newspaper clippings. Finally, both A. Ward and A. Ward's book had been straightened out, the latter edited and published; and G. W. Carleton had the pleasure of giving in exchange for the green baize bag $6,000 as the author's share of the profits.

To the artist, Carleton, Artemus had appeared like a caricature of Uncle Sam. To Artemus, the publisher became "Dear Carl," and to his "Dear Carl" the humorist announced, "You and I will get out a book next spring, which will knock spots out of all comic books in ancient or modern history. And the fact that you are going to take hold of it convinces me that you have one of the most *massive* intellects of this or any other epoch. Yours, my pretty gazelle, A. Ward." When the "pretty gazelle" made too many alterations in A. Ward's manuscripts, however, the author, with tongue—where it usually was—in cheek, declared, "The next book I write I'm going to get *you* to write."

In the guise of an itinerant showman, "Artemus Ward" tilted at the windmills of sentimentality and insincerity, exposing, by means of graphic caricatures, execrable spelling, colossal exaggerations, and tall tales, the absurdities of American life. He was part and parcel of the Yankee tradition, from his own long, impassive face to the terse humor he purveyed. With calm mendacity he spun his brief stories about "New England Rum, and its Effects," "The

Shakers," or a "Celebration at Baldinsville in Honor of the Atlantic Cable." The Negro question was simply solved—the "Afrikan" "wooden't be sich a infernal noosanse if white people would let him alone." As for politics, Artemus had "no politics. Nary a one. I'm not in the bisiness. . . . I'm in a far more respectful bisniss nor what pollertics is." At all events, whether he laughed at Brigham Young or Ossawatomie Brown, Oberlin College or the "Sences taker," he was "Yours for the Pepetration of the Union, and the bringin of the Goddess of Liberty out of her present bad fix."

At the height of his popularity Artemus was often to be seen lying on a sofa in Carleton's office at Broadway and Lispenard, puffing a cigar and framing witticisms. Carleton enjoyed the witticisms almost as much as the profits. As *Artemus Ward; His Travels* and *Artemus Ward In London* and *Artemus Ward's Panorama* rolled from the press, the anecdotes rolled also, until the publisher had collected a fund of Wardiana. By 1898, long after G. W. Dillingham had succeeded Carleton, *The Complete Works of Artemus Ward* was still a valuable item on the publisher's list. More than 100,000 copies had been printed, and the plates had become "so worn as to render it unreadable, yet the sale kept on."

"Artemus Ward" did more for Carleton than provide him with profits and witticisms. Having read a manuscript by Henry Wheeler Shaw, he recommended it to the publisher, who issued *Josh Billings, Hiz Sayings* and struck another bonanza in the comic treasury. In place of the itinerant showman, "Josh" impersonated the itinerant lecturer. In place of "Artemus Ward's" stories, "Josh Billings" depended upon brief essays. His prose was peppered with the same exaggerated misspellings that Ward had popularized, and with ludicrous sententiousness he gravely addressed "The Billingsville Sowing Sosiety" or "A Wimmin's League Meetin." At "Female Eddikashun" or Saratoga Springs, "War and Army Phrazes" or Long Branch, he tossed his gentle darts. "Yankee Noshuns" were "a kind ov noshuns that reside in Nu England, but travel awl over the world." Manifest destiny was simply "the science ov going tew the devil, or enny other place before yu git thare." Sparse of build, sharp of features, with rustic, unpolished demeanor, Henry Wheeler Shaw was himself transformed into the comic lecturer, "Josh Billings."

Josh Billings' Proverbs and *Josh Billings on Ice* cleared the way in time for *Josh Billings' Farmer's Allminax.* Carleton had suggested a burlesque of the popular old farmer's almanac, and Billings' manuscript, written on newspaper wrappings, was transformed into a book which eventually sold more than half a million copies. Although it started off slowly, taking nearly a year to exhaust the first edition of 2,000, it suddenly struck fire and turned the year with 150,000 copies to its credit. The twenty-five-cent paper volume was succeeded by an annual comic *Allminax,* the author writing five or six little paragraphs, stuffing them into his hat, and reading the sayings aloud to his friend and publisher. Finally, the wit and wisdom of all the *Allminaxes* from 1870 to 1879 were gathered together as "Josh Billings' " *Old Probability,* bound in one volume and priced at $1.50. The laughter of Carleton and Billings must surely have been as hearty as the public's. Josh Billings' arrows were not dipped in gall. His wit was rather a "Feejee club that makes those who feel it grin while they wince." His victims might be slaughtered, but they expired with a smile upon their faces, for his shafts against humbug and pretension were genial, and though the highfalutin received a mortal wound from his darts, it died laughing at itself.

If "Artemus Ward" and "Josh Billings" anticipated to some degree the humor of Will Rogers, another "comic fellow" whom Carleton added to his list foreshadowed the Private Hargrove of a later generation. "Private Miles O'Reilly" (Charles G. Halpine) of the 47th Regiment of New York Volunteers was feted at Delmonico's and pardoned by the President for his breach of decorum in publishing songs relative to the joint naval and military operations against Charleston. *The Life and Adventures . . . of Private Miles O'Reilly* was advertised as one of the funniest and most satirical collections of military and political humor the war had produced. Certainly, in the guise of an Irish private in the Union Army, the author was able to spin his gentle satire about a visit to the White House or the Miles O'Reilly caucus, city politics or the war itself. This "Irish Pickwick" followed his success with *Baked Meats of the Funeral,* and Carleton found that he had once more tickled the funny bone of the public.

Carleton was able to produce the same effect not only as publisher but as artist and author in his own right. Urged by Morris Phillips to issue his sketches of Havana in book form, Carleton had offered to the public *Our Artist in Cuba,* consisting of fifty drawings on wood depicting G. W. C., after a nautical departure entitled "Sick Transit," struck dumb with admiration at the sights he had witnessed. "Our Artist" enjoyed an equally fruitful sojourn in Peru, where he trapped with his comical pen the streets and the fleas of Lima, the boiled monkeys and pretty women of South America; and *Our Artist in Peru* was followed in 1877 by a composite volume of sketches from Cuba, Peru, Spain, and Algiers, which brought the author-publisher a clear profit of $10,000 and the public a humorous run for its money.

To Charles H. Webb, "author of books too humorous to mention," Carleton suggested a burlesque of one of his most successful ventures, a novel by Augusta Evans Wilson entitled *St. Elmo*. The burlesque, *St. Twel'mo* (published by Webb), sold fast, at the same time increasing the sale of the novel. In the course of *St. Twel'mo; or, the Cuneiform Cyclopedist of Chattanooga,* Webb took occasion to describe what happened when Etna, the heroine, produced a bestseller:

This thing must be kept up, thought Etna, and she next published a book. This made a hit—striking the publisher favorably, as he announced in a series of fantastic advertisements. Type of the most wonderful characters had to be cast expressly for the production of this work, and the services of the Learned Blacksmith were engaged as chief proof-reader—he should be kept well up in tongs, said Etna. Fifteen cylinder presses were kept running night and day to supply the demand, and the publisher was so broken down in health by the labor of writing advertisements, answering questions, . . . that he took in a partner and sailed himself for an uninhabited island to recuperate his shattered constitution.

Carleton indeed had had experience with best-sellers. The humor he published appealed to the American public, and readers plunged their hands into their pockets to pay for the privilege of laughing at themselves or their current enthusiasms. Carleton had taught the American eagle to pluck out a feather and tickle itself.

The publisher's Arabic symbol was a portent of good fortune not only upon the title-pages of humorous books but upon many a "sensational" novel and "meteoric" volume with which his trademark also came to be associated. When Carleton was described as the "largest publisher of sensational books by native American authors," the intention was to link his name not with blood-and-thunder works, but rather with novels that were sensationally successful. Priced at $1.50 or $1.75, the effusions of such best-selling authors as Mary J. Holmes, "Marion Harland" (Mrs. M. Virginia Terhune), Miriam Coles Harris, and Julie P. Smith were successfully launched by the publisher, along with "brilliant love stories" by "Ouida" (Marie Louise de la Ramée), Epes Sargent's *Peculiar,* and May Agnes Fleming's *Terrible Secret, Wonderful Woman,* and *Mad Marriage.* Most of Carleton's bonanzas in this line were society novels, "depicting the flirtations and follies of the married and single," spicy books that titillated nineteenth-century taste for hammock literature.

With an eye toward his pocketbook, Carleton collected and published in uniform style the popular but "moral" novels of A. S. Roe, launched "Brick" Pomeroy's *Sense* and *Nonsense* "of which thousands and thousands will be sold," and struck a goldmine in the works of Augusta Evans Wilson, whose contemporary reputation for brilliant genius, magnificent word-painting, powerful plot, and intensity of interest established her as the "mother of *St. Elmo.*" In addition, Carleton published under a joint imprint with Street and Smith the "cream of the contributions" to *The New York Weekly: Thrown on the World* by "Bertha M. Clay," *Peerless Cathleen* by Cora Agnew, *Faithful Margaret* by Annie Ashmore, and Mrs. George Sheldon's *Forsaken Bride.* The *Weekly* was said to have paid Mary Jane Holmes between four and six thousand dollars for a story, and with the royalties paid by Carleton for the book version she collected "a larger sum than that received by any other American authoress, with the possible exception of the author of Uncle Tom's Cabin." May Agnes Fleming's stories in turn yielded $100 an installment from the *Weekly,* and a fifteen per cent royalty from Carleton. Though they differed in content from *The New York Weekly* Series, the novels of Mayne Reid were equally "meteoric," and Carleton purchased the entire list of his romances in 1868. His *Scalp Hunters* and *Rifle Rangers* appealed to a different section of the public, but appealed none the less sensationally, while his magazine, *Onward,* brought to the youth of America the romance of the Rocky Mountains and Texan hunters, and to its publisher, Carleton, his share of the profits from yearly subscriptions at $3.50.

Another magazine published by Carleton reflected his third publishing interest. The *Record of the Year,* edited by Frank Moore, was a reference scrapbook, a compendium of important events selected from the most noteworthy articles in current newspapers and journals. This digest of information was similar in many ways to other treasuries of knowledge sponsored by Carleton, his *Tales from the Operas, Pulpit Pungencies, 100 Legal Don'ts, Popular Readings, Handbook of Popular Quotations,* and *Condensed Classical Dictionary.* Like his *Household Encyclopædia and Handbook of General Information,* these works were reference books that gave to a public eager for a shortcut to knowledge "infinite riches and much learning in a little space."

Only a step removed from his digests of information were Carleton's courtesy books, advertised as "Handbooks of Society," and offering for those who wished to be agreeable talkers or listeners *The Art of Conversation,* for those interested in self-improvement *The Arts of Writing, Reading, and Speaking,* for those desirous of learning the nice points of taste and good manners *The Habits of Good Society.* For those who wished all three accomplishments a new diamond edition was available consisting of three volumes in one box at $3. *The Art of Amusing* gave party-minded readers hints on home amusements, while *The Ladies and Gentlemen's Etiquette Book* instructed the curious in the habits of the best fashionable society. For the ladies exclusively *Female Beauty and the Art of Pleasing* was translated from the French for American circulation.

Carleton added to his varied list many translations from the French, some of which were as "sensational" as his humorous books and "meteoric" novels. The works of Michelet and Hugo, Renan and Houssaye, for example, found a ready market. The publisher's handling of these translations indicates his methods of "streamlining" the trade, for Carleton seems to have established a nineteenth-century record in speed of publishing and liberality of advertising. Michelet's *La Femme* was translated in three days, while the 450-page volume was set, cast, printed, bound, and 20,000 copies were sold in less than thirty days. The publisher had engaged Dr. John W. Palmer to do the translation, offering him $1,000 if the work were completed in seventy-two hours, and demanding a forfeit of $10 an hour for every hour's delay. Fortified by coffee and a wet towel round his forehead, Palmer dictated the translation to his wife and delivered the manuscript according to contract. Though he trailed behind such a twentieth-century speed record as was set by the *Roosevelt Memorial* pocket book, Carleton vigorously applied assembly-line methods to the nineteenth-century trade. His advertising was also decidedly modern both in tone and in expenditure. Ten thousand dollars was spent to advertise *Les Misérables,* and results were achieved, for one dealer bought 25,000 copies at the trade sale of George A. Leavitt and Company. Edmund Kirke's *Down in Tennessee* was advertised in the following modern terms: "Enormous advance orders. Thousands of copies swept off on publication day. Subsequent orders will be executed as soon as printers and binders can turn out the books."

Carleton not only was in advance of his times in his business methods, but demonstrated in his dealings with authors tact, courage, generosity, and integrity. When he purchased the stereotype plates of Augusta Evans Wilson's earlier books, he informed the author that he had been obliged to pay so much for the plates of *Macaria* that he could allow only a moderate percentage on future sales. Subsequently, after the successful publication of *St. Elmo* and *Vashti,* Carleton on his own initiative suggested an increase in the writer's percentage on *Macaria* and earned for himself Mrs. Wilson's encomium as "a Prince of Publishers." Alice Cary also declared him "very generous . . . wide-awake and liberal." To Edmund Clarence Stedman he allowed ten per cent royalties on *The Prince's Ball* and to "Artemus Ward" fifteen cents on each copy of his work sold. When "Josh Billings" offered to sell his *Farmer's Allminax* outright for $250 and to supply one for each of ten succeeding years at the same price, Carleton "with disinterestedness rare among publishers" advised the humorist to accept instead a royalty of three cents on each copy. Outright payment would have netted the author $2,500 in ten years. The royalty arrangement brought him $30,000 in the same time. Carleton's views on copyright also indicated his generous attitude toward authors, for he upheld a "universal, absolute right and control throughout the world to eternity of the author's brainwork to the author, his heirs, executors and assigns."

Like every publisher, Carleton made mistakes. The translation of Balzac was as total a failure as that of Hugo was a success. He erred in refusing to handle "Marion Harland's" *Common Sense in the Household,* which became a Scribner bonanza, and in declining B.

L. Farjeon's *Grif,* which over the Harper imprint was a great success. He added error to error by jumping at the next Farjeon book, *Solomon Isaacs,* which proved a failure. Carleton was brought to law by one Fannie Bean, who claimed that publication of her novel, *Dr. Mortimer's Patient,* had been delayed and was neither advertised nor placed on sale, except in the publisher's offices, after she had paid $900 which was to be returned after the first 2,000 copies had been sold. The breach of contract was decided in favor of the plaintiff. Perhaps the gravest mistake ever made by Carleton is revealed in a terse note written by Mark Twain about his "Jumping Frog" story: "Wrote this story for Artemus [Ward]—his idiot publisher Carleton, gave it to Clapp's Saturday Press."

Carleton upon several occasions had himself faced the difficulties of delay and postponement. *The Suppressed Book about Slavery!,* for which the stereotype plates were made in 1857, could not be published until 1864, when it at last disclosed "the hideous skeleton of the institution." The correspondence of Alexander von Humboldt had been prepared for production when it was learned that Appleton and Harper were ready to go to press with the same work, and the competing firms had to be compensated before publication could proceed. *The Love-Life of Dr. Kane,* the explorer who had brought fortune to G. W. Childs, was in press in 1862, but its publication was "stopped by a compromise with the brothers and executor of Dr. Kane," and the history of the explorer's "secret marriage" to Margaret Fox, of "Rochester Rappings" fame, did not see the light of day until four years later.

Despite such disappointments and failures, Carleton's career was both honorable and lucrative. In 1869 he was able to open a new Fifth Avenue Bookstore for which he had leased the Worth House, and the magnificence of his quarters almost defied description. In the first story salesroom frescoes reproduced the decorations of the Pompeian Library, while pillars and griffins, bronze statues and gilded moldings vied with books to attract the public. In the ceiling of his own inner sanctum appeared his trademark, the Arabic symbol denoting books, and a French stationery department was added to make of the old Worth House "one of the finest bookstores in the world." Meanwhile, the upper section of the building was kept, under Carleton's control, as a hotel, or, in the terms of contemporary wits, as a "home for indigent authors." While still in

business, half as publisher and half as hotel-keeper, in 1871, he took
into partnership his head clerk, George Dillingham, and converted
his house into G. W. Carleton and Company. In consequence of the
increasing magnitude of its publishing business, the firm was compelled, a year later, to open a still larger establishment under the
Fifth Avenue Hotel, and there, at 192 Fifth Avenue, G. W. Carleton
remained for more than a decade. In 1883, when the landlord raised
the rent by $4,000, the firm decided to abandon its retail trade and
limit itself to its own publications. At West 23rd Street, over Dutton and Company, in quarters equipped with steam heat and freight
and passenger elevators, Carleton terminated his association with
the company he had founded. In 1886 he retired from business, taking with him a name that for more than a quarter of a century had
been identified with American books and authors, and especially
with humorous American books. G. W. Dillingham succeeded
Carleton, continuing to offer to the public the "meteoric" volumes
and the humor that had been launched by his predecessor.

Meanwhile, Carleton spent "half his life in exploring far-off lands
and the other half in telling about them." From Egypt he sent letters
to his friends about the Sphinx and the Pyramids, the seraglios and
"the forty centuries of book-publishers looking down upon him"
from the "hieroglyphical banks" of the Nile. The trade did not be-
grudge him the pleasures of his retirement. "During his long business
career," *Publishers' Weekly* warmly affirmed, "Carleton had the
happy knack of making friends of all the authors whose books he
published, and they will rejoice to know that he is enjoying the
fortune which he won through their talents. There is at least one publisher whom even Lord Byron would not desire to kill, and his name
is Carleton." Fifteen years after his retirement, on October 11, 1901,
the publisher died, marking the end to a full and successful career.

Most of the authors and humorists who had rallied at Carleton's
office had long since scattered and died, but the seed they had
planted in American soil was still fruitful. The wit and wisdom of
"Artemus Ward" and "Josh Billings" had given way to the grander
wit and profounder wisdom of "Mark Twain," but it was they who
had helped clear the ground for the humor that was to become one
of the nation's most characteristic and most flourishing products.
Without their publisher, however, they would have been voices
laughing in the wilderness.

The little Arabic symbol that conceals the monogram of George W. Carleton should not be forgotten, for it impressed "hys Marke" upon books that filled an urgent need in nineteenth-century America. During and after the Civil War, when the nation was rent by disunion, hatred, and embitterment, that Arabic sign became a symbol not merely for books in general, but for books of good humor touched with a mild and genial satire. America learned to look at itself and its absurdities through a mirror that reflected clearly while it distorted. The effect was comic, but somehow sound. America, beholding itself, laughed at what it saw. And so, through the humorous books that bore upon their title-pages a little Arabic symbol that concealed the initials of a publisher, a nation smiled and came of age.

XIII. THE CALL OF THE WILD

Elliott, Thomes & Talbot

AND THEIR BLUE BACKS

A NATION come of age is a nation whose boundaries are set. By the time the nineteenth century was sixty or seventy years old, the westward-moving pioneers, having leaped the Great Plains, had established themselves upon the Pacific Coast. The wild frontiers of the far West were conquered, and no matter how undisturbed a wilderness might remain in the great expanse of the trans-Missouri region, that fact alone was sufficient to assure the nation that it was approaching its maturity. There was room, in the sixties and the seventies, for conquest—in the land of the Sioux and the Crow, the Ute and the Comanche, in the Great Plains of Buffalo Bill and Texas Jack; yet the fact that the Pacific Coast no longer lay open to adventurer and trailer in buckskin brought to the country even then a sense of its past.

Through what remote wilderness of that Pacific West could the hunter stalk, armed with powder horn and double-barreled rifle? Along which of its unexplored mountain passes could the scout in buckskin and wolfskin cap guide his "unfaltering" steed? Where were the painted Indians of the far West, whose shower of arrows could be scattered by the grape and canister of the pale dogs? Where were the panthers to bring down; where were their trackless woods? Where were the buccaneers with their ingots of gold and silver— where were the pirates and brigands and sharpshooters? From the far western slopes, as from the West Indian seas, romance was all but gone. The remote West was wild no longer, but the call of the wild still echoed in the generation that had followed the conquerors. Some of that generation answered the call by pushing forward into the wilderness of the trans-Missouri region. Others of that generation answered the call vicariously, through the well-thumbed pages of paper-backed dime novels that were already transforming history into romance and drama into melodrama.

For a nation self-conscious, nostalgic, there was much to remember. There were colonial tales—the witch trials of Massachusetts Bay Colony, the romance of Louisiana when Louisiana was a French colony and New Orleans a settlement of log huts on the west bank of the Mississippi. There was the Revolution, and there were closer wars to remember—the War of 1812, the Seminole War, the Mexican War. In the gun-toting West of the Great Plains, the present turned quickly into the past. Its wilderness was so swiftly being tamed that what was the region for adventure one day became the background for romance the next.

And if the remote or immediate past should pale, there was always the lure of the distant. There were Florida pirates and buccaneers of the "Isle of Spain"; there were the bloody exploits of the West Indian seas; there were Brazilian men-of-war and brigands of the Spanish Main. Always there was the wild and far-off West, whose call was wilder than any call of history. And beyond the Americas, from the Turks and the Moors to Ferdinand and Isabella, from the remote eastern world to the Fenians of old Ireland, from Galway Bay to Moorish Spain—there were tales to be told, tales that would answer the call of the wild, the distant in time or in space, for a nation self-conscious, come of age.

There was a trio of gentlemen in Boston who knew this well. In their own ears the call of the wild still echoed, for one had edited the tales that embodied it, another had yielded to the call by sailing to New Granada aboard the *Crescent City,* and still another had himself been the hero of a dime novel which, if written, would have included chapters on the conquest of California, digging for gold at Bidwell's Bar, a jaunt to the Sandwich and the Fiji Islands, Guam and the Philippines, China and Australia. Their firm was known as Elliott, Thomes and Talbot. It published dime novels for a nation whose farthest frontiers were conquered but whose sons still hearkened to the call of the wild.

William Henry Thomes, the hero of the unwritten dime novel which would have vied with the most thrilling paper-backs published by his firm, was born in Portland, Maine, in 1824, and was soon orphaned. The boy was reared by a guardian in Boston, but not taking well to schooling, he shipped at the age of eighteen aboard the *Admittance* to engage in the California hide trade. After he had seen some military service during the conquest of California, he returned to Boston, where he served as printer on the *Boston Daily Times* and married the daughter of Captain Peter Peterson, his old master on the *Admittance*. Neither the captain's daughter nor the *Boston Times* was sufficiently alluring to rival Thomes's gold fever, for in January, 1849, having joined the Boston and California Joint Stock Mining and Trading Company, the young adventurer sailed on the *Edward Everett* for San Francisco. On board ship he helped edit *The Barometer,* a weekly news sheet, until, in July, the *Edward Everett* expedition, the first organized contingent to leave Boston, arrived in California. There Thomes dug for gold at Bidwell's Bar, as Anton Roman did at Scott Bar, and, in addition, he encountered enough Indians, coyotes, and grizzlies to people his imagination for the rest of his days. Thomes, however, was insatiable as far as the allure of exotic places and exciting adventure was concerned. His wild oats were sown not only in the West, but in remoter regions. Besides an episode aboard an opium smuggler plying between China and California, he enjoyed the experiences of working in the gold mines of Victoria and keeping a store at Ballarat. When Thomes returned to the United States, he brought with him enough adventure stories to fill his own as yet unwritten books, and to offer innumerable authentic suggestions to the authors whose thrilling romances he would one day publish. Between 1854 and 1860 he was sufficiently settled to appear in the Boston *Directories* as reporter for the *Daily Times* and the *Herald*. The following year he felt equipped to enter upon his career as publisher.

Meanwhile, his partner-to-be, James R. Elliott, had also been laying the foundations for successful ventures in dime novels. A native of Mason, New Hampshire, he became typical of the local boy who made good, for he was to return to his home town in 1868 to speak, as a native son held in highest esteem, at Mason's centennial celebration. Since 1852 he had been a member of the firm of Moulton, Elliott, and Lincoln, publishers of the *True Flag* at 22 School Street in Boston, a weekly magazine which for two dollars a year offered to its avid subscribers the type of story Elliott's future partner had been living. Thomes through his adventures and Elliott through his armchair activities as editor had each in his own way prepared the groundwork for the career that lay ahead of them. They needed only to join forces to lay siege to a public now eager to answer the call of the wild when it was couched in extravagant phrases and sandwiched between the paper backs of a book.

This they did in 1861, a year after the New York firm of Beadle had introduced the thrills of the dime novel to America with the saffron-backed *Malaeska: the Indian Wife of the White Hunter* by Ann Stephens. Forming the firm of Elliott and Thomes at 100 Washington Street, Boston, they published *The American Union,* a periodical taken over from Graves and Weston. Within two years the young firm had so established itself that it was able to move to the Journal Building, at number 118 opposite Crosby and Nichols, and to attract a third partner into the organization.

Like Elliott and Thomes, Newton Talbot was prepared to offer many personal and business assets upon the altar of literary adventure. Born at Stoughton, Massachusetts, he, like Thomes, was early orphaned; he was raised in his native village as a farmer boy. At the age of twenty-one he went to Boston to seek his fortune, and after varied activities as a shoe dealer and inspector in the Custom House, he also yielded to the call of the wild and sailed in 1849 on the *Crescent City* for New Granada. Reaching Panama, he took passage up the coast to San Francisco, where he may possibly have encountered the wandering Thomes. Returning to Boston, his active wanderlust apparently satisfied, Talbot soon became a cashier in the Publishing Hall of Frederick Gleason, maintaining his connections as business manager when Maturin M. Ballou took over the Gleason publications. A western addict himself, Talbot doubtless enjoyed exchanging yarns with Thomes, and in addition he could offer to the firm ever-needed advice in the financial mysteries of publishing .

By 1863 the three gentlemen of Washington Street were described as "well-known in Boston as having been long connected with the newspaper press of this city, as editors and publishers. . . . The new firm, lacking neither capital nor experience, will . . . introduce new and timely improvements."

The new firm gave much of its attention to the expansion of its periodicals. *The American Union* was by this time, according to its proprietors, a first-class family journal, one of the best literary papers in the country, replete with charming tales and sketches, anecdotes, wit and humor, fun and fancy, and—needless to say—thrilling adventures. Its distinguishing feature was its lack of serials and advertisements. Yet even without such lures the journal seems to have found a host of readers at 5¢ a copy or $2 a year.

Besides having taken over Ballou's business manager, the publishers had also taken over Ballou's periodical, *The Flag of Our Union,* which had yielded Gleason, its founder, an annual income of $25,000. A miscellaneous weekly designed for the home circle, it had become "a 'household word' from Maine to California, gladdening the fireside of the rich and poor." Though it contained, according to the publishers, "not one vulgar word or line," and though it was free from "politics and all jarring topics," its emphasis upon violent narratives peopled with convicts and opium addicts, its turbulent sea stories and tales of discoveries scarcely suited it to "the family circle." Yet, with a history more distinguished than that of *The American Union, The Flag,* with its satin-surfaced paper, new type, and super-royal pages, was indeed a weekly visitor to many an American home. Whether or not it gladdened the fireside of the rich and poor, it did bring flamboyant adventure to the armchair subscribers who in turn must have filled the purses of its three new proprietors.

To their growing chain of story periodicals, the firm added, in April, 1863, *Ballou's Dollar Monthly Magazine.* In that issue Ballou inserted his own valedictory, stating that he had disposed of all right and title in his publishing business to Messrs. Elliott, Thomes and Talbot, who added their own salutatory, assuring the subscribers that the new publishers would have "the valuable advice and counsel of Mr. Ballou." Described as a family magazine catering "to the best feelings of the community, and not to the worst, like some of the journals of the day," the monthly included set sections such as Ruthven's Puzzle Page, The Housekeeper, Curious Matters, Facts and Fancies, Parlor Amusements, and the Young People's Story-Teller. Editorial Notes, or Chats with Correspondents, offered the editors the opportunity of advertising their other publications as well as giving advice to the lovelorn. But, in addition to its regular features, *Ballou's Monthly Magazine,* under the aegis of the new firm, regaled its subscribers with such thrilling tales as "The Persecuted Deacon," "The Maniac Lover," "The Ogilvie Pride," and, in time, with William H. Thomes's own serial effusions, "The Belle of

Australia" and "On Land and Sea." It carried the works of Horatio Alger, Jr., Amanda M. Hale, and James Franklin Fitts, whose productions were guaranteed to be "highly sensational, interspersed with charming home scenes and sweet glimpses of domestic life." With original engravings illustrating such respectable institutions as Warwick Castle and the Fruit Sellers of Rio de Janeiro, and with enticing advertisements of Fragrant Sozodont and Kidder's Pastilles, the monthly delighted not only its subscribers but its publishers, who enthusiastically promised each year that the next volume would excel the previous one, "if such a thing is possible."

Elliott, Thomes and Talbot attracted purchasers to their chain of periodicals not only through advertisements but through the formation of "clubs," a common enough device that offered a year's subscription free to any pioneering reader who obtained ten subscribers. Various combinations were sold at reduced prices, and wholesale agents were engaged from New Orleans to Albany, from Denver to New York. The purveyors of pulp magazines had established a lively business by selling adventure periodically in black and white.

It was from Ballou also that the firm took over another venture in periodicals, one directly connected with their publication of dime novels. *The Novelette,* originally issued by Ballou as a weekly specializing in four-part stories, was converted into a magazine that contained one long story, complete, written especially for the establishment, and from three to five short stories, along with miscellaneous matter. Thirteen numbers were issued at two dollars a year, and the complete stories included such piercing calls of the wild as Sylvanus Cobb, Jr.'s *White Hand! or, The Natchez Captive* and "Lieutenant Murray's" [Maturin M. Ballou's] *Pirate Smugglers.* Illustrations depicting The Ruse of the Robber or The Pirate Traitor's Doom titillated the taste of the reader and increased the firm's profits, as did the revenues from advertisements of Turner's Tic Douloureux, or Universal Neuralgia Pill. With a certain unconscious wit, the publishers announced that after January 1, 1871, they would convert *The Novelette* into "a first class magazine."

With such a line of periodicals the firm might have rested content. Yet they knew that the call of the wild could be tuned not only to magazine subscribers but to purchasers of cheap books. In a copious stream, therefore, dime novels that brought adventure and romance and limitless vistas of distant frontiers to a nation fast closing its actual frontiers flowed from the offices of *The Novelette, The Flag of Our Union, Ballou's Monthly Magazine,* and other roots of the pulp paper family tree.

In 1860 Erastus F. Beadle had begun his long and flourishing series of dime novels with the publication of Mrs. Stephens's *Malaeska.* When his success with this enterprise became apparent, several competitors appeared in the field. By 1863 Sinclair Tousey, Irwin P. Beadle (brother of Erastus), and Elliott, Thomes and Talbot each determined to issue a run of dime novels in competition with the original series, and the three houses were engaged in a minor civil war of their own to see who could launch the first of the rival issues. The gentlemen of Washington Street won the laurels, for on November 10, 1863, with the publication of Sylvanus Cobb, Jr.'s *Golden Eagle,* their Ten Cent Novelettes made their bow to the public, one day in advance of Irwin Beadle's and two in advance of Tousey's.

The Ten Cent Novelettes issued by Elliott, Thomes and Talbot were described as the largest and handsomest ten-cent books ever published. A new one appeared on the last Monday of every month, bound in pink and later in blue paper, well printed, containing from 100 to 128 pages. For one dollar the eager subscriber would receive twelve complete choice novels a year, written expressly for the firm by well-known American authors. According to the publishers, the Novelettes were larger than any other dime novels in the country, although they were furnished at the same price. Actually, the Elliott, Thomes and Talbot publications were similar to Beadle's in size, if somewhat larger, though the rival firm refrained from imitating the already well-known orange covers and used pink and then blue instead. In addition many of the Novelettes were reprints of the Shilling and Two Shilling series issued by Gleason-Ballou between 1844 and 1860.

Besides their Ten Cent Novelettes the firm of Elliott, Thomes and Talbot placed on the market a group of similar publications known as Brilliant Novelettes, richly illustrated in bound form, each containing a complete story, short stories, anecdotes and original engravings, priced at twenty cents. As *The North American Review* put it, "The success of Messrs. Beadle & Co.'s undertaking has led other publishers . . . to engage in similar enterprises. . . . we wish them all success, and regard the competition thus established as

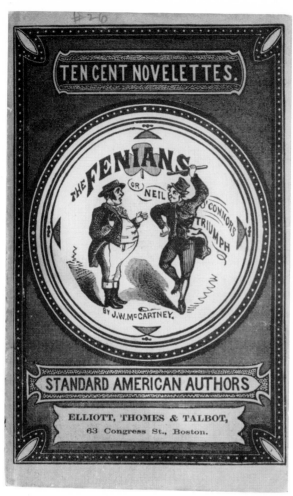

THE FENIANS, NO. 26 OF THE ELLIOTT, THOMES & TALBOT
TEN CENT NOVELETTES [1865]

EDITORIAL ROOM OF THE FRANK LESLIE PUBLISHING HOUSE

likely to be of service in raising the character of cheap literature generally." Though this roseate opinion was destined for some revision, there is no doubt that the cheap novels purveyed by Elliott, Thomes and Talbot served a timely purpose. For a country from whose borders romantic adventure was fast disappearing, they offered the lure of the distant in time and in space, the excitement of exploration and conquest, the color of the gun-toting West; and at the same time they reminded a nation of its roots and its turbulent, swift-passing history. There was room, for a time, for all the rival publishers of dime novels, for they rose to meet the need of a nation still hearkening to the call of the wild.

The "Standard American Authors" published by Elliott, Thomes and Talbot required, as did all dime novelists, a riotous imagination, a dramatic instinct, and an indefatigable right hand. In return for these capabilities they generally received approximately two dollars for a short column of print or three dollars run inside length, a sum that netted them about $50 or $75 for a story published in a periodical and probably a slightly higher price for one issued as a Novelette. The first Ten Cent Novelette published by Elliott, Thomes and Talbot was the work of Sylvanus Cobb, Jr., whose *Golden Eagle* was issued in a special edition of 25,000 copies printed for the New York trade. Thomes had known Cobb personally, and invited him to contribute to the new venture and thus continue the connections he had made with Gleason and Ballou. The prolific Cobb obliged, following *The Golden Eagle* with *The Bravo's Secret, The Yankee Champion, The Ducal Coronet,* and other effusions appropriately sub-titled.

The austere and retiring Maturin M. Ballou also continued his interest, not only offering his advice to the publishers of *Ballou's Monthly Magazine,* but contributing to their series of Ten Cent Novelettes such thrilling tales as *The Duke's Prize, The Turkish Slave,* and *The Child of the Sea,* all issued under the pseudonym of "Lieutenant Murray."

Another favorite of Elliott, Thomes and Talbot was Ben Perley Poore, the genial and talented newspaper correspondent, whose Revolutionary story, *The Scout,* was offered as a Brilliant Novelette, and whose *Mameluke; or, The Sign of the Mystic Tie* appeared as a Ten Cent Novelette.

E. Z. C. Judson, who was to make Buffalo Bill famous, lent his martial bearing and fluent storytelling to the task of supplying *The Volunteer* and *The Black Avenger* by "Ned Buntline" to the firm, while Jane G. Austin emerged from her Concord, Massachusetts, retreat to adorn the press with *The Novice, The Outcast,* and *Kinah's Curse.* Francis A. Durivage, the graceful poet, novelist, and historian, and Dr. J. H. Robinson, one of the first writers of "Westerns," were also among the firm's contributors, their violent effusions appearing both as Ten Cent and as Brilliant Novelettes.

Perhaps the most famous of the Elliott, Thomes and Talbot authors was Louisa M. Alcott, who supplied the firm with three thrillers, the first under the pseudonym of "A. M. Barnard" and the last two under her own name. *V. V.: or, Plots and Counterplots* was reprinted in 1865 from *The Flag of Our Union* as a Ten Cent Novelette, a tale in which the author of *Flower Fables* and *Hospital Sketches* let down her literary tresses and, secure in her pseudonymous retreat, indulged in her passion for the "lurid" and the exotic. Drugged coffee, an iron ring, disguises, suicide, and revenge were boiled in her sulphurous cauldron to produce one of the most bloody and most thunderous of the thrillers. *The Skeleton in the Closet* appeared as Number 49 of the series along with Perley Parker's *Foundling,* while *The Mysterious Key* followed as Number 50, narrating for insatiable purchasers the dubious delights of a union with an idiot and the secret of a hidden marriage.

Many of the Ten Cent or Brilliant Novelettes were, indeed, similar tales of horror. The titles alone were sufficient to dissuade the wary from purchase or to whet the appetite of the blood-and-thunder addict. *The Fatal Casket; or, The Poisoners of Paris; The Black Adder; Mr. Warburton's Ghost; The Bauer Murder; The Dwarf Fiend; Long Sim, the Idiot Pauper*—all rolled from the press to be well thumbed by those who hearkened to a ghoulish and ghostly call of the wild.

By far the most interesting of the Elliott, Thomes and Talbot dime novels, however, served up a different fare for readers in whose ears the call of the wild rang sharp and clear. For them, the publishers traced the country's past, embroidering its history with the thread of romance. Yet, though they wove fancy upon the web of fact, the framework was still solid enough to remind a multitude of readers of their historic heritage. Did they wish a tale of the Massachusetts Colony? They had but to purchase Number 31 of the Ten Cent

Novelettes, for the story of *Zelda* by Miss Jane Howard, and they would be transported to a Boston whose Common was "a vast extent of pasture-land, over which cattle feed undisturbed," to a time when the "Indian scalping-knife can do its work as neatly as the legalized halter!"—and they would be enthralled by the thrilling trial of a witch who had thrown her spells over a minister's son. If they preferred a story of the Louisiana Colony, Dr. J. H. Robinson's *White Rover* would introduce to them a hunter hero, "standing thoughtfully upon the margin of Lake Ponchartrain," a hero replete with hunting frock of dressed deerskin, Indian moccasins, and foraging cap, ready with powder-horn and ball pouch, hunting knife and double-barrelled rifle. Pierre Moran could "meet the red man two to one, and live through the fight"; he could "bring down the panther at two hundred yards"; he could "battle successfully with the howling wolf." Through trial and escape, abduction and grand denouement, readers of Number 2 of the Ten Cent Novelettes could be carried for the price of a dime to the thrilling days when New Orleans was a settlement of log huts on the west bank of the Mississippi and Louisiana was a French colony.

For Revolution addicts, the first of the Ten Cent Novelettes had been issued: Sylvanus Cobb, Jr.'s *The Golden Eagle; or, The Privateer of 1776*. Ben Perley Poore's Brilliant Novelette, *The Scout*, and Sylvanus Cobb's Ten Cent Novelette, *The Patriot Cruiser*, appealed to a similar audience. In *The Scout* armchair adventurers into the past could sally to the Talloosah trail in 1780, meeting Major Rupert Loudon in his otterskin cap and buckskin leggings, mounted on his "gallant steed" and prepared for the victorious march of the Sharpshooters that ended in Yorktown. Revengeful Cherokees, betrayal and a web of crime would culminate in love and patriotism, victory and wedlock for the Major of the Sharpshooters Battalion, Morgan's Brigade, who added to his military conquests the conquest of Aurora of the raven hair and full black eyes that "glowed with heartfelt thought." And what reader could remain unmoved by Ben Perley Poore's patriotic eulogy of the sons of freedom? "The sharpshooters! When the future historians of the Revolutionary struggle shall attempt to analyze the origins of the various classes of citizens who took up arms in defence of their liberties, it will be a hard matter to decide whether Celtic, Saxon or Indian blood was predominant in the veins of those hardy backwoodsmen." For patriotism equally ardent and adventure equally bold, readers could lose themselves in Number 52 of the Ten Cent Novelettes, Sylvanus Cobb, Jr.'s *Patriot Cruiser,* set in the eve of the Revolution, "the struggle which has since filled the noblest page in the history of nations," when the British army was quartered in Boston, and the hero "had seen the patriot's blood spilled by the foe—he had seen the hireling soldiers of the tyrant king trampling upon the dearest liberties of his country-men, and from that moment his life was pledged by an oath to the cause of that liberty which all true hearted Americans prayed for."

The Mexican War was less remote but no less colorful for sub-scribers whose call of the wild echoed from the past. For them, Number 16 of the Ten Cent Novelettes, "Ned Buntline's" *The Vol-unteer,* brought "a story of thrilling scenes, daring deeds, and stirring times," when the hero, a "noble specimen of a backwoodsman," who "stood just six feet and one inch . . . straight as one of his own forest maples," was mustered in to join in the attack upon Monterey in which "our brave troops" met the foe "hand to hand and knife to knife." Giving himself leeway for romance, the astute author re-minded his public that "The pages of American history have already received the records of the glorious five days which were occupied in the siege and capture of Monterey, yet there were many incidents that occurred in that siege, which never have been registered on the historian's scroll." On the dime novel scroll "Ned Buntline" pro-ceeded to register them, mingling with facts of the Texas Rangers and the Battle of Buena Vista the romance of a false accusation and a court martial, a death sentence and a happy ending that found the hero united with a Mexican wife.

For those who favored the remote in space to the distant in time, "Ralph The Reefer" would carry them to Florida in *The Florida Pirate,* and J. W. McCartney would transport them to Ireland in his story of *The Fenians: or, Neil O'Connor's Triumph.* The lure of the West Indies was couched in the pages of "Lieutenant Murray's" *Red Rupert* or Dr. John B. Williams's *Joaquin,* and its sequel, *The Buccaneers,* tales that told of brigands and the "Isle of Spain," and of a Spanish nation which, as "master of the Indies, could ballast their galleons with ingots of gold and silver." Tales of the sea, ocean spectres and ocean waifs, pirates and fishermen, rovers of the Irish Sea and cruisers of the English Channel conveyed readers to the far away, while William Henry Thomes planned his own accounts of

The Whaleman's Adventures in the Sandwich Islands and California, or *Running the Blockade.* Neither publisher nor reader could resist the wanderlust of *The Gold Robbers. A Story of Australia, The Pearl of Panama,* and *Zuleika; or, The Castilian Captive.*

Perhaps the greatest appeal, the fullest answer to those who heeded the call of the wild, lay in the books that combined the distant in time and in space, those that centered upon America's old West. William H. Bushnell, author of *Hack, The Trailer,* knew this well. He began his *Story of The Shoshonee Indians* with a few captivating paragraphs:

On an early June morning, many years ago, the lookouts at Fort Bridger were startled to see a single wagon advancing very slowly towards them—one apparently tenantless, for nothing of human kind was to be discovered in connection with it.

During the years that have followed, such a thing has become common, and is thought no more of than the sight of a stray Indian pony or the howling of a wolf was then. The overland route and the mountain passes, where the steel-muscled and steam-pulsating heart of the locomotive is now dashing unchecked along, were then little known. It was at the time when the first daring spirits had turned their backs upon civilization; when they banded together to resist the attacks of the Indians . . . and to see a lone wagon was at once a wonder and a mystery.

There was, of course, no mystery that Bushnell's hero could not eventually solve, for he was Hack, The Trailer—"all bone and muscle," his face "swarthy from exposure to sun and wind," his tall frame clothed in "well-worn and stained buckskin," his cap "formed of the shaggy skin of a wolf." The name of Hack, The Trailer, was "familiar to all who have travelled through Dacotah Territory." It was the name of a "man amongst men," who guided his "unfaltering steed" through the "trackless wood." His story made the Wild West come alive again, for its ingredients were painted Indians and showers of arrows, rifles that belched flame and lead, cannons that thundered, sending their loads of grape and canister abroad—the great " 'fire gun' of the white man." Its ingredients were squaws and hatchets, and dialogue that included such grim pronouncements as Fire-Flint's "Let the pale dog prepare for death!" An emigrant wagon and a bluff, war-worn veteran who commanded a little frontier fort, a band of Shoshonees who had attacked the wagon train, became irresistible when they were combined with that rare guide and trailer, Hack, who boldly answered the call of the wild in every reader's heart and who, in the trackless wood of Western literature still guides his unfaltering steed.

The Texan Bravo and *The Arkansas Ranger, The Mysterious Miner; or, The Gold Diggers of California* joined the flourishing line of Brilliant or Ten Cent Novelettes, surely stirring in the minds of the publishers as in the minds of their readers some nostalgia for the days of forty-nine. The Mexican War, the California gold rush were scarcely two decades past when they became subjects for historical romance. For the original forty-niners recalling their own adventures, as well as for the generation that had followed them or was close upon their heels, the dime novels of the West embodied the lure of a remembered past and a distant scene—a happy combination to satisfy the call of the wild to which a nation at home still hearkened.

During the period of their Ten Cent and Brilliant Novelettes, the firm of Elliott, Thomes and Talbot had moved to 63 Congress Street in the printers' rather than the publishers' headquarters of Boston. In 1870 Thomes and Talbot severed their connections with Elliott, who established himself as the publisher of *The Western World,* a "large, handsomely illustrated quarto journal, devoted to choice original literature by the most distinguished American authors." James R. Elliott described his undertaking as "A First-Class Literary Family Journal" boasting a circulation of over 20,000 and advertisements of it in the astounding number of 2,500 different papers and magazines. To canvass it, he advertised for local agents "in every town and village in the country," offering a "Magnificent $5 Premium Steel Engraving to every subscriber" as well as a liberal cash commission to agents, who could "easily" earn "$1 to $10 . . . in an evening." Just before Elliott's departure the firm had published, perhaps in his honor, its only book outside the domain of cheap literature—John B. Hill's *Proceedings at the Centennial Celebration of the One Hundredth Anniversary of the Incorporation of the Town of Mason, N.H.* This cloth octavo was doubtless issued in recognition of Elliott's presence at the celebration and his connections with the town of Mason. At the same time it heralded his departure to *The Western World.*

Elliott abandoned the firm at an opportune time. The fire of 1872 in Boston ruined many of their publications, temporarily at least, and Thomes and Talbot removed to 36 Bromfield Street—Elliott's own address as proprietor of *The Western World*—and finally to 23 Hawley Street, where they remained until the dissolution of the concern in the mid-eighties.

By the time the eighties had rolled around, critics were a little less optimistic about the possibilities of high literary standards in dime novels than they had been in the sixties. The Hon. Abel Goddard, member of the New York Assembly from St. Lawrence, was moved to make his bid for immortality by introducing into that body a bill declaring that "Any person who shall sell, loan, or give to any minor under sixteen . . . any dime novel . . . without first obtaining the written consent of the parent or guardian of such minor, shall be deemed guilty of a misdemeanor, punishable by imprisonment or by a fine not exceeding $50." Anticipating, perhaps, a possible ebbing in the dime novel tide, the partners were prepared to dissolve their firm. Like Elliott, Thomes was eager to pay a visit to a "Western World" of his own, returning in 1885 to California as president of the New England Society of California Pioneers. Talbot, too, was ready to abandon the financial direction of a publishing firm to take over the position of treasurer of Tufts College.

To George W. Studley, who had long worked both as clerk and publisher at 23 Hawley Street, the publications of Thomes and Talbot were turned over. It was he who revived in the Novelette Library the works of Dr. J. H. Robinson, and it was he who reprinted in his Owl Library the earlier series of Elliott, Thomes and Talbot.

Thomes returned at length to Boston, to 23 Hawley Street, where he shared his advice and his experience with Studley, and to his house in Concord Square, where his whiskered, mustachioed face brought visible reminders of the Wild West to the boys of the Hub. As past president of the Martin Association and past master of St. John's Lodge he could regale his Masonic listeners with the oral dime novel that was the story of his life. Talbot, plain-spoken and brusque, of "antique sternness and firmness of character," offered to Tufts College, the Ancient and Honorable Artillery, and the Universalist Club the practical sagacity for which he had gained a reputation.

While Thomes and Talbot rested thus upon their laurels, the laurels themselves flowered once more in the well-thumbed pages of George Studley's reprints known as the Novelette or Owl Library.

Indeed, the laurels they helped to foster cannot turn to seed so long as an eager public continues to seek escape from a weary present into a romantic past, or from a tamed and frontierless continent into remote and exotic lands where one unconquered frontier stretches beyond another, where the East is still mysterious and the West is still wild. For a public that hears the call of the wild, the call can still be answered in those Ten Cent Novelettes of Elliott, Thomes and Talbot, that offered, neatly bound in blue backs, the historic romance that was shaped from a nation's romantic history.

XIV. RAILROADS &
RAILROAD LITERATURE

The Leslies

OF PUBLISHERS' ROW

I N A spectacular manner, the United States became literally united on May 10, 1869. On that day, at Promontory Point, Utah, two railroads, the Union Pacific which had built westward from Iowa, and the Central Pacific which had built eastward from California, met. Laborers had been imported from China, supplies had been hauled in great sleds over the snowdrifts of the Sierras, and through a wilderness miles of track had been laid. The gigantic task was at last completed, and the event was signalized by the driving of a golden spike with a silver mallet at Promontory Point, the meeting place of the two lines. The jubilation of a continent was signalized by ringing bells and loud cheers, parades and fireworks, hundred-gun salutes and thanksgiving services.

It did not take long for the nation to realize that this had been more than a feat of engineering. Two plus two equaled, as they so often did in nineteenth-century America, five. The historic rendezvous of the Union Pacific and the Central Pacific meant more than the completion of a railroad that spanned the continent. It meant an end to remote outposts and to isolation. It heralded, in this visibly unified nation, an end to those spatial frontiers that had beckoned the hardy adventurer. On the positive side, it meant expansion and building and exploitation. With the seventies, the Age of the Pioneer gave way to the Age of Steel—the Railway Age—in a continent knit together by parallel bands of track. In its simplest terms, the ushering in of the Railway Age meant the ushering in of a form of literature with a new name and a new purpose—railroad literature. Many a publisher responded to the new need, but one typified more colorfully than all the others together those spectacular, silver seventies that had brought the need for railroad literature to a nation bound together with threads of steel. Frank Leslie—and his fascinating, passionate, incredible wife—were themselves the silver seventies.

He had not always been called Frank Leslie. Born Henry Carter in Ipswich, England, in 1821, he had adopted the pseudonym of Frank Leslie because his father, a glove-manufacturer, had not looked kindly upon the boy's interest in such affairs as woodcuts and engravings. As Frank Leslie he had had some success on *The Illustrated London News,* where he had learned a few of the "secrets" of pictorial printing, but in 1848 he had decided to settle in America. Ruddy-faced, black-bearded, the dynamic young man had worked for P. T. Barnum when the King of Humbugs took Jenny Lind on tour, and had served as wood engraver in Frederick Gleason's Publishing Hall in Boston. He had been managing foreman of Barnum and Beach's *Illustrated News,* and in January, 1854, he had set up as publisher of *Frank Leslie's Ladies Gazette of Fashion,* edited by the "intense" novelist, Ann Stephens. Nearly two years later, on December 15, 1855, he had commenced publication of *Frank Leslie's Illustrated Newspaper,* a project that was to make him a power on New York's Publishers' Row. With its graphic cuts of murders, assassinations, prize fights, and fires, that paper was to dominate the field of illustrated journalism for nearly three-quarters of a century. It sported just enough text to float the pictures instead of just enough pictures to float the text. Moreover, by the clever and ingenious device of dividing a block into small sections so that a number of engravers could work on the same picture at the same time before the wooden squares were screwed together, Frank Leslie could complete huge double-page engravings in a single night instead of in two weeks. This man of many projects had his hand on the public pulse. He knew what the people wanted, and he gave it to them, in the form of flaming double-page engravings that graphically exposed every *cause célèbre* of the country.

By 1876, when the Railway Age had become a reality, Frank Leslie's Publishing House had expanded into a pictorial factory from which a dozen different periodicals emerged to titillate the varied fancies of the public. There were papers for children and for the ladies, there were scandal sheets and news sheets, story papers and joke papers, papers to satisfy every appetite, except perhaps the publisher's. Daring and exuberant, Frank Leslie was not content with being a pioneer in illustrated journalism and a household word in every home where magazines were read. Too vital to confine his interests to periodicals, he wanted a finger in every publishing pie. The flourishing of America's Railway Age gave him the perfect opportunity. Frank Leslie's motto was "Never shoot over the heads of the people." It might just as well have been "He who runs may read."

He had long been fascinated by America's railroads. In the fall of 1869 he had sent a staff artist, Joseph Becker, to make pictorial records of the transcontinental journey by rail, and his views "Across the Continent" had emblazoned the pages of *Frank Leslie's Illustrated Newspaper* for months. By 1877 the publisher was prepared to make the same journey himself, in the most elaborate luxury that the spectacular seventies had as yet devised. He would be accompanied by a retinue of writers, artists, and photographers. He would also be accompanied by his second wife, Miriam Florence Leslie, a woman with a mysterious past, a brilliant present, and an intriguing future.

Born in New Orleans in 1836—a year which she usually altered to 1851 when asked for a close reckoning—Miriam had been educated in most of the foreign languages and polished in all of the foreign graces so that she would shine as a glittering descendant of a family of Creole *émigrés* who had once been noble French Huguenots. Actually she needed little polish, for she had a captivating beauty of her own. Gray-eyed, sunny-haired, subtly charming, she exhibited the loveliest shoulders in town, and she walked with a gracious ease that was impossible for a masculine eye not to follow. Miriam was the mistress not only of language but of many a bedazzled gentleman, and not only of gentlemen, but of every occasion that fortune might offer.

Leslie had survived one unfortunate marriage before he pledged his troth to the seductive Miriam. She had survived two, the first a short-lived affair with a jeweler's clerk, the second a fifteen-year union with the celebrated archeologist, Ephraim George Squier. Sandwiched between these marital enterprises had been an episode on the stage during which she had appeared as "sister" of that vivid adventuress, Lola Montez. By 1874, when she married Frank Leslie, she had become a *grande dame* in her own right, an enchanting hostess in the publisher's Fifth Avenue establishment and in his country seat at Saratoga. If she sported a scarlet stocking on one leg, however, she sported a blue stocking on the other. Her fingers were bedecked with diamonds, but they also bore traces of printer's ink; for Miriam, observing that the pen in Leslie's hand was often mightier than the sword in Napoleon's, had enjoyed a brilliant apprenticeship as fashion editor at the Leslie Publishing House. She was equipped for the task, for she had been acknowledged—in Leslie's paper at least—as belle of the Lincoln inaugural ball; and if there was anything she knew better than fashions, it was the women who wore them and the men who admired them.

Certainly there had been many men who had admired Mrs. Frank Leslie. She had played hostess, at the side of her successful and distinguished husband, to Dom Pedro, Emperor of Brazil, Don Carlos, and General Grant. She had been presented to Governor Tilden with what was estimated as $70,000 worth of diamonds on her person. She had captivated the Poet of the Sierras, Joaquin Miller, and she had completely captivated her third husband, Frank Leslie.

She was a forcible power behind his now considerable throne. The huge five-story publishing house at 537 Pearl Street had so expanded during the seventies that thousands of dollars each week went to pay three or four hundred employees. Tremendous amounts of money—at times two or three thousand dollars—were tied up in postage stamps from customers of what had become a prodigious mail-order business. The erstwhile fashion editor had developed into literary critic of the entire domain, who could write on "Types Of Lovers" or "dreams of dresses," select stories, correspond with contributors, and enjoy a fruitful "intercourse with foreign personages." By the beginning of 1877 Frank Leslie bestrode Publishers' Row like a colossus, flinging weeklies and monthlies, pictorials and story papers down to the man on the street from the pinnacle of his publishing domain. For these magnates of Publishers' Row, the year 1877 seemed destined to be an *annus mirabilis,* and what was more fitting at that time than to take a transcontinental excursion that would glorify the Railway Age for all America.

The various railroads that threaded the country astutely offered their services free to those who could advertise them so well. The Leslie Excursion of 1877 across the continent would be the most lavish gesture yet made by the fabulous couple of Pearl Street, a gesture that would dramatically announce to a world avid for travel that the Railway Age was rolling its heady course. They would go wherever the railroads would take them. They would sketch the towns and scenery of the West for their *Illustrated Newspaper*. Miriam would write up her views of California from a woman's standpoint, and Leslie would gauge the popular taste for what had come to be known as railroad literature.

On Tuesday evening, April 10, 1877, the travelers assembled at New York's Grand Central Depot. The group of nine men, three women, and Miriam's Skye terrier included Bracebridge Hemyng, their star juvenile writer; Edwin A. Curley, historian of the expedition; three artists, a staff photographer, and a business manager. Over a hundred friends gathered to bid farewell to the railroaders. Champagne baskets and hampers were loaded on the sumptuous Palace car that had been named the "Frank Leslie." When the last whistle sounded, loud cheers rose from the platform, hands and handkerchiefs waved, and the signal torpedoes which Wagner, the railroad king, had placed on the tracks, exploded in a deafening chorus. The Leslies had fired their own salute and were on their way.

At Chicago the Wagner Palace car, with its divans and mirrors and sofas, was exchanged for the "President," a hotel on wheels that had been exhibited at the Centennial. Mr. Pullman arrived in person to explain its virtues to the distinguished visitors. The kitchen of the "President" was equipped with every convenience, from a mammoth roaster to a charcoal broiler. For breakfast the travelers could enjoy fish caught at the last station. As they sped across country at the thrilling rate of twenty miles an hour, they could partake of Delmonican repasts magically concocted from a refrigerator and larder that were merely boxes underneath the car.

From the "Phenix City of the Lakes" to Omaha, the train whistled on. Emigrants bound for the Black Hills, border ruffians and gambling sharps, pickpockets and grizzle-haired miners, a lonely band of Omahas flashed by as the great plains rolled away on either side. The West sat for its portrait as the Leslie Excursion train steamed on to Fremont, through the Platte Valley, to Cheyenne, Magic City of the Plains. The rolling prairie gave way to low bluffs. Through snowsheds and blinding snowstorms the coyote howled as the nineteenth century flew upon the coach wheel. Canyons and buttes made way for the grand sweep of mountains. Chinese laborers appeared along the railroad. Cinnamon bears and a stream of Mormons joined the flashing pictures at Ogden. The vignettes of western life accumulated. Indians in calico rags and red paint lounged on the planked sidewalks of Carson City. From the snows of the Sierras the "President" reached the green valley of the Sacramento, and the City of the Golden Gate lay at the other end of a railroad track in the silver seventies.

The transcontinental jaunt, which included a stay at San Francisco's fabulous Palace Hotel, a dinner at former Governor Stanford's mansion, excursions to Los Angeles and the Yosemite, a visit to the mining town Virginia City, Nevada, and an interview with Brigham Young, ended on June 7, 1877, when the Leslies were back in Gotham. The journey had cost $15,000. It had provided material for Mrs. Leslie's book, *California A Pleasure Trip from Gotham to the Golden Gate,* and for Mr. Leslie's assorted newspapers. It had proven in lavish, gaudy, dramatic fashion that the Railway Age was part of America's history. It had also given Frank Leslie an opportunity to review his thoughts and achievements as a provider of railroad literature for a Railway Age.

Early in his career, in 1855, *Frank Leslie's Portfolio of Fancy Needlework,* edited by Ann Stephens, had appeared over the imprint of Stringer and Townsend. Perhaps it was then that Leslie had determined he could profit more from his books if he published them himself. At any rate, after a few minor pictorials, he had begun his venture in book publishing with the simple device of issuing his *Pictorial History of The War of 1861* and *of the American Civil War,* edited by E. G. Squier, then Mrs. Leslie's husband, between 1861 and 1862. Consisting of thirty-three numbers altogether, the *Pictorial History of the American Civil War* recalled in its format and appearance the serial, and perhaps one of the most interesting features of all the Leslie books is that, no matter what their layout, they still suggest the magazine. For the railway traveler suspended between East and West as he spanned the continent, reading matter that appeared like a transition between periodical and book seemed, perhaps, an appropriate device for railroad literature.

After a Series of New Novels in 1863 and 1864, a *Pictorial Life of Abraham Lincoln,* and a venture in the dime novel field with his *Boy's & Girl's Weekly,* Leslie issued his *Historical Register of the . . .*

Centennial Exposition, for which agents canvassed in connection with souvenir lottery tickets. Although the work resulted in a libel suit, the undaunted magazine magnate entered the lists in 1877 as a full-fledged publisher of books, especially of such books which those who traveled on rails might read.

The year 1877 was Leslie's *annus mirabilis* not only in railway excursions but in book publishing. Despite the sums of money spent on the grand jaunt to the Pacific and on the magnificent "at homes" at his baronial estate in Saratoga, Frank Leslie and his wife did not hesitate to plunge into further expense by continuing to publish, on a larger scale than ever, books for those who rode the rails.

All those books were arranged in series, and in whatever format they appeared, they reminded the reader that the publisher was also in the magazine business. They are important not only because of their interest in this respect, but because of their place in the history of the cheap reprint designed especially for railroad literature.

From his imposing offices at 537 Pearl Street, Frank Leslie's Home Library of Standard Works by the Most Celebrated Authors appeared in 1877. The Home Library was designed, according to the enthusiastic publisher, to place within the reach of all (and especially—despite its domestic heading—of all who traveled through the country on the growing network of railroads) "the best works of the best authors." Books usually sold for $1.50 or $2.00 could now be furnished for 10¢ or 20¢, and the standard authors of all time could be picked up as traveling companions for all America. Though the series was aimed to include all the authors made famous by the test of time and none of unknown or untried popularity, the list offered, among the more classic works of Charles Reade, Bulwer-Lytton, and Wilkie Collins, such less-established but perhaps equally delectable items as *Good-by, Sweetheart!* by Rhoda Broughton, Mrs. Annie Edwards's *Vagabond Heroine,* and *Murphy's Master* by James Payn. The astute publisher obviously applied his motto, "Never shoot over the heads of the people," to his books as well as to his magazines. The price of the series depended upon size, double numbers fetching twenty cents and single numbers ten. A copy of *Hannah* by Miss "Muloch," better known today as Dinah Craik, author of *John Halifax, Gentleman,* is one of the few that has survived through the years. Appearing as it does, without hard covers, it resembles not only such enterprises as Lupton's Leisure Hour

Library, but Leslie's own magazine serials. It stands as one of the small number of extant specimens of the type of novel that Frank Leslie purveyed for readers en route in a Railway Age.

The Home Library was not the only venture of this publisher who had always preferred to run twenty magazines with 1,000 circulation each to one with a distribution of 20,000. Having based still another series upon the title of one of his periodicals, the *Chimney Corner,* which had been planned, started, and edited by Mrs. Leslie, he continued his Chimney Corner Series (begun in 1876) with books in duodecimo boards at fifty cents each, in which readers could enjoy the delights of *Living or Dead, Wife in Name Only,* or *Woman's Victory,* and experience the pleasures of the fireside as they sped on wheels across the continent.

For a time at least these series paid dividends, for they included, in addition, Frank Leslie's Popular Library Series issued in octavo between 1876 and 1877, illustrated, and bound in heavy covers, for twenty-five cents. In this compact format appeared Verne's *Michael Strogoff, Reaping the Whirlwind* by Mary Cecil Hay, and the effusions of Charles Gayler from *Fritz, The Emigrant* to *Montague: or, The Belle of the Matinee.*

For the boys who took to the railroad Leslie added a fourth series between 1876 and 1877, Frank Leslie's Boys Library Series, consisting of paper-covered editions of the *Jack Harkaway* stories by Bracebridge Hemyng, along with *Three Yankee Boys* by "Commodore Ah-Look of New Bedford," and a variety of thrillers concerned with Apache chiefs and Pawnee ranges.

Nearly every book bearing the Leslie imprint was in the class of cheap railroad literature and was handled by the American News Company, which had served as agents for his periodicals also. Through that Company's system, and with the development of railroads throughout the country, cheap, popular literature could be retailed at newsstands, station kiosks, and on the trains themselves, where train boys included books among the wares they shouted. Canvassing agents themselves rode the rails, purveying Leslie's periodicals, while the American News Company distributed Leslie's book reprints. The railroad had united the country not only geographically but culturally, too. On miles of steel track sped the popular novels of the day. Fireside companions had become traveling companions. Hammock literature had a new name—it was known as railroad literature.

Leslie was one of many publishers who realized what the railroads meant in terms of national literary consumption. In one or two years, between 1876 and 1877, he tripled his book production of the preceding twenty years, sending along the lines of a transcontinental railroad his reprints of "Ouida's" *Granville de Vigne* and Victor Hugo's *Hunchback of Notre Dame,* William Black's *In Silk Attire* and Bulwer-Lytton's *Eugene Aram.* In this particular enterprise of providing railroad literature for a Railway Age he should have succeeded, for a mass market was developing for his cheap reprints for the train. Other factors intervened, however, and instead of the success that was due him for his astute seizure of America's moment, failure lay in wait for Frank Leslie.

The crisis of seventy-seven broke in upon America's exuberant seventies and upon the *annus mirabilis* of a publishing magnate. Real estate values had declined, and Leslie had made imprudent speculations at Saratoga and elsewhere. Promissory notes could not be collected. The circulation of his periodicals had fallen off. The sumptuous *Historical Register of the . . . Centennial* proved a heavy trade loss. The expensive editorial staff, the purchase of a press for nearly $70,000, the enormous sums spent upon diamonds and Worth gowns for his fashionable wife, as well as the cost of the great transcontinental excursion—all contributed to the decline and fall of the grandiose prince of Pearl Street, who had provided railroad literature for a nation on coach wheels.

Early in September Frank Leslie was forced to make an assignment of his property, for the benefit of his creditors, to Isaac W. England, publisher of the *Sun.* A committee appointed to investigate Leslie's affairs reported that he had been overdrawing his account for some time and recommended that five trustees should control the business, the publisher to receive only twenty per cent of the profits. His publishing house would be restored to him within three years from January 1, 1878, or sooner if his debts were paid before that time. Meanwhile he would act as general manager of the establishment he had founded.

His humble status did not last long. On March 20, 1879, Frank Leslie entered into a composition deed with his creditors, who agreed to accept the payment of fifty per cent of the balance of his debts as full settlement of the claims against him. By January 10 of the following year the publisher had paid thirty-five per cent of that fifty per cent balance, leaving a debt of only about $100,000. Doubtless in a short time, with the help of the growing demand for railroad reading, he would have recovered his business. The dynamic publisher's hopes were thwarted, however, for on that very day—January 10, 1880, Frank Leslie died.

To his brilliant and seductive wife, now assigned the unaccustomed role of widow, he left his debts, his business, and his name, bequeathing to her the challenge to pay the first, continue the second, and vindicate the third. She accomplished all three in a style worthy of a nineteenth-century *grande dame* and Napoleon rolled into one. Borrowing $50,000 from a philanthropic woman, she paid the last cent due to her creditors on May 23, 1881. On June 4, the Leslie property was transferred by the assignee to Mrs. Leslie, who promptly changed her name, at a special term of the Court of Common Pleas, to "Frank Leslie." From that time on the magnate of Publishers' Row and the purveyor of railroad literature to a nation bore a man's name but was in reality a beautiful and fascinating and apparently ageless woman. With the help of the Garfield assassination—an event which she seized upon with ruthless determination and prompt decision and regaled in all its gory detail to a sensation-hungry public—the new "Frank Leslie" was able to pay the $50,000 debt to her benefactress before the first installment was due.

The second "Frank Leslie," the lady of glittering shoulders and sinuous form, fast became a legend on Publishers' Row. As queen of Park Place, where the Leslie House had removed, she fascinated a public who acclaimed her a "commercial Joan of Arc" who could wield with equal ease a drawing-room fan or a quilled pen. In a black silk or cashmere dress, she seated herself at her desk to attend to her vast correspondence, her editorial work, her dealings with foreign literary men and artists, her contracts for supplies, proofs, make-up, money orders, and checks. She overhauled and reorganized every department until her publishing house was the most effective and extensive one of its kind in the world. Sixteen presses rumbled in the pressroom; the paper consumed each year by her House would stretch to over 8,000 miles; in a week it amounted to some seventeen tons. The establishment used a miniature lake of ink, ranking third among the ink consumers of the country. Over 3,000 square inches of boxwood were needed each week, one and one-half million ems of type were set in the composing room, and every hour 1,500 wrappers were addressed in the mailing department. The aggregate circulation of her periodicals exceeded one-fourth of a million copies of each edition. Over this domain reigned the most fascinating "newspaper man" in America.

"Frank Leslie" did not abandon her late husband's interest in railroad literature. Although her experiments in that line were not so extensive as his, they are of some interest as little-known attempts at book publishing by a woman in the nineteenth century. As early as 1881 her imprint appeared on *Frank Leslie's Bubbles and Butterflies,* described by the flowery publisher as "a quite too too and too tenderly utter book for summer travellers with aesthetic illustrations to be lived up to by Du Maurier." This twenty-five-cent traveling companion was followed in the eighties by other books: *Frank Leslie's Holiday Book; Queen Titania's Book of Fairy Tales,* in an elegant illuminated cover for one dollar, *Amusing Adventures, Afloat and Ashore, of Three American Boys; Frank Leslie's Christmas Book* for 1888, also listed at one dollar, with colored plates. The Frank Leslie Publishing House, in its impressive five-story building at the corner of Park and College Place, apparently had room for a book publication office in addition to its engraving, editorial, composing, and electrotyping departments—which were all under the shrewd supervision of a woman in an immaculate French costume seated at a white oak desk. As late as 1896 the siren of Publishers' Row lent her name to *Frank Leslie's Illustrated Famous Leaders and Battle Scenes of the Civil War.*

By that time, however, the dashing Mrs. Leslie had married and divorced her fourth husband, Willie Wilde, brother of Oscar, and was soon to substitute for her absorbtion in books and railroad literature an interest in her celebrated salon, over which she reigned as Baroness de Bazus, a titulary heritage from her noble Huguenot forebears. One of the most talked-of women in New York, she continued to engage the interest of Gotham long after she had abandoned Publishers' Row. As author of a variety of books on the social scene, as hostess of a salon in her elaborate suite at the Gerlach or the Chelsea, as an intimate of foreign nobles and domestic celebrities, she held the public eye until her death on September 18, 1914.

And even after her death, her will became the topic for as animated speculation as the European war. Mrs. Leslie bequeathed the bulk of her fortune, a matter of some two million dollars, to Carrie Chapman Catt for the cause of woman suffrage. Once again her name was in the limelight. Her life was fittingly climaxed by the dramatic controversy that ensued over the terms of the will, and Mrs. Leslie would have been gratified by the excitement that attended her effective exit from this world to the next.

Her life had been no less effective than her death. With her third husband, Frank Leslie, she had typified those spectacular seventies that had followed the driving of a golden spike with a silver mallet at the meeting place of two great railroads. Both Frank Leslie and the "Frank Leslie" who succeeded him had realized the impact of the Railway Age upon nineteenth-century America. For a nation on coach wheels they had provided old wine in new bottles, by sending to the farthest reaches of the country cheap reprints known as railroad literature. They had lived and they had embodied America's splendid Railway Age, and for the needs of that age they had helped provide books that would transform train carriages into firesides. In the wake of the railroad kings came the publishing magnates, knitting the nation together with the literature they purveyed. With the help of the one, nineteenth-century America learned to run upon the coach wheel. With the help of the other, nineteenth-century America learned that he who runs may read.

XV. IMMIGRATION & THE BOOK TRADE

Ernst Steiger

GERMAN-AMERICAN PUBLISHER

TO COMPLETE the herculean task of building a transcontinental railway, about ten thousand coolies were imported from China in one of the many mass immigrations that enriched America throughout the nineteenth century. From about 1820 until after the turn of the century immigrants came, in varying and swelling tides, escaping from religious persecution or military service or poverty, seeking in their place freedom of worship, a peaceful and democratic society, opportunity and wealth. During the first half of the century they came, as Robert Fergus, James Redpath, and Frank Leslie had come, from the British Isles; or, as Anton Roman had come, from Germany. During the later decades of the century they poured into the country from the villages and farms of Italy, Austria, and Poland. For them all, whatever their origin, the New World became the Promised Land, the "Mother of Exiles" who raised her shining lamp beside "the golden door." And the New World in turn became the "Melting Pot," simmering with immigrants who transformed the face of the nation, until the very name *America* became a synonym for those heterogeneous, teeming masses who had adopted a country and claimed it for their own. In time immigration would become a "problem," and restrictions would be imposed that dimmed the promise of the Promised Land; but now—in the mid-nineteenth century—the door stood open and the lamp shone bright.

They brought more than their strength and their skills to their new country, those immigrants streaming from across the seas. They laid the tracks for the great transcontinental railroad, but they brought more than the product of their physical toil to the country that welcomed them. They brought to it their songs and their music,

233

their color and their beauty, their wit, their romance, their scholarship. They brought, too, the reminder that native Americans were descended of immigrants.

Sometimes a wave of immigration rose to a crest after a foreign revolution, and in the decade after the Revolution of 1848 in Germany, the tides of newcomers swelled with the German men and women who had hoped to trade oppression for liberty, poverty for riches, a limited outlook for the larger opportunities of the New World. Migrating to the United States, they brought with them their physical strength, their intellectual cultivation, the color of their foreign background. Most important of all, they brought with them their transcendent purpose—to leave a country already shadowed by Teutonic militarism and to embrace a country dedicated to the individual man whoever or whatever he might be.

For the liberty of this larger opportunity, one such German crossed the seas in 1855. His journey took him from Leipzig to Liverpool, where he embarked on the *Baltic;* on the twenty-first of February he landed at New York's Canal Street dock. Although he was only twenty-two years old, he was well endowed not only to face the New World but to enrich it, for he brought with him a fluency in many languages and a deep admiration for the country he would make his own. He could teach America much of the languages and ways of the Old World, and at the same time he could teach the immigrants who had preceded him and who would follow after him the language and the literature, the customs and the laws of their adopted country. Such were his desires and his purposes, and for their execution he held in his hands the most powerful of weapons —books that advanced understanding. For Ernst Steiger was a bookseller and a publisher as well as a German immigrant. The books he sold and published would be, for the most part, the books that helped America to understand immigrants and the books that helped immigrants to understand America. Upon this dual purpose his long career was founded. An immigrant who worked both for immigrants and for the country they had adopted, Ernst Steiger, dealing in the printed word, was prepared to heighten the promise of the Promised Land.

A farmer's son, he had been born in Gastewitz, a small village in Saxony, in October, 1832, and his early interests and pursuits conformed to the pattern that moulded the careers of many immigrant

German bookdealers of his time. After his studies in Dresden and a short period in high school the boy was apprenticed, in 1848, to the book jobbing and commission firm of Bernhard Hermann in Leipzig. The terms of his five-year apprenticeship were simply stated by his employer: "You pay me nothing and I pay you nothing." The terms covered the hours from seven to twelve and from two to six. First as errand boy and later as clerk, Ernst Steiger familiarized himself with the workings of the House, which acted as packing and forwarding agent for out-of-town retail booksellers and as distributing agent for out-of-town publishers. At the same time Steiger's ambition was fired to found in the future a "renowned international book establishment." To prepare himself for the fruition of his dream, he systematically devoted his free time to the study of languages: Italian, Bohemian, Russian, French, English, Latin, and Greek, and in 1853 he moved on to Dresden, entering the retail business of Woldemar Türk, who was to characterize him as the "perfect example of employee" who would become the "perfect example of employer."

The groundwork had been laid, the pattern set, the characteristics moulded. Ernst Steiger demonstrated early in life those typically Teutonic interests and abilities that he would shortly apply to his career in America. He had a genius for unremitting toil and methodical industry; upholding Carlyle's doctrine of work, he used every moment unsparingly, wringing from it some small measure toward the advancement of learning. His business was and would be his prime joy, and he would sit happily at his desk for the many years ahead, priding himself on taking no vacation from the work that was his life. He did not drink or smoke or keep late hours in company. He was systematic and economical. He had been born a bibliographer, a master of detail, and his interests in language, bibliography, and education would not only dominate his career for the remainder of his long life, but provide him with the means for increasing the mutual understanding of Americans and foreigners. A man of strong, positive character, he would plod along a straight and narrow and Teutonic path toward the fulfillment of a dream. It was America's good fortune that the dream was a wise and fruitful one, for Ernst Steiger was a man of purpose whose dream was destined to be fulfilled.

With the arrival of a letter in December, 1854, from Steiger's former employer, Bernhard Hermann, the dream began to take shape:

There will be a vacancy, in February, in the business of my brother-in-law, Bernhard Westermann, in New York, which I am called upon to fill. I offer you this position. Three years' contract; free passage; salary, first year, 400 dollars; second and third years, 500 dollars.

My advice is: You accept this position.

Steiger's reaction was overwhelmingly favorable. His ambition had been to establish a book house in Europe, in England or France, Italy or Russia, Austria or Hungary. He "had not dared to think of America. Now the offer came from there; it was too good, and even before reading the letter to the end I had decided to accept." The offer, moreover, had come from B. Westermann & Company, a German-American firm established in 1848 and one of the earliest and best-known importers of books in continental languages.

Armed with his ambitions, fortified with his systematic perseverance, Ernst Steiger landed in New York, one of some 70,000 German immigrants who arrived in 1855, and was received by August Buechner, Westermann's partner. To improve his English conversation, he boarded with an American family in Brooklyn. To increase his general language abilities, he attended courses in French and Spanish at the Mercantile Library. For his Sunday morning walks he selected a companion with whom he could converse in French, Spanish, or English, and in the evenings he worked alone at the store or in his room in the interests of Westermann & Company. Westermann appreciated his labors and returned the compliment by making Steiger a silent partner in the concern when the young man announced that he intended starting into business for himself. Yet, his ambitions could not be stilled.

In September, 1863, while a member of Westermann's firm, Ernst Steiger struck the first blow toward an independent career. From his friend, Frederick W. Christern—who had formed the firm of Garrigue and Christern, foreign booksellers in New York, and who had employed the young immigrant, Frederick Leypoldt—Steiger purchased a small German News Agency which had been established as early as 1852. Christern, who had taken over the Agency at a sheriff's sale in part satisfaction of a loan, gave notice of the transfer:

. . . I have this day sold the German News Agency, Bookselling, and Publishing Business, located at No. 17 North William Street, up stairs, which has, since May 10th, 1861, been conducted by Mr. Joseph Wieck, as my Agent, and for my sole account, together with all the debts due to the said business to Mr. Ernest Steiger, of this city.

From September, 1863, until February, 1864, the business was managed by Joseph Wieck, acting as Steiger's agent, while Steiger himself divided his time between Westermann's and 17 North William Street. In February, 1864, the German News Agency was metamorphosed into the firm of E. Steiger, who would "endeavor by prompt and careful attention to the interests of his correspondents to give complete satisfaction to all who might favor him with their orders." Although Steiger continued to work for Westermann until the last day of 1865, his own long-lived firm would be dated from 1864, when the upstairs room of 17 North William Street, opposite the office of the Loyal Publication Society, took on the name of its actual proprietor. At the end of 1865, after the close of the Civil War, Steiger finally left Westermann's and took over his Agency completely, arriving there at seven every morning and remaining there till six at night. It had been run up to that time with the assistance of three employees. Within five years it was to develop into a business that boasted a personnel of ninety.

The history of his firm is far less significant than the story of his publications; yet it, too, was inextricably interwoven with the annals of the small but important group of German bookdealers who emigrated to America in the period that followed the Revolution of 1848. For a time Steiger handled the German textbooks of S. R. Urbino, who had started in business with the purchase of Elizabeth P. Peabody's famous circulating library on Boston's West Street, an early and colorful meeting ground of Europe and America—and the name of Elizabeth Peabody would reappear significantly in Steiger's career. Decades later Steiger was to purchase the German book business of L. W. Schmidt of Barclay Street, one of the oldest concerns in New York's German book trade and a well-known importer of European literature. At the end of the century when Lemcke and Buechner transferred their export department to Ernst Steiger the circle would be completed, for Lemcke and Buechner had once been known as B. Westermann & Company. And so, his career is linked with the first German-American booksellers who supplied their patrons through direct communication with Leipzig and other European publishing centers, and who began the circulation of German books in America. Steiger was one, not of many, but of few—a small group of German immigrants who gave to their new country as much as they took from it, for they happened to deal in books that gave voice to an international exchange of thought.

From 1864, the date that appears below his device that bears a pen crossing a sword with the motto in German: "The pen is mightier than the sword," almost until his death shortly after the United States entered the First World War, Ernst Steiger continued in a business that furthered that international exchange of thought. His firm history, during his lifetime, is briefly told, for it includes but three removals and one fire. In 1869 Steiger moved to Frankfort Street, one door east of William Street, not far from the *Sun* Building, French's Hotel, and the office of the *New-Yorker Staats-Zeitung,* "where with better facilities and an ever-increasing stock of German Books And Periodicals," he was enabled "to fill all orders with the greatest promptness and regularity." By 1872 his "ever-increasing stock" was matched by a personnel of some one hundred twenty assistants, including about sixty clerks. Six years later he carried his business to 25 Park Place, a "spacious and advantageously located building," where his now huge stock could be properly displayed, and there he remained until the move in 1910 to Murray Street. The small upstairs room on North William Street had been transformed with the years into a bustling emporium thronged by German or American writers with manuscripts, exponents of the latest concepts in German-American literature, news agents, expressmen, and messengers —all personally supervised by Ernst Steiger. The Steiger co-partnership, E. Steiger & Company—largely a family affair—was formed in 1880, and in 1898 the proprietor celebrated his fiftieth anniversary as bookseller and publisher, dating his jubilee from the year of his apprenticeship in Germany. Not until 1915 did he resign as president of the company he had founded, when he was succeeded by his son and transferred much of his attention to the Steiger Trading Company for general commercial development in Mexico. During all those years Ernst Steiger, German emigrant to America, had lived the fulfillment of a youthful dream. He had established in New York an international book concern that became a meeting place for Europe and America, a common ground for the exchange of ideas in print. By his importations and his publications he had advanced the mutual understanding of Germans and Americans so that immigrants would learn to know their adopted country and Americans would learn to know the foreigners who had made that country their own. This he had accomplished primarily through the books he published and sold—books that were designed either for the German emigrants to the New World or for the Americans who welcomed them there.

To answer the needs of German immigrants in America, especially of those who ventured to this country in the decade following the Revolution of 1848, Ernst Steiger published books that were by, for, or about those newcomers to the Promised Land. The so-called German-Americans, many of whom had brought to the New World a background of culture and learning, needed a medium for self-expression. They found it in Steiger's establishment, for he was ever eager to publish books by German-Americans or by Germans familiar with America. To his office on North William Street and later on Park Place they brought their manuscripts, sure of a favorable reception, and by publishing their works Steiger filled a double need, providing the authors with the means of being read, providing readers with a fund of information about the New World. As early as July of 1864 the publisher announced that he was "ready to make arrangements for the publication and sale, on commission, of German Books And Pamphlets. His connections with all the dealers in German Books throughout the Union offer unsurpassed facilities for giving new publications the widest publicity. He has his own printing-office, with new German types, and can bestow especial care upon correct composition and good printing." The "Typographical Composition of matter for publication in the German Language" would be "executed in the best style" in Steiger's printing office, where electrotype and stereotype plates were prepared and careful and reasonable presswork and pamphlet binding were assured. He was liberal in the payment of "honorarium and royalties" and "careful in the get-up of his books, all of which were printed from plates." "I acted upon the principle," he announced, "not to publish a book or pamphlet that was not worth making plates of."

Reflecting such methods and principles, Ernst Steiger's office became a kind of headquarters for German authors in America or for German authors familiar with America. For them he published his *Deutsch-amerikanische Bibliothek,* a collection of ten volumes by

Reinhold Solger, Karl Dilthey, and Friedrich and Rudolph Lexow, literary romances and novels priced at fifty cents in paper and seventy-five cents in boards, many of which had some bearing upon life in America. Over Steiger's imprint in 1867 appeared *Californien* by Karl Rühl, who had been a journalist in San Francisco for about ten years, and who proceeded to supply German-Americans with an account of the social and political, commercial and industrial life of California. Like Rühl, Theodor Kirchhoff had settled in San Francisco, and his *Reisebilder und Skizzen aus Amerika,* emerging from Steiger's office, supplied a lively account of the Mormons and the Northwest, the Pacific and Texas. German travelers in America found a mouthpiece in Steiger's press, from which rolled accounts of Rudolph Schleiden's journeys through the United States, in which that German diplomat in Washington strove for a better understanding of American life by providing information about the states and territories of the West. The German poems of Konrad Krez bore the self-explanatory title, *Aus Wiskonsin,* and Steiger was never reluctant to publish the verses of his fellow German-Americans, issuing an anthology of *Heimathgrüsse aus Amerika, Dornrosen,* the first collection of German-American lyrics, as well as the poems of Johann Straubenmüller, who exalted in his lines Washington's birthday, a flower from Lincoln's grave, and the Fourth of July, besides translating into German the poems of Longfellow and Poe, Emerson and Whittier. Indeed, in most of Steiger's German publications there was usually embedded substantial information about life in the New World. His publications for the Deutschen Gesellig-Wissenschaftlichen Vereine von New York included discourses on the city's public schools, Johns Hopkins University, and the life and work of Franz Lieber. *Steiger's Illustrirter Volks-Kalender* for 1865 and subsequent years was an illustrated German almanac designed for "all classes of Germans" in America, for a free people; it covered the history of the Civil War and statistics of the United States, as well as details about German consuls in America. Alexander Schem's *Deutsch-amerikanisches Conversations-Lexicon,* many volumes of which appeared over the Steiger imprint, was far more than a dictionary, for, written with the co-operation of German writers in America, it became a cyclopedia of information vital for Germans living in America.

As Steiger published the books of German-Americans about

America in general, he published another type of Americana more closely related to the lives of German emigrants to the New World —books about the newcomers who had made the Promised Land their own. In May of 1870 he announced that he was offering a prize of $800 for the best historical sketch, fifty pages in length, octavo in size, on the subject of the independent intellectual life of Germans in America, with special reference to the German-American press and its influence upon the development of ideas in the Union. Among the judges were Oswald Ottendorfer of the *New-Yorker Staats-Zeitung* and Willy Wallach, Commissioner of Emigration. Through the years Steiger published and continued to publish the books that would display to German-Americans the part that they themselves had played in evolving a free America. His *Bilder aus dem Amerikanischen Leben von Deutschen in Amerika* consisted of two important volumes: Johann Rittig's *Federzeichnungen aus dem Amerikanischen Stadtleben,* pen sketches of German-American city life, and Stürenburg's *Klein-Deutschland,* pictures of everyday New York customs. Gustav Körner's work on the German element in the United States covered the period from 1818 to 1848 and included the history of Germans in most of the states and sections of the Union, while Rattermann's history would be restricted to the annals of the German element in the State of Maine.

Perhaps the most important of Steiger's publications about German immigrants and their history in the United States was the two-volume *Geschichtsblätter* edited by Carl Schurz. The Germans, according to Schurz, having migrated to America and settled there as simple immigrants, were immediately conscious of a strong community spirit among themselves. They had lost their political connections with the old country, and their interests in the New World were familial rather than national. Language differences increased their isolation from the political development of the United States, and the German group was soon reduced to a minor position in American cultural and national life. By the second third of the nineteenth century, German migrations had brought to this country only a small number of educated men who could give to the German element in America its rightful place in the new land. The two hundredth anniversary of the first German settlement in Pennsylvania had, however, aroused a new interest in the history of German immigration, which had given rise to the publication of new and valuable works in the field. Such was the purpose of the *Geschichts-blätter,* which would epitomize for the present generation of German-Americans, through biographical sketches, histories of individual communities, and stories of remarkable incidents, the part their forebears had played in the development of the New World.

Schurz's promise was borne out in Steiger's publication. The *Geschichtsblätter* included a new and revised edition of Friedrich Kapp's *Die Deutschen im Staate New York,* which Steiger had originally published in 1867 as the first volume of a history of German immigration in America. The work revealed the history and character of the German immigrants in New York State, covering their role in the American Revolution as well as the lives of such notable German-Americans as Nicholas Herkimer and John Peter Zenger. As the second volume of the *Geschichtsblätter,* Steiger published Oswald Seidensticker's *Bilder aus der Deutsch-pennsylvanis-chen Geschichte,* a history of German immigration in Pennsylvania from the time of the settlement of Germantown in 1683 to the end of the Revolution, with colorful accounts of Franz Daniel Pastorius and Christoph Sauer.

At the same time as Steiger published such volumes as these, calculated to stimulate a pride in the part that German immigrants had played in their adopted country, he issued, for The German Society, Anton Eickhoff's all-inclusive volume, *In der Neuen Heimath.* The German Society, founded in 1784 by Baron Steuben, existed to protect the interests of German immigrants and was actively supported by the German-American book trade in general and by Ernst Steiger in particular. As he had been secretary of the German Society for the Benefit of Widows and Orphans, and of the German Lieder-kranz, he also served as secretary of The German Society, and in conjunction with their one-hundredth anniversary, Steiger issued for that Society Eickhoff's record of German immigration in the United States, a work that covered the historical and statistical annals of over three million German-Americans in nearly every state of the Union.

It was for The German Society also that Steiger published a book that played a significant part in the lives of Germans in America. As he had lent his imprint to books by German-Americans and to books about German-Americans, so he placed his device upon books designed for German-Americans, and particularly for German-Americans to learn something of American customs and citizenship. The *Praktische Rathschläge und Mittheilungen für deutsche Einwanderer* consisted of a body of information assembled by The German Society for German immigrants. It covered almost every need of German-Americans, from their voyage across the seas to regulations for the inspection of immigrants, from rates of money exchange to immigrant trains throughout the country. And its map of lower New York marked the location not only of The German Society and the German *Emigranten-haus,* but of Steiger's *Deutsche Buchhandlung.* From Steiger's press appeared other volumes designed to enlighten German newcomers about life in the New World, from Drebing's treatise on common law in the United States to Luther Cushing's work on parliamentary law. And, in 1888, the publisher turned author on behalf of his fellow German-Americans by collaborating with Caspar Stürenburg in editing a volume of *Auskunft und Rath für Deutsch-Amerikaner.* Consisting primarily of answers to questions that had been posed in the *New-Yorker Staats-Zeitung,* the book contained a variety of useful information for the daily life of Germans as yet unfamiliar with American customs. From the history and laws of the United States to the rights and duties of citizens, from business and exchange to postage rates, from internal revenue taxes to civil service rules, from marriage and divorce laws to United States passports, the *Auskunft* was a mine of information for German immigrants in America. Steiger had not only published it but helped edit it as well, for who was in a better position to understand the needs of German-Americans than a German-American who happened to be a publisher?

There were other books that German-Americans needed, and these, too, Ernst Steiger was quick to provide. One of their prime needs was obviously related to language, and Steiger's press proceeded to fill that need. Supplying to the trade a wide range of English grammars for Germans, and English and German dictionaries—"the best books for Germans to learn English"—he published one of the most valuable works in the field, *Ahn's American Interpreter* "for Germans To Learn English Without A Teacher." As Steiger announced, "It *sells in large lots* because it is not only for Germans recently immigrated and for laborers, factory hands, and other servants [sic], but also for others who have been in this country some time already, and who think they can speak English.

. . . It is useful also for American employers of immigrated Germans." It was so useful, indeed, that it was succeeded later on by *Ahn's New American Interpreter,* "an *up-to-date* edition at a *very low* price, of our Interpreter which has been so favorably known throughout the United States and Europe, for decades, in consequence of its great practical value for Germans intending to emigrate to this country and also for immigrants not yet conversant with the English language."

The needs of German-Americans were not entirely filled by books that taught them American customs and the English language. The generation of immigrants, of which Steiger was one, needed books that provided them with study and enjoyment not only in their role as German-Americans but in their role as Germans. The process of assimilation would take almost a generation to complete itself, and while they were learning the American way of life, the newcomers needed study and diversion as Germans. By 1866, with the increasing German emigration to America, German schools had sprung up all over the country and were playing such an important part in the educational system of the United States that Ernst Steiger could announce:

There is at present a large and very rapidly increasing demand for School and Academic Textbooks and works of General Literature in the *German language.*

Numerous responsible persons, in all parts of the country, are turning their special attention to dealing in the same.

German Schools and Literary Organizations are so rapidly springing into existence that this department of publication must ere long become of far greater importance than heretofore.

For the German schools in the United States Steiger proceeded to publish German textbooks. "I strive," he declared, "to meet all wants of the German Schools of the country." By 1870 his German schoolbooks were in such demand that they netted him nearly $14,000 a year. For those schools he published Deghuée's *Arithmetic* in German and English on opposite columns, as well as Reffelt's series of primers, copybooks, and readers which "by a Committee of Teachers . . . appointed to report upon the various German School Books, was pronounced The Best. . . . they have been introduced into almost all the German Schools of the Eastern States, as

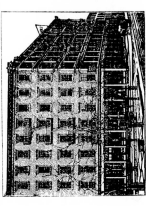

LONDON (ENGLAND) OFFICE:
2 DEAN'S YARD,
WESTMINSTER, S. W.

LOVELL'S AMERICAN NOVELISTS.
LOVELL'S POLITICAL & SCIENTIFIC.
LOVELL'S LITERATURE SERIES.
LOVELL'S FOREIGN SERIES.

LOVELL'S INTERNATIONAL SERIES.
LOVELL'S OCCULT SERIES.
LOVELL'S ILLUSTRATED SERIES.
LOVELL'S AMERICAN AUTHORS.

JOHN W. LOVELL COMPANY,

PUBLISHERS.

LOVELL'S RUGBY 12-MOS.
LOVELL'S RED LINE POETS.
LOVELL'S STANDARD SETS.
LOVELL'S MISCELLANEOUS WORKS.

LOVELL'S LEATHER-CLAD TALES.
LOVELL'S DETECTIVE SERIES.
LOVELL'S STANDARD 12-MOS.
LOVELL'S OXFORD 12-MOS.

TEN DIFFERENT SERIES PUBLISHED REGULARLY WITH PAPER COVERS.

New York, 774 .... 189c

LOVELL LETTERHEAD SHOWING NEW YORK AND
LONDON OFFICES

NEW YORK:
142, 144, 146, 148 AND 150 WORTH STREET,
AND 3, 4, 5, 6 MISSION PLACE.

POST OFFICE BOX: 1892.

STEIGER ESTABLISHMENT, ABOUT 1868

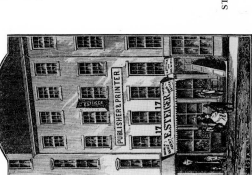

PUBLISHER & PRINTER

17 17

E. STEIGER

INTERIOR VIEW OF APPLETON'S BOOK STORE ABOUT 1855

THE COUNTING-ROOM OF THE HARPER ESTABLISHMENT

also into many of the West." Reffelt's arithmetical aid and fractional frame, Grauert's readers, Douai's *Turner-Schulbücher,* all rolled from Steiger's press onto the desks of Germans in America who were studying their lessons in the German schools in America.

Both German-American children and German-American parents needed entertainment as well as instruction, and this Steiger also supplied. Often purchasing the copyright and plates of German books, he offered, for the enjoyment of Germans in America, books in the German language. One "Library" after another appeared over his imprint: *Steiger's Haus-Bibliothek,* a fifteen-volume collection of novels by Brachvogel, Hartmann, Grimm, and others; *Steiger's Deutsche Bibliothek* in two hundred numbers; *Steiger's Humoristische Bibliothek,* priced at $6 the year for fifty-two numbers and including the humorous tales of Hackländer, Honthumb, and Friedrich Gerstäcker, whose *Flatbootmann* had appeared over Steiger's imprint, as well as one number in Plattdeutsch. For the children Steiger issued not merely textbooks but over thirty volumes at twenty-five cents each of *Steiger's Jugend-Bibliothek,* a charming series of "strictly moral, but entirely unsectarian" tales for children bound in illustrated covers and offering the stories of "W. O. von Horn" [Wilhelm Oertel] about Benjamin Franklin, John Jacob Astor, and the burning of Moscow. For the whole family the firm provided in time *Steiger's German-American Cookbook,* elucidating the mysteries of "cooking in the thrifty German manner . . . with due regard to American market products."

In his capacity as publisher alone Steiger could not, however, satisfy all the literary needs of Germans in America. To supply books for their enjoyment, therefore, he imported on such a vast scale that his office became the central depot, not only for all the German books published in the United States, but for foreign publications as well. Not without reason he boasted that "I have business connections with Germans in all parts of the Union, and have secured the assistance of all dealers in German books, by becoming their New York Agent, and in making my establishment the central depot for all German books published in the United States. By these connections I am enabled to aid, to no inconsiderable extent, the sale and introduction of any book published in the German language." As special agent for Brockhaus in Leipzig, as well as for other large German firms, Steiger could offer their publications along with his own. His popular importations came from Germany by steamer every week, semi-weekly, and even three or four times a week, until this German News Agent, Importer and Bookseller, Publisher and Printer could advertise "The Fullest and Best Selected Stock of German Books In All Departments," "the largest *retail* stock of German books in the world" selected for the most part "with special regard to the Wants of Book-Buyers in America"—so extensive a stock that it attracted customers from all parts of the country. With the aid of his one hundred and twenty assistants he carried on, it was said, "the largest German publishing and bookselling business out of Germany," keeping the *"largest Stock in America* of German Books" and advertising the "Quickest Importation" either direct from the publishers in Germany or through his agents in Leipzig and Stuttgart.

It is little wonder that his store was a scene of intense activity at all times, where news agents brushed shoulders with authors and expressmen with messengers. For out-of-towners who could not browse in person through his tremendous stock, Steiger issued catalogue after catalogue of the books he could supply. Catalogues of medical literature and theology, philosophy and pedagogy, the theater and gift books flowed from his office until Steiger had spent $50,000 issuing them and could offer an "elegant Patent Self-Binder" to hold them. A Guide through Steiger's stock of German books consisted of an alphabetical index to about eight hundred departments and specialties. He could announce for sale a German circulating library containing five thousand volumes. General agent in the United States for the most important German political newspapers, he could also offer periodicals of every variety, from *Leslie's Illustrirte Zeitung* to the *Deutsche Roman-Zeitung.* There was little in the line of German books and periodicals that Steiger could not supply. From the cheapest editions of pocket-size standard German books in paper covers priced at five or ten cents to superbly illustrated gift books, from German plays for amateurs to German almanacs, Steiger's emporium was the headquarters in America. And if one type of almanac needed at home was not available from abroad, Steiger simply published it himself, issuing his own *Jahrbuch der Deutschen in Amerika.* Beginning in May of 1869 he also published a *Literarischer Monatsbericht,* or monthly record of recent German publications "designed to be a Continuous Monthly Register of the movements in the German Literary and Publishing World, and in German Journalism." The first publication of its kind on this side of the Atlantic, 19,000 copies were sent free "to all who desire to receive it," and it listed a variety of publications, all of which the indefatigable Steiger could supply.

In one volume of Alexander Schem's *Deutsch-amerikanisches Conversations-Lexicon,* a section was devoted to the accomplishments of Ernst Steiger. Since Steiger published that volume, there is little doubt that he saw and approved the passage devoted to himself. There it was stated that among his greatest achievements might be counted his publications that helped Germans understand American customs, his publications that revealed the literary accomplishments of Germans in America, and his publications that advanced the interests of German-American culture. Through his books by, for, and about German-Americans, Steiger had fulfilled these purposes. The books that bore his device of the sword crossed with the pen had taught German immigrants to know themselves and to know their adopted country. He had given them a medium for self-expression, and he had given them the means for understanding themselves and their new land. He had accomplished an end more than sufficient for one career and one lifetime. Yet, Steiger's task, as he saw it, was not finished. For the circle of understanding would not be complete until he had helped Americans to understand the foreigners who flocked to the New World.

As he had sold and published books to overcome the language barrier of Germans, Steiger also published books that would teach Americans to understand German. He strove unceasingly to encourage the study of German in public schools until in 1869 he could state that it was "a branch of study which is constantly receiving increased attention from the American public, and now required by law in several States." When, in 1875, a mass meeting was held at Cooper Institute to discuss *The German Language in the Public Schools,* Steiger was on hand to publish the addresses delivered. He was on hand, too, to provide texts for such instruction—a wide variety of "Books for Americans Studying the German Language."

The works of Johann Franz Ahn, Doctor of Philosophy at the College of Neuss, had been published by John Weik of Philadelphia, with whom Steiger's friend and colleague, Frederick W. Christern, had been connected. Now Steiger took over the numerous Ahn textbooks revised and edited by Henn or Fischer "to fulfil the requirements of the most rational graded course of instruction, . . . in the Public Schools of New York City." From his press were issued *Ahn's New Practical and Easy Method Of Learning The German Language, Ahn's Rudiments of the German Language,* Grauert's *Manual of the German Language,* Deghuée's German readers, to which was added *Steiger's Colloquial Method of learning the German Language.* "Though well aware that there is no 'royal road' to German," the publisher announced that he had "at least endeavored to offer a road which is free from needless difficulty, and as easy as it can be made by the aid of suitable typographical arrangement." Indeed, it was, he boasted as early as 1867, "in consequence of his sending out a few specimen copies" of *Ahn's Rudiments* and *Method* that those works had "recently been largely introduced into Public Schools and Private Institutions in various parts of the country." And for students who could not "procure the assistance of a teacher," *Ahn's New . . . Method* might be followed "with perfect confidence that, by paying proper attention thereto, they will acquire a correct pronunciation of the language and be understood wherever German is spoken." Steiger's German Series of Ahn's texts was designed "to furnish young learners . . . with such an available means as shall give them a fair mastery of German for the ordinary uses of life," and the Ahn-Henn German Course, it was declared, met "the expectations of the friends of German instruction" since it combined "all the qualities needed to make the study of German easy and popular. . . . No other method . . . can present so many acceptable arguments in favor of the continued study of the language in the Public Schools." Produced with "a special view to the requirements of American schools," Steiger's German Series along with his German script charts did much toward breaking down the language barrier between native Americans and German immigrants during the 1860's and 1870's.

There were other ways also through which Americans might be taught a more complete understanding of the foreigners in their midst. Time and again the industrious Herr Steiger spoke or wrote on the repeal of duty on foreign books, the reprinting and circulation of German books in America, the copyright law of the United States. Although in time he favored international copyright, he did not believe that manufacture in America should be an essential part of an international copyright grant. The contention of German authors and publishers that American publishers were guilty of literary piracy in reprinting non-copyright material was, he held, unfounded. To *The Evening Post* he addressed a letter, signed "Progress," in which he advocated "in the interest of the scholars and other persons in this country who must keep themselves informed of the progress of science and literature abroad, and who, therefore, require foreign publications," the removal of the twenty-five per cent duty on all foreign books. From the viewpoint of the German-American publisher, Ernst Steiger, imported publications were not luxuries but necessities, and levying a duty upon them was "entirely out of keeping with the free, liberal, and advanced institutions" of the United States.

In line with such principles Steiger published and served as general agent in the United States for many volumes of the monthly journal, *The Workshop . . . Devoted to Progress of the Useful Arts*. A translation of the German *Gewerbehalle,* the periodical, copiously illustrated, introduced Americans to the latest developments in ornamental and useful arts as practiced in Germany, from book binding to mural painting, from the decoration of firescreens to the manufacture of bedsteads. The periodical was one more means of extending mutual understanding between Americans and Germans.

Perhaps the most effective aspect of Steiger's long struggle to advance that understanding arose from his profound interest in the theories and practices of the German educator, Friedrich Froebel, inventor of the kindergarten system. Through the publicity he gave to that system, paying for it at his own expense, and through the books he imported and published, Ernst Steiger was largely responsible for the spread of Froebel's "New Education" throughout the United States, and thus he introduced yet another connecting link between Americans and Germans in the New World.

Froebel's kindergarten system, "analogous to the treatment of plants by a skilful gardener," aimed to develop the child in a natural manner and to educate simultaneously the head and the hand. By issuing leaflets and tracts, catalogues and pamphlets, many of them for gratuitous distribution, Steiger helped to introduce the "New Education" into the United States. At the Philadelphia Centennial Exhibition his collection of kindergarten material was awarded a medal and, in time, educators could obtain from Steiger's establishment all the kindergarten "gifts" and "occupation material"—much of it designed and manufactured by the publisher himself—that advanced the Froebel method. Beads and blocks and crayons, tablets, pegs, and rings, spheres, cylinders, and cubes, paper frames and Leporello Books—all the attractive materials and devices for paper-folding, modeling and ring-laying, weaving, plaiting, and cork work—were supplied by Steiger, along with the terrestrial and celestial globes of Joseph Schedler, until it was said that

> After many years of earnest labor for the introduction, into this country, of the Kindergarten system, E. Steiger has now become the largest publisher of Kindergarten Books and Material in America. All his productions are the direct issue of Froebel's own ideas or the results of thoughtful study by Froebel's pupils.

Froebel's pupils were often spurred to set their ideas to paper, and they doubtless could be found scurrying with their manuscripts under their arms to Herr Steiger's office. They were sure of a favorable reception, for the publisher, announcing "Books and Pamphlets Published and Sold on Commission for Authors, Societies, etc.," stressed his particular predilection for "Books . . . of interest to the educational . . . public."

> It is hardly necessary to say that printing and binding a book and making it ready for the market comprise but a small portion of the expense and trouble attached to its successful publication. To the mere mechanical labor succeeds the necessity of making the book known and creating the desired demand for it. This is a work that can only be properly done by a publisher whose connections enable him to secure for the book general attention and a positive market.
>
> The fact that large educational interests and information centre in the establishment of the undersigned is sufficient to assure authors of meritorious educational works that their interests can best be furthered by such a connection.

Froebel's pupils were inclined to agree with Steiger. When Elizabeth P. Peabody returned from a European tour in the course of which she had studied the kindergarten method, she revised her *Guide to the Kindergarten and Intermediate Class* to exalt Froebel as *"the discoverer of the method of Nature"* and submitted the work to Ernst Steiger, who published it along with her sister, Mary Mann's

Moral Culture of Infancy. Many of the Froebel disciples were, of course, like Steiger, German-Americans, and their studies found a hearty acceptance at his establishment. From his press was issued as a series *The Kindergarten Guide* of Maria Kraus-Boelte and John Kraus, who had established a model kindergarten in New York that combined the methods of Pestalozzi and Froebel. Matilda H. Kriege's *The Child, Its Nature and Relations* was published by Steiger to elucidate Froebel's principles of education—"a subject, almost new to this country"—and particularly his motto, "Come, let us live for our children!" The publisher of that work, which was a free rendering of the German of Baroness Marenholtz-Bülow, declared that he

is resolved to expend his best energies in the interest of Education. He has witnessed with lively satisfaction the progress of education in this country; but while appreciating the good that has been done, he agrees in the opinion of many that the system at work is susceptible of improvement. He has embraced the cause of the Kindergarten System, therefore, as best calculated, in his judgment, to inaugurate a thorough educational reform; and he will gladly entertain proposals for the publication of other valuable works on the subject.

Volume after volume elucidating the "New Education" of Froebel appeared over Steiger's now familiar imprint, from Matilda Kriege's biographical sketch of Froebel to Alma Kriege's *Rhymes and Tales for the Kindergarten and Nursery,* from Heinrich Hoffmann's *Kindergarten Toys* to *The Kindergarten. A Manual for the Introduction of Froebel's System* by Dr. Adolf Douai, founder of the first American kindergarten in Boston (a private school for Germans), whose work was enthusiastically endorsed by Elizabeth Peabody in a letter to the publisher. Douai's rational readers, combining the Pestalozzi and Froebel methods and introducing the "developing system of instruction, as practiced in the best Swiss and German schools," found a ready publisher in Steiger, as did Watson's *Manual* of musical calisthenics and Jane Hoxie's *Book of Programs.* For his Manual Training Series he published *Steiger's Elementary Sewing Designs,* containing object teaching charts and actual practice cloth and colored threads—an animated book in every sense of the word. Through his series of *Papers on Education* the publisher mined yet another educational source that revealed to Americans the progress made by Germans in kindergarten instruction.

Perhaps his most ambitious undertakings in the educational field were the works edited by Henry Kiddle, city public school superintendent, and Alexander J. Schem, assistant superintendent. Their *Cyclopædia of Education* began with a flourish. "The first three printings," Steiger declared, "sold remarkably well, and it looked as if the publisher would become a rich man through this book. But then there came a financial panic, with a scarcity of money that nearly killed bookbuying. To add to this . . . Henry Kiddle avowed his adherence to spiritualism and made himself impossible as City School Superintendent. He resigned, and that discredited the book." Before that unhappy outcome, however, Steiger had also published, as a supplement to *The Cyclopædia of Education,* the Kiddle and Schem *Year-Book of Education,* the contributors to which included Elizabeth Peabody and Mary Mann, as well as the Kiddle and Schem *Dictionary of Education,* for which "propositions from booksellers, agents, and others intending to thoroughly canvass certain limited territory" were invited.

There is no doubt that Ernst Steiger's office had become a headquarters not merely for German immigrants but for German and American educators as well. To advance still further the mutual understanding of Germans and Americans and to give yet another impetus to progressive education in the United States, Ernst Steiger set up in his publishing establishment a Free Educational Bureau. In the early 1870's he announced that

having established a Free Bureau for suiting Kindergarteners and German Teachers with situations, and supplying Schools and Families with Teachers of the German and other Modern Languages,

teachers and kindergartners in search of positions should answer application Form *A* and private persons and corporations in search of teachers should answer Form *B,* both supplied by Steiger. In 1878, when he moved to 25 Park Place, he reminded the public that he was

enabled to make additions to the various Departments of his Business and would call attention to the fact that, . . . he has established a Free Educational Bureau, through the medium of which Teachers and Kindergartners desiring positions, Institutions needing Teachers, and Parents or Guardians seeking information respecting Educational Institutions or Private Teachers, may all be accommodated—without being charged the customary fee.

Steiger's own *Educational Directory For 1878* advertised the Educational Bureau, where application forms were filed and free access to them was given to principals of educational institutions, parents and guardians. By the end of the decade Steiger's establishment on Park Place bustled with activity, between the calls of Froebel disciples with manuscripts and teachers and kindergartners seeking positions. Steiger's Free Educational Bureau, the proprietor announced, "is accommodating *Teachers* and *Kindergartners* with positions, *Schools* and *Colleges* with Teachers and Professors, *Parents* and *Guardians* with Tutors and Governesses . . . *all without charge* to any party." What is more, Steiger himself was not merely proving that "as faithful service may be rendered in the publisher's office as at the teacher's desk," but was helping Americans to understand and appreciate the direct contributions made by Germans and German-Americans to progressive education in particular and to the cultural development of the country in general.

The circle of his twofold purpose was all but complete. Through the books he published and imported, Steiger had increased the mutual understanding of Germans and Americans until each could "assimilate what is best in the other." His aims, however, were still more ambitious and far-reaching, for Steiger believed not only in the exchange of German-American ideas, but in an international exchange of thought. "Steam and electricity," he agreed, had "brought the extreme ends of the Earth nearer together," and "the whole human family" had been "drawn more closely together." Publisher and bookseller were both, "in a peculiar sense, conservators of an advancing civilization. Upon no other department of purely commercial enterprise do the enlightenment and intelligence of the world so largely depend. It is especially through their active agency that a continued impulse is given to all educational interests; and to their method of adapting the means and capacities of trade to the needs of the people much of the intellectual progress of the world is due. . . . The publisher, . . . has for his sphere of action the whole world." Ernst Steiger recognized the all-important fact that "an exchange of international thought is as necessary as the establishment of international commerce," and to advance that international exchange of

thought he embarked upon publishing projects that would help all
the foreigners of the world to understand Americans.

Especially effective in fulfilling such a purpose was Steiger's grandiose design of collecting and exhibiting at the Vienna Exhibition
of 1873 the periodical literature of the United States. The enormous
task of assembling six thousand specimen copies of American periodicals was undertaken single-handed, without remuneration, and
at a personal expense of $5,000 by the untiring publisher. Journals
from nearly every state and territory of the Union were collected in
one hundred nineteen uniform volumes to demonstrate to the European world that

whatever military hectors . . . may think to the contrary, 'the pen is
mightier than the sword.' . . . At least so in the transatlantic country of
liberty, whose population of forty millions needs an army of only
30,000, but enjoys . . . the luxury of 8000 periodicals.

Eight thousand periodicals are issued between the Gulf of Mexico
and the great Canadian Lakes! . . . Spaniards, Portuguese, Frenchmen,
Italians, Bohemians, Scandinavians, Poles, Russians, Welsh and Dutch,
have their papers printed in their own vernaculars, wherever their immigration has formed large settlements. Of all these periodicals the
Steiger Collection exhibits about three fourths.

The gigantic enterprise, undertaken to inform the world of the "extent, power and influence of the American Periodical Press, the
young but sturdy outgrowth of the free institutions of this country,"
succeeded, taking not only Europe but America itself by surprise,
"pointing as it did to the fact that, in numbers at least, the Periodical
Press of this country stands at the head of the World." For his monumental work in promoting the international exchange of literature,
Steiger was awarded the Medal of Merit and the Order of the Crown
as well as, later on, the Order of Franz Josef, replicas of which were
soon placed beneath his device of the pen crossed by the sword. But
Steiger did not stay to rest upon his laurels.

Teutonic in his love of systematic bibliography, he proceeded to
catalogue *The Periodical Literature of the United States of America*,
complementing the actual physical collection he had amassed for
the Vienna Exhibition, and including a polyglot index that ranged
from Accidents to Zoology, Adventists to Yachting, and Ale to
Woman's Rights. In conjunction with this work Steiger attempted

also "a small specimen catalogue of original American works" for the purpose of "drawing the eyes of the whole world to the value— hitherto mostly underestimated—of original American books other than works of poetry, fiction, education, & c." In 1873 the attempt was so far ahead of its time that it was destined to failure. Of over two thousand applications for information sent to American authors and publishers, only three hundred succeeded in eliciting answers. Yet, Steiger's specimen catalogue of American books, despite the fact that it remains merely a miscellaneous and incomplete specimen appended to his catalogue of periodical literature, was a noteworthy and early attempt to prove that "There are many American Books . . . so *interesting, important, special* and *unique,* . . . that there would . . . be a considerable demand for them in foreign countries, if public attention were there properly directed to them." As Steiger, the German-American, working in the then comparatively "barren field of American bibliography," was one of the first to attempt a catalogue of Americana for European enlightenment, it was left to another foreigner in America, the Polish Leon, to produce the first catalogue of American first editions.

In addition to his descriptive catalogues designed for circulation in Europe and America, Ernst Steiger entered the field of "International Publishing," offering to authors his services and facilities "for *publishing* on commission (for their account) *their writings* in book or pamphlet form. By means of our extended connections we can make such publications known, and forward them to the booksellers, . . . not only in America, but also in all parts of Europe."

Translation naturally became a significant factor in Steiger's international publishing schemes. "The American Copyright Law," he announced,

is such that any one may make and publish a translation of any book that he may see fit.

There are hundreds of American books . . . that could be translated into German with decided advantage and sure profit to their proprietors. . . .

In view of the growing demand for books of this kind I have secured the services of competent translators, who will work under my immediate supervision. The books can be stereotyped or electrotyped from *new and elegant German Type,* in my own establishment, and the proof read by me personally.

To testify to his "superior facilities for translating, printing, binding, and selling works of this kind," Steiger referred his customers to a letter from Benjamin B. Russell & Company of Boston, affirming that

Mr. E. Steiger has furnished us, ready for the press, the plates of a German translation of Mrs. Hanaford's Life of Abraham Lincoln. He has had the entire matter in his hands, has acted judiciously in selecting a competent and able translator, and had the plates ready before the time agreed upon. His charges were moderate.

In his efforts toward the international exchange of ideas, Steiger worked not only as publisher but as bookseller. As he had imported books for Germans in America, so he also exported American books for foreign circulation. As American agents for hundreds of booksellers in London, Paris, Brussels, Rotterdam, Leipzig, Vienna, St. Petersburg, Moscow, Stockholm, Copenhagen, Athens, Rome, and Cape Town, Steiger & Company solicited prospectuses and catalogues of important new books and periodicals that were likely to find a market abroad. American periodicals and books were exported "to the Continent of Europe" at first twice a month and later every week, and arrangements were made for exchanges with European journals and literary institutions. Steiger's deliveries by steamer were made "both ways," and he could declare that he brought before the European market American books and periodicals "at a much lower price" than had heretofore been offered by way of England. By 1899 his company announced that they "are now the only firm in America making weekly shipments of American books and periodicals to Germany and all the northern, eastern, and southern countries of Europe."

One particular publication undertaken in 1879 by Steiger bears full evidence upon its title-page of the international character of his establishment. Hermann Schumacher's *Petrus Martyr, Der Geschichtsschreiber des Weltmeeres* carries the imprint of Steiger of New York, the publisher's former employer, B. Hermann of Leipzig, Sampson Low of London, Gaspar y Alba of Madrid, Hoepli of Milan, and Hachette of Paris. Moreover, the work itself, having what Steiger called "peculiar attractions for all interested in the history of the discovery of America," served to make foreigners aware of American traditions and hence understand them.

After 1880 the emphasis on German immigrants in America was giving way before other mass immigrations. As a result of this, and perhaps also of the recent Panic, the demand for German importations slackened in the United States. Several German periodicals were suspended, many newspapers were merged with others, and their circulation decreased considerably. Steiger, whose stock of German books was therefore "larger than necessary," turned his indefatigable efforts toward providing the needs of other emigrants to this country. Books were imported not merely from Germany and Austria, but from Switzerland and England, France and Spain, Portugal and Italy, Belgium and Holland, Denmark and Sweden, Russia and Brazil, Japan and Turkey, Egypt and the East Indies. When necessary, orders were sent by cable, and through Steiger's agents in every major city of the world, from Warsaw to Bucharest, from Calcutta to Shanghai, works were imported to meet the needs of the teeming tides of new emigrations to the United States. The languages that could be studied from Steiger's texts came to include Bohemian and Bulgarian, Danish and Dutch, Hungarian and Italian, Swedish and Polish, Russian and Servian, Czechoslovakian and Roumanian, Spanish and Turkish, Chinese and Japanese, as well as the French and German and Hebrew that had been carried before. By 1903 books for learning more than two hundred fifty foreign languages from Abyssinian to Zulu-Kaffir were kept on hand, and his emporium featured books for Dutchmen to learn English, for Bohemians, Roumanians, Hungarians, Italians, Poles, Portuguese, Russians, Spaniards and Swedes to learn English. For Spanish immigrants Brockhaus's *Coleccion* of "Autores Espanoles" was circulated and Steiger's *Kindergarten Manual* reappeared as the Spanish *Manual Steiger*. Hebrew prayer books, Bibles, schoolbooks, and publications "for the use of Jewish children and of students of Hebrew" were supplied, and at length the firm could even offer textbooks in the universal languages of Volapük, Esperanto, and Ido.

Foreign language texts and the polyglot books that facilitated the exchange of international thought continued as the specialty of the Steiger House until the First World War. The proprietor, who had married "as early as his circumstances permitted" Bertha Krehbiel, the daughter of a prominent German physician, had proceeded to train his children to take part in his enormous business. But with the First World War, and especially with America's entrance into the war, the Steiger emporium suffered a felling blow. "Empty benches" confronted "teachers of the German language all over the United States," and instruction in that tongue declined until it was near the vanishing point in elementary classes. Steiger & Company, no longer able to import German publications regularly, announced in 1917 that

Importations of foreign books and periodicals are, in consequence of conditions, which have arisen in the course of the last two or three years, subject to more or less delay, if at all feasible. . . .
Import orders are accepted only subject to delay and possible loss in transit at purchaser's risk.

On August 2 of that year, not quite four months after the United States had entered the war, Steiger died at the age of eighty-four. His firm continued in existence until, in 1934, it filed a petition of bankruptcy, after which it was reorganized as The Steiger Company. If the First World War had crippled the firm, the Second apparently delivered the death blow, for not long after the suicide of Ernest Steiger, Jr., in 1943, the concern, after nearly eighty years of active business, disappeared from publishing annals.

Its founder had received many honors and distinctions in his day, but the medal of merit and knightly crosses he was awarded are but scant testimony to his actual accomplishments. A German immigrant in the United States, he labored untiringly for the advancement of mutual understanding between Germans and Americans, and for an even broader exchange of international thought. He helped to overcome the barriers of foreign emigrants to the New World and to increase American understanding of foreigners. His publications remain his greatest distinctions, for they exalted the promise of the Promised Land.

XVI. THE ADVANCEMENT OF LABOR & WOMAN'S RIGHTS

John W. Lovell

HIS SOCIAL CONSCIENCE

THE mass immigration which enriched this country so magnificently during the nineteenth century created its problems, too. Primarily they were problems of labor, for the immigrants, often content to work at cheaper rates, for longer hours, and under the most devastating conditions, were a source of keen competition to native workers. But immigration was only one factor that governed the needs and the welfare of labor, and competition was only one of its many problems. The lack of regulation of wages and hours and working conditions, the disapproval of labor unions, the scorn for any combination of labor, the exploitation of women and children were major problems of the nineteenth century. Against such abuses the workingmen and idealists of the country gradually took their stand.

The rights of labor, and with them the rights of women, became causes to which crusaders flocked. The Noble Order of the Knights of Labor under the leadership of Terence Powderly agitated during the 1880's "to secure to the toilers a proper share in the wealth that they create." Henry George, struggling to uphold the Single Tax, announced that there was "but one way of solving the labor question, . . . and that is by securing to all men their inalienable right to live and to work," an end that could be accomplished only by "abolishing the private ownership of land." Co-operative settlements, organized by visionaries and socialists, were formed basically to "dignify labor, to abolish the curse of wage-slavery," and to give to men and women equal pay for equal work as well as an equal voice in the government. The Sociologic Society, founded by a group of women, propagated the "principles of co-operation," raised the standard of the productiveness of labor as the measure of reward, and asserted that the "community is responsible" for the condition of its members. The Twilight Club discussed over its convivial dinners the future of the labor movement, strikes, and trade unions, while the Manhattan Liberal Club, affording a platform for the exposition of new ideas and the exchange of free thought, took time to consider a co-operative colony that would serve as the "model to a better system of government when the great revolution so rapidly approaching demands a change." In cheap books that could be circulated among the masses, the Labor Library of the Socialist Labor Party incorporated volumes that strove for the rights of labor and the rights of women. And gradually, after violence and strikes, organization and legislation, by the early part of the twentieth century the basic rights of both had been at least potentially assured.

Perhaps one of the greatest paradoxes that evinced itself in the struggle for those rights was that the crusaders emerged not only from the working classes themselves but occasionally from the ranks of the capitalists. For, when their altruism had possibilities of boomeranging to their own advantage, or, more infrequently, when their social conscience made itself felt, the capitalists sometimes rallied to labor's standard and preached the cause of woman's rights. The wide circulation of cheap books that advanced those causes might profit the men who published them, for example, as much as they benefited the masses for whom they were intended. It is perhaps a typically nineteenth-century paradox, therefore, that one such publisher, who gave a greater impetus than had yet been given to the printing and distribution of cheap books, raised his voice in the cause of labor's rights and woman's rights and lent his presses to their advancement. For John W. Lovell, the publisher, was not only a capitalist, but a "plunger," a business magnate, a "Svengali" in commerce, who was accused from time to time of piracy and sharp practice and who organized one of the largest and most extraordinary book trusts in the history of publishing. But he was also a socialist who became a prime mover in a co-operative colony in Mexico, and he was a theosophist who dreamed of Universal Brotherhood. He was a member of the Twilight Club that cogitated the labor problems of the day, and before the Manhattan Liberal Club he delivered an address on the co-operative city where work would be "made honorable in both sexes." He was, depending upon

who considered his many-faceted character, a schemer or a visionary, a capitalist or a socialist, a juggler of millions or an idealist.
Actually, he was all of these, for John W. Lovell, book trust organizer and publishing mogul, was also the man who distributed
cheap books on the rights of women and the rights of labor among
the millions. A man of perfect self-confidence, whose powers of
persuasion were rendered almost irresistible by his personal mag-
netism, John W. Lovell, genius of finance, ambitious, grasping,
greedy, had also been endowed with a social conscience. He was
a nineteenth-century phenomenon and in his colorful career were
embodied the paradoxes of his age. The story of his business empire
is as interesting as the story of his social conscience. But it was the
latter that gave an impetus to reform and so made its mark upon
history.

John W. Lovell was born in 1851 with printer's ink in his veins
and the hum of printing presses in his ears. His father, John Lovell,
had founded the Lovell Printing and Publishing Company at Montreal in 1835—an establishment still active today as John Lovell &
Son. As publisher of the first Canadian Directory, pioneer in Canadian schoolbooks, and importer of the first steam press into Canada,
he became a resourceful master to his many sons, including the
versatile and ambitious young John Wurtele Lovell. After instruction at Miss Fisher's school on Aylmer Street and at the high school
affiliated with McGill University, the boy, aged thirteen, was apprenticed to his father to learn the printing trade. By the time he
reached his majority he had learned more than enough to manage
the vast establishment planned by his shrewd and enterprising father
at Rouses Point on the American-Canadian border.

The buildings of Lovell's Lake Champlain Press on the border
would eventually cost over $60,000, and the presses, types, stereo-
type apparatus and bindery material would approximate another
$100,000. The establishment on the banks of Lake Champlain would
give employment to at least five hundred persons and, since it was
located on the American side of the boundary line, it would be "an
American industry, planted on American soil." By 1873 the plant
was in operation, printing the sheets of British copyright works in
the United States and circulating them in Canada through the Montreal firm. It took no time at all for the founder to be accused of
the " 'cute' dodge" of defrauding "the revenue of both countries"

and underselling "all the traders who pay their honest dues." Lovell, who paid the required duty on American reprints at the Canadian customhouse, replied to the "unsavory slanders" and "offensive libel" and blithely continued to operate the five-story factory where, in time, over eight hundred people were employed in typesetting, plate-making, printing, and binding good books at cheap prices. The plant, equipped with foundry and electrotyping apparatus, also boasted an auditorium and running track, and soon became known as the largest New York printing and publishing establishment north of Albany. As manager of the Rouses Point branch, John W. Lovell was gaining experience in the conduct of enormous publishing enterprises. He was his father's son, however, and therefore could not linger long in an establishment founded by another. Versatile, aggressive, visionary, he determined to go forth and shape his destiny as publisher in his own right.

His capital consisted of experience, youth, and energy when, having married and declared his intention of becoming an American citizen, John W. Lovell set up the New York firm of Lovell, Adam & Company in 1876. With G. Mercer Adam of the Toronto wholesale bookseller-publishers, Adam, Stevenson & Company, young Lovell and his father formed a co-partnership for the purpose of reprinting British copyright books in editions priced as cheaply as possible. From the very beginning of his career, therefore, Lovell recognized the importance of the wide distribution of cheap books both to the publisher and to the masses of readers. "One feature," it was announced,

which will steadily be kept in view will be the issue of all works at as cheap a retail price as will be consistent with the expense of their production.

Lovell, Adam & Company was shortly transformed, by the admission of Francis L. Wesson of the Springfield small arms manufacturing firm, into Lovell, Adam, Wesson & Company, publishers of the Lake Champlain Press Series and re-issuers of English and foreign classics, with branches in Montreal and Rouses Point, and offices at 764 Broadway. Yet even this association seemed too confining for the ambitious Lovell. By 1877 the co-partnership had been dissolved and John W. Lovell, aged twenty-six, was really on his own, ready to make publishing history.

There is no doubt that, when he opened his office on New York's Bond Street as a publisher of books the following year, he began business as a pirate. Actually, the publishing scene was such that, endowed as he was with aggressive and ambitious plans, he could do nothing else. Although the cost of production had fallen, the established publishing houses still maintained "war prices" for the books they printed. They upheld their exorbitant rates by means of the "Courtesy of the Trade," an agreement among the principal publishers that secured to one of them the exclusive right to reprint certain English or foreign books. By a " 'priority claim' advertisement" of their intention to reproduce a specified work, the publishers obtained a monopoly on the reprint rights, a monopoly that was respected through "Courtesy of the Trade." In the days before international copyright, therefore, the business of publishing strikingly resembled a "close corporation" whose members had no intention of admitting outsiders into their self-satisfied ranks. Faced with such a situation, John W. Lovell determined to make a new departure in the publishing field by the wide circulation of cheap books. His plans served a double purpose. He would make sizable inroads upon the sales of the long-established publishing houses, and at the same time he would bring within the reach of the masses the best literature of the time.

In order to do so, however, he was forced to the piracy of reprints. Beginning with what he advertised as the first American edition of Charles Knight's *Popular History of England,* he extended his list until it included cheap editions of Dickens and Thackeray, Coleridge and Milton. A variety of inexpensive series rolled from his presses: The Popular Twelvemos, Standard Histories, Caxton Classics, and Lovell's Editions of the Poets. Observing that most of the cheaper editions of such books were imported from England, he

determined to issue them here in such styles, and at such prices as to render their future importation unnecessary and unprofitable. Possessing extensive works at Rouses' Point, N.Y., he has made entirely new electrotype plates of the books, thus keeping many people employed in making plates, paper, printing and binding.

Accused of sharp practice, he could retort that he was simply encouraging "home manufacture." Condemned for cut-throat competition, he replied that "only an international copyright based on the royalty scheme can find favor with the people of this country. Cheap books are what are wanted, and if we can give cheap books and at the same time fairly remunerate foreign authors for their brainwork, the desired end is attained. . . .

Go in heartily for the 'courtesy of the trade' and—starve. . . . I prefer to follow the examples that led to success in the past."

The royalty scheme of copyright which Lovell advocated at the time was, he declared, a protest against the monopoly of any one publisher in the works of a given author. A ten per cent royalty would give the author "a fair remuneration," and the competition thus allowed for would keep the price at the lowest possible figure. The same publisher, he reminded his attackers, could print both a fine and a cheap edition from the same set of plates. "I believe," he announced, "with the late Charles Knight that the mass of the people should be our first consideration, and our aim be the diffusion among them of the best literature at the cheapest possible price." The young publisher's royalty scheme of copyright was scorned as the creed of the "Revolutionists" and branded as "legalized freebooting." He himself was charged with violation of rights on several publications, with outright piracy, and with a "preference for printing unauthorized cheap editions of such works as have been tested at the risk . . . of authorized publishers." Moreover, his proposals to pay royalties were frequently greeted with hints that his proposals had never been realized.

There is no doubt that there was some justice on both sides. There is even less doubt that John W. Lovell gained for himself, almost at the beginning of his career, an "unenviable notoriety" that is difficult to equate with his developing interest in the welfare of the masses. He was aggressive and irrepressible. He was also plausible and magnetic. By 1881 he had failed in business, but by the next year he had reorganized as John W. Lovell Company, and the man who had first appeared in New York as a pirate was on his way to becoming one of the largest distributors of important books at cheap prices that publishing history had ever witnessed.

The year 1882 was a significant one in the career of John W. Lovell, for it saw the inception of what he called Lovell's Library, a series of cheap paper books priced at ten, twenty, or thirty cents, and destined to exert a powerful influence upon the reading habits of the masses of people in the United States. The type would be larger, the print clearer, the paper better than in the cheap series that had preceded it. The size would be "more pleasant and convenient to handle." The "handsome paper cover" would make each issue "worthy of preservation." The contents of each number would be taken from "the vast field of Fiction, including, besides all the Standard works, the best current Literature of the day: the leading works in History, Biography, Travels, and Belles-Lettres." Announced as a weekly publication, the series grew until, as a tri-weekly, it included by 1890 nearly 1,500 numbers. Moreover, by one of his cleverest coups, Lovell obtained for his Library a second-class postal rate that carried it to all sections of the country at the same price as newspapers. When cloth-bound issues were requested, he met the demand by issuing two editions of the same work, one in paper and another, at a slightly higher price, in cloth. In time the publisher came to be known as "Book-A-Day Lovell." He boasted a yearly sale of seven million cheap books, carried four million in stock, and actually published a new book each day. The man who had started as a literary pirate had already succeeded in eliminating some of his rivals, was gradually beginning to pay a royalty for "authorized" editions, and showed every indication that he had been born a century before his time.

There seemed no end to his expansion. In 1888 he purchased for a quarter of a million dollars all the plates and stock of the famous Munro Library. To Lovell's Library were added other series: Lovell's American Authors' Series, Lovell's American Novelists' Series, the Occult and Illustrated, the Foreign Literature edited by Edmund Gosse, the Rugby, the Universal, the Franklin, the Red Line; and many of them were "published by arrangement with the author, to whom a royalty is paid." With his brothers he formed associations or subsidiary firms, Frank F. Lovell & Company representing him in Boston as well as in New York, and Charles W. Lovell serving conveniently as president of the bookbinding firm known as the Lovell Manufacturing Company. Lovell had branches not only in Boston but in Chicago, and in 1888 he set up an office in London that was to make history on its own.

As London representative Lovell chose a remarkable young man named Wolcott Balestier, who had edited a Lovell magazine, *Tid-Bits,* and who was as richly endowed with explosive ideas as his employer. At 2 Dean's Yard, Westminster, Balestier opened the quarters that became in an incredibly short time the literary oasis of London. This slight, intense, spare and stooping, "young-old man" of the pallid complexion and deep-set eyes was destined to become the close and valued friend of Henry James, Edmund Gosse, and Rudyard Kipling, the last of whom was to marry Balestier's sister. He was destined also for an early death, and his magnificent schemes were almost all to be realized within the three years that were left to him.

On the day of his arrival in London Balestier obtained a copy of Mrs. Humphry Ward's *Robert Elsmere* from Mudie's Library and had it in the American mails that night. As a result of his enterprise, John W. Lovell became the first American publisher of Mrs. Humphry Ward, to whom he paid $500 for the honor and earned for himself the slightly altered epithet of "moral pirate." It was through the efforts of Wolcott Balestier also that John W. Lovell became the first American publisher of Rudyard Kipling and, later on, of James M. Barrie. Many of those cheap American reprints that bear the imprint of Lovell or his subsidiary firms have been invested with a considerable monetary value and have found their way to the treasure rooms of American libraries. That, however, was neither Lovell's nor Balestier's intention. Their plan was simply to offer to English authors substantial payments for the use of advance sheets of their forthcoming books. In that manner Lovell could anticipate the pirates at the same time that he salved his conscience and lined the purses of the English literati. The erstwhile pirate, Lovell, now published authorized editions by arrangement with the writers, and the little office in Dean's Yard became the source whence flowed the first American editions of some of the most important literary works of the nineteenth century.

Throughout Lovell's career his primary motive was at all times the circulation of cheap books. Cheap books were designed for distribution among the masses. And, during the 1880's and 1890's, the masses had begun to rise up in revolt. John W. Lovell enjoyed revolt and understood the masses. His humming printing presses stood ready. Although he had been accused of cutthroat competition and sharp practice, he was ready to join the forces of labor and serve as reformer-publisher to the masses.

Lovell's Library was an excellent medium in which, now and then, to include some item of revolutionary economic interest, and the publisher was aware of it. Of one such work he announced that it "has such an important bearing upon the financial and political state of the country to day that the publishers are justified in issuing it in a cheap form, thus placing it within the reach of all who are interested in the industrial problem." But Lovell was never one to concentrate his efforts in a single series, and the bulk of his labor publications were included in yet another "Library"—Lovell's Political and Scientific Series. Issued either weekly or monthly at from 10¢ to 35¢ for individual items or $5 to $15 for an annual subscription, the Series embraced "Interesting and instructive works by distinguished writers at home and abroad" published by "special arrangement with the authors." Either in Lovell's Library or in Lovell's Political and Scientific Series—and occasionally in both—appeared some of the most important labor publications of the eighties. Cheap American books, it had been noted, "would open new avenues among the poorer classes, . . . would quicken national life and educate and elevate the taste of the people." In his role as reformer, "alert to advance some movement or some society which may make mankind better," John W. Lovell seized the power afforded him by his presses and gave to the masses the books that advanced their causes.

Perhaps the most interesting of his economic publications was one that occupied twelve semi-monthly numbers of Lovell's Library and consisted of a translation of the work of Jean Baptiste André Godin, founder of the socialistic *Familistère* in Guise, France. The translator, Marie Howland, who had spent a year in Godin's community and who was a friend of Lovell, came directly to the point in her preface, which was incorporated in another edition of the work:

One of his [Godin's] radical doctrines is that the great capitalist has no moral right to use his fortune for personal aggrandizement, whether he inherited it from others or built it up himself through industrial enterprise. The fact remains the same, that it has been all created . . . by labor. . . .

That a man has not a moral right to do what he pleases with his 'own' is to-day as radical a doctrine as was that promulgated a century ago and more, that the true sovereignty rests in the body of the people.

Social Solutions, describing in the fullest detail the principles and practical applications of the Social Palace at Guise, marked, according to Lovell, "an era in the growth of the labor question. It should serve as the manual for organized labor in its present contest, since its teachings will as surely lead to the destruction of the wages system as the abolition movement lead [sic] to that of chattel slavery." It was, in short, "The Best Utterance on The Labor Question." With publisher and translator, the editor, Edward Howland, Marie Howland's husband, joined forces, declaring in an explanatory note:

The purpose of the present publication is to iterate and reiterate, to explain and re-explain, how definite and simple is the exit of society, from the cannibalistic competition of the present, to a higher form of civilization. That a new heaven and a new earth are lying at our very doors, is a truth we cannot expect those whose material existence is absolutely dependent upon the support of the present order of things, to either believe or promulgate.

The work, which appeared as a semi-monthly pamphlet at ten cents a number or one dollar complete, was arranged so that each part would form an "inside core, paged continuously from the beginning to the end, about which will be folded, . . . an irregular number of pages. . . . used for the printing of such matter, . . . as . . . will be of advantage in exciting public attention, to this most important subject." The subjects discussed were indeed important: The Co-Operative Movement At Work; The Co-Operative Traveller Abroad; The Growing Co-Operative Character of the Social Movement; The Integration of Society; The American Co-Operative Union; The Railroads And Socialism. It was clear that *Social Solutions* was designed to illustrate "Socialism In Action." "It is the distinguishing feature of the Labor Movement," Lovell advertised, "that strives after the attainment of a social state for every human being, such as shall be the healthy stimulation of all his good qualities." Lovell had shown courage in undertaking its publication, and was proud enough of his part in the distribution of the work among the masses to permit his efforts to be trumpeted abroad:

. . . when it first appeared in French, it seemed the most important duty to translate it into English. . . . To find some publisher who should look upon its publication as a pleasant duty, was the impossible task undertaken at that time. This was some dozen years ago. . . .

It was hopeless to find, in all these years, a publisher. One house announced it as in preparation, but soon abandoned the idea of issuing it, on the ground that the *Labor Question was too exciting.*

Finally, however, Mr. Godin himself agreed to advance the cost of an edition, should it be necessary, and Mr. John W. Lovell, who had identified his house with the effort for the establishment of Integral Cooperation, . . . took an active interest in the publication of "Social Solutions," as the manual of the new philosophy that holds out such definite and cheering promise of a new life for organized labor.

As Lovell himself put it,

Though the translation of this most important demonstration of the new life for labor was announced when it was prepared, by one of the chief publishers of this country, . . . it remained in manuscript until, in the course of events, a more progressive publisher was found.

That Lovell was a "progressive publisher" was, if anything, an understatement. Over his imprint appeared some of the most revolutionary labor tracts of the times. *Integral Co-Operation* by Albert K. Owen, socialist, engineer, and friend of Mexico as well as of Lovell, outlined a fiery doctrine:

The peon system has been abolished by law just as our slavery system has been; but both in Mexico and the United States the law is one thing and the practice quite another. There are gangs of chained negroes driven to work, to-day, in the pine lands of North Carolina. . . .

Negroes in the south and the wage slaves of the north have no power to exercise their rights to vote against the dominant whites in the one instance or against their employers or taskmasters in the other.

Labor And Capital by Edward Kellogg showed succinctly "how and why capitalists get so large a part of the yearly productions of labor, and why the producers get so small a part." It asserted that "The laboring classes of all civilized nations have been, and are, as a body, poor. Nearly all wealth is the production of labor; therefore, laborers would have possessed it, had not something intervened to prevent this natural result." Kellogg's solution, a new monetary system, was hailed by Wendell Phillips as the "easiest . . . remedy for our troubles and dangers."

Other remedies and points of view were advanced in other Lovell publications, from John A. Grier's disquisition on *Our Silver Coin-*

age to Kemper Bocock's *Tax The Area,* from Goldwin Smith's *False Hopes,* which laid bare all the fallacies in the various plans for "emancipating labor from the dominion of capital," to Cook's *True Solution of the Labor Question.* Socialistic and co-operative commonwealths were analyzed at length in the paper-backed issues that appeared over Lovell's imprint. In *Socialism,* by Starkweather and Wilson, "Every important phase of the great labor movement which now shakes the foundations of the world is here for the first time in one brief essay presented to the public." The authors waved a crimson banner, declaring that "The thoughtful men of earth, . . . foresee that these questions can be decided finally and forever by no other means than by the sword of war. . . .

Let us bend every energy to the education of the people, that they may, when clangs the fateful hour, know how and where to strike for liberty or death." In the new republic of governmental co-operation, the hours of labor would be shortened with "less work for each and more work for all." The iron law of wages was castigated and "Equal Pay for Equal Time and Equivalent Services" upheld. Trade unions and strikes were advocated as a means to an end, the means being education, the end emancipation.

There never was a strike, however 'unsuccessful,' that was not morally worth millions, not only to those immediately interested, but to the remotest toiler on the world's wide rim. . . . capital (in the hands of individuals) and labor are not, and never can or will be, friends. . . .
. . . To . . . remedy these evils the abolition of private property . . . is the first necessity; the next is . . . seizure for common use for the collective benefit of the producing community.

Similar themes were pursued in Gronlund's *Coöperative Commonwealth* and Schellhous's *New Republic,* while a translation of Friedrich Engels's *Condition of the Working Class in England in 1844* offered an historical perspective to Americans of the 1880's, and "Stepniak's" *Underground Russia* reminded them that "The people themselves, rendered the arbitrators of their own destinies, can alone improve their own condition." Even a novel—*Papa's Own Girl* by Marie Howland—could be centered about the socialistic "palace" in Guise, and even in the innocuous Lovell magazine, *Tid-Bits,* "a compendium of the choicest gems of literature, . . . and humorous entertainment," there could be inserted in the same issue with palmistry and handwriting coupons a plea for trade unions as "schools for self-government and mutual self-help."

In yet another Lovell publication nearly every aspect of the labor problem was covered. Charles Wingate's edition of *Twilight Club Tracts* presented the most significant "Questions of the Day" that had been discussed by the Club, of which John W. Lovell was, of course, a member. The volume included, therefore, essays on labor, wages, trade unions, the hours of labor, the Negro and Indian problems—all the vital economic questions of the time, from social forces in the United States to the future of the labor movement.

Twilight Club Tracts included also a significant discussion of strikes and arbitration by Terence Powderly, Grand Master Workman of the Holy and Noble Order of the Knights of Labor. Lovell helped publicize the efforts of the Knights of Labor, just as he helped publicize the doctrines of the socialists. In *Social Solutions* there had been incorporated the Preamble and Declaration of Principles of the Knights, as well as Powderly's important Labor Circular.

The final section of *Social Solutions* was devoted to yet another aspect of the labor problem in which John W. Lovell was deeply and personally involved. One plank in the Industrial Brotherhood's platform called for the establishment of co-operative institutions. It is apparent that Lovell, the pirate publisher, was also a socialist. Moreover, he was an active socialist who took part in one of nineteenth-century America's most promising co-operative schemes. The scheme was elaborated in the twelfth section of *Social Solutions,* where the so-called Crédit Foncier of Sinaloa was described.

On Topolobampo Bay in Sinaloa, Mexico, a community would be established, planned by Albert K. Owen, the visionary engineer who sought to reorganize society by substituting "Integral Co-Operation" for free enterprise. The Crédit Foncier of Sinaloa meant simply that credit was based upon real rather than personal estate, and the term was used in contradistinction to the Crédit Mobilier. The city to be built on the Mexican harbor would be called "Pacific City," and there "evolution and not . . . revolution," "interdependence and not . . . independence," "co-operation and not . . . competition," "State responsibility for every person" would be espoused. An uncompromising exponent of socialism, the communal settlement would be a co-operative society, a "City of Peace by the Sea," where private interests were merged into one great system of public equity, where taxes and rent were abolished, where labor was the source of wealth and public utilities were used for the public. This New Eldorado would be a co-operative city filled with co-operative homes, co-operative factories, and co-operative farms. Since land and all other natural resources were regarded as the gift of God, they must be the common property of all.

The Crédit Foncier of Sinaloa was endowed with more than mere principles. Through Owen's work as a railroad engineer, it had concessions for railroads in Mexico. It boasted two newspapers, *The Credit Foncier of Sinaloa* edited by Marie and Edward Howland, and *The New City* edited by Albert K. Owen. It had a library— the Topolobampo Library—which included the publications of John W. Lovell. It had a Constitution, drawn up in 1886. And it had behind it a company, the Credit Foncier Company, of which John W. Lovell served as treasurer. Located at first in the Mutual Life Building and later in the Washington Building at 1 Broadway, the Credit Foncier Company published books on integral co-operation which were sold by the treasurer, who offered also, as an "Object Lesson in Co-Operation," fifty-two novels a year and a subscription to *The New City* for $1.50. The Credit Foncier Company had been created primarily to finance Pacific City and, under the aegis of Treasurer Lovell, it proceeded to offer shares of stock in the New Eldorado at $10 a share. The concessions were not to be opened for occupancy until $150,000 had been subscribed.

John W. Lovell, who helped found the community and who visited it, served it not merely as publisher and as treasurer but as author as well. Before the Manhattan Liberal Club on November 19, 1886, he delivered an address, later condensed and published by the Credit Foncier Company, entitled "A Co-Operative City," in which he described that "dream of Sir Thomas More, the hope of the Socialist, the *Ultima Thule* of those who look forward to a higher and better civilization than the world has seen." Its great aim would be to "dignify labor, to abolish the curse of wage-slavery," and insure the equitable division of profits. In Pacific City there would be the greatest freedom of speech and of thought. Doctors would work on salary. Lawyers would be almost unknown, since there would be no litigation. Work would be limited to eight hours a day. "This country could," the inspired Lovell concluded, "by making each county and municipality a business corporation organized in the interests of all the inhabitants instead of special classes, attain to a degree of prosperity as yet undreamed of. Should we succeed, perhaps our pioneer work may serve as a model to a better system of government when the great revolution so rapidly approaching demands a change." Yet again, in the supplement of his edition of Owen's *Integral Co-Operation,* the publisher elaborated the hopes and dreams of the Sinaloa experiment.

I should like to be present at that birth of a new city, destined, I believe, to play such an important part in the future destiny of this country and of the world. For if Integral Co-operation proves the success we anticipate may it not be the example that will be adopted by this country, when that Revolution comes we are so rapidly nearing. That it will be some form of Socialism is certain. . . . The plan of the Credit Foncier of Sinaloa aims at . . . giving to labor what it is justly entitled to, while, . . . holding out rewards to satisfy the most able and industrious, practicing interdependence.

To Owen, Lovell submitted his prospectus for the Crédit Foncier, suggesting, "from a business standpoint," that a joint stock company be incorporated with a capital of one million dollars in 100,000 shares at $10 each. His plans were as ever grandiose, and indeed, in the 1892 *Copartnership Directory* the Credit Foncier Company is listed with a capital of one million dollars. Had the colonists waited until a small number of selected pioneers prepared the groundwork, the New Eldorado might well have succeeded.

As it was, eager and foolish settlers rushed to Sinaloa—several hundreds of them—before the co-operative industries could be practically organized. The Topolobampo colonists, *Harper's Weekly* reported in 1887, "are a peculiar people." Dressed as Kansas farmers, they lived in tropical *casas* and tents and were called to breakfast at six in the morning by a tune on the clarinet. For eight hours a day every colonist worked for the community, receiving in return for his labor $3 in fiat money. Despite their enthusiasm, the stress of frontier life had radically reduced their ranks by 1890. By 1891, it was said, only a wharf had been constructed. Finally, alterations were made in the terms of the concessions forbidding any further co-operative experiment, and by 1895 the Credit Foncier Company had made its exit from the New York City *Directories*. In January, 1897, a curious agreement was drawn up between Albert K. Owen and John W. Lovell's wife, assigning to her, "in consideration of large sums of money which have from time to time been advanced to him" for use in connection with the Crédit Foncier settlement, one half of his interest in the Mexican concessions and properties. Lovell alone apparently refused to abandon hope in the scheme that would "help forward the evolution of our world." In 1897 he journeyed to Japan, negotiating with Mr. Komura, assistant minister to Count Okuma, "A Maker of New Japan," for the Japanese colonization of Mexico and the founding of a new Japan on the shores of Topolobampo Bay. There is no doubt that Lovell wished not only to protect his own interests in the abandoned colony but to promote yet another scheme for the reformation of the laboring world.

His career had been peppered with such schemes. Lovell, publishing magnate and socialist, was a staunch Single-Taxer as well, and in the works of Henry George he found still another means of giving to labor labor's due. As he was a friend of Albert K. Owen, he was also a personal admirer of the distinguished economist. Indeed, it was at Lovell's home that Karl Marx's daughter, Eleanor Marx Aveling, and her husband, who were to discuss "The Sinaloa Folk" in a chapter of their book on *The Working-Class Movement in America*, met Henry George. Lovell was, in addition, the first American publisher to seize the opportunity of issuing a popular-priced edition of *Progress And Poverty*. The story of the enterprise was recounted by George's son:

The English cheap edition of "Progress and Poverty" was doing so well that the author was set on a cheap American edition. He thought of importing a duplicate set of the English plates, but abandoned this to put the book in the hands of John W. Lovell, a publisher of standard books in cheap form, who had just started a serial library, with a complete book in each number. They were paper covered, compact, attractive volumes. "Progress and Poverty," . . . was sold for twenty cents. . . . Mr. George was to get ten per cent. royalty, the same as from Appleton for the better edition; but this in effect amounted to very little, for the author gave away so many copies and made such large personal discounts to those who bought quantities for educational purposes, that the Lovell edition brought small return to him, considering the great sale.

Lovell outlined the plans for publication in a detailed letter to Henry George:

We will publish in "Lovell's Library" your work Progress and Poverty, making the price 20¢ retail. We will make new electrotype plates at our own expense and in consideration of this we are to have the right to continue the publication of the work in the Library on the following conditions

That we pay to you 10% of the retail price, that is (2¢) two cents per copy for every copy sold of the work.

That we furnish to you all copies you may require for your own use, or for sale to any person or persons, except booksellers, (our agreement with the Am. News Cy who handle the Library gives them the exclusive sale to the Book and News Trade), at the lowest price we sell to the Am. News Co.

That statements of such sales shall be rendered to you quarterly, on the first days of Jany, April, July and October of each year and payment of Royalty made to you on those dates.

Should the publication of the Library be discontinued at any time, you are to have the option of purchasing the plates at a reasonable price that may be agreed upon, and it is now agreed and understood that we will publish the work only in the "Library" form and continue to do so, unless we receive instructions from you or your permission to publish in some other form.

Progress And Poverty appeared for thirty-five cents as No. 1 of Lovell's Political and Scientific Series, and also for twenty cents as No. 52 in Lovell's Library. The publisher advertised it as a "great book" treating "of the cause of industrial depression, and of increase of want with increase of wealth, and the remedy." With its discussions of wages and capital, the laws of distribution, the injustice of private property in land, George's epoch-making treatise announced that the enslavement of labor was the ultimate result of private property in land and that the "right of ownership that springs from labor excludes the possibility of any other right of ownership. If a man be rightfully entitled to the produce of his labor, then no one can be rightfully entitled to the ownership of anything which is not the produce of his labor." The author stated that he would "be glad to hear from those who share the views expressed in this book, and who desire to advance them" if such champions would address him in care of John W. Lovell Company. Because of Lovell's forthright and courageous enterprise, Henry George's inflammatory doctrine was spread among the people of this country who, at the price of twenty or thirty-five cents, were able to buy *Progress And*

Poverty in the tens of thousands. As Henry George himself put it,

"Progress and Poverty" is going magnificently. It is going better than
any book Lovell publishes, even his most successful novels. His man-
ageing [sic] man is confidant [sic] that they will sell 250 000 copies
before the rush stops.

For only ten cents the public was offered *The Land Question,* in
which Henry George asserted that landlords' right is labor's wrong
and concluded that "Until we in some way make the land, what
Nature intended it to be, common property, . . . we have not established the Republic in any sense worthy of the name." Like *Progress
And Poverty, The Land Question* appeared both in Lovell's Political
and Scientific Series and in Lovell's Library, where "the remarkable
pamphlet" was presented "to those who wish to get at a glance some
intelligent idea of theories now beginning to revolutionize thought,
. . . the low price of ten cents at which we have issued it will enable
those who have read it in its previous form to extend its circulation
among those not yet alive to the importance of the great question it
treats."

As No. 3 in his Political and Scientific Series Lovell published yet
another tract by Henry George, *Social Problems,* in which was laid
bare "the heart of all the great questions which are now beginning to agitate the public mind"; and subsequently his firm issued
George's *The Condition Of Labor,* an open letter to Pope Leo XIII,
reminding the pontiff that "men have made land private property,
and thus given into the exclusive ownership of the few the provision
that a bountiful Father has made for all."

In addition to the books by Henry George, Lovell served as publisher of a book *about* the revolutionary economist, *An Account of
the George-Hewitt Campaign in the New York Municipal Election
of 1886*—"the first serious contest at the polls between those who
aim to eradicate social injustice and those who profit . . . by its per-
petuation." While Abram S. Hewitt was, it was said, the candidate
of the class that depends for its living upon "the sweat of other
men's brows," Henry George stood as "the candidate of men who
believe that we must live by the sweat of our own brows." The circulation of the *Account* left much to be desired, however. After
forty copies had been printed, Lovell's printing press broke down,
no more were issued, and the work was then withdrawn.

Despite this misfortune, John W. Lovell had done much, through his publications, to advance the ideas of the great Single-Taxer. He advanced them also through his advertisements, for in Lovell's paper volumes, where the back covers were frequently adorned with glowing accounts of the Hardman Piano and Pond's Extract, Singer Sewing Machines and Pears's Soap, Vitalized Phos-phites and Colgate's Cashmere Bouquet, there appeared also advertisements of the publications of Henry George & Company as well as of the Hand To Hand Club, which existed for the purpose of circulating George's works. Lovell used this means to publicize many of the reforms of the day. His series carried advertisements of the Labor Library, published by the Labor News and Publishing Association and including Karl Marx's *Capital*. He advertised, needless to say, the publications of the Credit Foncier as well as the tenets of the Sociologic Society. The People's Co-Operative Supply Association or the Family Supply Union, housed in Lovell's building and aimed at the cheap distribution of commodities, found Lovell's publications an excellent medium for advertisements, as did *Truth,* the revolutionary organ of the working people of America and advocate of the rights of man in all the lands of the earth.

The "Lovell Library Advertiser" reflects clearly Lovell's political interests and reforming efforts. In the same way, a remarkable document found among the publisher's papers forms a revealing index to the questions of the day that so deeply engrossed him. It is headed "Memories," and the "Memories," listed one by one, include Socialism and the Single Tax, Mexico and Japan, Henry George and Albert K. Owen. They include also a rather unusual item, which at first glance seems scarcely compatible with Lovell's fiery and progressive interests—Theosophy. Yet the basic tenet of Theosophy was the Universal Brotherhood of Man, and so that strange faith, endorsed by the many-faceted publisher, takes a comprehensible if singular part in a life that was colored by so many revolutionary faiths and inspired by so many zealous creeds.

In September, 1875, the Theosophical Society, whose headquarters would be in India, was founded in the rooms of Madame Helena Petrovna Blavatsky. Its aims were to form a nucleus of a Universal Brotherhood, to promote the study of Aryan and Eastern literatures and religions, and to investigate the unexplained laws of nature. Of these tenets the first only was compulsory, the other two being optional. Among the earliest members was John W. Lovell, in whom, apparently, the "principle of brotherhood" had already become "so commonplace a fact of life that it had ceased to be a virtue." Lovell served the society for many years both as faithful adherent and as publisher. He was interested in "Spiritualistic Phenomena," but he was consumed with the doctrine of Universal Brotherhood. In an unusual manuscript entitled "The World Within" outlining his conceptions of the subconscious mind and the solar plexus, he noted particularly that

The trained mind knows that every transaction must benefit every person who is in any way connected with the transaction and any attempt to profit by the weakness, ignorance, or necessity of another will inevitably operate to his disadvantage. This is because the individual is a part of the Universal. A part cannot antagonize any other part, but, on the contrary the welfare of each part depends upon a recognition of the interest of the whole.

His altruism had its practical side, however, for Lovell also declared that

Self denial is not success. We cannot give unless we get; we cannot be helpful unless we are strong. If we wish to be of service to others we must have power and more power, but to get it we must give it, we must be of service. . . . we must become a channel whereby the Universal can express activity.

To his fellow Theosophists Lovell was certainly of service. For Mabel Collins, the authoress who could leave her physical body at will and who left it almost daily for the purpose of studying under an Egyptian master, he proved a ready publisher, issuing her strange tale of *The Blossom And The Fruit,* "wild in theme and rhapsodical in treatment," a story which, according to the author, had "come from a far country and was brought in a mysterious manner." There were other colorful figures who joined Lovell in the Universal Brotherhood—Emma Hardinge Britten, the spiritualist and trance medium who was used as a messenger by a group of Rosicrucians of which Sir Edward Bulwer was a member, and who was controlled by the spirits of Emanuel Swedenborg for knowledge and Daniel Webster for eloquence. And, of course, there were William Q. Judge and Colonel Henry S. Olcott, the Buddhist and mesmerist, as well as several of the Crédit Foncier enthusiasts.

When Mr. Judge informed Lovell that the work of the society could be advanced by the circulation of cheap books dealing with occultism, the publisher promptly added to his numerous series a monthly "library" entitled Lovell's Occult Series, to be issued in paper covers for 50¢ a copy or $5 a year and in cloth bindings for $1 each. "The books of the Occult Series are called forth," it was announced, "by the increasing demand for enlightenment upon occult themes." It was thought proper to add that "the authors are remunerated for their consent" to the American reprints. The first number in the Series, Mabel Collins's *The Blossom And The Fruit,* was followed in time by a succession of books all of which advanced in their astral and magical way the concept of the Universal Brotherhood of Man; and "If Mr. Lovell had done nothing else than this," the Theosophists concluded, "he had done enough to regenerate the world had the world been ready and willing to listen." *Clothed With the Sun, The Idyll Of The White Lotus, Magic White and Black, The Talking Image of Urur* all received the Lovell endorsement as well as, subsequently, the works of the remarkable Ursula N. Gestefeld, who was to transfer from the Theosophical to the Christian Science approach. The royalty offered to Mabel Collins for her *Light on the Path* evoked a response that revealed something of a lapse in Universal Brotherhood among the publishing fraternity:

I do not expect any thing at all from you for "Light on the Path" for it has already been pirated largely, and can be of no pecuniary value to you. It has never brought me a farthing, and I do not expect it ever to.

In John W. Lovell, however, the doctrine of Universal Brotherhood theosophically interpreted burned strong for many years. At a seance in 1890 the medium reported not only that the Queen of Sheba and a spirit from Arabia stood beside him, but that he could "come in communication with spirits from all the planets" if he wished. Because of his extended range of thought, he was a perfect magnet to attract spirits. The medium, possibly aware of Lovell's profession, saw, moreover,

enormous piles of paper, and different countries; France, England, and others, all round this. Mr. Lovell is inside of this, and they all go up to him; and the spirit says, "he will control them all. A second Archimedes." They show a great roll of paper, and they say, *that* is the lever. . . . The spirit now turns to Mr. Lovell and says, You will receive, through spirit power, knowledge of the planets; which you will give to the world; and would you have more?

. . . If you only make all the countries bow to this one:—and you, you, will make them by this work you have begun. This present condition must be changed. It's the great revolution that is coming;—not through swords,—but in a different manner. . . . Mr. Lovell; you are putting props under the lever all the time;—the lever that is to do this great work.

. . . When it comes, it will be like an avalanche; and it is not so far off as people think. . . .

Lovell, who certainly continued to place a variety of props under the lever, announced that he was watched over and aided in his business by a "spirit guide" named "Rosie" or "Josie." In 1896 he was admitted as a probationer to the Eastern School of Theosophy, and as late as 1913 he suggested to Mabel Collins that a *Light on the Path* bookplate be sold to all who owned a copy of the book, offering to donate his services freely "through the great love I bear you, and the debt I must ever owe to you for what this Book has been to me."

The magnanimity that Lovell displayed to one woman was simply a minor indication of the respect he fostered for all women. Every cause he had upheld, from the rights of labor to the co-operative society of Sinaloa, from socialism to Theosophy, included in its credo, either tacitly or expressly, the rights of women, and as Lovell had struggled to champion the progressive movements of his time, he labored also in the crusade for woman's rights. Among the "Memories" listed on his document of "Memories" is included Woman Suffrage and in his home, where he held seances for Theosophists, he tendered receptions to the members of Sorosis and the Woman Suffrage Society.

It was primarily as a publisher that John W. Lovell endorsed the rights of women. In his labor publications an important place was given to utterances for the equality of women, and in *Socialism* by Starkweather and Wilson it was boasted that

Socialism was the first, and is still, the only political, social, or religious organization which recognizes the perfect equality of woman with man. . . .

We . . . advocate that the conditions and opportunities for betterment shall be the same for woman as for man; that she shall receive equal remuneration for equal time and service; that every trade, profession, and occupation shall be open to her, and no other impediment or conditions imposed than those that are placed upon man, viz.: her *fitness.*

The Sinaloans also advocated woman suffrage, Albert K. Owen quoting the statement that "Liberty is always depicted as a woman. This is prophetic, for liberty will come when woman assumes her rightful place." At Sinaloa she assumed that rightful place, for, protesting against the disfranchisement of women and denouncing as "damnable any and all managements which tax, imprison and hang women to whom it denies the right of representation," the colonists of Pacific City placed the female sex on an equal level with the male—a condition that was "required by the eternal fitness of things." In his own address on "A Co-Operative City" Lovell had promised that there

Women will receive equal pay with men for equal work, and be given occupations for which they are best fitted. They will also have an equal voice in the government, enjoying the franchise equally with men, and be eligible for any office.

Even in *Tid-Bits,* and in its very first number, he incorporated among the "Miscellaneous Tid Bits" a witticism that exposed the senselessness in the disfranchisement of women, quoting a female advocate of the cause who brought down the house with her clever argument: "I have no vote, but my groom has, whose rent I pay; I have a great respect for that man in the stables, but I am sure if I were to go to him and say, 'John, will you exercise the Franchise,' he would reply, 'Please, mum, which 'orse be that?' " *Tid-Bits* could always be relied upon for its "Good Words For And About Women," but it was especially in his role as publisher of cheap books that John W. Lovell advanced their cause and helped realize their emancipation.

Lovell's Library, which had found a place for many of the cheap Lovell labor publications, proved an equally successful and low-priced medium for books that championed woman's rights. It included August Bebel's *Woman,* dealing with the legal status of women along with the social revolution and socialistic society, as well as Margaret Lee's *Divorce,* a "powerful American Novel" concerned with the problems of the "marriage state." It included, most significantly, the work of Lillie Devereux Blake, ardent and lifelong crusader in the cause. After Dr. Morgan Dix, the rector of New York's Trinity Church, had exposed his "amazingly reactionary" attitude toward modern woman in his Lenten Lectures, Lillie Devereux Blake replied to his observations in a series of addresses at Frobisher's Hall. As soon as Dr. Dix's sermons had been published by Appleton, John W. Lovell "requested Mrs. Blake's replies for publication." Prepared from her notes and from newspaper reports, the lectures were issued under the title of *Woman's Place To-Day* and, bound in cloth and in paper covers, the volume was widely sold, becoming "a handbook of arguments for woman suffrage workers on both sides of the Atlantic." Mrs. Blake, pleading a wider mission for modern women, demanded through her arguments "direct power" for women so that they could "come among men, not to sit subordinate as women so often do now, . . . but with authority." "Women in this country to-day," she reminded her public with perhaps a touch of historic licence, "are only asking for the liberties they enjoyed in Egypt 4000 years ago." *Fettered for Life* followed Mrs. Blake's lectures in Lovell's Library, while under the publisher's aegis appeared other works designed to exalt the new woman. Even a treatise on *The Woman's Club* could proclaim that "Before our civilization can progress farther, woman must be fitted to stand beside her mate and do her share." In *The Woman Who Dares,* by that theosophical incarnation of the new woman, Ursula N. Gestefeld, was incorporated the author's concept of the "broad-minded, self sufficient woman who realizes that she is a *woman first* and man's adjunct afterwards; realizes what she owes to *herself* as well as to him and is *not* content to live for him alone, the world well lost." John W. Lovell endorsed not only Mrs. Gestefeld's beliefs, but Mrs. Gestefeld herself, becoming her associate in one of his many publishing enterprises.

Although it was difficult at first to perceive in the pirate publisher of cheap reprints the exponent of a Universal Brotherhood that included a Universal Sisterhood as well, John W. Lovell frequently practiced what he preached. The publisher of revolutionary socialistic and labor doctrine applied his credo in the community at Sinaloa. The publisher of radical precepts on woman's rights would one day set up a subsidiary firm in association with a woman who upheld those rights. The social conscience that was occasionally to appear paradoxical in the future juggler of millions seemed at other times quite consistent with his personal activities. Lovell's social conscience—whether paradoxical or consistent—served its purpose, for it was surely a factor in his publication of those cheap editions of progressive volumes that advanced the rights of labor and the rights of woman and that were circulated so widely among the Universal Brotherhood of which he felt himself a part.

Some of those volumes, particularly those published between 1890 and 1893, bear the imprint not of John W. Lovell, but of the United States Book Company, Successors to John W. Lovell Company. The seemingly unimportant change in imprint actually reflects one of the publisher's most audacious schemes and one of the most amazing and significant events in the annals of American publishing. For the United States Book Company, by and large a Lovell combination, was a gigantic book trust whose history is as fascinating as any of the novels it published.

Lovell had many excellent reasons for promoting such an enterprise, although the primary one may well have been his inability to resist grandiose schemes for juggling millions. In the absence of an international copyright, the competition in cheap reprints had increased to such an extent that price-cutting was the order of the day. A book originally priced at thirty cents would appear on another publisher's list at twenty-five and shortly thereafter over yet another imprint at ten. A slot machine, in use at Long Branch, produced a book in inferior style for a nickel! One of Lovell's reasons for organizing a book trust was, therefore, to keep the publishing business from "sinking to the nickel-in-the-slot level." It was his design to draw all the publishers of cheap reprints together in one large "combine" that would concentrate the business, stabilize prices, stop the suicidal discounts along with the deterioration in quality of manufacture, pool profits, and thus end the ruinous competition that threatened to exterminate publishers of cheap paper-covered reprints. He believed, too—or declared he believed—that such a plan would hasten some form of international copyright, "for when the works of popular authors can be protected and published exclusively by a single house, the author can be rewarded by a very small addition to the cost of a book, while his publisher is unassailed by competition."

When, however, publishers refused to consolidate voluntarily, Lovell resorted to the far more drastic scheme of buying them out by purchasing or renting the plates of all available competitors. As he had bought Munro's Library, now he proceeded to buy an enormous collection of duplicate plates from one house after another until he controlled "more than one-half the yearly output of cloth-bound books handled by the trade (school-books excepted) and over three-fourths of the paper-covered books"—until, indeed, his firm had become a giant octopus regulating the majority of the cheap "Libraries." From Worthington, Estes and Lauriat, W. L. Allison and De Wolfe, Fiske, Hurst & Company, Pollard and Moss, and numerous other houses in Albany and Chicago, Boston and New York, including of course Frank F. Lovell & Company, Lovell accumulated plates, attempting to realize the supreme coup of cornering the market.

In July, 1890, shortly after the organization of the schoolbook merger, the American Book Company, Lovell's giant octopus that aimed at controlling the entire output of cheap literature in the United States was incorporated under New Jersey State laws as the United States Book Company, with a capital of three and a quarter million dollars in preferred and common stock. An additional issue of stocks and bonds was to bring the firm's indebtedness to five million dollars. Among the directors of the gigantic enterprise, of which Lovell appeared as vice-president, were Horace K. Thurber, and Edward Lange of the Trow Printing Company, which was heavily involved in the scheme. According to the prospectus,

The business of the United States Book Co. is the manufacture, publishing, and sale of books. It has acquired by purchase . . . an enormous publishing plant consisting of stereotype and electrotype plates to the number of more than 1,250,000. Its stock of books consists of more than 7,000,000 volumes, of the value at cost of manufacture of more than $1,000,000.

Reaction to Lovell's daring plan was varied. "Whatever its outcome," however, it was remarked that it gave the organizer "a strong position in the trade, and makes him at once an important figure in trade history." To some it was "one of the best things that has happened to the book trade in years"; to others it was a trust formed "for the sake of commanding the market for stolen literature." None could have failed to agree that it was one of the most important trade events of the time, whose magnitude was worthy of Lovell's overwhelming efforts and grandiose ambitions, "the most stupendous publishing undertaking which perhaps the booktrade of any country has ever witnessed." To many, certainly, it was clear that Lovell was a genius of finance who, if he wanted a quarter of a million dollars, could start the presses printing stock blanks and with a valise full of them bring back the cash in exchange for the stock in short order.

The United States Book Company, which made so flourishing a bow into the book trade, enjoyed a short but colorful history. Over its imprint appeared a wide range of Series—the Westminster and the Columbus, the Canterbury and the Metropolitan, the Leather Clad and the Seaside Library, the Oxford Edition of Twelvemos and the Universal, along with Lovell's Political and Scientific Series and Occult Series. Its standard sets formed "the Most Complete List of Standard Sets ever Published." From "Doré Gift Books" to "The Home Library" its imprints flooded the country. Under the aggressive leadership of John W. Lovell, the company swiftly acquired additional plates, controlling the various series of J. S. Ogilvie —a formidable competitor who had previously refused to enter into agreement with Lovell but who consented to do so for the price of $200,000—and subsequently becoming the agents of the Belford Company publications. In the firm's offices were trained such promising men as John Hovendon, dean of American book travelers, Alexander Grosset, and George Dunlap. In branches at Boston and Chicago, as well as in London, where plans were hatched for the first American editions of James M. Barrie and arrangements were made with Marie Corelli and Mrs. Hungerford, author of sentimental three-deckers by "The Duchess," the United States Book Company extended its far-reaching tentacles. Naturally it became necessary to meet such expansion with augmented capitalization, for it was evident to John W. Lovell that "the increase in the business of printing and selling books will be as steady and sure as the increase of the population of the country." An assessment was made on the stockholders, the Manhattan Trust Company in one of the largest personal mortgages ever put upon record in Boston lent one million dollars to the trust, and the firm's assets were placed at $5,350,000.

It had become essential that the United States Book Company, that outsize planet in the publishing firmament, form satellite firms as depots for the distribution of its books which could be numbered now in none but astronomical figures. The longest-lived of those subsidiaries was Lovell, Coryell & Company, with Vincent M. Coryell as president and offices on East 10th Street, organized in 1892 primarily for the publication of well-made books in cloth or leather, many of which were adorned with headbands and silk ribbon markers. In March of that year the new firm purchased from the United States Book Company the stock on hand and the right to publish certain of the Lovell series. Later on, moving uptown to 20th Street, it housed its stock and samples in a wareroom and boasted a million and a half books on a single floor. As Coryell & Company, the firm was to outlast the parent organization by many years. Other offshoots with less happy destinies included the Wayside Publishing Company at the United States Book Company's headquarters on Worth Street, the Seaside Publishing Company, and the National Book Company, with Edward Lovell as president, specializing in the latest copyright editions of the best works of fiction by well-known authors. John Hovendon became manager of yet another branch, the International Book Company, which was succeeded by the Hovendon Company on Waverly Place, while Frank F. Lovell served as president of the Empire Publishing Company until he subsequently founded, with his brother Charles, the Home Book Company at the old Worth Street address. Still later, Lovell Brothers & Company was organized by the family, and the Prudential Book Company was established by Frank F. Lovell, a firm that inserted slips advertising its books in packages of tea, cocoa, or coffee. One issue of *The American Bookseller* in 1892 seems to be given over entirely to Lovell enterprises, for it carries advertisements not only of the United States Book Company but of its satellites, the National and International, the Hovendon and Lovell, Coryell—an almost complete literary family tree.

By far the most interesting of the satellites was Lovell, Gestefeld & Company, a concern organized by John W. Lovell in association with his theosophist friend, Ursula N. Gestefeld. In August, 1892, the firm took great pleasure in informing the trade that they had opened an office at 125 East 23rd Street, New York, where "in addition to their Miscellaneous and Standard Works, they will make a specialty of Occult, Metaphysical and Christian Science publications, of which they will carry a large and complete stock at all times." As Lovell himself put it, "I rented a building . . . the first floor and basement for a Publishing House which I organized . . . giving Mrs. Gestefeld the upper floors for her residence and fitting up the first floor as a Hall for the meetings of her Society" (the Exodus Society for the exposition of the science of being and the leading questions of the new thought movement). It was Lovell, Gestefeld & Company which, in addition to its occult and metaphysical publications, continued to circulate the progressive labor and woman's rights tracts that had appeared in Lovell's Political and Scientific Series. Along with works on mental science and palmistry, astrology and hypnotism, theosophy and the occult, the company carried not only the free thought writings of Ursula N. Gestefeld, but the radical productions of Henry George, Edward Kellogg, and the Howlands. Transformed into the Gestefeld Library and Publishing Company, it continued to reflect "All Representative Modern Thought" until, in 1896, the firm's stock was purchased by the Metaphysical Publishing Company.

By that time the outsize bubble formed by the United States Book Company and its satellites had burst. In March of 1893 a receiver was appointed for the property of the United States Book Company, and the proceedings involved its sub-companies, whose offices were occupied by deputy sheriffs. The gradual liquidation of the United States Book Company had begun. A bonded indebtedness of one million dollars was secured by a mortgage on 1,254,000 electrotype and stereotype plates and most of the publishing plant. The stock and plates of the parent firm and its subsidiaries were sold, the receiver carrying on the business while the United States Book Company's retail and jobbing departments were gradually discontinued. Curtains were down at the great book company's establishment. It was, depending upon how the bankruptcy was interpreted, the "End of Another Dream" or the "End of the Great Book Trust." Lovell, it was said, had been over-ambitious, "continually reaching out for more, . . . congesting the plant and in many cases rendering it inoperative." In spite of his "appetite for large affairs," he had displayed a genius better attuned to "ruining than running" his enterprises. He had been both too lavish and too acquisitive. He had gone so far as to arrange with authors, "at no insignificant prices," for more than two hundred new novels in one year, a number which "might have satisfied all our publishing houses put together." None the less, there were other reasons for the demise of the enormous book trust. The passage of the International Copyright Act, as well as the Panic of 1893, had been a contributing factor, but whatever the causes, the bankruptcy of the United States Book Company marked an end both to the trust itself and to the publishing career of its founder.

Those directly involved at first refused to admit that fact. The United States Book Company was succeeded, under the direction of its creditors but without the participation of John W. Lovell, by the American Publishers Corporation, better known in Wall Street as the "Publishers' Corpse" since it had started business "with more liabilities than assets." Despite the fact that it advertised itself as "The Largest Publisher Of Books In The United States," the American Publishers Corporation followed in the footsteps of the United States Book Company, going into receivership and being reorganized yet again as the Publishers Plate Renting Company for the sale and rental of plates. In 1904 the remainder of those plates was sold at public auction by Coryell & Company, and with that transaction were buried the relics of the great book trust that had died more than a decade before.

The founder's career in the book trade was over also, although, still "full of hope, of success," he refused to concede the fact. John W. Lovell, undaunted by the history of the United States Book Company, conceived the idea of a great magazine trust and attempted to obtain a controlling interest in *Godey's*. As promoter of the so-called Auto Book Concern and as a member of Lovell Brothers, printers on Lafayette Place, with an interest in the Lovell Company on Duane or Chambers Street, he continued for a time to put a finger into the publishing pie. The plums, however, had vanished. In 1900 John W. Lovell "for many years connected with the book trade, but . . . now described as sales agent and promoter, . . . filed a petition in bankruptcy" with no assets except a lot in Woodlawn Cemetery.

He was not to occupy that lot for another thirty-two years. During most of them the man who had once earned the title of book-a-day Lovell spent his inexhaustible energies as a "real estate developer." His taste for grandiose negotiations had not diminished, for one of his final ambitions as late as 1930 was a plan for a Ford Motor Building on Times Square that would cost approximately thirty-eight million dollars—a singular design perhaps for the Crédit Foncier enthusiast and Single-Taxer.

In April, 1932, at the age of eighty, John W. Lovell died. His obituaries refer to him as the speed king of publishers, the founder of Lovell's Library, the book trust magnate who had introduced Kipling and Barrie into the United States. They had forgotten that he was also a pioneer socialist, laborite, and exponent of woman's rights, a man who gave to the masses the cheap paper-covered volumes that advanced their causes. At least one side of his many-faceted career had been dominated by a social conscience that had upheld in all its varied phases the Universal Brotherhood of Man. Through this he stakes a claim in the emancipation of the oppressed.

But in every aspect of his extravagant and paradoxical life he stakes a claim in memory. The grandiose schemer who organized one of the most audacious book trusts in history colored his times with the flash of his exuberant, aggressive, magnetic personality. The distributor of cheap books for the millions, the socialist of Sinaloa, the Single-Taxer, the publisher of works on the rights of labor and the cause of woman suffrage impressed upon his times the power of the social conscience with which he was endowed. The schemer joins the vivid, irrepressible magnates of the past. The Utopian shares a place with the idealists and visionaries of the future.

Dick & Fitzgerald

THE TROUPERS OF ANN STREET

To the nostalgic, reminiscing twentieth-century mind, the nineteenth century has become above all the time when the family was the supreme unit of the nation and the home was the hub of America. For all of its great accomplishments, struggles, and adventures, the nineteenth century has come to mean the century of hearth and home, when people were born at home, and lived at home, and died at home.

Especially they lived at home. In its kitchen they prepared the foods now lost to an impatient age, and in its parlor they assembled to seek their joys and entertainments. In memory they assemble there again—dancing their quadrilles, the lancers and the polonaise, playing their games, patience and cribbage and whist. From the kitchen they carry their home-made rum shrub, their taffy and their caramels, those "delicious cream confections," before they settle down to watch a home-made shadow pantomime or a parlor tableau entitled "Popping the Question." Around a nineteenth-century piano they gather for songs from *Tony Pastor's Bowery Songster* or the *Bones and Banjo Melodist*. Before a nineteenth-century curtain they join to applaud a parlor theatrical entitled *Ten Nights in a Barroom* or *A Dental Engagement*. And after the performance a wealth of entertainment still awaits them, from amateur magic and fortune-telling to round and forfeit games, from puzzles to recitations, from dialogues to riddles and conundrums.

From the viewpoint of its own comparative homelessness, the twentieth century so envisions the nineteenth, romanticizing the past, over-simplifying it perhaps, but drawing an authentic picture none the less. To the twentieth century that has "let others sing, dance and perform" for it and has grown "more empty" in the process, the nineteenth century in America has become this picture of a nation at home, framed in the gold of a golden age.

There is proof that the picture is authentic, and the proof lies in those well-thumbed books of parlor tableaux and theatricals, social pastimes and songsters that the nineteenth century needed for its winter evenings' entertainments. The books, indeed, are all that is left of this vanished age, and for a later time they recreate the picture, evoke the nostalgia, restore the yesterday.

For all its varied purposes and accomplishments, the nineteenth century needed and found its publishers, those dealers in the printed word who so often shaped history while they recorded it. Two of them, joining forces on New York's Ann Street, were known as Dick and Fitzgerald, publishers extraordinary to the nineteenth-century American fireside. Across the years their books still reflect the warmth and glow of a hearthfire that has turned to ash.

William Brisbane Dick was a fortunate man whose life was marked by many auspicious days. Born in Philadelphia in 1826, the son of John and Arabella Dick, he was fortunate in claiming a close relationship with Wesley Burgess, for Burgess was to become head of the firm of Burgess, Stringer & Company, publishers and booksellers in New York. Dick was fortunate, too, in his friendship with Lawrence R. Fitzgerald, born like him in Philadelphia in 1826, a young man who had received a thorough training in the mercantile business and had served as salesman with the firm of Burgess and Zieber.

On one of Dick's auspicious days in the 1840's, he ventured to New York with his friend, embarking upon what was to become a long and prosperous career. The two young men accompanied Wesley Burgess to New York when Burgess, Stringer was being organized, and they served a useful apprenticeship with a company that dealt in periodicals, music, and books of a general nature. After Stringer retired to form the firm of Stringer and Townsend, Ransom Garrett took his place as co-partner, and the two promising young men from Philadelphia were as fortunate in their connection with Garrett as they had been with Burgess. Burgess and Garrett became, after the withdrawal of Burgess, Garrett & Company, publishers of popular fiction and games at 18 Ann Street, until the "& Company" were starred in title roles and the firm became Garrett, Dick &

Fitzgerald. Garrett had only to retire for the names of Dick and Fitzgerald to stand alone in publishing history—an event signalized by the articles of co-partnership which were executed on June 30, 1858.

The New York City *Directories* of 1858/59 record the change in the firm name, listing simply Dick and Fitzgerald, books, 18 Ann Street. That narrow thoroughfare, only three blocks long and divided by Theatre Alley, was a mecca not only for gentlemen of the book trade but for sharpers, gamblers, and fireladdies. If Messrs. Dick and Fitzgerald wished diversion from their literary pursuits, they could visit Barnum's American Museum a few doors away with its famous "egress" on Ann Street, or enjoy a hearty meal with neighboring printers and booksellers at Windust's eating-house. In the Paternoster Row of America, Dick and Fitzgerald were at home. A good location and a thorough training augured well for their success in publishing.

Instead of issuing the miscellaneous books that had appeared in Burgess's lists, the two young publishers of Ann Street decided to specialize along the lines previously laid down by Ransom Garrett. They would cater almost exclusively to the mid-century's desires for entertainment and self-improvement, and since in mid-nine-teenth-century America the hub of social enjoyment was the home, it was for entertainment in all the homes of America that their books were published.

Even before the execution of their articles of co-partnership, Dick and Fitzgerald had issued a monthly journal whose title alone is indicative of their purposes. *The Home Circle,* priced at three cents a copy, was "Devoted to Literature, News, Fun, Poetry, & c."; but it was devoted above all to readers who gathered at a nineteenth-century fireside, and it contained, therefore, nuggets for every member of the family. For the daughter there were poems—"The Old Clay Pipe" or "My Flora"; for the son there were tales of adventure and animals—"The Ghost Raiser," "The Western Stage Driver," or an "Adventure with Sharks." For the father there were informative articles on "Alcohol in Wine," the "Origin of Paper Money," or "Ancient Glass Manufactures." And the mother of the family would doubtless enjoy the story entitled "George Durand; or, The Profligate," a revealing account of "Quack Medicines," or the useful receipts in the "Housekeeper's Department." For them all there was a section devoted to "Family Pastime," where riddles and charades, rebuses and parlor pastimes might be found, and for them all, too, there were advertisements of other Dick and Fitzgerald publications, from the firm's Shilling Library to a series of books on the "Exploits of Highwaymen," from *The Magician's Own Book* to *The Ladies' Guide to Beauty*.

Certainly it was the "home circle," and more specifically the parlor of the home that provided the background for nineteenth-century recreation, and at least half the books appearing under the imprint of Dick and Fitzgerald may be classed as "parlor entertainments." In one of his illuminating prefaces William Brisbane Dick wrote, "There is nothing more delightful than . . . to devote the whole or part of an evening to social amusement." He had in mind, as did his readers, social amusement at home. So it was that he published several general books of parlor entertainment, *What Shall We Do To-Night? or Social Amusements for Evening Parties* by "Leger D. Mayne" (William B. Dick himself), *The Sociable; or, One Thousand and One Home Amusements, Fireside Games; for Winter Evening Amusement,* and *Uncle Josh's Trunk-Full of Fun*—books that taught the willing host the secrets of round and forfeit games, ingenious puzzles, innocent sells, musical pastimes, startling illusions, gallantry shows, and mirth-provoking exhibitions. In their pages both hosts and guests would find explained such family games as "Selling Statues" or "The Magic Handkerchief," a "Musical-Merry-go-Round" or "The Needle and Thread Trick." From "Hocus Pocus" to "Living Flowers," from "Tableaux Vivants" to "Mrs. Jarley's Wax-Works," from "Bout Rhymes" to "Hunt The Hare," there were pastimes for young and old, witty and agile, for those who loved games of action and for those who preferred games requiring memory. For all the games the setting was the home—at "merry Christmas-time, or on a wet day in the country or in the city too, . . . or on a winter's evening, when the fire is burning cheerily, pussy purring on the hearth, and the lamps lighted." The apparatus required was simple, for these parlor pastimes demanded only a family endowed with "good temper, good spirits, and gentleness, so that at any moment amusement for an evening can be obtained by anybody who wills it." And if the Dick and Fitzgerald books for the home circle were purchased, the entire winter season, including a social gathering every week, could be passed harmoniously and pleasantly by customers throughout the country.

Having once decided to limit their publications to books that would raise the spirit and improve the mind, Dick and Fitzgerald introduced a variety of works within their specialty. One of the most popular entertainments of the nineteenth century arose, in all probability, from the combination of the average person's desire to shine in society and the general ubiquity of elocution teachers. Recitation, dialogue, and joke books would meet the requirements of both, and the publishers proceeded to flood the market with collections, many of them arranged by William B. Dick himself, offering "new and bright little pieces" for "small children" or "young Thespians," and ready-made speeches for the gallant slashers of the day. When Dick's ingenuity failed him, the firm could always resort to Frost's *Dialogues for Young Folks,* Barber's *Ready-Made Speeches,* or Mc-Bride's *All Kinds of Dialogues.* While Dick and Fitzgerald flourished no program would be wanting for Washington's Birthday, no master of dialect would be unable to con the lines of "Der Drummer" or "Vat You Please," and no sharp young card would lack a joke to quote from *Yale College Scrapes; or, How the Boys Go It at New Haven.* With *Chips from Uncle Sam's Jack Knife,* "a broad grin" was guaranteed "for the domestic hearth, or boarding-house parlor, for the whole winter." From 18 Ann Street flowed recitations suited to every occasion and every elocutionist, from "The Palmetto and the Pine" to "Curfew Must not Ring To-night," from "The Blue and the Gray" to "The Drunkard's Dream," from "Aunt Patience's Doughnuts" to "The Baby's Kiss." Besides writing many of the firm's reciters, William B. Dick offered, without increasing the charge of thirty cents for a book in paper and fifty for the same in boards, some excellent advice on elocution: "Each child must so perfectly memorise its part that the text will be recited without hesitation. When this is accomplished, it is time to attend to gesture and emphasis. Let both of these be merely improvements . . . of their own natural efforts. . . . When one person is speaking, it adds greatly to the effect if the listeners seem to appreciate what is said by appropriate gestures . . . in a perfectly natural manner." As an authority on the subject, Dick was able to issue in the 1870's a series entitled *Dick's Recitations and Readings,* in which he had the re-

markably good sense to render some poetical effusions in prose form
to help readers avoid a sing-song inflection. While he catered to the
demands of an elocuting world, William Brisbane Dick did his best
to raise the standards of the art.

Almost as popular among parlor entertainments were card games,
and Dick profitably explained to a world devoid of radios, television,
and motion pictures the varieties of patience, cribbage, and whist.
The result of two years of consultations with the best players in
the country, *The American Hoyle,* appearing under the pseudonym
of "Trumps," was given to an eager public. When Dick wearied of
his role as "Trumps," he could publish Professor Proctor's medita-
tions on draw-poker or an exposition of games and tricks with cards
by the reformed gambler, J. H. Green. In addition to elucidating
the mysteries of bezique and euchre, commercial pitch and whisky
poker, the firm produced new card games—cards for courtship and
fortune-telling, for popping the question or for Leap Year, the last
of which were "intended more to make fun among young people
than for any practical utility."

There were other games that nineteenth-century America enjoyed. Gathered in the parlor, the young folks could put on a lively
exhibition of legerdemain if they had studied *The Fireside Magician*
or *The Great Wizard of the North's Handbook of Natural Magic.*
They could indulge in a thrilling session of mesmerism if they were
equipped with De Laurence's *Hypnotism,* or amaze one another with
vocal feats if they had bought *Ventriloquism Self-Taught* by Professor Ganthony. With *The Magician's Own Book* they could find
"amusement sufficient to occupy the evenings of a family for three
or four years, and give a new source of enjoyment each evening."
While the book *"amuses,* it also *instructs,"* and with it "a man could
amuse the great and small members of his family, or make himself
the lion of a party, for an indefinite period." Best of all, the family
could read one another's palms if they possessed a copy of *Dick's
Mysteries of the Hand; or, Palmistry Made Easy.*

Reading palms was only one way of fortune-telling. Dick and
Fitzgerald knew all the ways, and for nineteenth-century America's
fireside evenings they published their fortune-tellers and dream-
books, from *Mother Shipton's Oriental Dream Book* to *Madame Le
Normand's Unerring Fortune-Teller* (with a Chart of Fate), from
The Golden Wheel Dream Book by Felix Fontaine, Professor of

Astrology, to *Le Marchand's Fortune-Teller and Dreamer's Dictionary* by the celebrated Parisian seer. Fortunes could be told, as Dick and Fitzgerald advised an avid public, from the white of an egg or from apple-parings, from moles, fingernails, and dreams. The firm's dream books have the distinction of having introduced for the first time the lucky number device, an innovation devoutly cherished by guileless addicts.

To shine in the parlor was a worthy feat, but to shine in the ballroom was every nineteenth-century gentleman's desire. Who could master the devious steps of the polonaise, the lancers, or the caledonians without having studied *Dick's Quadrille Call-Book, and Ball-Room Prompter?* Who could bow gallantly or step gracefully through the redowa or schottische without the aid of Professor De Walden's *Ball-Room Companion* or General Ferrero's *Art of Dancing* as executed at the author's private academies? From 18 Ann Street flowed complete directions for calling figures or executing round dances, as well as for learning the intricacies of the Parisian Varieties or the Prince Imperial Set. From jigs to contra dances, from the german to the galop, instructions were available in a form at once concise, lucid, and reasonable. And for those who wished to strum a banjo while their friends enjoyed the dancing, Frank Converse's *Complete Banjo Instructor* (without a master) might be ordered for fifty cents the copy.

For only ten cents, the firm sent through the mails their song books, *Tony Pastor's Bowery Songster, Christy's Bones and Banjo Melodist, The Shamrock,* the *Camp-Fire, The Arkansas Traveller's,* the *Plantation.* From tent and forecastle to hearth and home there were songs for every occasion, even to *William Lingard's On the Beach at Long Branch Song Book.* There were love songs and sentimental songs, Ethiopian and comic songs, patriotic and convivial songs, and as the quartet gathered round the upright piano—a copy of *Tony Pastor's "444" Combination Songster* propped on the ledge —the strains of "Life on the Bloomingdale Road" or "The Angel Dressed in White" floated sweetly to nineteenth-century ears. With the help of the Ann Street publishers, the tunes of "She Smiled When I Had Done It" or "I Always Take It Cool," "Hunkydory" or "Humbug Now is All the Go" were familiar melodies in the parlors of yesterday.

Perhaps, in that leisurely yesterday when the home held more charms than the street, the most popular social pastime was the parlor theatrical. With wigs, a dab of grease paint, and some histrionic inclination, a group of young Thespians could convert the parlor into a magic fairyland or a dark forest, a French boulevard or an American saloon. Like Louisa May Alcott's Little Men and Little Women, they could tread the boards of a home-made stage and win the applause of their audience—provided, of course, that they owned the texts of their plays. The firm of Dick and Fitzgerald willingly supplied those scripts, sending across the country, at fifteen or twenty-five cents a copy, the farces and comediettas, dramas and vaudeville sketches that would set a stage-struck America to conning its lines. Their stock of New Plays and Entertainments was varied, ranging from *Ten Nights in a Barroom* to *Freezing a Mother-in-Law,* from *A Dental Engagement* to *Josiah's Courtship.* There were Ethiopian acts and monologues, mock trials and initiations, tableaux and shadow pantomimes, acting charades and plays—plays Irish and rural, western and temperance and military—plays to fulfill every desire of a century bent on barnstorming. For those who preferred western drama, there was *Crawford's Claim,* a play in three acts requiring nine male and three female performers and two and a quarter hours acting time. For those who inclined to farce, there was the *Darkey Wood Dealer* in one act, requiring only three male actors and twenty minutes playing time. For comedy, *Standing Room Only* might be selected—one act, three males and one female, thirty-five minutes. From colonial drama to vaudeville, from playlet to farce, Dick and Fitzgerald could recommend a variety of intriguing titles. For those who wished a ready reference theatre book, there was T. Allston Brown's *History of the American Stage,* while for those less ingenious than Miss Alcott's characters the firm facilitated matters by providing wigs and beards, Weldon's *Fancy Costumes,* colored fires, and tableau-lights, as well as a make-up box for five dollars, which contained hare's foot and nose putty, spirit gum and moustache-cosmetique, together with an assortment of crimped hair and other theatrical sundries. The parlor stage need never languish for winter evenings' entertainments while Dick and Fitzgerald flourished on Ann Street.

If half the publications of the firm centered round the parlor of the home, the other half might be said to center round the kitchen. If the upper middle classes profited most from the varied entertainments concocted by Dick and Fitzgerald, it was the so-called lower classes, the domestics, nursery-maids, and butlers, who must have proved the best customers for the firm's books on self-improvement. With these nineteenth-century courtesy books on hand, the denizens of the kitchen could rise to parlor status, in their mastery of the social amenities, by learning what William B. Dick eagerly taught: "to say or do the proper thing at the proper time and in a proper manner." For them Dick's etiquette books were bound in paper and sold at ten, twenty-five, or thirty cents, from *How to Behave in Society* to *The Art of Dressing Well,* from *Blunders in Behavior Corrected* to *Dinner Napkins, and How to Fold Them.* Doubtless for them, too, as well as for the ladies and gentlemen of the parlor, the firm published its aids to beauty and love, revealing the secrets of pomades and cosmetics in *The Ladies' Guide to Beauty* by the private physician to Queen Victoria, whose work had been revised by an American colleague, or offering "amusing" and "sarcastically instructive" hints on the art of fascinating in Madame Lola Montez's *Arts of Beauty.* For a nominal fee the willing pursuer could learn *How to Win and How to Woo,* or encompass the entire *Art and Etiquette of Making Love,* from curing bashfulness to commencing a courtship, from popping the question to acting suitably after an engagement. For those already wooed and won, of course, *Bridal Etiquette* was available at only ten cents the copy. Dick and Fitzgerald did not neglect the feminine arts. For the fair sex, the "most discriminating and exacting portion of an intelligent public," they offered works on crochet and fancy work or painting on china, and Franz Thimm's *French, German, Spanish,* and *Italian Self-Taught* to those still in need of "finishing." To meet the more urgent needs of ladies in "society, household duties, and business," a series of *Letter-Writers* was projected, the *Society,* the *Commercial,* and the *Sensible,* so that one might with perfect propriety introduce a Sunday School scholar to a clergyman in another city or thank a friend for the loan of an umbrella. The type of publication that centered most about the kitchen was naturally the cookbook, and of these the Ann Street firm offered a wide assortment, ranging from *The American Housewife and Kitchen Directory* to *How to Cook and How to Carve,* from *Dick's Home Made Candies* to *How to Cook Potatoes, Apples, Eggs, and Fish Four Hundred Different Ways.* With such indispensable reference books on hand, the mysteries of terrapin and puddings, pickles and catsups need remain mysterious no longer.

In addition to their kitchen receipts and their parlor entertainments, Dick and Fitzgerald published their Reason Why Series and their Shilling Library of reference books, "intended . . . for the use of persons whose means are limited, but who desire to . . . form their habits and character, so as to fit them for mingling in the best society." With manuals on ready reckoning and phonography, taxidermy and horse training, masonic ritual and printing, punctuation and health, the family aquarium and household pets, the firm aided both home and business. They catered to outdoor amusements with their books on sports—bowling and wrestling, calisthenics and yachting. They appealed to a more solitary type of indoor amusement with their series of cheap novels, their "Hand and Pocket Library," narratives of border adventure, detective stories, exploits of celebrated highwaymen, and, at twenty-five cents each, such Prize Novels as *The Midnight Queen* or *The Matricide's Daughter, The Rescued Nun* or *Belle of the Bowery,* tales that doubtless whetted the appetite of parlor and kitchen alike.

At the Centennial Exhibition in Philadelphia the well-known handbooks of Dick and Fitzgerald were on display, with "sample lines of their publications, which go all over the country." Though not always advertised in those terms, the firm actually was, by and large, a mail-order house. It was forced to that status by the very nature of its books, most of which were priced cheaply at thirty cents in paper or fifty cents in boards, and all of which were designed to appeal to families in Kansas or Maine, Illinois or Virginia. One needed only a parlor and a kitchen to subscribe with pleasure to the works issued from Ann Street; it did not matter where the parlor and kitchen were located. It was for that reason that Dick and Fitzgerald took such pains to recommend clarity in mail orders. "We have done a large book trade through the mails. . . . We receive so many letters every day that it is impossible for us to remember the Post-Office, County, and State where any particular person receives books. . . . Put on a plain direction." It was for that reason also that the firm reminded its patrons that "it is easier and cheaper to get books from New York than people generally imagine. You have only to write a few words . . . and the book comes free of postage, and arrives by return mail."

Because it was a mail-order house, Dick and Fitzgerald adopted a rather stringent policy in regard to payments. There was a time when books could be sent C.O.D. from Ann Street, provided five or ten dollars were sent in advance to cover freight charges. For the most part, however, no orders were filled unless sufficient money accompanied them. Remittances were to be made by express or post-office money order, a draft on a New York bank, or cash in a registered letter. Postage stamps would be accepted only if they were clean and covered sums less than one dollar. In addition to their strict policy on payments, the Ann Street firm upheld stringent rules on exchanges. No books could be exchanged, and under no circumstances could they be sent subject to approval. In spite, or perhaps because of these restrictions, the mail-order house flourished, and at their P. O. Box 2975 orders flowed in, while books, free catalogues ("no charge for catalogues or information") and stationery, playing-cards and music were supplied to booksellers and peddlers at lowest wholesale prices, and flowed out "to any part of the United States or Canada." Customers were urged to see how promptly a cash order would be executed by "the great publishing house of Dick and Fitzgerald." The catalogues themselves served as incentives to purchasers, for they were often made as attractive as possible by the inclusion of charming illustrations, delightful cuts depicting card games, banjo playing, puzzles, parlor tricks, etiquette, and even the gentle art of courtship.

Selling books was perhaps simpler for Dick and Fitzgerald than buying them, or the rights to them. When William B. Dick did not himself write the firm's handbooks or collections, he produced them after consultations with experts in the field, or ordered original selections written expressly for the works. The house was always "glad to read manuscripts (which were to be accompanied by a statement of the price demanded) . . . by any author, known or unknown, with a view toward publication." Music, needed in the ten-cent songsters, was published by W. A. Pond or William Hall of New York. Occasionally plates were purchased from such companies as Street and Smith, and occasionally, in spite of the firm's favorable attitude toward international copyright, books were pirated. Interrupted by only one lawsuit brought by an English pugilist, Dick and Fitzgerald went their smooth and merry way of supplying entertainment and self-improvement to the parlors and kitchens of American homes.

Their progress was reflected in the lives of the partners, both of whom were substantial men of affairs. While Lawrence Fitzgerald boasted membership in the Neptune Club along with a close friendship with President Arthur, William B. Dick proceeded to amass a fine dramatic library adorned with extra-illustrated books, and to join such clubs as the Lotos, The Grolier, The Church, and, since he had served as a captain in the Gettysburg Campaign, the Lafayette Post of the G.A.R. A member of St. Bartholomew's parish and a resident of the Park Avenue Hotel, the tall, fair, blue-eyed William B. Dick lent tone to his mail-order house on Ann Street.

Meanwhile, the firm was altered by changes not in its publications but in its personnel. Fitzgerald's death in 1881 was followed by a dissolution of the co-partnership, although William B. Dick continued the business under the same style until his retirement in 1898. It was then that Dick's son, Harris, who was to become one of the anomalies of nature, a "millionaire publisher," took over the affairs of 18 Ann Street, carrying on the traditions established by his father both in his business and his personal life.

Born in 1855, Harris Brisbane Dick had been trained in the ways of Dick and Fitzgerald, and now, as head of the firm, the tall, presentable, mustachioed gentleman continued to compile or edit the later series of card games and reciters first launched by his father. "Trumps" had been altered to "Trumps, Jr." and cribbage to Russian bank, but little else was changed by the stately bachelor who found time for The Union League, The Players, and his fine collection of prints, as well as for the parlor theatricals and letter-writers of Dick and Fitzgerald, and who met with equal ease the demands of the Social Register and of 18 Ann Street.

So, catering to the American hearth and home, the firm continued, aided by such faithful and steadfast employees as Rudolph Behrens and William Train, until Harris Dick died suddenly in the Boston subway in 1916. When the will of the "millionaire publisher" was probated, it was learned not only that he had bequeathed over one million dollars, much of which had stemmed from private sources, to The Metropolitan Museum of Art, but that he had directed his executor to "convert into money . . . the good-will and assets (but not the firm name) of the book publishing business now carried on . . . under the firm name of 'Dick & Fitzgerald.' "

Though the letter of the will was abided by, its spirit was not.

The firm of Dick and Fitzgerald was reorganized in 1917 as the Fitzgerald Publishing Corporation, Successor to Dick and Fitzgerald, and as such it continued to do business until 1940, sending forth, from Vesey Street and later from East 38th Street, reciters and dream books and amateur theatricals. But the parlor had given way to the playhouse, and, to advance with the times, the new firm issued a series of "Playhouse Plays." For many years, under the guidance of Harris Dick's friends, Arthur Howard Abendroth and Rudolph Behrens, and his cousin, Thomas Leggett, the Fitzgerald Publishing Corporation persisted. It continued for a short time under the aegis of the Walter H. Baker Company, Theodore and Carl G. A. Johnson, President and Treasurer respectively of that firm, and William M. Sloane, playwright, later of William Sloane Associates, taking over its dramatic publications, and Rudolph Behrens of Danbury, Connecticut, its handbooks. A notation in the *New York Copartnership and Corporation Directory,* however, shows the way the wind was blowing. The firm's capital, which in 1931 had been only $18,000, had risen, under the Johnson brothers, to $50,000 by 1933. By 1934 the firm's capital had fallen to $18,000. In 1940 the Fitzgerald Publishing Corporation was dissolved.

For over eighty years the publications of Dick and Fitzgerald and its successor had brought entertainment to the American home. Doubtless it was because the center of entertainment shifted gradually away from the home that the business declined. The parlor itself has become obsolete, and with it has vanished the need for Fireside Magicians and Parlor Theatricals. 18 Ann Street has vanished, too, engulfed by a branch building of a bank. Still, the stray paper copies priced at thirty cents and bearing the old Dick and Fitzgerald imprint arouse nostalgia for the days of upright pianos and forfeit games, of gallantry shows and innocent sells, of euchre, bezique, quadrilles, and polonaises. When those paper copies can still be found, they help to brush the dust from yesterday's bandbox, revealing a way of life and a state of mind that have become historic. It was for that way of life that the firm of Dick and Fitzgerald existed, and from that way of life that it flourished. Although both have gone, the twentieth century can still recall them, for, in the paper-bound handbooks bearing the Dick and Fitzgerald imprint, yesterday is reenacted. The cast of characters is the family; the time—the latter half of the nineteenth century; the place—the parlor with warmly glowing fireside. And the curtain rises on a nation at home.

3

SURVIVAL OF TRADITION

The Twentieth-Century Survivals

SOMEWHERE along the line—certainly not at the turn of the century, but more probably around 1914—the nineteenth century became the twentieth. The century of continental expansion and manifest destiny which had pushed relentlessly from east to west, broken down the wilderness, and cleared frontiers until a nation stretched in space from one sea to another, was metamorphosed gradually into a century whose frontiers were national no longer, but stretched instead into planetary space. The century of civil war, out of which a nation had been constructed into a union south to north across the map, had turned into a century of global war out of which sprang fully armed the science of destruction.

As the frontiers of space had changed, so, too, had the concepts of the mind. The age of confidence that had believed in the self-made man and his climb from rags to riches, from log cabin to the White House, had been transformed into the age of collective insecurity, the age of anxiety, the "aspirin age," whose ministering angels were the doctors of the mind. The century when a nation learned to laugh at itself had turned into the century when a nation learned to whistle in the dark. The time when the pioneer of the wild West sprawled and rioted across the pages of books about the plains slipped into the time when Buck Rogers straddled his rocket for a trip into space in the pages of what were euphemistically known as comic books. The Silver Age and the Railroad Age had become the Atomic Age—the age of technology for technology's sake. The Promised Land for the immigrant receded into an asylum for the refugee. Woman's rights had ceased to be a rallying cry, and labor's rights, having been won, needed only to be guarded and extended.

Such rallying cries as arose in the new century were echoes of fear rather than of courage, and called to their standard not the champions of the oppressed but the hunters of shadows. And in the home that had been the hub of nineteenth-century America, the hearthstone had turned into a twenty-one-inch screen around which gathered the silent worshipers of mechanized entertainment. The vibrant, exuberant, expanding nineteenth century, whose possibilities had seemed endless and whose whole had been more than the sum of its parts, was over. It had given way to a century whose technological possibilities seemed indeed limitless, but whose other possibilities had narrowed into one—the possibility of survival.

And yet, despite the changes, there has been continuity. Despite the enormous shifts in outlook and perspective, there has been some survival of tradition. Though the soldier of the Alamo and Gettysburg would search in vain for the arms he bore on the distant fields of a warring twentieth century, his purposes were not altogether dissimilar to the purposes of those who fought the later global wars. If the pioneer and the settler who had helped to cultivate a continent and make it whole would find no wilderness to break, no frontiers to conquer, still they would recognize in some who followed after them the will to break a wilderness and the spirit to conquer a frontier.

Especially the publisher of the nineteenth century could find himself at home in the nation of the twentieth century. For he can still, if he will, help shape while he reflects the living history of his country. If the gulf between the individual publisher and the affairs of his times has widened somewhat, yet the publisher, by the very nature of his profession, is still empowered to determine those affairs and guide the history that he lives. One by one publishers of the nineteenth century have faded from the annals of their trade, some ending with success and some with failure. Yet others have pushed on, their firms enduring from one century to the next, a patent demonstration of continuity within change and of survival of tradition within an altered age. More than one hundred ninety such houses have lived on from the nineteenth century or before, working in the present, still shaping to some extent the history that they continue to reflect. Their story is the mirror not only of yesterday, but of today.

If the "average" man exists only in the reports of statisticians, the "average" publisher can hardly be said to exist at all, much less an "average" publisher whose business has survived from the nineteenth century or even earlier into the present time. Yet a composite portrait of such a publisher can be drawn, wearing the clothes of one, serving the apprenticeship of another, starting out in business as a third, developing the philosophy of most, and living out his life against the background of nearly all. From the varied stories of one hundred ninety-one American publishing houses that survive from before 1900, a single "biography" can be sketched that reanimates the lives of most of the founders, and a single history can be told that epitomizes the history of all.

He was born—this composite founder—somewhere in New England, perhaps on a farm in Acton, Massachusetts, like James Brown, perhaps in Cape Cod like Thomas Crowell (who in his youth went to sea where he scrubbed decks and furled flags), or in Vermont like Henry Oscar Houghton, or in Maine, like George Palmer Putnam. He was born, too, in an early nineteenth century that would seem to him, as he reminisced later in life, a less blatant, less extravagant, less competitive age than the present. His schooling would probably have been meager, although he might have entered Yale, as Henry Holt did, or Harvard, as John Allyn did. He probably would not have led so varied a life as did the Irish immigrant, John Kenedy, who worked in a Baltimore quarry and poled a raft down the Ohio as a frontier trader before he finally founded a publishing house that would endure from 1826 until the present. He certainly could not ordinarily trace his beginnings as far back as Lafayette's friend, Mathew Carey, who assisted Franklin in his print shop at Passy before establishing a firm that would become the oldest surviving house in America. But, at all events, early in life he would have served an apprenticeship, acting as printer's devil in a newspaper office or a job printing establishment, starting as the local agent for a penny press, or tending a bookstore that was also a news depot and carried a side branch of wallpaper, stationery, and window shades. And then, having accumulated a small capital (even though, if his name was Putnam, he had worked for only $25.00 a year and keep) and having developed a strong respect for Yankee ethics, the erstwhile apprentice would decide to go into business for himself.

The founding of his firm might possibly date from the rejection of a manuscript, as Henry Holt's is said to have done, when Leypoldt's refusal of a Holt translation led to a warm friendship and later to a business association; or again, it might have started with a casual meeting such as Fleming H. Revell's chance encounter with Dwight L. Moody, who was to influence his publishing career so strongly. But however it began, there is little doubt that the new enterprise was set up in a dingy room or a small corner of a loft in Boston or New York, and that the young publisher was also a printer and bookseller on the side. His first publication was sure to have been a theological item, such as Appleton's earliest venture, *Crumbs from the Master's Table,* for religious books were far less speculative than the literature in any other field. To sell his wares, he would eventually engage itinerant book peddlers, although only Mathew Carey could claim to have hired as his agent the celebrated Parson Weems; or he might go himself from village to village selling books, traveling by country stages, on horseback, or in private conveyances. Later on he would engage agents to canvass sets from house to house or to sell subscription books on the installment plan. At the great New York trade sales he would augment his stock, and of course he would early begin the importation of books from England, dispatching a messenger to board a packet, obtain the sheets of popular English novels, and hasten back with them. He might even include among his services that of general export agent and like Appleton be forced to purchase and forward a hearse for a demanding customer. In his printing factory the first motive power of his presses would probably derive, as Harper's did, from a horse harnessed to a beam, driving the shaft that worked the presses, from which emerged the popular sets and select novels that titillated popular taste.

The founder, very likely adorned in a blue coat with bright buttons, a light buff waistcoat, and blue pantaloons, would be rapidly developing an ability to gauge that popular taste. Besides theology —the ever-steady seller—he would find that the educational field was a fertile one, and that his country's demand for readers and arithmetics, geographies and histories was constantly increasing. If he were as fortunate as Appleton, he would acquire Webster's famous "blue-back" *Speller* and would keep one of his largest presses running day after day, year after year, on that book alone until the press was worn out and thirty-five million copies had been sold—sold in cases to drygoods and supply houses, furnished to crossroads stores, and handled along with calicoes and ginghams. Developing a backlog of books in religion, education, and juveniles, he would come to understand that such publications were of far greater importance to his concern than any other books. Literature, of course, was of interest, too. If his name were Putnam, he could boast a first list that included Irving, Poe, and Lowell. Indeed, he would then one day recall that Poe had walked into his office and had there written *Eureka,* later signing an I O U to the effect that in consideration of seven dollars received he would ask for no further advances on the work. Indeed, if his name were Putnam, he would find the name immortalized in that *Fable for Critics* where Lowell had written:

> SET FORTH IN
> *October, the 21st day, in the year* '48,
> BY
> G. P. PUTNAM, BROADWAY.

For the most part, however, he would content himself with the literary productions brought over from England, and, in time, would issue elegant editions of Bacon and Carlyle, Macaulay and Scott. He could, of course, start a magazine such as Harper's or Appleton's, Putnam's, Lippincott's, or Scribner's, following serial publication of a story with the book version and thus finding both a new source of supply and a new market. He himself might enter the literary field, a publisher turned author, writing pseudonymous juveniles as Edward Mead did, or anonymous novels as Henry Holt was to do.

In time, his business would expand and he would be forced to move to larger quarters, preferably in New York where the book trade was centering, setting up anew against a background of marble fireplaces and carved woodwork, Corinthian columns and frescoed walls. From these loftier and more expanded quarters, he could look back upon what had passed and contemplate what was yet to be. He had probably lived through the Mexican War, and almost certainly through the Civil War. During the draft riots in New York he would have been ordered by a mob to close his buildings and would have barricaded his entrance. After the Civil War he would have found his accounts with southern booksellers a loss, but would have proceeded in time to publish the recollections and autobiographies of the heroes both in blue and in gray. He had survived at least one fire, and possibly more; he had weathered the panic of 1857, when he had probably made a temporary assignment, and he —or his house—would weather later panics.

Gradually his business had undergone a transformation. His functions as publisher, bookseller, and printer had been separated, and he had decided to confine himself principally to the publishing of books. His magazines had been discontinued. He had formed one or two strong and lasting friendships with authors, with whom at times no formal contract was needed to set forth the terms of mutual agreement, and with whom any contract was, in all events, couched in the simplest words. After the Philadelphia Centennial Exhibition of 1876, he had probably indulged in a series of successful art books, and he had doubtless augmented and strengthened his list by the purchase of or merger with another firm, as Houghton purchased Osgood and thus acquired the Ticknor & Fields American classics, as Little, Brown would, toward the turn of the century, acquire Roberts Brothers, or as Appleton would still later merge with Century.

Full of years, satisfied with the achievement of having built up a business of large proportions from the proverbial shoestring, the founder was ready to retire, leaving to his sons—now his partners— the house he had established. And so the house, and the sons or the grandsons, faced the new century. Upon the walls of the office was hung the portrait of the founder. And there, too, the treasured mementoes were framed: souvenirs like Mathew Carey's check returning to Lafayette in 1824 the sum of $400 with which he had started his business, or the token of a later age in the Putnam office, the canceled check for $100,000 which had been the initial royalty payment for Charles Lindbergh's *We*. The heritage left by the founder was not always untrammeled. With the turn of the century, the firm that had withstood the panic of 1893 might face bankruptcy and reorganization. Appleton's experiment in installment sales, the large number of Harper family retainers at inflated salaries had both brought about insolvency and the decline of family control; but none the less, the firm—now a corporation—had persisted. With the turn of the century, too, the cost of business had increased. The International Copyright Law of 1891, for which the founder had probably campaigned, had restricted the cheap reprinting of popular English novels. The panic of 1907 would follow that of 1893, and the concern in the twentieth century would face and survive the far greater disaster of a depression couched between two world wars.

With the changing times, the house itself had changed. The Scribner firm that had rejected Arnold Bennett's *Old Wives' Tale* because of its "unpleasant and sordid details" and that had declined Gertrude Atherton on moral grounds, would find itself publishing F. Scott Fitzgerald, Thomas Wolfe, and Ernest Hemingway. The age of wholesale advertising for a few best-sellers, the age of the "boomed book" was at hand. With one or two popular successes, the firm could weather almost any storm, it believed. Indeed, for Harold Bell Wright, the house of Appleton established a special department for the manufacture, promotion, and distribution of his works alone. According to the witticism, American literature had passed from the age of [Hamilton Wright] Mabie to the era of Canby. It was passing, at all events, from the sweetness and light authors of the early twentieth century, from the Myrtle Reeds, the George Barr McCutcheons, the Gene Stratton Porters, the John Fox, Jrs., to Hemingway and Faulkner, from romance and uplift to "naturalism" and realism.

Transferred to more modern quarters, where the click of the typewriter supplanted the scratch of the quill pen, the house that had survived from the early nineteenth century learned to survive the later time. With the First World War had come an increase in commodity prices and in price schedules; with the Second World War had come paper shortages and frozen prices. The firm had faced inflation and depression and strikes as well as war. It had seen the country pass from an agricultural to an industrial economy, from the era of rugged individualism to the era of managed economy. And although it continued to publish the books that reflected the past, its major concern was with the present and the future. Its device, along with its foundations, was a heritage from the past. But it entered the present enormously expanded, sometimes with as many as seven large departments and a London branch. In its offices might be trained others who would start their own publishing houses. And so the firm looked to the present and the future.

To celebrate its centenary, however, it might reflect for a while upon the past, recording the career of its founder in a brochure for limited distribution, or reprinting its first publication in an equally limited edition. The story of its first century was indeed the epitome of the literary and publishing history of America. In its lists could be read the steady expansion and growth of the country. What Franklin Roosevelt said of Harper might have been said of all the surviving firms: "The activities of your house have been contemporary with a long and notable period in our national life. There are few businesses that are so intimately interwoven with the national fabric as a publishing house."

The surviving firms give evidence on every hand that they have helped to weave that national fabric when its pattern altered and when its pattern remained unchanged. Strikingly, in some instances, they bear witness to the continuity of the pattern. The history of William Hilliard, who helped to enrich the golden age of Harvard University, is repeated to some extent in the later career of John Allyn, who, having studied at Harvard, championed, like his predecessor, the advancement of learning by publishing the classical lexicons and textbooks of the Harvard professors.

The life of that self-made man, George W. Childs, was not unlike the life of Henry O. Houghton, who, having begun as a printer's devil and entered college with a purse containing three York shillings, saw his Riverside Press develop into a magnificent factory that employed six hundred hands. And James Harper's career had been still another version of the success of rugged individualism based upon the moral precepts of Benjamin Franklin; for Harper, the barefoot boy who grew up on a Long Island farm, the son of a country carpenter, who was practically self-educated, lived not only to found a great publishing house but to become mayor of New York City. Impressed by Franklin's *Autobiography,* he had chosen the printing trade as his profession and, in his homespun clothes and heavy cowhide boots, had served his apprenticeship with Paul & Thomas before he established a firm that was to become an American institution. Indeed, a full-length statue of Franklin adorned the facade of the Harpers' Franklin Square building, where the iron staircase came to be known as "the ladder to literary fame." Despite the story that, when asked which was the Harper and which the Brothers, the reply was that any one was the Harper and the rest the Brothers, surely it was the eldest, James, who most resembled a "Poor Richard" hoisting himself to success by his own bootstraps.

The Railroad Age that so deeply influenced the Leslie publications was a motive force in the development of Rand McNally—a firm that produced railroad maps because they were essential for railroad travel, and paperback novels because they were distributed by hawkers on the nation's railroads. And even today, when the company issues textbooks, juveniles, and general publications, it repeats the nineteenth-century theme with twentieth-century variations by printing not only railroad but bus and airline tickets, and highway maps for those who cross the country in automobiles.

The immigrations that created the demand for Ernst Steiger's books are reflected, too, in the work of the surviving houses. For the Jewish immigrants to the New World, The Jewish Publication Society issues its narratives of American Jewry, its stories of Jewish pioneers and patriots and pilgrims in the new land. For the Irish immigrants, the Catholic publications of P. J. Kenedy & Sons provided and still provide a means for their preservation of faith in their adopted country.

The Lovell imprints that championed the advancement of women are not dissimilar to the Putnam imprint upon Ellen Key's revolutionary works on feminism or Dr. Marie Stopes's equally revolutionary works on marriage. And, since bridges, though often intangible, exist across every channel, the bridge between the economic advancement of women in the early twentieth century and the growth of the Gregg and Pitman publishing concerns can be crossed directly and surely.

The great Lovell book trust that was known as the United States Book Company was simply a variation on the theme of the American Book Company, an enormous textbook house that grew from the merger of other concerns, became a giant in the field, and set up subsidiary firms. Like Lovell's organization, it, too, was castigated as a monopoly worse than the notorious Standard Oil Company. Charged with bribery and the use of political machinations, it was accused also of publishing a textbook on sociology that gave merely scant mention of the nature of trusts. But whatever its motives or its nature at the founding, the American Book Company did stave off Federal or State control of textbooks and, unlike Lovell's establishment, survived to provide texts for the twentieth century.

The popular entertainment to which the firm of Dick & Fitzgerald catered was the foundation stone also of the houses of Samuel French and Walter H. Baker. While they, too, may have begun with farces and melodramas and rural plays for domestic production, they survived to issue the flag-waving dramas of the First World War and the plays that provided the staple fare for the little theaters that boomed in the lush twenties. They persisted—Baker producing an all-time favorite in *Aaron Slick from Punkin Crick,* a play that has been viewed by five million people and has had some 50,000 performances, or more than all the plays seen in New York in any five-year period. Though they no longer publish dramas for home consumption, these houses still flourish by sending across the country plays for school commencements and church groups—the less domestic, but no less popular entertainments of a later age.

The surviving houses that have helped to continue the pattern of the national fabric have helped to change it also. The transformations in science and economics that mark the new era were woven in part by the publishers, who helped to introduce the twentieth century to those who lived it. Indeed, they often began that task in the nineteenth century. When Edward L. Youmans walked into the house of Appleton and asked to borrow a scientific book which the firm had just published, an association was formed that was to develop into one of the most dynamic forces in the advancement of scientific thought in America. As a result of that association, the firm of Appleton was to publish the works of Darwin, Spencer, Huxley, and Tyndall, was to launch the *Popular Science Monthly* to popularize the progress of science, and was to serve as interpreter of science for the people. In Appleton's International Scientific Series appeared Draper's *History of the Conflict between Religion and Science,* a paean to science that was placed upon the Index. Indeed, most of these early scientific Appleton publications were greeted with condemnation by the religious press, and although the firm took the somewhat equivocal view that a publisher's imprint was not necessarily an endorsement of the contents of a book, they continued to introduce the new science into America. In its way, Harper's publication of Chambers's *Vestiges of the Natural History of Creation,* which had cleared the ground for Darwin, had been equally significant, though it, too, was criticized by conservative authorities. With Holt's American Scientific Series and Putnam's International Science Series, these publications prepared the way for the blossoming of a newer science in the twentieth century.

The twentieth century has its scientific series also, notably that undertaken by The University of Chicago Press under Robert A. Millikan and including his work on *The Electron*. The new physics, the new chemistry, the new theory of matter are all reflected in the later imprints of the surviving houses. The scientific advances of the twentieth century were introduced not only to the specialist, but to the layman in such works as Duncan's *The New Knowledge* (Barnes), Conant's *Modern Science and Modern Man* (Columbia University Press), Heisenberg's *The Physical Principles of the Quantum Theory* (University of Chicago Press), and a symposium entitled *Alternatives to the H-Bomb* (Beacon Press).

The technological developments that grew with two World Wars are reflected in Putnam's publication of William Mitchell's *Winged Defense,* for which the publisher, with his profound personal interest in aviation, wrote a foreword, and for which the author, who held that aircraft would make seacraft obsolete, was court-martialed. Similarly, Macmillan's Air Age Education Series, published for the Civil Aeronautics Administration, demonstrates the skill with which the publisher helps to weave the national fabric of which he is a part. Less spectacularly, but no less notably, the advances in technology are mirrored in the continuing revisions of the Merriam Dictionaries, whose added words are an index to the accelerated rate of growth in the complexity of modern life. Radio and television, radar and air transportation are there defined for the denizens of a new age, who find that the ancient word *atomic* has now become endowed with one current, direful meaning. Technological progress is naturally best reflected in the publications of seven surviving houses that specialize in scientific and technical books, such as Van Nostrand and Wiley. Having published its Library of Modern Science during the twenties, and issued works on atoms, X-rays, and electrons, Van Nostrand joined the mobilization program by producing volumes on radio, navigation, and aircraft engineering. Following World War II, Wiley began its ambitious long-range Nuclear Science Program. The gap between Darwin's *Origin of Species* (Appleton) and Hans A. Bethe's *Elementary Nuclear Theory* (Wiley) or Reichenbach's *Philosophic Foundations of Quantum Mechanics* (University of California Press) is wide, but it is bridged by the surviving publishing houses which laid the foundations for scientific progress in the nineteenth century and carried it on into the twentieth.

In the science of psychology, the surviving firms have been especially active. Through the efforts of Longman and of Holt, the works of William James were introduced to the American public, while Appleton undertook publication of G. Stanley Hall's monumental treatise on *Adolescence* as early as 1904 when the firm faced financial difficulties. Little, Brown may be credited with that pioneer book in its field, Healy's *The Individual Delinquent,* and Dodd's purchase of the Moffat, Yard list brought to the concern the great works of Adler, Freud, and Jung. From The Childhood and Youth Series of Bobbs-Merrill to the serial publications in comparative psychology undertaken by The Johns Hopkins Press, from the works on maternal overprotection and the rights of infants issued by Columbia University Press to the manual on child psychology of Wiley, the advances in psychology have found significant support in the imprints of the surviving publishers.

Even more notable, however, has been their part in shaping the changing economic patterns of the twentieth century, an enterprise that also frequently had its beginnings in the preceding age. It was the publisher Crowell who suggested to Richard Ely as early as 1886 the subject of his *Labor Movement in America,* a work that was followed by other books from which grew Crowell's Library of Economics and Politics. It was Charles Scribner, who, although he personally detested socialism, issued Howe's *Privilege and Democracy in America,* Veblen's *Theory of Business Enterprise,* and the writings of Max Eastman. From that firm emerged also such a revealing exposé as Jacob Riis's *How the Other Half Lives,* as well as a compendium on the Bok world peace plan entitled *Ways to Peace.* Over the Harper imprint appeared Lloyd's *Wealth Against Commonwealth,* while Macmillan published Jack London's *War of the Classes* and Spargo's *Bitter Cry of the Children.* From Bellamy's *Equality* (Appleton) to Gilman's *A Dividend to Labor* (Houghton Mifflin), from Baker's *Following the Color Line* (Doubleday) to Harris's *Inequality and Progress* (Houghton Mifflin), the significant works that exposed racial and industrial inequality in both centuries frequently made their disturbing appearance into the world with the imprints of the surviving publishers upon them. Columbia University Press, which had served as agency for the publications bureau of the League of Nations, now handles the publications of six United Nations agencies. Bloch Publishing Company, through the works that bear its imprint, succeeded in awakening Jewish self-awareness after Hitler's rise to power, and now continues to issue the volumes that record the attainment of Israel's Statehood and America's part in that pioneer land. Shifts in economic and political thought are reflected in the very titles of such books as *The Spirit of Democracy* of 1914 (Beacon Press), *Pressure Politics* of 1928 (Columbia University Press), and *The World of the Four Freedoms* of 1943 (Columbia University Press). Upon them all the imprints of surviving publishers are stamped, testifying to their role in the weaving of the changing economic patterns that have become part of the national fabric.

As those publishers had issued the recollections of heroes of the Civil War, they undertook also the books that clarified for the public the two World Wars of a later century. They may not have taken so direct a part in those wars as the Merriams did in the Spanish-American War, when a cable sent to that office was found to contain a coded message from the Dictionary regarding Spanish transport movements, but there is no doubt that they helped reflect the events and ideologies of the later conflicts. The reminiscences of Seward and Porter gave way to those of Admiral Sims (Doubleday) and Brand Whitlock (Appleton), Wilson's minister to Belgium, whose notes had been sent to London in embassy mail pouches before they became a primary document of the First World War. As early as 1913 Usher's *Pan-Germanism* (Houghton Mifflin) had exposed the German plan for world aggression, and subsequently histories of the Great War emerged from the presses of the surviving publishers: Buchan's (Houghton Mifflin), Simonds's five-volume work (Doubleday), McMaster's (Appleton). The war was reflected not only in the histories but in the literature of the times, and as a result at least two of the houses found themselves with best-sellers on their hands—Putnam with Empey's *Over the Top,* which had been ghost-written with the help of Robert Gordon Anderson, and Little, Brown with Remarque's *All Quiet on the Western Front,* which became the most famous novel of World War I, although the publishers had deleted from it the too-realistic hospital chapter.

The role of the survivors was repeated with the Second World War, Bloch publishing the story of the fate of the Jews under the Nazis and the drama of Jewish resistance, Harper introducing the analyses of John Gunther, Winston issuing a history of World War II as the firm had issued a history of World War I, and Doubleday stamping its imprint upon Eisenhower's *Crusade in Europe.* The aftermath of the war was reflected in their work also, notably in *The Threat of Soviet Imperialism* (The Johns Hopkins Press) and Aron's *The Century of Total War* (Doubleday). Even a textbook house (Silver Burdett) could recognize the existence of a new and global world by publishing a post-war geography entitled *A World View* and achieving the translation of *Our Big World* into the Thai language.

While the part that the surviving houses played in introducing the twentieth century to those who lived it is clear and definite, the reasons for their taking that part may be less so. Did they publish these epoch-making and often controversial works simply to fill their coffers, or rather to assume the responsibility they felt they owed to the world in which they lived? While they had no desire to lose money by their enterprises, there is little doubt that the surviving publishers had developed a conception of their profession that viewed it not only as a business but as a public trust. A book was a commodity, but it was something more, and, as Walter H. Page put it, "the moment it is treated as a mere commodity it takes severe revenge on its author and on its publisher." Although James Brown once advised Henry Houghton, "Never hesitate to stop any enterprise which is not paying," the firm of Little, Brown has thought of itself as "something more than a business organized and intended primarily for immediate profit." Despite the fact that George H. Doran considered that in the Doubleday economy of publishing the auditor-in-chief and not the editor-in-chief was the final arbiter of policy, the house of Doubleday held that to be a publisher is something akin to holding public office. While Henry Holt seldom read the manuscripts that streamed into his office, he nevertheless believed that "the *belles-lettres* branch has got to be conducted as a profession, or there is no money in it. . . . Apparently the fine flavor of literature will not stand being dragged through the deeper mires of competition." John Harper may have remarked that "to a merchant the commodity in which he deals is always merchandise," but it was also his view that the Harper publishing mission must not merely meet existing demands but create those demands "by the suggestive power" of its own initiative.

Many of the most significant books undertaken by the surviving houses were certainly suggested by the publishers themselves, who recognized that a moral responsibility attached to the nature of their business and that any extension of their business could and should be an extension of public knowledge. As Van Nostrand put it, "The good publisher . . . creates books out of his own vision of markets." Frank Dodd went so far as to say that, because of his responsibility to the public, a publisher should issue twenty or thirty books a year "for the credit of the house, even if they did not pay," and Walter H. Page concluded that "a book that has any sterling quality . . . ought never to have the imprint of a publisher who is not really a sharer of its fortunes, a true partner with the author." To Scribner's, on the other hand, a publishing house was a forum which should present all sides of a controversial issue; but although this view differed from Page's, it stemmed from the same realization of responsibility to the public.

Publishing, certainly, is not an exact science. It is a property, but it is also a responsibility. It is a money-making machine, but it is something more than that. It is a business, but it is also a cultural trusteeship. That the surviving publishers were aware of this double nature of their unique profession is indicated not only by their own words, but by the activities of their houses. In the final analysis they have come to understand with Archibald MacLeish that "To honor a book is to honor civilization." It is their peculiar privilege to honor the books that help shape the civilization of their country.

It is possible, though not probable, that this conception of their profession—this twofold view that saw a publishing house as both a business and a public trust, each benefiting and profiting the other—was one of the reasons why one hundred ninety-one organizations founded before 1900 still survive. It is a possibility to be reckoned with, but never to be proved by facts and figures.

Other reasons for their survival present themselves, however, which can be substantiated by their own histories. Of one hundred ninety-one houses that survive from before 1900, fifty-three, or twenty-seven per cent, are still in control of the families that founded them. The percentage becomes greater when it is remembered that several of those houses—the religious book societies, the university presses, scholarly institutions, and the American Book Company, a merger—were established not by founders of families at all, but usually by various publications committees. When these houses have been eliminated from the count, the proportion of surviving firms still controlled by the original family rises to thirty-five per cent. The inclusion of Lippincott, which began with control of the present family in 1836, of Putnam, which remained in the charge of the original family from 1838 to the early 1930's, and of Harper, which continued in family control from 1817 to 1900, would further increase the percentage. But since it was primarily because of the large number of family retainers in the house of Harper that the establishment suffered temporary financial difficulty, that firm must be eliminated from the register and regarded as one of the few exceptions that prove the rule. America's oldest publishing firm—Lea & Febiger—has persisted in the hands of founder Mathew Carey's family since 1785. John Wiley & Sons, founded in 1807, is today represented by the fifth generation of the original family. P. J. Kenedy & Sons traces family continuity back to 1826, William H. Sadlier, Inc., to 1832, and A. S. Barnes & Company to 1838, while Dodd, Mead & Company, founded in 1839, may boast itself the oldest general publishing house in New York still in the control of the founder's family. From these facts alone it becomes apparent that one obvious element in the formula for survival is the establishment not only of a sound business but of a dynasty to carry it on.

A second ingredient in the survival formula is evidenced by the large number of specialist firms among the surviving houses, a proportion that may be gauged at one hundred sixty-six to twenty-five. There were, of course, shifts in the history of these houses from the general to the specialist field, as in the cases of Blakiston and Lea & Febiger, which began as general houses but were subsequently transformed into medical firms, and of Wiley, which turned from general publishing to science and technology. And there was the shift from one specialty to another, as in the case of Barnes, which began as a textbook concern but was converted into a publishing house for books on sport and physical education when, after the

First World War, health education became mandatory in some states. By and large, however, the houses that began as specialist houses have continued with their specialties. And, since eighty-six per cent of the surviving organizations are specialist houses, the second element in the formula for survival becomes clear. Having established a dynasty, a firm might do well to choose a specialty for which there is an enduring demand.

The surviving specialist houses might be said to supply the needs of man's soul, man's intellect, and man's body, but of all the trinity, the soul emerges with the strongest and most abiding requirements. Of the one hundred sixty-six surviving specialist houses, forty-seven supply those needs in one way or another, primarily by the publication not merely of the Bible but of a variety of denominational tracts and theological and religious books. Through its system of colportage by which religious publications were distributed by sale or gift to the accompaniment of spiritual conversation and prayer, the American Tract Society circulated its works through the farthest reaches of the country, while The American Baptist Publication Society has in a similar manner distributed the Bible among the destitute poor. When immigrants arrived in the United States, they were greeted with evangelical literature, and when they moved on to the Middle West, the church—and its publishing agencies—moved west with them. Religious books have sold well in good times and in bad times, too, when people apparently needed the comfort that such literature could supply. The panic year of 1893 was the most prosperous in the history of Fleming H. Revell. The entry of the United States into two World Wars heightened the demand for religious books, as well as for related books on mind mastery and self-help—a demand that was reflected in the output not only of firms that specialized in such productions but of the general publishing houses as well, many of which organized religious book departments for that purpose. Even L. C. Page, a general concern with a strong line of juveniles, can undertake Tolstoy's *The Kingdom of God Is Within You* with a foreword of appreciation by Mary Martin!

Closely linked to the needs of man's soul is his desire for immortality, a desire that is most tangibly brought to fruition in his children. Twenty-seven of the surviving specialist houses are built upon the needs of the nation's children, twenty-two as textbook and educational concerns and five as producers of juveniles. As Daniel

Heath astutely remarked, "Let me publish the text books of a nation and I care not who writes its songs or makes its laws." McGuffey, Webster, and Spencer have formed an educational trinity that is a living heritage in the country. Indeed, Webster's "blue-back" *Speller* is older than the country itself, a declaration of independence for the American language. So enormous were the profits in providing textbooks for the nation's children that a so-called schoolbook "adoption," involving thousands of copies of books, was formerly attended with violent competition and with methods better adapted to political conventions than to institutions of learning. Saloon keepers in the West and Middle West often acted as members of local school boards, with obvious results, and one luckless publisher's representative, whose competitors had set a trap for him, was forced to flee a St. Louis "adoption" in the dead of night minus overcoat and shoes. Although such colorful procedures have ended, the textbook industry has extended both its resources and its influence. It has also followed the dictates of the changing times. When a Quaker school objected that a chapter on choice and chance in an algebra schoolbook might encourage gambling, the chapter was eliminated. When the Woman's Christian Temperance Union advocated the passage of laws requiring instruction in the deleterious effects of alcohol and narcotics, new physiology textbooks were provided for the purpose. The Spanish-American War led not only to the wider use of Spanish texts, but to the development of the American educational system in Cuba, Puerto Rico, and the Philippines, with the aid of publishers' representatives. The textbook publishers have followed with profit the changing trends of the times, reducing their production of German schoolbooks after the First World War, keeping pace by supplying the literature of the new education—the project method—by which children of a later generation learn to do by doing.

Texts facilitate the education of children and juvenile literature provides the pleasure of children. To twenty-seven specialist houses that supply the means for that education and that pleasure must be added the many general publishing firms which have established textbook or juvenile departments. Macmillan was in the vanguard with its Children's Books Department, founded in 1919 to give special attention to books for boys and girls, but others have followed, recognizing the ever-enduring needs of the nation's children as well as the profits that can be derived from supplying them.

To fill man's intellectual needs, seven university presses founded before 1900 survive today, when they have been joined by the great spate of newer university presses that produce scholarly and significant books both for layman and specialist. To these firms might be added five other houses that concentrate upon scholarly publications, including Barnes & Noble and Hafner Publishing Company, as well as eleven specialist organizations that provide trade and reference books: Funk and Merriam with their dictionaries, Gregg and Pitman with their shorthand and business books, Bowker and Wilson with their reference works and bibliographies for libraries and the book trade, the American Library Association, together with F. E. Compton, The Grolier Society, A. N. Marquis, and James T. White, with their encyclopedias and biographical reference books. And surely serving the mind of man are the thirteen houses that specialize in music, the four that concentrate upon drama, and the three whose output is confined primarily to art.

The demands of man's body are supplied by five houses specializing in medicine: The Blakiston Division of McGraw-Hill, Lea & Febiger, Williams & Wilkins, F. A. Davis Company, and W. B. Saunders Company, all of which have contributed to the medical progress of the twentieth century. In such a category also might be placed the seven scientific and technical specialists, including Van Nostrand and Wiley, Frederick J. Drake and Norman W. Henley, as well as the houses of Barnes and Stackpole with their books on sport and physical education.

Eleven law book publishing firms, seven houses catering to the needs of industry, four directory publishers, three Masonic concerns, two whose publications serve the farmer and the agriculturist, two which produce gift and record books, and the remaining miscellaneous houses that emphasize such diverse interests as transportation, socialism, genealogy, Orientalia, and maritime literature complete the list of specialist houses which, quantitatively at least, dominate the field of the surviving publishers. Their history suggests a tentative formula for endurance in the trade: dynastic control coupled with a strong specialty that fulfills unceasing requirements, notably religious literature or texts for children. Of the making of books there is no end, but apparently of the making of books for man's soul and of books for man's children there never will be an end. Neither war nor peace, prosperity nor depression, motion pictures nor television can set a finis to books that lure men from the chimney corner with words to lift their souls and that lure children from play with words to rouse the mind and touch the heart.

The long-established firms, whether specialist or general, have survived not only the fluctuations of the times but the errors of their own ways. Mistakes of rejection have never been catastrophic; yet in the annals of publishing they must be recorded on the debit side of the ledger. Macmillan's refusal of Ellen Glasgow's first book, *The Descendant,* was regarded as one of the two greatest mistakes ever made by the president, George Brett, who later acknowledged that had he read the manuscript personally instead of leaving the decision to others, it would not have been declined. One of the most golden of opportunities was lost by Fleming H. Revell when the house turned down Charles M. Sheldon's *In His Steps.* Putnam must confess the refusal of *All Quiet on the Western Front* before it became a Little, Brown best-seller, while Scribner must bear the ignominy of having declined not only Bennett's *Old Wives' Tale* and Gertrude Atherton, but all but one of Emily Dickinson's poems. Dreiser's *Sister Carrie* was rejected by Harper and when later accepted by Doubleday was so poorly regarded that it was published in a small edition to minimize circulation.

The declinations that preceded the publication of other books cannot be assigned to specific houses, but there is little doubt that the rejections were made by at least a few of the long-established firms. Louisa Muhlbach's historical novel, *Joseph II,* had been almost universally declined and had been printed in Mobile during the Confederacy and bound in wallpaper before it was taken over by Appleton and became an astonishing success. Half a dozen refusals preceded the same firm's acceptance of Westcott's *David Harum,* and by the time it became a best-selling novel of 1898 it was also a posthumous one. Upton Sinclair's *The Jungle,* having been rejected by five houses, appeared as a best-seller of 1906. At least six declinations were received by Zona Gale before Appleton published *Miss Lulu Bett* in 1920, and five houses had turned down Mary Roberts Rinehart's *The Circular Staircase* before it emerged over the Indianapolis imprint of Bobbs-Merrill. Benét's *John Brown's Body* is said to have been refused by dozens of publishers before it enriched the list of Doubleday, Doran.

Mistakes of acceptance are more devastating than mistakes of rejection, but they can neither be counted nor recorded. Yet, was it a mistake for Lea & Blanchard to have issued Poe's *Tales of the Grotesque and Arabesque* in 1839, although by 1841 the book had not yet returned the expense of publication? Was it an error for Putnam to have published the 1851 edition of Hawthorne's *Mosses from an Old Manse,* which two years after its appearance had not sold more than 750 copies?

To the mistakes of the surviving firms must be added, also on the debit side of their ledgers, an attitude that sometimes does less than honor to a book. The piracies that preceded the passage of the International Copyright Law are over, but they have upon occasion been followed by other "piracies." The sub-standard contracts offered to the young author of a first book by such long-established firms as Dutton or Macmillan may be condoned by their auditor-in-chief but surely not by their editor-in-chief. The rather casual disregard of a contract that discredits the history of such a house as Houghton Mifflin is less an error of judgment than a perversion of ethics.

Yet all these mistakes and blots upon the 'scutcheon are canceled out by the achievements of the publishers who have survived them. For these publishers have not only contributed to the civilization of which they are a part but garnered the rewards they merit. Upon their lists have appeared many of the significant books of the times and many of the best-sellers of the day. Among the "Golden Multitudes" recorded by Frank Luther Mott there appear time and again the imprints of Carey & Lea or Lea & Blanchard, Wiley and Putnam, Harper, Scribner, Appleton, Dodd, Mead. To them belongs the glory attendant upon the publication of Cooper's *The Spy* (Wiley & Halsted), Dana's *Two Years Before the Mast* (Harper), Poe's *The Raven* (Wiley & Putnam), Melville's *Moby-Dick* (Harper), Joel Chandler Harris's *Uncle Remus* (Appleton), and Stephen Crane's *The Red Badge of Courage* (Appleton).

The best-sellers of a later day, however, lend themselves more readily to exact quantitative analysis. Moreover, they form a better index to the accomplishments of the long-established houses, since in their case those firms faced the competition less of other nineteenth-century firms which have since fallen by the wayside than of the newer companies founded after 1900. What proportion of the later best-sellers can be assigned to the surviving houses when they

faced the keener competition of new publishing blood? Alice Payne
Hackett in her *Fifty Years of Best Sellers* has listed, in order of sales,
the American best-sellers from 1880 to 1945. Of fifty-five titles that
sold a million or more copies each, thirty-four bore the imprints of
the surviving houses, including, in order of popularity, Margaret
Mitchell's *Gone with the Wind* (Macmillan), Lew Wallace's *Ben
Hur* (Harper), and Marion Hargrove's *See Here, Private Hargrove*
(Holt). Of the one hundred fourteen best-selling titles that sold less
than one million copies each, sixty-seven were published by the long-
established firms. Of the total one hundred sixty-nine titles recorded,
in other words, one hundred one—or sixty per cent—bore the imprints of the survivors. In the lead, with ten best-sellers to the credit
of each, are Doubleday, with the novels of Gene Stratton Porter and
Tarkington's *Penrod;* Houghton Mifflin with the works of Kate
Douglas Wiggin, Lloyd C. Douglas, and Ben Ames Williams; and
Little, Brown, with *Quo Vadis* and volumes by "Ethel Vance,"
James Hilton, Cronin, and Marquand. Tying for second place, with
nine best-sellers each, are Macmillan, Scribner, and Dodd, Mead,
while Harper emerges as runner-up with eight titles. The survivors
who hit the best-seller lists frequently include Lippincott (six), Putnam (five), Holt and Revell (four each), Dutton and Winston (three
each), Appleton, Crowell, and McClurg (two each). Five firms appear with only one title each: Lothrop, with Margaret Sidney's
Five Little Peppers of 1880; The Pilgrim Press, with a religious best-
seller of 1903, William Allen Knight's *Song of Our Syrian Guest;*
Judson Press, the trade name of The American Baptist Publication
Society's printing plant, with Marshall Saunders's *Beautiful Joe* of
1911; Funk & Wagnalls, with Emily Post's *Etiquette* of 1922; and
Abingdon-Cokesbury, the publishing division of The Methodist
Publishing House, with another religious best-seller, Norman Ny-
gaard's *Strength for Service to God and Country* of 1942. To the
surviving firms go the credit and the rewards for having published
such notable best-sellers as Jerome K. Jerome's *Three Men in a
Boat* (Holt), Edward Westcott's *David Harum* (Appleton), Owen
Wister's *The Virginian* (Macmillan), Jack London's *The Call of the
Wild* (Macmillan), and Betty Smith's *A Tree Grows in Brooklyn*
(Harper). The proportion of best-sellers contributed by the surviv-
ing firms is increased when Edward Weeks's "Modern Estimate of
American Best Sellers" is used as a basis for consideration. That list,

excluding such best-sellers as the Bible, Fannie Farmer's *Cook Book,* and *The Book of Etiquette,* lists sixty-five American best-sellers from 1875 to 1933. Of the sixty-five, fifty-eight—or nearly ninety per cent—were published by the survivors.

That the credit for so many of the nation's best-sellers belongs to the long-established houses is partially explained by their standing in output of books. In 1954 they led the lists quantitatively, Doubleday first, Macmillan second, Harper third, and Oxford fourth, with Lippincott, Dodd, Mead, and Little, Brown not far behind.

The publisher rather than his country gathers the rewards of the best-seller. What, then, of those books which may or may not have been best-sellers, but which are regarded as the most significant literary productions of the twentieth century? Any listing of such works is sure to be at best arbitrary and at worst misleading, but one such summary exists which is perhaps less arbitrary and misleading than most. In 1951, The Grolier Club placed on exhibition what were called "The Important Books in English" published between 1901 and 1950. The one hundred eighteen books selected included sixty-seven that were by American authors and were primarily of a high literary quality, embracing novels, poetry, essays, juveniles, short stories, biographies, drama, history, and one philosophical work. During the first half of the twentieth century, when the surviving houses faced primarily the competition of their newer rivals, what proportion of the so-called important books bore their long-tried imprints? Of the one hundred eighteen books exhibited, sixty—or fifty per cent—were published by the surviving concerns. Leading them all, with twelve books to its credit, was the house of Scribner, which published volumes by Edwin Arlington Robinson, Edith Wharton, F. Scott Fitzgerald, Ernest Hemingway, and Thomas Wolfe. The firms of Harper and Doubleday (Doubleday, Page and Doubleday, Doran), represented by ten volumes each, tied for second place, Harper joining the list with works by John Dos Passos and Edna St. Vincent Millay, Doubleday with the novels of Upton Sinclair, Booth Tarkington, and Ellen Glasgow, as well as with Benét's epic poem, *John Brown's Body.* Macmillan, with eight imprints, gained fourth place, its name appearing upon the novels of Owen Wister and Jack London and the poems of Vachel Lindsay, Edgar Lee Masters, and Marianne Moore. The remaining survivors who issued the "important" books of the half-century included Holt and Houghton Mifflin (five each), Dutton (three), Dodd, Mead and Little, Brown (two each), and Putnam's, Oxford, and Warne (one each). Among the great American books bearing their imprints were Frost's *North of Boston* (Holt), Sandburg's *Chicago Poems* (Holt), *The Education of Henry Adams* (Houghton Mifflin), Brooks's *Flowering of New England* (Dutton), and Marquand's *The Late George Apley* (Little, Brown).

Leading in quantitative output, with a goodly proportion of best-sellers to their credit, the surviving firms have also been leaders among the publishers of significant twentieth-century works. If they have left to the newer houses, whose antiquity sits more lightly upon their structures, the task of introducing to the public the more radical writings of the times, nevertheless they have succeeded in paying the debt they owe to their profession and to the civilization of which it is a part. They have woven into the present the strong, conservative threads of the past. They have helped to mould the twentieth century, but they have not forgotten the century that preceded it. And so they reflect an age that is marked both by change and by continuity. In an era that is often unmindful of its beginnings, they throw upon the screen of today the shadow of yesterday. In a catastrophic time they are active reminders that civilization has roots as well as branches. It is the privilege of all publishers to shape and to color the national fabric. But only to these long-established houses belongs the special privilege of linking today with yesterday in an age that must look to the past before it can turn to the future.

SUPPLEMENT

UNITED STATES BOOK PUBLISHING FIRMS

Surviving from Before 1900

This Supplement covers, for the most part, only those firms founded prior to 1900 which devote their major activities to the publishing of books. Thus, a concern such as N. W. Ayer & Son is not included, for although it publishes an important *Directory of Newspapers and Periodicals* and was founded before 1900, it is primarily an advertising agency and not a book publishing business. Organizations such as The Grolier Club which publish books only occasionally are also excluded. Museums and institutions are not represented except in a few cases where their publishing output is of great relative significance.

In all other respects, the Supplement aims to include all book publishing firms in the United States, whether general or specialist, surviving from before 1900. Yet such is the tenacious nature of the profession of publishing that, after this Supplement goes to press, there is little doubt that other small but sturdy specialist publishing firms will crop up too late for inclusion. The fact that completeness in this survey may be an objective almost impossible to realize simply adds another feather to the caps of the many old publishers who will not fade away.

1. AFRICAN METHODIST EPISCOPAL SUNDAY SCHOOL UNION. Founded 1882 and incorporated 1889. The Union, located in Nashville, Tennessee, continues to specialize in religious publications.   S*

2. ALLYN AND BACON, Inc. Founded 1868 in Boston as John Allyn, Publisher and Importer, specializing in classical textbooks, most of them derived by purchase of the rights of publication from the Harvard University Bookstore, the previous publisher. Partnership with Dr. George Andrew Bacon formed 1888, when the style was changed to Allyn and Bacon, but emphasis upon the classics continued. Under the influence of Bacon's sons, Charles

* *S* indicates a specialist house; *G* a general publishing house.

Edward Bacon and Paul Valentine Bacon, who became sole partners in 1930, the firm's interests broadened to advance humanistic
studies in America. Now strong in the Social Studies. A merger
effected with Prentice-Hall of New York in 1951, the original
organization of Allyn and Bacon remaining intact.   S

3. THE AMERICAN ACADEMY OF ARTS AND SCIENCES.
Founded 1780 in Boston "to cultivate every art and science which
may tend to advance . . . a free, independent, and virtuous people." James Bowdoin served as first president, followed in 1791
by John Adams. The Academy published the first of its *Memoirs*
in 1785 and a new series was begun in 1833. The Academy began
publication of its *Proceedings* in 1848. Through the Publications
Funds, administered by a Committee of Publication, the Academy
publishes both serial and separate works in the arts and sciences. S

4. THE AMERICAN BAPTIST PUBLICATION SOCIETY.
Founded 1824 in Washington, D. C., as the Baptist General Tract
Society to publish and circulate tracts for American Baptists. In
1826 headquarters were transferred to Philadelphia, and in 1839
the first book publications were issued: Booth's *Reign of Grace,*
Backus's *Church History,* and *Memoirs of Distinguished Chris-
tians.* In 1840 the Society was reorganized and called The American Baptist Publication and Sunday School Society (shortened in
1845 to The American Baptist Publication Society), serving as the
official publishing house for American Baptists. In 1856, the concern purchased the New England Sabbath School Union, and until
the early 1890's The American Baptist Publication Society was
the only Baptist publishing house in existence. The Judson Press
is the trade name of the Society's printing plant and now publishes teaching materials for Sunday church schools, in addition
to books.   S

5. AMERICAN BIBLE SOCIETY. Founded 1816 in New York "to
encourage a wider circulation of the Holy Scriptures, without note
or comment." Elias Boudinot served as first president. In 1822 the
Society established its own Bible House. Incorporated 1841. By
means of auxiliary societies, domestic and foreign agents, and colporteurs, the Society circulates the Bibles, which it prints and publishes, both in the United States and abroad. Has published the
Bible in 206 languages, and issues a monthly organ, *Bible Society
Record.*   S

6. AMERICAN BOOK COMPANY. Founded 1890 as merger of
four major textbook houses: D. Appleton & Co., A. S. Barnes &
Co., Ivison, Blakeman, Taylor & Co., and Van Antwerp, Bragg

& Co. Later took over Harper schoolbook list, acquired textbooks of other publishing houses, and set up subsidiary companies. In 1908 reincorporated under the much stricter laws of the State of New York and dropped its subsidiary companies to remove the basis for charges that it was a "trust." Is today one of the largest publishers of textbooks only in the world, including in its list three great names in the history of education: McGuffey, Webster, and Spencer.   S

7. AMERICAN LIBRARY ASSOCIATION. Founded 1876 in Philadelphia by about one hundred librarians, including Melvil Dewey, "for the purpose of promoting the library interests of the country." Incorporated 1879. In 1909 headquarters were established in Chicago. Since 1886 the Association has conducted a publishing program for libraries "and in the interest of library progress and education generally." The Association specializes, therefore, in the publication of professional tools for libraries and librarians.   S

8. THE AMERICAN PHILOSOPHICAL SOCIETY. Founded 1769 in Philadelphia as a merger of Benjamin Franklin's Junto (begun in 1727) and his American Philosophical Society (begun in 1743), with Franklin as president. The Society's *Transactions*, the oldest scientific journal in America with a continuous history, was launched in 1769. The Society's *Proceedings* was begun in 1838 and *Memoirs* in 1935. In addition to its serial publications, the Society publishes separate works and miscellaneous publications in the field of scholarship.   S

9. THE AMERICAN SABBATH TRACT SOCIETY (RECORDER PRESS). Founded 1843 in New York City as The General Sabbath Tract Society by a group of individuals acting for members of the Society, "to promote the observance of the Bible Sabbath . . . by the publication and circulation of . . . periodicals, tracts, treatises, and books." In 1844 the name was changed to The American Sabbath Tract Society. Incorporated 1856. In 1872 the Society moved its publishing interests to Alfred, N.Y., and at that time the Society assumed printing and publication of *The Sabbath Recorder*, which had been launched in 1844. Another removal took place in 1894, to Plainfield, N.J. The Recorder Press, the publishing house of The American Sabbath Tract Society, is still an organ of the Seventh Day Baptist Denomination and continues to print and publish denominational works as well as to carry on commercial printing.   S

10. AMERICAN TECHNICAL SOCIETY. Founded 1898 in Boston by R. T. Miller, Jr., to make available to workers information on

technical and vocational subjects. The founder retired in 1940, and the Society was then incorporated "not for profit under the laws of the State of Illinois." The Society, now in Chicago, publishes mainly works in the fields of industrial arts and vocational education. **S**

11. AMERICAN TRACT SOCIETY, Inc. Founded 1825 by S. V. S. Wilder and others through merger involving New York Religious Tract Society, New England Tract Society, and about forty smaller groups engaged in publishing and distributing evangelical literature—its purpose, "to diffuse a knowledge of . . . Jesus Christ as the Redeemer of sinners, and to promote the interests of vital godliness and sound morality, by the circulation of religious tracts." Published *Pilgrim's Progress* in twenty-five languages and through its system of colportage has reached families in remote sections of the country. In five major wars has published and distributed free evangelical literature to the armed services. In 1948 discontinued book publication and now aims at annual distribution of from fifteen to twenty million gospel tracts. **S**

12. APPLETON-CENTURY-CROFTS, Inc. Founded 1825 as Daniel Appleton, book department of Daniel Appleton's drygoods business in New York City. Entered publishing field 1831 with a religious item: W. Mason's *Crumbs from the Master's Table*. Style changed to D. Appleton & Company 1838 when William Henry Appleton became his father's partner. Daniel Appleton retired in 1848 (died 1849) and William Henry Appleton became president. The latter resigned from the presidency in 1894 and died in 1899. His son, William Worthen Appleton, succeeded him as president (died 1924). In 1900, the firm was reorganized, and another reorganization took place in 1917. The concern was consolidated in 1933 with The Century Company, and the firm name was changed to D. Appleton-Century Company, Inc. The Century Company had been founded 1870 with magazine venture of Roswell Smith and Josiah Gilbert Holland, and was organized as The Century Company 1881. Purchased stock of F. S. Crofts, Inc., which was merged with the firm in 1948 to form Appleton-Century-Crofts, Inc. The house has several major departments, including Trade, Medical, College, and Reference Book. **G**

13. ARCHITECTURAL BOOK PUBLISHING CO., Inc. Founded 1895 in New York by Paul Wenzel for the purpose of publishing and promoting the sale of architectural and industrial art books. The firm's first book publications were Keppler's *Modern Jewelry* and Hartmann's *Modern American Sculpture*. The company be-

came a partnership in 1914 with the admission of Maurice Kra-
kow. Incorporated 1924. The firm, still specializing in architecture
and industrial arts, continues in the control of the original family,
now under Walter W. Frese, grandson of the founder.   S

14. AUGSBURG PUBLISHING HOUSE. Founded 1891 in Minneapolis, Minnesota, by the United Norwegian Lutheran Church to
publish the papers and textbooks of the Church, to make available
English translations of Norwegian religious works, and to serve as
an outlet for Lutheran authors in America. In 1917, the House
absorbed the Lutheran Publishing House and the Hauge Printing
and Publishing Society, both of which had been established in
1878. The firm specializes in publications for The Evangelical
Lutheran Church.   S

15. AUGUSTANA BOOK CONCERN. Founded 1884 as a private
stock company to do part of the printing for the Augustana Synod
(now the Augustana Evangelical Lutheran Church). Since it was
a continuation of the "Ungdomens Vänner" and the Augustana
Tract Society, its history may be indirectly traced back to 1854,
when three pioneer pastors, Esbjörn, Hasselquist, and Carlsson,
planned a newspaper for Swedish Lutheran immigrants. [The
Swedish Lutheran Publication Society, organized in 1858, was
taken over in 1874 by the Engberg-Holmberg Publishing Company, and in 1877 a new publication society, the "Ungdomens
Vänner," was started at Augustana College, later incorporated as
the Augustana Tract Society]. In 1889, the Lutheran Augustana
Book Concern was established at the convention of the Augustana
Synod at Rock Island, Illinois, as the official publication house of
the Synod. In 1903 its name became the Augustana Book Concern,
and in 1917 it purchased the remainder of the business of the
Engberg-Holmberg Publishing Company. The Concern continues
to propagate religious truth through the circulation of Lutheran
literature and to encourage Swedish-American endeavor.   S

16. THE AVE MARIA PRESS. Founded 1865 at Notre Dame, Indiana, by the Congregation of Holy Cross, under the Rev. Edward Sorin, C.S.C., for the purpose of publishing a weekly home
magazine, *The Ave Maria,* as well as Catholic books. The house
continues its publications for Catholics, now emphasizing pamphlets.   S

17. WALTER H. BAKER COMPANY. A direct descendant of Herbert Sweet Company, established 1845 in Boston for the purpose
of publishing plays. In 1851 the Sweet Company was sold to William H. Spencer, who carried on the enterprise until his death in

1870, when his brother, Charles H. Spencer, entered the firm, later merging his holdings with Lee & Shepard. From 1872 to 1885 the play business was carried on under the name of George M. Baker & Company. Walter H. Baker, a brother of George M. Baker, was given charge of the play department of Lee & Shepard in 1874 and, from that time until 1892, carried on both the retail and mail order departments. In the latter year Walter H. Baker formed a partnership with Frank E. Chase, with whom the business was carried on until 1920, when Chase's interest passed to Theodore Johnson. Theodore Johnson and Walter H. Baker incorporated the concern in 1920 under the style of Walter H. Baker Company. In 1929, after Baker's death, Theodore Johnson purchased the Baker holdings. In 1951 Theodore Johnson retired, selling his share to New York interests. Specialists in drama, the firm established the Baker International Play Bureau in 1924 and the following year opened a religious department issuing plays for church groups.   S

18. BAKER, VOORHIS & CO., Inc. Founded 1820 in New York City by Oliver Halsted for the selling and publishing of law books. In 1830, when John S. Voorhies became Halsted's partner, the firm name was changed to Halsted & Voorhies, and upon Halsted's death in 1842 the business was continued by Voorhies. After the death of Voorhies in 1865, the firm was continued as Baker, Voorhis & Co. Incorporated 1889. In 1894 the firms of L. K. Strouse & Company, law booksellers and publishers, and Baker, Voorhis & Co. were consolidated. The concern was affiliated with The Lawyers Co-operative Publishing Company in 1940. It continues to specialize in the publication of law books.   S

19. BANCROFT-WHITNEY COMPANY. Founded 1856 in San Francisco by Hubert Howe Bancroft under the name of H. H. Bancroft for the publication of books and the wholesale and retail supply of books, stationery, office supplies, and musical instruments. The firm's first publication was a revised *Clerk's Assistant for California* by Henry J. Labatt. In 1870 the firm name was changed to A. L. Bancroft Company. In 1886 the establishment was destroyed by fire and was merged with Sumner Whitney Co., law publishers of San Francisco, the firm being renamed the same year Bancroft-Whitney Company. The following year the concern launched its important Annotated Reports System, selecting and annotating significant decisions from all courts. In 1919 The Lawyers Co-operative Publishing Company acquired a controlling interest in the firm. The concern continues to specialize in modern tools of legal research for all lawyers.   S

20. BANKS-BALDWIN LAW PUBLISHING COMPANY. Founded 1804 in New York and Albany by David Banks and William Gould under the name of Gould & Banks, the first American house engaged exclusively in the sale and publication of law books. Banks had charge of the New York house, Gould of the Albany branch. In 1857 when David Banks, Jr., and his brother, Charles Banks, became partners, the firm name was changed to Gould, Banks & Gould. The following year David Banks and the Goulds retired, and David Banks, Jr., and his brothers, Charles Banks and A. Bleecker Banks, continued the firm under the name of Banks & Brothers. In 1880 Charles Banks retired. During the 1890's two distinct corporations were formed: Banks & Company in Albany (after the dissolution of Banks, Gould & Company) with A. Bleecker Banks as president, and the Banks Law Publishing Company, successor to Banks & Brothers, in New York. In 1910 the Albany firm was acquired by Matthew Bender & Company. The New York firm was reorganized in 1923 by David Banks, 3rd, who associated with himself William E. Baldwin. Two years later Baldwin purchased the Banks Law Publishing Company, and in 1932 the firm was merged with the Baldwin Law Publishing Company as Banks-Baldwin Law Publishing Company of New York and Cleveland.   S

21. A. S. BARNES & COMPANY, Inc. Founded 1838 by Alfred Smith Barnes as textbook publishing firm in Hartford, Connecticut. In 1840 the concern was moved to Philadelphia, where its name was changed to A. S. Barnes & Burr, and five years later it was transferred to New York City, becoming A. S. Barnes & Company, educational publishers. In 1890 the American Book Company took over a large portion of the firm's educational books, and a new company was organized to extend the list of miscellaneous publications. The purchase of the educational books and periodicals of E. L. Kellogg & Co. in 1906 led the firm to return to the educational field. The company was incorporated in 1909 as the A. S. Barnes Company, under Henry B. Barnes as president, with the policy of continuing and enlarging the textbook line. A reorganization took place in 1918, with John Barnes Pratt as president, and the following year Pratt took over the firm's hymn books and physical education, folk dance, and game books, as well as the name A. S. Barnes & Company. That firm, incorporated in 1930, claims to be the world's largest publishers of books on physical education, sport, and allied fields. It has continued in the control of the original family (though not of the immediate family).   S

22. BARNES & NOBLE, Inc. Founded 1874 in Wheaton, Illinois, by Charles Montgomery Barnes for the purpose of jobbing used textbooks. Incorporated 1894 as C. M. Barnes Company. The founder retired in 1902, and his son, W. R. Barnes, became president. In 1907 the firm's name was changed to C. M. Barnes-Wilcox Company. Ten years later William R. Barnes sold his interest in that company and came to New York City, where he bought a partnership in Noble and Noble (formerly Hinds and Noble). The store name was then changed to Barnes & Noble with W. R. Barnes as president and G. Clifford Noble as secretary-treasurer. In 1929 Noble withdrew, selling his interest to John Wilcox Barnes, grandson of both C. M. Barnes and J. W. Wilcox. W. R. Barnes died in 1945, and his son, John W. Barnes, president since 1942, continues in that office. The firm did not enter the publishing field until 1932, when it issued *An Outline of the History of Europe 1500-1848* by Henry W. Littlefield. Specializing in educational and scholarly publications, the concern continues in the control of the original family, the third generation of which is now represented.   S

23. BEACON PRESS, Inc. Founded in Boston in 1854, when the executive committee of the American Unitarian Association proposed to raise $50,000 for the "printing, distribution and sale of religious books and pamphlets." Published its first book that year: Bartol's *Grains of Gold,* under imprint of American Unitarian Association. For some years after, outside houses issued many of the Unitarian books, but the precedent of official American Unitarian publishing had been established. In 1914 Beacon Press imprint was introduced and publishing program was broadened to include books dealing not only with religious matters, but with ethical, sociological, and philanthropic subjects. A second expansion of publishing was begun in the mid-1940's, and the firm may be regarded as a "university press" for liberal religious thought. Beacon Press now publishes books of general interest, with a second publishing operation, The Starr King Press, for books of more narrowly denominational concern.   S

24. BEHRENS PUBLISHING COMPANY. An offshoot of the firm of Dick & Fitzgerald, established in New York City in 1858 by William B. Dick and Lawrence R. Fitzgerald. In 1917 that firm was reorganized as the Fitzgerald Publishing Corporation, continuing until 1940. At that time Rudolph Behrens of Danbury, Connecticut, took over the Dick & Fitzgerald handbooks under the name of Behrens Publishing Company. The concern, con-

tinued by his son, now specializes in fraternal books and prepared speeches, as well as many of the original Dick & Fitzgerald handbooks.   S

25. MATTHEW BENDER & COMPANY, Inc. Founded 1887 in Albany, N.Y., by Matthew Bender for the publication of law books. Incorporated 1915. The firm acquired the stock of Banks & Company, Fallon Law Book Company, and other partnerships. The concern, still specializing in law and tax publications, continues in the control of the original family, now represented by two sons, two grandsons, and a great-grandson of the founder.   S

26. CHAS. A. BENNETT CO., Inc. Founded 1899 in Peoria, Illinois, by Charles A. Bennett for the publication of the *Manual Training Magazine*. In 1903 the firm name was changed to Manual Arts Press, and two years later the concern published its first book, Murray's *Problems in Woodworking*. Incorporated 1909 as The Manual Arts Press. The magazine was discontinued in 1939, and the firm emphasized its school shop texts, craft books, art books, and homemaking books. In the same year L. L. Simpson succeeded the founder as president, Bennett continuing as chairman of the board until his death in 1942. On the firm's fiftieth anniversary, October 1, 1949, the name was changed to Chas. A. Bennett Co., Inc. to allow for a broader publishing scope. Upon L. L. Simpson's death in 1952 Richard H. Simpson became president. The concern specializes in the publication of textbooks and technical books.   S

27. BENZIGER BROTHERS, Inc. Founded 1853 in New York, an offshoot of the Swiss firm established in 1792 by Joseph Charles Benziger. In 1860 the United States firm became independent under J. N. Adelrich Benziger and Louis Benziger, grandsons of the founder. Branches were opened in Cincinnati in 1860, Chicago in 1887, San Francisco in 1929, and Boston in 1937, with units in Brooklyn consisting of a complete book manufacturing plant and a plant for the production of ecclesiastical metalware. Vestments and statuary are manufactured. Publications cover the complete Catholic field, and the firm continues in the control of the original family.   S

28. BERLITZ PUBLICATIONS, Inc. Founded 1878 in Providence, R.I., by Maximilian D. Berlitz, to publish books for the Berlitz School of Languages. The scope of publishing activity has so widened that, besides the books designed for the Berlitz language teaching method, the firm publishes self-instruction language books for home study as well as travel phrase books, and issues phonograph records for language teachers. The concern claims to have

published some forty million copies of its language textbooks. Now a New York corporation, the firm still specializes in language publications and numbers among its executives members of the original family.	S

29. ALFRED M. BEST COMPANY, Inc. Founded 1899 in New York City by Alfred M. Best for the purpose of publishing a volume of insurance reports. The firm, still in the control of the founder, continues to specialize in insurance publications, reports, and directories.	S

30. THE BLAKISTON DIVISION of the McGRAW-HILL BOOK COMPANY, Inc. Founded 1843 in Philadelphia by Presley Blakiston and Robert Lindsay under the style of Lindsay and Blakiston. In 1882, with Lindsay's retirement, Blakiston purchased the entire interest in the firm, which became P. Blakiston Son and Company. Upon Blakiston's death in 1898 the name was changed to P. Blakiston's Son and Company. The firm was incorporated in 1929 and reorganized ten years later as The Blakiston Company. It was purchased by Doubleday in 1944, and by the McGraw-Hill Book Company, Inc., in 1954. Having begun as a general publishing and bookselling house with religious books and imports, the concern soon began to specialize in medical and dental works. It now publishes only books in medicine and allied fields.	S

31. BLOCH PUBLISHING CO., Inc. Founded 1854 in Cincinnati as Bloch and Company, Publishers and Printers, by Edward Bloch and Rabbi Isaac M. Wise. Chicago branch established 1885 under the founder's son, Charles E. Bloch, as The Bloch Publishing and Printing Co. In 1901 the Cincinnati and Chicago firms were transferred to New York as the Bloch Publishing Co., "The Jewish Book Concern." Since 1929 the firm has issued *Bloch's Book Bulletin*—edited by Solomon Kerstein—a guide to Jewish books in all languages, "the only one of its kind published." In 1940 the founder's grandson, Edward H. Bloch, took over management. Continuity of family interest and firm policy are represented in this company, America's oldest Jewish publishing house.	S

32. BOARD OF CHRISTIAN EDUCATION OF THE UNITED PRESBYTERIAN CHURCH OF NORTH AMERICA (THE GENEVA PRESS). Founded 1863 in Pittsburgh, Pennsylvania, by the United Presbyterian Board of Publication, subject to the control of the General Assembly of the United Presbyterian Church of North America, for the printing and circulating of Holy Scriptures and the publishing of tracts, papers, periodicals, and

books. In 1944 the present name was adopted. The concern continues to specialize in publication of denominational materials.   S

33. THE BOBBS-MERRILL COMPANY, Inc. Founded 1838 in Indianapolis by E. H. Hood and Samuel Merrill as a book and
stationery store. The following year Merrill acquired Hood's interest, and after the former's death the business was left to his son,
Samuel Merrill, and his son-in-law, Charles W. Moores. The firm's
first venture into the publishing field was a legal work, *Indiana
Reports* (Volume 5). After the Civil War the name became Merrill,
Meigs & Co. In 1884 the firm merged with Bowen, Stewart & Co.
to form the Bowen-Merrill Company, a corporation. Important
events in the company's history included the purchase in 1899 of
the Houghton Mifflin law book list and the purchase in 1912 of
125 law volumes of The American Publishers Company of Norwalk, Ohio. In 1903 the name was changed to The Bobbs-Merrill
Company. The firm, having discontinued both its wholesale paper
department and retail bookselling department, now publishes trade,
law, and schoolbooks.   G

34. BOSTON MUSIC COMPANY. Founded 1885 in Boston, for the
purpose of publishing music, by Gustave Schirmer, Jr., son of the
founder of G. Schirmer, Inc. The firm, which continues to specialize in the publication of music, is still in the control of the
original family, now under Gustave Schirmer, 3rd, son of the concern's founder.   S

35. R. R. BOWKER COMPANY. Founded 1872 as *The Publishers and Stationers' Weekly Trade Circular* (renamed *Publishers'
Weekly* 1873) by Frederick Leypoldt. Both Leypoldt and Richard
Rogers Bowker worked for the founding of the American Library
Association, and the first number of *The Library Journal* was issued in 1876. The firm's long labors for international copyright
began in the 1880's. In 1911 the concern became R. R. Bowker
Company under the presidency of R. R. Bowker, the owning and
operating agency for all Leypoldt and Bowker publications. Beginning as the office of the *Publishers' Weekly,* organ of the book
trade, the company has grown with the growth of the trade, issuing
numerous bibliographic tools and directories and expanding its
directions to record, interpret, and serve the book trade and the
library field.   S

36. THE BRUCE PUBLISHING COMPANY. Founded 1891 in Milwaukee, Wisconsin, by William George Bruce and conducted under his own name until 1914, when the firm was incorporated
as The Bruce Publishing Company. Publishers of general trade

books and Catholic religious books as well as of textbooks for college and school use, including books for industrial arts and vocational education, the firm continues in the control of the original family. G

37. THE BURCH DIRECTORY COMPANY. Founded 1868 in Akron, Ohio, by Nathan H. Burch for the purpose of publishing city directories. The firm's first publication was the Akron, Ohio, *City Directory*. In 1889 the firm became a partnership between Nathan H. Burch and David W. Bowman. With the founder's death in 1897, David W. Bowman became sole owner until 1936, when the firm became a partnership between David W. and Byron W. Bowman. Since David W. Bowman's death in 1945, Byron W. Bowman has operated the firm alone. It continues to specialize in the publication of city directories. S

38. JOHN BYRNE & COMPANY. Founded 1892 in Washington, D.C., by John Byrne and Charles Gulentz, specializing in law books. After Byrne's death in 1923, his interest was purchased by Gulentz, and subsequently the firm was acquired by Callaghan & Company. S

39. CALLAGHAN & COMPANY. Founded 1864 in Chicago by Andrew Callaghan under the name of Callaghan & Cutler, a legal publishing firm for the Middle West. In 1870 the name was changed to Callaghan & Cockroft, and in 1873, to Callaghan & Company. In 1949 a printing plant was constructed in Mundelein, Illinois. The firm continues to specialize in the publication of legal and allied works. S

40. THE CHRISTIAN EDUCATION PRESS. Founded 1828 in Chambersburg, Pennsylvania, as the Board of Christian Education and Publication of the Evangelical and Reformed Church by the General Synod, to publish *The Magazine of the Reformed Church*. In 1849 three preachers formed a company to carry on the business as a private enterprise, but in 1864 it was returned to the Synod. After a fire that year in Chambersburg, it was moved to Philadelphia. From 1899 until 1940 Heidelberg Press was the trade name for the books and other materials published by the Board; in 1940 the present name was adopted. S

41. CHRISTIAN PUBLICATIONS, Inc. Founded 1886 as a private enterprise by Dr. A. B. Simpson to publish periodicals and, later, books concerning his missionary work. The first book publication was Dr. Simpson's *The King's Business*. In 1912 Dr. Simpson relinquished personal control of the business, which was incorporated that year as The Christian Alliance Publishing Company

(changed in 1932 to Christian Publications, Inc.). Although a New York corporation, the firm's headquarters are in Harrisburg, Pennsylvania. The firm is the denominational publishing house for The Christian and Missionary Alliance. S

42. THE CHRISTIAN SCIENCE PUBLISHING SOCIETY. Founded 1898 in Boston by Mary Baker Eddy for the purpose of "more effectually promoting and extending the religion of Christian Science" as taught by the Founder. The Society's first book publication was the *Christian Science Hymnal*. Under control of a Board of Trustees, the Society continues to specialize in the publication of Christian Science literature. S

43. COLUMBIA UNIVERSITY PRESS. Founded 1893 at a meeting of Columbia College trustees "to promote the study of economic, historical, literary, scientific and other subjects; and to promote and encourage the publication of literary works embodying original research in such subjects." Until 1907 its books were published under a contract arrangement with Macmillan, and its sales were handled by Macmillan until 1911. Reorganized in 1923 by Frederick Coykendall, one of its trustees, the Press began to develop its present form and program in 1927, with the appointment of Charles G. Proffitt as its executive officer. In 1928 it began to do the University's printing, in 1934 it started its house organ, *Pleasures of Publishing,* and in 1940 a subsidiary imprint, King's Crown Press, was established, at first to provide economical printing facilities for Ph.D. theses, now to serve as an economical publication service for scholars. The Press's publishing program includes scholarly books for the specialist, books by scholars for educated lay readers, advanced university textbooks, reference books, and books issued or distributed by the Press as agent for other organizations. S

44. F. E. COMPTON & COMPANY. Founded 1893 in Chicago by Chandler B. Beach, under the name of Chandler B. Beach & Company, for the purpose of publishing and distributing *The Students' Cyclopedia*. During the summer of 1893 Dr. Beach was joined by Frank E. Compton, who served as salesman and in 1905 purchased the sales rights. In 1907 the firm name was changed to F. E. Compton & Company. Incorporated 1912, when Compton purchased the manufacturing rights. Ten years later the firm launched its *Compton's Pictured Encyclopedia,* which has constantly been revised and rebuilt since that time. The concern specializes in the publication of that work. S

45. CONCORDIA PUBLISHING HOUSE. Founded 1869 by the Evangelical Lutheran Church of Missouri, Ohio, and other States (present name: The Lutheran Church—Missouri Synod), for the purpose of producing religious materials, promoting religious education among its members, and extending knowledge among people generally. Its purpose was accomplished by the publication and distribution of Bibles, church books, hymnals, religious periodicals, and the collected works of Luther. The latter is considered the most ambitious single undertaking in the firm's history. The company may be regarded as a Lutheran ministry of print.   S

46. EZRA A. COOK PUBLICATIONS, Inc. Founded 1867 in Wheaton and Chicago, Illinois, by Ezra A. Cook, for the purpose of publishing works in opposition to secret societies. Later the firm policy changed, and in addition to continuing the publication of such material, the concern began to publish rituals and Masonic books generally. About 1910 the firm acquired the publications of the Rev. T. B. Arnold. Specializing in fraternal publications, the business is now a corporation.   S

47. CORNELL UNIVERSITY PRESS.* Founded 1869 with Prof. Willard Fiske as director, but discontinued in 1884 "during a period of economic stringency." Re-established in 1930 by the Board of Trustees. Meanwhile, the Comstock Publishing Company (established 1893 by Profs. John Henry Comstock and Simon Henry Gage) had fulfilled, in part, the function of a university press at Cornell. In 1931 the Comstock Publishing Company was merged with the newly re-established Press under the management of Woodford Patterson, publishing text and reference volumes in natural science and scholarly books in the humanities, the classics, economics, and political science. In 1951 the name became Cornell University Press, including Comstock Publishing Associates. Special interests of the Press are books about the Middle East, civil liberty, chemistry, and evolution of civilization, as well as series, joint imprints, and scholarly works of merit. The Comstock imprint is used in fields of the life sciences. Great Seal Books, another division of the Press, provides inexpensive editions of "out-

---

* A university press with a history similar to that of Cornell University Press is the University of Pennsylvania Press. As early as 1870 *The Penn Monthly* carried the imprint of "University Press Company" and in 1889 a University of Pennsylvania Press was organized which published the *University Medical Magazine*. Over thirty years later, a new corporation was formed. The Press is not described in a separate sketch because it traces its own origin to the year 1921 and not to 1870 or 1889 (See *The Association of American University Presses Directory* 1954, p. 35).

standing writings of past years." The first university press founded in America.   S

48. COYNE ELECTRICAL SCHOOL. Founded 1899 as a trade school in Chicago by three Coyne brothers. The School was purchased in 1914 by Bennett W. Cooke. A separate publishing division, specializing in the publication of technical books, was started in 1941.   S

49. THOMAS Y. CROWELL COMPANY. Founded 1870 as a book-bindery in Boston by Thomas Y. Crowell, under the style of Thomas Y. Crowell, Successor to Benjamin Bradley, a Boston bookbinder for whom Crowell had worked and whose firm had been established in 1834. In 1875 Crowell purchased the stock, bound books, and sheet stock of Warren & Wyman of New York, a firm specializing in religious books, and this transaction started the gradual evolution of his business from binding to publishing. A publishing branch was opened in New York in 1876, and the Boston bindery was moved there in 1900. The firm has continued in the control of the Crowell family.   G

50. F. A. DAVIS COMPANY. Founded 1879 in Philadelphia by F. A. Davis for the purpose of publishing medical and scientific books. Still concentrating in that field, the firm continues in the control of the original family.   S

51. DAVISON PUBLISHING COMPANY. Founded 1885 in New York by Alvah E. Davison for the purpose of publishing *Davison's Textile Blue Book*. In 1920 the firm purchased Dockham's *American Report and Directory* (begun 1866 in Boston) and merged it with the *Blue Book*. The concern, now in Ridgewood, New Jersey, specializes in textile publications, registers, directories, guides, and catalogues, and continues in the control of the original family (now managed by the founder's son, Harold M. Davison).   S

52. T. S. DENISON & COMPANY. Founded 1876 in Chicago by Thomas S. Denison, playwright, for the publication of amateur plays. After the founder's death in 1911, Eben Holmes Norris, who had joined the firm in 1892, succeeded him. In 1944 L. M., E. M., and K. M. Brings acquired the concern. Now in Minneapolis, the firm does some general book publishing but specializes in dramatic publications, operettas, entertainment and speech books.   S

53. THE DIETZ PRESS, Inc. Founded 1890 by August Dietz, Sr., in Richmond, Virginia, under the name of The Dietz Printing Co., as a printing and publishing house. Incorporated 1942 as The Dietz

Press, Inc. The firm, which publishes general trade books, emphasizes Americana and Southern historical works and continues in the control of the original family. G

54. DODD, MEAD & COMPANY, Inc. Founded 1839 by Moses Woodruff Dodd and John S. Taylor in New York under the style of Taylor & Dodd, their first imprint appearing that year upon Dr. Gardiner Spring's *The Obligations of the World to the Bible.* In 1840 the partners separated, M. W. Dodd publishing principally theological works. Upon Dodd's retirement in 1870, Frank H. Dodd, his son, formed a partnership with his cousin, Edward S. Mead, as Dodd & Mead, general publishers. The firm's largest single project was the *New International Encyclopaedia,* begun in 1885 and frequently revised. After Frank H. Dodd's death in 1916, the business was incorporated with Edward H. Dodd, the founder's grandson, as president. Important subsequent events included five purchases and three alliances: purchase of the American branch of John Lane Company (1922), of the Moffat, Yard list (1924), of Small, Maynard (1926), of Duffield & Green, and of Sears (both in 1934); alliances with F. S. Crofts Company, college textbook publishers (1924), with John Martin (1926), and with De La Mare, publishers of garden books (1933). In the early 1930's the *Encyclopaedia* was sold to Funk & Wagnalls, and the firm, along with Harper, Harcourt, Brace, and Little, Brown, instituted the reprint house of Blue Ribbon Books. The oldest general publishing house in New York still in the control of the original family, with Edward H. Dodd, Jr., as president and Frank C. Dodd as Chairman of the Board. G

55. F. W. DODGE CORPORATION. Founded 1891 in Boston by Frederick W. Dodge, under the name of F. W. Dodge & Co., in order to supply construction news services. In 1896 The F. W. Dodge Company of New York was organized by Dodge and Clinton H. Sweet, who had established the Record & Guide Co. in New York in 1868. The Dodge firm purchased from Sweet the *Real Estate Record & Builders' Guide, Architectural Record,* and *Sweet's Indexed Catalogue* in 1906, and six years later purchased shares held by Sweet and others. Upon Dodge's death in 1915 his interest was taken over by his widow and his half-brother, Franklin T. Miller. In 1923 their interests were bought by the F. W. Dodge Corporation, and various subsidiary corporations were merged. The firm continues to specialize in news and marketing services and publications for industry, principally in the construction field. In 1952 a regular book department was organized. S

56. DODGE PUBLISHING COMPANY. Founded 1897 in San Francisco as the Dodge Book and Stationery Company for the manufacture of gift books and calendars. The following year the firm appeared in New York as Dodge Stationery Company, and in 1899 as Dodge Publishing Company. In 1927 the concern was acquired by Robert M. McBride and has since then been associated with Robert M. McBride and Company (now The McBride Company, Inc.) as a separate corporation. Although the firm published general trade books for two or three years in the mid-1930's, it now specializes once again in gift books and calendars.   S

57. THE REUBEN H. DONNELLEY CORPORATION. Founding traced to 1864, when Richard R. Donnelley established a printing business in Chicago. In 1881, as the printing of directories became an important part of the firm's operations, R. R. Donnelley & Sons Company established a branch, the Chicago Directory Company, where Reuben H. Donnelley, son of Richard R. Donnelley, began work in 1882. A contract signed in 1886 for the publication of the Chicago Telephone Directory launched the firm into the telephone directory publishing field, and in that year the Reuben H. Donnelley concern was established. Incorporated 1917 as The Reuben H. Donnelley Corporation. The firm, which also concerns itself with mail advertising and other activities, continues to specialize in the publication of telephone directories, and is still in the control of the original family, now represented by the third generation.   S

58. M. A. DONOHUE & CO. Founded in 1861 as Cox & Donohue, bookbinders. Shortly after, the firm's style was changed to Donohue, Wilson & Henneberry, and about 1880 to Donohue & Henneberry, during which period the concern entered the printing as well as the binding business and started publishing books. In 1901, when M. A. Donohue bought out Henneberry, the firm became M. A. Donohue & Co. Its original object in publishing was to issue children's books and sets. In the early 1900's the firm decided to deal exclusively in children's books. It is probably the oldest juvenile publishing firm in the country which throughout its history has been controlled by one family.   S

59. DOUBLEDAY & COMPANY, Inc. Founded 1897 in New York City by Frank N. Doubleday and S. S. McClure under the style of Doubleday, McClure Company. The firm's first book publication was *Romance, Vol. I Tales from McClure's*. With the withdrawal of McClure and the admission to partnership of Walter Hines Page, the name was changed in 1902 to Doubleday, Page &

Company. McClure, Phillips & Company, which had been formed by McClure and John S. Phillips, passed into the hands of Doubleday, Page & Company, and in 1910 the Country Life Press was established in Garden City, Long Island. A merger with the George H. Doran Company in 1927 resulted in another change of name —to Doubleday, Doran & Company, Inc. In 1946 the style became Doubleday & Company, Inc. The firm, now owning and operating The Literary Guild of America and several other book clubs, is still in the control of the original family.   G

60. FREDERICK J. DRAKE & CO. Founded 1899 in Chicago by Frederick J. Drake for the purpose of publishing semi-technical books. After the founder's death in 1912, the firm was managed by L. Brent Vaughan. Retiring in 1930, Vaughan was succeeded by Stafford W. Drake, the founder's son, who became president in 1945. In 1949 the company was moved to Wilmette, Illinois. The firm, still specializing in semi-technical books—how-to-do-it books, works on carpentry and building, refrigeration, electricity, aviation, radio and electronics, commercial art, etc.—continues in the control of the original family.   S

61. THE DRAMATIC PUBLISHING COMPANY. Founded 1885 in Chicago by Charles H. Sergel for the purpose of publishing plays and acting as agent on performing rights. Incorporated 1887. Between 1897 and 1918 various publishing firms were purchased and merged with the concern, which continues to specialize in the publication of plays and allied works.   S

62. E. P. DUTTON & CO., Inc. Founded 1852 in Boston by Lemuel Ide and Edward P. Dutton under the name of Ide & Dutton, distributors of schoolbooks and supplies. By the end of the first year the firm had bought out Charles S. Stimpson's church bookstore in Boston, an acquisition which brought the concern important connections with the Episcopal Church. The first imprint appeared in 1855 upon Horace Mann's *Lectures on Education*. In 1858 Dutton bought out Ide's interest and the firm became E. P. Dutton & Company, publishing principally denominational works. The company acquired the Old Corner Book Store (previously famous as Ticknor & Fields) in 1864, and four years later, when they took over the business of the General Protestant Episcopal Sunday School Union and of the Book Society, established a branch office in New York. In 1869, after James R. Osgood & Co. offered Dutton its New York business in exchange for Dutton's Boston business, the company's offices were transferred to New York City. Subsequently the publishing program was expanded from the early

emphasis upon theology to general literature, education, and fiction, and through a connection with J. M. Dent of London, the firm became publishers of *Everyman's Library,* beginning in 1906. After Edward P. Dutton's death in 1923, John Macrae became president; following the latter's death in 1944, his son, Elliott B. Macrae, became president. Incorporated 1928. G

63. EDEN PUBLISHING HOUSE. Founded 1895 in St. Louis, Missouri, by the German Evangelical Synod of North America to print and publish works for the Evangelical Church. The charter was amended in 1945 to broaden the scope of activity. The House continues to specialize in religious publications for the Evangelical and Reformed Church since its merger in 1934. S

64. THE EDUCATIONAL PUBLISHING CORPORATION. Founded 1883 in Dorchester, Massachusetts, by William Norris for the purpose of publishing a magazine and books for use by teachers in the elementary grades. Sold in 1932. In 1949 changed from a Massachusetts to a Connecticut corporation. Now in Darien, Connecticut, the present owner is M. E. Walker. The firm specializes in publishing books and *Grade Teacher,* a professional magazine for elementary teachers. S

65. EDWARDS BROTHERS, Inc. Founded 1893 in Ann Arbor, Michigan, by John J., Thomas, and Daniel Edwards, for the purpose of mimeographing schoolbooks. Incorporated in 1930, the firm changed the same year from mimeographing to lithoprinting by Rotoprint press. In 1942 the publishing activities were assumed by J. W. Edwards, Publisher, Inc., a wholly-owned subsidiary. The concern, specializing in scientific and technical titles and a music reprint program, continues in the control of the original family. All books published by this firm are manufactured by the photo-offset method (lithoprinting). S

66. THE EVANGELICAL PRESS. Founded 1895 in Harrisburg, Pennsylvania, as the Board of Publication of the United Evangelical Church, to issue Church publications and literature. In 1935 the publishing houses of the Church in Cleveland and Harrisburg were consolidated in the latter city. The Harrisburg plant has been directed by the Rev. S. L. Wiest (1895-1910), J. J. Nungesser (1911-1922), and Dr. Roy H. Stetler from 1922 to the present. The Press has broadened its scope, and while it still specializes in religious publications, it also does printing for other companies. S

67. CARL FISCHER, Inc. Founded 1872 by Carl Fischer in New York as a retail music business primarily to supply European

music at lower domestic prices. In 1885 the firm established a journal, *The Metronome,* and in 1907, *The Musical Observer* (now *Musical Courier*), both still published under other auspices. The scope of publication was broadened to include every department of musical activity. In 1892, when the founder's sons entered the business, the firm became a partnership. Incorporated 1923. Following the founder's death in the same year, management continued under the direction of his son, Walter S. Fischer, as president; and after the latter's death in 1946, his son-in-law, Frank Hayden Connor, succeeded him. Still specializing in music publications including not only music for schools, sheet music, choral, piano, and vocal publications, but also books on music and masterwork editions, the concern continues in the control of the original family.   S

68. J. FISCHER & BRO. Founded 1864 in Dayton, Ohio, by Joseph Fischer, music publisher. In 1875 the firm was transferred to New York City. The founder died in 1901 and the business was continued by his sons, George and Carl T. Fischer. Incorporated 1906. The firm's early publications were confined to music for the Catholic Church, but the list has gradually expanded to include all forms of music. Since 1923 a house organ, *Fischer Edition News,* has been published periodically. After Carl T. Fischer's death in 1952 Joseph A. Fischer became president, and the firm continues in the control of the original family.   S

69. SAMUEL FRENCH, Inc. Founded 1850 in New York by Samuel French as a branch of the English firm which had been established in 1830 by the English actor, Thomas Hailes Lacy, for the purpose of publishing plays and acting as authors' agent. In 1872 French bought out Lacy. French died in 1898 and the firm, incorporated in 1899, continues to publish and handle plays for all purposes.   S

70. FUNK & WAGNALLS COMPANY. Founded 1876 by Isaac Kaufman Funk, who shortly thereafter was joined by Adam Willis Wagnalls, under the name of I. K. Funk & Company. In its early years the company published principally reference books and theological works. In 1890 it was incorporated as the Funk & Wagnalls Company, and in 1894 issued the first edition of *A Standard Dictionary of the English Language,* revised and enlarged in 1903. In 1913 a new dictionary was published. Although the house specializes in reference books and publications in the educational field, it has in recent years also published juvenile books and fiction.   S

71. C. R. GIBSON & COMPANY. Founded 1872 in New York City by John Gibson as John Gibson & Company for the purpose of printing business forms and practicing commercial lithography. Incorporated in 1903 in New York City as C. R. Gibson & Company, and in 1940 in Norwalk, Connecticut. The firm publishes booklets and pamphlets for the pre-school child and specializes in the publication of record or memory books in which the user records information. The concern continues in the control of the original family.   S

72. GINN AND COMPANY. Founded 1867 in Boston by Edwin Ginn for the purpose of publishing textbooks. From 1870 until 1877 the firm operated as Ginn Brothers (Edwin Ginn and Fred B. Ginn). With the admission to partnership of Daniel C. Heath, the name was changed to Ginn and Heath, which, with the admission of George A. Plimpton, became Ginn, Heath and Company in 1881. With Heath's withdrawal in 1885 the firm name was altered to Ginn and Company. Incorporated 1939. From 1896 until 1950 the company owned and operated the Athenaeum Press in Cambridge. Throughout its existence the firm has published school and college textbooks.   S

73. GOSPEL TRUMPET COMPANY. Founded 1881 by Daniel S. Warner in Rome City, Indiana, for the publication of a periodical, *Gospel Trumpet,* for the Church of God Reformation Movement. The plant was moved several times, including removals to Grand Junction, Michigan (1886), Moundsville, West Virginia (1898), and finally to Anderson, Indiana (1906). Meanwhile the publishing scope was broadened and, as the publication board of the Church of God, the company publishes books, periodicals, tracts, and pamphlets, as well as the *Gospel Trumpet*—all serving the Church of God.   S

74. THE H. W. GRAY COMPANY, Inc. Founding traced to 1894, when H. Willard Gray set up the American agency of the London music publishing firm, Novello, Ewer & Co. (established 1811) in New York. In 1906 the present H. W. Gray Company was formed, purchasing the American branch of Novello, Ewer & Co., and the following year the firm published Frederick S. Converse's *The Pipe of Desire,* the first American opera produced by the Metropolitan Opera Company. The firm, still in the control of the original family, continues to specialize in the publication of music for the church and choir music by American composers.   S

75. GREGG PUBLISHING DIVISION, McGRAW-HILL BOOK COMPANY, Inc. Founded 1899 in Chicago under the name of

the Gregg Publishing Company by John Robert Gregg for the purpose of issuing and promoting his *Gregg Shorthand* (which had first been published by the author in Boston in 1893). The firm was incorporated 1907, when a New York office was established and the concern expanded with an extensive line of shorthand books as well as textbooks in other commercial subjects. The firm was purchased in 1948 by McGraw-Hill Book Company, Inc., and is now the Gregg Publishing Division of that firm, comprising McGraw-Hill's Business Education Department and the original Gregg organization.   S

76. THE GROLIER SOCIETY Inc. Founded 1895 in Boston as The Grolier Society, a Maine corporation, by Walter M. Jackson, for the purpose of publishing "good books in fine bindings." Moved to New York in 1900, and in 1910 the firm began publication of *The Book of Knowledge*. The name was changed in 1936 to The Grolier Society Inc. Acquired the *Encyclopedia Americana* in 1945. The firm specializes in the publication of reference books and encyclopedias, chiefly in sets.   S

77. GROSSET & DUNLAP, Inc. Founded 1898 in New York by George T. Dunlap and Alexander Grosset under the name of Dunlap & Grosset. The following year the style was changed to Alexander Grosset & Co., and in 1900 to Grosset & Dunlap. The firm specialized at first in "rebinds" and later in reprint fiction, beginning with Paul Leicester Ford's *Janice Meredith*. Incorporated in 1918, the concern subsequently expanded into the fields of reference books and juvenile series, but the popular price idea was the rock upon which it was founded. In 1944 the original family holdings were sold to a combination: Book-of-the-Month Club, Random House, Harper, Little, Brown, and Scribner's.   G

78. HAFNER PUBLISHING COMPANY. History traced to 1872, when Gustav E. Stechert and F. Wolff organized the firm of Stechert & Wolff in New York "for the purpose of importing and selling all kinds of European literary works." In 1876, with Wolff's withdrawal, the firm name was changed to Gustav E. Stechert, shortened to G. E. Stechert around 1897, and again changed to G. E. Stechert & Co. in 1904. After Stechert's death in 1899 Alfred Hafner, a partner since 1897, administered the business, and by 1914 he had become sole owner. In 1919 Hafner's sons, Walter A. and Otto H. Hafner, joined the firm. In 1946 the company's name became Stechert-Hafner, Inc., with Walter A. Hafner as president, and at that time the Hafner Publishing Company was

organized, with Otto H. Hafner as president, for the purpose of taking over the publishing functions of the former G. E. Stechert & Co. The firm specializes in scholarly works in linguistics, natural sciences, mathematics, and statistics, and the third generation of Hafners is now represented. S

79. HARPER & BROTHERS. Founded 1817 in New York as J. & J. Harper by James and John Harper, who printed their first book that year: *Seneca's Morals,* published by Evert Duyckinck. The following year the firm issued its own first publication, Locke's *Essay concerning Human Understanding.* In 1823 a third brother, Joseph Wesley Harper, joined the concern, followed in 1825 by the fourth Harper brother, Fletcher; in 1833 the name was changed to Harper & Brothers. The publication of *Harper's Magazine* was begun in 1850, of *Harper's Weekly* in 1857, of *Harper's Bazar* in 1867, and of *Harper's Young People* in 1879. Following James Harper's death in 1869, five Harper sons were admitted to the firm: John W., Philip J. A., Joseph W., Jr., Fletcher, Jr., and Joseph Abner. The three remaining Harpers of the first generation died in the '70's (Joseph Wesley in 1870, John in 1875, and Fletcher in 1877). Subsequently, several members of the third generation became associated with the business. In 1896 the firm, which had remained in the family for three generations, became a stock company. Financial difficulties necessitated the reorganization of the house in 1900, when it emerged as a new corporation with George B. M. Harvey as its head. In 1922 the firm gave up its own printing establishment, and in 1923 it was again reorganized under stock ownership. G

80. THE HARRISON COMPANY. A descendant of The Franklin Printing House, established 1859 in Atlanta, Georgia. In 1873 James P. Harrison & Company, formed by James P. Harrison and others, acquired the Franklin Steam Printing House. Both concerns served as State printers and published trade books. In 1906 the Franklin Printing & Publishing Company was sold, and the following year the present Harrison Company was organized as a successor to its two predecessors by George W. Harrison, George W. Harrison, Jr., and J. T. Doonan, specializing in the publication of law books. George W. Harrison and George W. Harrison, Jr., both died in 1936, and the firm passed into the hands of J. T. Doonan. After Doonan's death in 1951 the company was acquired by John M. Elliott and other old employees. The firm now emphasizes local law books for the southeastern states and is also planning gradually to expand in the general law field. S

81. HARVARD UNIVERSITY PRESS. An outgrowth of the printing office for the University established in 1871. After 1896 the office expanded in the general publishing field. In 1913 it was organized by the President and Fellows of Harvard College as Harvard University Press, for the purpose of publishing scholarly works. In 1943 the printing and publishing functions were separated, Harvard University Press and Harvard University Printing Office becoming entirely independent of each other and both being regarded as departments of the University. The Press, strictly a publishing concern, buys its printing from the Printing Office as well as from perhaps a dozen other book manufacturers. The Press is governed by an editorial board (Board of Syndics) and a finance board (Board of Directors), both appointed by the President and Fellows of Harvard College.   S

82. D. C. HEATH AND COMPANY. Founded 1885 in Boston by Daniel Collamore Heath, who dissolved his partnership in Ginn, Heath to establish his own educational publishing house for the purpose of providing "the tools of the new education." Beginning with only twenty-four titles, the firm expanded rapidly. In 1888 Charles H. Ames was admitted to partnership, later partners including William E. Pulsifer and Dr. Winfield S. Smyth. Incorporated 1895. In 1910 Pulsifer, Smyth, and William H. Ives purchased the concern, Pulsifer becoming president. Later presidents include Mr. Winfield S. Smyth, son of Dr. Winfield S. Smyth (1925), Dudley R. Cowles (1937), and Marvin B. Perry (1946). The firm continues to specialize in pedagogical works and in textbooks from the primary grade through the university. Its list comprises nearly three thousand titles, almost one-third of which are modern foreign language publications.   S

83. HEBREW PUBLISHING COMPANY. Founded 1883 in New York by Joseph L. Werbelowsky and others, forming the firm of Rosenbaum and Werbelowsky. Incorporated 1901 for the purpose of publishing Jewish books. Continuing in the control of the original family, the concern specializes in Judaica for all Jews.   S

84. THE NORMAN W. HENLEY PUBLISHING COMPANY. Founded 1890 in New York City by Norman W. Henley for the purpose of publishing technical and scientific books. The firm purchased Henry Carey Baird & Company, Inc., of Philadelphia, and still sells titles under that imprint. The founder died in 1945, and the company is continued by his nephew, Charles E. Henley. Still specializing in scientific and technical books, the firm continues in the control of the original family.   S

85. HERALD PUBLISHING HOUSE, A TRUST ESTATE. Founded 1860 in Plano, Illinois, under the name of Herald Publishing House, Inc., by the Reorganized Church of Jesus Christ of Latter Day Saints for the purpose of printing religious literature for church members. The firm's first book publication was the Inspired Version of the Holy Scriptures. In 1921 the publishing house was moved to Independence, Missouri. The House still specializes in religious literature for church members, issuing six magazines including the official church organ, *The Saints' Herald*, in addition to books.   S

86. B. HERDER BOOK CO. American branch of the German firm of Catholic publishers (established by Bartholomäus Herder in 1801) founded in 1873 in St. Louis under the management of Joseph Gummersbach. In 1917 it became independent of the German firm, and continues to specialize in Catholic publications.   S

87. A. J. HOLMAN COMPANY. Founded 1872 in Philadelphia by A. J. Holman and George S. Lare for the purpose of publishing the King James Bible. Through Holman's association in 1839 with Jesper Harding, however, the house may be traced back to the firm of Solomon Conrad (1801), which became Kimber, Conrad & Co. (1806), Kimber, Sharpless (1816), Jesper Harding (1817), Jesper Harding & Son (1856), and William W. Harding & Company (1859-1872). Moreover, the firm owns the charter and stock of the house of Sower (direct successors to Christoph Sauer, who published the first German Bible in this country in 1743). Specializing only in Bibles, the firm continues in the control of the original family.   S

88. HENRY HOLT AND COMPANY, Inc. Founded 1866 in New York under the name of Leypoldt & Holt by Frederick Leypoldt and Henry Holt. The firm's first publication was Charles Godfrey Leland's translation of Joseph von Eichendorff's *Memoirs of a Good-for-Nothing*. In 1870, with the admission to partnership of R. O. Williams, the style was changed to Leypoldt, Holt & Williams. Two years later Leypoldt retired to devote himself to the *Literary Bulletin*, which had been launched by the firm in 1869 and which developed under Leypoldt into *Publishers' Weekly*. The firm name then became Holt & Williams. With Williams's retirement in 1873 the style was changed to Henry Holt & Company. Henry Holt's brother, Charles Holt, became a partner in 1878. The firm was incorporated in 1903 as Henry Holt & Company, and in 1926 the founder died. The concern was re-incorporated in

1928 as Henry Holt & Company, Inc., and since then it has been publicly owned. Two magazines were acquired: *Field & Stream* in 1951 and *Popular Gardening* in 1955. At present about eighty per cent of the book business consists of the distribution of texts to high schools and colleges, the remainder consisting of the distribution of general books to jobbers and retailers.   G

89. HOUGHTON MIFFLIN COMPANY. Founded 1852 in Cambridge, Massachusetts, by Henry Oscar Houghton, as the printing firm of H. O. Houghton & Company, the press being known as The Riverside Press—its policy to do the best printing and binding available in America at the time. Still continuing H. O. Houghton & Company, the founder in 1864 formed a partnership with Melanchthon M. Hurd under the style of Hurd & Houghton for the purpose of publishing books, especially standard literature and law books, with offices in Boston and New York. In 1872 George H. Mifflin became a member of Hurd & Houghton, and the following year *The Atlantic Monthly* was acquired. In 1878 Hurd retired, and at the same time the house formed a combination with James R. Osgood & Co. (successors to Ticknor & Fields), the style being changed to Houghton, Osgood & Co., with headquarters in Boston. Upon Osgood's retirement in 1880 the firm became Houghton, Mifflin & Co. Eight years later Henry O. Houghton, Jr., was admitted to partnership. Houghton Mifflin Company was incorporated in 1908. The founder's goals in printing have been enlarged in an attempt to apply his motto, "Tout bien ou rien," to the concern's publishing enterprises.   G

90. HOUSE OF THE CHURCH OF THE BRETHREN. Founded 1897 in Mt. Morris, Illinois, by Joseph Amick and D. H. Miller as the Brethren Publishing House, to provide the Church of the Brethren with religious literature. The publishing house was officially organized as a separate entity in 1916, and the present name was adopted in 1946. Now in Elgin, Illinois, the House still specializes in publications for the Church of the Brethren.   S

91. INTERNATIONAL TEXTBOOK COMPANY. Founded 1889 in Scranton, Pennsylvania, as The Colliery Engineer Company, by Thomas Jefferson Foster and others, to publish instruction texts in coal mining as part of a correspondence course in that field. Incorporated 1890. In 1901 the name was changed to International Textbook Company; the purpose, as stated in its charter, was to publish textbooks for the "dissemination of literary, technical, educational and other information." The firm also received a charter for its subsidiary corporation, International Correspond-

ence Schools, which was to offer home study courses from instruction texts published by the International Textbook Company. Another subsidiary, The Haddon Craftsmen, Inc., prints and manufactures texts for the International Textbook Company and other publishers and distributors. The firm has expanded its publishing activities to include textbooks in engineering, business, and mathematics for resident teaching in colleges and universities. It operates correspondence schools to provide job-related instruction in the industrial and business fields and publishes and prints instruction texts and material for that program.   S

92. THE INTERSTATE PRINTERS AND PUBLISHERS, Inc. Founded 1896 in Danville, Illinois, for the purpose of job printing, under the name of Commercial Printing Co. The firm name was changed to Interstate Printing Co. in 1908 and to The Interstate Printers and Publishers, Inc. in 1939. The concern, which now prints and publishes books, specializes in books for agriculture, physical education, and special education.   S

93. THE JEWISH PUBLICATION SOCIETY OF AMERICA. Founded 1888 in Philadelphia, a successor organization to the American Jewish Publication Society which had been established in 1845. Its first publication appeared in 1890, a revised edition of Lady Magnus's *Outlines of Jewish History*. Among the numerous books which have appeared since then are works in theology, history, biography, poetry, and fiction, and a considerable number of juveniles. The purpose of the Society, to spread the knowledge of Jewish history and of Jewish religious teachings and practices especially among American Jews and non-Jews, has been steadily upheld so that it has become "a great force for unity in American Jewry," strengthening "the loyalties of Jews to the faith of their fathers and to the land of which they are devoted citizens."   S

94. JOHN KNOX PRESS. Founded 1838 in Philadelphia by the General Assembly of the Presbyterian Church, as the Presbyterian Board of Publication, for the purpose of furnishing "the churches under its care with suitable tract, Sabbath School and other publications." At the time of the Civil War, when the Presbyterians split into two groups, northern and southern, the General Assembly of the Presbyterian Church in the Confederate States (now known as the Presbyterian Church, U.S.) set up a Committee of Publication for that body in Richmond, Virginia. The name of this publishing house was later changed to Onward Press, and in 1938 to John Knox Press. It is still the publishing unit of the

Board of Christian Education of the Presbyterian Church, U.S. With headquarters in Richmond, the Press aims "to contribute to and stimulate the advancement of Christian thought . . . by the publication and distribution of books and other printed materials."   S

95. THE JOHNS HOPKINS PRESS. Founded 1878 as the Publication Agency of Johns Hopkins University to encourage "professors and lecturers to give to the world in print the results of their researches." Launched the *American Journal of Mathematics* 1878 and its first book, Freeman's *Introduction to American Institutional History,* 1882. Name changed to The Johns Hopkins Press 1890. The Press, which boasts an uninterrupted history, "now provides for the publication of scholarly writing . . . for the advancement of scholarship; and the publication of books and magazines . . . which present the findings . . . of scholars for the education of the lay, or non-professional reader."   S

96. ORANGE JUDD PUBLISHING CO., Inc. Founded 1836 in New York by Charles M. Saxton, bookseller and publisher of agricultural books. Partnership with Early E. Miles reflected in change of imprint until Miles sold out his interest to Saxton and the firm became Charles M. Saxton, Agricultural Book Publishers. After Saxton's death the business was bought by Orange Judd, publisher of the *American Agriculturist,* in 1864, when the Saxton and Judd lists were combined and the firm was renamed Orange Judd & Co. Later passed into hands of creditors, but was reorganized in 1883 with David W. Judd, brother of Orange Judd, as president, and extended its activities. In 1921 George E. Eiermann, who died in 1951, purchased the book department. His son, George E. Eiermann, Jr., is now president. Continues to specialize in farming, agricultural, gardening, and pet books.   S

97. P. J. KENEDY & SONS. Founded 1826 by John Kenedy, Irish immigrant in Baltimore, as small bookselling business. With removal to New York City in 1836, the firm concentrated upon serving Irish Catholic population by issuing catechisms, prayerbooks, and devotional works, with sideline in religious goods and articles. Style of firm changed to John Kenedy & Son 1865 and business was continued under Patrick J. Kenedy. House expanded, acquiring plates and stock of other firms, becoming a potent influence in Catholic publishing. Incorporated 1904 as P. J. Kenedy & Sons. Only remaining link with early American phase of Catholic publishing, with continuous family ownership.   S

98. CHARLES H. KERR & COMPANY. Founded 1886 in Chicago by Charles H. Kerr and a group of socialists as a co-operative

publishing house. Incorporated 1893. In 1900 the firm issued the *International Socialist Review*. The concern specializes in the publication of books on scientific socialism, working class books on economics, history, social sciences, labor, etc.   S

99. THE LAWYERS CO-OPERATIVE PUBLISHING COMPANY. Founded 1882 in Newark, New York, by three lawyers—James E. Briggs, his son William H. Briggs, and Ernest Hitchcock—to manufacture, publish, and sell reprints of American or English Law Reports, textbooks, and digests. The following year Hitchcock's interest was purchased by the printer, Ezra R. Andrews, and in 1885 headquarters were transferred to Rochester, New York. The firm began publication of *Case and Comment—The Lawyers' Magazine* in 1894. Several mergers and acquisitions have subsequently marked the company's expansion: purchase of a controlling interest in Bancroft-Whitney Company (1919), absorption of the White Binding Company (1936), merger of the E. R. Andrews Printing Company and the Aqueduct Building Company with the concern (1938), acquisition of Baker, Voorhis & Co. of New York and of Bender-Moss Company of San Francisco (1940). The firm continues to specialize in the publication of law books. S

100. LEA & FEBIGER. Founded 1785 in Philadelphia by Mathew Carey, who established a daily newspaper and two monthly magazines, and thus entered into the publishing of books in general including literature, religion, science, and medicine. The firm has since undergone over a dozen changes in style, reflecting various owners' names. The Carey name continued until 1836, having appeared as M. Carey & Son in 1817 (with the association in the firm of the founder's son, Henry C. Carey); M. Carey & Sons in 1821 (with the admission to partnership of the founder's son-in-law, Isaac Lea); H. C. Carey & I. Lea in 1824 (with the retirement of Mathew Carey); Carey, Lea & Carey in 1826 (with the admission of Edward L. Carey); Carey & Lea in 1829 (when the retail and publishing departments were divided); Carey, Lea & Blanchard in 1833 (with the partnership of William A. Blanchard). In 1836, upon the retirement of Henry C. Carey, the Carey name was dropped and the style became Lea & Blanchard, changing to Blanchard & Lea in 1851 when Isaac Lea retired in favor of his son, Henry Charles Lea. A brief reversal to Lea & Blanchard occurred in 1865 when Blanchard retired and was succeeded by his son Henry, and this was followed the same year by a change to Henry C. Lea upon the withdrawal of the younger Blanchard. In 1880 the style became Henry C. Lea's Son & Co., in 1885 Lea

Brothers & Co., and in 1907 Lea & Febiger, reflecting the association of Charles M. and Arthur H. Lea and Christian C. Febiger. These three partners retired in 1915, the business being continued by Van Antwerp Lea, great-great-grandson of Mathew Carey, and Christian Febiger, son of Christian C. Febiger. Following the death in 1945 of Christian Febiger, his place was taken by Henry Lea Hudson, Christian C. F. Spahr, and John F. Spahr, grandsons respectively of Charles M. Lea and Christian C. Febiger. In 1955 Francis C. Lea, nephew of Van Antwerp Lea, joined the partnership. During the 1840-1850 decade, the policy of the house had gradually changed from general publishing to a concentration upon medicine. It has now excluded from its list all except works in the medical field and allied professions. The oldest publishing house in America, the firm continues in the control of the original family.   S

101. J. B. LIPPINCOTT COMPANY. Founding traced by purchase to 1792, when Jacob Johnson established a small bookstore and printing plant in Philadelphia. Between 1792 and 1849 the business underwent several changes of name, reflecting the admission of various partners: Johnson & Warner (with the association in the firm of Benjamin Warner), Warner & Grigg (with the admission of John Grigg), Grigg & Elliot (with the admission of Hugh Elliot), and Grigg, Elliot & Company. In 1849 the concern was purchased by J. B. Lippincott & Company, established in 1836 by Joshua Ballinger Lippincott, specializing in religious publications. After the acquisition of Grigg, Elliot & Company, the name was changed temporarily to Lippincott, Grambo & Company, and the firm expanded to cover practically every field of literature including medical and educational textbooks. In 1868 the house founded a London agency and began publication of *Lippincott's Magazine,* continued until 1914 when it was sold to McBride, Nast and Company. In 1885 a joint stock company was formed under the name of J. B. Lippincott Company. Upon the founder's death the following year, his son, Craige Lippincott, succeeded him as president; Craige Lippincott was succeeded after his death in 1910 by his brother, J. Bertram Lippincott; in 1926 the latter's son, Joseph Wharton Lippincott, became president. In 1941 the company acquired two New York firms: the Frederick A. Stokes Company, and Carrick & Evans. The house, with three medical journals and three major publishing divisions—a school and college textbook department, a medical, nursing, and pharmaceutical book department, and a complete department of general literature in-

cluding juveniles—continues under the control of the Lippincott family, a member of the fourth generation, Joseph Wharton Lippincott, Jr., being now executive vice-president while his father remains chairman of the board.   G

102. LITTLE, BROWN & COMPANY. Founded 1837 in Boston by Charles C. Little and James Brown, who entered into partnership for the purposes of publishing and selling books. Indirectly, through the partners' previous association with Hilliard, Gray & Co., the firm's roots may be traced back to 1784 when Ebenezer Battelle opened the bookstore in Boston which eventually passed into the hands of Jacob A. Cummings and William Hilliard, whose concern in 1827 took the style of Hilliard, Gray & Co. Many of the Hilliard, Gray & Co. assets, including legal publications, were secured in 1837 by Little and Brown. In 1847 the style of the firm was changed to Little, Brown and Company, with Augustus Flagg as junior partner. John Bartlett of *Familiar Quotations* became a partner in 1865. During the 1890's, under James Brown's son, John Murray Brown, the company began to expand in the general publishing field. Two major events in its history were the purchase in 1898 of the general list of Roberts Brothers of Boston, and the alliance in 1925 with the Atlantic Monthly Company through which Little, Brown and Company became the publishers of all Atlantic Monthly Press books. A similar association made in 1951 with the New York publishing firm of Duell, Sloan & Pearce was terminated in 1956.   G

103. LONGMANS GREEN & CO., Inc. The New York agency of the House of Longman (founded by Thomas Longman in London in 1724) established in 1875 under C. J. Mills and converted into a New York partnership in 1889. At that time its original purpose, to promote the sales of books published in England, was broadened to include the publication of works by American authors in a wide field of interest. Since then the American publishing program, especially in the fields of higher education and of junior, religious, and general books, has outgrown the representation of English titles, although the latter function remains a part of the company's mission today. In 1935 the partnership became a New York corporation.   G

104. LOTHROP, LEE & SHEPARD CO., Inc. Founded 1868 in Boston by Daniel Lothrop, who as early as 1850 had "experimented in publishing" in New Hampshire, and N. P. Kemp. The following year the firm, publishers of Sunday school and other books, became D. Lothrop & Co. In 1870 John C. and James E. Lothrop

were firm members, and the following year the company was known as Daniel Lothrop & Co. In 1887 W. H. Arnold, E. S. Brooks, and E. H. Pennell were admitted to the firm, which became D. Lothrop Company. Daniel Lothrop died in 1892, and Mrs. Lothrop helped manage the business for a time. In 1895, with Pennell as president, the style was changed to Lothrop Publishing Co. In 1904 the firm's assets were purchased by Lee & Shepard, which had been established in Boston in the early '60's by William Lee and Charles A. B. Shepard as general publishers with a strong line of juveniles; by 1905 the firm was styled Lothrop, Lee & Shepard Company. In 1943 the company was taken over by its present owners, Crown Publishers, Inc., and, as Lothrop, Lee & Shepard Co., Inc., in New York, publishes only juveniles. S

105. LUTHERAN PUBLISHING HOUSE. Founded 1893 in Blair, Nebraska, by the Danish Evangelical Lutheran Church Association in America, under the name of Danish Lutheran Publishing House, to publish literature for the Church. In 1943 the present name was adopted. The House continues to publish religious literature and song books for the United Evangelical Lutheran Church. S

106. LYONS & CARNAHAN, Inc. Founded 1887 in Chicago as O. M. Powers & Company, publishers of commercial education books. The name was changed, when James A. Lyons joined the firm, to Powers and Lyons. With Powers's withdrawal, the firm name became J. A. Lyons and Company. In 1912 James W. Carnahan joined James A. Lyons in a partnership, Lyons & Carnahan, textbook publishers. Lyons died in 1920 and Carnahan purchased his interest. The firm was then incorporated as Lyons & Carnahan, Inc. The concern specializes in the publication of school textbooks. S

107. A. C. McCLURG & CO. Founded 1844 in Chicago by William W. Barlow under the name of W. W. Barlow & Co. as a small retail store offering Bibles, books, stationery, and writing instruments. In 1849 Barlow sold the business to William Bross, who subsequently disposed of it to Samuel C. Griggs. Griggs retired in 1871, selling his share to two employees, Alexander C. McClurg and Egbert Jansen, who formed the new firm of Jansen, McClurg & Co. In 1886 Jansen retired and the style was changed to A. C. McClurg & Co. After McClurg's death in 1900, his son, Ogden T. McClurg, became president. In 1923 the company discontinued its retail store, continuing as book publishers and job-

bers. The firm was one of the first publishers of Zane Grey and Clarence E. Mulford (originator of Hopalong Cassidy), and the first book publisher of Edgar Rice Burroughs. In the mid-1940's the concern discontinued its publishing activities except for a few new editions of older books, and since that time has been engaged as wholesalers of books, stationery, and other merchandise.   (Until mid-1940's) G

108. DAVID McKAY COMPANY, Inc. Founded 1882 in Philadelphia by David McKay. The firm's first book publication was a seventh edition of Walt Whitman's *Leaves of Grass* (1882). Important events in the company's history included the taking over in 1888 of the business of H. C. Watts & Co., the purchase in 1896 of the publishing plant of Charles De Silver & Sons, the absorption of the business of Edward Meeks (successor to E. Claxton & Co.), and the purchase in 1903 of the American branch of George Routledge & Sons. Upon the founder's death in 1919 the business was incorporated and carried on by his sons. Alexander McKay became president, continuing in that office until 1950, when the firm was sold to its present owners and moved to New York, with Kennett L. Rawson as president. The firm has published foreign language textbooks and dictionaries, juveniles, chess books, how-to books, and from 1936 to 1950 also published a series of comic books under an arrangement with King Features Syndicate. Since 1950 the firm has expanded its activities in the general trade field of fiction, biography, world affairs, and religion, while continuing the previous specialties except for comics, which have been discontinued.   G

109. McLOUGHLIN BROTHERS, Inc. Founded 1828 in New York by John McLoughlin, Scottish immigrant, as a print shop. Entered publishing field with tracts or "leaflet stories of a semi-religious character" for young readers, which were expanded into the "McLoughlin Books for Children." Shortly before 1840 the firm was merged with John Elton's publishing concern and adopted the style of John Elton and Company. With the retirement of McLoughlin and of Elton before 1848, John McLoughlin, Jr., succeeded his father. In the early 1850's Edmund McLoughlin became a partner, and the firm name was changed to McLoughlin Brothers, specialists in children's books. After the death of John McLoughlin, Jr., in 1907, he was succeeded by his sons, James G. and Charles McLoughlin. The latter died in 1914, and in 1920 James McLoughlin sold the business to Milton Bradley Company. A subsidiary company, retaining the name of McLoughlin Brothers, Inc.,

was formed for the reorganization and continuation of the publishing business in children's books. The company and its publication rights and other assets were acquired in 1954 by Grosset & Dunlap, Inc., who plan to continue the publication of titles originally issued by McLoughlin Brothers and to add appropriate new titles. McLoughlin Brothers, Inc., continues to exist as a separate corporate entity, but with its business managed by Grosset & Dunlap, Inc.   S

110. THE MACMILLAN COMPANY. Founded 1869 in New York as an American agency of the London House of Macmillan (which had been established in 1843 by Daniel and Alexander Macmillan) under the management of George Edward Brett, with the principal purpose of acquainting the American public with the publications of the London house. George E. Brett died in 1890 and was succeeded by his son, George Platt Brett. In 1896 two distinct companies were organized: Macmillan & Co., Ltd., of London, and The Macmillan Company of New York, the latter ceasing to be an agency solely for the sale of the English Macmillan's books and becoming a separate publishing house. Branch offices were established and the company expanded further. In 1931 George Platt Brett, Jr., succeeded his father in the presidency. In 1950 the firm became a wholly American-owned company, and in 1954 a London office was opened. The concern has five principal departments: Trade (with subdivisions in children's books, religious books, and outdoor books), Medical-Public Health, College, Educational, and Technical. The family continuity persists, and the firm has become one of the largest general book publishers, with extensive distributive facilities.   G

111. MACOY PUBLISHING & MASONIC SUPPLY COMPANY, Inc. Founded 1849 in New York City by two Masons, Robert Macoy and John W. Simons, under the name of Macoy & Simons, for the purpose of publishing Masonic books. *The Master Workman* by Robert Macoy was the firm's first book publication. In 1859 Macoy and Daniel Sickels formed a partnership under the name of Macoy & Sickels. Simons retired, and in 1865 William T. Anderson and A. S. Archer joined the firm which in 1869 became Macoy Publishing and Manufacturing Company. In 1876 William T. Anderson bought out Macoy and changed the firm name to Masonic Furnishing Company. The same year John Hoole bought the business from Anderson, joining with three partners under the name of Masonic Publishing and Furnishing Company. In 1897 Sherwood Bradley Robertson, who since 1887 had been operating

the Masonic Publishing and Supply Company, purchased the D. H. Howell Manufacturing Company and the Robert Macoy Publishing Company (formed by Robert Macoy in 1877 after the sale of his business to Anderson). All three businesses—the Macoy firm, the Robertson concern, and the D. H. Howell Manufacturing Company—were consolidated in 1898 and incorporated under the name of Macoy Publishing and Masonic Supply Company. Between 1901 and 1902 another firm, the Masonic Publishing and Furnishing Company (successors to the original Macoy & Simons partnership) was merged with the corporation, which now specializes in the publication of fraternal literature and the manufacture of fraternal regalia.   S

112. EDWARD B. MARKS MUSIC CORPORATION. Founded 1894 in New York City under the name of Jos. W. Stern & Co. by Edward B. Marks and Joseph W. Stern, for the publication of music. In 1920 the firm name was changed to Edward B. Marks Music Company, and in 1932 to Edward B. Marks Music Corporation. The concern, still specializing in the publication of music, continues in the control of the original (Marks) family.   S

113. THE A. N. MARQUIS COMPANY. Founded 1897 in Chicago by Albert Nelson Marquis as A. N. Marquis & Company for the compilation and publication of *Who's Who in America.* The firm's first book publication was *Who's Who in America,* Volume I (1899-1900). In 1908 the firm name became Albert Nelson Marquis and in 1926, The A. N. Marquis Company, incorporated 1953 as Marquis-Who's Who, Inc. (a nonprofit foundation). In 1939 the concern assumed publication of *Who's Who in Commerce and Industry* and in 1953 established the Library of American Biography. The firm continues to publish *Who's Who in America* and the biographical reference works supplemental thereto, as well as to maintain and expand the Library of American Biography. It specializes in the publication of biographical reference dictionaries.   S

114. MENTZER, BUSH & COMPANY. Founded 1898 in Chicago by John P. Mentzer and Charles F. Atkinson, under the name of Atkinson & Mentzer, for the purpose of publishing school textbooks. In 1904 the firm name was changed to Atkinson, Mentzer & Grover, in 1912 to Atkinson, Mentzer & Co., and in 1922 to Mentzer, Bush & Company. Still specializing in textbook publishing, the firm continues in the control of the original (Mentzer) family.   S

115. G. & C. MERRIAM COMPANY. Founded 1831 as a printing office and bookstore in Springfield, Massachusetts, by George and Charles Merriam. The firm acquired the rights to Webster's *American Dictionary* in 1844 and published a revised enlargement of it in 1847—the first *Merriam-Webster*. The great revision of the *Merriam-Webster Dictionary* appeared in 1864 and has since been followed by a succession of important revisions. In 1855 Homer Merriam joined the firm. In 1877 Charles Merriam sold his interest to Ivison, Blakeman, Taylor & Co., in 1880 George Merriam died, and in 1904 Homer Merriam relinquished the presidency. The post was then occupied by Orlando M. Baker, followed by a line of men in the Websterian succession, whose story is that of "respected devotion" to the ideals of the great lexicographer and the firm known as publishers of *Merriam-Webster Dictionaries*.   S

116. CHARLES E. MERRILL BOOKS. Founded 1842 by William G. Webster, son of Noah Webster, and Lucius E. Clark, under the name of Webster & Clark, for the purpose of publishing educational books. Changes in firm name until the 1860's were as follows: Clark & Austin (with the retirement of Webster and the association in the firm of Jeremiah B. Austin); Clark, Austin & Smith (with the partnership of Cornelius Smith); Clark, Austin, Maynard & Company in 1859 (with the death of Smith and admission to partnership of Effingham Maynard and Livingston Snedeker). During the Civil War the firm faced extreme financial difficulties, but in 1865 the business was resumed by Clark & Maynard. Clark retired in 1888, and the concern was renamed Effingham Maynard & Company by Maynard and Everett Yeaw. In 1893 the firm consolidated with Charles E. Merrill & Company (Charles E., Sr., and Edwin C. Merrill) and was incorporated as Maynard, Merrill & Company. Maynard died in 1899, and in 1907 Charles E. Merrill, Sr., bought the Maynard interest, the corporation's name being changed to Charles E. Merrill Company. Merrill, who died in 1930, was succeeded as president by Charles E. Merrill, Jr., who held the office until his death in 1942. Two years later the capital stock was acquired by W. C. Blakey, Eleanor M. Johnson, Harold S. Brown, and The Educational Printing House, Inc. In 1946 the capital stock was acquired by stockholders of American Education Press, Inc., and three years later by the Wesleyan University Press, Inc. The corporation was dissolved and the business continued under the name of Charles E. Merrill Company as a division of Wesleyan University Press, Inc. In 1952, under the same arrangements, the firm name became Charles E. Merrill

Books. Throughout its history the concern has specialized in American educational publications and textbooks. With headquarters in Columbus, Ohio, the firm continues that specialty. S

117. THE METHODIST PUBLISHING HOUSE. Founded 1789 as the Methodist Book Concern, the publishing agency of the Methodist Episcopal Church, with Rev. John Dickins as Book Steward in Philadelphia. The Concern's first book publication was John Wesley's *Christian's Pattern*. In 1804 headquarters were transferred to New York. The first branch house was opened in Cincinnati in 1820 and chartered in 1839 as the Western Book Concern of the Methodist Episcopal Church to serve the Middle West. Though actually never separate from the eastern Concern, the two were merged in 1912 as the Methodist Book Concern. Meanwhile two other Methodist publishing houses had been established: the Methodist Protestant Book Concern, founded after the Methodist Protestant Church was organized in 1828, and the Methodist Publishing House of the Methodist Episcopal Church, South, founded after the sectional split in the Methodist Episcopal Church in 1844, and in 1924 adopting the Cokesbury Press imprint. In 1914 the Methodist Book Concern began using the Abingdon Press imprint. In 1940, after the unification of the Church and the formation of The Methodist Church, all three publishing organizations were united to form the present Methodist Publishing House, its book publishing division known as Abingdon-Cokesbury Press (altered in 1954 to Abingdon Press). The Methodist Publishing House— the oldest denominational publishing house in America—is still the publishing agency of The Methodist Church as it was in 1789. It operates through publishing headquarters in New York City and Nashville, Tennessee, and retail outlets in fifteen cities. S

118. THE METROPOLITAN MUSEUM OF ART. Founded 1870 in New York City by a group of citizens. Printing activity in the name of the Museum was undertaken almost immediately, and the first formal publication, a Museum *Catalogue*, was issued in 1872. The Editorial Department of the Museum was established in 1908. The Department publishes scholarly monographs and picture books, as well as catalogues, handbooks, and guides to the collections. It is an affiliated member of the Association of American University Presses. S

119. MOODY PRESS. Founded 1894 in Chicago by Dwight L. Moody under the name of The Bible Institute Colportage Association, for the distribution of Christian literature. The first book published was C. H. Spurgeon's *All Of Grace*. In 1941 the name was changed

to Moody Press, which, still controlled by the Moody Bible Institute, continues to specialize in Christian literature.　　S

120. MOREHOUSE-GORHAM CO., Inc. Founded 1884 in Milwaukee, Wisconsin, as The Young Churchman Co., by Linden H. Morehouse, who in 1870 had begun publication of a religious periodical, *The Young Churchman*. The firm's first book publication was the Rev. Arthur Wilde Little's *Reasons for Being a Churchman* (1885). Incorporated 1885. Important events in the company's history were alliances with the London firms of Messrs. A. R. Mowbray & Co., The Faith Press, and the Dacre Press. Upon Morehouse's death in 1915, his son, Frederic C. Morehouse, succeeded him, and the firm's name was changed in 1918 to Morehouse Publishing Co. After the death of Frederic C. Morehouse in 1932, Linden H. Morehouse II, grandson of the founder, became president. In 1938, when the Morehouse Publishing Co. and Edwin S. Gorham, Inc., of New York were combined, publishing headquarters were transferred to New York, and the firm name was again changed to Morehouse-Gorham Co. Publishers of Sunday school textbooks, Episcopal Church books, and religious books for church, church schools, and churchmen, with a vestment division and retail branches in Chicago and San Francisco, the firm continues in the control of the original family.　　S

121. THE MOSHER PRESS. Founded 1891 by Thomas Bird Mosher in Portland, Maine, for the purpose of publishing literary works in choice and limited editions. The first Mosher book was George Meredith's *Modern Love* (1891). After the founder's death in 1923 The Mosher Press was supervised by Flora Lamb, and in 1942 the Press was purchased from Mrs. Thomas Bird Mosher by J. G. Williams of Williams Book Store, at which time it was moved to Boston. The Press is now continued by his daughter, Harriet E. Williams, and specializes in "literary and scholarly works."　　S

122. MUHLENBERG PRESS. Founded 1855 as The Lutheran Publication Society of the General Synod, in Philadelphia. The first publication was *The Blind Girl of Wittenberg*. In 1919 the Society merged with the Board of Publication of the General Council and the Board of Publication of the United Synod of the South to form the Board of Publication of the United Lutheran Church in America. In 1953 the Board established the Lutheran Readers Club. The Muhlenberg Press is the book publishing division of the United Lutheran Publication House, which also issues magazines, lesson courses, and other printed material for use in churches.　　S

123. MUSEUM OF FINE ARTS, BOSTON. Founded 1870 in Boston by the founding Trustees of the Museum "to afford instruction in the Fine Arts." The first book publication was a *Descriptive Catalogue of Casts of Greek and Roman Sculpture* by Edward Robinson (1887). The Museum continues to specialize in scholarly and popular art publications, with special emphasis upon material in the Museum's collections.   S

124. NATIONAL BAPTIST PUBLISHING BOARD. Founded 1897 in Nashville, Tennessee, by Dr. Richard Henry Boyd, for the printing of religious literature for the National Baptist Convention of America. The Board, still specializing in religious publications, denominational literature, and Sunday school requisites, continues in the control of the original family.   S

125. NATIONAL PUBLISHING COMPANY. Founded 1863 in Philadelphia by Joshua R. Jones. Incorporated at the time of the founder's death in 1915. During its early years the firm published books of general interest as well as Bibles. The Bible publishing activities were expanded, until now the company specializes in the publication of Bibles and religious books, besides doing extensive manufacturing for other publishers in the medical and textbook fields. S

126. THOMAS NELSON & SONS. American branch of Thomas Nelson & Sons, Ltd. (established at Edinburgh in 1798) founded 1854 in New York by Thomas Nelson II, with the purpose of carrying on a general publishing business and publishing Bibles in "quality binding," as well as low-priced editions for wide distribution. Through the years the firm has been known as publishers of encyclopedias, medical books, and juveniles. The firm's greatest publishing venture was the Revised Standard Version of the Bible in 1952.   S

127. NOBLE AND NOBLE, PUBLISHERS, Inc. Founded 1883 in New York by Arthur H. Hinds. When G. Clifford Noble became a partner in 1887, the firm name was changed to Hinds and Noble, operated both as a bookstore and as a publishing concern specializing in textbooks. Subsequent changes of the incorporated Publishing Department were Hinds, Noble and Eldredge, and Hinds, Hayden and Eldredge. The partnership of Hinds and Noble operating as a bookseller and jobber continued until 1917, when the partnership was dissolved and assets purchased by G. Clifford Noble, who changed the name to Noble and Noble. In 1914 or 1915 G. Clifford Noble had organized a separate publishing company named after his son, Lloyd Adams Noble. Lloyd Adams Noble withdrew in 1917, and in 1921, when another son, J. Ken-

drick Noble, joined the business, the publishing firm name of Lloyd Adams Noble was changed to Noble and Noble. Incorporated 1934 as Noble and Noble, Publishers, Inc. In 1925 the firm purchased the publishing concern of F. A. Beatty and in 1942, that of Simons Peckham. Still specializing in the publication of textbooks for elementary and high schools, the concern continues in the control of the Noble family. S

128. THE OPEN COURT PUBLISHING COMPANY. Founded 1887 by Edward C. Hegeler of La Salle, Illinois, for the purpose of "establishing ethics and religion upon a scientific basis." Has published two periodicals—*The Monist,* devoted to the philosophy of science, and *The Open Court,* devoted to religion and science—as well as books on philosophy, mathematics, evolution, the history of religion, comparative religion, science and religion, to bring about "a reformation of religious life on the basis of science." S

129. OTTENHEIMER: PUBLISHERS. Founded 1890 in Baltimore, Maryland, by Isaac and Mose Ottenheimer, under the name of I. & M. Ottenheimer. In 1955 the firm's name was changed to Ottenheimer: Publishers. Originally known for its publication of ten-cent joke books, the concern is now known for its low-priced nonfiction, travel books, language books, and Vest Pocket Library of dictionaries and reference books. It continues in the control of the original family. G

130. THE OTTERBEIN PRESS. Founded 1833 in Circleville, Ohio, as the printing establishment of the United Brethren in Christ, to publish a paper devoted to religious, moral, and literary intelligence. In 1837 the first book—a hymn book—was published. In 1853 the concern was moved from Circleville to Dayton, Ohio, by boat, railway boxcar, and wagons. The present name was adopted in 1935. The firm continues to specialize in denominational religious publications, primarily for the Evangelical United Brethren Church. S

131. OXFORD UNIVERSITY PRESS, Inc. The American branch of Oxford University Press (founded at Oxford in 1478), established 1896 under the management of John Armstrong, as a distributive agency to promote the sale of Oxford Bibles. Its main function continued to be that of "keeping the American public acquainted with Oxford books, both sacred and secular, and of supplying the books without avoidable delay," but by the time of the early 1930's it had begun to expand its functions until it has become a publishing house in its own right as well, issuing many significant original American publications. G

132. L. C. PAGE & COMPANY, Inc. Founded as a subsidiary of the firm of Estes & Lauriat, which was established in Boston in 1872 by Dana Estes and Charles E. Lauriat. The subsidiary concern was formed in 1892 as the Joseph Knight Company. In 1896 Joseph Knight resigned and Lewis C. Page became president. The following year the firm name was changed to L. C. Page & Company. In 1898 the original Estes & Lauriat partnership was dissolved, being followed by two distinct concerns, Charles E. Lauriat Co., successors to the retail department, and Dana Estes & Co., successors to the publishing division. In 1914 the Page firm purchased the list and plant of Dana Estes & Co. Lewis C. Page died in May, 1956. The concern publishes standard works, travel books, and nature stories, but is especially strong in its juvenile series.   G

133. PARKER & SON, Inc. Founded and incorporated 1898 in Los Angeles, California, under the name of Spencer & Parker, for the purpose of legal printing, by Tom Spencer and Robert Parker. C. H. Stone purchased the Spencer interest, and the firm name became Parker & Stone, followed by other changes: Parker, Stone & Baird (1919), Parker & Baird (1935), Parker & Company (1939), and Parker & Son, Inc. (1954). In 1953 the Parker interest purchased all outstanding stock. The firm, specializing in legal and financial printing and publications, continues in the control of the original (Parker) family.   S

134. THE PAULIST PRESS. An outgrowth of The Catholic Publication Society established in 1866 in New York by the founder and first superior of the Paulist Fathers, Isaac Hecker, as the printing apostolate of the Missionary Society of St. Paul the Apostle. Publishes pamphlets and booklets aiming to "teach religion by means of the printed word."   S

135. THE PILGRIM PRESS. Founded 1832 in Boston as the Congregational Sunday-School and Publishing Society in conjunction with the establishment that year of the Massachusetts Sabbath-School Society. United in 1868 with the Congregational Board of Publication (which had been established in 1829 as the Doctrinal Tract and Book Society) under the name of The Congregational Sabbath-School and Publishing Society. In 1919 the legal name of the Society became the Congregational Publishing Society and its trade name, The Pilgrim Press, the publishing and supply house of the Congregational Christian churches.   S

136. PITMAN PUBLISHING CORPORATION. Founded 1890 by Charles A. Pitman in New York under the name of Isaac Pitman & Sons, a branch of Sir Isaac Pitman & Sons (established 1837 in

London). After 1923 the New York house began to issue a greater proportion of American books, and since 1933, when the Pitman Publishing Corporation was formed, expansion has proceeded further. Now an independent company, Pitman Publishing Corporation publishes not only business education books, but college, technical, arts and crafts, and general nonfiction books.   S

137. R. L. POLK & CO. Founded 1870 in Detroit by Ralph Lane Polk for the purpose of publishing a business directory of towns on the Detroit & Milwaukee Railway and a Michigan State Gazetteer. The firm expanded and issued its first *Detroit City Directory* in 1874. Incorporated 1885. After the founder's death in 1923 his son headed the firm, and the latter was succeeded in the presidency after his death in 1950 by the third Ralph L. Polk. The concern, with approximately 760 active publications, now has five major divisions—City Directory, Bank Directory, Direct Mail and Motor List, Motor Statistics, and Special Services. It continues in the control of the original family.   S

138. PRANG PUBLISHERS DIVISION of THE AMERICAN CRAYON COMPANY. Founded 1856 in Boston by Louis Prang and Julius Mayer as Prang & Mayer, lithographic and copperplate press manufacturers. Within a few years the partnership was dissolved and the firm became L. Prang & Co., lithographers and fine art publishers. In 1865 Prang introduced to the American public the chromo and about a decade later the artistic Christmas card. In 1874 the Prang Educational Company was formed, with Louis Prang as president, to promote and publish materials for art instruction in the public schools. The Company was sold to a syndicate after the founder's death in 1909. Edwin O. Grover became president of the Company in 1912, when he changed its name to The Prang Company. In 1926 The American Crayon Company of Sandusky, Ohio, bought the right to use the Prang name on art materials, and now publishes art textbooks over the Prang name. S

139. THEODORE PRESSER CO. Founded 1883 at Lynchburg, Virginia, by Theodore Presser, who began publication of *The Etude,* a music magazine. The following year Presser moved to Philadelphia and branched out into the publication of music and music books under the name of Theo. Presser, Music Publisher and Dealer. Upon the founder's death in 1925 James Francis Cooke became president. In 1930 the Presser Company purchased the John Church Company of Cincinnati (established in 1860), and the following year the firm purchased the Oliver Ditson Company of Boston. In 1953 Arthur A. Hauser became president. The con-

cern, now in Bryn Mawr, Pennsylvania, continues to specialize in music publications. S

140. THE PRICE & LEE COMPANY. Founded 1873 in New Haven, Connecticut, by William W. Price and Wilson H. Lee for the purpose of publishing city directories and guides. In 1878 the firm published a telephone directory. Incorporated 1891 as The Price & Lee Company. Price sold his interest to Lee in 1910, and the latter sold his interest in 1919. The concern continues to specialize in the publication of city directories, maps, and guides. S

141. FREDERICK PUSTET COMPANY, Inc. Founded 1865 in New York as a branch of the German Catholic publishing house established by Friedrich I. Pustet in Passau in 1819. Another branch was set up in Cincinnati (1867). Incorporated in the United States in 1917. Still affiliated with the mother house, now at Regensburg, the firm, publishers of the Ratisbon breviaries, missals, and other liturgical publications, continues in the control of the original family, and in the United States has been under the management of the Tapke family since 1903. S

142. G. P. PUTNAM'S SONS, Inc. Founded 1838 in New York under the style of Wiley & Putnam by John Wiley and George Palmer Putnam. In 1848 the firm was dissolved, Wiley concentrating upon scientific and technical books, and G. P. Putnam setting up as an independent publisher, issuing the writings of Irving, Poe, Lowell, Bryant, Cooper, Hawthorne, *et al.* In 1852, with the admission of John W. Leslie, the firm name was changed to G. P. Putnam & Company. An assignment was made in 1857, and for a period during the early '6o's an arrangement was made with Hurd & Houghton to publish and sell the Putnam books on commission. Active publishing was again begun in 1866, when the founder's son, George Haven Putnam, entered the firm and the style became G. P. Putnam & Son. Two years later, with the admission of John Bishop Putnam, the firm name was changed to G. P. Putnam & Sons. A third son, Irving Putnam, was admitted in 1871, and the following year, with the death of George Palmer Putnam, the style became G. P. Putnam's Sons, incorporated in 1892. A printing plant, the Knickerbocker Press in New Rochelle, was established 1874 and sold 1932. In 1884 Theodore Roosevelt was made a special partner. Subsequently, five grandsons of the founder entered the firm, and in 1930, after the death of George Haven Putnam, the concern was reorganized. George Palmer Putnam, the founder's grandson, sold his interest to Palmer Putnam, and Earle H. Balch and Melville Minton of Minton, Balch & Co. entered

the firm, their company being merged with Putnam's. Irving Putnam died in 1931, Palmer Putnam retired in 1932, and in 1934 Minton and Balch acquired a controlling interest, family control having ceased. Mr. Balch retired in March, 1946. Mr. Minton, who bought Mr. Balch's stock, died in 1955 and was succeeded by his son, Walter J. Minton.   G

143. RAND McNALLY & COMPANY. Founded 1856 in Chicago as a print shop by William H. Rand, job printer. Shortly after, consolidated with the *Chicago Tribune* job printing department, and in 1864 Andrew McNally and Rand purchased the shop from the *Tribune* and formed a partnership. The firm was incorporated in 1873 as Rand McNally & Company. Original specialization in railroad printing evidenced by the firm's first publication, *Western Railway Guide,* in 1869, and through its connections with the nation's railroads the company was naturally led into the map-making essential in railroad literature. The adoption of the wax engraving method of map-making in 1872 ultimately made the firm's name synonymous with maps and map-making. However, it ranks high both as textbook and trade publisher, and is also one of the oldest of the publishing houses to specialize in juveniles.   S

144. FLEMING H. REVELL COMPANY. Founded 1869 in Chicago by Fleming H. Revell for the purpose of publishing a Christian magazine, *Everybody's Paper,* at the suggestion of the founder's brother-in-law, Dwight L. Moody. Advancing to book publications from periodicals (the first book publication being W. P. MacKay's *Grace and Truth*), the concern became one of the first wholly independent and undenominational publishing houses in America aiming at "the promotion of Christian principles and the faith and the furtherance of world-wide Evangelism." A branch office was set up in New York in 1887, and in 1904 headquarters were transferred to that city, the Chicago office being subsequently discontinued. In 1881 the firm purchased the stock of W. G. Holmes Company and in 1893, the Toronto Willard Tract Depository. The company, incorporated in 1890 and now in Westwood, New Jersey, is still in the control of the original family.   S

145. REVIEW AND HERALD PUBLISHING ASSOCIATION. Founded 1855 in Battle Creek, Michigan, by James White for the purpose of publishing health, educational, and religious literature. The firm's first book publication was Uriah Smith's *Daniel and the Revelation.* Incorporated 1861 under the name of the Seventh-day Adventist Publishing Association. In 1902 the plant was destroyed by fire, and four years later it was transferred to Washington, D.C.

The firm continues to specialize in health, educational, and religious literature. S

146. G. RICORDI & CO., Inc. Founded 1897 in New York City as the agency of the Italian firm of music publishers, which had been established in Milan in 1808. In 1899, under the management of George Maxwell, the firm began the publication of American compositions. Incorporated 1911. During World War II the company's stock and copyrights, which had been sold to the Milan firm, were seized by the Alien Property Custodian, and the company's publishing activities ceased, being resumed after the war. The concern continues to specialize in music publications, particularly operas, symphonic works, and choral music. While the New York Ricordi does not publish books on music, the Milan firm does. S

147. THE ROUGH NOTES COMPANY, Inc. Founded 1878 in Indianapolis by Henry L. Martin for the publication of an insurance journal, *Rough Notes*. Incorporated 1881. Following the founder's death in 1916, the stock was sold and the new management took over in 1917. Reincorporated 1931. The firm, which provides insurance office systems and supplies and insurance sales services, specializes in the publication of insurance magazines and books. S

148. THE H. M. ROWE COMPANY. Founded 1867 in Baltimore, Maryland, by Warren H. Sadler as W. H. Sadler, Publisher, for the publication of textbooks in commercial subjects. In 1892 Dr. H. M. Rowe associated himself with the founder in a partnership, and in 1898 the business was incorporated as Sadler-Rowe, Inc. In 1907 the present name was adopted. The firm continues to specialize in the publication of textbooks in the field of business education and since 1898 has issued *The Rowe Budget*. Dr. Charles G. Reigner has been president of the Company since 1927. S

149. THE SAALFIELD PUBLISHING COMPANY. Founded 1899 in Akron, Ohio, by Arthur James Saalfield, who purchased the book publishing department of the Werner School Book Company. Beginning as general publishers of trade books, premium books, and subscription books, the firm in 1902 entered the field of children's books. Today it specializes in children's books, continuing in the control of the original family. S

150. WILLIAM H. SADLIER, Inc. Founded 1832 in New York City by Denis and John Sadlier under the name of D. & J. Sadlier for the purpose of publishing Catholic books. About 1874 John's son, William H. Sadlier, established the firm of William H. Sadlier, publishing books for use in Catholic schools. After William H.

Sadlier's death the business was carried on by his widow, Annie M. Sadlier. Incorporated 1928, with Annie M. Sadlier as president. After her death in 1930 her son, Frank X. Sadlier, became president. The original firm of D. & J. Sadlier came into his hands and was disbanded. Upon his death in 1939 Mrs. Frank X. Sadlier succeeded him. The firm, continuing in the control of the original family, now specializes in the publication of textbooks.   S

151. BENJ. H. SANBORN & CO. Founded 1898 in Boston by Benjamin H. Sanborn when the firm of Leach, Shewell & Sanborn was divided. By assignments and purchases, however, the company's publications may be traced back to the eighteenth-century Boston firm of Manning & Loring. Incorporated 1899 in Maine. Its home office has been in Chicago since 1912, when the late W. F. Young acquired control. The firm's important purchases included the acquisitions of Thos. R. Shewell & Company (1902), Sibley & Co. (1916), and the Augsburg Publishing Co. (1940). From its beginnings the company has specialized in educational publications, school and college textbooks.   S

152. W. B. SAUNDERS COMPANY. Founded 1888 in Philadelphia by Walter Burns Saunders to serve as publisher to the medical profession and to publish books in the whole area of medical science. The firm's first publication (1888) was Hobart Amory Hare's *Quiz Compend of Physiology*. In 1900 a London office was opened. The firm, still specializing in medicine, the biological sciences, nursing and dentistry, publishes textbooks, book journals, annual volumes, and manuals in medicine and surgery. It continues in the control of the original family.   S

153. G. SCHIRMER, Inc. Founded 1861 in New York City under the name of Beer & Schirmer by B. Beer and Gustav Schirmer, who purchased the firm of Kerksieg & Breusing (established 1848 in New York). In 1866, when Schirmer obtained complete control, the concern was named G. Schirmer. The founder's sons, Gustave, Jr., and Rudolph E., managed the business jointly since 1885. In 1893 the founder died and the business was incorporated as G. Schirmer, Inc., with Rudolph E. Schirmer as president. The latter died in 1919 and was succeeded by his nephew, Gustave Schirmer, 3rd (1919-1921), William Rodman Fay (1921-1929), Carl Engel (1929-44), and again by Gustave Schirmer (1944-   ). The firm continues to specialize in music publications and some books on music and musicians.   S

154. THE ARTHUR P. SCHMIDT CO., Inc. Founded 1876 in Boston by Arthur P. Schmidt for the purpose of publishing music.

The firm became Arthur P. Schmidt Co. in 1916. Incorporated 1949. This concern published the first American symphony, John Knowles Paine's *Spring Symphony* (1880), and continues to specialize in educational musical publications. **S**

155. SCHROEDER & GUNTHER, Inc. Founded 1879 in New York City by John H. Schroeder, under the name of J. H. Schroeder, for the purpose of publishing and distributing educational music, with a special interest in the American composer. In 1920 a partnership was formed with Emil A. Gunther under the name of Schroeder & Gunther. Incorporated 1924. The firm, in Rhinebeck, New York, since 1947, has published both sheet music and music books and specializes in the publication of piano teaching material by American composers. **S**

156. SCOTT, FORESMAN AND COMPANY. Founded 1896 in Chicago by E. H. Scott and H. A. Foresman for the purpose of publishing textbooks. The firm had been preceded by a partnership known as Albert, Scott and Company, established in 1890 by E. H. Scott and C. J. Albert. Still specializing in school and college textbooks, the house continues in the control of the original families. **S**

157. CHARLES SCRIBNER'S SONS. Founded 1846 in New York by Charles Scribner and Isaac D. Baker as Baker & Scribner, issuing as its first publication the Rev. Edwin Hall's *The Puritans and Their Principles*. After Baker's death the style of the firm was changed in 1851 to Charles Scribner, and an importing house was organized in 1857 as Scribner & Co., later Scribner & Welford. After the death of Charles Scribner and the admission of Andrew Armstrong, the firm became in 1872 Scribner, Armstrong & Co. (the importing house known as Scribner, Welford & Armstrong), under Charles Scribner's son, John Blair Scribner. In 1878, when John Blair Scribner bought out Armstrong's interest, the style was changed to Charles Scribner's Sons (as importers, Scribner & Welford). In 1891 the firm in both its branches became Charles Scribner's Sons. Incorporated in 1904, the company still continues in the control of the family that founded it, a Charles Scribner having succeeded his father, Charles Scribner, who succeeded his father, Charles Scribner. **G**

158. J. D. SHELDON CO. Founded 1864 in New York City by J. DeWitt Sheldon, Augustus Sheldon, and Clarence D. Sheldon, for the purpose of publishing a weekly giving price changes in cotton goods. The firm's first book publication was *Sheldon's Buyers' Reference Book* by Clarence D. Sheldon (1872). Since 1921 the concern's actual publishing has been done by the partnership of

J. S. Phelon & Company (nephews of the founders), established in 1908, although J. D. Sheldon Co. holds the copyrights. The firm, which thus continues in the control of the original family (nephews of the founders and their descendants), specializes in the publication of business directories in the drygoods and kindred trades.   S

159. THE SHIELD PRESS. Founded 1848 in Madison, Indiana, by William P. Levey, as a bookbinding concern. In 1870, with the admission of the founder's son, William M. Levey, the firm name became William P. Levey & Son, and in 1878, with the admission of another son, Louis H. Levey, the firm name was changed to Levey Bros. & Company. In 1883 the concern was transferred to Indianapolis. With the retirement of Louis H. Levey in 1916, the style was changed to Levey Printing Company, and in 1937, to Shield Press, Inc. Upon the acquisition of the firm in 1955 by the Indiana Catholic Press, Inc., the title was changed to The Shield Press. In addition to its binding, printing, and lithographic activities, the Press specializes in the publication of interest-computing works.   S

160. SILVER BURDETT COMPANY. Founded 1885 in Boston by Edgar O. Silver as publisher of *The Normal Music Course.* The following year a partnership was formed with M. Thatcher Rogers under the name of Silver, Rogers and Company. In 1888 Rogers sold his interest to Frank W. Burdett, and the firm became Silver, Burdett and Company, expanding in the schoolbook line for the purpose of publishing and distributing textbooks which "incorporate sound learning and teaching techniques." Incorporated 1892 as Silver, Burdett and Company, becoming Silver Burdett Company 1935. In 1903 and 1904 the stocks and lists of the Morse Company and of the Potter and Putnam Company were acquired, and headquarters were moved to New York. At the death of the founder in 1909 control of the firm was divided. Currently concentrating upon elementary and high school texts.   S

161. SMITHSONIAN INSTITUTION. Founded 1846 in Washington, D.C., by act of Congress, according to the terms of the bequest of James Smithson to the United States government for "the increase and diffusion of knowledge among men." Joseph Henry was the first secretary. In 1848 the first volume of the *Smithsonian Contributions to Knowledge,* Squier and Davis's *Ancient Monuments of the Mississippi Valley,* was published and distributed, and the following year a system of international exchanges was inaugurated. Important series of publications have included *Smithsonian Miscellaneous Collections* (begun in 1862), *Bulletins of*

the United States National Museum (begun in 1875), *Proceedings of the National Museum* (begun in 1879), *Bulletins of the Bureau of American Ethnology* (begun in 1887), *Annals of the Astrophysical Observatory* (begun in 1900), and *Annual Reports of the Board of Regents to Congress.* The Institution continues to specialize in scientific, technological and art publications for the "diffusion of knowledge." S

162. THE STACKPOLE COMPANY. Founded 1831 by Theophilus Fenn, in Harrisburg, Pennsylvania, under the name of The Telegraph, as a newspaper and job printing shop, succeeding the Harrisburg Statesman. Book publishing operations were commenced in 1937 by The Telegraph Press, under the name of Stackpole Sons. Activities were suspended during World War II, and in 1946 the firm resumed publishing under the name of The Stackpole Company, a division of The Telegraph Press, Edward J. Stackpole, President. The company specializes in books on guns, hunting, fishing, and other outdoor sports, broadened in the last few years to include Americana. S

163. THE STANDARD PUBLISHING FOUNDATION. Founded 1866 in Cleveland, Ohio, by Isaac Errett, James A. Garfield, later President of the United States, and T. W. Phillips, under the name of The Standard Publishing Company, for the purpose of teaching the principles of Biblical Christianity on a nonsectarian basis. In 1955 the present name was adopted. Now in Cincinnati, the firm specializes in the publication of religious books and Sunday school material. S

164. STANFORD UNIVERSITY PRESS. Founded 1893 in Stanford, California, by Julius Andrew Quelle as a student-operated print shop. In 1917 the plant was purchased by the University, and the publishing department was established in 1925. The Press publishes scholarly trade books, textbooks, reference books, and series. S

165. STREET & SMITH PUBLICATIONS, Inc. Founded 1855 in New York City by Francis S. Street and Francis S. Smith under the name of Street & Smith, for the purpose of publishing a weekly family paper, *New York Weekly Dispatch* (changed in 1858 to *New York Weekly*). Upon Street's death in 1883 Ormond Gerald Smith, Francis Smith's son, bought out Street's interest. When Francis Smith died in 1887, the business was continued by his sons, George Campbell Smith and Ormond Gerald Smith. Under their direction the firm began the publication of dime novels in 1889 with the Log Cabin Library and the Nugget Library, followed by

the Nick Carter Detective Library and the Diamond Dick Library. The concern issued the Merriwell Series in paperbacks, as well as standard English and American works both in paper and cloth. In 1915 the publication of dime novels gave way to an emphasis upon magazines. Ormond and George Smith died in 1933, and the latter's son, George Campbell Smith, Jr., became president, succeeded in 1937 by Artemas Holmes, who was in turn succeeded by Allan L. Grammer. Gerald H. Smith, grandson of the founder, was president from 1948 until his death on June 18, 1955. He was succeeded as president by Arthur Z. Gray. The firm, now publishing specialized magazines directed to specific audiences, as well as annuals, continues in the control of the original Smith family.   S

166. CLAYTON F. SUMMY CO. Founded 1888 in Chicago by Clayton F. Summy for the purpose of publishing educational music materials for piano teachers. In 1931 the business was reorganized with John F. Sengstack as president, and the following year the founder died. The firm publishes music books as well as educational piano, choral (sacred and secular), organ, and instrumental music.   S

167. THE SUNDAY SCHOOL BOARD OF THE SOUTHERN BAPTIST CONVENTION. Founded 1891 in Nashville, Tennessee, by the Southern Baptist Convention to serve "the churches through the development of curricula for Bible study and Christian training." The Board's first book publication was Charles E. Taylor's *The Story of Yates the Missionary*. In 1932 the Board adopted the press name of Broadman Press for the publication of general religious books, while curriculum materials were published under the imprint of the Board. For the books designed specifically for Southern Baptist churches, the name of Convention Press was selected in 1955. The organization is still controlled by the Southern Baptist Convention.   S

168. THOMAS LAW BOOK COMPANY, Inc. Founded 1885 in St. Louis, Missouri, as The F. H. Thomas Law Book Company, Inc., publishers and dealers in law books, by F. H. Thomas (who had previously formed a partnership as Soule, Wentworth and Thomas, dealers in law books), J. G. Lodge and A. M. Thomas. In 1920 the firm name was changed to Thomas Law Book Company. The concern continues to specialize in the law book field.   S

169. THOMAS PUBLISHING COMPANY. Founded 1890 in Philadelphia by H. Mark Thomas and others for the purpose of publishing directories. Incorporated 1898. The firm, now in New York City, is still in the control of the founder and continues to

specialize in industrial publications, directories, and purchasing guides. S

170. CHARLES E. TUTTLE COMPANY. History traced to 1832, when George Albert Tuttle worked as a printer in Vermont. In 1833 he published a newspaper at Rutland. In 1850 George A. Tuttle & Co. was formed as a general job printing and publishing concern. When the founder retired in 1872, the business was divided among his four sons as The Tuttle Company. At the death of Harley Tuttle in 1893, Egbert C. Tuttle assumed sole control of the company, and with the latter's death in 1928 the firm was retained by the Estate and later divided among his children. The Charles E. Tuttle Company was established in 1935 by Charles E. Tuttle, primarily as an antiquarian book firm, although some publishing was done. Charles E. Tuttle, Jr., great-grandson of George Albert Tuttle, inherited the concern in 1943. In 1948 a branch was established in Tokyo, Japan. The firm, now specializing in the publication of books in Japan on Oriental life, history, language, and art in English, is individually owned by Charles E. Tuttle, Jr.

S

171. THE TUTTLE PUBLISHING COMPANY, Inc. History traced to 1832 (for details see sketch of CHARLES E. TUTTLE COMPANY). Incorporated 1885. After Harley Tuttle's death in 1893, the firm was operated by Egbert C. Tuttle, until his death in 1928, as a publishing and printing business, specializing in genealogies and town histories. Upon Egbert C. Tuttle's death the firm was retained by the Estate, and in 1935 Berenice R. Tuttle, granddaughter of George Albert Tuttle, became president. It has since 1944 been leased to Edwin F. Sharp, still under the name of The Tuttle Publishing Company and specializing in the publication of genealogies, and continuing in the control of the original family. S

172. THE UNITED STATES NAVAL INSTITUTE. Founded 1873 at The United States Naval Academy, Annapolis, Maryland, as a private, nonprofit association of members, by a group of officers and professors attached to the Naval Academy, for the furtherance of scientific, professional, and literary knowledge in the Navy. Its first president was Admiral David D. Porter. Since its founding the Naval Institute has published a periodical, *United States Naval Institute Proceedings,* and in 1899 began publishing books of general naval interest. An affiliate of the Association of American University Presses, the Institute specializes in the publication of textbooks, training manuals, and histories for use in the Navy, Marine Corps, Coast Guard, and Merchant Marine. S

173. UNIVERSITY OF CALIFORNIA PRESS. Founded 1893 as an outgrowth of the University's Committee on Publications of 1886. Its first publications of 1893 included Lawson's *The Geology of Carmelo Bay* and Shinn's *Notes on the Development of a Child, Part I.* In 1915 the printing office and the Press were housed in the same building, and in 1933 were consolidated into a single organization. After that time the policy of the Press expanded to include in its program both scholarly works and books of general interest, with emphasis upon distinguished printing. The printing office is now once more operated as a separate department of the University.   S

174. THE UNIVERSITY OF CHICAGO PRESS. Planned in 1891 with the establishment of the University of Chicago by President William Rainey Harper; operated as a private corporation under Daniel C. Heath from 1892 to 1894, and since then as a department of the University under control of the Chancellor and a Board of University Publications chosen from the faculty. The Press has always confined its work to the printing and publication of scholarly books and materials useful in university teaching.   S

175. THE UNIVERSITY PUBLISHING COMPANY. Founded 1899 in Lincoln, Nebraska, by George L. Towne for the publication of textbooks. The firm, still in the control of the founder, continues to specialize in textbooks.   S

176. THE UNIVERSITY SOCIETY, Inc. Founded 1897 in New York by George Bryan for the purpose of publishing and distributing educational books. The concern was moved to Ridgewood, New Jersey, in 1952, and still specializes in educational publications.   S

177. D. VAN NOSTRAND COMPANY, Inc. Founded 1848 in New York by David Van Nostrand under his personal imprint. After his death in 1888 the style of the firm was changed to D. Van Nostrand Company. From the beginning the firm specialized in technical and scientific books, not venturing outside of those fields until 1927, when the company was reincorporated, and when it broadened its scope.   S

178. FREDERICK WARNE & CO., Inc. Founded 1881 in New York City as an agency of Frederick Warne & Co., Ltd., of London (established 1865). Incorporated 1920. Still owned by the London concern, the firm continues to specialize in juveniles, particularly picture books, publishing some American titles, but the bulk of publishing is done in conjunction with the London house.   S

179. THE WARTBURG PRESS. Founded 1881 in Columbus, Ohio, as the Lutheran Book Concern, by the Evangelical Lutheran Joint Synod of Ohio and other States, to publish literature for the church body. In 1930 the Lutheran Book Concern and the Wartburg Publishing House (established 1883 in Waverly, Iowa, by the Evangelical Lutheran Joint Synod of Iowa and other States) were merged as a result of the formation that year of the American Lutheran Church. The present name was adopted in 1944. The concern, controlled by the American Lutheran Church, with its home office in Columbus, Ohio, continues to specialize in Lutheran publications. S

180. WEST PUBLISHING COMPANY. Founded 1876 in St. Paul, Minnesota, by John B. and Horatio D. West to provide "better service to the lawyer than he is now receiving." The firm's first publication (1876) was a pamphlet, *The Syllabi*, a forerunner of *The National Reporter System*. In 1924 the Congress of the United States commissioned West Publishing Company in conjunction with Edward Thompson Company of Northport, Long Island, to compile and prepare *The Code of the Laws of the United States*, and in 1946 both firms were commissioned to revise the federal Criminal Code and the federal Judicial Code. The firm also publishes annotated statutes for the various states and through its law school department co-operates with all law schools in the country. S

181. THE WESTMINSTER PRESS. Founded 1838 in Philadelphia by the General Assembly of the Presbyterian Church, as the Presbyterian Board of Publication, for the purpose of furnishing "the churches under its care with suitable tract, Sabbath School and other publications." The first book publication was *The Way of Salvation Familiarly Explained* by the Rev. Archibald Alexander. In 1887 the Board was styled the Presbyterian Board of Publication and Sabbath School Work, and in 1923 the name was changed to Board of Christian Education of the Presbyterian Church in the United States of America. The Westminster Press is the imprint of the publication division of that Board, publishing Church school curricula, hymnals, official Church books, and general religious books, as well as a general line of trade books. S

182. WHEELER PUBLISHING COMPANY. Founded 1897 in Chicago by William H. Wheeler for the purpose of publishing schoolbooks. The founder died in 1936. The firm continues to specialize in the publication of textbooks, and the Wheeler family has been in control of the business since its inception. S

183. JAMES T. WHITE & COMPANY. Founded 1873 in San Francisco by James Terry White for general book publishing. Incorporated 1902 in the State of New York. In 1887 headquarters were transferred to New York City, and the following year the firm began compilation of the first volume of *The National Cyclopedia of American Biography,* a continuous publication now in forty-seven volumes. Specializing in the publication of that work, the firm continues in the control of the original family.   S

184. WILCOX & FOLLETT CO. Founded 1874 in Wheaton, Illinois, by C. M. Barnes, as a jobbing business in second-hand schoolbooks. The firm was moved to Chicago and, in 1894, incorporated as C. M. Barnes Company. In 1898 J. W. Wilcox became associated as treasurer. Barnes retired in 1902, his son, W. R. Barnes, becoming president. In the same year, Charles W. Follett entered the firm, later becoming president. In 1907 the firm name was changed to C. M. Barnes-Wilcox Company, and ten years later, with the withdrawal of W. R. Barnes, to J. W. Wilcox & Follett Co., and in 1943 to Wilcox & Follett Co. In 1942 the company started trade book publishing and the following year entered the field of juveniles. In addition to its wholesaling of books and its trade publishing department, the firm has associated with it a textbook publishing company, Follett Publishing Company.   G

185. W. A. WILDE COMPANY. Founded 1868 in Boston by William Allan Wilde, who obtained the New England distribution of Ivison, Blakeman, Taylor & Co. of New York for the purpose of publishing and circulating religious books. Under the name of W. A. Wilde & Company the firm obtained from Henry Hoyt Company Peloubet's *Select Notes.* Incorporated 1899 in Maine as W. A. Wilde Company. The firm, continuing in the control of the original family, specializes in "fundamental religious publications."   S

186. JOHN WILEY & SONS, Inc. Founded 1807 in New York City by Charles Wiley, bookseller and printer, who branched into the publishing field prior to 1814. In 1821 the firm name was Wiley & Halsted; in 1828 the founder died and was succeeded by his son, John Wiley; in 1832, with the partnership of George Long, the style was changed to Wiley & Long. John Wiley entered into a partnership with George Palmer Putnam in 1838, when the firm became Wiley & Putnam, general publishers. Upon the dissolution of the partnership in 1848 Wiley continued under his own name and began to specialize in scientific and technical works. Charles and William H. Wiley, sons of John Wiley, entered the firm, which in 1875 became John Wiley & Sons. Incorporated 1904. William

H. Wiley, the first president of the corporation, died in 1925 and was succeeded by William O. Wiley, great-grandson of the founder. The company, specializing in all the major branches of engineering, the pure and applied sciences, business, and the social sciences, continues as a private corporation in the control of the original family, the fifth generation of which is now represented in the firm.   S

187. THE WILLIAMS & WILKINS COMPANY. Founded 1890 in Baltimore by John H. Williams as a small printing shop. With admission of Harry B. Wilkins to partnership in 1893, the firm became Williams & Wilkins, later passing into the ownership of Edward B. Passano. Incorporated in 1925 as an independent publishing house, distinct from the printing firm of Waverly Press, Inc., Williams & Wilkins Company specialized in scientific books and periodicals. In 1932 took over assets of William Wood and Company, which had been founded in New York in 1804 by Samuel Wood, and which became William Wood and Company in 1863, specializing in medical publications. From 1932 to 1946 known as the William Wood Division of Williams & Wilkins. Today the Baltimore firm combines the two specialties of scientific and medical publications.   S

188. THE H. W. WILSON COMPANY. Founded 1898 in Minneapolis by Halsey William Wilson, who in 1889 had formed a partnership with a fellow student at the University of Minnesota to deal in student textbooks and supplies. All of its publications, including the *Cumulative Book Index* begun in 1898, the *Readers' Guide to Periodical Literature* commenced in 1901, and the *Book Review Digest* founded in 1905, are outgrowths of definite library needs. In 1913 the company was moved to White Plains, New York, and four years later to New York City. The house, issuing major indexes and reference works for research and library scholarship, claims to be the world's largest reference publishing concern—with over 400 employees—performing all publishing operations under one roof.   S

189. THE JOHN C. WINSTON COMPANY. Founded 1884 in Philadelphia by John C. Winston. Entered the textbook field in 1918, but continues to publish books in a wide range of categories, as well as Bibles.   G

190. M. WITMARK & SONS. Founded 1883 in New York by Isidore Witmark and his brothers (all of whom were under age), as a printing firm. The concern proceeded to specialize in the publication of music. In 1928 M. Witmark & Sons was purchased by

Warner Brothers, and the firm, still specializing in music, is part of the Music Publishers Holding Corporation owned by Warner Brothers. S

191. THE B. F. WOOD MUSIC CO., Inc. Founded 1893 in Boston by B. F. Wood and John Aiken Preston for the purpose of publishing music teaching material especially for piano teachers. Preston died in 1914 and Wood in 1922. The firm was continued by nephews of the founders and was in the control of the original families until 1950, when the old company was sold to Mills Music, Inc., of New York City. The new company then established continues under the name of The B. F. Wood Music Co., Inc., in Boston, its executives being Mills Music, Inc., with Mr. Jack Mills, President and Treasurer. The firm publishes music books, including "Edition Wood." S

NOTE: According to the 1956-1957 edition of *Literary Market Place,* published after this book went to press, other specialist firms which may qualify as houses surviving from the nineteenth century are: American Sunday School Union, Americana Corp., Binfords & Mort, P. F. Collier & Son Corporation, R. D. Cortina Co., Fairchild Publications, Inc., F. W. Faxon Co., Inc., McKnight & McKnight Publishing Co., Pacific Press Publishing Assn., Popular Science Publishing Co., Sports Afield, and The Writer, Inc.

1769 The American Philosophical Society

1780 The American Academy of Arts and Sciences

1785 Lea & Febiger (first actual firm)

1789 The Methodist Publishing House

1792 J. B. Lippincott Company

1804 Banks-Baldwin Law Publishing Company

1807 John Wiley & Sons, Inc.

1816 American Bible Society

1817 Harper & Brothers

1820 Baker, Voorhis & Co., Inc.

1824 The American Baptist Publication Society

1825 American Tract Society, Inc.
Appleton-Century-Crofts, Inc.

1826 P. J. Kenedy & Sons

1828 The Christian Education Press
McLoughlin Brothers, Inc.

1831 G. & C. Merriam Company
The Stackpole Company

1832 The Pilgrim Press
William H. Sadlier, Inc.
Charles E. Tuttle Company
The Tuttle Publishing Company, Inc.

1833 The Otterbein Press

1836 Orange Judd Publishing Co., Inc.

1837 Little, Brown & Company

1838 A. S. Barnes & Company, Inc.
The Bobbs-Merrill Company, Inc.
John Knox Press
G. P. Putnam's Sons, Inc.
The Westminster Press

1839 Dodd, Mead & Company, Inc.

1842 Charles E. Merrill Books

1843 The American Sabbath Tract Society (Recorder Press)
The Blakiston Division of the McGraw-Hill Book Company, Inc.

1844 A. C. McClurg & Co.

1845 Walter H. Baker Company

1846 Charles Scribner's Sons
Smithsonian Institution

1848 The Shield Press
D. Van Nostrand Company, Inc.

1849 Macoy Publishing & Masonic Supply Company, Inc.

1850 Samuel French, Inc.

1852 E. P. Dutton & Co., Inc.
Houghton Mifflin Company

1853 Benziger Brothers, Inc.

1854 Beacon Press, Inc.
Bloch Publishing Co., Inc.
Thomas Nelson & Sons

1855 Muhlenberg Press
     Review and Herald Publishing
       Association
     Street & Smith Publications,
       Inc.

1856 Bancroft-Whitney Company
     Prang Publishers Division of
       The American Crayon Com-
       pany
     Rand McNally & Company

1858 Behrens Publishing Company

1859 The Harrison Company

1860 Herald Publishing House, A
       Trust Estate

1861 M. A. Donohue & Co.
     G. Schirmer, Inc.

1863 Board of Christian Education
       of the United Presbyterian
       Church of North America
       (The Geneva Press)
     National Publishing Company

1864 Callaghan & Company
     The Reuben H. Donnelley Cor-
       poration
     J. Fischer & Bro.
     J. D. Sheldon Co.

1865 The Ave Maria Press
     Frederick Pustet Company, Inc.

1866 Henry Holt and Company, Inc.
     The Paulist Press
     The Standard Publishing Foun-
       dation

1867 Ezra A. Cook Publications,
       Inc.
     Ginn and Company
     The H. M. Rowe Company

1868 Allyn and Bacon, Inc.
     The Burch Directory Company
     Lothrop, Lee & Shepard Co.,
       Inc.

     W. A. Wilde Company

1869 Concordia Publishing House
     Cornell University Press
     The Macmillan Company
     Fleming H. Revell Company

1870 Thomas Y. Crowell Company
     The Metropolitan Museum of
       Art
     Museum of Fine Arts, Boston
     R. L. Polk & Co.

1871 Harvard University Press

1872 R. R. Bowker Company
     Carl Fischer, Inc.
     C. R. Gibson & Company
     Hafner Publishing Company
     A. J. Holman Company
     L. C. Page & Company, Inc.

1873 B. Herder Book Co.
     The Price & Lee Company
     The United States Naval Insti-
       tute
     James T. White & Company

1874 Barnes & Noble, Inc.
     Wilcox & Follett Co.

1875 Longmans Green & Co., Inc.

1876 American Library Association
     T. S. Denison & Company
     Funk & Wagnalls Company
     The Arthur P. Schmidt Co.,
       Inc.
     West Publishing Company

1878 Berlitz Publications, Inc.
     The Johns Hopkins Press
     The Rough Notes Company,
       Inc.

1879 F. A. Davis Company
     Schroeder & Gunther, Inc.

1881 Gospel Trumpet Company
     Frederick Warne & Co., Inc.
     The Wartburg Press

1882 African Methodist Episcopal Sunday School Union
The Lawyers Co-operative Publishing Company
David McKay Company, Inc.

1883 The Educational Publishing Corporation
Hebrew Publishing Company
Noble and Noble, Publishers, Inc.
Theodore Presser Co.
M. Witmark & Sons

1884 Augustana Book Concern
Morehouse-Gorham Co., Inc.
The John C. Winston Company

1885 Boston Music Company
Davison Publishing Company
The Dramatic Publishing Company
D. C. Heath and Company
Silver Burdett Company
Thomas Law Book Company, Inc.

1886 Christian Publications, Inc.
Charles H. Kerr & Company

1887 Matthew Bender & Company, Inc.
Lyons & Carnahan, Inc.
The Open Court Publishing Company

1888 The Jewish Publication Society of America
W. B. Saunders Company
Clayton F. Summy Co.

1889 International Textbook Company

1890 American Book Company
The Dietz Press, Inc.
The Norman W. Henley Publishing Company
Ottenheimer: Publishers

Pitman Publishing Corporation
Thomas Publishing Company
The Williams & Wilkins Company

1891 Augsburg Publishing House
The Bruce Publishing Company
F. W. Dodge Corporation
The Mosher Press
The Sunday School Board of the Southern Baptist Convention

1892 John Byrne & Company
The University of Chicago Press

1893 Columbia University Press
F. E. Compton & Company
Edwards Brothers, Inc.
Lutheran Publishing House
Stanford University Press
University of California Press
The B. F. Wood Music Co., Inc.

1894 The H. W. Gray Company, Inc.
Edward B. Marks Music Corporation
Moody Press

1895 Architectural Book Publishing Co., Inc.
Eden Publishing House
The Evangelical Press
The Grolier Society Inc.

1896 The Interstate Printers and Publishers, Inc.
Oxford University Press, Inc.
Scott, Foresman and Company

1897 Dodge Publishing Company
Doubleday & Company, Inc.
House of the Church of the Brethren
The A. N. Marquis Company
National Baptist Publishing Board

G. Ricordi & Co., Inc.
The University Society, Inc.
Wheeler Publishing Company

1898 American Technical Society
The Christian Science Publishing Society
Grosset & Dunlap, Inc.
Mentzer, Bush & Company
Parker & Son, Inc.
Benj. H. Sanborn & Co.
The H. W. Wilson Company

1899 Chas. A. Bennett Co., Inc.
Alfred M. Best Company, Inc.
Coyne Electrical School
Frederick J. Drake & Co.
Gregg Publishing Division, McGraw-Hill Book Company, Inc.
The Saalfield Publishing Company
The University Publishing Company

NOTES ON SOURCES

I. JAMES D. BEMIS

Postriders, Newspapers, & Pioneer Printing Methods
   The Albany Register (January 3, 1800); *The Centennial History of Chautauqua County* (Jamestown, N.Y., 1904), II, 96; [Franklin Ellis], *History of Columbia County, New York* (Philadelphia, 1878), p. 117; Frederick Follett, *History of the Press of Western New-York* (Rochester, 1847), p. 67; William H. Hill, *A Brief History of the Printing Press in Washington, Saratoga and Warren Counties* (Fort Edward, N.Y., 1930), p. 95; Eber D. Howe, *Autobiography and Recollections of a Pioneer Printer* (Painesville, Ohio, 1878), p. 20; John W. Moore, *Moore's Historical, Biographical, and Miscellaneous Gatherings, . . . relative to Printers* (Concord, N.H., 1886), pp. 23, 143; Joel Munsell, *Chronology of the Origin And Progress of Paper And Paper-Making* (Albany, 1876), p. 64; J. Munsell, *The Typographical Miscellany* (Albany, 1850), p. 146; Elliot G. Storke, "History of the Press of Cayuga County," *Cayuga County Historical Society Collections*, No. 7 (Auburn, 1889), pp. 53, 55; Harriet A. Weed, ed., *Autobiography of Thurlow Weed* (Boston, 1883), I, 22.

Bemis's Letter Describing His Journey
   James D. Bemis to Mr. and Mrs. Daniel Ward, January 1804. The letter is included in Henry O'Reilly, "A few Remarks concerning James D. Bemis, the Patriarchal Editor of Western New York," Henry O'Reilly Materials, Rochester Historical Society (courtesy Blake McKelvey). There is a copy in the O'Reilly Collection, Typographical Mementos I, New York Historical Society (courtesy Oscar Wegelin). The letter is printed in O. Turner, *History of the Pioneer Settlement of Phelps and Gorham's Purchase* (Rochester, 1851), p. 492.

The Western Repository Advertisement
   Western Repository (Canandaigua) I:41 (February 7, 1804), photostat in New York Public Library.

Bemis's Early Life
   Details of Bemis's early life appear in his autobiographical letter of November 17, 1846, printed in the *Ontario County Times* (June 30, 1897) and reprinted in Thomas W. Draper, *The Bemis History and Genealogy* (San Francisco, 1900), pp. 133-36. Further details appear in [W. H. McIntosh], *History of Ontario County* (Philadelphia, 1876), pp. 33, 66; Charles F. Milliken, *A History of Ontario County, New York and Its People* (New York, 1911), I, 289; information from Dorothea E. Spear, American Antiquarian

Society. The writer is grateful also to Rollo G. Silver and Barrows Mussey for suggestions relating to Bemis.

The Bemis-Holley Sale

Follett, *History of the Press in Western New-York* (Rochester, 1847, reprinted New York, 1920), p. 4.

Bemis's Activities as Newspaper Publisher

James D. Bemis to Thurlow Weed, January 13, 1823 (courtesy Margaret Butterfield, University of Rochester); Clarence S. Brigham, *History and Bibliography of American Newspapers 1690-1820* (Worcester, 1947), I, 562-63, 714; *The Daily Messenger* [Canandaigua] (December 9, 1947), Sec. III, p. 2 and IV, p. 5; Follett, *op. cit.* (1920), pp. 3, 5; Follett, *History of the Press of Western New-York; . . . Together with the Proceedings of the Printers' Festival, Held . . . January 18, 1847* (Rochester, 1847), p. 5 of the *Proceedings;* Milton W. Hamilton, *The Country Printer New York State, 1785-1830* (New York, 1936), pp. 84, 214; *Ontario Repository, and Western Advertiser* X:12 (July 7, 1812) (New York Public Library).

Bemis's description of the postrider is reported in Follett, *op. cit.* (1920), p. 6.

At one time Bemis planned to branch out also into magazine publishing. According to J. Munsell, *The Typographical Miscellany* (Albany, 1850), pp. 125-26, on August 20, 1816, Bemis issued proposals for publishing a monthly magazine under the title of the *Western Magazine and Monthly Miscellany,* to contain 80 pp. a month and to be priced at $5 a year. This magazine was not published, however, but was replaced by the *American Monthly Magazine* in 1817, published in New York.

Bemis's Public Offices

Lewis Cass Aldrich, *History of Ontario County New York* (Syracuse, 1893), p. 220; *Catalogue of the Trustees, Teachers and Pupils, of the Ontario Female Seminary* (Canandaigua, 1827), p. 2; *The Daily Messenger* [Canandaigua] (December 9, 1947), Sec. II, p. 4 and V, p.3; Edward Hungerford, *Men And Iron The History of New York Central* (New York, 1938), p. 49; O'Reilly, "A few Remarks concerning James D. Bemis."

Bemis's Training and Setting Up of Apprentices

For information regarding this phase of Bemis's activity, the writer is indebted to Harry C. Durston, Onondaga Historical Association. For the terms of agreement with Loomis, see Charles James Smith, "Our Missionaries," *Centennial Celebration of the Congregational Church of Rushville New York,* New Age Print (1902), p. 27 (courtesy Robert Moody, Rushville, N.Y.) and Albertine Loomis, *Grapes of Canaan* (New York, 1951), p. 318. This phase of Bemis's career is discussed in *The Daily Messenger* [Canandaigua] (December 9, 1947), Sec. IV, p. 5; Milton W. Hamilton, *The Country Printer,* pp. 36 ff., 83; Milton W. Hamilton, "The Spread of the Newspaper Press in New York Before 1830," *New York History* XIV:2 (April 1933); Henry Wayland Hill, ed., *Municipality of Buffalo, New York* (New York & Chicago, 1923), I, 460-61; Frank M. Hollister, "Some Early Buffalo Characters," *Publications of the Buffalo Historical Society* XVII (1913), p. 180; John Clyde Oswald, *Printing in the Americas* (New York, 1937), pp. 227-28; Guy H. Salisbury, "Early History of the Press of Erie County," *Publications of the Buffalo Historical Society* II (1880), p. 201; Laurentius G. Sellstedt, "Roswell Willson Haskins," *ibid.* IV (1896), pp. 263-64. In a letter to the writer, Dr. R. W. G. Vail states, "Bemis . . . was undoubtedly the father of the press of Western New York and more printers were trained in his shop than in any other shop I know of, outside of that of Isaiah Thomas in Worcester."

For details regarding the setting up of Redfield, the writer is indebted to Dr. Clarence S. Brigham, American Antiquarian Society. See also Dwight H. Bruce, *Onondaga's Centennial* (Boston, 1896), II, 189; W. W. Clayton, *History of Onondaga County, New York* (Syracuse, 1878), p. 192; L. H. Redfield to Henry O'Riley [sic], Syracuse, January 30, 1858 (courtesy Blake McKelvey, Rochester Historical Society); "Lewis H. Redfield," *Syracuse Evening Herald* (July 15, 1882), courtesy Harry C. Durston, Onondaga Historical Association, and Raymond E. Sparks, Syracuse Public Library.

The Reputation of the Ontario Repository & Its Proprietor
Draper, *The Bemis History*, p. 136.

Bemis's Bookselling Methods & Activities
Draper, *op. cit.*, p. 134; advertisement in *The Farmer's Diary, Or, Beers' Ontario Almanack, For 1823;* Follett, *op. cit.* (1920), p. 4. The books and stationery sold are advertised in *The Farmer's Diary* for 1816, 1817, 1823, 1824, 1827-1830, as well as in the *Ontario Repository* (July 7, 1812, April 6, 1819, and March 27, 1821), courtesy Mrs. Ralph O. Stratton, Ontario County Historical Society, and the *Rochester Telegraph* (August 18, 1818), courtesy Blake McKelvey, Rochester Historical Society. The writer is indebted to Mrs. Stratton and Dr. McKelvey for considerable information relating to Bemis.

The Rushville Order
Benjamin Loomis to J. D. Bemis, Rushville, April 13, 1832 (courtesy Mrs. Edith M. Fox, Collection of Regional History, Cornell University).

Bemis as Wholesaler for the Western Country
Follett, *op. cit.* (1920), p. 4; Hamilton, *The Country Printer*, p. 73; General Friend Palmer, *Early Days in Detroit* (Detroit, 1906), p. 474.

The Bemis Bindery, Agency for Typefounders & Miscellaneous Activities
All these phases of Bemis's activity are noted in the Bemis book labels found in MS record books of Quaker meetings (courtesy Society of Friends, Records Committee), which describe the proprietor as "Printer, Bookseller and Bookbinder," who "keeps for sale, Ledgers, Journals, and all other kinds of Account and Blank Books; Cyphering and Writing Books, Memorandum do. Blank do. rul'd for Music; Attorney's Registers, & c. Books for Recording

Deeds, Town business, & c. and all work in the Binding line, executed in a neat and faithful manner."

See also advertisements in *Buffalo Gazette* (April 1, 1812), courtesy Alice J. Pickup, Buffalo Historical Society, and *Ontario Repository* (July 7, 1812); Follett, *op. cit.* (1920), p. 4; Hamilton, *The Country Printer*, p. 13; [W. H. McIntosh], *op. cit.*, p. 64; Turner, *op. cit.*, p. 459.

Bemis's Personal Characteristics & Expression of His Hopes

Bemis's autobiographical letter of November 17, 1846, reprinted in Draper, *op. cit.*, pp. 135-36; Follett, *History of the Press of Western New-York; . . . Together with the Proceedings of the Printers' Festival* (1847), p. 6 of *Proceedings.*

The Bemis Publications

It may be that a work of more general interest takes precedence as the first book published by Bemis. The second edition of [Charles Williamson], *A Description of the Genesee Country. Printed for the Author*, 1804 was probably printed at Canandaigua by Gould & Post or by their successors, Gould & Bemis. See *New York State Library 125th Annual Report 1942*, p. 44.

The Bemis publications are listed in Alexander V. Blake, *The American Bookseller's complete Reference Trade List* (Claremont, N.H., 1847), p. 152 (where the Bemis & Shepard imprints are also listed) and in Douglas C. McMurtrie, *A Bibliography of Books, Pamphlets and Broadsides Printed at Canandaigua, New York 1799-1850* (Buffalo, 1939). See also advertisement in *The Farmer's Diary, Or, Beers' Ontario Almanack, For 1823* and Roorbach, *Bibliotheca Americana 1820 to 1848*. Many of the titles are owned by the New York Historical Society and the New York Public Library. In addition, the New York Public Library has photostats of the title-pages of numerous Bemis publications. A few additional titles were supplied by Mary B. Brewster, New York State Library.

For the Washington Benevolent Society, see Dixon Ryan Fox, "The Washington Benevolent Society," *Columbia University Quarterly* XXI:1 (January 1919), pp. 27-37, and E. F. Hanaburgh, "News for Bibliophiles," *The Nation* (October 30, 1913), pp. 405-6.

Bemis's Partners

Bemis's autobiographical letter of November 17, 1846, reprinted in Draper, *op. cit.*, p. 135.

Almanacs Published by Bemis

The Farmer's Diary; or, Western Almanac made its bow in 1812. According to McMurtrie, the issue for that year is unknown save for an advertisement in the *Ontario Repository*, but copies of the 1812 and 1813 *Almanacs* are now in the Rochester Public Library. A copy of the 1813 *Almanac*, lacking the title-page, is owned by the Rochester Museum of Arts and Sciences, and the New York Public Library boasts a copy of the 1814 issue.

In addition to McMurtrie's *Canandaigua Bibliography*, see *Almanacs Now In The Possession Of The Rochester Museum Of Arts And Sciences* (Rochester, 1935, typescript in New York Public Library), and Alexander J. Wall, *A List of New York Almanacs 1694-1850* (New York, 1921). For information regarding the *Almanacs* at the Rochester Public Library, the writer is indebted to Mr. Percy Clapp, formerly of the New York Public Library, and Emma Swift of the Rochester Public Library.

Pickering's Political Essays

Hamilton, *The Country Printer*, p. 78; *Ontario Repository* (July 7, 1812); O'Reilly, "A few Remarks concerning James D. Bemis, . . . accompanied by the presentation of a copy of the 'first bound book,' printed between Seneca Lake and the Pacific Ocean," New York Historical Society and Rochester Historical Society.

For the Redfield letter, see L. H. Redfield to Henry O'Riely [sic], Syracuse, March 10, 1858 (courtesy Blake McKelvey, Rochester Historical Society). In a letter to O'Reilly of November 7, 1841, Bemis had written, "Of Pickering's letters, it was the first bound volume printed west of *Utica*." (Rochester Historical Society). The copy presented to the New York Historical Society by O'Reilly is said to have been given to O'Reilly by Bemis.

Seaver's Narrative of the Life of Mrs. Mary Jemison

Isabel Ayrault, in "The True Story of Mary Jemison The White Woman of the Genesee," *The Rochester Historical Society Publication Fund Series* VIII, 196, states without further ado that Banister accompanied Seaver to the home of Mrs. Jennet Whaley and there met Mary Jemison. Elmer Adler, in a letter of April 12, 1948, to the writer, remarked, "The statement in the Ayrault article seems to me to be little more than a misreading of the Introduction." Dr. R. W. G. Vail, in a letter of April 22, 1948, to the writer, stated, "I have re-read the introduction and am still rather puzzled by what it says, just as you were. . . . It is possible that Banister encouraged Seaver to write Mrs. Jemison's life. I would guess from the introduction that Bemis, the printer, and Seaver, perhaps with Banister as well, went to see Mrs. Jemison."

There are three variations of the first edition that indirectly tell the tale of the book's early popularity. The first variation shows the verso of the title-page blank, without copyright notice, indicating that the sheets of the entire edition were printed before copyright had been secured and that a few copies were bound up without the copyright leaf. The second variation contains the copyright notice on an extra leaf following the title-page. Apparently because of its success, the *Narrative* was copyrighted on May 8, 1824, when James D. Bemis deposited the title of the book, the right whereof he claimed as proprietor. Bemis therefore printed a separate copyright leaf which was inserted after the title-page in those copies which had already been bound but which remained unsold. The third variation has the copyright leaf pasted on the verso of the title-page and represents the remainder of the edition that was still unbound and in sheets. For details regarding the first edition and its variants, see James E. Seaver, *A Narrative of the Life of Mary Jemison. Revised by Charles Delamater Vail* (New York: American Scenic and Historic Preservation Society, 1932), pp. 274 ff.; Elmer Adler, "An Adventure in

Americana," *Quarto Club Papers* 1928:1929 (New York, 1930), pp. 14-31; Elmer Adler, "The Persistent Re-blossoming of Mary Jemison," *Rochester Historical Society Publication Fund Series* III, 119-26; *American Book-Prices Current 1941-1945,* p. 829; James E. Seaver, *A Narrative of the Life of Mary Jemison* (New York, 1925), pp. 276-77; [Frederick Strecker], *Tabulation of Editions and Issues of "The Life of Mary Jemison" By James Everett Seaver* (single leaf).

For further details regarding the *Narrative,* the writer is indebted to Margaret Butterfield, University of Rochester, and Dr. R. W. G. Vail. See also Wright Howes, *U.S.-Iana* (New York, 1954), No. 9138; Howard H. Peckham, *Captured By Indians* (New Brunswick, N.J., 1954), pp. x and 78 f.; James E. Seaver, *A Narrative of the Life of Mrs. Mary Jemison* (Canandaigua: J. D. Bemis and Co., 1824), pp. ix-x.

Bemis's Journey to Europe & Decline

Bemis's autobiographical letter of November 17, 1846, reprinted in Draper, *op. cit.,* pp. 135-36. The New York State Library owns five letters from Bemis to Oliver Phelps at Canandaigua, written in 1835 from Paris and alluding to Franco-American relations (courtesy Edna L. Jacobsen, New York State Library).

Printers' Festival of 1847

Follett, *History of the Press of Western New-York; . . . Together with the Proceedings of the Printers' Festival, . . . January 18, 1847* (1847), p. 5 of *Proceedings.*

Bemis's Infirmity

Dr. George A. Elliott, Superintendent of Brattleboro Retreat, to the writer, March 22, 1948. For information regarding Bemis's stay at the Utica State Hospital, the writer is indebted to Dr. Arthur W. Pense. See also O'Reilly, "A few Remarks concerning James D. Bemis."

Bemis's Ambitions & Achievements

Bemis's autobiographical letter of November 17, 1846, reprinted in Draper, *op. cit.,* p. 135; Turner, *op. cit.,* p. 460.

II. WILLIAM HILLIARD & HIS FIRM

William Hilliard

William Allen, *The American Biographical Dictionary* (Boston & Cleveland, 1857), pp. 433 f.; T. W. Baldwin, *Vital Records of Cambridge* (Boston, 1914), I, 356; G. S. Hillard, *A Memoir of James Brown* (Boston, 1856), p. 10; "Francis Hilliard," *DAB;* Abiel Holmes, "The History of Cambridge," *Collections of the Massachusetts Historical Society for . . . 1800.* Series I, Vol. VII, 19 n.; Alexander McKenzie, *Lectures on the History of the First Church in Cambridge* (Boston, 1873), p. 176; S. E. Morison, *Harvard College in the Seventeenth Century* (Cambridge, 1936), I, 352 n. 2; L. R. Paige, *His-*

tory of Cambridge (Boston, 1877), pp. 45 n. 1, 303, 305; *Proceedings of the Cambridge Historical Society* (Cambridge, 1915), p. 10.

According to Arthur P. Morley, Hilliard's print shop "flourished for generations as the most famous printing plant in America." See his "Cambridge—The Great Unknown City of America," *Boston Evening Transcript* (June 13, 1936), Sec. 6, p. 11 (courtesy Frederick H. Pratt and Rollo G. Silver). For further details on Hilliard's Cambridge press, see *Stephen Daye and His Successors* (Cambridge, 1921), pp. 22 ff. and Note on *The Firm's Collateral Connections*.

Jacob Cummings

Boston Directory 1810 (courtesy Oscar Wegelin, New York Historical Society); A. O. Cummins, *Cummings Genealogy* (Montpelier, 1904), p. 258; Florence W. Newsome, *The Publishing and Literary Activities of the Predecessors of Ticknor & Fields,* Masters Thesis, Boston University, 1942, p. 25.

Notice of the dissolution of copartnership between Andrews & Cummings appears in *Columbian Centinel* (March 4, 1809), p. 3 (courtesy Edward G. Freehafer, New York Public Library), and in *Independent Chronicle* (March 27, 1809), p. 3 (courtesy Dr. Clarence S. Brigham, American Antiquarian Society).

Formation of Cummings & Hilliard; Stand at 1 Cornhill

Announcement of the firm's formation appears in *Columbian Centinel* (May 16, 1812), p. 1 (courtesy Boston Public Library and Rollo G. Silver). The announcement is dated May 13, 1812.

The stand at 1 Cornhill had an interesting history, "its origin dating back to 1784, when Ebenezer Battelle kept a bookstore in Marlborough Street. . . .

Three years later, in 1787, Benjamin Guild purchased the Battelle business, and carried it on as the Boston Book Store, at 59 Cornhill, . . . and afterwards at No. 1 Cornhill, on the north corner of Spring Lane. In 1792 Samuel Cabot became the proprietor, and continued the business until 1797, when William P. and Lemuel Blake, who succeeded him, began a publishing business in addition to selling books and stationery. They were succeeded in 1806 by William Andrews." "Little, Brown & Co. In A New Home," *Publishers' Weekly* LXXVI:15 (October 9, 1909), p. 1025. See also Charles K. Bolton, *Circulating Libraries In Boston, 1765-1865* (The Colonial Society of Massachusetts, February 1907), pp. 202 f. and "Little, Brown & Co.," *Publishers' Weekly* LIII:24 (June 11, 1898), p. 934.

For the facilities and customers of Cummings & Hilliard, see E. M. Bacon, "Old Boston Booksellers," *The Bookman* V:5 (July 1897), p. 374; *English and Foreign Books for Sale by Cummings & Hilliard* (Boston, n.d.), courtesy American Antiquarian Society; R. L. Rusk, *The Letters of Ralph Waldo Emerson* (New York, 1939), I, 23.

Textbooks of Cummings & Hilliard

See *Catalogue of Valuable Books, for Sale by Cummings & Hilliard* (n.d.), courtesy American Antiquarian Society, and the firm's list at end of J. A.

Cummings, *An Introduction to Ancient and Modern Geography* (Boston & Cambridge, 1821).

Harvard's Augustan Age

For Harvard at this period, see S. E. Morison, *Three Centuries of Harvard* (Cambridge, 1936), pp. 216 ff. The firm's publications of Harvard works are listed in *Catalogue of Valuable Books, for Sale by Cummings & Hilliard.*

Bigelow's American Medical Botany

G. E. Ellis, *Memoir of Jacob Bigelow* (Cambridge, 1880), pp. 50 f. See also C. E. Goodspeed, *Yankee Bookseller* (Boston, 1937), p. 286; *The Month at Goodspeed's* XIII:6 (March 1942), p. 193; Rollo G. Silver, *The Boston Book Trade 1800-1825* (New York, 1949), p. 13.

Books Sold By Cummings & Hilliard

Catalogue of Latin, Greek, French, and English Classics (Boston, 1825), courtesy Boston Public Library; *Catalogue of Latin, Greek, and Hebrew Books, Lately Received from Germany* (Cambridge, 1825), courtesy American Antiquarian Society; *English and Foreign Books for Sale by Cummings & Hilliard; Foreign Books . . . an invoice of . . . French, Spanish, Italian, and Latin Books* (n.d.), courtesy Boston Public Library.

Timothy Harrington Carter

See C. A. and S. A. Carter, *Carter A Genealogy* (Clinton, 1887), pp. 111 f.; Newsome, *op. cit.*, appended to which is a photostatic copy of Carter's Autobiography. (The writer is indebted to Miss Newsome for many suggestions used in the preparation of this chapter.) See also "Obituary. Timothy Harrington Carter," *Publishers' Weekly* XLVI:4 (July 28, 1894) and "The Old Corner Book-Store," *The New England Magazine* XXIX:3 (November 1903), pp. 305 f.

Formation of Cummings, Hilliard & Company

See Notice in *Columbian Centinel* (March 26, 1823), p. 3 (courtesy Edward G. Freehafer, New York Public Library).

Jacob Cummings had died on February 24, 1820. Announcement of his death is in *Independent Chronicle* (March 1, 1820), p. 1 (courtesy Boston Public Library and Rollo G. Silver).

For the firm's law books, see the list at end of Cummings, *An Introduction to Ancient and Modern Geography* (Boston & Cambridge, 1821).

Richard Bridge Carter

J. L. Blake, *A Biographical Dictionary* (Philadelphia, 1856), pp. 250 f.; Newsome, *op. cit.*, p. 28.

Hilliard, Jefferson & The Library of The University of Virginia

Jefferson's letters to Hilliard and his firm have almost all been published in Elizabeth Cometti, ed., *Jefferson's Ideas On A University Library* (Charlottesville, 1950), where some citations are also given, pp. 3 ff., from Hilliard's letters to Jefferson.

Jefferson's Catalogue reflected his views that "Great standard works of established reputation, too voluminous and too expensive for private libraries, should have a place in every public library," that "Indifferent books are sometimes inserted, because none good enough are known on the subject," and that "Nothing of mere amusement should lumber a public library." Jefferson's desire was for the largest sum obtainable—$40 or $50,000—"to purchase the most essential books of text and reference for the schools." The Proctor in the year of Jefferson's death had paid, on account of the library and apparatus, $35,947.78. For details of the Catalogue and expense of books and apparatus, see Randolph G. Adams, *Three Americanists* (Philadelphia, 1939), p. 73; Arthur Bestor, "Thomas Jefferson and the Freedom of Books," *Three Presidents And Their Books* (Urbana, Ill., 1955), pp. 7 f.; *A Catalogue of the Library of the University of Virginia* (Charlottesville, Va., 1828 and 1945 reprint), *passim; Early History of the University of Virginia, as contained in the letters of Thomas Jefferson and Joseph C. Cabell* (Richmond, Va., 1856), pp. 289, 291, 355, 363; F. W. Page, "Our Library," *The* [University of Virginia] *Alumni Bulletin* II:3 (November 1895), pp. 78 ff.; *Report of The Rector And Visitors of the University of Virginia, to the President And Directors of the Literary Fund* (Richmond, 1826) appended to *Journal of the House Of Delegates of . . . Virginia, Begun . . . December 1826* (Richmond, 1826), p. 27; information from John Cook Wyllie. A manuscript copy of Jefferson's Catalogue of Books for the University of Virginia Library, 1825, is in the Alderman Library, University of Virginia.

The Hilliard side of the correspondence, never published in its entirety, from which copious quotations appear here, consists primarily of 14 letters from Hilliard or his firm to Thomas Jefferson, dated between July 14, 1824 and May 8, 1826, owned by The Huntington Library. They are quoted by permission of The Huntington Library, San Marino, California, where they are catalogued as HM 9230, 9236, 9260, 9279, 9287, 9291, 9297, 9300, 9306, 9323, 9338, 9339, 9346, 9351. In addition, one letter from Cummings, Hilliard & Company to Jefferson, October 7, 1825, is owned by the Alderman Library, University of Virginia, along with the firm's Invoices Nos. 1 and 3.

The Memorandum of Agreement between Jefferson and Hilliard, April 8, 1825, is owned by the Manuscripts Division, Library of Congress, as well as the Bond by Hilliard and his surety, May 7, 1825.

For further details, see Arthur Bestor, "Thomas Jefferson and the Freedom of Books," *Three Presidents And Their Books* (Urbana, Ill., 1955), pp. 1-44; P. A. Bruce, *History of the University of Virginia* (New York, 1920-22), II, 40, 190 ff.; Harry Clemons, *The University of Virginia Library 1825-1950* (Charlottesville, 1954), pp. 5, 12, 145; Thomas Jefferson to Joseph Coolidge, Jr., January 15, 1825 and April 12, 1825, in *The Writings of Thomas Jefferson. Monticello Edition* (Washington, D.C., 1904), XVIII, 335 f., 337 ff.; Thomas Jefferson to F. W. Gilmer, June 6, 1825, in Richard Beale Davis, ed., *Correspondence of Thomas Jefferson and Francis Walker Gilmer 1814-1826* (Columbia, S.C., 1946), p. 146; *The Jefferson Papers of the University of Virginia A Calendar* (Charlottesville, Va., 1950), *passim;* information from Mr. John Cook Wyllie, Alderman Library, University of Virginia.

The books in the Charlottesville branch were sold to C. P. McKennie & M. W. D. Jones, who disposed of some of the stock at auction. See *Virginia Advocate* (December 11, 1829).

Cummings, Hilliard & Co. & The Raising of Standards of The American Press

Columbian Centinel (October 13, 1824), p. 2 (courtesy Mrs. Dorothea E. Spear, American Antiquarian Society); *Independent Chronicle* (October 13, 1824), p. 4 (courtesy Boston Public Library and Rollo G. Silver).

Boston Type & Stereotype Foundry

Established in 1817, the Boston Type Foundry was purchased by T. H. Carter in 1822. In 1823 a stereotype foundry was added and a few years later it was organized as the Boston Type and Stereotype Foundry. See *Boston Directory* 1823; "History of the Boston Type Foundry," *Printer's Bulletin*, Extra Number (June 1867); Newsome, *op. cit.*, p. 25.

Charles C. Little

Bacon, "Old Boston Booksellers," *The Bookman* (July 1897), p. 374; "Charles C. Little," *DAB;* George T. Little, *The Descendants of George Little* (Auburn, 1882), p. 208; Little, Brown & Company, *One Hundred Years of Publishing* (Boston, 1937), pp. 12 ff.; *New-England Historical and Genealogical Register* XXIII:4 (October 1869), p. 477; "Obituary. Mr. Charles C. Little," *American Literary Gazette* XIII:8 (August 16, 1869), p. 225. His admission as a partner is announced in *Columbian Centinel* (October 13, 1824), p. 2 (courtesy Mrs. Dorothea E. Spear, American Antiquarian Society) and in *Independent Chronicle* (October 13, 1824), p. 4 (courtesy Boston Public Library and Rollo G. Silver).

John Hubbard Wilkins

Newsome, *op. cit.*, p. 25; Notice of John H. Wilkins reprinted from *The New Jerusalem Magazine* (January 1862).

For the rather inadequate catalogue described, see *Catalogue of Books Recently Purchased in London, and For Sale by Hilliard, Gray, & Company* (Boston, 1833), courtesy American Antiquarian Society.

Harrison Gray

Allen, *The American Biographical Dictionary*, p. 394; *Boston Directory* 1816 and 1825 (courtesy Boston Public Library); Newsome, *op cit.*, p. 25.

Carter & The Old Corner Bookstore

Newsome, *op. cit.*, p. 75.

The returns of Cummings, Hilliard & Company appear in *ibid.*, pp. 25 f.

Carter's name appears on the imprint of many works by Jacob Abbott between 1836 and 1845. See Carl J. Weber, *A Bibliography of Jacob Abbott* (Waterville, Maine, 1948), *passim*.

Hilliard, Gray & Co. & Their Publications & Stock

Boston Directory 1827; *Catalogue of Law Books for Sale by Hilliard, Gray*

& Company (Boston, n.d.), courtesy American Antiquarian Society; *A Catalogue of School and Classical Books, published by Hilliard, Gray, Little, & Wilkins* (Boston, 1828), p. 32 and *passim;* Little, Brown & Company, *One Hundred Years of Publishing,* pp. 12 f.; *A Select Catalogue of Books, Chiefly Published or Imported by Hilliard, Gray, and Co.* (Boston, 1837).

For a time, the firm name was Hilliard, Gray, Little, & Wilkins.

Publisher & Author: Longfellow's Outre-Mer No. I

L. S. Livingston, *A Bibliography of . . . the Writings of Henry Wadsworth Longfellow* (New York, 1908), pp. 3, 16 f., 19; S. Longfellow, *Life of Henry Wadsworth Longfellow* (Boston, 1886), I, 194 and 194 n. 1; L. Thompson, *Young Longfellow* (New York, 1938), pp. 187 f., 388.

The letter containing Longfellow's stipulations to Hilliard, Gray was written on June 30, 1833, and clearly indicates that the book had been printed before a publisher was found. Since the publisher's name appears on the title-page, it seems obvious that the title-page signature was printed last. Thompson points out that the title-page signature of *Outre-Mer No. I* was printed last, after the book had been printed.

Longfellow's *Miscellaneous Poems Selected from the United States Literary Gazette* had been published by Cummings, Hilliard & Company, and Harrison Gray in 1826.

Another interesting example of the firm's relationships with authors is furnished by the planned publication of Elizabeth Peabody's *Key to History.* According to Louise Hall Tharp, *The Peabody Sisters of Salem* (Boston, 1950), pp. 69, 87, "She [Elizabeth Peabody] was to raise the capital and they would give her ten per cent on the retail price, which she considered a very favorable proposition. 'The whole cost will be 4770 dollars for paper, stones, letter press and printing but besides that there will be baggage and wagoning for 100 stones, each weighing, I fancy, about an hundred pounds. This will be not short of fifty dollars more.'

. . . When the splendid scheme of having Sophia for illustrator fell through, Hilliard, Gray and Company lost interest."

Sparks's Library of American Biography & Ripley's Specimens of Foreign Standard Literature

For Sparks, see Herbert D. Adams, *The Life and Writings of Jared Sparks* (Boston & New York, 1893), II, 195 ff.; Van Wyck Brooks, *The Flowering of New England* (New York, 1936), p. 122.

For Ripley, see O. B. Frothingham, *George Ripley* (Boston, 1882), pp. 97 f.; "In Memoriam George Ripley," *New-York Tribune,* Extra No. 63 (July 1880), p. 4; "George Ripley," *DAB.*

Later Development of Boston Type & Stereotype Foundry

Boston Directory 1829, advertisement of Boston Type and Stereotype Foundry; *ibid.,* 1837.

It is interesting to note that, "In 1820 or 1821, Crocker & Brewster planned the publication of Thomas Scott's *Family Bible* in six volumes. Crocker suggested stereotyping the edition, but when this project was submitted to Cummings & Hilliard, Manning & Loring, and Lincoln & Edmands, the three firms rejected the proposal." Rollo G. Silver, *op. cit.,* p. 8.

The Literary Advertiser

Hilliard, Gray & Co's Literary Advertiser No. 4 (January 1832), courtesy Harvard College Library.

Patrons of Hilliard, Gray

The patrons may be determined from the MS Account Book of Brown, Shattuck, & Company, a firm associated with Hilliard, Gray (courtesy Jack Neiburg). For Peter Force, see Hilliard, Gray & Co. to Peter Force, Boston, August 31, 1833 and September 10, 1835 (Library of Congress).

The books and articles sold appear in *A Select Catalogue of Books, Chiefly Published or Imported by Hilliard, Gray.*

James Brown

Bacon, "Old Boston Booksellers," *The Bookman* (July 1897), p. 374; "James Brown," *DAB;* J. C. Derby, *Fifty Years among Authors* (New York, 1884), p. 670; G. S. Hillard, *A Memoir of James Brown;* Little, Brown & Company, *One Hundred Years of Publishing,* pp. 20 f.; *Norton's Literary Gazette* II:6 and 7 (March 15 and April 2, 1855), pp. 131, 154.

It is of interest that John Bartlett of *Familiar Quotations* was employed in 1836 at the University Bookstore in Cambridge and in 1849 became the owner of the establishment.

Charles Brown

Hillard, *A Memoir of James Brown,* p. 15.

The Firm's Collateral Connections

Bacon, *op. cit.,* p. 374; *Books Lately Published by Hilliard and Brown* (Cambridge, n.d.), courtesy American Antiquarian Society; MS Account Book of Brown, Shattuck & Company (courtesy Jack Neiburg); Hillard, *op. cit.,* pp. 14 f.; Hilliard and Brown's *Catalogue of Books, with the Prices Annexed at which They Are Furnished to the Students of Harvard College* (Cambridge, 1828), courtesy Harvard College Library; *List of Books, Published . . . By Brown, Shattuck, & Company* (Cambridge, March 1833), courtesy American Antiquarian Society; Rusk, *op. cit.,* I, 250 n. 92; Lemuel Shattuck, *Memorials of the Descendants of William Shattuck* (Boston, 1855), p. 302; "Lemuel Shattuck," *DAB;* "Lemuel Shattuck," *Memorial Biographies of The New England Historic Genealogical Society,* III, 293 f.; *Town of Cambridge. Statement of the Treasury,* 1833, pp. 5, 8; W. F. Willcox, *Studies in American Demography* (Ithaca, 1940), pp. 466, 479; *Works Recently Published by Hilliard and Brown* (Cambridge, n.d.), courtesy American Antiquarian Society; *Works Recently Published by Hilliard and Brown* (Cambridge, January 1828).

According to "The University Press, Cambridge," *The Bookmakers. Reminiscences and Contemporary Sketches of American Publishers. From the New York Evening Post. 1875,* William Hilliard and Eliab W. Metcalf set up a small printing office on Holyoke Street about 1823. Actually, Hilliard had printed, as early as 1802, a college commencement broadside, with the imprint, "University Press, William Hilliard."

For Charles Folsom, and further details of the University Press of Cambridge, which dates back to 1639 when Stephen Daye set up the first press in this country, and which is still active and distinct from the Harvard University Press, see *Stephen Daye and His Successors* (Cambridge, 1921), pp. 22 ff.; "Charles Folsom," *DAB;* John Clyde Oswald, *Printing in the Americas* (New York, 1937), p. 87; information from Foster M. Palmer, Harvard College Library; Theophilus Parsons, *Memoir of Charles Folsom* (Cambridge, 1873), pp. 4, 13; information from Charlotte R. Truitt of the University Press of Cambridge, Inc.

Changes in & End of Hilliard, Gray

For the disposal of much of the stock to Little & Brown, see Bacon, *op. cit.,* p. 375; Hillard, *op. cit.,* p. 15; Little, Brown & Company, *One Hundred Years of Publishing,* pp. 14 f.

For the firm's announcement, see *Boston Directory* 1837.

For Harrison Gray's subsequent activity, see *Boston Directory* 1843.

For the disposal of stock to James Munroe, see Roorbach, *Bibliotheca Americana 1820-1852,* which lists Munroe & Company as publishers of Ripley's Specimens of Foreign Literature.

For the street named after Hilliard, see L. M. Hastings, *The Streets of Cambridge* (1921), p. 38.

III. JAMES P. WALKER & HORACE B. FULLER

Transcendental New England

Two of the best definitions of Transcendentalism in New England appear in Octavius B. Frothingham, *Transcendentalism in New England* (New York, 1880), pp. 136-37, and Vernon Louis Parrington, *Main Currents in American Thought* (New York, [1930]), II, 317 f., 379 f.

Horace B. Fuller's End

"Obituary Notes," *Publishers' Weekly* LV:3 (January 21, 1899), p. 56. I am indebted to Mr. George L. McKay, Librarian of The Grolier Club, and to Mr. Rollo G. Silver for the use of the latter's notes deposited at The Grolier Club.

Hickling, Swan and Brown

For this firm, see "Brewer & Tileston," *The Bookmakers. Reminiscences and Contemporary Sketches of American Publishers. From the New York Evening Post. 1875,* p. 107, and "Obituary. Charles Hickling," *Publishers' Weekly* XXXIII:24 (June 16, 1888), p. 940.

For Swan's death, see *American Literary Gazette and Publishers' Circular* IV:3 (December 1, 1864), p. 76.

James P. Walker & His Early Career & Appearance

Walker is described, and his early career narrated in [Thomas B. Fox, ed.], *Memoir of James P. Walker* (Boston, 1869), *passim*. Walker's letter of December 23, 1858 appears in *ibid.*, p. 24.

The American Unitarian Association had in 1854 proposed raising $50,000 for printing, distributing and selling religious books and pamphlets. See Jeannette Hopkins, *Books that will not burn* (Boston, [1954]), pp. 8 ff.

Henry May Bond

Bond died May 14, 1864, of wounds received in the Battle of the Wilderness. See *Harvard Memorial Biographies* (Cambridge, 1866), II, 12 ff.

Walker, Wise Imprints

See, besides the books themselves, the firm's advertisements and announcements in *American Literary Gazette* II:7 (February 1, 1864), p. 254, II:10 (March 15, 1864), p. 355, III:1 (May 2, 1864), p. 31, III:10 (September 15, 1864), pp. 338-39, III:11 (October 1, 1864), p. 351, IV:3 (December 1, 1864), p. 97, IV:5 (January 2, 1865), p. 155, IV:8 (February 15, 1865), p. 231; their listings in Orville A. Roorbach, *The Bibliotheca Americana, 1858-1861, passim* and in *The American Catalogue, 1861-1866, passim;* and their catalogues: *Catalogue of Standard Books chiefly by Eminent Unitarian Divines, for sale by Walker, Wise, & Co.* (Boston, n.d.) and *Catalogue of Sunday-School Manuals; . . . And Books Suitable for Sunday-School Libraries, for sale by Walker, Wise, And Company* (Boston, 1859)—both courtesy of Mrs. Dorothea E. Spear, American Antiquarian Society.

Walker's Early Life, Apprenticeship, & Employments

[Fox, ed.], *op. cit., passim.*

Stock of Walker, Wise

See *Catalogue of Standard Books chiefly by Eminent Unitarian Divines, op. cit.*

Civil War Imprints of Walker, Wise

American Literary Gazette III:10 (September 15, 1864), p. 338; "Publisher's Advertisement" in Wendell Phillips, *Speeches, Lectures, and Letters* (Boston: Walker, Wise, and Co., 1864), p. iv. The same advertisement appears in the Redpath 1863 edition of Phillips's *Speeches* but is quoted here since the attitude is particularly characteristic of Walker, Wise.

Juvenilia of Walker, Wise

Catalogue of Sunday-School Manuals, op. cit., p. 7; *Standard Books for the Young Published by Walker, Wise, & Co.* (Boston [1862]).

The Pioneer Boy by William M. Thayer, published in 1863 by Walker, Wise and republished by Walker, Fuller, has a particular claim to fame. "Written *by the permission of the President himself, and from material furnished by him,"* [*American Literary Gazette* III:1 (May 2, 1864), p. 31] it takes its place as one of the earliest appearances of the Lincoln story in juvenile literature. Josiah G. Holland refers to it as "a singularly faithful statement of the early experiences of Abraham Lincoln" [J. G. Holland, *The Life of Abraham Lincoln* (Springfield, Mass., 1866), p. 25 n.]. According to a late edition of the work [W. M. Thayer, *Abraham Lincoln The Pioneer Boy And How He Became President* (London, 1906), p. v]: "The author of this volume wrote the *first* Life of Abraham Lincoln—The Pioneer Boy, And How He Became President—which, after a very large sale, passed out of print in consequence of the destruction of the plates by fire, . . . 'The Pioneer Boy' was the first complete biography of the man." Despite this exaggeration, the Thayer work does mark one of the earliest treatments of Lincoln's life in literature for children.

On July 18, 1862, Thayer had written a remarkable letter to Senator Orville Hickman Browning (The Lincoln Papers, Library of Congress, Vol. 81, ff. 17179-17184, courtesy David C. Mearns, Chief, Manuscripts Division) regarding his preparation of the book and his desire for anecdotes about the President: ". . . Mr. Wise is one of the publishing house in Boston, known as Walker & Wise, a very enterprising and popular firm, & they put into my hands, a month since, some letters and documents from J. Scripps Esq. of Chicago with the request that I should prepare a volume for boys upon President Lincoln's early life. . . . my object is to show that 'the boy is father of the man,' showing the young that pluck and not luck makes the man. . . ."

Senator Browning read a portion of Thayer's letter to Lincoln, who "asked me [to] leave it with him which I did." [*The Diary of Orville Hickman Browning* (Springfield, Ill., 1925), I, 564.]

The Library of Congress owns the subject's copy of the book, inscribed on the flyleaf:

Abraham Lincoln.
President of the
United States.
With the respects of
the Publishers
May. 1. 1863.

For this information, the author is deeply indebted to Mr. David C. Mearns.

General Publications of Walker, Wise

"Publishers' Note" in Henri Martin, *The Age of Louis XIV* (Boston: Walker, Wise, and Co., 1865), I, vii; "Publishers' Note" in Harriet Martineau, *History of the Peace* (Boston: Walker, Wise, and Co., 1864), I, v.

Walker, Fuller Imprints

See, besides the books themselves, the firm's advertisements and announcements in *American Literary Gazette* V:2 (May 15, 1865), p. 33, V:10 (September 15, 1865), p. 221, VI:1 (November 1, 1865), p. 29, VI:3 (December 1, 1865), p. 101, VI:11 (April 2, 1866), pp. 302, 316; and their listings in *The American Catalogue*, 1861-1866, *passim*.

Massachusetts in the Rebellion

In his preface, the author, P. C. Headley, remarked, "The publishers have clearly done their part to make the volume acceptable to the people; and it is committed to them in the hope that it will be." See P. C. Headley, *Massachusetts in the Rebellion* (Boston: Walker, Fuller & Co., 1866), p. vii.

Youth's History of the Rebellion & Objections to It
American Literary Gazette VI:8 (February 15, 1866), p. 228, and VI:9 (March 1, 1866), p. 249.

Sales Figures of Walker, Fuller Juveniles
For these figures, see "Sketches of the Publishers. Walker, Fuller & Co., Boston," *The Round Table* III:30 (March 31, 1866), p. 203.

Withdrawal of Support by American Unitarian Association
American Literary Gazette VI:8 (February 15, 1866), p. 223; "Sketches of the Publishers," *The Round Table* III:30 (March 31, 1866), p. 202.

Walker's Failure, Later Life, & Death
[Fox, ed.], *op. cit.*, pp. 29, 50 f., 82, 97.

Horace B. Fuller Imprints
See, besides the works themselves and the advertisements listed therein, Fuller's advertisements and announcements in *The American Booksellers' Guide* I:9 (July 1, 1869), p. 35, I:11 (September 1, 1869), p. 32, II:1 (November 1, 1870), p. 33, II:5 (May 1, 1870), pp. 222, 224, II:6 (June 1, 1870), pp. 246, 272, II:7 (July 1, 1870), p. 318, II:9 (September 1, 1870), p. 406, II:10 (October 1, 1870), p. 472, II:11 (November 1, 1870), p. 545, II:12 (December 1, 1870), pp. 574, 578, III:2 (February 1, 1871), p. 75, III:3 (March 1, 1871), p. 115, III:4 (April 1, 1871), pp. 134, 154, III:7 (July 1, 1871), p. 235, III:8 (August 1, 1871), p. 277, V:8 (August 1, 1873), p. 191; *American Literary Gazette* IX:11 (October 1, 1867), pp. 297-98, X:5 (January 1, 1868), p. 162, XI:1 (May 1, 1868), p. 39, XVI:9 (March 1, 1871), p. 175, XVI:11 (April 1, 1871), p. 228; *Merry's Museum* LIV:4 (October 1867), N.S. I:1 (January 1868), I:6 (June 1868), I:8 (August 1868), I:10 (October 1868), III:4 (April 1870), IV:10 (October 1871), advertisements; Fuller listings in *The American Catalogue*, 1866-1871, *passim*, and *Uniform Trade List Circular* (August 1867), p. 148.

Morning Glory Series
Mrs. Follen's *The Well-Spent Hour* was announced as a "wholesome little story—old-fashioned in its matter of fact tone, and sober account of a little girl's life, into which no thread of romance is woven"—an early appeal for realism in juvenile stories. See advertisement at end of Mary G. Darling, *Battles at Home* (Boston: Horace B. Fuller, 1871). The Alcott book, *Morning Glories, and Other Stories,* gave the Series its title.

Merry's Museum
For details of *Merry's Museum* under Fuller's aegis and Louisa May Alcott's editorship, see L. M. Alcott to her uncle, Boston, January 22 [1869] (Houghton Library, courtesy Mr. William A. Jackson); *American Literary Gazette* IX:11 (October 1, 1867), p. 298, and X:6 (January 15, 1868), p.

177; *Merry's Museum* LIV:4 (October 1867), verso of cover, LIV:5 (November 1867), Prospectus for 1868, verso of cover, LIV:6 (December 1867), pp. 1, 2, N.S. I:12 (December 1868), Prospectus . . . for 1869, verso of front cover; Madeleine B. Stern, "The First Appearance of a 'Little Women' Incident," *American Notes & Queries* III:7 (October 1943), pp. 99-100.

Miss Alcott recorded in her Journal for January 1868: "F. pays me $500 a year for my name and some editorial work on Merry's Museum." See Ednah D. Cheney, ed., *Louisa May Alcott Her Life, Letters, and Journals* (Boston, 1889), p. 193, and Madeleine B. Stern, *Louisa May Alcott* (Norman, Okla., 1950), pp. 168 ff.

Dirigo Series

The Series was so named because "Dirigo" (I direct) was the motto of the State of Maine, and the first volume concerned "Six Months in the Forests of Maine." The existence of the Alcott juvenile, *Will's Wonder Book,* remained unknown until it was discovered as a volume in this Series. For a more detailed treatment, see Jacob Blanck, *Bibliography of American Literature* (New Haven, 1955), I, 32; Madeleine B. Stern, "Louisa's *Wonder Book:* A Newly Discovered Alcott Juvenile," *American Literature* XXVI:3 (November 1954), pp. 384-90. I am indebted to Mr. Frederick R. Goff, Chief, Rare Books Division, Library of Congress, for permission to examine the Series.

The Boston Fire

The American Booksellers' Guide IV:12 (December 1, 1872), p. 408.

Later Career of Horace B. Fuller

In 1877 Fuller is listed in the Boston Directory as a clerk at 340 Washington Street, where the bookseller, William B. Clarke, is also located.

In 1879 Horace Fuller is listed in the Boston Directory as a salesman at 336 Washington Street, where Albert W. Lovering is located. For details about Lovering see "The Boston Failure," *Publishers' Weekly* IX:6 (February 5, 1876), p. 170; Adolf Growoll Scrapbooks, *American Book Trade History,* VIII, 125 (courtesy *Publishers' Weekly*); *Publishers' Weekly* IX:8 (February 19, 1876), p. 229, XV:17 (April 26, 1879), p. 491, XV:24 (June 14, 1879), p. 648.

Horace B. Fuller is listed in the Boston Directories 1883-85 as superintendent, 450 Washington Street, where Jordan, Marsh was located. (Information courtesy Mr. Paul North Rice, formerly of New York Public Library, and Mr. Richard G. Hensley and Mr. Frank P. Bruno, Boston Public Library.)

IV. JOHN RUSSELL

The Ante-Bellum South

See Parrington, *op. cit.,* II, 99.

Russell's Bookstore & The Literary Gatherings There

Van Wyck Brooks, *The Times of Melville and Whitman* (New York,

1947), p. 71; Virginia P. Clare, *Harp of the South* (Oglethorpe University, Georgia, 1936), p. 51; Sidney J. Cohen, "Three Notable Ante-Bellum Magazines of South Carolina," *Bulletin of the University of South Carolina*, No. 42, Part II (July 1915), pp. 38 f.; "The Death of Mr. John Russell," *Charleston Daily News* (November 23, 1871), courtesy Dorothy Smith, South Caroliniana Library, University of South Carolina; Charles Duffy, *The Correspondence of Bayard Taylor and Paul Hamilton Hayne* (Baton Rouge, 1945), p. 4; Paul Hamilton Hayne, "Ante-Bellum Charleston," *The Southern Bivouac* N.S. I:6 (November 1885), pp. 327 ff.; "The Late John Russell," *The Charleston Daily Courier* (November 23, 1871), courtesy B. E. Powell and Mrs. Anne C. Orr, Duke University, and Kathleen Blow, University of Texas; Edgar Long, *Russell's Magazine As An Expression of Ante-Bellum South Carolina Culture* (Doctoral Dissertation in typescript, University of South Carolina, 1932), pp. 42 ff.; Frank Luther Mott, *A History of American Magazines 1850-1865* (Cambridge, 1938), p. 488; Alfred T. Odell, "William Gilmore Simms in the Post-War Years," *Bulletin of Furman University* XXIX:3 (May 1946), p. 73; La Salle C. Pickett, *Literary Hearthstones of Dixie* (Philadelphia & London, 1912), pp. 82 f., 109, 141; *The South in the Building of the Nation* (Richmond, 1909), VII, 453-54; Samuel G. Stoney, "The Memoirs of Frederick Augustus Porcher," *The South Carolina Historical and Genealogical Magazine* XLIV:2 (April 1943), p. 65; Henry T. Thompson, *Henry Timrod* (Columbia, S.C., 1928), p. 26; William P. Trent, *William Gilmore Simms* (Boston & New York, 1892), pp. 228 f.

Russell's Life

"The Death of Mr. John Russell," *Charleston Daily News* (November 23, 1871) states that Russell was born in 1813. His death certificate, however, records that he died on November 21, 1871, at the age of 59 years and 8 months, thus placing his birth in March, 1812. For other biographical details about Russell see *The Charleston Directory* 1835-1836; *Charleston Directory and Stranger's Guide* 1840 and 1841 (courtesy Dorothy Smith, South Caroliniana Library, University of South Carolina); Hayne, "Ante-Bellum Charleston," *The Southern Bivouac* (November 1885), pp. 327 ff.; Long, *Russell's Magazine As An Expression of Ante-Bellum South Carolina Culture*, pp. 43 ff.; information from A. S. Salley, Columbia, S.C.; William Gilmore Simms to Hon. R. T. Conrad, Charleston, October 19, 1847, and William Gilmore Simms to E. A. Duyckinck, Charleston, September 3, 1849, Miscellaneous Collection, Manuscript Division, New York Public Library.

Russell's Personal Characteristics & Reputation

"The Death of Mr. John Russell," *Charleston Daily News* (November 23, 1871); J. C. Derby, *Fifty Years among Authors, Books and Publishers* (New York, 1884), p. 674; Hayne, "Ante-Bellum Charleston," *op. cit.*, pp. 330, 335; Paul H. Hayne, ed., *The Poems of Henry Timrod* (New York, 1873), p. 23; Long, *Russell's Magazine*, pp. 43 f.; Mott, *History of American Magazines 1850-1865*, p. 488; A. S. Salley, Jr., "Southern Magazines," *The* [Charleston] *Sunday News* (August 27, 1899), courtesy Mr. John Cook Wyllie, University of Virginia.

Simms's Letters re Russell
The Letters of William Gilmore Simms Collected and Edited by Mary C.
Simms Oliphant, Alfred Taylor Odell, T. C. Duncan Eaves (Columbia, S.C.,
1953), II, 150 f., 271, 546, 559. See also Simms to Duyckinck, Woodlands,
February 25 [1847], Charleston, September 3, 1849, and Charleston, September 27, 1849, Miscellaneous Collection, Manuscript Division, New York Public Library.

Facilities Provided for Russell's Customers
Information from Ellen M. Fitzsimons, Charleston Library Society, and
A. S. Salley; *The Letters of William Gilmore Simms,* II, 129, 168, 340; Simms
to Conrad, Charleston, October 19, 1847, Miscellaneous Collection, Manuscript Division, New York Public Library.

Books Sold by Russell
See Russell's advertisements in *The Charleston Mercury* (May 3, 1855–
September 5, 1855, May 12, 1857, December 8–29, 1860, April 17, 1861–
June 14, 1862), courtesy Oscar Wegelin, New York Historical Society; *Part
First Of A Catalogue of rare, curious, and useful Books! For Sale By Russell
& Jones, No. 251 King Street,* University of Chicago, courtesy B. E. Powell,
Duke University Library.

Fraser's Paintings
The Letters of William Gilmore Simms, II, 546. See also Simms to E. A.
Duyckinck, Charleston, September 3, 1849, Miscellaneous Collection, Manuscript Division, New York Public Library.

Russell's Magazine
For details of the periodical, see Kate H. Becker, *Paul Hamilton Hayne:
Life and Letters* (Belmont, N.C., 1951), pp. 16 ff.; Cohen, *Three Notable
Ante-Bellum Magazines of South Carolina, passim;* information from Georgia
H. Faison, University of North Carolina; Irving Garwood, *American Periodicals From 1850 To 1860* (Macomb, Illinois, 1931), p. 72; William S. Hoole,
A Check-List and Finding-List of Charleston Periodicals 1732-1864 (Durham, N.C., 1936), pp. 5, 63 f.; Jay B. Hubbell, *The Last Years of Henry
Timrod, 1864-1867* (Durham, N.C., 1941), p. 4; Fronde Kennedy, "Russell's
Magazine," *The South Atlantic Quarterly* XVIII:2 (April 1919), pp. 125-44;
Long, *Russell's Magazine, passim;* Daniel M. McKeithan, *A Collection of
Hayne Letters* (Austin, Texas, 1944), *passim;* Frank McLean, *Periodicals
Published in the South Before 1880,* University of Virginia Dissertation, 1928,
p. 46, courtesy Jack Dalton, University of Virginia; Mott, *A History of American Magazines 1850-1865,* pp. 488 ff.; John Russell to Miss Dickson, May 4,
n.y. (Duke University, courtesy B. E. Powell); *Russell's Magazine* I:1 (April
1857), p. 82, I:2 (May 1857), p. 178, I:1–VI:6 (April 1857–March 1860),
annotated copy in New York Public Library; slip dated October 1, 1859, and
sent out with the October 1859 issue of *Russell's Magazine* (courtesy A. S.
Salley, Columbia, S.C.); "Russell's Magazine," *The Charleston Daily Courier*
(January 1, 1857), p. 2 (courtesy B. E. Powell, Duke University, and Kath-

leen Blow, University of Texas); *The South in the Building of the Nation*, VII, 453; *The Southern Literary Messenger* (October 1856), p. 306, (May 1857), p. 392; George A. Wauchope, *The Writers of South Carolina* (Columbia, S.C., 1910), p. 15.

For Simms's appraisal, see "Our Literary Docket," *The Charleston Mercury* (July 12, 1859), p. 1, and information from Mrs. Albert D. Oliphant.

Status of Southern Publishing

Russell's Magazine II:6 (March 1858), p. 566, IV:4 (January 1859), p. 370, V:5 (August 1859), p. 395; [W. G. Simms], "Literary Prospects of the South," *Russell's Magazine* III:3 (June 1858), pp. 199 ff.; Yates Snowden, *Confederate Books*, no t.p., unpaged; "Southern Publications," *De Bow's Review*, N.S. I:2 (August 1852), p. 211.

Books Published by Russell and by Russell & Jones

See, in addition to the books themselves, *The American Catalogue*, 1866-1871; Charles N. Baxter and James M. Dearborn, *Confederate Literature* (Boston, 1917), p. 106; *Catalogue of the Salley Collection of the Works of William Gilmore Simms* (Columbia, S.C., 1943), *passim;* William A. Courtenay, *A Catalogue of the Portraits, Books, . . . Presented to the Charleston Library Society* (Columbia, S.C., 1908), *passim;* James G. Johnson, *Southern Fiction Prior to 1860* (University of Virginia, 1909), p. 82; *The Letters of William Gilmore Simms* (Columbia, S.C., 1954), III, 155, 158; "Notices of New Works," *Southern Literary Messenger* XX:3 (March 1854), pp. 191 f.; *Proceedings of the Elliott Society of Natural History of Charleston, S.C.*, I, 4; "Publishers' Circular," *The Literary World* IX:237 (August 16, 1851), p. 131; Roorbach, *Bibliotheca Americana*, 1820-1852, 1852-1855; John Russell to Duyckinck, Carlton House, October 7, 1854 and Charleston, January 5, 1855, Manuscript Division, New York Public Library (courtesy Robert W. Hill); James F. Shearer, "French and Spanish Works Printed in Charleston, South Carolina," *The Papers of the Bibliographical Society of America*, XXXIV (1940), p. 169; M. Tuomey and F. S. Holmes, *Pleiocene Fossils of South-Carolina* (Charleston: Russell and Jones, 1857), preface; information from Robert J. Turnbull, Yemassee, S.C.; Oscar Wegelin, *A List of the Separate Writings of William Gilmore Simms Of South Carolina 1806-1870* (Hattiesburg, 1941), *passim.*

The Jones Brothers

For details, see Beatrice St. J. Ravenel, *Architects of Charleston* (Charleston, 1945), pp. 215, 296 n. 49.

Value of Firm's Stock

List of the Tax Payers of the City of Charleston for 1860 (Charleston, 1861), p. 247.

Death of James C. Jones & of Russell's Mother

James C. Jones died on March 17, 1861. Jones's death record, courtesy Beatrice St. J. Ravenel, Charleston; information from A. M. Gayer, Magnolia Cemetery, Charleston.

Russell & The Civil War

"The Death of Mr. John Russell," *Charleston Daily News* (November 23, 1871); "The Late John Russell," *Charleston Daily Courier* (November 23, 1871); Snowden, *Confederate Books,* unpaged.

According to F. M. Hutson, Chief Clerk, Historical Commission of South Carolina, however, the index to Confederate rolls does not list a John Russell as adjutant.

Sale of Russell's Stock

Long, *Russell's Magazine,* p. 65.

Russell's Death, Will, & Appraisal of Stock

Copy of Russell's death certificate and abstract of Russell's Will, courtesy Ellen M. Fitzsimons, Charleston Library Society; Inventory of Goods and Chattels of John Russell, Deceased, in Office of Judge of Probate, Charleston.

V. JAMES REDPATH

Redpath's Creed

Charles F. Horner, *The Life of James Redpath and The Development of the Modern Lyceum* (New York & Newark, [1926]), p. 91; James Redpath, *The Roving Editor: Or, Talks with Slaves in the Southern States* (New York, 1859), pp. v ff.

Redpath's Life

The American Bookseller XXIX:5 (February 28, 1891); Horner, *op. cit., passim; New York Tribune* (February 11, 1891), p. 12; Major J. B. Pond, *Eccentricities of Genius* (London, 1901), pp. 533 ff.; *Publishers' Weekly* XXXIX:7 (February 14, 1891), p. 291; Helen Beal Woodward, *The Bold Women* (New York, 1953), pp. 217 ff.

Publishers' Weekly and the *Tribune* give the year of his birth as 1835.

Articles on Redpath in the *Dictionary of American Biography* and in Appleton's *Cyclopedia of American Biography* omit any mention of his publishing activities. According to Pond, *op. cit.,* p. 535, "In 1863 Mr. Redpath began business as a publisher; but finding it uncongenial to his tastes, he soon abandoned it." Helen Beal Woodward, *op. cit.,* p. 227, simply states that "in 1863 he took a flier at publishing with a book of nursing experiences by Bronson Alcott's daughter, Louisa." [Mary V. H. Terhune], *Marion Harland's Autobiography* (New York & London, 1910), discusses Redpath without mentioning his career as publisher.

Redpath's Reform Activities

The Land League Testimonial to James Redpath at Delmonico's June 1, 1881 (New York, 1881); James Redpath and Richard J. Hinton, *Hand-Book to Kansas Territory and the Rocky Mountains' Gold Region* (New York, 1859); James Redpath, *The Roving Editor* (New York, 1859); James Redpath, *Talks About Ireland* (New York, 1881); F. B. Sanborn, ed., *The Life*

And Letters of John Brown (Boston, 1891), p. 294; F. B. Sanborn, *Recollections of Seventy Years* (Boston, 1909), I, 207; Woodward, *op. cit.*, p. 223.

Redpath & Haiti

James Redpath, ed., *A Guide to Hayti* (Boston: Thayer & Eldridge, 1860) and (Boston: Haytian Bureau of Emigration, 1861).

The Haytian Bureau's address appears in *Boston Directory* 1861 and 1862. Redpath also had offices at 55 Liberty Street in New York. See *Trow's New York City Directory* 1862/63.

The first number of *Pine and Palm* is recorded as of May 18, 1861. Redpath also had a New York office for *Pine and Palm* at 48 Beekman Street. See *Trow's New York City Directory* 1861/62. For Redpath's letter to Cameron, see *The War of the Rebellion: A Compilation of the Official Records of the Union And Confederate Armies* (Washington, 1899), Series III, Vol. I, 244 f.

Thayer & Eldridge and Redpath's Writings

James Redpath, *Echoes of Harper's Ferry* (Boston: Thayer & Eldridge, 1860), p. 9; James Redpath, *The Public Life of Capt. John Brown* (Boston: Thayer & Eldridge, 1860), p. 8; [James Redpath], *Southern Notes for National Circulation* (Boston: Thayer & Eldridge, 1860); Ralph L. Rusk, ed., *The Letters of Ralph Waldo Emerson* (New York, 1939), V, 218 n. 153.

The firm of Thayer & Eldridge is listed as booksellers and publishers in the *Boston Almanacs* of 1860 and 1861.

The Atlantic Monthly, reviewing *The Public Life of Capt. John Brown,* stated that "It would have been well, had this book never been written." It was "written in the spirit and style of an Abolition tract." [See *The Atlantic Monthly* V:29 (March 1860), pp. 378 f.]

Frank Leslie's Illustrated Newspaper was more caustic: "The names of the hero and his biographer render it unnecessary to explain the character of his volume; the one has expiated his crimes upon the gallows, the other has fled the country to avoid an investigation upon which he did not desire to throw any light. . . . In every point of view this is a detestable book. . . . It expounds the most ultra-fanaticism. . . . We trust that we have seen the last of Mr. Redpath on American soil, either in person or through his works. He is a dangerous, meddlesome and designing man, a foreign plague spot." [See *Frank Leslie's Illustrated Newspaper* IX:221 (February 25, 1860), p. 193.]

According to information received from Mr. Rollo G. Silver of Simmons College, Thayer & Eldridge owed Redpath $3642.68 for cash, not merchandise. It appears that Redpath endorsed a few notes for the firm, in return for which favor he collected 5.1 cents on the dollar. See Thayer & Eldridge Insolvency #704, Suffolk County Probate Court and Court of Insolvency, Boston.

Redpath's "Schemes" & Personality

Horner, *op. cit.*, p. 90; Mary A. Livermore, *The Story of My Life* (Hartford, 1898), pp. 485 f.

Redpath's Publishing Office
Boston Almanac 1864, p. 114; *Boston Directory* 1863-64.

"Books for the Times"
American Publishers' *Circular and Literary Gazette* I:9 (September 1, 1863), pp. 346, 348, I:10 (September 15, 1863), p. 378, I:12 (October 15, 1863), p. 439; advertisement of Redpath's "Books for the Times" in *Boston Almanac* 1864, p. 282. Redpath's publisher's circular also appears at the end of *Shall We Suffocate Ed. Green?* (Boston: Redpath, 1864) and [J. R. Beard], *Toussaint L'Ouverture: A Biography and Autobiography* (Boston: Redpath, 1863), pp. 367-72. Prices are given in these sources.

Shall We Suffocate Ed. Green? By a Citizen of Malden was doubtless written by Redpath himself, who, in 1864, at the time of publication, lived in Malden.

Handling of Hospital Sketches
Miss Alcott's *Hospital Sketches* appeared first in *The Commonwealth* I:38, 39, 41, 43 (May 22, May 29, June 12, June 26, 1863). Both Redpath and the firm of Roberts Brothers sought permission to reprint the work in book form, but Louisa favored the former.

For the publication and appearance of *Hospital Sketches,* see Louisa Alcott's letters (undated) to James Redpath, in the New York Historical Society (courtesy Miss Dorothy Barck, former Librarian); Ednah D. Cheney, ed., *Louisa May Alcott Her Life, Letters, and Journals* (Boston, 1889), pp. 139, 151 ff.; F. B. Sanborn, *Recollections of Seventy Years* (Boston, 1909), II, 387; Odell Shepard, ed., *The Journals of Bronson Alcott* (Boston, 1938), p. 357; Madeleine B. Stern, *Louisa May Alcott* (Norman, Okla., 1950), pp. 133 ff.

The amount of $200 represents, apparently, payments on all editions.

William Ellery Channing's *Thoreau: The Poet-Naturalist* was not published until 1873, when Roberts Brothers issued it.

"Books for the Camp Fires"
Ralph Admari, "The House That Beadle Built 1859 to 1869," *The American Book Collector* IV:6 (December 1933), p. 290; Louisa Alcott to James Redpath, December 2, n.y., mentioning the "dime set," and January 24, 1864, mentioning the arrival of "the little green backs" (courtesy New York Historical Society); American Publishers' *Circular and Literary Gazette* II:9 (March 1, 1864), p. 318; Albert Johannsen, *The House of Beadle and Adams* (Norman, Okla., [1950]), I, 48; *Legends of the Infancy and Boyhood of Jesus Christ* (Boston: Redpath, n.d.), verso of front cover and recto of back cover, where the series is described and opinions of the press are quoted; *Shall We Suffocate Ed. Green?,* list of "Books for the Camp Fires" at end.

The first of the series, *On Picket Duty,* was published January 23, 1864.

Redpath's General Publications
American Publishers' *Circular and Literary Gazette* I:12 (October 15, 1863), p. 439, II:4 (December 15, 1863), p. 153, II:12 (April 15, 1864), p. 426. See also *The American Catalogue,* 1861-1866.

Redpath's last advertisement appears in *American Publishers' Circular* II:12 (April 15, 1864), p. 426.

Redpath's Later Activities

Frank Leslie's Illustrated Newspaper LVII:1464 (October 13, 1883), p. 123; Horner, *op. cit.,* p. 227; Albert Bigelow Paine, *Mark Twain: A Biography* (New York & London, 1912), I, 441; Pond, *op. cit.,* p. 194; Eron Rowland, *Varina Howell Wife of Jefferson Davis* (New York, 1931), II, 526.

Redpath's lecture agency was first called the Boston Lyceum Bureau and later the Redpath Lyceum Bureau. According to Helen Beal Woodward, *op. cit.,* p. 218, "So potent was the very word 'Redpath,' . . . that, fifty years after his heyday, half the Chautauquas touring the corn belt and the Western plains were calling themselves 'Redpath Chautauquas.' "

Varina Davis's *Jefferson Davis, . . . A Memoir* was published in 1890 by the Belford Company of New York.

VI. CHARLES W. CLARK

Reconstruction in Louisiana

John R. Ficklen, *History Of Reconstruction In Louisiana (Through 1868)* (Baltimore, 1910), *passim;* Ella Lonn, *Reconstruction In Louisiana After 1868* (New York & London, 1918), *passim;* Allan Nevins and Henry Steele Commager, *The Pocket History of the United States* (New York, 1951), pp. 236 f., 244, 249; Edward Larocque Tinker, *Creole City* (New York, London & Toronto, 1953), p. 118.

Clark's Personal Life

When Clark died in New Orleans in 1907, he was 86 or 87 years of age and had been a resident of the city for over fifty years. According to the records of Masonic Cemeteries, New Orleans (courtesy Ben Weaver, Superintendent), where Clark is buried, Clark was a native of Pennsylvania. He was, therefore, apparently born in Pennsylvania ca. 1820 and came to New Orleans shortly before 1857. Unfortunately, Pennsylvania birth records were rarely compiled until after 1860.

There is a possibility that Clark was the Charles Clark who is listed at 120 S. 8th Street in the 1854 Philadelphia Directory. At that home address are also located a John Clark and John C. Clark & Son, book and job printers of Dock Street. The son in that concern was John Ross Clark. It may possibly be inferred that Charles Clark was a younger son of the printer, John C. Clark, and that, after finding no room for expansion in his father's firm, he moved to New Orleans. John C. Clark, printer, appears in the Philadelphia Directories as early as 1819 and 1820, the period of Charles Clark's birth. John C. Clark Company of Philadelphia has "no information available" on the subject.

To increase the confusion regarding Clark's early life, there is a statement in the *Daily Picayune* (December 20, 1907), p. 6 (courtesy Lucy B. Foote, Librarian, Louisiana Room, Louisiana State University) to the effect that Clark was a native of Harrisonburg, Virginia, and that he had resided in

New Orleans for the last 58 years, dying at the age of 86. Virginia birth records do not begin until 1853. There is no New Orleans Directory listing for Clark as early as 1849. Since the Cemetery Records are taken from the Board of Health permits, they are undoubtedly more reliable than the newspaper source.

For Clark's masonic and typographical affiliations, his residence of "over fifty years" in New Orleans, and mention of his son, see "Charles W. Clark, Dead," [New Orleans] *Times-Democrat* (December 20, 1907), p. 5 (courtesy John Hall Jacobs, Librarian, New Orleans Public Library); *Daily Picayune* (December 20, 1907), p. 6 (courtesy Lucy B. Foote); "Funeral of Mr. Charles W. Clark," *New Orleans Item* (December 20, 1907), p. 5 (courtesy John Hall Jacobs). According to *Proceedings of the M.'.W.'.Grand Lodge of F.'.and A.'.Masons, of the State of Louisiana, . . . February 8, 1858* (New Orleans, 1858), p. 150, Clark was initiated into Quitman Lodge, No. 76 on February 8, 1858. However, he had received his Entered Apprentice degree on October 2, 1857, at which time he stated his age as 33. He was advanced to the degree of Fellowcraft on November 13, 1857, and raised to the degree of Master Mason on November 27, 1857. Eventually he was elected to life membership. (Information from Adam F. Huhner, Jr., Worshipful Master, Quitman Lodge No. 76, New Orleans.)

Clark & Brisbin

The firm is listed in the New Orleans Directories 1857-1861 (courtesy Lucy B. Foote, Rosa M. Oliver, Louisiana State Museum, and Evangeline Thurber, Chief Reference Librarian, Howard-Tilton Memorial Library, Tulane University). The firm appears in 1857 as proprietors of the Crescent Job Office at 70 Camp. In 1859 the firm address was 19 Commercial Place.

For firm advertisements, see *New Orleans Daily Crescent* (1857-59), *passim* (courtesy Evangeline Thurber). A full-page advertisement appears in *Daily Commercial Advertiser* (June 1, 1858), p. 4.

For Clark & Brisbin imprints, see Max L. Griffin, "A Bibliography of New Orleans Magazines," *The Louisiana Historical Quarterly* XVIII:3 (July 1935), p. 546 [this mentions *The Volunteers' Friend*, which, although dated November 23, 1861, after Clark's enlistment in the army, may have been prepared before]; Shelf List of New Orleans Imprints at New York Public Library; Donald E. Thompson, *A Bibliography of Louisiana Books and Pamphlets in the T. P. Thompson Collection of the University of Alabama Library* (University, Ala., 1947), Nos. 698, 2970. These, as well as many of the Clark, and Clark & Hofeline imprints were examined through inter-library loan with the University of Alabama.

Civil War Service of Clark & Brisbin

Andrew B. Booth, *Records of Louisiana Confederate Soldiers and Louisiana Confederate Commands* (New Orleans, 1920), II, 120, 339.

Clark & The Crescent Job Office

In the New Orleans Directory for 1867 Clark is listed as foreman of the Crescent Job Office, and Brisbin as foreman of the Bulletin Job Office.

For details regarding the *Crescent,* its history and policy under James O. Nixon, see Fayette Copeland, "The New Orleans Press And The Reconstruction," *The Louisiana Historical Quarterly* XXX:1 (January 1947), pp. 152 ff.

For the lithographic business installed as the Crescent Job Office, see "The Crescent," *The New Orleans Crescent* (December 21, 1866), p. 6.

For the imprints of the Crescent Job Office, and of Nixon as state printer, see, besides the works themselves, Lucy B. Foote, compiler, *Bibliography of the Official Publications of Louisiana 1803-1934,* American Imprints Inventory No. 19, The WPA Historical Records Survey Program, *passim;* Thompson, *op. cit.,* Nos. 692, 1888, 2929.

For *The Phonographic Magazine,* see *The Phonographic Magazine* I:2 (November 15, 1868), verso of cover and pp. 17-18, and I:3 (December 1, 1868).

Clark's Lithographic, Book & Job Printing House

The firm's advertisement appears in *Graham and Madden's [New Orleans] City Directory For 1870.*

For Clark imprints, see, besides the works themselves, Thompson, *op. cit.,* Nos. 205, 461.

Albert D. Hofeline

For personal details of Hofeline I am indebted to information from Rosa M. Oliver, Louisiana State Museum. See also *Times Picayune* (December 30, 1928), p. 2 (courtesy Lucy B. Foote and John Hall Jacobs).

Clark & Hofeline

The firm appears in the New Orleans Directories 1874-1882 and is included in *The American Catalogue 1876-1884.* According to a Clark & Hofeline advertisement in *The Strangers' Guide and Crescent City Business Centre Directory For 1881-'82* [New Orleans:] Clark & Hofeline, [1881], the firm was "Established 1871." This statement, however, is not borne out by the New Orleans Directories, where the firm first appears in 1874, nor by the firm imprints, which begin in 1873. The 1871 New Orleans Directory lists Clark's individual firm, and 1871 imprints are of Clark's individual firm.

For the firm imprints, see, besides the works themselves, Foote, *op. cit.,* pp. 62, 512; Thompson, *op. cit., passim.*

For quoted passages, see [Napier Bartlett], *A Soldier's Story of the War* (New Orleans: Clark & Hofeline, 1874), unpaged; James Dugan, *Doctor Dispachemquic* (New Orleans: Clark & Hofeline, 1879), p. iii; *History Of The Riot At Colfax* (New Orleans: Clark & Hofeline, 1874), pp. 5, 14; Randell Hunt, *An Appeal In Behalf Of Louisiana, . . . for . . . a republican form of government* (New Orleans: Clark & Hofeline, 1874), pp. 1, 6, 7, 25; *The Muse, As I Have Found Her* (New Orleans: Clark & Hofeline, 1878), p. x; *Public Debt Of Louisiana. Argument of Delegate B. R. Forman* (New Orleans: Clark & Hofeline, 1879), p. 21; *Spofford vs. Kellogg. Arguments of Henry M. Spofford, before The Senate Committee on Privileges and Elections* (New Orleans: Clark & Hofeline, 1877), Dedication; Hon. F. C. Zacharie,

A Review of The Constitutional Points in the Louisiana Case (New Orleans: Clark & Hofeline, 1874), p. 1.

The New Orleans Monthly Review

The *Review* ran from April 1874 to August 1876, with two periods of suspension from September 1874 to December 1874 and from May 1876 to June 1876. Between April and August 1874 it was printed by Weed; from January 1875 to August 1876 it was printed by Clark & Hofeline. It was superseded, January 1878, by the *New Orleans Quarterly Review*.

See *The New Orleans Monthly Review* I:1 (April 1874)–III:5 (July 1876), *passim.* "Editor's Salutatory" appears in I:1 (April 1874), pp. 7 ff.

Noteworthy articles reflecting Reconstruction include, in chronological order, "The Grand Army of the Republic. Opinion of the Negro As A Constitution Maker," I:6 (January 1875), p. 472; "Were The Confederates Guilty Of Treason?" II:1 (February 1875), pp. 56 ff.; "Progress Of Absolutism In The United States," II:2 (March 1875), pp. 81 ff.; "Review of Right Rev. J. P. B. Wilmer, Bishop of Louisiana: Defence of Louisiana," II:3 (April 1875), pp. 166 f.; "The Future And Duty Of The Young South," II:3 (April 1875), pp. 214 f.; "The New Republican Organization," III:3 (March 1876), pp. 165 ff.; "Decision Of The Supreme Court Of The United States On The Enforcement Act," III:4 (April 1876), p. 450.

For difficulties involved in its publication, see "To Our Friends and Patrons of 'The New Orleans Monthly Review,'" I:6 (January 1875), p. 478; "To The Friends Of The New Orleans Monthly Review," III:4 (April 1876), p. 324.

For further details, see Griffin, *op. cit.,* pp. 526 f.; information from John Hall Jacobs; Frank McLean, *Periodicals Published in the South Before 1880,* University of Virginia Dissertation, 1928, p. 51, courtesy N. Harvey Deal, Reference Librarian, Alderman Library, University of Virginia; Frank Luther Mott, *A History of American Magazines 1865-1885* (Cambridge, Mass., 1938), p. 45.

For information regarding the *Southern Quarterly Review,* the writer is indebted to Julia Harris, Humanities Reading Room, University of Texas Library.

Other Clark & Hofeline Periodicals

These are known only by their listings in the New Orleans Directories, where they appear as issued from 112 Gravier, the Clark & Hofeline address. The *Daily City Item* is so listed in 1878, the *New Orleans Observer* in 1881 and 1882, the *Southwestern Churchman* in 1881, and *Southern Knight* in 1881 and 1882. In 1882 it is noted that Clark & Hofeline were proprietors of *Southern Knight.* For *Southern Knight* see also *Farley's Reference List of the Stationers, Booksellers, Printers and Paper Dealers in the United States. . . . 1882* (Philadelphia, [1882]), p. 79.

Later Careers, & Deaths of Clark & Hofeline

Clark's association with L. Graham & Son is indicated in the New Orleans Directory for 1883. For that firm, see *The Industries of New Orleans, Her*

Rank, Resources, Advantages (New Orleans, 1885), p. 109 (courtesy Lucy B. Foote); Adolf Growoll Collection, *American Book Trade History* VI, 87 (courtesy *Publishers' Weekly*).

For the post-Reconstruction careers of Clark and of Hofeline, see the listings for Clark in the New Orleans Directories 1883-1907, and for Hofeline 1883-1929. The firm of Malus & Hofeline is listed 1888-1898, and Albert D. Hofeline 1899-1929. In 1887 Hofeline and E. T. Adams, the photographer, issued a *Photographic album of the city of New Orleans, comprising the principal business houses and views of the City.*

Clark died in New Orleans at the age of 86 or 87, on December 18, 1907, and was buried in the Masonic Cemeteries. Hofeline died at the age of 80, on December 29, 1928, and was buried in Greenwood Cemetery. In his Will, dated March 16, 1918 ("Succession of Albert D. Hofeline," Docket 178-805, Civil District Court for the Parish of Orleans), Hofeline ordered his "printing plant . . . to be sold to the best advantage and the amount derived therefrom to be equally divided" among his sisters. See "Charles W. Clark, Dead," [New Orleans] *Times Democrat* (December 20, 1907), p. 5 (courtesy John Hall Jacobs); information from Mrs. Naomi M. Drake, Bureau of Vital Statistics, New Orleans; "Funeral of Mr. Charles W. Clark," *New Orleans Item* (December 20, 1907), p. 5 (courtesy John Hall Jacobs); *Times Picayune* (December 30, 1928), p. 2 (courtesy Lucy B. Foote); information from Mr. Ben Weaver, Superintendent, Masonic Cemeteries, New Orleans.

VII. ROBERT FERGUS

Early Chicago Background

J. S. Buckingham, *The Eastern and Western States of America* (London & Paris, [1842]), pp. 262, 275; Elias Colbert and Everett Chamberlin, *Chicago and the Great Conflagration* (Cincinnati & New York, 1872), pp. 54 f., 66; Paul Gilbert and Charles Lee Bryson, *Chicago And Its Makers* (Chicago, 1929), pp. 68 f.; Thomas Hoyne, *Biographical Memoir of the Hon. George Manierre* [Chicago, 1878], pp. 19 ff.; Lloyd Lewis and Henry Justin Smith, *Chicago The History Of Its Reputation* (New York, [1929]), pp. 39 ff.; Ernest Poole, *Giants Gone Men Who Made Chicago* (New York & London, [1943]), p. 22; Henry Justin Smith, *Chicago's Great Century* (Chicago, 1933), pp. 24, 28; David Ward Wood, ed., *Chicago and its Distinguished Citizens* (Chicago, 1881), p. 28.

Fergus's Early Life & Apprenticeship; Voyage to America

A. T. Andreas, *History of Chicago* (Chicago, 1884-1886), II, 485-86; Biographical Card on Fergus in Clipping File, Chicago Historical Society (courtesy Miss Elizabeth Baughman, to whom the writer is indebted for considerable information on Fergus); information from Mr. John Easton of Robert Maclehose & Co., Ltd., Glasgow; "Robert Fergus Cut Down," *The Chicago Daily Tribune* (June 24, 1897), pp. 1, 3 (original in Chicago Historical Society); information from Mr. George L. McKay, The Grolier Club; James

Maclehose, *The Glasgow University Press 1638-1931* (Glasgow, 1931), pp. 232-33; Manuscript Biographical Sketch of Fergus (Illinois State Historical Library, courtesy Mr. Harry E. Pratt, State Historian); Necrology Form filled out by Robert Collyer Fergus for Chicago Historical Society.

A search made by R. T. Rivington, Clerk of Stationers' Hall, London, failed to disclose any mention of Fergus in the records from 1825 to 1840.

Fergus's Early Employment in Chicago

"Chicago's Oldest Printing House Thrown Into The Street A Wreck," *Chicago Times-Herald* (October 21, 1900) (original in Chicago Historical Society, Robert Fergus Scrapbook); [Z. Eastman], "Early Printers of Chicago," *Rounds' Printers Cabinet* XXV:4 (October 1880), p. 1 (original in Chicago Historical Society).

The signers of a caution in the *Weekly American* of July 31, 1840, warning printers not to come to Chicago as there were sufficient workmen in the city, included Robert Fergus. See Andreas, *op. cit.*, I, 417.

Ellis's Early Life

Andreas, *op. cit.*, I, 417; [Z. Eastman], *op. cit.;* "Obituary. Death of William Ellis," *The Chicago Daily Tribune* (May 18, 1873), p. 16 (original in Chicago Historical Society).

Chicago's First Business Directory

Andreas, *op. cit.*, I, 412-13; "Corporation Proceedings," *Daily Chicago American* (January 2 and January 29, 1840), p. 2 (courtesy Mr. Harry E. Pratt, Illinois State Historical Library); J. Seymour Currey, *Chicago: Its History and Its Builders* (Chicago, 1912), I, 314; *Fergus' Directory of the City of Chicago, 1839. Compiled by Robert Fergus* (Chicago: Fergus Printing Co., 1876) [No. 2 of Fergus Historical Series], *passim;* Henry H. Hurlbut, *Chicago Antiquities* (Chicago, 1881), pp. 7-8; Douglas C. McMurtrie, *A Bibliography of Chicago Imprints 1835-1850* (Chicago, 1944), p. 29; *Story of Chicago In Connection with the Printing Business* (Chicago, 1912), pp. 102-103.

Ellis & Fergus "Firsts" & Other Imprints

Andreas, *op. cit.*, I, 383-84, 413-14, III, 833; Card File of Chicago Imprints in New York Public Library; "Celebration Of Franklin's Birth Day," [Chicago] *Daily Democrat* (January 19, 1848), p. 2 (original in Chicago Historical Society); "Chicago's Oldest Printing House Thrown Into The Street A Wreck," *Chicago Times-Herald* (October 21, 1900); *Directory of the City of Chicago Illinois, for 1843. Compiled by Robert Fergus* (Chicago: Fergus Printing Co., 1896) [No. 28 of Fergus Historical Series], pp. 3-4; "Robert Fergus Cut Down," *op. cit.;* Mrs. John H. Kinzie, *Wau-Bun The "Early Day" in the North-West* (Chicago, 1932), p. l; Joseph Kirkland, *The Story of Chicago* (Chicago, 1892), p. 57; Moses Kirkland, *History of Chicago* (Chicago & New York, 1895), II, 144; McMurtrie, *Bibliography of Chicago Imprints 1835-1850, passim;* Douglas C. McMurtrie, "Books and Pamphlets Printed in Chicago, 1835-1850," *Bulletin of the Chicago Historical Society* I:1-4 (No-

vember 1934, February, May and August 1935), *passim;* Douglas C. Mc-
Murtrie, *The First Printers of Chicago* (Chicago, 1927), *passim;* J. W. Norris,
General Directory and Business Advertiser of the City Of Chicago, For . . .
1844 (Chicago: Ellis & Fergus, 1844), *passim;* J. W. Norris, *Norris' Business
Directory . . . of . . . Chicago, For 1846* (Chicago: Fergus Printing Co., 1883)
[No. 25 of Fergus Historical Series], p. 56; Sabin 12660, 37940, 77443; Frank-
lin William Scott, *Newspapers And Periodicals of Illinois 1814-1879* (Spring-
field, Ill., 1910), pp. 54 ff.; Hon. John Wentworth, *Early Chicago* (Chicago:
Fergus Printing Co., 1881) [No. 16 of Fergus Historical Series], p. 17.

The 1844 Chicago *Directory* was reprinted not only by Fergus but also by
T. F. Bohan as a souvenir publication in 1902.

A copy of Mrs. Kinzie's *Narrative* was offered for sale by Goodspeed for
$250 [see *The Month at Goodspeed's* XVI:1 (October 1944), p. 9]. The
Paullin copy fetched $130 in 1929 [see *Part I of the Rare & Desirable Ameri-
can Collection From the Library of George W. Paullin* (New York, 1929),
p. 85]. The Paullin copy of *The Rosarist's Companion* fetched $60 [*ibid.*, p.
86].

The extremely rare *Quid Nunc* appears to have been published in a daily
and a weekly edition, the former established July 4, 1842, and the latter,
July 12, 1842 (information from Mr. Paul L. Berry, Chief, Serials Division,
Library of Congress).

Dissolution of Ellis-Fergus Partnership

[Z. Eastman], *op. cit.,* p. 1; "Obituary. Death of William Ellis," *The Chicago Daily Tribune* (May 18, 1873), p. 16 (original in Chicago Historical
Society).

Ellis died in 1873, "a man of strict integrity and a good printer," leaving
"a handsome fortune behind him."

For the fire that destroyed Fergus's paper warehouse, see "Destructive
Fire," *Chicago Daily Democrat* (May 24, 1849), p. 2 (courtesy Miss Elizabeth Baughman, Chicago Historical Society).

Fergus Activities During the 1850's & 1860's

Card File of Chicago Imprints, New York Public Library; *Check List of
Chicago Ante-Fire Imprints 1851-1871.* American Imprints Inventory No. 4
(Chicago, 1938), *passim; Midland Notes* No. 14 (Midland Rare Book Com-
pany, Mansfield, Ohio), No. 47.

For Fergus's early friendship with Pinkerton, the writer is indebted to information from Mrs. Thatcher Hoyt, Fergus's granddaughter. See also Joan
Pinkerton Chalmers, "When the Pinkertons Came to Chicago," *Midweek* [Chi-
cago] (May 27, 1931), courtesy John O. Camden, Pinkerton's National Detective Agency, Inc.; Poole, *op. cit.,* pp. 60-61; Richard W. Rowan, *The
Pinkertons* (Boston, 1931), p. 7.

The Fergus Historical Series

In the Introduction of the first number, the following tribute was paid to
Fergus: "He has grown even faster than the city; from being a simple citizen,
he has expanded into a corporation, and I am told it requires a large building

to contain the Fergus Printing Company. May his shadow never be less, and may he earn the gratitude of future generations by rescuing from oblivion the history of Ancient Chicago—part of which he was."

The tribute to the Series appears in No. 19, p. 53, where it is quoted from the *Chicago Tribune* of May 5, 1881.

A listing of the Fergus Historical Series follows. All imprints are of Chicago, Fergus Printing Company.

1. Joseph N. Balestier, *The Annals of Chicago*. 1876.
2. *Fergus' Directory of the City of Chicago, 1839. Compiled by Robert Fergus*. 1876.
3. John Dean Caton, *The Last of the Illinois*. 1876.
4. Hon. William H. Brown, *An Historical Sketch of the Early Movement In Illinois For The Legalization of Slavery*. 1876.
5 & 6. [William H. Bushnell], *Biographical Sketches of some of the Early Settlers of the City of Chicago*. 1876.
7 & 8. Hon. John Wentworth, *Early Chicago*. 1876.
9. Henry Brown, *The Present and Future Prospects of Chicago*. 1876.
10. Hon. J. Young Scammon and Hon. Isaac N. Arnold, *Addresses delivered at the Annual Meeting of the Chicago Historical Society, . . . 1868*. 1877.
11. James N. Hyde, *Early Medical Chicago*. 1879.
12. Edward G. Mason, *Illinois in the Eighteenth Century*. 1881.
13. Hon. Joseph Gillespie, *Recollections of Early Illinois*. 1880.
14. *Early Illinois*. [1881].
15. Hon. Isaac N. Arnold, *Abraham Lincoln* [&] Hon. James W. Sheahan, *Stephen A. Douglas*. 1881.
16. Hon. John Wentworth, *Early Chicago. Fort Dearborn*. 1881.
17. Hon. Isaac N. Arnold, *William B. Ogden*. 1882.
18. *Chicago River-And-Harbor Convention. . . . Compiled by Robert Fergus*. 1882.
19. Charles Cleaver, *Early Chicago Reminiscences*. 1882.
20. Charles Fenno Hoffman, *A Winter In The West*. 1882.
21. Robert Fergus, *Biographical Sketch of John Dean Caton*. 1882.
22. *Chicago Bar Association Lectures*. [1882].
23. William K. Ackerman, *Early Illinois Railroads*. 1884.
24. John Wentworth, *Congressional Reminiscences*. 1882.
25. J. W. Norris, *Norris' Business Directory . . . of . . . Chicago, For 1846. . . . Revised . . . By Robert Fergus*. 1883.
26. William Henry Harrison, *A Discourse on the Aborigines Of The Ohio Valley*. 1883.
27. Hiram W. Beckwith, *The Illinois And Indiana Indians*. 1884.
28. *Directory of the City of Chicago Illinois, for 1843. Compiled by Robert Fergus*. 1896.
29. Julia Duncan Kirby, *Biographical Sketch of Joseph Duncan*. 1888.
30. [Juliette Augusta Kinzie], *Narrative of the Massacre at Chicago*. 1914.
31, 32, 33, & 34. [E. G. Mason, ed.], *Early Chicago*. 1890.
35. William Ward Wight, *Eleazer Williams*. 1903.

Reynolds's My Own Times
   Reynolds' *History of Illinois. My Own Times* (Chicago, 1879), "Publishers' Argument."

Fergus Job Orders
   The Chicago Historical Society owns the Fergus Job Order Books of the
firm's later history.

Death of Robert Fergus
   "Robert Fergus Cut Down," *The Chicago Daily Tribune* (June 24, 1897),
pp. 1, 3 (original in Chicago Historical Society).

Collapse of Firm
   "Chicago's Oldest Printing House Thrown Into The Street A Wreck,"
Chicago Times-Herald (October 21, 1900), original in Chicago Historical
Society; "Collapse of the Fergus Printing Company," *Publishers' Weekly*
LVII:5 (February 3, 1900), p. 295.
   None the less, there are a few works bearing the Fergus imprint after 1900,
e.g., Nos. 30 and 35 of the Fergus Historical Series; and the Job Order Books
and List of Supplies Purchased (owned by the Chicago Historical Society)
also indicate that the firm did resume some activity after its "collapse."

VIII. JACOB W. CRUGER

The Texas Revolution, The Republic of Texas, & Annexation
   Ed Bartholomew, *The Houston Story*. . . . *1836-1865* (Houston, 1951), pp.
10, 185; Charles Edwards, *Texas and Coahuila* (New York, 1834), *passim;*
Llerena Friend, ed., "Notes and Documents. Contemporary Newspaper Accounts of the Annexation of Texas," *The Southwestern Historical Quarterly*
XLIX:2 (October 1945), pp. 280 f.; *The Handbook of Texas* (Austin, 1952),
II, 554, 757; Francis Moore, Jr., *Description of Texas* (New York, 1844), p.
28; Nevins and Commager, *op. cit.,* p. 195; Col. Edward Stiff, *The Texan
Emigrant* (Cincinnati, 1840), p. 336; *Telegraph and Texas Register* (March
4, 1846), p. 2 (courtesy Robert L. Peterson, Newspaper Collection, University
of Texas Library, to whom I am indebted for many of the subsequent references from the *Telegraph and Texas Register* and other Texas newspapers);
Texas Centennial Exhibition Held at The Library of Congress (Washington,
1946), pp. 2 ff., 7; David Woodman, Jr., *Guide to Texas Emigrants* (Boston,
1835), *passim.*

Cruger's Early Life; Connection with Daniel Cruger, Jr.
   S. W. Geiser, "Note on Dr. Francis Moore (1808-1864) Texas Collection,"
The Southwestern Historical Quarterly XLVII:4 (April 1944), pp. 420 f.; A.
C. Gray, "History of the Texas Press," in Dudley G. Wooten, ed., *A Comprehensive History of Texas 1685 to 1897* (Dallas, 1898), II, 384 [The statement there made that Cruger had been a cadet at West Point Military Academy is not corroborated by the Academy's Registers. According to Col. W. J.

Morton, Librarian of the Academy, "He was never a cadet at West Point."];
The Handbook of Texas I, 441.

For Daniel Cruger, Jr., see *Biographical Directory of the American Congress* (Washington, 1950), pp. 1039 f.; Clarence S. Brigham, *History and Bibliography of American Newspapers 1690-1820* (Worcester, Mass., 1947), I, 715, 747 f.; W. W. Clayton, *History of Steuben County, New York* (Philadelphia, 1879), pp. 65 ff., 77 f.; Milton W. Hamilton, *The Country Printer* (New York, 1936), pp. 55, 267; Guy H. McMaster, *History Of The Settlement of Steuben County, N.Y.* (Bath, 1853), pp. 173 f.; Irvin W. Near, *A History of Steuben County, New York* (Chicago, 1911), I, 448; Millard F. Roberts, *Part First. Historical Gazetteer of Steuben County, New York* (Syracuse, 1891), p. 149.

A Daniel Crugu [sic] is listed as a Texas landowner in *Abstract of Land Certificates* (Austin, 1841), p. 106. The name appears as Daniel Crugur in *Abstract of Valid Land Claims* (Austin, 1859), p. 100.

Francis Moore, Jr.: Early Life & Departure for Texas with Crugers

Biographical Directory of the Texan Conventions and Congresses (Austin, [1941]), p. 142; Herbert Gambrell, *Anson Jones* (Garden City, N.Y., 1948), p. 98; Geiser, *op. cit.*, pp. 419 ff.; *The Handbook of Texas* II, 229. Having seen extracts of an attack against Moore, John T. Andrews and others of Bath, N.Y., wrote a letter to President Lamar giving full particulars of Moore's early life and describing his departure for Texas. The letter appears in *The Papers of Mirabeau Buonaparte Lamar* [ed. by Charles Adams Gulick, Jr.] (Austin, n.d.), V, 202.

The Buckeye Rangers; Cruger in War Department

For the service of Moore and Cruger with the Buckeye Rangers, see D. W. C. Baker, *A Texas Scrap-Book* (New York, Chicago, etc., [1875]), p. 273; *Biographical Directory of the Texan Conventions*, p. 142; *The Handbook of Texas* I, 237; *Houston A History And Guide* (Houston, 1942), p. 202; A. B. Norton, "History of Journalism in Texas," in F. B. Baillio, *A History of the Texas Press Association* (Dallas, 1916), p. 325; Mrs. S. C. Red, *The Medicine Man in Texas* (Houston, [1930]), p. 242; Ben C. Stuart, *The History of Texas Newspapers from the Earliest Period to the Present*, 1917 (MS in Rosenberg Library), p. 193; Homer S. Thrall, *A Pictorial History of Texas* (St. Louis, 1879), p. 595.

Moore's service with the Buckeye Rangers is questioned in Geiser, *op. cit.*, p. 421. Although the names of Cruger and Moore do not appear in the Muster Roll of Captain Allen's Buckeye Rangers (General Land Office), this does not obviate the possibility that they may have served with the Rangers. According to the Commissioner of the General Land Office, "It is possible that the Muster Roll is not complete."

There is some confusion regarding the date of Moore's first arrival in Texas. According to the [Bath] *Constitutionalist* (July 17, 1839), p. 3, he left Bath in 1836 and "the war terminated soon after his arrival." The *Telegraph and Texas Register* (August 7, 1839), p. 3, reprints an extract from the notice in the Bath paper, prefacing it with the statement: "We find the following flattering notice of *Dr. Moore* in the *'Constitutionalist'* published at Bath, N. Y., from whence he came to this country, early in the Spring of 1836." According to *Official Correspondence of the Texan Revolution 1835-1836 Edited by William C. Binkley* (New York & London, [1936]), II, 600 n. 3, he had been an assistant surgeon in the volunteer army in December 1835. Moreover, this work includes (p. 599) a letter from D. G. Burnet to Stephen Richardson dated April 7, 1836, assigning Moore to superintend the transportation of cattle. According to *Biographical Directory of the Texan Conventions and Congresses* (Austin, [1941]), p. 142, he joined the volunteer army October 1, 1835. Perhaps Moore made two trips to Texas in 1835 and in 1836. Mr. Thomas W. Streeter feels the evidence is conclusive that Moore was in Texas as early as April 1836.

An Audited Military Claim is filed in the Archives Division, Texas State Library (courtesy Seymour V. Connor, State Archivist) under the name of Jacob W. Cruger. It is a $50 draft dated January 6, 1837, for military services. According to the Audited Civil Claims, Cruger served as a clerk in the War Department, September–December of 1836. According to the records of the General Land Office (courtesy Bascom Giles, Commissioner), Jacob W. Cruger received a grant of 320 acres of land in Limestone County by Certificate No. 594 for service in the Army of the Republic from June 6 until September 22, 1836.

Journey to Houston; Early Houston

Bartholomew, *op. cit.*, pp. 32 f.; Richard S. Hunt and Jesse F. Randel, *Guide to the Republic Of Texas* (New York, 1839), pp. 45 f.; Adele B. Looscan, "Harris County, 1822-1845," *The Southwestern Historical Quarterly* XIX:1 (July 1915), pp. 39 f.; Francis R. Lubbock, *Six Decades In Texas* (Austin, 1900), pp. 46 f.; "Notes On Texas," *The Hesperian: or, Western Monthly Magazine* I:6 (October 1838), pp. 428 ff.; *Telegraph and Texas Register* (October 11, 1837), p. 4, (October 21, 1837), p. 3, (May 19, 1838), p. 4.

Cruger Abandons Merchandising; Cruger & Moore Purchase Telegraph

Joe B. Frantz, *Gail Borden* (Norman, Okla., [1951]), pp. 126 f.; Mary Glasscock Frazier, *Texas Newspapers During the Republic,* Masters Thesis, University of Texas, 1931, pp. 91 f., courtesy Kathleen Blow, Reference Department, University of Texas Library; Geiser, *op. cit.,* p. 421; Gray, *op. cit.,* II, 371, 384; *The Handbook of Texas* I, 189, 441, and II, 229, 721; Douglas C. McMurtrie, "Pioneer Printing In Texas," *The Southwestern Historical Quarterly* XXXV:3 (January 1932), p. 186; Addie Roy, *History of the Telegraph and Texas Register 1835-1846,* Masters Thesis, University of Texas, 1931, *passim,* courtesy Mrs. Jule Oppermann, University of Texas Library.

Notice of dissolution of the firm of G. & T. H. Borden and continuance of the *Telegraph* by Borden & Moore appears over date of March 9, 1837, in the *Telegraph and Texas Register* (May 30, 1837), p. 4. Notice of dissolution of the Borden & Moore copartnership and authorization to settle accounts with

Moore or Cruger appears over date of June 20, 1837, in the *Telegraph and Texas Register* (June 24, 1837), p. 4 (courtesy Robert L. Peterson).

Early History of the Telegraph and Texas Register

Sam Acheson, *35,000 Days In Texas* (New York, 1938), p. 5; Hubert Howe Bancroft, *History of the North American States And Texas* (San Francisco, 1889), II, 549; Eugene C. Barker, "Notes On Early Texas Newspapers, 1819-1836," *The Southwestern Historical Quarterly* XXI:2 (October 1917), pp. 141 ff.; Bartholomew, *op. cit.*, p. 67; John Henry Brown, *History Of Texas* (St. Louis, [1893]), II, 522 f.; Ethel Mary Franklin, "Joseph Baker," *The Southwestern Historical Quarterly* XXXVI:2 (October 1932), pp. 130, 136; Gambrell, *op. cit.*, p. 97; Gray, *op. cit.*, II, 370; *The Handbook of Texas* II, 720 f., 944; L. W. Kemp, "The Capitol (?) at Columbia," *The Southwestern Historical Quarterly* XLVIII:1 (July 1944), pp. 6 f.; Looscan, "Harris County," *The Southwestern Historical Quarterly* XVIII:3 (January 1915), p. 279 n. 18; Lubbock, *op. cit.*, pp. 50 f.; McMurtrie, *op. cit.*, pp. 183 ff.; Lewis W. Newton and Herbert P. Gambrell, *A Social and Political History of Texas* (Dallas, [1932]), pp. 116 f.; Norton, *op. cit.*, pp. 324 f.; *The South in the Building of the Nation* (Richmond, Va., [1909]), VII, 423; Stuart, *op. cit.*, pp. 14 ff., 19 ff.; *Telegraph and Texas Register* (May 2, 1837), p. 2 (courtesy Robert L. Peterson); *Texas Newspapers 1813-1939* (Houston, 1941), p. 115; Clarence R. Wharton, *Gail Borden, Pioneer* (San Antonio, 1941), p. 69; Ernest W. Winkler, "The Seat of Government of Texas," *The Quarterly of the Texas State Historical Association* X:2 (October 1906), p. 169; H. Yoakum, *History of Texas* (New York, 1856), II, 196 f.

Pioneer Houston Printing Office

Bartholomew, *op. cit.*, pp. 87 ff.; Gambrell, *op. cit.*, pp. 97 f.; Lubbock, *op. cit.*, p. 51; Norton, *op. cit.*, p. 47; *Telegraph and Texas Register* (May 2, 1837), p. 2; Winkler, "The Seat of Government of Texas," pp. 169 f.

Telegraph and Texas Register under Cruger & Moore

Bartholomew, *op. cit.*, p. 203; H. Bailey Carroll, "Texas Collection," *The Southwestern Historical Quarterly* L:1 (July 1946), p. 130; "Centennial of Statehood Documents," *The Library Chronicle of the University of Texas* I:4 (Fall 1945), p. 36; [Bath] *Constitutionalist* (July 17, 1839), p. 3; "Diary of Adolphus Sterne edited by Harriet Smither," *The Southwestern Historical Quarterly* XXXII:3 (January 1929), p. 256; Gambrell, *op. cit.*, pp. 98, 410; William R. Hogan, "Rampant Individualism in the Republic of Texas," *The Southwestern Historical Quarterly* XLIV:4 (April 1941), pp. 468, 472; William R. Hogan, *The Texas Republic* (Norman, Okla., [1946]), p. 221; *Houston A History And Guide* (Houston, 1942), pp. 202 f.; *The Papers of Mirabeau B. Lamar* II, 499; information from Robert L. Peterson, University of Texas Library; Ashbel Smith, *Reminiscences of the Texas Republic* (Galveston, 1876), p. 48; Justin H. Smith, *The Annexation of Texas* (New York, 1911), p. 443; *Telegraph and Texas Register* (October 11, 1837—May 26, 1838), *passim*, (March 19, 1845), p. 2, (April 23, 1845), p. 2; *The Writings of Sam Houston 1813-1863* (Austin, 1940-1943), IV, 205, and VI, 11 f.

Extra Facilities & Attractions of Telegraph Office; Job Printing

Looscan, "Harris County," *The Southwestern Historical Quarterly* XIX:1 (July 1915), p. 58; Lubbock, *op. cit.*, p. 84; Norton, *op. cit.*, p. 334; *Telegraph and Texas Register* (October 11, 1837), p. 4, (February 24, 1838), pp. 1, 3, (May 12, 1838), p. 4, (May 19, 1838), p. 3, (May 26, 1838), p. 4.

Public Printing in Texas (1838)

Gray, *op. cit.*, II, 374; *Telegraph and Texas Register* (May 12, 1838), p. 3.

Telegraph Imprints

For the Republican and Statehood imprints of Cruger and his Telegraph office, here and hereinafter discussed, see, besides the works themselves, *Fifty Texas Rarities Selected from the Library of Mr. Everett D. Graff* (Ann Arbor, Mich., 1946), No. 22; C. W. Raines, *A Bibliography of Texas* (Austin, 1896), *passim;* Sabin XXV, 25 ff. [Nos. 94948–95126]; Shelf List of Houston and Austin imprints at New York Public Library; Thomas W. Streeter, *Bibliography of Texas 1795-1845 Part I. Texas Imprints* (Cambridge, Mass., 1955). This noteworthy work includes "A Brief Sketch of Printing in Texas Through the Year 1845," which summarizes printing in Texas for the period year by year, as well as an Appendix on "Texas Newspapers Through 1845." See also *Texas Centennial Exhibition* . . . (Washington, 1946), Nos. 73, 82, 164; E. W. Winkler, "Check List Of Texas Imprints, 1846-1876," *The Southwestern Historical Quarterly* XLVI:4–XLIX:4 (April 1943–April 1946), *passim.*

Morning Star & Texas Centinel

Bancroft, *op. cit.*, pp. 549 f.; Bartholomew, *op. cit.*, p. 128; Brown, *History Of Texas*, pp. 523 f.; Joe B. Frantz, *The Newspapers of the Republic of Texas*, Masters Thesis, University of Texas, 1940, pp. 115 f., courtesy Kathleen Blow; Gray, *op. cit.*, II, 374 ff., 384 f.; *The Handbook of Texas* II, 236, 760; *Houston A History And Guide* (Houston, 1942), p. 203; Walter McCausland, "Some Early Texas Newspapers," *The Southwestern Historical Quarterly* XLIX:3 (January 1946), p. 384; McMurtrie, *op. cit.*, pp. 184, 186, 190; Norton, *op. cit.*, pp. 330, 336; *The Texas Almanac & State Industrial Guide* (Dallas, 1936), p. 483; *Texas Newspapers 1813-1939*, pp. 16, 112.

The *Morning Star* was first published by E. Humphreys & Co. As Gray points out (II, 374), "circumstances and subsequent events point strongly to the conclusion that Jacob W. Cruger was the real owner, or at least one of the partners." Upon Humphreys' death in November, 1839, it was announced that the publication of the *Star* would be continued as usual by J. W. Cruger.

Cruger's Partners

For George W. Bonnell, see Brown, *History Of Texas*, p. 524; *The Encyclopedia of The New West* (Marshall, Texas, 1881), p. 574; *The Handbook of Texas* I, 186 f.; Lubbock, *op. cit.*, p. 85; Norton, *op. cit.*, pp. 330 f.

For Martin Carroll Wing, see Brown, *History Of Texas*, p. 524; *The Handbook of Texas* II, 924; Norton, *op. cit.*, p. 331.

Bid on Public Printing; Contract for Spanish Translation of Texas Laws

Bonnell & Cruger, Bid on Public Printing (December 6, 1839); Contract with Cruger (December 18, 1839) (Public Printing Papers, Archives Division, Texas State Library, courtesy Seymour V. Connor, State Archivist).

Public Printing Services & Remunerations

J. W. Cruger, Bid on Binding 600 Copies of the Laws (February 4, 1840); Cruger & Bonnell, Account for Public Printing (February 24, 1840); J. W. Cruger, Account for Public Printing (September 4, 1841); Cruger & Moore to State Department, Account for Subscriptions, Stationery & Binding (February 3, 1843) (Public Printing Papers, Archives Division, Texas State Library).

Printing prices of 1849 are revealed by the agreement of Cruger & Moore to print a weekly edition of 1,000 copies of a paper of imperial size for $2,500 a year, for the Methodists of Texas—the *Texas Wesleyan Banner,* which became the *Texas Christian Advocate.* See *The Handbook of Texas* II, 766 [where it is said the contract was made with James F. Cruger & Moore]; Anne Ayers Lide, *Robert Alexander and the Early Methodist Church in Texas* (Austin, 1934), p. 117; Stuart, *op. cit.,* p. 125.

Cruger & Moore, Public Printers (1844)

Cruger & Moore to Committee on Public Printing, Bid for Public Printing (January 6, 1844); Contract with Cruger & Moore as Public Printers (February 12, 1844) (Public Printing Papers, Archives Division, Texas State Library); *The Handbook of Texas* I, 441; *Journals of the House of Representatives of the Eighth Congress of the Republic Of Texas* (Houston: Cruger & Moore, 1844), p. 345 (courtesy Llerena Friend, Librarian, Barker Texas History Center, University of Texas Library); *Laws Passed By The Eighth Congress of the Republic Of Texas* (Houston: Cruger & Moore, 1844), pp. 109 f.; *The Northern Standard* (February 24, 1844), pp. 2, 3 (courtesy Robert L. Peterson); *The Writings of Sam Houston* III, 530 f.

Public Services of Cruger & Moore

Bartholomew, *op. cit.,* pp. 79, 204; *Biographical Directory of the Texan Conventions,* pp. 29, 31, 33, 41, 142 f.; information from Granville W. Elder, Postmaster, Houston, Texas; Geiser, *op. cit.,* p. 422; *The Handbook of Texas* II, 229; *Laws passed by The Second Legislature of the State Of Texas. Volume II* (Houston: Telegraph Office, 1848), p. xlviii; Looscan, "Harris County," *The Southwestern Historical Quarterly* XIX:1 (July 1915), pp. 54, 57; Lubbock, *op. cit.,* pp. 57 f., 165, 171; Annie Middleton, "The Texas Convention of 1845," *The Southwestern Historical Quarterly* XXV:1 (July 1921), p. 31.

There is no corroboration of the frequently repeated statement (see, e.g., *The Handbook of Texas* I, 441), that J. W. Cruger was assistant secretary of the Texas Senate.

For Cruger's land titles, see *Abstract of Land Certificates* (Austin: Cruger & Wing, 1841), p. 107; *Abstract of Valid Land Claims* (Austin, 1859), pp. 122 f. Cruger had bounty warrants for 320 acres. As early as August 16, 1838, he had 1–3 Leagues, Second Class, in Harris County. According to the records of the General Land Office (courtesy Bascom Giles), Cruger received a grant of 320 acres of land in Limestone County (Certificate No. 594) for service in the Army of the Republic of Texas, patented August 4, 1862. By Certificate No. 29/52, dated January 18, 1847, he received another grant of 247 acres of land in Coryell County.

Joel Miner
The Handbook of Texas II, 204; Norton, *op. cit.*, pp. 334 f.

Public Printing in Texas (1848)
Laws passed by The Second Legislature of the State Of Texas. Volume II, 59 ff.

Changes in Houston & the Telegraph
Bartholomew, *op. cit.*, pp. 138, 229; Gambrell, *op. cit.*, p. 98; *Houston A History And Guide*, p. 203. For the want of ink in an early issue of the *Telegraph*, see *Telegraph and Texas Register* (June 20, 1837), p. 2. Front page of this issue is dated June 13, 1837, but date line above editorial is June 20.

Cruger Sells Out to Moore; Later History of the Telegraph
Acheson, *op. cit.*, p. 27; Bartholomew, *op. cit.*, p. 233; Geiser, *op. cit.*, p. 421; Gray, *op. cit.*, II, 384; The Handbook of Texas I, 449, II, 721; McCausland, *op. cit.*, p. 385; Norton, *op. cit.*, p. 332; *Texas Newspapers 1813-1939*, pp. 114 f.; S. O. Young, *A Thumb-Nail History of the City of Houston* (Houston, 1912), p. 86.

Moore's Later Career, & Death
Geiser, *op. cit.*, pp. 421, 424 f.; The Handbook of Texas II, 229; Norton, *op. cit.*, p. 334; Mrs. S. C. Red, *op. cit.*, p. 243; *The Writings of Sam Houston* VIII, 125 f. Moore left a son named Francis Cruger Moore.

Cruger's Civil War Service, & Death
Basil W. Duke, *Morgan's Cavalry* (New York & Washington, 1906), p. 103; Gray, *op. cit.*, II, 385; The Handbook of Texas I, 441, 669 f.; *The Houston Tri-Weekly Telegraph* (December 8, 1864), p. 2 (courtesy Llerena Friend).
Cruger's brother James died in Houston, June 1874 (Obituary File, courtesy Richard L. Ducote, Librarian, Texas Room, Houston Public Library).

End of the Telegraph Press
"An Interesting Story For Kyle," *The Kyle News* (March 10, 1939), p. 1; "Texas Collection," *The Southwestern Historical Quarterly* XLII:4 (April 1939), p. 410.

IX. ANTON ROMAN

Opening of Far West
See Allan Nevins and Henry Steele Commager, *The Pocket History of the United States* (New York, 1951), pp. 197, 314 f.

Roman's Appearance

A photograph of Anton Roman is reproduced in Noah Brooks, "Bret Harte: A Biographical and Critical Sketch," *The Overland Monthly* XL:3 (September 1902), p. 205.

Roman's Early Life & Mining Activities

For the early phases of Roman's life, see Idwal Jones, "The Man From Scott Bar," *Westways* (June 1948), pp. 8-9; Robert O'Brien, *California Called Them* (New York, London, Toronto, [1951]), pp. 162, 234; "Anton Roman," *San Francisco Chronicle* (June 22, 1903), p. 2 (courtesy Mabel R. Gillis, formerly of the California State Library); "Anton A. Roman, Romance Of Early Days In His Life," *San Francisco Examiner* (June 22, 1903), p. 3 (courtesy Mabel R. Gillis); Charles H. Shinn, *Mining Camps A Study in American Frontier Government* (New York, 1885), pp. 219 ff.; Franklin Walker, *San Francisco's Literary Frontier* (New York, 1939), p. 259.

There is a possibility that Roman was in New Mexico in 1846. In the Huntington Library is a summons to the constable of Santa Fe commanding him to summon Marcus Quintane [Marcos Quintana?] before the justice of the peace to testify concerning an assault and battery made on the person of Maubrecie Duran by A. Roman. The summons is signed by John R. Tulles and is dated December 22, 1846 (courtesy Ernest R. May, and Haydée Noya of the Huntington Library).

Details of the rich Scott Bar gravels appear in H. H. Bancroft, *History of California* (San Francisco, 1884-90), VI, 365 ff., 494. See also *History of Siskiyou County, California* (Oakland, 1881), p. 217. An account of the arbitration effected between rival mining camps at "Scotch" Bar may be found in Shinn, *op. cit.*, pp. 220-23.

Roman's Bavarian origin is shown by his registration record in *Index to San Francisco Great Register of Voters,* 1898, 42d assembly district, 10th precinct (courtesy Mabel R. Gillis). Special acknowledgment is due to Mabel R. Gillis, Rollo G. Silver, and Neal Harlow for their aid in the preparation of this chapter.

A brief sketch of Roman's life appears in Robert E. Cowan, *Booksellers of Early San Francisco* (Los Angeles, 1953), pp. 11 ff.

The Purchase from Burgess, Gilbert & Still

"Reminiscences of Bret Harte (a symposium: 'The Genesis of the Overland Monthly,' signed by Anton Roman)," *The Overland Monthly* XL:3 (September 1902), p. 220; Henry R. Wagner, "Commercial Printers of San Francisco From 1851 To 1880," *The Papers of the Bibliographical Society of America* XXXIII (1939), p. 76.

Roman's Migratory Bookselling & Shasta Book Store

"Reminiscences of Bret Harte," p. 220; George R. Stewart, Jr., *Bret Harte Argonaut and Exile* (Boston & New York, 1931), p. 130.

Roman's advertisement is reprinted in M. H. B. Boggs, *My Playhouse Was A Concord Coach* (Oakland, 1942), p. 155.

Further details of Roman's book business in Shasta and his finances appear in Anton Roman, "The Beginnings of the Overland As Seen By The First Publisher," *Overland Monthly*, 2nd Series, XXXII:187 (July 1898), p. 72.

Roman in San Francisco

Roman, "The Beginnings of the Overland," *Overland Monthly* (July 1898), p. 72 and "Reminiscences of Bret Harte," *ibid.* (September 1902), p. 220.

Between 1862 and 1871 Roman is listed in the San Francisco *Directory* at 417 and 419 Montgomery Street, and later at 11 Montgomery. For these listings thanks go to Mabel R. Gillis, Neal Harlow of the University of California Library, William Ramirez of the San Francisco Public Library, and Dorothea E. Spear of the American Antiquarian Society.

According to "Notes On Books And Booksellers," *American Literary Gazette and Publishers' Circular* V:6 (July 15, 1865), pp. 121-22, Roman "first started in this city by selling books at auction in 1859. He leased for that purpose a portion of W. B. Cooke & Co.'s store, on Montgomery Street. After remaining there about a year, he removed into the old stand of J. G. Gilchrist, now occupied by the Telegraph Company. . . . After staying in this store about a year and a half, his success was secured beyond peradventure, and so rapid was the increase of his business that he was obliged to look out for a larger store. In the beginning of the year 1862 he obtained the store now occupied by him on Montgomery Street, between California and Sacramento Streets, which is the largest and most elegant single room occupied for such purposes in San Francisco."

Californiana Published by Roman

See, besides the books themselves, *American Literary Gazette* IX:3 (June 1, 1867), p. 73; Ethel Blumann and Mabel W. Thomas, eds., *California Local History A Centennial Bibliography* (Stanford, 1950), *passim;* Robert E. and Robert G. Cowan, *A Bibliography of the History of California 1510-1930* (San Francisco, 1933), *passim;* Ruth Doxsee, "Book Publishing in San Francisco (1848 to 1906)," Special Study (MS in University of California, School of Librarianship), 1931, pp. 13-16 (courtesy Ruth Doxsee); list of books bearing the Roman imprint in *Overland Monthly* (July 1898), p. 72 n. 2; Roman's advertisements in many of his publications, as well as in *Publishers' Trade List Annual* 1877 and 1878, *Publishers' Weekly* III:14 (April 5, 1873), p. 359, VIII:1 (July 3, 1875), p. 56; San Francisco *Directory* 1868-69, between pp. 80 and 81; C. F. Tiffany and A. C. Macdonald, *The Pocket Exchange Guide of San Francisco* (San Francisco [1875]), p. 10; *Uniform Trade List Circular* (September 1867), p. 181.

Hittell's preface appears in John S. Hittel [sic], *The Resources of California* (San Francisco: A. Roman & Co., and New York: W. J. Widdleton, 1863), p. v. For the affidavit in the third edition of 1867, the writer is indebted to Neal Harlow, University of California. See also Robert E. Cowan, *A Bibliography of the History of California . . . 1510-1906* (San Francisco, 1914), pp. 111-12.

For Cremony's dedication, see John C. Cremony, *Life Among the Apaches* (San Francisco & New York: A. Roman & Co., 1868), Dedication.

For the publisher's note in Hutchings, see J. M. Hutchings, *Scenes of Wonder and Curiosity in California* (New York & San Francisco: A. Roman & Co., 1872), prefatory note from publisher.

Roman's Works for Miners

Guido Küstel, *Nevada and California Processes of Silver and Gold Extraction* (San Francisco: Frank D. Carlton, 1863), p. 3; "List of Valuable Works on Mining . . . For Sale by A. Roman & Co.," advertisement in William Barstow, *Sulphurets* (San Francisco & New York: A. Roman & Co., 1867), p. 118.

Roman's Orientalia & Farming Books

T. A. Kendo, *Treatise on Silk and Tea Culture and Other Asiatic Industries Adapted To The Soil And Climate Of California* (San Francisco & New York: A. Roman & Co., 1870), Preface; at the end of this work is the list of "Important Books for Farmers, for sale by A. Roman & Co." Benoni Lanctot, *Chinese and English Phrase Book* (San Francisco & New York: A. Roman & Co., 1867), Preface; at the end of Lanctot is the list in which "A. Roman & Co. invite particular attention to the following works on China and Japan." A. W. Loomis, ed., *Confucius and the Chinese Classics* (San Francisco & New York: A. Roman & Co., 1867), pp. vii-viii. See also advertisement of Loomis's work at the end of John Franklin Swift, *Going to Jericho* (New York & San Francisco: A. Roman & Co., 1868). Loomis's work was announced as "the first book printed from Stereotype Plates in California," in *Publishers' Weekly* VIII:1 (July 3, 1875), p. 56.

Juveniles & Schoolbooks Published by Roman

Publishers' Weekly VIII:1 (July 3, 1875), p. 56, X:5 (July 29, 1876), *passim;* advertisement of Roman's "California Juvenile Books" at end of Hutchings, *op. cit.* (1871); Roman's list at end of Gregory Yale, *Legal Titles to Mining Claims* (San Francisco & New York: A. Roman & Co., 1867).

For the juveniles and texts, and school apparatus sold by Roman, see *The California Mail Bag* I:5 (December 1871), p. 112; Roman's advertisement at end of Hittell, *op. cit.* (1874); *San Francisco Business Directory and Mercantile Guide* 1864-65, p. 31.

Roman's Literary Publications

Besides the works themselves, see Edgar J. Hinkel, ed., *Bibliography of California Fiction, Poetry, Drama.* W.P.A. Project (Oakland, 1938), I, *passim;* list of Roman imprints at Huntington Library (courtesy Lyle H. Wright); *Madrona Etc. By D.T.C.* (San Francisco: A. Roman & Co., 1876), Note; A. W. Patterson, *Onward: A Lay of the West* (New York & San Francisco: A. Roman & Co., 1869), Remarks; information from Jacob Zeitlin, Los Angeles.

For discussions of Charles Warren Stoddard's *Poems,* edited by Bret Harte and published by Roman in 1867, see Francis O'Neill, "Stoddard, Psalmist of the South Seas," *The Catholic World* CV:628 (July 1917), p. 511; Charles

H. Shinn, "Early Books, Magazines, and Book-Making," *The Overland Monthly*, 2nd Series, XII:70 (October 1888), p. 347; Walker, *op. cit.*, p. 230.

Outcroppings

For the preparation and journalistic reception of *Outcroppings*, edited by Bret Harte for Roman in 1865 but dated 1866, see Bret Harte to Anton Roman, San Francisco, January 8, 1866, in Geoffrey Bret Harte, ed., *The Letters of Bret Harte* (Boston & New York, 1926), pp. 3-4; Bret Harte, "My First Book," California edition of *Works* (Boston & New York, 1929), III, 427 ff.; *Outcroppings: Being Selections Of California Verse* (San Francisco & New York: A. Roman & Co.—W. J. Widdleton, 1866), p. 3; "Outcroppings of California Verse," *San Francisco Evening Bulletin* (January 6, 1866), p. 1; "Reminiscences of Bret Harte," p. 220; Stewart, *op. cit.*, pp. 129 ff.; Walker, *op. cit.*, pp. 211 ff.

Roman's Reputation

Titus F. Cronise, *The Natural Wealth of California* (San Francisco: H. H. Bancroft & Co., 1868), pp. 683-84.

The Overland Monthly; Bret Harte & Anton Roman

H. H. Bancroft, *Essays and Miscellany* (San Francisco, 1890), p. 600; Henry J. W. Dam, "A Morning with Bret Harte," *McClure's Magazine* IV:1 (December 1894), pp. 44-45; Charles S. Greene, "Magazine Publishing in California," *Publications of the Library Association of California* (San Francisco, 1898), No. 2, pp. 3 ff.; George Wharton James, "The Founding of the Overland Monthly," *Overland Monthly* LII:1 (July 1908), pp. 5, 10; Idwal Jones, *Ark of Empire* (Garden City, N.Y., 1951), pp. 204 ff.; B. E. Lloyd, *Lights and Shades in San Francisco* (San Francisco, 1876), pp. 301 ff.; Henry Childs Merwin, *The Life of Bret Harte* (Boston & New York, 1911), pp. 44-45; Frank Luther Mott, *A History of American Magazines 1865-1885* (Cambridge, Mass., 1938), III, 56, 402 ff.; *The Overland Monthly* (July 1898, September 1902), *passim;* "Overland Reminiscences," *Overland Monthly*, 2nd Series, I:1 (January 1883), p. 1; T. Edgar Pemberton, *The Life of Bret Harte* (London, 1903), pp. 82, 87-88; "Reminiscences of Bret Harte," pp. 220 ff.; Roman, "The Beginnings of the Overland," p. 73; "A. Roman," *San Francisco Alta California* (August 4, 1879), p. 1 (courtesy Mabel R. Gillis); Stewart, *op. cit.*, pp. 162-63; Charles Warren Stoddard, "Early Recollections of Bret Harte," *The Atlantic Monthly* LXXVIII:469 (November 1896), pp. 675-76; Walker, *op. cit.*, pp. 259 ff.

See also *The Overland Monthly* I:1 (July 1868), p. 99, I:4 (October 1868), p. 385.

For details of its later history, see " 'The Overland Monthly' Sold," *Publishers' Weekly* LVIII:10 (September 8, 1900), p. 484.

There is some confusion regarding the story behind "The Luck of Roaring Camp." In "Reminiscences of Bret Harte," prepared for *The Overland Monthly* of September 1902, Roman indicated that he had read the proofs before he received word of the tale's "immorality." In an interview with Roman reported in the *San Francisco Alta California* of August 4, 1879, p. 1, however, he states that he read the proofs after he had received a letter from his partner denouncing the story as "indecent." Moreover, according to James Howard Bridge, *Millionaires and Grub Street* (New York, 1931), p. 214, Roman occasionally remarked that the lady proofreader was a "fanciful creation." There was also some difference of opinion between Harte and Roman regarding Mrs. Roman's part in "The Luck." See Harte's letter to Nan, August 29, 1879, in Geoffrey Bret Harte, ed., *op. cit.*, pp. 152-53: "Do you remember the day you lay sick at San José and I read you the story of 'The Luck,' and took heart and comfort from your tears over it, and courage to go on and *demand* that it should be put into the magazine. And think—think of fat Mrs. Roman claiming to be its sponsor!!!" This explosion was doubtless a result of the *Alta California's* report of the interview with Roman (August 4, 1879), in which Roman stated, "I told my wife that she was truly the sponsor of Bret Harte."

Other Magazine Projects of Roman

Information from Dr. Archibald Malloch, New York Academy of Medicine. Roman also reprinted articles from the *California Medical Gazette* (San Francisco), such as Arthur B. Stout's "Hygiene, as regards the Sewerage of San Francisco," in 1868 and 1869.

For details about *The Californian*, see *The Californian* I:1 (January 1880), p. 90, II:7 (July 1880), p. 100, VI:33 (September 1882), p. 291; Greene, *op. cit.*, p. 7; Mott, *op. cit.*, III, 56, 406; "Reminiscences of Bret Harte," p. 222; Roman, "The Beginnings of the Overland," p. 75. *The Californian* (1880-82) superseded *The Overland*, which was suspended 1876-82 and the second series of which, begun in 1883, in turn superseded *The Californian*.

Roman's Books for the Million

Roman's books "for the million" are advertised in *The California Mail Bag* I:5 (December 1871), p. 112. His *Catalogue raisonné: a general and classified list of the most important works in nearly every department of literature and science, published in the United States and England, with a bibliographical introduction* (San Francisco, 1861) is owned by the California State Library.

See also "Notes On Books And Booksellers," *American Literary Gazette* V:6 (July 15, 1865), pp. 121-22, where the stock is summarized as follows: "Standard and miscellaneous books, 50,000 volumes; medical works, 3,000 volumes; theological works, 8,000 volumes; scientific books, 5,000 volumes; military books, 500 volumes."

For the wide variety of his stock, see also *San Francisco Business Directory and Mercantile Guide* 1864-65, pp. 30-31.

The eastern publications sold by Roman are listed in "Books of the Month," *The Overland Monthly* V:1 and 2 (July and August 1870), pp. 104, 200; in *The California Mail Bag* II:3 (June-July 1872), pp. 11, 41; and at the end of *The Californian* II:9 (January 28, 1865). According to William McDevitt of San Francisco, Roman had his name appended to the title-pages of some of the books of which he procured quantities. His agents are mentioned in J. Price and C. S. Haley, *The Buyers' Manual and Business Guide; being a de-*

scription of the Leading Business Houses . . . Of The Pacific Coast (San Francisco, 1872), p. 48.

Roman & Widdleton

For Roman's connections with W. J. Widdleton, see *The American Bookseller*, N.S. I:10 (May 15, 1882), p. 226; Bret Harte to James R. Osgood & Co., May 30, 1870, in *Concerning "Condensed Novels" By Bret Harte Introduction And . . . Notes By Nathan Van Patten* (Stanford University, 1929), pp. xix-xx; "Obituary. W. J. Widdleton," *New-York Tribune* (May 3, 1882), p. 5; "Obituary. William J. Widdleton," *Publishers' Weekly* XXI:18 (May 6, 1882), p. 478; "Sketches of the Publishers. William J. Widdleton," *The Round Table* IV:54 (September 15, 1866), pp. 107-8.

Roman's Business Methods & Associates

See Roman's advertisements on the covers of the San Francisco *Directory* 1861 and 1862 (courtesy Neal Harlow and Dorothea E. Spear); his advertisements at the end of Barstow, *op. cit.,* Hittell, *op. cit.* (1874), *A Sketch of the Route to California, China And Japan, via the Isthmus of Panama* (San Francisco & New York, 1867); Price and Haley, *op. cit.,* p. 48; *San Francisco Business Directory and Mercantile Guide* 1864-65, p. 30. San Francisco *Directory* 1859-1865, listings for Frank D. Carlton, and 1863-1872, listings for Joseph A. Hofmann (courtesy Dorothea E. Spear, American Antiquarian Society, and Oscar Wegelin, New York Historical Society).

For Roman's letter about Charles Reade, see A. Roman & Co. to the publishers of the *New-York Tribune,* February 8, 1876, MS Division, New York Public Library (courtesy Robert W. Hill).

The Lick House Block Store

American Booksellers' Guide III:12 (December 1, 1871), p. 446; *American Literary Gazette* (December 1, 1871), p. 23; *The California Mail Bag* I:5 (December 1871), p. 112; Price and Haley, *op. cit.,* p. 48.

Roman's Failure & New Start

"The Affairs of A. Roman & Co.," *American Bookseller* VII:8 (April 15, 1879), p. 309; *The Californian* IV:22 (October 1881), p. 358.

Roman's Later Years & Death

In 1894 he was an unsuccessful non-partisan candidate for recorder. See *San Francisco Chronicle* (June 22, 1903), p. 2 (courtesy Mabel R. Gillis).

For Roman's death, see also "Death of Anton Roman," *The Argonaut* LII:1372 (June 29, 1903), p. 427; *Sacramento Union* (June 23, 1903), p. 1 (courtesy Mabel R. Gillis); *San Francisco Examiner* (June 23, 1903), p. 6 (courtesy William Ramirez, San Francisco Public Library).

X. GEORGE W. CHILDS

The Anonymous Review

Review of George W. Childs. A Biographical Sketch. By James Parton, George W. Childs, Publisher. [From Frank Leslie's "Self-Made Men of our

Times"], Anecdotes of Public Men. No. C. By Col. J. W. Forney. Supplement to Public Ledger, Saturday, March 1, 1873, Journalism in the United States from 1690 to 1872. By Frederic Hudson. New York: Harper & Bros. A copy of this anonymous pamphlet is owned by the New York Historical Society. For the attribution of authorship to Peterson, see the *DAB* article on Childs.

For the pictures of Childs, see clipping from *Truth* [New York] (April 14, 1894) at New York Historical Society.

Childs as Front-Page News

See, for example, "George W. Childs Dead," *New-York Tribune* (February 3, 1894), p. 1.

For Childs and the Alderney calf, see Edward Robins, "Men and Things Reminiscences of a Famous Publisher," clipping in Rollo Silver's notes deposited at Grolier Club.

Childs's Origins

Elias Child, *Genealogy of the Child, Childs and Childe Families* (Utica, 1881), p. 750; information from John J. Proud, Superintendent of Laurel Hill Cemetery Co. Childs's death record does not contain the names of his parents (information from Registrar of Vital Statistics, Philadelphia).

Childs's Early Life & Appearance

Character Studies in American Biography. George W. Childs. Reprinted from The American Biographical Cyclopaedia (New York, 1911); "George William Childs," *DAB;* "George William Childs," *The National Cyclopaedia of American Biography* II, 272; *Memorial Service in Honor of the Late George W. Childs . . . Held in the Temple of the Reform Congregation Keneseth Israel* (Philadelphia, 1894), p. 17; Frank H. Norton, *Sketch of George W. Childs. From Frank Leslie's Historical Register 1877; Review, passim.*

Childs's Association with Thomson

"George W. Childs," *The American Bookseller* XVIII:7 (October 1, 1885), pp. 201 f.; "George W. Childs," *Publishers' Weekly* XLV:6 (February 10, 1894), p. 307; George W. Childs, *Recollections* (Philadelphia, 1890), pp. 10 ff.; J. C. Derby, *Fifty Years among Authors, Books and Publishers* (New York, 1884), pp. 334 f.; John T. Faris, *Men Who Conquered* (New York, [1922]), p. 111; James Parton, *George W. Childs. A Biographical Sketch* (Philadelphia, 1870), *passim; Review*, p. 4; "Sketches of Publishers," *The Round Table* III:37 (May 19, 1866), *passim;* Thomson's advertisement at end of *Philadelphia Described to the Stranger and Citizen* (Philadelphia, 1848) and in *Public Ledger* (December 29, 1849), p. 2.

Childs's Confectionery & Patent Medicine Business

Childs's advertisements in *Public Ledger* (November 18, 1848), p. 3, (December 18, 1848), p. 3, (July 25, 1849), pp. 2, 3; *Review;* "G. W. Childs," *DAB;* Frederic B. Hudson, *Journalism in the United States from 1690 to 1872* (New York, 1873), p. 512.

For erroneous information about Childs, see, for example, the article on Childs in *The Encyclopaedia Britannica,* where it is stated that "in 1847 he established a book-shop in Philadelphia."

Childs's Connections with Peterson

W. Brotherhead, *Forty Years among the Old Booksellers of Philadelphia* (Philadelphia, 1891), pp. 28 ff.; "G. W. Childs," *DAB;* "Obituary. Dr. Robert Evans Peterson," *Publishers' Weekly* XLVI:18 (November 3, 1894), p. 697; *Review,* p. 8.

Publications of R. E. Peterson, R. E. Peterson & Company, & Childs and Peterson

Peterson's advertisement in *Norton's Literary Advertiser* I:6 (October 15, 1851), p. 65; R. E. Peterson & Company's list at end of *Peterson's Familiar Science* (Philadelphia, 1854); advertisements of Childs and Peterson in *American Publishers' Circular* I:1–III:18 (September 1, 1855—May 2, 1857), *passim.* See also Roorbach, *Bibliotheca Americana,* 1850, 1820-52, 1852-55, 1855-58, 1858-61.

Establishment of Peterson & Company & Childs and Peterson

Partnership notice of R. E. Peterson & Company appears in *Norton's Literary Gazette* II:3 (March 15, 1852), p. 54. See also "Changes Among the Trade," *ibid.* II:4 (April 15, 1852), p. 72.

Partnership notice of Childs and Peterson appears in *ibid.* N.S. I:23 (December 1, 1854), p. 607. See also *Review,* p. 9.

Expansion of Law Book Line

"Sketches of Publishers," *The Round Table* (May 19, 1866), p. 314.

Childs's Views on Public Taste

G. W. Childs to the Reverend Francis L. Hawks, Philadelphia, February 8, 1858 (New York Historical Society). Childs was discussing a planned quarterly, "America—Past & Present," which apparently never materialized.

Childs & The Publication of Kane

The Kane–Childs Correspondence (Historical Society of Pennsylvania) consists of some 50 letters written between January and October of 1856. Quotations from the letters are made through the courtesy of R. N. Williams, 2nd, Director of the Historical Society of Pennsylvania.

See also G. W. Childs, *Recollections,* pp. 12 f.; "G. W. Childs As An Advertiser," *Publishers' Weekly* XLV:14 (April 7, 1894), p. 566; G. W. Childs to Dr. Griswold, Philadelphia, October 23 and November 22, 1856 (Boston Public Library, courtesy Zoltán Haraszti); Childs and Peterson to T. B. Thorpe, Philadelphia, September 9, 1856 (Miscellaneous Papers, New York Public Library); *The Congressional Globe* (December 23, 1856), p. 161, (January 27, 1857), p. 463, (March 4, 1857), p. 997; William Elder, *Biography of Elisha Kent Kane* (Philadelphia, 1858), pp. 216, 218, 223 ff., 249; E. K. Kane to Hon. J. K. Kane, Delmonicos, Saturday 4 P.M. (courtesy

Mrs. Fayette B. Dow, Washington, D.C.); E. K. Kane to John Pendleton Kennedy, Philadelphia, January 6, 1856 and February 9, 1856 (Peabody Institute Library); E. K. Kane, *Arctic Explorations* (Philadelphia, 1856), I, 5 f.; "Elisha Kent Kane," *DAB;* "Dr. E. K. Kane, U.S.N., Commander Of The Arctic Exploring Expedition," *Frank Leslie's Illustrated Newspaper* II:38 (August 30, 1856), p. 178; "The Kane Resolution—The Course of Senator Brodhead," *Philadelphia Ledger* (January 10, 1857), p. 1 (courtesy Mrs. Fayette B. Dow); *The Love-Life Of Dr. Kane* (New York, 1866), p. ix n.; Jeannette Mirsky, *Elisha Kent Kane and the Seafaring Frontier* (Boston, [1954]), pp. 179 ff.; E. P. Oberholtzer, *The Literary History of Philadelphia* (Philadelphia, 1906), p. 371; *Passages From The Correspondence and other papers of Rufus W. Griswold* (Cambridge, Mass., 1898), pp. 306 f.; *Review,* p. 9; "Sketches of Publishers," *The Round Table* (May 19, 1866), pp. 313 f.

Childs & The Publication of Allibone

Advertisements of the work at end of *The National Almanac and Annual Record for . . . 1863* (Philadelphia, 1863) and Francis J. Grund, *Thoughts and Reflections on the Present Position of Europe* (Philadelphia, 1860); "S. A. Allibone," *DAB; American Literary Gazette* XIV:10 (March 15, 1870), pp. 277 f.; Brotherhead, *op. cit.,* pp. 30 f.; "George W. Childs," *The American Bookseller* (October 1, 1885), p. 202; *Norton's Literary Gazette* N.S. I:23 (December 1, 1854), p. 607; *Passages From The Correspondence . . . of Rufus W. Griswold,* p. 307; *Review,* pp. 8 f.; "Sketches of Publishers," *The Round Table* (May 19, 1866), p. 314; Talcott Williams, "Childs, the Giver," *The Review of Reviews* IX:3 (March 1894), pp. 287 f.

Peterson's Retirement & Childs's Connection with Lippincott

George W. Childs to Edward McPherson, Philadelphia, February 20, 1861, containing newspaper clipping on *Union of Publishers,* and July 15, 1861 (The McPherson Papers, Library of Congress); "George W. Childs, The Philadelphia Publisher," *American Phrenological Journal* XLIX:10 (October 1869), p. 366; "George W. Childs," *Public Ledger Almanac* (Philadelphia, 1895), p. 68; *Review,* p. 10.

Childs's Publishing Credo

Childs to the Reverend Francis L. Hawks, Philadelphia, February 8, 1858 (New York Historical Society).

Childs's Publications

Advertisements in *American Literary Gazette* II:2–XII:12 (November 16, 1863—April 15, 1869), *passim,* and in *American Publishers' Circular* VIII:1 —N.S. I:8 (January 1862—August 15, 1863), *passim; The American Catalogue* 1861-66 and 1866-71; Carl J. Weber, *A Bibliography of Jacob Abbott* (Waterville, Maine, 1948), p. 71.

Childs & The Publication of Brownlow

For Childs's handling of *Parson Brownlow's Book, Sketches of the Rise, Progress, and Decline of Secession* (Philadelphia, 1862), see *American Pub-*

lishers' Circular VIII:4 (April 1862), p. 41, VIII:7 (July 1862), p. 73; E. M. Coulter, *William G. Brownlow* (Chapel Hill, 1937), pp. 219 ff., 235 ff.

The National Almanac

The National Almanac and Annual Record (Philadelphia, 1863), pp. 5 f. and (Philadelphia, 1864), p. 3.

Childs & The Publication of Lossing

G. W. Childs to J. F. Callan, January 20, 1863 (New York Historical Society); G. W. Childs to B. J. Lossing, Philadelphia, November 4, 1863, July 17, 1865, December 6, 1865 (A. W. Anthony Collection, New York Public Library); G. W. Childs to Edward McPherson, February 27, 1862 and Philadelphia, October 3, 1863 (McPherson Papers, Library of Congress); Alexander Davidson, Jr., "How Benson J. Lossing Wrote His 'Field Books,'" *Papers of the Bibliographical Society of America* XXXII (1938), p. 63; Derby, *op. cit.*, p. 691; Benson J. Lossing, *Pictorial History of the Civil War* (Philadelphia, 1866), I, 6.

American Publishers' Circular

Founded in 1851 as *Norton's Literary Advertiser,* with the title changed the next year to *Norton's Literary Gazette and Publishers' Circular,* the trade paper became known on September 1, 1855 as the *American Publishers' Circular and Literary Gazette,* issued by the Book Publishers' Association with Charles B. Norton serving as "assistant secretary and librarian." In April, 1857, Charles R. Rode took Norton's place, continuing his connection with the paper until proprietorship was transferred to George W. Childs. On November 2, 1863, the title was changed once again to the *American Literary Gazette and Publishers' Circular,* which was purchased from Childs in 1872 by Frederick Leypoldt, who merged it with his *Weekly Trade Circular* and dubbed it the following year *The Publishers' Weekly.*

For the history of the *Circular,* and Childs's policy as its proprietor, see advertisement on last page of *American Literary Gazette* (Christmas 1870); *American Publishers' Circular* N.S. I:6 (April 1, 1863), p. 49, and Octavo Series I:1 (May 1, 1863), p. 2; G. W. Childs to E. A. Duyckinck, Philadelphia, April 15, 1863 and July 6, 1863 (Miscellaneous Papers, New York Public Library); F. Hudson, *Journalism in the United States* (New York, 1873), p. 514; F. L. Mott, *American Magazines 1865-1880* (Iowa City, 1928), p. 66; F. L. Mott, *A History of American Magazines* (Cambridge, 1938), II, 158 f. and III, 491 f.; "The New Year," *Publishers' Weekly* IX:1 (January 1, 1876), pp. 10 f.; "The Publisher of Three Journals," *American Literary Gazette* VI:2 (November 15, 1865), p. 44; "Sketches of Publishers," *The Round Table* (May 19, 1866), p. 314.

The Paris correspondence, furnished by Dr. John Dunlap Osborne over the initials "G.S.," was a notable feature of the *Circular.* For his contributions, see "The Identity of 'G.S.' Revealed," *Publishers' Weekly* XLV:25 (June 23, 1894), p. 910.

Holmes's testimonial appears in the advertisement in *American Publishers' Circular* I:9 (September 1, 1863), p. 351.

Childs's Valedictory was printed in *The Publishers' and Stationers' Weekly Trade Circular* N.S. I:2 (January 25, 1872), p. 35.

Childs Abandons Book Publishing

American Literary Gazette VI:10 (March 15, 1866), p. 275, and VIII:10 (March 15, 1867), pp. 292, 316.

For Childs's retention of proprietorship in Sharswood, see Derby, *op. cit.,* p. 337.

For the Frank Leslie article on Childs, see "The Self-made Men of our Times. George W. Childs," *Frank Leslie's Chimney Corner* III:71 (October 6, 1866), pp. 296 f.

The Ledger Almanacs

G. W. Childs to Edward McPherson, December 31, 1863 (McPherson Papers, Library of Congress); Hudson, *op. cit.,* p. 100; *Public Ledger Almanac 1870* (Philadelphia, [1869]), verso of front cover.

Childs's Success

Richard D. Altick, *The Scholar Adventurers* (New York, 1950), p. 214 n.; *American Literary Gazette* XIV:12 (April 15, 1870), p. 335; "Ein amerikanischer Buchhändler. George W. Childs," [Leipzig] *Illustrirte Zeitung* LIX: 1529 (October 19, 1872), pp. 291 f.; "Mr. Childs' Library and Curios," *The No Name Magazine* II:12 (September 1891), *passim;* Clipping File, Biographical Section, Begun by Talcott Williams, Journalism Library, Columbia University, courtesy Wade A. Doares, Librarian (The following articles in that collection should particularly be indicated: "G. Washington Childs, A.M."; "George W. Childs' Career," *The World;* "G. W. Childs' Two Wills," (October 2, 1894); "Men of Quakerdom. George W. Childs," *The Quaker;* "The Printers And Mr. Childs," *Printer's Circular* [Philadelphia] (May 1888); "The Recollections Of A Famous Editor. Julian Hawthorne's Letter on George W. Childs," (May 31, 1891); "Rising From The Ranks"); *The City Item* I:12 (December 30, 1882), p. 4; *The Daily Graphic* (January 10, 1888), p. 498 and (May 12, 1888), p. 552; *Entertaining A Nation The Career of Long Branch* (Long Branch, 1940), pp. 45 f.; *Executors' Sale. Autographs, Rare Books and Historical Documents in the Collection of the late George W. Childs* (Philadelphia: Freeman, 1928), *passim;* John W. Forney, *Anecdotes of Public Men* (New York, 1873), p. 430; *Frank Leslie's Illustrated Newspaper* XXXVIII:966 (April 4, 1874), p. 59, LVII:1462 (September 29, 1883), p. 91, LXII:1602 (June 5, 1886), p. 247; *Harper's Weekly* (clipping, Miscellaneous Papers, Manuscript Division, New York Public Library); *The Journalist* II:16 (July 11, 1885), pp. 1 f., VII:8 (May 12, 1888), p. 8, XI:11 (May 31, 1890), p. 9, XII:8 (November 8, 1890), p. 9, XII:16 (January 3, 1891), p. 8, XVIII:26 (March 10, 1894), p. 14; "The Lounger," *The Critic* (February 27, 1892), p. 131; Edward D. McDonald and Edward M. Hinton, *Drexel Institute of Technology* (Philadelphia, 1942), pp. 8 ff.; F. L. Mott, *A History of American Magazines 1741-1850* (New York & London, 1930), I, 549, 554; *New York Sun* (September 13, 1887), p. 2; *Publishers' Weekly* II:21 (November 21, 1872), p. 544; F. W. Robinson, *The Library of George*

W. Childs (Philadelphia, 1882), *passim;* "Stampatori Esteri," *L'Arte Della Stampa* IV:1-2 (July–August 1872), p. 12; "The Story of Two Men," *Adolf Growoll Collection. American Book Trade History* IV, 43 (courtesy *Publishers' Weekly*); *Town Topics* XVIII:15 (October 13, 1887), p. 4.

Childs's Recollections

"Recollections of Mr. Childs," *The Evening Bulletin* (May 24, 1889), Clipping File, Journalism Library, Columbia University.

Childs's book might well have been included among the success stories discussed by Irvin G. Wyllie in *The Self-Made Man in America* (New Brunswick, N.J., 1954). Although Mr. Wyllie points out (p. 174) that "Through all our history the self-made man was the exception not the rule," he emphasizes also that "Belief in the self-made man requires only an act of faith." See also Kenneth S. Lynn, *The Dream of Success* (Boston, [1955]), p. 253: "More obsolete than the Model T, Alger continues to be our mythmaker."

XI. A. K. LORING

Loring's Library

Charles K. Bolton, *Circulating Libraries In Boston, 1765-1865* (The Colonial Society of Massachusetts, February 1907), p. 207; *English Division. Catalogue of Loring's Select Circulating Library* (Boston, 1863) and Aaron K. Loring, *Catalogue of Loring's Select Library. Established June 1859* (Boston, n.d.), both catalogues courtesy Boston Public Library.

For Loring's addresses here and subsequently given, see *Boston Almanac and Business Directory.* For many addresses the writer is indebted to Paul North Rice formerly of the New York Public Library.

Loring's Origins

C. H. Pope, *Loring Genealogy* (Cambridge, 1917), p. 162.

Loring's Apprenticeship

Boston Directories 1855-1860; *Boston Transcript* (September 27, 1911), p. 15.

Loring's Characteristics

E. D. Cheney, ed., *Louisa May Alcott Her Life, Letters, and Journals* (Boston, 1889), p. 161; "Aaron K. Loring," *Publishers' Weekly* LXXX:14 (September 30, 1911), p. 1284.

G. W. Dillingham

"Jubilee Of G. W. Dillingham Co.," *Publishers' Weekly* LXXII:6 (August 10, 1907), pp. 346 f.; "Obituary. George Wellington Dillingham," *ibid.* XLIX:1 (January 4, 1896), p. 10; *Town Topics* XVIII:11 (September 15, 1887), p. 7.

Loring's Publishing Credo
    A. K. Loring to Louisa M. Alcott, n.p., n.d. [1864] (courtesy the late Carroll A. Wilson).

Horatio Alger, Jr., & Aaron K. Loring
    Advertisement of *The Schoolmate* in *Boston Almanac* for 1870, p. 125; "Horatio Alger," *DAB;* Frederick Lewis Allen, *The Big Change* (New York, [1952]), pp. 63 f., 69; J. Blanck, *Peter Parley to Penrod* (New York, 1938), p. 29; Grace Williamson Edes, *Annals of the Harvard Class Of 1852* (Cambridge, 1922), pp. 5 ff.; information from Mr. Frank Gruber; Loring's list in *The Publishers' Trade-List Annual* (New York, November 1875); H. R. Mayes, *Alger A Biography Without a Hero* (New York, 1928), *passim.*
    Some of Mayes's statements are subject to question. According to him (p. 45), Loring made "discreet inquiries" regarding the authorship of *Ragged Dick* and decided that he "would not be averse to bringing it out." Since Loring was already Alger's friend and publisher, the "discreet inquiries" would appear to have been rather superfluous.
    For quoted Alger passages, see Horatio Alger, Jr., *Frank's Campaign; or, What Boys can do on the Farm for the Camp* (Boston: Loring, 1864), pp. v f.; *Ragged Dick; or, Street Life In New York With The Boot-Blacks* (Boston: Loring, [1868]), p. vii; *Struggling Upward And Other Works* (New York, [1945]), pp. 203, 280; *Fame And Fortune; or, The Progress Of Richard Hunter* (Boston: Loring, [1868]), p. viii; *Rough And Ready; or, Life Among The New York Newsboys* (Boston: Loring, [1869]), p. 7; *Rufus And Rose; or, The Fortunes Of Rough And Ready* (Boston: Loring, [1870]), pp. vii f.; *Bound To Rise; or, Harry Walton's Motto* (Boston: Loring, [1873]), p. viii; *The Young Miner; or, Tom Nelson In California* (Boston: Loring, [1879]), pp. 5 f.
    For the Alger bibliography, see Frank Gruber, "The Books of Horatio Alger, Jr.," *Antiquarian Bookman* II:20 (November 13, 1948), pp. 874 ff.

Loring's Juvenile Publications
    Advertisement of Alger's *Shifting For Himself* in *Publishers' Weekly* X:12 (September 16, 1876), p. 515; Blanck, *op. cit.,* p. 45; *Publishers' Trade-List Annual,* 1875.
    For the price of Louisa M. Alcott's separate *Proverb Stories: Kitty's Class Day, Aunt Kipp,* and *Psyche's Art,* see *The American Catalogue . . . July 1, 1876.* When first issued the Tales of the Day were priced at ten cents. See R. H. Shove, *Cheap Book Production in the United States, 1870 To 1891* (Urbana, 1937), pp. 141 f.

L. M. Alcott & Loring
    Cheney, *op. cit.,* pp. 235 f.; Loring to L. M. Alcott, n.p., n.d. [1864] (courtesy the late Carroll A. Wilson); reports of Loring's payment to L. M. Alcott for *Moods* (courtesy the late Carroll A. Wilson); O. Shepard, ed., *The Journals of Bronson Alcott* (Boston, 1938), p. 408; Madeleine B. Stern, *Louisa May Alcott* (Norman, Okla., 1950), pp. 140 f., 158, 203, 217, 296.

For Louisa Alcott's remarks on Loring's characteristics, see Cheney, *op. cit.*, p. 161.

Popular Novels Published by Loring

The *American Booksellers Guide* IV:5 (May 1, 1872), p. 149, and IV:10 (October 1, 1872), p. 330; *American Literary Gazette and Publishers' Circular* XII:10 (March 15, 1869), p. 245, and XIII:11 (October 1, 1869), p. 336; Loring's list in *Publishers' Trade-List Annual* (November 1875); *Publishers and Stationers Trade List Directory for 1869*, p. 412; *Publishers' Weekly* XI:12 (March 24 ,1877), p. 363.

Loring's Home Manuals & Practical Stories

Publishers and Stationers Trade List Directory for 1869, p. 412; *Publishers' Trade-List Annual*, 1875; *Publishers' Weekly* XI:12 (March 24, 1877), p. 363.

Loring Publications in the Loring Library

In his list of publications in *Publishers' Trade-List Annual*, 1875, Loring states, "In Circulating Libraries, no other novels published have such enduring popularity." See also *Books Most Called for at Loring's Library* (Boston, n.d.), courtesy Boston Public Library, which includes the works of Alcott, Alger, George Macdonald, Mrs. Warren, and others whose books Loring had published.

For Loring's library patrons, see *Publishers' Weekly* LXXX:14 (September 30, 1911), p. 1284.

Loring's Coffee House

Loring is listed under Restaurants in the *Boston Almanac* 1876-1881. His coffee rooms are listed in the 1875 Boston Directory at 1 Bromfield (courtesy Edward G. Freehafer, New York Public Library). See also *Publishers' Weekly* XII:1 (July 7, 1877), p. 6; *Town Topics* XVIII:11 (September 15, 1887), p. 7.

Loring was also in business as a newsdealer. See his letter to G. L. Ford of the *New-York Tribune*, November 26, 1879 (Ford Collection, New York Public Library), in which he bemoans the late arrival of the New York papers. "Consequently when todays came I had 32 of yesterdays left."

Loring's Bankruptcy & Sale of His Plates

Advertisement of the trade sale in *The American Bookseller* XII:6 (September 20, 1881), p. 134 (courtesy Rollo G. Silver); *The American Bookseller* XI:12 (June 15, 1881), p. 355 [Here Loring's assets are put at $14,000 and his liabilities at $20,000] and XII:5 (September 1, 1881), p. 115 (courtesy George L. McKay and Rollo G. Silver); *Publishers' Weekly* XX:1 (July 2, 1881), p. 3, XX:17 (October 22, 1881), p. 510, LXXX:14 (September 30, 1911), p. 1284; Receipt of December 8, 1881 (courtesy Dr. Clarence S. Brigham, American Antiquarian Society); Transfer of Copyright on *Moods* (courtesy the late Carroll A. Wilson).

Loring's Later Life, & Death
"Jubilee Of G. W. Dillingham Co.," *Publishers' Weekly* LXXII:6 (August 10, 1907), pp. 346 f.; Letterhead of undated note from Loring at 542 Washington Street to "Friend Sheperd," courtesy Dr. Clarence S. Brigham; *Publishers' Weekly* XXV:6 (February 9, 1884), p. 177, XXXIV:18 (November 3, 1888), p. 650, LXXX:14 (September 30, 1911), p. 1284; information from Mrs. F. J. Walton, Superintendent of the Home for the Aged.

XII. GEORGE W. CARLETON

Early Nineteenth-Century American Humor
Walter Blair, *Native American Humor* (New York, Cincinnati, Chicago, etc., [1937]), pp. 9 f., 124; *The Cambridge History of American Literature* (New York, 1927), II, 155 ff.; David Donald, ed., *Inside Lincoln's Cabinet The Civil War Diaries of Salmon P. Chase* (New York, 1954), pp. 149, 162; Parrington, *op. cit.*, III, 92; Constance Rourke, *American Humor* (New York, [1931]), pp. 221 ff.

Carleton's Visit to Cuba & His Appearance
George W. Carleton, *Our Artist in Cuba* (New York: Carleton, 1865), *passim;* "G. W. Carleton," *The American Bookseller* XXIV:8 (October 15, 1888), picture opp. p. 263; J. C. Derby, *Fifty Years among Authors, Books and Publishers* (New York: Carleton, 1884), p. 48.

Carleton's Early Life
"G. W. Carleton & Co.," *New-York Evening Post* (April 28, 1875), photostat courtesy Mr. Frederic Melcher; "George W. Carleton Retires," *Publishers' Weekly* XXIX:21 (May 22, 1886), p. 651; Derby, *op. cit.*, pp. 235-44; "Jubilee of G. W. Dillingham Co.," *Publishers' Weekly* LXXII:6 (August 10, 1907), p. 345; "Obituary. George W. Carleton," *ibid.* LX:16 (October 19, 1901), p. 857.

Rudd & Carleton: Their Activities; Carleton's Trademark
American Catalogue 1855-1858, *passim;* [William Allen Butler], *Nothing to Wear: An Episode of City Life* (New York: Rudd & Carleton, 1857), pp. 9, 67; *The Cambridge History of American Literature* II, 156; "G. W. Carleton," *The American Bookseller* (October 15, 1888), p. 263; "G. W. Carleton & Co.," *New-York Evening Post* (April 28, 1875); "G. W. Carleton, Retiring from Business, Tells Some of His Experiences," *Adolf Growoll Collection. American Book Trade History* IV, 10-12 (courtesy *Publishers' Weekly*); Derby, *op. cit.*, pp. 233, 235-44; Q. K. Philander Doesticks [Mortimer Thomson], *Nothing to Say* (New York: Rudd & Carleton, 1857), *passim;* Ferris Greenslet, *The Life of Thomas Bailey Aldrich* (Boston & New York, 1908), pp. 36, 52; George C. Holt, *Memorial of William Allen Butler Read before the Association of the Bar of the City of New York, March 10, 1903, passim;* "Jubilee of G. W. Dillingham Co.," *Publishers' Weekly* (August 10, 1907),

p. 345; "Literary Intelligence," *American Publishers' Circular and Literary Gazette* III:9 (February 28, 1857), p. 131, and VII:32 (December 5, 1861), p. 285; "Obituary. George W. Carleton," *Publishers' Weekly* (October 19, 1901), p. 857; Morris Phillips, "The Late George W. Carleton," (October 19, 1901), *Growoll Collection. American Book Trade History* IV, 10-12; Frederic F. Sherman, *A Check List of First Editions of the Works of Thomas Bailey Aldrich* (New York, 1921), p. 5; Laura Stedman and George M. Gould, *Life and Letters of Edmund Clarence Stedman* (New York, 1910), I, 218; Ernest James Wessen, "Campaign Lives of Abraham Lincoln 1860," *Papers In Illinois History . . . For . . . 1937* (Springfield, Ill., 1938), No. 1. According to Wright Howes, *U.S.-Iana* (1700-1950) (New York, 1954), No. 6159, *The "Wigwam Edition"* was "the first life of Lincoln in book form."

Fletcher Harper had refused to publish Butler's poem in book form after he had sold 80,000 copies of *Harper's Weekly,* where the poem had run, since he believed there would be no further demand. Rudd and Carleton, who asked for and received permission to publish it in book form, later claimed to have sold 20,000 copies, although the author stated he received no benefit. For details about *Nothing to Wear,* see Blanck, *Bibliography of American Literature* I, 449 f.; William Allen Butler, *A Retrospect of Forty Years* (New York, 1911), pp. 278 ff.; John A. Kouwenhoven, "Some Ado About Nothing," *The Colophon* N.S. II:1 (Autumn 1936), pp. 101-13.

Carleton's Office Personnel

American Literary Gazette VIII:6 (January 15, 1867), p. 191, XI:6 (July 15, 1868), p. 152, XI:7 (August 1, 1868), p. 169, XI:8 (August 15, 1868), p. 177; "G. W. Carleton & Co.," *New-York Evening Post* (April 28, 1875); "G. W. Carleton, Retiring from Business, Tells Some of His Experiences," *Growoll Collection. American Book Trade History* IV, 10-12; "George W. Dillingham," *The American Bookseller* XXIV:9 (November 1, 1888), pp. 298 f.; Greenslet, *op. cit.,* p. 61; "Obituary. George Wellington Dillingham," *Publishers' Weekly* XLIX:1 (January 4, 1896), pp. 10 f.; *Publishers' Weekly* LI:15 (April 10, 1897), p. 664; *Town Topics* XVIII:11 (September 15, 1887), p. 7.

Carleton's Humorous Publications

American Literary Gazette II:5 (January 1, 1864), p. 196, II:10 (March 15, 1864), p. 354, V:3 (June 1, 1865), p. 62, V:5 (July 1, 1865), p. 110, V:9 (September 1, 1865), p. 200, V:10 (September 15, 1865), p. 223, VII:2 (May 15, 1866), p. 43; [Charles F. Browne], *Artemus Ward His Book* (New York: Carleton, 1862), pp. 79 f., 176, 179, 205, and *passim;* [Charles F. Browne], *The Complete Works of Artemus Ward* (New York, [1898]), pp. 11, 26, and *passim;* G. W. Carleton, *Our Artist in Cuba, Peru, Spain and Algiers* (New York: Carleton, 1877), *passim;* G. W. Carleton, *Our Artist in Peru* (New York: Carleton, 1866), *passim;* "G. W. Carleton," *The American Bookseller* (October 15, 1888), p. 263; "G. W. Carleton & Co.," *New-York Evening Post* (April 28, 1875); "G. W. Carleton, Retiring from Business, Tells Some of His Experiences," *Growoll Collection. American Book Trade History* IV, 10-

12; Carleton's Catalogue at end of Mary E. Tucker, *Life of Mark M. Pomeroy* (New York: Carleton, 1868); Cyril Clemens, *Josh Billings, Yankee Humorist* (Webster Groves, Mo., 1932), pp. 51 ff., 115, 128, 156; Derby, *op. cit.*, pp. 235-44; [Charles G. Halpine], *The Life and Adventures, Songs, Services, and Speeches of Private Miles O'Reilly* (New York: Carleton, 1864), *passim;* "Jubilee of G. W. Dillingham Co.," *Publishers' Weekly* (August 10, 1907), p. 346; "Obituary. George W. Carleton," *ibid.* (October 19, 1901), pp. 857 f.; Morris Phillips, "The Late George W. Carleton," (October 19, 1901), *Growoll Collection. American Book Trade History* IV, 10-12; *Publishers' Trade-List Annual* 1873, 1874, 1879; "Return of Private Miles O'Reilly," *New York Herald* (October 20, 1863), clipping at New York Public Library; Don C. Seitz, *Artemus Ward* (New York & London, [1919]), pp. 117 ff.; [Henry W. Shaw], *Josh Billings, Hiz Sayings* (New York: Carleton, 1866), pp. 47, 58, and *passim;* [Henry W. Shaw], *Josh Billings: His Works, Complete* (New York: Carleton & Co., 1880), pp. xxiv, xxviii ff., and *passim;* C. H. Webb, *St. Twel'mo* (New York, 1867), p. 55.

Carleton's "Sensational" Books & Novels

American Catalogue 1876-1884, p. xxvi; *American Literary Gazette* II:3 (December 1, 1863), p. 108, VIII:3 (December 1, 1866), p. 117, VIII:11 (April 1, 1867), p. 335, IX:2 (May 15, 1867), p. 52, X:5 (January 1, 1868), p. 168, X:8 (February 15, 1868), p. 217, XI:4 (June 15, 1868), p. 106, XII:2 (November 16, 1868), p. 44, XII:4 (December 15, 1868), p. 127; "G. W. Carleton," *The American Bookseller* (October 15, 1888), p. 263; "G. W. Carleton & Co.," *New-York Evening Post* (April 28, 1875); Carleton's list at end of *Carleton's Classical Dictionary* (New York: Carleton, 1882); Derby, *op. cit.*, p. 239; Mary Noel, *Villains Galore* (New York, 1954), pp. 114, 192; La Salle C. Pickett, *Literary Hearthstones of Dixie* (Philadelphia & London, 1912), p. 293; *Publishers' Trade-List Annual* 1875; *Mayne Reid's Magazine Onward. For the Youth of America* (New York: Carleton, January 1869— February 1870); Elizabeth Reid, *Mayne Reid* (London, 1890), p. 239.

Carleton purchased the copyrights of "Marion Harland's" novels from Sheldon & Co. See *American Literary Gazette* XIV:2 (November 15, 1869), p. 57.

Carleton's Treasuries of Information & Society Handbooks

American Literary Gazette VII:3 (June 1, 1866), p. 70; *Carleton's Household Encyclopædia and Handbook of General Information* (New York: Carleton, 1879); "George W. Dillingham," *The American Bookseller* (November 1, 1888), pp. 298 f.; *Publishers' Trade-List Annual* 1875, 1878, 1879, 1880, 1881; *Record of the Year. A Reference Scrap Book* (New York: Carleton, 1876, 1877).

Carleton's Translations from the French

"G. W. Carleton," *The American Bookseller* (October 15, 1888), p. 263; "G. W. Carleton & Co.," *New-York Evening Post* (April 28, 1875); "G. W. Carleton, Retiring from Business, Tells Some of His Experiences," *Growoll*

Collection. American Book Trade History IV, 10-12; Derby, *op. cit.*, pp. 235-244; "George W. Dillingham," *The American Bookseller* (November 1, 1888), pp. 298 f.

Carleton's Advertising, Dealings with Authors, & Views on Copyright

American Literary Gazette III:9 (September 1, 1864), p. 263; "G. W. Carleton," *The American Bookseller* (October 15, 1888), p. 263; "G. W. Carleton & Co.," *New-York Evening Post* (April 28, 1875); Clemens, *op. cit.*, p. 115; Derby, *op. cit.*, pp. 251 f., 397; *Publishers' Weekly* XV:7 (February 15, 1879), p. 197; Seitz, *op. cit.*, p. 120; Stedman and Gould *op. cit.*, I, 218.

Carleton's Mistakes & Disappointments

Derby, *op. cit.*, pp. 235-244, 566 f.; "Literary Intelligence," *American Publishers' Circular and Literary Gazette* VI:19 (May 12, 1860), p. 246; *The Love-Life of Dr. Kane* (New York: Carleton, 1866), p. viii; "The Mistakes of a Publisher," *Growoll Collection. American Book Trade History* IV, 10-12; *Publishers' Weekly* XXXVII:25 (June 21, 1890), p. 825; Donald Sheehan, *This Was Publishing* (Bloomington, Indiana, 1952), p. 63; *The Suppressed Book about Slavery!* (New York: Carleton, 1864), p. 6; *Mark Twain's Notebook* (New York & London, 1935), pp. 7, 55.

Carleton's Store, Control of Hotel, Dillingham's Partnership, & Later Firm Locations & Activities

American Literary Gazette XIII:8 (August 16, 1869), p. 219, XIV:1 (November 1, 1869), pp. 5 f., XVI:8 (February 15, 1871), p. 150; "G. W. Carleton & Co.," *New-York Evening Post* (April 28, 1875); "G. W. Carleton, Retiring from Business, Tells Some of His Experiences," *Growoll Collection. American Book Trade History* IV, 10-12; "Obituary. George W. Carleton," *Publishers' Weekly* (October 19, 1901), pp. 857 f.; "Obituary. George Wellington Dillingham," *ibid.* XLIX:1 (January 4, 1896), pp. 10 f.; *Publishers' Weekly* I:12 (April 4, 1872), p. 302, XXIII:23 (June 9, 1883), p. 689, XXVIII:4 (July 25, 1885), p. 141, XXXIII:6 (February 11, 1888), p. 333; *Trow's New York City Directory* 1869/70—1886/87.

Carleton's Retirement & Death

The American Bookseller XIX:10 (May 15, 1886), p. 255; Clipping File, Biographical Section, begun by Talcott Williams, Journalism Library, Columbia University, courtesy Wade A. Doares, Librarian; "Literary and Trade Notes," *Publishers' Weekly* XXXIII:26 (June 30, 1888), p. 989; "Obituary. George W. Carleton," *ibid.* (October 19, 1901), p. 857.

A copy of the notice of "Dissolution of Co-Partnership," dated May 8, 1886, is deposited in the Ford Collection, New York Public Library.

G. W. Dillingham Company

Announcement of the incorporation of the G. W. Dillingham Company, after Dillingham's death, appears in *Publishers' Weekly* XLIX:23 (June 6, 1896), p. 957. This company was incorporated with John H. Cook as president and John W. Hesse as secretary and treasurer, both men having worked for Carleton. The G. W. Dillingham Co. in 1906 had a capital stock of $115,000. In 1907, when it celebrated its fiftieth jubilee, *Publishers' Weekly* announced that the firm "bids fair to outlast another fifty years." In 1916 the firm was bankrupt, with liabilities of $50,000 and assets slightly more than $5,000. For details, see "G. W. Dillingham Co. Bankrupt," *Publishers' Weekly* XC:10 (September 2, 1916), p. 677; *Adolf Growoll Collection. American Book Trade History* IV, 112; "Jubilee of G. W. Dillingham Co.," *Publishers' Weekly* (August 10, 1907), pp. 345 ff.

XIII. ELLIOTT, THOMES & TALBOT

The Call of the Wild

The precise timing of the closing of physical frontiers and the consequent substitution of literary for actual adventure is, of course, impossible to determine accurately. Many historians would place the shift of emphasis later than the present writer. Nevertheless, the stories speak for themselves, and most frequently those stories were based upon adventures, explorations, or wild events that had already occurred and were part of the nation's past.

Interesting recent remarks upon the subject appear in Hoffman Birney, "Speaking of Books," *The New York Times Book Review* (August 2, 1953), p. 2, where the author discusses the "growth of . . . culture heroes and of Western fiction," and in Edwin Corle's review of Wallace Stegner's *Beyond The Hundredth Meridian* in the *New York Herald Tribune Book Review* (September 19, 1954). Mr. Corle states that "About the year 1885 the curtain began to come down . . . on the old 'wild' and gun-toting West and the stage was gradually taken over by the scholar and the scientist." The present writer feels that the curtain had come down earlier, except, of course, in the trans-Missouri region, and knows that the stage had long before 1885 been taken over by the dime novelist.

William Henry Thomes

Nicholas Ball, *The Pioneers of '49* (Boston, 1891), pp. 50 f.; Hubert Howe Bancroft, *History of California* (San Francisco, 1886), V, 746; *Boston Transcript* (March 7, 1895), p. 10 (courtesy Boston Public Library); C. W. Haskins, *The Argonauts of California* (New York, 1890), pp. 394, 456; Octavius Thorndike Howe, *Argonauts of '49* (Cambridge, 1923), pp. 50 f.; Oscar Lewis, *Sea Routes to the Gold Fields* (New York, 1949), pp. 31, 43; George R. Stewart, *Take Your Bible in One Hand. The Life of William Henry Thomes* (San Francisco, 1939), *passim;* "William Henry Thomes," *DAB.* Letters to George R. Stewart from Clarence H. Carter and George P. Tilton (courtesy Bancroft Library, University of California) contain material on Thomes.

James R. Elliott

James Romanzo Elliott was the son of Andrew and Sally (Warren) Elliott (information from T. A. Eaton, Greenville, N.H.). See also *Boston Direc-*

tories 1852-1860; information from Mrs. Harold F. Elliott, Librarian of the Mason Public Library; John B. Hill, *Proceedings at the Centennial Celebration of . . . Mason, N.H., August 26, 1868* (Boston, 1870), p. 82.

Newton Talbot

Hosea Starr Ballou, "Hon. Newton Talbot, A.M.," *New-England Historical and Genealogical Register* (October 1904), LVIII, 329-34.

The Firm of Elliott, Thomes & Talbot and Their Periodicals

Ballou's Monthly Magazine XVII:4 (April 1863), p. 338, XXXII:6 (December 1870), advertisement of *The Novelette,* (July-December 1877), XLVI, iv; *Boston Almanac* 1864, pp. 52 f.; George Waldo Browne, "Pioneers of 'Popular Literature,'" *Granite State Magazine* III:2 and 3 (February and March 1907), pp. 51 ff.; "Illustrated Journalism in the United States," *The Newsman* IV:10 (December 1887), p. 2; F. L. Mott, *A History of American Magazines* (Cambridge, 1938), II, 31, 35 f.; *The Novelette* No. 159, prospectus of the 1870 *Ballou's;* Leona Rostenberg, "Some Anonymous and Pseudonymous Thrillers of Louisa M. Alcott," *Papers of the Bibliographical Society of America* XXXVII:2 (1943), *passim.*

The Flag of Our Union is deposited in the Library of Congress. The New York Public Library has a fairly complete run of *Ballou's Monthly Magazine* and several issues of *The Novelette.*

The Firm's Ten Cent Novelettes & Brilliant Novelettes

Besides the works themselves, see Ralph Admari, "The House That Beadle Built 1859 to 1869," *The American Book Collector* IV:6 (December 1933), pp. 288 f. and V:2 (February 1934), p. 60; *The American Catalogue 1861-1866; The Beadle Collection of Dime Novels Given to The New York Public Library by Dr. Frank P. O'Brien* (New York, 1922), pp. 16 f., 75; "Beadle's Dime Books," *North American Review* (July 1864), XCIX, 309; *Boston Almanac* 1864, p. 53; Charles Bragin, *Dime Novels Bibliography 1860-1928* (Brooklyn, N.Y., 1938), p. 28; *The Ralph F. Cummings Standard Dime and Weekly Novel Catalogue* (Grafton, Mass., 1936), p. 12; Albert Johannsen, *The House of Beadle and Adams* (Norman, Okla., [1950]), I, 45 [According to Johannsen, the first 24 of the Ten Cent Novelettes were bound in pink. No. 25, Charles Cutterfield's *Tip: or, The Bridal of Death,* was the first of the original blue backs]; W. C. Miller, *Dime Novel Authors 1860-1900* (Grafton, Mass., 1933), *passim;* Edmund Pearson, *Dime Novels* (Boston, 1929), p. 83; Ten Cent Novelettes advertisement on cover of *The Novelette* No. 151; Lists of Novelettes on covers of Ten Cent Novelettes owned by the New York Public Library; their run is good, though far from complete.

Some of the Elliott, Thomes & Talbot Novelettes were reprints. For example, Dr. J. H. Robinson's *The White Rover: or The Lovely Maid Of Louisiana,* published as No. 2 of the Ten Cent Novelettes, had been published by Gleason in 1852.

Quoted passages appear in Ned Buntline [E. Z. C. Judson], *The Volunteer: or, The Maid of Monterey* (Boston: Elliott, Thomes & Talbot, [1865] [No. 16 of Ten Cent Novelettes], pp. 3, 4, 8; William H. Bushnell, *Hack, The Trail-*

er. A Story of The Shoshonee Indians (Boston: Elliott, Thomes & Talbot, [1869]) [No. 68 of Ten Cent Novelettes], pp. 7, 17, 49, 71, 87, 88; Sylvanus Cobb, Jr., *The Patriot Cruiser. A Revolutionary Story* (Boston: Elliott, Thomes & Talbot [1868]) [No. 52 of Ten Cent Novelettes], pp. 7, 12; Miss Jane Howard, *Zelda. A Tale of the Massachusetts Colony* (Boston: Elliott, Thomes & Talbot, [1866]) [No. 31 of Ten Cent Novelettes], pp. 12, 58; Ben Perley Poore, *The Scout; or, Sharpshooters of the Revolution* (Boston: Studley, n.d.) [Brilliant Novelette of Elliott, Thomes & Talbot], pp. 4, 7, 20; Dr. J. H. Robinson, *The White Rover: or The Lovely Maid Of Louisiana* (Boston: Gleason, 1852) [Reprinted as No. 2 of Ten Cent Novelettes], pp. 7, 9; Dr. John B. Williams, *Joaquin: or, The Brothers of the Coast* (Boston: Elliott, Thomes & Talbot, [1869]) [No. 72 of Ten Cent Novelettes], p. 7.

The Firm's Authors & Rates Paid Them

Ralph Admari, "Ballou, the Father of the Dime Novel," *The American Book Collector* IV:3-4 (September-October 1933), p. 126; Admari, "The House That Beadle Built," *ibid.* IV:6 (December 1933), p. 289; George W. Browne, "Pioneers of 'Popular Literature,'" *Granite State Magazine* III:2 and 3 (February and March 1907), pp. 54, 109, 111 ff.; Gelett Burgess, "Confessions of a Dime Novelist," *The Bookman* (August 1902), XV, 532 f.; Ella Waite Cobb, *A Memoir of Sylvanus Cobb, Jr.* (Boston, 1891), p. 123 and *passim;* Jay Monaghan, *The Great Rascal* (Boston, 1952), *passim;* Mary Noel, *Villains Galore* (New York, 1954), p. 46; Edmund Pearson, *Dime Novels* (Boston, 1929), p. 83; Fred E. Pond, *Life And Adventures Of "Ned Buntline"* (New York, 1919), *passim;* Leona Rostenberg, "Some Anonymous and Pseudonymous Thrillers of Louisa M. Alcott," *op. cit., passim.*

The discovery of Louisa M. Alcott's pseudonymous and anonymous effusions was made by Leona Rostenberg and reported in her "Some Anonymous and Pseudonymous Thrillers of Louisa M. Alcott," *op. cit.* See also L. M. Alcott, *The Mysterious Key, and What It Opened* (Boston: Elliott, Thomes & Talbot, [1867]) (courtesy the late Carroll A. Wilson); L. M. Alcott, *The Skeleton in the Closet* in Perley Parker, *The Foundling* (Boston: Elliott, Thomes & Talbot, [1867]) (courtesy P. D. Howe); A. M. Barnard, *V.V.: or, Plots and Counterplots* (Boston: Thomes & Talbot, [1865]) (copy in New York Public Library); Madeleine B. Stern, *Louisa May Alcott* (Norman, Okla., 1950), pp. 144 f., 170, 383 f.

Elliott & "The Western World"

Boston Almanac 1871, advertisement of *The Western World* opp. p. 127; *Evans' Advertising Hand-Book* (Boston, 1871), unpaged advertisement (courtesy Miss Mary Noel); *Frank Leslie's Illustrated Newspaper* XXXI:790 (November 19, 1870), p. 159.

Through 1869 and for part of 1870, *The Illuminated Western World* (later *The Western World*) had been published by the Western World Company of New York (information from the Chief, Serials Division, Library of Congress, and David R. Watkins, University of Minnesota Library).

The *Boston Directories* from 1870 to 1885 list the firm as Thomes and Talbot instead of Elliott, Thomes and Talbot.

Elliott & the Mason Celebration
Elliott responded, at the celebration, to the toast to "The Flag of Our Union and its Literary Namesake." See John B. Hill, *Proceedings, op. cit.,* p. 82.

The Boston Fire
Ball, *op. cit.,* p. 51; Bancroft, *op. cit.,* V, 746; "A Literary Career," *Ballou's Monthly Magazine* (January-June 1884), LIX, 397 f.

Attempted Censorship of Dime Novels
"Prohibition of Dime Literature," *Publishers' Weekly* XXIII:17 (April 28, 1883), p. 500.

George W. Studley
The Beadle Collection of Dime Novels Given to The New York Public Library, *op. cit.,* pp. 71 f.; *Boston Directories* 1877-1890; Bragin, *op. cit.,* p. 28; Miller, *op. cit., passim.*

Thomes's Appearance & Later Activities
Ball, *op. cit.,* p. 51; *Boston Directories* 1888-1890; pictures of Thomes on title-pages of his works published by Lee and Shepard.

Talbot's Characteristics & Later Activities
Ballou, "Hon. Newton Talbot," *op. cit., passim; Boston Directories* 1889-1890; George H. Emerson, *Life of Alonzo Ames Miner* (Boston, 1896), pp. 166 f., 174 f.; excerpt from the regular meeting of Trustees of Tufts College, March 8, 1904 (courtesy Harvey E. Averill, Secretary of the Corporation, Trustees of Tufts College). [This record, made at the time of Talbot's death, mentions "his clear and strong intelligence, his breadth of view; his keen human interest in all questions and movements of the world; his large and deep faith in God; and, above all, his tenderness, sympathy and friendliness of spirit."]

XIV. THE LESLIES

The Railway Age
Nevins and Commager, *op. cit.,* pp. 312 f.; Mary Noel, *Villains Galore* (New York, 1954), pp. 3, 67, 142; Parrington, *op. cit.,* III, 7 f.

Frank Leslie: His Characteristics & Early Life
Madeleine B. Stern, *Purple Passage The Life of Mrs. Frank Leslie* (Norman, Okla., [1953]), pp. 33 ff.

Frank Leslie's Publishing House
Stern, *op. cit.,* pp. 35, 56.

Leslie's Interest in Railways
Robert Taft, "The Pictorial Record of the Old West XI. The Leslie Ex-

cursions of 1869 and 1877," *The Kansas Historical Quarterly* XVIII:2 (May 1950), pp. 118 ff. Reprinted in Robert Taft, *Artists and Illustrators of the Old West: 1850-1900* (New York, 1953).

Mrs. Leslie's Appearance & Early Life
Stern, *op. cit., passim.*

Frank Leslie's Expanded Publishing House
Stern, *op. cit.*, pp. 78 f., 231.

The Leslie Excursion Across the Continent
Stern, *op. cit.*, pp. 79-88, 232 f.; Taft, *op. cit., passim.*

The start of the journey is described in *Frank Leslie's Illustrated Newspaper* XLIV:1126 (April 28, 1877), pp. 140 f. The series, "Across the Continent," ran in *Frank Leslie's Illustrated Newspaper* between XLIV:1136 (July 7, 1877) and XLVI:1182 (May 25, 1878), with some Western features running even later.

Mrs. Leslie's version is given in her *California A Pleasure Trip from Gotham to the Golden Gate. (April, May, June, 1877.)* (New York, 1877)—a book which remains a valuable contribution to Western Americana.

Frank Leslie as a Publisher of Books
Charles Bragin, *Dime Novels Bibliography 1860-1928* (Brooklyn, 1938), p. 25; *New-York Daily Tribune* (August 25, 1877), p. 6; *The New-York Times* (September 10, 1877), p. 5; Stern, *op. cit.*, pp. 192 ff. [This contains a check list of Leslie book publications]. See also Madeleine B. Stern, "The Frank Leslie Publishing House," *Antiquarian Bookman* VII:24 (June 16, 1951), pp. 1973-1975.

A few additional Leslie imprints appear in *List and Description of Illustrated Publications and Premium Chromos issued by Frank Leslie* [New York, 1876] (Catalogue in author's possession).

Frank Leslie's Home Library
Since he had first set up as a publisher, Leslie had issued 11 books, excluding pictorials. In the short span between 1876 and 1877 he published at least 35, for the most part reprints of novels which had run in his journals. About half of those publications were items in Frank Leslie's Home Library.

A full advertisement of the Home Library appears in *Frank Leslie's Illustrated Newspaper* XLIV:1144 (September 1, 1877), p. 448. The series is mentioned in Raymond H. Shove, *Cheap Book Production in The United States, 1870 To 1891* (Urbana, 1937), pp. 5, 57.

Chimney Corner & Other Leslie Book Series
Frank Leslie's Chimney Corner, Popular Library, and Boys Library Series are advertised in *Publishers' Trade List Annual 1877*. An advertisement of *Michael Strogoff* published by Frank Leslie's Publishing House appears in *Publishers' Weekly* XI:4 (January 27, 1877), p. 128. See also Stern, *op. cit.*, pp. 193 f.

American News Company as Leslie Agents

See *Publishers' Trade List Annual* 1873, where the American News Company advertises that it handles Frank Leslie's magazines. *Publishers' Trade List Annual* 1877 lists Frank Leslie's Library Series under the general heading of the American News Company. The connection with the News Company has perhaps dimmed the realization that these many books were actually Leslie publications. See also The American News Company, Inc., *Covering a Continent A Story of Newsstand Distribution and Sales* (New York, 1930), p. 13.

Leslie Assignment & Death

New-York Daily Tribune (September 10, 1877), p. 8; *The New-York Times* (September 13, 1877), p. 8, (September 14, 1877), p. 8, (September 30, 1877), p. 2; Stern, *op. cit.*, pp. 89, 96 ff., 233 f.

Mrs. Frank Leslie, Publisher

Stern, *op. cit.*, pp. 100 ff., 106 ff., 237 ff.

Mrs. Leslie's Book Publications

Advertisements in *Frank Leslie's Illustrated Newspaper* LIII:1355 (September 17, 1881), p. 47, LXIV:1663 (July 30, 1887), p. 395; *The American Catalogue* 1884-1890, pp. 14, 421; *The New-York Times* (July 14, 1895), p. 15; *Publishers' Trade List Annual* 1887 and 1888; *Publishers' Weekly* XLVIII:3 (July 20, 1895), p. 115.

An interesting account appears in *A Brief History of Frank Leslie's Publishing House* (New York [ca. 1887]) in *Growoll Collection. American Book Trade History* VIII, 75 (courtesy *Publishers' Weekly*). See also "The Frank Leslie Publishing House," *Frank Leslie's Illustrated Newspaper* LVI:1435 (March 24, 1883), p. 81. A description of Mrs. Leslie at work appears in "General Gossip of Authors and Writers," *Current Literature* II:2 (February 1889), p. 104.

Mrs. Leslie's Later Life

Stern, *op. cit., passim.*

XV. ERNST STEIGER

Mass Immigrations to the United States

Nevins and Commager, *op. cit.*, pp. 241, 267, 289, 302, 304 ff.

Ernst Steiger's Early Life, Characteristics, & Arrival in America

"Ein deutscher Buchhändler in Amerika," *Buch der Welt* XXXI:28 and 29 (1872), pp. 447 f., 464 [For the translation of this article, as well as for all German translations required in this chapter, the writer is deeply indebted to Miss Leona Rostenberg of New York City]; "An Honorable Career" and "Ernst Steiger," *Publishers' Weekly* LXXXII:3 (July 20, 1912), pp. 133 ff.; "Obituary Notes," *ibid.* XCII:6 (August 11, 1917), pp. 489 f.; Ernst Steiger,

Dreiundfünfzig Jahre Buchhändler in Deutschland und Amerika (New York, [1901]), *passim;* "Ernst Steiger," *Publishers' Weekly* LIII:10 (March 5, 1898), p. 440.

Steiger Firm History

The American Bookseller V:11 (June 1, 1878), p. 493, XXII:4 (August 15, 1887), p. 105; *American Literary Gazette and Publishers' Circular* II:9 (March 1, 1864), p. 318, VI:8 (February 15, 1866), p. 236, XII:9 (March 1, 1869), p. 238; "Business Changes," *The American Bookseller* X:7 (October 1, 1880), p. 257; "Business Notes," *Publishers' Weekly* XIII:18 (May 4, 1878), p. 440, XVIII:14 (October 2, 1880), p. 440, LVI:25 (December 16, 1899), p. 1279, LXXVII:13 (March 26, 1910), p. 1414; "Ein deutscher Buchhändler in Amerika," *op. cit.,* pp. 447 f., 464; leaflet in R. R. Bowker Letters, Manuscripts Division, New York Public Library; Theodor Lemke, *Geschichte des Deutschthums von New York* (New York, 1891), pp. 164 ff.; "Literary And Trade Notes," *Publishers' Weekly* XXVI:26 (December 27, 1884), p. 983; "Notes On Books And Booksellers," *American Literary Gazette* XII:9 (March 1, 1869), p. 222; "Obituary Notes," *Publishers' Weekly* XCII:6 (August 11, 1917), pp. 489 f.; *Publishers' Weekly* XIII:21 (May 25, 1878), p. 514; Steiger, *Dreiundfünfzig Jahre Buchhändler,* pp. 44 f.; "Ernst Steiger," *Publishers' Weekly* LIII:10 (March 5, 1898), p. 440, LXXXII:3 (July 20, 1912), p. 135.

Steiger's Publications by, about, & for German-Americans

Besides the books themselves, and the advertisements they carry, see *American Bookseller* XV:3 (February 1, 1884), p. 117; *American Literary Gazette* II:11 (April 1, 1864), p. 390, II:12 (April 15, 1864), p. 424, III:2 (May 16, 1864), p. 69, III:4 (June 15, 1864), p. 130, III:6 (July 15, 1864), p. 183, III:10 (September 15, 1864), pp. 301, 303, IV:2 (November 15, 1864), p. 53, VI:8 (February 15, 1866), p. 238, VIII:7 (February 1, 1867), p. 233, XI:7 (August 1, 1868), p. 168, XI:11 (October 1, 1868), p. 286, XIII:5 (July 1, 1869), p. 136, XIV:3-4 (December 1, 1869), p. 614, XIV:7 (February 1, 1870), p. 190; *Books for the Study of Languages* (New York: E. Steiger & Co., n.d.), *passim;* "Ein deutscher Buchhändler in Amerika," *op. cit.,* pp. 447 f., 464; Anton Eickhoff, *In der Neuen Heimath* (New York: E. Steiger & Co., 1884) [the advertisements printed therein are particularly inclusive]; Friedrich Kapp, *Die Deutschen im Staate New York* (New York: E. Steiger & Co., 1884), introduction by Carl Schurz; Lemke, *op. cit.,* pp. 165 f.; *Publishers' Trade List Annual* 1885, 1886, 1889, 1895; *Publishers' Weekly* XX:27 (December 31, 1881), p. 888, XXV:5 (February 2, 1884), p. 155, XXVII:13 (March 28, 1885), p. 375, XXX:6 (August 7, 1886), p. 191; information from Mr. Otto H. Rutgers of The German Society; [Ernst Steiger, ed.], *Deutscher Buchhandel und Presse* (New York, 1869), advertisements at end; E. Steiger, *Medicinische Bibliothek* (New York, 1872), advertisements at end; "Ernst Steiger," *Publishers' Weekly* (July 20, 1912), pp. 135 f.; *Steiger's Literarischer Monatsbericht* II:6 (January and February 1871), announcement at end; *Uniform Trade List Annual* 1873.

Steiger as Importer & Bookseller

American Literary Gazette IV:2 (November 15, 1864), p. 53, VI:7 (February 1, 1866), p. 215, VI:8 (February 15, 1866), p. 238, IX:2 (May 15, 1867), p. 55, XII:11 (April 1, 1869), p. 277, XII:12 (April 15, 1869), p. 301, XIII:5 (July 1, 1869), p. 117, XIV:2 (November 15, 1869), p. 76, XIV:3-4 (December 1, 1869), unpaged note, XV:3 (June 1, 1870), p. 91; "Ein deutscher Buchhändler in Amerika," *op. cit.,* p. 464; leaflet in R. R. Bowker Letters, Manuscripts Division, New York Public Library; "Notes On Books And Booksellers," *American Literary Gazette* XIII:5 (July 1, 1869), p. 117; *Publishers' Trade List Annual* 1878 & 1883; *Publishers' Weekly* IX:21 (May 20, 1876), p. 678, X:1 (July 1, 1876), p. 86, XII:2-3 (July 14, 1877), p. 94, XX:27 (December 31, 1881), p. 888, XXXI:5-6 (January 29, 1887), p. 203, XXXII:18 (October 29, 1887), p. 609, XLII:3 (July 16, 1892), p. 120, XLVI:18 (November 3, 1894), p. 710, LI:5 (January 30, 1897), p. 288, LVIII:2 (July 14, 1900), p. 222; Jos. Schedler, *An Illustrated Manual for the use of the Terrestrial and Celestial Globes* (New York: E. Steiger, 1875), advertisement at end; E. Steiger to R. R. Bowker, New York, June 25, 1872, and E. Steiger & Co. to R. R. Bowker, New York, January 22, 1915, in R. R. Bowker Letters, Manuscripts Division, New York Public Library, letterheads; Steiger, *Dreiundfünfzig Jahre Buchhändler,* p. 128; "Ernst Steiger," *Publishers' Weekly* (July 20, 1912), p. 136; *Uniform Trade List Annual* 1873; *The Year-Book of Education For 1879* (New York: E. Steiger, 1879), p. 479.

Steiger's Accomplishments

Alexander J. Schem, *Deutsch-amerikanisches Conversations-Lexicon* (New York: E. Steiger, 1873), X, 463.

Steiger's Publications & Activities to Further American Understanding of Germans

For the language texts for Americans published by Steiger, see, besides the works themselves and the advertisements they carry, *Ahn's Complete Method of the German Language by Dr. P. Henn* (New York: E. Steiger & Co., [1876]), Preface; *Ahn's First German Reader. . . . By Dr. P. Henn* (New York: E. Steiger, 1875), p. iii; *Ahn's Fourth German Book* (New York: E. Steiger, 1876), advertisement at end; *Ahn's New Practical and Easy Method Of Learning The German Language* (New York: E. Steiger, 1873), pp. iii f.; *Ahn-Oehlschlaeger's Pronouncing Method of The German Language* (New York: E. Steiger, 1880), p. iv; *Ahn's Rudiments of the German Language. By Dr. P. Henn* (New York: E. Steiger & Co., [1873]), p. iii; *American Literary Gazette* III:1 (May 2, 1864), p. 25, VIII:8 (February 15, 1867), p. 253, IX:6 (July 15, 1867), p. 175, XII:10 (March 15, 1869), p. 258, XIII:4 (June 15, 1869), p. 101, XIII:7 (August 2, 1869), p. 207, XIII:10 (September 15, 1869), p. 320, XIV:7 (February 1, 1870), p. 191; *Books for the Study of Languages* (New York: E. Steiger & Co., n.d.), *passim; Publishers' Trade List Annual* 1878; *Publishers' Weekly* IV:2-3 (July 1873), p. 101, XL:3 (July 18, 1891), p. 123.

For Steiger's writings on the reprinting of German books in America and the repeal of duty on foreign books, as well as his views on international copyright, see *The Evening Post* [New York] (August 22, 1882), p. 3; *Adolf Growoll Collection. American Book Trade History* XI, 103 (courtesy *Publishers' Weekly*); "Literary And Trade Notes," *Publishers' Weekly* LXXV:2 (January 9, 1909), pp. 51 f.; "Notes On Books And Booksellers," *American Literary Gazette* XIV:3-4 (December 1, 1869), unpaged note; *Publishers' Weekly* XXV:13 (March 29, 1884), p. 383; Alexander J. Schem, *Deutsch-amerikanisches Conversations-Lexicon* (New York, 1873), X, 463; [Ernst Steiger, ed.], *Deutscher Buchhandel und Presse* (New York, 1869), *passim;* E. Steiger, *Mittheilungen über den Vertrieb deutscher Bücher und Zeitschriften in den Vereinigten Staaten* (New York, 1868), *passim;* E. Steiger, *Der Nachdruck in Nordamerika* (New York, 1866), *passim;* E. Steiger, *On The Removal Of The Duty On Books* ([New York], 1882), *passim;* Ernst Steiger, *Urheberrecht und Nachdruck in Nord-Amerika* (New York, 1908), *passim.*

For *The Workshop,* see *American Literary Gazette* X:11 (April 1, 1868), p. 303; *The Workshop* I (1868)—XI (1878) and XVII (1884), *passim.*

For Steiger's educational publications, support of the Froebel system, and his Educational Bureau, see, besides the publications themselves, "Ein deutscher Buchhändler in Amerika," *op. cit.,* pp. 447 f., 464; Adolf Douai, *The Kindergarten* (New York: E. Steiger, 1872), letter from E. P. Peabody to publisher at beginning; Adolf Douai, *The Rational Phonetic Primer* (New York: E. Steiger, 1872), p. iii; *Growoll Collection. American Book Trade History* XI, 103; Henry Kiddle and A. J. Schem, *The Dictionary of Education* (New York: E. Steiger & Co., 1882), Notice, verso of title-page; Maria Kraus-Boelte and John Kraus, *The Kindergarten Guide No. 2* (New York: E. Steiger, 1877), advertisement at end; Matilda H. Kriege, *The Child, Its Nature and Relations* (New York: E. Steiger & Co., [1872]), Notice, verso of title-page; leaflet in R. R. Bowker Letters, Manuscripts Division, New York Public Library; Joseph Payne, *Froebel and The Kindergarten System* (New York: E. Steiger, 1874), announcement at end; Elizabeth Peabody, *Guide to the Kindergarten and Intermediate Class, . . . and Moral Culture of Infancy, by Mary Mann* (New York: E. Steiger, 1877), pp. iii, 10; *Publishers' Trade List Annual* 1882; *Publishers' Weekly* X:1 (July 1, 1876), p. 26, XIII:21 (May 25, 1878), p. 514, XV:4 (January 25, 1879), p. 116, XVI:3-4 (July 26, 1879), p. 111, XXI:24 (June 17, 1882), p. 647, XLVI:20–21 (November 17–24, 1894), p. 190, LVI:2 (July 8, 1899), p. 101; E. Steiger to R. R. Bowker, New York, June 21, 1872, in R. R. Bowker Letters, Manuscripts Division, New York Public Library; "Ernst Steiger," *Publishers' Weekly* (July 20, 1912), p. 136; *Steiger's Educational Directory For 1878* (New York: E. Steiger, 1878), p. [322]; *The Year-Book of Education For 1879* (New York: E. Steiger, 1879), p. 551.

Steiger's Work to Help Foreigners Understand America: His Periodical Collection, International Publishing, Exports

"American Bibliography," *Publishers' Weekly* V:22 (May 30, 1874), p. 512; *American Literary Gazette* VI:7 (February 1, 1866), p. 215, VI:8 (February 15, 1866), p. 238, X:2 (November 15, 1867), p. 44, XIII:2 (May 15, 1869), p. 45; "Business Notes," *Publishers' Weekly* LVI:25 (December 16, 1899), p. 1279; *Growoll Collection. American Book Trade History* XI, 103; leaflet in R. R. Bowker Letters, Manuscripts Division, New York Public Library; [Ernst Lemcke], *Skat* (New York, 1886), p. ii; "Notes On Books And Booksellers," *American Literary Gazette* XIII:2 (May 15, 1869), p. 31; *Publishers' Weekly* IV:1 (July 5, 1873), p. 3, VI:2 (July 11, 1874), p. 41, XXI:8 (February 25, 1882), p. 199; Schedler, *op. cit.,* p. 1; Hermann A. Schumacher, *Petrus Martyr, Der Geschichtsschreiber des Weltmeeres* (New York, etc.: E. Steiger, *et al.,* 1879), New York Public Library copy containing inserted letter from Steiger to the Literary Editor of *The New York Tribune,* New York, February 12, 1879, regarding the work; E. Steiger, *The Periodical Literature of the United States of America* (New York: E. Steiger, 1873), *passim;* "Ernst Steiger," *Publishers' Weekly* LXXXII:3 (July 20, 1912), p. 136; "Mr. Steiger's Attempt," *ibid.* V:23 (June 6, 1874), p. 531; "Mr. Steiger's Vienna Collection," *ibid.* IV:4 (July 26, 1873), p. 117.

Steiger's Work for Non-German Emigrants to the United States

Books for the Study of Languages, passim; Publishers' Trade List Annual 1880, 1883, 1885, 1886, 1889, 1890, 1905; *Publishers' Weekly* XVIII:4-5 (July 24, 1880), p. 125, XXII:3-4 (July 22, 1882), p. 109, XXIV:4 (July 28, 1883), p. 131, XXV:20 (May 17, 1884), p. 578, XXV:21 (May 24, 1884), p. 607, XXV:22 (May 31, 1884), p. 622, XXVII:8 (February 21, 1885), p. 239, XXXII:15 (October 8, 1887), p. 523, LVII:21 (May 26, 1900), p. 1082, LXIII:17 (April 25, 1903), p. 1074, LXVIII:2 (July 8, 1905), p. 69, LXIX:13 (March 31, 1906), p. 1098, LXXXVIII:4 (July 24, 1915), p. 316; "Ernst Steiger," *Publishers' Weekly* (July 20, 1912), p. 136; *Steiger's Monthly Gazette of English Literature No. 10* (February 1902), advertisement at end.

Steiger's Marriage

"Ernst Steiger," *Publishers' Weekly* (July 20, 1912), p. 135.

The First World War

Publishers' Trade List Annual 1917; *Publishers' Weekly* XCII:4 (July 28, 1917), p. 396; "A Survey of the Country's Action against the German Language," *ibid.* XCIV:4 (July 27, 1918), p. 189.

Steiger's Death

"Obituary Notes," *Publishers' Weekly* XCII:6 (August 11, 1917), pp. 489 f.

Firm's Bankruptcy & Later History

Information from Miss E. Marie Becker, Reference Librarian, New York Historical Society; "Obituary Note," *Publishers' Weekly* CXLIV:2 (July 10, 1943), p. 136; "Publisher A Suicide," *The New York Times* (July 1, 1943), p. 12; "Steiger in Bankruptcy," *Publishers' Weekly* CXXVI:24 (December 15, 1934), p. 2144.

XVI. JOHN W. LOVELL

Labor Problems & Solutions
George E. McNeil, ed., *The Labor Movement* (New York, 1891), p. 573; Nevins and Commager, *op. cit.*, pp. 255, 267, 286, 289 f., 292 f., 295, 298 f., 306.

Lovell's Early Life; Rouses Point Printing Establishment
"Business Notes," *Publishers' Weekly* IX:13 (March 25, 1876), p. 409; Alfred H. Dymond, "International Copyright," *The Canadian Monthly and National Review* I:4 (April 1872), p. 298; "Like Humpty Dumpty," *The World* [New York] (January 31, 1893), pp. 1 f.; [John W. Lovell], "Earlier Years," MS (courtesy Mr. John K. Lovell); "J. W. Lovell Dead," *The New York Times* (April 22, 1932), p. 17; "John Lovell's Printing Office," *Publishers' Weekly* III:5 (January 30, 1873), pp. 107 f.; Lovell Papers [Collection of Personal & Business Notes, Pamphlets, MSS, Clippings, Letters, etc.], courtesy Mr. John K. Lovell of Yonkers, N.Y., to whom the writer is indebted for detailed information regarding his father; [Sarah Lovell], *Reminiscences of Seventy Years* (Montreal, 1908), p. 83 (courtesy Mr. John K. Lovell); "Obituary Notes John W. Lovell," *Publishers' Weekly* CXXI:18 (April 30, 1932), pp. 1888 f.; Raymond H. Shove, *Cheap Book Production in The United States, 1870 To 1891* (Urbana, Ill., 1937), p. 75.

Firms of Lovell, Adam & Lovell, Adam, Wesson
"Business Changes," *The American Bookseller* II:5 (September 1, 1876), p. 172; "Business Changes," *Publishers' Weekly* X:9 (August 26, 1876), p. 365; "Business Notes," *ibid.* XII:19 (November 10, 1877), p. 558; *Publishers' Weekly* XI:4 (January 27, 1877), p. 116, XII:19 (November 10, 1877), p. 558.

Publishing Conditions in 1870's; Lovell's Publishing Principles & Early Career as Publisher
The American Bookseller X:4 (August 16, 1880), pp. 91 f.; "Business Notes," *Publishers' Weekly* XIII:24 (June 15, 1878), p. 576; "The Canadian Incursion," *ibid.* XV:15 (April 12, 1879), p. 439; "The Courtesy of the Trade," *The Times* [Philadelphia] (April 22, 1879), clipping, courtesy Mr. John K. Lovell; J. W. Lovell, "The Royalty *vs.* The Monopoly Scheme of Copyright," *Publishers' Weekly* XV:21 (May 24, 1879), pp. 580 ff.; Lovell Papers; "John W. Lovell," *The New City* I:5 (February 8, 1893), pp. 7 ff.; "The 'Monopoly' of Copyright," *Publishers' Weekly* XV:18 (May 3, 1879), p. 508; "Obituary Notes John W. Lovell," *ibid.* CXXI:18 (April 30, 1932), pp. 1888 f.; *Publishers' Trade List Annual* 1880; *Publishers' Weekly* XV:16 (April 19, 1879), pp. 462, 470 f., XVII:5 (January 31, 1880), p. 132, XVIII:6 (August 7, 1880), pp. 146 f., XVIII:8 (August 21, 1880), p. 216, XVIII:11 (September 11, 1880), pp. 302 f., XIX:5 (January 29, 1881), pp. 110 f., XIX:13 (March 26, 1881), p. 369, XXI:15 (April 15, 1882), p. 406; Shove, *op. cit.*, pp. 37, 75 f., 81, 99.

John W. Lovell Co.; Lovell's Library; Firm's Expansion

The American Bookseller XIII:8 (April 15, 1882), p. 167, XVII:5 (March 2, 1885), p. 152, XXV:7 (April 1, 1889), p. 140; *Boston Directory* 1887–1888; "Business Notes," *Publishers' Weekly* XXXIII:19 (May 12, 1888), p. 752; *Chicago Directory* 1887–1889; "A Large Transaction," *The American Bookseller* XXIII:9 (May 1, 1888), pp. 234, 242; "The Late John W. Lovell," *The North Countryman* (April 28, 1932), clipping in Lovell Papers; "Like Humpty Dumpty," *The World* (January 31, 1893), pp. 1 f.; Lovell Papers; "J. W. Lovell Dead," *The New York Times* (April 22, 1932), p. 17; *New York City Copartnership Directory* 1885 and 1889; *New York City Directories* 1883-1889; "Obituary Notes John W. Lovell," *Publishers' Weekly* CXXI:18 (April 30, 1932), pp. 1888 f.; *Publishers' Trade List Annual* 1884, 1885, 1886, 1887, 1889; *Publishers' Weekly* XXXV:13 (March 30, 1889), p. 497, XXXVI:23 (December 7, 1889), p. 873, XXXVII:4 (January 25, 1890), pp. 186 f., XXXVIII:1 (July 5, 1890), p. 24; Shove, *op. cit.,* pp. 13, 38, 77 ff.; "Special Notice to the Trade," *Publishers' Weekly* XXXIII:19 (May 12, 1888), p. 757.

Lovell's London Branch

Balestier formed a partnership with William Heinemann and projected the "English Library" for the publication of English and American books on the Continent. While in Dresden on a business trip in December 1891 he died, and Arthur Waugh succeeded him as Lovell's agent. For Balestier's brief but remarkable career and his accomplishments for Lovell, see "Charles Wolcott Balestier," *DAB;* Mary R. Cabot, *Annals of Brattleboro 1681-1895* (Brattleboro, Vt., 1922), II, 979 ff.; C. E. Carrington, *The Life of Rudyard Kipling* (Garden City, N.Y., 1955), pp. 134-52; B. D. Cutler, *Sir James M. Barrie A Bibliography* (New York, [1931]), pp. 64 f.; Edmund Gosse, "Wolcott Balestier," *The Century Magazine* XLIII:6 (April 1892), pp. 923 ff.; Edmund Gosse, *Portraits And Sketches* (London, 1912), pp. 215-225; Amy Hanmer-Croughton, "The Wife of Rudyard Kipling," *The Rochester Historical Society Publication Fund Series* VI (1927), pp. 231 ff.; Henry James, "Wolcott Balestier," *The Cosmopolitan* XIII:1 (May 1892), pp. 43 ff.; "Obituary. Mr. Henry James's Tribute to the Memory of Wolcott Balestier," *The American Bookseller* XXXI:12-13 (June 15 and July 1, 1892), pp. 222 f.; Howard C. Rice, *Rudyard Kipling in New England* (Brattleboro, Vt., 1936), pp. 10 f.; Arthur Waugh, *One Man's Road* (London, 1931), pp. 172-211.

See also, for Lovell's foreign policy and first American editions of Kipling, *The American Bookseller* XXIV:8 (October 15, 1888), p. 263; "The Author of Robert Elsmere," *The Critic* XIII:249 (October 6, 1888), p. 167; *The . . . Collection of . . . Kipling made by G. M. Williamson* (New York: Anderson Galleries, 1915), Sale No. 1140, Item 18; Rudyard Kipling, *Mine Own People* (New York: United States Book Company, [1891]), facsimile letter from Kipling; Rudyard Kipling, *Soldiers Three* (New York: John W. Lovell Co., [1890]), facsimile letter from Kipling; Flora V. Livingston, *Bibliography of the Works of Rudyard Kipling* (New York, 1927), *passim;* Lovell Papers; *Publishers' Weekly* XXXVIII:11-12 (September 20 and 27, 1890),

p. 345; Janet Penrose Trevelyan, *The Life of Mrs. Humphry Ward* (New York, 1923), p. 74.

Lovell's Labor Publications

The American Bookseller XXI:7 (April 1, 1887), p. 205; Kemper Bocock, *Tax The Area* (New York: John W. Lovell Co., [1887]), *passim* and advertisement at end; "Cheap Books," *Publishers' Weekly* XXIII:18 (May 5, 1883), p. 522; Bertha M. Clay, *From Out The Gloom* (New York: John W. Lovell Co., [1886]), advertisement at end; Charles H. W. Cook, *The True Solution of the Labor Question* (New York: United States Book Company, 1890), *passim; The Credit Foncier of Sinaloa* No. 3 (June 16, 1885), p. 27; J. B. A. Godin, *Social Solutions. Translated . . . by Marie Howland* (New York: John W. Lovell Co., n.d.), pp. iii f.; John A. Grier, *Our Silver Coinage* (New York: Frank F. Lovell & Co., 1889), *passim;* Edward Howland, ed., *Social Solutions* (New York: John W. Lovell Co., 1886), Nos. 1-12, *passim;* Edward Kellogg, *Labor And Capital* (New York: John W. Lovell Co., 1884), *passim;* "Like Humpty Dumpty," *The World* (January 31, 1893), pp. 1 f.; Lovell Papers; *Ninety Dinners. A Three Years' Record of Ye Twilight Club* (n.p., 1886), p. 80; Mary Noel, *Villains Galore* (New York, 1954), p. 280; Albert K. Owen, *Integral Co-Operation* (New York: John W. Lovell Co., [1885]), *passim;* J. Harris Patton, *The Democratic Party* (New York: Lovell, Gestefeld & Co., n.d.), advertisement at end; *Publishers' Trade List Annual* 1884, 1885, 1886, 1892; *Publishers' Weekly* XXXI:13 (March 26, 1887), p. 444, XXXIII:3 (January 21, 1888), pp. 140 f., XXXVII:4 (January 25, 1890), p. 187; Goldwin Smith, *False Hopes* (New York: United States Book Company, 1890), *passim;* A. J. Starkweather and S. Robert Wilson, *Socialism* (New York: John W. Lovell Co., 1884), *passim;* Stepniak [Sergyei M. Kravchinski], *Underground Russia* (New York: John W. Lovell Co., 1883), *passim; Tid-Bits* I:1 (August 23, 1884), p. 8, II:52 (August 8, 1885), pp. 411, 415; Charles F. Wingate, ed., *Twilight Club Tracts* (New York: United States Book Company, [1889]), *passim.*

Lovell & Sinaloa

"As It Is In Topolobampo," *The Sun* (February 8, 1891), p. 25; Clay, *op. cit.,* advertisement at end; *The Credit Foncier of Sinaloa* No. 3 (June 16, 1885), p. 32; Howland, *op. cit.,* No. 1, pp. 15, 33 ff., No. 2, p. 6; Leopold Katscher, "Owen's Topolobampo Colony, Mexico," *The American Journal of Sociology* XII:2 (September 1906), pp. 145-163; information from Mrs. L. O. Kellogg, Carmel, California; Rev. Alexander Kent, "Cooperative Communities in the United States," *Bulletin of the Department of Labor* No. 35 (July 1901), pp. 640 f.; "Like Humpty Dumpty," *The World* (January 31, 1893), pp. 1 f.; John W. Lovell, *A Co-Operative City and The Credit Foncier Company* (New York, [1886]), *passim;* Lovell Papers; "John W. Lovell," *The New City* I:5 (February 8, 1893), pp. 7 ff.; Memorandum Of Agreement between Albert K. Owen, . . . and Carrie F. Lovell (January 14, 1897) in Lovell Papers; *The New City* I:1 (December 8, 1892), I:2 (December 22, 1892), I:7-9 (March 8—April 8, 1893), *passim; New York City Directories* 1887–1895; *New York Copartnership Directory* 1892 (courtesy E. Marie

Becker, Reference Librarian, New York Historical Society); Owen, *op. cit.,*
pp. 199 ff., 207; Thomas A. Robertson, *A Southwestern Utopia* (Los Angeles, 1947), *passim;* "The Topolobampo Colony," *Harper's Weekly* XXXI:
1593 (July 2, 1887), pp. 475 ff.; *Topolobampo Library (Howland Collection)*
(Topolobampo, 1893), *passim;* Wingate, *op. cit.,* pp. 305-320.

Lovell & Henry George

Edward and Eleanor Marx Aveling, *The Working-Class Movement in
America* (London, 1891), p. 193; Charles Albro Barker, *Henry George* (New
York, 1955), p. 423; Henry George to James McClatchy, New York, March
28, 1883 (Henry George Collection, New York Public Library); Henry
George, *The Condition Of Labor* (New York: United States Book Company,
1891), *passim;* Henry George, *The Land Question* (New York: John W.
Lovell Co., 1884), *passim;* Henry George, *Progress And Poverty* (New York:
John W. Lovell Co., [1883]), *passim;* Henry George, Jr., *The Life of Henry
George* (Garden City, N.Y., 1930), pp. 404 f.; Howland, *op. cit.,* No. 3,
advertisement at end; John W. Lovell to Henry George, November 28, 1882
(Henry George Collection, New York Public Library); Lovell Papers; Louis
F. Post and Fred. C. Leubuscher, *An Account of the George-Hewitt Cam-
paign* (New York: John W. Lovell Co., n.d.), *passim* and typed note by James
P. Archibald inserted at end of New York Public Library copy; Starkweather
and Wilson, *op. cit.,* advertisements at beginning and end.

Lovell's Advertisements

Henry George, *The Condition Of Labor* (New York, 1891), advertisements
at beginning; Howland, *op. cit.,* No. 1, advertisement at end, No. 3, pp. 40 ff.
and inside back cover, No. 12, advertisement; Starkweather and Wilson, *op.
cit.,* advertisements at end; *Tid-Bits* IV:90 (May 1, 1886), p. 191, V:112
(October 2, 1886), p. 15.

"Memories"

"Memories," Lovell Papers (courtesy Mr. John K. Lovell).

Lovell & Theosophy

Mabel Collins, *The Blossom And The Fruit* (New York: Frank F. Lovell
& Co., [1889]), *passim* and p. 290 n.; Mabel Collins, *The Idyll Of The White
Lotus* (New York: Lovell, Gestefeld & Co., [1890]), p. 315; Mabel Collins,
Suggestion (New York: Lovell, Gestefeld & Co., [1892]), advertisement at
end; Basil P. Howell, ed., *The Theosophical Society The First Fifty Years*
(London, 1925), pp. vii, 25, 45, 49; "Like Humpty Dumpty," *The World*
(January 31, 1893), pp. 1 f.; "Literary Notes," *The Path* IV:7 (October
1889), p. 229; John W. Lovell, "Reminiscences of Early Days of the The-
osophical Society," *The Canadian Theosophist, passim,* in Lovell Papers;
John W. Lovell to Mrs. Cook [Mabel Collins], New York, January 15, 1913,
in Lovell Papers; "John W. Lovell," *The Rag* I:5, pp. 2 f., in Lovell Papers;
"John W. Lovell," *The Theosophical Messenger* XX:6 (June 1932), p. 143;
"J. W. Lovell Dead," *The New York Times* (April 22, 1932), p. 17; Lovell

Papers; Medium's Report of Seance, October 19, 1890, in Lovell Papers; The World Within (MS) in Lovell Papers.

Lovell & Woman's Rights

Katherine Devereux Blake and Margaret Louise Wallace, *Champion Of Women The Life of Lillie Devereux Blake* (New York, [1943]), pp. 151 ff., 158; Lillie Devereux Blake, *Woman's Place To-Day* (New York: John W. Lovell Co., [1883]), *passim;* Ursula N. Gestefeld to John W. Lovell, Chicago, January 5, 1891, in Lovell Papers; Howland, *op. cit.,* No. 1, p. 15; Margaret Lee, *Divorce* (New York: Frank F. Lovell & Co., [1889]), *passim;* information from Mr. John K. Lovell; Lovell, *A Co-Operative City,* p. 15; Lovell Papers; "Memories," Lovell Papers; Olive Thorne Miller [Harriet Mann Miller], *The Woman's Club* (New York: United States Book Company, [1891]), p. 18 and *passim; The New City* I:7 (March 8, 1893), p. 9; Owen, *op. cit.,* pp. 188 f.; Starkweather and Wilson, *op. cit.,* pp. 59 f.; Stepniak, *op. cit.,* advertisement at end; *Tid-Bits* I:1 (August 23, 1884), p. 1, II:33 (April 4, 1885), p. 101.

Rise & Fall of United States Book Company & Its Subsidiary Concerns

The magnitude of the trust is reflected by the multitude of contemporary references to it. See especially "The Abuse of Receivership," *Publishers' Weekly* XLV:18 (May 5, 1894), p. 681; "The Affairs Of The American Publishers Corporation," *ibid.* LII:6 (August 7, 1897), pp. 213, 215; "The Affairs of the United States Book Company," *ibid.* XLIII:5 (February 24, 1893), pp. 268 ff., XLIII:6 (February 11, 1893), p. 300, XLIII:13 (April 1, 1893), pp. 558 f., XLIII:16 (April 22, 1893), p. 646, XLIII:17 (April 29, 1893), p. 671, XLIII:20 (May 20, 1893), p. 754, XLIV:9 (August 26, 1893), pp. 256 f.; *The American Bookseller* XXVII:7 (April 1, 1890), p. 196, XXVIII:15 (September 1, 1890), p. 139, XXIX:3 (January 31, 1891), p. 119, XXXII:1-2 (July 15 and August 1, 1892), *passim;* "A Book Trust," *New York Herald* (June 23, 1889), p. 22; "Business Notes," *Publishers' Weekly* XLI:6 (February 6, 1892), p. 293, XLI:11 (March 12, 1892), p. 426, XLI:12 (March 19, 1892), pp. 449 f., XLIII:4 (January 28, 1893), pp. 193 f., XLIII:11 (March 18, 1893), p. 457, XLIII:12 (March 25, 1893), p. 504, XLIII:13 (April 1, 1893), p. 557, XLIII:18 (May 6, 1893), p. 706, XLIII:22 (June 3, 1893), p. 852, XLV:7 (February 17, 1894), p. 331, XLIX:8 (February 22, 1896), p. 361, XLIX:25 (June 20, 1896), p. 1011, LIII:4 (January 22, 1898), p. 84, LVII:2 (January 13, 1900), p. 35; *Committee on Stock List, New York Stock Exchange. United States Book Company. New York, May 25, 1891,* New York Stock Exchange Printing Office A-1074 (broadside in author's possession); "The Copyright Bill," *New-York Daily Tribune* (April 15, 1890), p. 6; [T. Irving Crowell], *Thomas Young Crowell* (New York, [1954]), pp. 38 ff.; Cutler, *op. cit.,* pp. 7 ff., 35 f., 41, 90; "Defeat of the Copyright Bill," *The American Bookseller* XXVII:10 (May 15, 1890), p. 259; George T. Dunlap, *The Fleeting Years* (New York, 1937), pp. 111 f., 119 f.; George T. Dunlap, "Genesis of a Publishing Business," *Publishers' Weekly* CXXVIII:5 (August 3, 1935), p. 277; "Exit The United States Book Co. Et Al.," *ibid.* LXV:4 (January 23, 1904), p. 107;

"Gifts For All The Year," *The New-York Times* (December 11, 1895), p. 10; *Adolf Growoll Collection. American Book Trade History* (courtesy *Publishers' Weekly*) VIII, 123 f., XII, 55 f.; Arthur S. Hamlin, *Copyright Cases* (New York & London, 1904), pp. 122 f.; "The Herald's Book Trust," *Publishers' Weekly* XXXVI:1 (July 6, 1889), p. 8; "The 'Library' Publishers' Combination," *ibid.* XXXVII:10 (March 8, 1890), p. 354; "The 'Library' Publishers' 'Combine,'" *ibid.* XXXVII:7 (February 15, 1890), pp. 274 f., XXXVII:8 (February 22, 1890), pp. 299 f.; "Like Humpty Dumpty," *The World* (January 31, 1893), pp. 1 f.; "Literary And Trade Notes," *Publishers' Weekly* XXXVIII:9 (August 30, 1890), p. 247, XLII:20 (November 12, 1892), p. 784, LVII:1 (January 6, 1900), p. 11; "The Lovell 'Book Trust,'" *The Critic* XVI:327 (April 5, 1890), p. 172; "Mr. Lovell on Cheap Books," *ibid.* XVI:328 (April 12, 1890), p. 185; "John W. Lovell on Cheap Books," *Publishers' Weekly* XXXVII:16 (April 19, 1890), p. 535; "The Lovell Combination," *ibid.* XXXVII:13 (March 29, 1890), pp. 458, 460 f.; "J. W. Lovell Dead," *The New York Times* (April 22, 1932), p. 17; "J. W. Lovell on International Copyright and the Book Trust," *The American Bookseller* XXVII: 9 (May 1, 1890), p. 240; Lovell Papers; *Minutes of the Annual Meeting of Stockholders of the Trow Directory, Printing And Bookbinding Company. . . . at . . . Jersey City, N.J. . . . July 17, 1894,* pp. 14 f.; "The New Book Trust," *The World* (July 11, 1890), p. 4; *New York Copartnership Directory 1892* (courtesy E. Marie Becker, Reference Librarian, New York Historical Society); "No Book Trust," *New-York Daily Tribune* (April 22, 1890), p. 7; "Obituary Notes John W. Lovell," *Publishers' Weekly* CXXI:18 (April 30, 1932), pp. 1888 f.; "The Proposed Reorganization of the United States Book Company," *ibid.* XLIX:4 (January 25, 1896), pp. 191 f.; *Publishers' Trade List Annual 1892, 1894, 1895, 1896, 1901, 1902; Publications of the United States Book Company* [New York, October 1890], *passim; Publishers' Weekly* XXV:13 (March 29, 1884), p. 382, XXXVII:15 (April 12, 1890), p. 508, XXXVII:17 (April 26, 1890), p. 557, XLI:13 (March 26, 1892), pp. 514 f., XLII:9 (August 27, 1892), p. 284, XLVIII:1 (July 6, 1895), p. 8, XLVIII:15 (October 12, 1895), p. 661, L:22 (November 28, 1896), p. 179, LXI:18 (May 3, 1902), p. 1045, LXIII:23 (June 6, 1903), p. 1320, LXIV:16 (October 17, 1903), p. 847, LXV:4 (January 23, 1904), p. 92; "Receiverships Again," *ibid.* XLV:24 (June 16, 1894), pp. 885 f.; "Reorganization Of The American Publishers Corporation," *ibid.* LIII:10 (March 5, 1898), p. 438; Shove, *op. cit.,* pp. 43, 45 f., 51, 82, 99 ff.; "The Trade of the Year," *The American Bookseller* XXIX:3 (January 31, 1891), p. 85; "The United States Book Company," *Publishers' Weekly* XXXVIII:2 (July 12, 1890), p. 32; "The United States Book Co. Agents For The Belford Co.," *ibid.* XXXIX:5 (January 31, 1891), p. 235; *United States Book Company Catalogue. Standard And Miscellaneous Books* (New York, n.d.), *passim;* Waugh, *op. cit.,* pp. 195-211; "Would A Book Trust Bind?" *New York Herald* (June 30, 1889), p. 13.

Lovell's Later Career, & Death

Information from S. L. Buckingham, Stephen Merritt Burial and Cremation Company; "Business Notes," *Publishers' Weekly* XLIV:25 (December 16,

1893), p. 1005, LVIII:10 (September 8, 1900), p. 488; *Growoll Collection.
American Book Trade History* XII, 56; "J. W. Lovell Dead," *The New York
Times* (April 22, 1932), p. 17; John W. Lovell to Edsel Ford, New York,
June 9, 1930, in Lovell Papers; Lovell Papers; *New York City Business Directory* 1895; "Obituary Notes John W. Lovell," *Publishers' Weekly* CXXI:18
(April 30, 1932), pp. 1888 f.; information from John C. Plumb, Superintendent, Woodlawn Cemetery; Shove, *op. cit.,* p. 105.

XVII. DICK & FITZGERALD

The Nineteenth-Century American Home

Details are based upon the Dick & Fitzgerald publications themselves. For
the quoted remark about the twentieth-century attitude toward entertainment,
see Ben Hecht, *A Child of the Century* (New York, 1954), p. 626: "The
more we let others sing, dance and perform for us, the more empty we become."

William B. Dick, Lawrence R. Fitzgerald, & Their Early Connections with Burgess & Garrett

American Publishers' Circular and Literary Gazette II:49 (December 6,
1856), p. 749; information from John J. Fitzgerald, City Clerk of Pittsfield,
Mass.; "Lawrence R. Fitzgerald," *The American Bookseller* XII:8 (October
15, 1881), p. 237 (courtesy Rollo G. Silver); *New York City Directories*
1853-1858; "Obituary. Lawrence R. Fitzgerald," *The New-York Times* (October 12, 1881), p. 5; "Obituary. Lawrence R. Fitzgerald," *Publishers' Weekly*
XX:17 (October 22, 1881), pp. 520 f.; "Obituary. William B. Dick," *New-York Tribune* (September 6, 1901), p. 14; "Obituary. William Brisbane
Dick," *Publishers' Weekly* LX:11 (September 14, 1901), p. 434.

The will of Lawrence R. Fitzgerald, at the Surrogate's Court of the County
of New York, gives the date of the co-partnership.

Ann Street

Before the move to No. 18, Ransom Garrett, William B. Dick, and Lawrence R. Fitzgerald are listed in the *New York City Directories* at No. 22 Ann
Street. Wesley F. Burgess is listed at the latter address from 1849 to 1854.

For details of Ann Street at the time, see Aaron Mendoza, "Some Associations of Old Ann Street, 1720-1920," *Valentine's Manual of Old New York,*
New Series, 1920-1921.

The Home Circle

See *The Home Circle* V:3 (March 1858), *passim* (courtesy Mrs. Dorothea
E. Spear, American Antiquarian Society). The periodical is listed under the
heading of Newspapers in Trow's *New York City Directory* 1859-1863, with
Dick & Fitzgerald as publishers.

The Firm's Publications for the Homes of America

Besides the books themselves, see advertisements in *American Literary
Gazette* II:10 (March 15, 1864), p. 366, III:1 (May 2, 1864), p. 33, III:9

(September 1, 1864), p. 269, IV:1 (November 1, 1864), p. 23, IV:4 (December 15, 1864), p. 130, V:4 (June 15, 1865), p. 86, VI:1 (November 1, 1865), p. 28, VII:11 (October 1, 1866), p. 267, VIII:12 (April 15, 1867), p. 367, IX:5 (July 1, 1867), p. 151, XVII:3 (June 1, 1871), p. 82, XVII:9 (September 1, 1871), pp. 272 f.; *American Publishers' Circular and Literary Gazette* VIII:7 (July 1862), p. 74; Charles Bragin, *Dime Novels Bibliography 1860-1928* (Brooklyn, 1938), p. 28; *Dick & Fitzgerald Catalogue* (New York, n.d.); *Dick & Fitzgerald's Descriptive Book Catalogue* (New York, n.d.); *Dick's Descriptive Catalogue of Dramas, Comedies, Farces* (New York, n.d.); *The Home Circle* V:3 (March 1858), *passim;* information from Albert Johannsen; Warren Elbridge Price, *Price's Catalogue of Paper Covered Books* (New York, 1905), p. 58; *Publishers' Trade List Annual* for 1875, 1876, 1886, 1888; *Publishers' Weekly* VI:24 (December 12, 1874), p. 661, Christmas Number, 1875, p. 853, IX:5 (January 29, 1876), p. 146, XII:13 (September 29, 1877), p. 382, XXXV:8 (February 23, 1889), p. 347, XLIII:4 (January 28, 1893), p. 247, XLV:4 (January 27, 1894), p. 73; R. H. Shove, *Cheap Book Production in the United States, 1870 To 1891* (Urbana, Ill., 1937), p. 140; *Uniform Trade List Circular* I:6 (April 1867), pp. 280-87; Harry B. Weiss, *Oneirocritica Americana* (New York, 1944), p. 15.

Quoted passages appear in *Dick's Little Dialogues for Little People* (New York: Dick & Fitzgerald, [1890]), pp. 3 f.; *Dick's Original Album Verses and Acrostics* (New York: Dick & Fitzgerald, [1879]), Preface, p. 4; *Dick's Society Letter-Writer for Ladies* (New York: Dick & Fitzgerald, [1884]), p. 19; *Fireside Games; for Winter Evening Amusement* (New York: Dick & Fitzgerald, [1859]), p. 3; *The Home Circle* V:3 (March 1858), pp. 2, 3; Leger D. Mayne [William B. Dick], *What Shall We Do To-Night?* (New York: Dick & Fitzgerald, [1873]), Preface, p. 5.

The Centennial Exhibition
Publishers' Weekly X:1 (July 1, 1876), p. 19.

Firm Policy & Mail-Order Techniques
Dick & Fitzgerald Catalogue (New York, n.d.); *Dick's Descriptive Catalogue of Dramas* (New York, n.d.); *Publishers' Trade-List Annual* for 1875; *Uncle Josh's Trunk-Full of Fun* (New York: Dick & Fitzgerald, [1869]), verso of title-page, pp. 2, 7, 12, 19, 58.

Firm Catalogues
The undated list of Dick & Fitzgerald publications deposited in the Library of the University of Missouri, for example, is charmingly illustrated.

Firm's Methods of Obtaining Material
The American Hoyle, for example, was a result of the consultation method [see *American Literary Gazette* IV:4 (December 15, 1864), p. 130], while *Dick's Diverting Dialogues* (New York: Dick & Fitzgerald, [1888]) contained material "written expressly" for the work. Other methods of obtaining plates, etc., are revealed in *Dick's Descriptive Catalogue of Dramas;* A. G. Doughty, "Haliburton," *Transactions of the Royal Society of Canada,* 3rd Series, Vol. III, Sec. II (1909), p. 62; "Judge Gildersleeve Decides in Favor of Dick and

Fitzgerald," *Publishers' Weekly* XLV:20 (May 19, 1894), p. 739; *Publishers' Weekly* XXV:13 (March 29, 1884), p. 381.

Personal Details regarding Dick & Fitzgerald

For such information the author is indebted to Margaret B. Harris, Charlotte Haynes of The Church Club, George L. McKay of The Grolier Club, and Andrew H. A. Thompson of the Lafayette Camp No. 140.

See also The American Art Association, *The Libraries of the Late Harris B. Dick and William B. Dick* (New York, January 24 and 25, 1918); announcement of Neptune Club regarding Fitzgerald's funeral in *The New-York Times* (October 12, 1881), p. 5; *The War of the Rebellion: . . . Official Records* (Washington, 1889), Series I, Vol. XXVII, Part 2, p. 215; J. G. Wilson, *The Memorial History of the City of New-York* (New York, 1893), IV, 130.

Dissolution of Co-Partnership & Dick's Retirement

Publishers' Weekly XX:23 (December 3, 1881), p. 799, LIII:17 (February 12, 1898), p. 349.

Harris B. Dick: His Personal & Business Life

For this information the author is indebted to Rudolph Behrens, Percy L. Hance, W. M. Ivins, Jr., John Knight of The Players, Aaron and the late Mark Mendoza, Harry C. Vail, Superintendent of the Green-Wood Cemetery, Brooklyn, and F. B. Whitlock of The Union League Club.

See also *Last Will and Testament of Harris Brisbane Dick, Deceased*, p. 3 (courtesy Stewart & Shearer); Metropolitan Museum of Art, *Forty-eighth Annual Report of the Trustees* (New York, 1918), pp. 12, 24 f.; newspaper clippings on Dick Bequest (courtesy Metropolitan Museum of Art); "Obituary Notes. Harris B. Dick," *The New-York Times* (September 22, 1916), p. 7; "Obituary Notes. Harris Brisbane Dick," *Publishers' Weekly* XC:14 (September 30, 1916), pp. 1112 f.; *Publishers' Weekly* XC:15 (October 7, 1916), p. 1161; *Social Register, New York* XII:1 (November 1897), p. 108.

At his death, Harris B. Dick bequeathed to The Metropolitan Museum of Art $1,069,298.98.

Fitzgerald Publishing Corporation

For details regarding this firm the author is indebted to Percy L. Hance, Theodore Johnson, the late Mark Mendoza, and William Sloane.

See also *Fitzgerald Publishing Corporation's Descriptive Catalogue of Plays, Entertainments and Books* (New York, n.d.); *New York City Directory* 1920/1921; *New York Copartnership and Corporation Directory* 1933 and 1934; "Obituary Notes. Arthur Howard Abendroth," *Publishers' Weekly* CI:6 (February 11, 1922), p. 358. The Minutes of the Fitzgerald Publishing Corporation are deposited with the Walter H. Baker Company, Boston. Mr. Theodore Johnson, formerly of the Walter H. Baker Company, writes: ". . . in 1931 the firm's capital was $18,000. By 1933 it had risen to $50,000. . . . One primary reason why we closed the New York office is that we found, through experience over several years, that we were merely competing with ourselves in publishing a play list both from New York and Boston."

Rudolph Behrens continued the Dick & Fitzgerald handbook line at Danbury, Connecticut, under the firm name of Behrens Publishing Company, Publisher of Dick & Fitzgerald Hand Books, and his son continues the Behrens Publishing Company.

XVIII. THE TWENTIETH-CENTURY SURVIVALS

Sources for the histories of the surviving firms are so numerous and so obvious that they do not require individual citation. They consist primarily of the books, pamphlets, and brochures issued by firms for centennials and other anniversaries, as well as the reports of their accomplishments in *Publishers' Weekly*. Of equal importance are the catalogues of the surviving houses, which reflect both the history of the country and the part taken by the publishers in shaping that history.

Among general sources, a few works merit specific mention. *The Bookmakers. Reminiscences and Contemporary Sketches of American Publishers. From the New York Evening Post. 1875* (photostat at New York Public Library) and J. C. Derby, *Fifty Years among Authors, Books and Publishers* (New York, 1884) both include accounts of the early histories of many of the surviving firms. A good survey is provided in Hellmut Lehmann-Haupt, *The Book in America* (New York, 1951). For the business of publishing during the nineteenth century, an excellent study is Donald Sheehan's *This Was Publishing* (Bloomington, Indiana, 1952).

Another important source consisted of answers to questionnaires circulated by the author among the long-established firms, questionnaires covering not only the histories of the concerns but their contributions to American civilization during the nineteenth and twentieth centuries. For the most part those questionnaires were answered by the publishers involved with the utmost cooperation. To list the names of all who responded with facts and opinions, pamphlets, brochures, and books, would require more space than can be allotted to such a pleasant task. The writer here wishes to thank most cordially the many publishers who replied to her numerous requests with helpful details and copious information, indicating that they have not forgotten their sense of the past despite their absorbing interest in the present and future of their concerns.

The capsule sketches of the surviving houses which appear in the Supplement of this book were based not only upon the materials mentioned but upon a smaller questionnaire circulated among the publishers involved. Upon completion, the sketches were sent to the individual publishers, who responded promptly with suggestions and with approvals. For this, too, the writer wishes to express her appreciation. The interest of most of the publishers in this historical work has been surpassed only by that of the writer herself, who has found their pleasure in the traditions of their firms both illuminating and gratifying.

For aid in selecting the surviving houses, the author is grateful to Jacob Blanck, Mary Ann Lee, Frederic G. Melcher, and Rollo G. Silver. See also Card File of publishers in office of *Publishers' Weekly* (courtesy Miss Rose Weinberg) and Etna M. Kelley, *The Business Founding Date Directory* (Scarsdale, N.Y., [1954]).

INDEX